# German Diplomatic Relations 1871-1945

# German Diplomatic Relations 1871-1945

✦

## The Wilhelmstrasse and the Formulation of Foreign Policy

*William Young*

iUniverse, Inc.

New York  Lincoln  Shanghai

# German Diplomatic Relations 1871-1945
## The Wilhelmstrasse and the Formulation of Foreign Policy

iUniverse books may be ordered through booksellers or by contacting:

iUniverse
2021 Pine Lake Road, Suite 100
Lincoln, NE 68512
www.iuniverse.com
1-800-Authors (1-800-288-4677)

ISBN-13: 978-0-595-40706-4 (pbk)
ISBN-13: 978-0-595-85072-3 (ebk)
ISBN-10: 0-595-40706-4 (pbk)
ISBN-10: 0-595-85072-3 (ebk)

Printed in the United States of America

For Great Friends,

Mark Massen
and
Martin Skotzke

# Contents

# *Abbreviations*

✦

## *(Used in the Footnotes)*

AMT      American Military Tribunal Transcript and Documents, Nuremberg, Germany, Elwyn B. Robinson Special Collections, Chester Fritz Library, University of North Dakota, Grand Forks, North Dakota.

APP      Historische Reichkommission, *Die Auswärtige Politik Preussens, 1858-1871*, 10 vols., eds. E. Brandenburg and others (Oldenburg: G. Stalling, 1932-39).

BWBB      British Foreign Office, *The British War Blue Book: Documents Concerning German-Polish Relations and the Outbreak of Hostilities Between Great Britain and Germany on September 3, 1939* (New York: Farrer and Rinehart, 1939).

DB      *Diplomat in Berlin 1933-1939: Papers and Memoirs of Jozef Lipski, Ambassador of Poland*, ed. Waclaw Jedrzejewicz (New York: Columbia University Press, 1968).

BDOW      *British Documents on the Origins of the War, 1898-1914*, 11 vols., eds. G.P. Gooch and H.W.V. Temperley (London: Her Majesty's Stationery Office, 1926-28).

DBFP      British Foreign Office, *Documents on British Foreign Policy, 1919-1939*, 65 vols. (London: Her Majesty's Stationary Office, 1946-86).

DGFP(C)      German Foreign Office, *Documents on German Foreign Policy 1918-1945, Series C (1933-1937)*, 6 vols. (Washington, D.C.: U.S. Government Printing Office, 1957-83.

| | |
|---|---|
| DGFP(D) | German Foreign Office, *Documents on German Foreign Policy 1918-1945, Series D (1937-1941)*, 14 vols. (Washington, D.C.: U.S. Government Printing Office, 1949-76). |
| FYB | Ministere des Affaires Etranqeres, *The French Yellow Book: Diplomatic Documents (1938-1939)* (New York: Reynal and Hitchcock, 1940). |
| GD | *Official German Documents Relating to the World War*, trans. Carnegie Endowment for International Peace, Division of Law, 2 vols. (New York: Oxford University Press, 1923). |
| GP | German Foreign Office, *Die Grosse Politik der Europäischen Kabinett, 1871-1914: Sammlung der diplomatischen Akten des Auswärtigen Amtes*, 40 vols., eds. Johannes Lepsius, Albrecht Mendelssohn Bartholdy, and Friedrich Thimme (Berlin: Deutsche Verlagsgellschaft für Politik, 1922-27). |
| HWD | *Blitzkrieg to Defeat: Hitler's War Directives, 1939-1945*, trans. and ed. Hugh Trevor-Roper (New York: Holt, Rinehart, and Winston, 1964). |
| IMT | International Military Tribunal Documents, Nuremberg, Germany, Elwyn B. Robinson Special Collections, Chester Fritz Library, University of North Dakota, Grand Forks, North Dakota. |
| NCA | United States, Chief of Counsel for the Prosecution of Axis Criminality, *Nazi Conspiracy and Aggression*, 8 vols. and 2 sups. (Washington, D.C.: U.S. Government Printing Office, 1946-48). |
| NMT | *Trials of War Criminals Before the Nuremberg Military Tribunals Under Control Council Law No. 10*, 15 vols. (Washington, D.C.: U.S. Government Printing Office, 1949-53). |
| NSR | German Foreign Office, *Nazi-Soviet Relations, 1939-1941: Documents from the Archives of the German For-* |

*eign Office*, eds. Raymond J. Sontag and James S. Beddie (Washington, D.C.: Department of State, 1948).

OWW        *Outbreak of the World War: German Documents Collected by Karl Kautsky*, eds. Max Montgelas and Walther Schucking (New York: Oxford University Press, 1924).

SDP          *Soviet Documents on Foreign Policy, 1917-1941*, 3 vols., ed. Jane Degras (Oxford: Oxford University Press, 1953).

TMWC      International Military Tribunal, Trial of the Major War Criminals before the International Military Tribunal, Nuremberg 14 November 1945—1 October 1946, 42 vols. (Nuremberg: International Military Tribunal, 1947).

# *Preface*

The "continuity" issue has been a theme in German historiography for half a century. Historians have examined the foreign policy and war aims of Wilhelmine and Nazi Germany. This study will examine the continuity, if any, of German Foreign Office influence in the formulation of foreign policy under the leadership of Otto von Bismarck (1862-90), Emperor William II (1888-1918), the Weimar Republic (1919-33), and Adolf Hitler (1933-45). The main purpose of this work is to examine the validity of the defense argument made at the International Military Tribunal, and later, the American Military Tribunal, held at Nuremberg in the late 1940s that members of the Foreign Office had little, if any, influence on decision-making in the realm of foreign policy. The military tribunals held key representatives from the German Foreign Office as defendants against charges of conspiracy to wage wars of aggression, the actual waging of wars, war crimes, and crimes against humanity. This work concentrates on the first charge, that of conspiracy. The International Military Tribunal found former German Foreign Ministers Constantin von Neurath (1932-38) and Joachim von Ribbentrop (1938-45) both guilty of conspiracy in spite of pleas of innocence due to their minimal influence over Hitler's foreign policy: Ribbentrop argued that Hitler was actually his own Foreign Minister and he only carried out orders as a technical specialist. Other members of the Foreign Office, including the State Secretary for Foreign Affairs,[1] Ernst von Weizsäcker, were also found guilty of this charge after lengthy trials by the American Military Tribunal.

Since its creation in 1870, the German Foreign Office has had a history of strict obedience to the head of German affairs, whether it be Imperial Chancellor Otto von Bismarck, who was also Prussian Foreign Minister, or Emperor Will-

---

1.  The German title of State Secretary for Foreign Affairs is more commonly referred to as Foreign Secretary in most countries. These titles will be used interchangeably throughout this study. It is important to note that before 1919 the Imperial Chancellor, under the authority of the Emperor and German constitution, was responsible for foreign affairs. The Chancellor also held the position of Prussian Foreign Minister. There was no Imperial Foreign Minister, but the Secretary of State served the Chancellor as the chief administrator of the Foreign Office. After 1919, the Weimar Republic created the position of Foreign Minister and promoted the previous post of Foreign Secretary to fill this position. At the same time the Under State Secretary became the new State Secretary.

iam II, carrying out, not formulating foreign policy. The parliamentary cabinets of the Weimar Republic controlled foreign policy after the First World War. But, the Wilhelmstrasse gained some influence in the formulation of foreign policy when Gustav Stresemann served as Foreign Minister from 1923 to 1929. Stresemann, who served for a short time as Chancellor (1923), became a focal point in European politics because of Germany's postwar situation, as well as the combined German civilian and military leaders quest to revise the Treaty of Versailles. Under the autocratic rule of Adolf Hitler, as Ribbentrop argued at Nuremberg, the Foreign Office was again forced into its traditional subservient role as a mere technical apparatus which carried out foreign policy decisions, but did not formulate them.

An examination of the history of the Foreign Office reveals the continuity of the ministry's function as an organization designed to carry out the instructions of German leaders. Bismarck, William II, and Hitler all practiced, to varying degrees, their desire to be their own Foreign Minister. In Bismarck's case, as the Imperial Chancellor and Prussian Foreign Minister, he had absolute control of foreign policy. He appointed civil servants and diplomats, who carried out his instructions without question, to key positions in the Foreign Office. In 1890, Emperor William II dismissed the Iron Chancellor and initially replaced him with men who knew little of world affairs so that he, himself, could greatly influence the direction of German foreign policy. Eventually William II appointed the diplomat Bernhard von Bülow as Foreign Secretary (1897-1900), and later as Imperial Chancellor and Prussian Foreign Minister (1900-9), to carry out his Weltpolitik. Although influenced by the military, especially Admiral Alfred von Tirpitz, William II took foreign policy initiatives on his own, sometimes contrary to the advice of Bülow and Friedrich von Holstein, who held much influence inside the Foreign Office, as well as a long succession of foreign secretaries. The Emperor strongly disliked professional diplomats. Ridding himself of foreign affairs experts, the Emperor approached the First World War under the military leadership's influence with little expert diplomatic advice, since the Imperial Chancellor and Prussian Foreign Minister, Theobald von Bethmann Hollweg, knew little of foreign affairs, and Foreign Secretary Gottlieb von Jagow took a back seat in the Emperor's circle of influential advisers.

Coming to power in 1933, Hitler kept Neurath, a conservative elite, as Foreign Minister while he consolidated his control over Germany. The Foreign Office, traditionally consisting primarily of aristocrats, under Neurath shared common aims, to a certain degree, with Hitler. They both wanted Germany to be rid of the Versailles restrictions and regain its status as a Great Power. For a while both the Chancellor and Foreign Minister worked together, especially since Hitler valued the need of maintaining German respectability in the diplomatic world. Hitler, however, had an additional agenda, eastward expansionism, and thus sought ultimate control over German foreign policy. The Führer, who greatly disliked professional diplomats, employed the ambitious and loyal champagne dealer, Ribbentrop, who knew little of world affairs beyond his travels, as a personal diplomat to not only challenge the authority of the Foreign Office, but to carry out his foreign policy initiatives. Neurath and the Foreign Office opposed Hitler's meddling in diplomatic affairs, but found the situation impossible. They swiftly lost the influence in the formulation of foreign policy that the ministry had acquired during the Weimar Republic. In early 1938, Hitler became his own Foreign Minister, dismissing Neurath, and replacing him with Ribbentrop as the token head of the Foreign Office. Thus, under the autocratic rule of Hitler, the Foreign Office came full circle and clearly resumed its traditional position as an agency meant to carry out the instructions of the German leadership with strict obedience as during the times of Bismarck and William II.

If the above thesis proves true, then the defense arguments of Ribbentrop and other diplomats at the Nuremberg trials had a ring of truth to them. Ribbentrop, although officially Reich Foreign Minister, professed that he had little influence in the formulation of foreign policy. He, in fear of his life during the Nuremberg proceedings, argued that Hitler, acting as his own Foreign Minister, and Hermann Göring were the conspirators planning wars of aggression.[2] Ernst von Weizsäcker, Ribbentrop's Foreign Secretary, insisted that the Foreign Office had no influence on policy.[3] Could these statements be mere arguments made by men in the shadow of the gallows? Bradley Smith has shown that the Allies were out to try and convict the much disliked Ribbentrop months before the end of the war. Evidence, no matter how circumstantial, pointing toward Ribbentrop's involvement in a Nazi conspiracy to wage wars of aggression was gathered during the

---

2.    Joachim von Ribbentrop, *The Ribbentrop Memoirs*, ed. A. von Ribbentrop, trans. Oliver Watson, introd. Allan Bullock (London: Weidenfeld and Nicolson, 1954), 31, 79; International Military Tribunal, *Trials of the Major War Criminals Before The International Military Tribunal, Nuremberg 14 November 1945—1 October 1946*, 42 vols. (Nuremberg: International Military Tribunal, 1947), 9:401, 10:416, 10:321; U.S. Chief of Counsel for the Prosecution of Axis Criminality, *Nazi Conspiracy and Aggression*, 8 vols. and 2 sups. (Washington, D.C.: U.S. Government Printing Office, 1946-48), L-74, 7:841; DeWitt C. Poole, "Light on Nazi Foreign Policy," *Foreign Affairs*, 25, (October 1946), 130.

3.    Ernst von Weizsäcker, *Memoirs of Ernst von Weizsäcker*, trans. John Andrews (Chicago: Henry Regnery, 1951), 106.

course of the war.[4] Norman Rich has pointed out that these documents, in their abundance, were overwhelming to any defense that Ribbentrop could manage.[5] These same documents that convicted the Foreign Minister, as Allied logic would have it, implicated other leading members of the Foreign Office and were used to try individual diplomats, who survived the war, at Nuremberg. Ribbentrop realized his own predicament. He wrote in his uncompleted memoirs, "Adolf Hitler is dead, and others must therefore be found responsible."[6] On 5 October 1946, shortly before his execution, Ribbentrop wrote to his wife:

> Everyone knows that the verdict is quite untenable, but I happen to have been Adolf Hitler's Foreign Minister and political considerations therefore call for my conviction. Fate willed that my principal witness, Adolf Hitler, is dead. Were he able to give evidence, the whole verdict would collapse. As it is, I must bear the fate of the followers of such a mighty and perhaps demoniac personality.[7]

Much has been written on German foreign policy during 1871 to 1945. However, there exist few studies of the German Foreign Office during this period.[8] In regards to the Foreign Ministers of the Third Reich, Neurath and Ribbentrop have received some recent attention.[9] This study of the Foreign Office adds to the already published research by including findings from the unpublished American Military Tribunal papers located in the Chester Fritz Library at the University of North Dakota.

The writing of this study was influenced by Professor (Emeritus) Playford Thorson of the University of North Dakota, Richard Langhorne, a former Fellow of St John's College and Director of the Centre of International Studies at Cam-

---

4.    Bradley Smith, *Reaching Judgment at Nuremberg* (London: Andre Deutsch, 1977), 183-84. Even among the Nazi elite, as Alan Bullock pointed out, Ribbentrop was much disliked (Ribbentrop, xi).

5.    Norman Rich, "Hitler's Foreign Policy," chap. in *The Origins of the Second World War Reconsidered: The A.J.P. Taylor Debate After Twenty-Five Years*, ed. Gordon Martel (Boston: Allen and Unwin, 1986), 120.

6.    Ribbentrop, 180.

7.    Ibid., 199.

8.    There are only two detailed studies that examine the German Foreign Office during this period. See Lamar Cecil, *The German Diplomatic Service, 1871-1914* (Princeton: Princeton University Press, 1976) and Paul Seabury, *The Wilhelmstrasse: A Study of German Diplomats under the Nazi Regime* (Berkeley and Los Angeles: University of California Press, 1954). Unfortunately there are no studies regarding the Weimar Republic.

9.    See John L. Heineman, *Hitler's First Foreign Minister: Constantin Freiherr von Neurath, Diplomat and Statesman* (Berkeley, Los Angeles, and London: University of California Press, 1979); John Weitz, *Hitler's Diplomat: The Life and Times of Joachim von Ribbentrop* (New York: Ticknor and Fields, 1992); and Michael Bloch, *Ribbentrop* (New York: Crown, 1992).

bridge University, and C. Edmund Clingan of Queensborough Community College at the City University of New York. The author would also like to thank David G. Rowley of the University of Wisconsin-Platteville. The staff of the Special Collections and Inter-Library Loan Office at the University of North Dakota Chester Fritz Library were extremely helpful in this endeavor.

The work could not have been completed without the support of my wife Patricia Young, Mark Massen, and Martin Skotzke. I also want to thank my parents, Kenneth and Marilyn Young, as well as my sisters, Joni Young, Jami Komatz, and Mary Schepp for their encouragement. Patricia, as always, served as my proofreader. Our children, Mark, William, Geoffrey, and Heather, also played a vital role.

William Young
Grand Forks, North Dakota
June 2006

# 1

# *Rise of Prussia to 1862*

## Hohenzollerns and Brandenburg-Prussia

The House of Hohenzollern began their rule over the Mark of Brandenburg with the reign of Frederick I (1417-40). The Margrave of Brandenburg was one of seven important German princes that had the right to elect Holy Roman Emperors as outlined in the Golden Bull of 1356. Two hundred years later, Elector John Sigismund (1608-19) acquired the Duchy of Cleves and the Principality of Ravenstein on the Lower Rhine River, as well as the Counties of Mark and Ravensberg on the Weser River in the Treaty of Xanten (1614). Then, in 1618, John Sigismund inherited the Duchy of Prussia (East Prussia) which lay outside the Holy Roman Empire. He held East Prussia as a vassal of the King of Poland-Lithuania. Overall, however, the lands of the Hohenzollerns were now referred to as Brandenburg-Prussia.[1]

The lands of the Hohenzollerns were trampled during the Thirty Years' War (1618-48).[2] Elector George William (1619-40) was too weak to defend his territories. By the time of his death his lands were in the hands of the Swedes, Dutch,

---

1. For the early history of Brandenburg-Prussia, one should consult F.L. Carsten, *The Origins of Prussia* (Oxford: Clarendon Press, 1954); H.W. Koch, *A History of Prussia* (London: Longman, 1978); Margaret Shennan, *The Rise of Brandenburg-Prussia* (London: Routledge, 1995); Hajo Holborn, *A History of Modern Germany*, 3 vols. (New York: Alfred A. Knopf, 1959-69); Sidney B. Fay and Klaus Epstein, *The Rise of Brandenburg-Prussia to 1786*, rev. ed. (Malabar, FL: Krieger, 1981); Michael Hughes, *Early Modern Germany, 1477-1806* (Philadelphia: University of Pennsylvania Press, 1992); and Peter H. Wilson, *The Holy Roman Empire, 1495-1806* (New York: St. Martin's Press, 1999). See also Alison Deborah Anderson, *On the Verge of War: International Relations and the Jülich-Kleve Succession Crises (1609-1614)* (Boston: Humanities Press, 1999).
2. For Germany during the Thirty Years' War, see C.V. Wedgwood, *The Thirty Years' War* (London: Jonathan Cape, 1938); Geoffrey Parker, ed. *The Thirty Years' War* (London: Routledge and Kegan Paul, 1984); Gerhard Benecke, *Germany in the Thirty Years' War* (London: Edward Arnold, 1978); Ronald G. Asch, *The Thirty Years' War: The Holy Roman Empire and Europe, 1618-1648* (New York: St. Martin's Press, 1997); and Herbert Langer, *The Thirty Years' War* (Poole: Blandford Press, 1980).

Hessians, and Imperial forces. But, he was succeeded by his son, Elector Frederick William I (1640-88). Frederick William gradually built up a power base and slowly won back Hohenzollern lands in the final stages of the Thirty Years' War. He acquired East Pomerania and several secularized bishoprics, including Minden, Cammin, Halberstadt, and the promise of the Bishopric of Magdeburg in the Treaty of Westphalia (1648). The Hohenzollerns were quickly becoming the second most important ruling family in Germany.[3]

In the 1650s, Frederick William became entangled in conflicts that threatened to destroy his electorate. In 1654, Muscovy invaded the Polish-Lithuanian Commonwealth beginning the Thirteen Years' War (1654-67). Then, Sweden invaded the Commonwealth starting the Second Northern War (1655-60). In these wars Elector Frederick William balanced his allegiance to the King of Poland-Lithuania concerning East Prussia with his desires to acquire West Prussia and West Pomerania. He had only 2,000 troops,[4] and was forced to change sides several times. In the Peace of Oliva, Frederick William acquired full sovereignty over East Prussia in 1660. He then defeated a Swedish army at Fehrbellin during the Pomeranian War (1674-79), earning the title "the Great Elector." Frederick William and his army of 12,000 men supported the Dutch Republic, Spain, and the Austrian Habsburgs in the struggle against French aggression in the Dutch War (1672-78/79).[5] The Great Elector made defensive alliances with the German Emperor, Dutch Republic, and Sweden in light of Louis XIV of France's aggression in 1685-86. His son, Elector Frederick III (1688-1701), and a force of 30,000 troops fought on the side the Grand Alliance against the Sun King during the Nine Years' War (1688-97).[6] In the War of the Spanish Succession (1701-1713/14), Frederick III allied with the Austrian Habsburgs and joined the Second Grand Alliance against Louis XIV in return for the German Emperor recognizing him as Frederick I, King in Prussia (1701-13). In the Peace of Utrecht (1713), Frederick I acquired the towns of Moers and Krefeld in the County of Moers, north of Düsseldorf; the County of Lingen in Westphalia; the

---

3.    There are several general studies about Germany that address Brandenburg-Prussia after the Thirty Years' War. See John Gagliardo, *Germany under the Old Regime, 1600-1790* (London: Longman, 1991), Rudolf Vierhaus, *Germany in the Age of Absolutism*, trans. Jonathan B. Knudsen (Cambridge: Cambridge University Press, 1988); Holborn, *A History of Germany*; and Peter H. Wilson, *German Armies: War and German Politics, 1648-1806* (London: University College London, 1998).

4.    David J. Sturdy, *Fractured Europe, 1600-1721* (Oxford: Blackwell, 2002), 370.

5.    Ibid.

6.    Ibid.

towns of Valengin and Neuchâtel in the Swiss Canton of Neuchâtel; Geldern; and part of Upper Guelders.[7]

In 1714, King Frederick William I (1713-40) of Brandenburg-Prussia quickly became involved in the Great Northern War (1700-21) against Sweden. He was allied with Russia, Denmark-Norway, Britain, and Hanover. The Prussians took control of Stettin, and then captured Stralsund, Rügen, and Wismar. In the Second Treaty of Stockholm (1720), Frederick William I acquired Wollin, Usedom, and West Pomerania south of the Peene River, including Stettin. Prussia now controlled both banks of the lower Oder River and possessed in Stettin a first-class Baltic port. During his reign Frederick William increased the size of the Prussian Army from 40,000 to 80,000 men, increasing the importance of Brandenburg-Prussia in international relations.[8]

## Frederick the Great

In 1740, King Frederick II of Prussia (1740-86) invaded the Austrian Habsburg possession of Silesia, beginning the War of the Austrian Succession (1740-48). Frederick II's chief diplomatic adviser, Heinrich von Podewils, was against such a brash move.[9] The invasion was a complete surprise to Maria Theresa of Austria and to Europe.[10] The war quickly grew into a conflict between Austria, Britain, Hanover, and the Dutch Republic against Prussia, France, Bavaria, Saxony, and Spain. The Austro-Prussian conflict was called the First Silesian War (1740-42). Frederick II's military success at the Battle of Chotusitz (1742), and the combined threat of her enemies, forced Maria Theresa to agree to the Peace of Breslau

---

7.   The reign of the Great Elector and Brandenburg involvement in European wars are examined in Derek McKay, *The Great Elector* (London: Longman, 2001); William Young, *International Politics and Warfare in the Age of Louis XIV and Peter the Great* (Lincoln: iUniverse, 2004); Derek McKay, "Small-Power Diplomacy in the Age of Louis XIV: The Foreign Policy of the Great Elector during the 1660s and 1670s," in *Royal and Republican Sovereignty in Early Modern Europe: Essays in Memory of Ragnhild Hatton*, ed. Robert Oresko, G.C. Gibbs, and H.M. Scott (Cambridge: Cambridge University Press, 1997) and Ferdinand Schevill, *The Great Elector* (Chicago: University of Chicago Press, 1947). Frederick III/Frederick I is examined in Linda Frey and Marsha Frey, *Frederick I: The Man and His Times* (Boulder: East European Monographs, 1984).

8.   Shennan, 54; Philip G. Dwyer, "The Rise of Prussia," in *The Rise of Prussia, 1700-1830*, ed. Philip G. Dwyer (London: Longman, 2000), 13. Frederick William I is examined in Robert Ergang, *The Potsdam Führer: Frederick William I, Father of Prussian Militarism* (New York: Columbia University Press, 1941) and Reinhold August Dorwart, *The Administrative Reforms of Frederick William I of Prussia* (Cambridge, MA: Harvard University Press, 1953).

9.   H.M. Scott, "Prussia's Emergence as a European Great Power, 1740-1763," in *The Rise of Prussia, 1700-1830*, ed. Philip G. Dwyer (London: Longman, 2000), 161.

10.  See H.M. Scott, *The Birth of a Great Power System, 1740-1815* (Harlow: Pearson, 2006), 48.

(1742). The Habsburgs made peace with Prussia at the cost of Silesia. However, Austrian military success in 1743 and 1744 led to Frederick II launching the Second Silesian War (1744-45) against the Habsburgs to protect Silesia. Prussian forces, numbering about 124,000, now faced the combined might of Austria, Saxony, Britain, and the Dutch Republic.[11] Frederick II invaded Saxony. The Prussians defeated the Austrians and Saxons at the Battle of Hohenfriedberg in Silesia; the Austrians at the Soor in Bohemia, Hennersdorf, and Görlitz; as well as the Saxons at the Battle of Kesseldorf in 1745. These victories resulted in the Peace of Dresden (1745). In this treaty, Austria confirmed the Prussian acquisition of Silesia.[12]

The Great Powers of Europe were alarmed at the growth in power of Prussia under Frederick II. The Prussian King spent the next decade strengthening the Prussian economy, increasing his war chest, improving the cavalry, building up an army of 143,000 men, and making an alliance with Britain.[13] In 1756, Austria, France, Russia, Sweden, and Saxony created a coalition to cripple or destroy Prussia. But, Frederick II made the first move. Prussian forces invaded Saxony in August 1756, beginning the Seven Years' War (1756-63). During the next seven years the Prussians defeated the Austrians at Lobositz and Prague (1757), the French at Rossbach (1757), Austrians at Leuthen (1757), Russians at Zorndorf (1758), as well as Austrians at Liegnitz and Torgau (1760) despite being heavily outnumbered during the entire war. These victories kept Prussia from defeat in the conflict. Nevertheless, Frederick the Great and the Prussians suffered setbacks

---

11.    Christopher Duffy, *The Army of Frederick the Great* (Newton Abbot: David and Charles, 1974), 162.

12.    Frederick II is treated in D.B. Horn, *Frederick the Great and the Rise of Prussia* (London: English Universities Press, 1964); Gerhard Ritter, *Frederick the Great: A Historical Profile*, trans. and intro. Peter Paret (Berkeley: University of California Press, 1968); Walther Hubatsch, *Frederick the Great: Absolutism and Administration*, trans. Patrick Doran (London: Thames and Hudson, 1975); Robert B. Asprey, *Frederick the Great: The Magnificent Enigma* (New York: History Book Club, 1986); Theodor Schieder, *Frederick the Great*, ed. and trans. Sabina Berkeley and H.M. Scott (London: Longman, 2000); and Giles McDonough, *Frederick the Great: A Life in Deed and Letters* (London: Weidenfeld and Nicolson, 1999). The military side of Frederick II is addressed in Christopher Duffy, *Frederick the Great: A Military Life* (London: Routledge and Kegan Paul, 1985); Dennis E. Showalter, *The Wars of Frederick the Great* (London: Longman, 1996); and Christopher Duffy, *Prussia's Glory: Rossbach and Leuthen, 1757* (Chicago: Emperor's Press, 2003). The War of the Austrian Succession is addressed in M.S. Anderson, *The War of the Austrian Succession, 1740-1748* (London: Longman, 1995) and Reed Browning, *The War of the Austrian Succession* (New York: St. Martin's Press, 1993).

13.    Duffy, *The Army of Frederick the Great*, 165.

against Austria at Kolin (1757), Russia at Gross-Jägersdorf (1757), Austria at Hochkirch (1758), Russia at Kay (Paltzig) (1759), Austro-Russian forces at Kunersdorf (1759), and Austria at Maxen (1759). Berlin was overrun by the enemy twice during the war. In 1761, Frederick II was too weak to afford battle and tried to keep his enemies at bay through a series of maneuvers. By December 1761 the Prussians were on the brink of defeat. But, the death of Empress Elizabeth I of Russia turned the situation in favor of Frederick II when Tsar Peter III allied with Prussia in 1762. Frederick II fought on, defeating the Austrians at the Battle of Burkersdorf, and forced Maria Theresa of Austria to agree to the Peace of Hubertusburg in 1763. Frederick the Great would keep Silesia. Moreover, as Hamish Scott has written, "it [the Seven Years' War] established the Hohenzollern state as a great power."[14]

Immediately after the Seven Years' War, Frederick the Great stood alone without allies in Europe. The Anglo-Prussian alliance had broken down toward the end of the war.[15] Prussia was suffering from the devastation of war. Prussia had to rebuild. The Prussian King now needed to avoid war at all costs. He knew that Prussia could easily lose its newly won Great Power status, which rested upon the strength of the Prussian Army. He therefore gradually built up the Prussian Army to 190,000 men.[16] He wanted to use the army as a strategic deterrent. Frederick the Great did not want war. He wanted to use the army to deter other Great Powers from attacking Prussia. Paul W. Schroeder has written that:

> fear underlay Prussia's policy and ambitions in general, a consciousness that its power base was fragile and its great-power status marginal. More than once Frederick remarked that Prussia's crest should feature a monkey rather than an eagle, for it could only ape the great powers.[17]

Frederick II controlled Prussian foreign policy and he sought peace in Europe. The most significant threat to Prussia was Russia under Empress Catherine II.

14.    H.M. Scott, "Aping the Great Powers: Frederick the Great and the Defence of Prussia's International Position, 1763-1786," *German History* 12 (1994), 286.

15.    See Karl W. Schweizer, *England, Prussia and the Seven Years' War: Studies in Alliance Policies and Diplomacy* (Lewiston, NY: Edwin Mellen, 1989); Patrick Francis Doran, *Andrew Mitchell and Anglo-Prussian Diplomatic Relations during the Seven Years' War* (New York: Garland, 1986); and Karl W. Schweizer, *Frederick the Great, William Pitt, and Lord Bute: The Anglo-Prussian Alliance, 1756-1763* (New York: Garland, 1991).

16.    Dennis E. Showalter, "Hubertusburg to Auerstädt: The Prussian Army in Decline?" *German History* 12 (1994), 311.

17.    Paul W. Schroeder, *The Transformation of European Politics, 1763-1848* (Oxford: Clarendon Press, 1994), 24.

Russian armies had achieved several notable victories over the Prussian Army in the Seven Years' War. After the conflict Russia was the most powerful state in East Europe. As such, Frederick II sought and achieved a defensive alliance with Russia in 1764. Catherine II needed the Prussian alliance to control the election of a new king to the Polish-Lithuanian Commonwealth. She wanted to control Poland-Lithuania through Stanislaw Poniatowski. But, the Empress feared Ottoman interference and a Turkish invasion of southern Russia. Catherine II got what she wanted, but then so did Frederick II with a Russian alliance to deter an Austrian attack against Prussia.

Despite the Prusso-Russian alliance, the Turks declared war against Russia in 1768. The armies of Catherine the Great crushed the Turks in the Russo-Turkish War (1768-74). The Russians quickly overran a vast amount of Ottoman territory. Consequently, Austria became alarmed at the increasing power of Russia. Austria demanded compensation for the territorial growth of the Russian Empire. To resolve the growing crisis, Austria, Russia, and Prussia negotiated the First Partition of Poland in 1772. Frederick the Great gained Ermland, the Netze district, and West Prussia. The partition was a significant action because it linked East Prussia to Pomerania and Brandenburg.[18]

The War of the Bavarian Succession (1778-79) was the one occasion in which Frederick II went to war in the late eighteenth century. In this conflict, which had no pitched battles, Prussia prevented Austria from annexing the Electorate of Bavaria after the death of the last Wittelsbach. In the Peace of Teschen (1779) the Habsburgs were forced to accept only a small strip of Bavarian territory.[19] Frederick the Great had established and upheld the balance of power between the Hohenzollerns and Habsburgs.

After the death of Frederick the Great, Prussia was heavily involved in international politics. In September 1787, the Ottoman Turks declared war against Russia. Catherine the Great had annexed the Crimea in 1783, and a buildup of Russian forces near the Turkish border encouraged the Sublime Porte to launch a preemptive strike. Austria and Prussia were busy with revolts in the Austrian Netherlands and United Provinces. Prussia and Britain cooperated in putting down the rebellion in the Dutch Republic in 1787. Even so, Austria

---

18.    See Herbert H. Kaplan, *The First Partition of Poland* (New York: Columbia University Press, 1962); Jerzy Lukowski, *The Partitions of Poland, 1772, 1793, 1795* (London: Longman, 1999); and H.M. Scott, *The Emergence of the Eastern Powers, 1756-1775* (Cambridge: Cambridge University Press, 2001).

19.    For the War ov the Bavarian Succession, see Paul P. Bernard, *Joseph II and Bavaria: Two Eighteenth Century Attempts at German Unification* (The Hague: Martinus Nijhoff, 1965).

joined the Russians against the Turks in February 1788. Initially, the Austro-Russian alliance had a difficult time against the Turks. In March, Count Ewald Friedrich von Hertzberg of the Prussian Department of Foreign Affairs suggested a Prussian alliance with Austria and Russia in exchange for a Second Partition of Poland. He wanted Danzig, Thorn, and the Palatinates of Poznan and Kalisz for Prussia.[20] Catherine II of Russia and Joseph II of Austria were not interested in this idea. They had no interest in the further growth of Prussian power. Then, in June 1788, Sweden attacked Russia. Hertzberg then offered a Prussian alliance with the Polish-Lithuanian Commonwealth. But King Stanislaw Poniatowski feared Prussian intentions. In 1789, Catherine the Great withdrew Russian forces from Poland-Lithuania to prevent the provocation of Prussia. Russian power in Poland was quickly collapsing. The Russians were at war with Sweden and the Ottoman Empire, facing the threat of Prussia, and experiencing a Polish rebellion against Russian dominance. Then, in 1789-90, the Russians and Austrians won a series of military victories against the Turks and Sweden. As a result, in March 1790, Prussia and Poland agreed to a defensive alliance. With the death of Leopold II, Austria bowed out of the war in the Peace of Reichenbach (1790). Russia continued the wars alone. Russian forces defeated the Swedes and forced the Peace of Verela (1790). This allowed the Russians to move troops to counter the Prussians on the Polish front. At this point, Frederick William II (1786-97) sought to improve relations with Catherine the Great. Russia agreed to consider a partition of Poland to remove the Prussian threat. As a consequence, a major revolt against Russian domination broke out in May 1791. The Poles created a constitution. Then, in 1791, the Russians achieved a series of victories against the Turks that resulted in the Peace of Jassy (1792).[21]

---

20.  Lukowski, 124.
21.  For international political relations during this period, see Isabel de Madariaga, *Russia in the Age of Catherine the Great* (London: Weidenfeld and Nicolson, 1981) and Hamish M. Scott, *The Birth of a Great Power System, 1740-1815* (London: Longman, 2005).

## Prussia in the Age of the
## French Revolutionary Wars and Napoleonic Wars

The era of the French Revolutionary Wars (1792-1802) and Napoleonic Wars (1803-15) were difficult for Prussia.[22] The French Revolution brought Prussia and Austria together. In August 1791, Frederick William II of Prussia and Leopold II of Austria (1790-92) issued the Declaration of Pillnitz threatening France that Austria and Prussia would intervene in the French Revolution to protect the French royal family. In February 1792, Austria and Prussia concluded a defensive alliance. Then, in April, the French government declared war against the new German Emperor, Francis II of Austria (1792-1835), and invaded the Austrian Netherlands. The Austrians defeated the French at the Battles of Mons and Tournai. Afterwards, an Austro-Prussian army assembled at Coblenz, and began its march, under the command of Duke Ferdinand of Brunswick, towards Paris in July 1792. The allied army defeated the French at Longwy and Verdun in early September, and the road seemed open to Paris. But, the allied army was defeated by the French at the Battle of Valmy in late September 1792. As a result, the allied army retreated to Germany. French forces conquered the Rhineland, Austrian Netherlands, and Savoy, and then invaded central Germany in late 1792.

In the meantime, Frederick William II had little interest in getting heavily involved in an anti-French coalition. Instead, the Prussian King sought territorial aggrandizement at the expense of Poland-Lithuania. Russian forces had invaded

---

22.    The French Revolution and Napoleon is examined in Owen Connelly, *French Revolution/Napoleonic Era* (New York: Holt, Rinehart, and Winston, 1979). Diplomatic relations are covered in Steven T. Ross, *European Diplomatic History, 1789-1815: France against Europe* (Malabar, FL: Robert E. Krieger, 1981) and Thomas M. Iiams, *Peacemaking from Vergennes to Napoleon: French Foreign Relations in the Revolutionary Era, 1774-1814* (Huntington, NY: Robert E. Krieger, 1979). The wars are the subjects of T.C.W. Blanning, *The Origins of the French Revolutionary Wars* (London: Longman, 1986); T.C.W. Blanning, *The French Revolutionary Wars, 1787-1802* (London: Arnold, 1996); Gregory Fremont-Barnes, *The French Revolutionary Wars* (Botley, Engl.: Osprey, 2001); Charles J. Esdaile, *The French Wars, 1792-1815* (London: Routledge, 2001); David Gates, *The Napoleonic Wars, 1803-1815* (London: Arnold, 1997); Charles J. Esdaile, *The Wars of Napoleon* (London: Longman, 1995); and David G. Chandler, *The Campaigns of Napoleon* (New York: Macmillan, 1966). Prussian policy is examined in Philip G. Dwyer, "Prussia during the French Revolutionary and Napoleonic Wars, 1786-1815," in *The Rise of Prussia, 1700-1830*, ed. Philip G. Dwyer (London: Longman, 2000). French policy towards the German states is treated in Sidney Seymour Biro, *The German Policy of Revolutionary France: A Study in French Diplomacy during the War of the First Coalition, 1792-1797*, 2 vols. (Cambridge, MA: Harvard University Press, 1957) and T.C.W. Blanning, *The French Revolution in Germany: Occupation and Resistance in the Rhineland, 1792-1802* (Oxford: Clarendon Press, 1983).

and occupied Poland-Lithuania while Prussia and Austria were busy with France in 1792. Catherine II then renewed the alliance with Austria and made an alliance with Prussia in August 1792. She feared the spread of the French Revolution throughout Europe. Two months later, after the Battle of Valmy, Frederick William II made territorial demands against Poland-Lithuania. He refused to further support Austria against France until Prussia gained Polish lands. As a result, in January 1793, Catherine II agreed to the Second Partition of Poland in the Convention of St. Petersburg.[23] Prussia gained Danzig, Thorn, as well as the Palatinates of Poznan and Kalisz.

After the acquisition of territory, Frederick William II committed troops to the War of the First Coalition (1792-97). An Austro-Prussian army under the Duke of Brunswick recaptured Mainz and pushed into the Rhine Palatinate and Alsace. The Prussians defeated the French at the Battle of Kaiserslautern in May 1794. Before long, however, a conflict in war strategy led to a deterioration of the Austro-Prussian war effort against Revolutionary France. Once again, Frederick William II became more interested in the Polish Question. In March 1794, a general revolt had broken out against foreign oppression in Poland. Russian, Prussian, and Austrian forces responded by suppressing the revolt. In January 1795, Russia and Austria agreed to the Third Partition of Poland. To satisfy Prussian demands concerning Poland, Russia and Austria ceded Warsaw and other Polish territories to Prussia in October 1795.[24] Meanwhile, in April 1795, Prussia had deserted the coalition against France in the Peace of Basle and declared neutrality. Prussia and France agreed to a demarcation line that roughly followed the Ems, Old Ijssel, and the Rhine Rivers, and included Frankfurt and all of Franconia where Prussia held the important lands of Ansbach and Bayreuth. The line was completed by following the northern boundaries of Bavaria, the Upper Palatinate, and Bohemia to Silesia. Frederick William II was to guarantee that no army would use the territories behind the line as a staging area for an attack against France. In return, France promised not to march any of its armies across this area in pursuit of the enemy.[25]

---

23.   See Robert Howard Lord, *The Second Partition of Poland: A Study in Diplomatic History* (Cambridge, MA: Harvard University Press, 1915).
24.   Lukowski, 179.
25.   Philip G. Dwyer, "The Politics of Prussian Neutrality, 1795-1805," *German History* 12 (1994), 351.

Frederick William III of Prussia (1797-1840) was cautious in his foreign policy.[26] He refused the join the coalition of Russia, Austria, Britain, Naples, Portugal, and the Ottoman Empire in the War of the Second Coalition (1798-1802) against Revolutionary France. He also declined the request for an alliance with France. Frederick William III could remain neutral because of the inflated reputation given to the Prussian Army by the other Great Powers.[27] As such, in 1802, France rewarded Prussia with territory in Westphalia and to the north of Thuringia.[28] With dreams of acquiring Hanover, Frederick William III wanted to remain neutral in the War of the Third Coalition (1805-7) against Napoleon I and France.[29] However, France had violated the north German neutrality by invading and occupying Hanover in 1803. Continued French violations of neutral north German territory by Napoleon I's troops resulted in Frederick William III, under the advice of Baron Karl August von Hardenberg, to sign the Agreement of Potsdam with Tsar Alexander I of Russia in November 1805. Frederick William III would offer armed mediation in the conflict, and if Napoleon I refused, Prussia would join the coalition against France. Napoleon I, nevertheless, defeated the Austrian and Russian armies at the Battle of Austerlitz in December 1805. Austria was forced out of the war in the Peace of Pressburg (Bratislava). Prussia quickly agreed to the humiliating Treaty of Schönbrunn with France two weeks later. Frederick William III would have to give up the Franconian principalities and Cleves in return for Hanover.[30] Prussia, however, was now at Napoleon I's mercy. By the Treaty of Paris (1806) Frederick William III was forced to promise to supply troops for the continuing French war against Russia. He was also required to join the Continental System and to close Prussian ports to British shipping.[31] At the same time, the French Army continued to threaten

---

26.   Frederick William III's foreign policy is examined in Brendan Simms, *The Impact of Napoleon: Prussian High Politics, Foreign Policy, and the Crisis of the Executive, 1797-1806* (Cambridge: Cambridge University Press, 1997). See also Brendan Simms, "The Road to Jena: Prussian High Politics, 1804-1806," *German History* 12 (1994).

27.   J.E. Stine, "Frederick William III and the Decline of the Prussian Army, 1786-1797" (Ph.D. diss., University of South Carolina, 1980) argues the growing weakness of the Prussian military.

28.   Showalter, "Hubertusburg to Auerstädt," 323.

29.   Prussian relations with Hanover are the topic of Guy Stanton Ford, *Hanover and Prussia, 1796-1803: A Study in Neutrality* (New York: AMS Press, 1967). See also Philip G. Dwyer, "Prussia and the Armed Neutrality: The Invasion of Hanover in 1801," *International History Review* 15 (November 1993), 661-87.

30.   Holborn, *A History of Modern Germany*, 2:381.

31.   Derek McKay and H.M. Scott, *The Rise of the Great Powers, 1648-1815* (London: Longman, 1983), 312-13.

Prussian lands.[32] Franco-Prussian relations quickly deteriorated, resulting in Frederick William III declaring war against France in August 1806. The result was the shattering defeat of the Prussian Army at the Battles of Jena and Auerstädt in October 1806.[33] French forces then overran the core of the Hohenzollern lands. As a result, the French "shattered the myth of Prussian invincibility which the victories of Frederick II had created."[34] Napoleon I took Berlin, but Frederick William III would not concede to French territorial demands. Frederick William III and his court moved to Königsberg and then to Memel in East Prussia. He agreed to a Russian alliance to drive the French back across the Rhine River in the Treaty of Bartenstein in 1807. But, Napoleon I defeated the Russians at the Battle of Friedland in June, with the consequence that Alexander I agreed to the Peace of Tilsit in July 1807. Decimated Prussia now lay at Napoleon I's mercy. Napoleon I allowed Frederick William III to keep his throne, but took away most of the Hohenzollern lands.

The Prussian Army was unprepared for war against Napoleon I. The army's deficiencies at Jena and Auerstädt reflected Prussian's failure to prepare for the inevitable, an all-out war against France. However, the era of the Prussian reform movement was already underway. The reform movement began with Frederick William III and the Prussian high nobility in the bureaucracy and army.[35] Baron Heinrich Friedrich Karl von Stein, Frederick William III's Chief Minister, began the reform of the Prussian government in 1807.[36] Napoleon I forced Frederick William III to dismiss Stein in 1808, but Prince Hardenberg as Prussian State Chancellor (Staatskanzler) (1810-22), a position without precedent in Prussian history, continued government reform after 1810. As for military reform, General Gerhard von Scharnhorst, the Prussian Minister of War, established the Militärische Gesellschaft in Berlin.[37] Even so, Scharnhorst's project for changing Prussia's military command structure and military was a long-term program. Prussian military reformers wanted to reform the ways of thinking about military

32.  For Napoleon's war aims in Germany, see Herbert A.L. Fisher, *Studies in Napoleonic Statesmanship, Germany* (Oxford: Clarendon Press, 1903).

33.  See David G. Chandler, *Jena 1806: Napoleon Destroys Prussia* (Botley: Osprey, 1996).

34.  McKay and Scott, 313.

35.  Holborn, *A History of Modern Germany*, 2:394-95.

36.  See Guy Stanton Ford, *Stein and the Era of Reform in Prussia, 1807-1815* (Princeton: Princeton University Press, 1922).

37.  Trevor N. Dupuy, *A Genius for War: The German Army and General Staff, 1807-1945* (Fairfax, VA: Hero, 1984), 18; Hajo Holborn, "The Prusso-German School: Moltke and the Rise of the General Staff," in *Makers of Modern Strategy from Machiavelli to the Nuclear Age*, ed. Peter Paret (Princeton: Princeton University Press, 1986), 283-84.

doctrine (how the army fought), improve the army's administration and logistics, and change the organization of the military (the creation of a divisional system).[38] Nonetheless, Prussia remained under French domination, and, as such, provided 20,000 military troops to support Napoleon I's invasion of Russia in 1812.[39]

Napoleon I's retreat from Russia provided a window of opportunity for Prussia. General Ludwig von Yorck boldly signed the Convention of Tauroggen, declaring Prussian neutrality, in the French war with Russia in December 1812. Shortly thereafter, in February 1813, Prussia allied with Russia against Napoleon I in the Treaty of Kalisch. Tsar Alexander I agreed that Prussia would gain Saxony in exchange for former Prussian lands in Poland.[40] In the upcoming struggle Frederick William III was able to mobilize 280,000 men for his army and established the Landswehr and Landsturm in 1813.[41] The Prussians were fueled by their hatred for Napoleon I. Field Marshal Gebhard Leberecht von Blücher commanded the Prussian Army. The Prussian General Staff included Gebhard von Scharnhorst and Neithard von Gneisenau. Austria joined the war against France in August 1813. The coalition defeated Napoleon I at the Battle of Leipzig in October, freeing all of Germany east of the Rhine River.[42] Soon Bavaria, Württemberg, and Baden joined forces against France. The allied armies, commanded by Prince Karl von Schwarzenberg, invaded France at the beginning of 1814.[43]

In March 1814, the Great Powers allied against Napoleon I established the Quadruple Alliance of Chaumont. It included Russia, Prussia, Austria, and Britain. Schwarzenberg and Blücher quickly captured Paris. At the end of March, Tsar Alexander I of Russia and King Frederick William III of Prussia

---

38.   The reforms are discussed in Gordon A. Craig, *The Politics of the Prussian Army, 1650-1945* (Oxford: Clarendon Press, 1955); William O. Shanahan, *Prussian Military Reforms, 1786-1813* (New York: Columbia University Press, 1945); Peter Paret, *Yorck and the Era of Prussian Reform, 1807-1815* (Princeton: Princeton University Press, 1966); and Martin Kitchen, *A Military History of Germany from the Eighteenth Century to the Present Day* (London: Weidenfeld and Nicolson, 1975).

39.   Holborn, *A History of Modern Germany*, 2:415.

40.   F.R. Bridge and Roger Bullen, *The Great Powers and the European States System, 1814-1914*, 2 ed. (London: Longman, 2004), 21.

41.   Holborn, *A History of Modern Germany*, 2:424.

42.   See Peter Hofschröer, *Leipzig 1813: Battle for the Nations* (Botley: Osprey, 1993); George Nafziger, *Napoleon at Leipzig: The Battle of the Nations, 1813* (Chicago: Emperor's Press, 1997); Peter Hofschröer, *Lutzen and Bautzen 1813* (Botley: Osprey, 2001); and J.P. Riley, *Napoleon and the World War of 1813: Lessons in Coalition Warfighting* (London: Frank Cass, 2001).

43.   The military alliance is examined in Gordon A. Craig, "Problems of Coalition Warfare: The Military Alliance against Napoleon, 1813-1814," in *War, Politics and Diplomacy* (London: Weidenfeld and Nicolson, 1966).

entered Paris as the victors. The Quadruple Alliance soon dictated the First Peace of Paris (May 1814). Representatives of the Great Powers met at the Congress of Vienna to decide the outstanding territorial issues in October 1814.[44] Prussia was represented by Frederick William III, Chancellor Hardenberg, and Wilhelm von Humboldt.[45] The Quadruple Alliance was most concerned about establishing a balance of power in Europe. Hardenberg sought to establish a role for Prussia that rewarded it for the Prussian Army's major contribution in defeatin Napoleon I. Frederick William III wanted to annex all of Saxony while Russia took control of Poland. But, Count Clemens von Metternich, the Austrian Foreign Minister, objected to Prussian control of all of Saxony. It was agreed, nevertheless, that Prussia would control Danzig and West Prussia, Thorn, and the Province of Poznan. Prussia also gained the northern half of Saxony, Upper and Lower Lusatia, land around Wittemberg, northern Thuringia with Erfurt, as well as Stralsund and the island of Rügen. Moreover, Prussia acquired much territory on the northern left bank of the Rhine River.[46] The Prussian Rhineland was separated from the rest of Prussia by Hanover and Hesse-Kassel. In the meantime, the German Committee of Five, consisting of Prussia, Hanover, Austria, Bavaria, and Württemberg, examined the possibility of a German constitution. In June 1815, in the Treaty of Vienna, the Great Powers established the German Confederation (Deutscher Bund). The Federal Diet at Frankfurt-am-Main became the main governmental tool of the association. The German Confederation consisted of thirty-five monarchial states and four city republics. Austria would become the dominant power in the German Confederation.

Towards the end of the Congress of Vienna, the Great Powers received word that Napoleon I had escaped from exile on the island of Elba and returned to France to raise an army in an attempt to restore the French Empire. Napoleon I had to act fast, and defeat the British and Prussian armies in Belgium before the arrival of Russian and Austrian forces. He defeated

---

44.    The Congress of Vienna is examined in C.K. Webster, *The Congress of Vienna, 1814-1815* (London: G. Bell and Sons, 1945); Harold Nicolson, *The Congress of Vienna: A Study in Allied Unity, 1812-1822* (New York: Harcourt, Brace and Company, 1946); Henry A. Kissinger, *A World Restored: Metternich, Castlereagh and the Problems of Peace, 1812-1822* (Boston: Houghton Mifflin, 1957); Douglas Dakin, "The Congress of Vienna, 1814-1815, and Its Antecedents," in *Europe's Balance of Power, 1815-1818*, ed. Alan Sked (London: Macmillan, 1979); and Tim Chapman, *The Congress of Vienna: Origins, Processes and Results* (London: Routledge, 1998).

45.    Lawrence J. Baack, *Christian Bernstorff and Prussia: Diplomacy and Reform Conservatism, 1818-1832* (New Brunswick: Rutgers University Press, 1980), 16.

46.    Holborn, *A History of Modern Germany*, 2:439-40.

Blücher and Gneisenau at the Battle of Ligny in June 1815.[47] Even so, two days later, British and Prussian forces defeated Napoleon I at the Battle of Waterloo. In September 1815, the Tsar, while at the Congress of Vienna, created the Holy Alliance of Russia, Austria, and Prussia to protect Europe against revolutionary forces. Moreover, as a result of Napoleon I's action in 1814-15, France was forced to accept the Second Peace of Paris (November 1815). In this treaty, Prussia gained Saarbrücken and Saarlouis.[48]

## Concert of Europe, German Confederation, and Customs Union

After the Napoleonic Wars, the Habsburg Empire dominated the politics of the German Confederation and the Italian states. The period from 1815 to 1848 is generally known as the Age of Metternich. Metternich was the Chancellor (1821-48) and Foreign Minister (1809-48) of Austria. Metternich and Austria played a key role in the diplomacy of the Concert of Europe.[49] Austria sought to restore the conservative order in Europe. The Habsburg Empire contained many different ethnic groups, including Germans, Poles, Croats, Serbs, Czechs, Italians, Magyars, Rumanians, Ruthenians, Slovaks, and Slovenes.[50] As such, the Austrian Foreign Minister and the Metternich System attempted to prevent the spread of nationalism and liberalism. What was the Metternich System? The historian Alan Sked has written:

> Essentially it is that Metternich strove to uphold the interests of an aristocratic, European social order through maintaining the 1815 Settlement by means of a repressive alliance of monarchical states, whose internal and external security were to be preserved by military and police co-operation as well as by efficient and centralised bureaucratic rule. In this way he hoped to exorcise the threat of revolution and so maintain the *status quo*.[51]

47.    Peter Hofschröer, *1815, The Waterloo Campaign: Wellington, His German Allies, and the Battles of Ligny and Quatre Bras* (London: Greenhill Press, 1998) and Peter Hofschröer, *1815, The Waterloo Campaign: The German Victory, From Waterloo to the Fall of Napoleon* (London: Greenhill Press, 1999) stress the Prussian contribution to the defeat of Napoleon.

48.    Holborn, *A History of Modern Germany*, 2:449.

49.    Austrian foreign policy is examined in Alan Palmer, *Metternich* (London: Weidenfeld and Nicolson, 1972); Paul W. Schroeder, *Metternich's Diplomacy at Its Zenith, 1820-1823* (New York: Greenwood, 1969); F.R. Bridge, *The Habsburg Monarchy among the Great Powers, 1815-1918* (New York: Berg, 1990); and Barbara Jelavich, *The Habsburg Empire in European Affairs, 1814-1918* (Hamden, CT: Archon, 1975).

50.    Jelavich, *The Habsburg Empire in European Affairs, 1814-1918*, 7.

51.    Alan Sked, "The Metternich System, 1815-1848," in *Europe's Balance of Power, 1815-1818*, ed. Alan Sked (London: Macmillan, 1979), 98.

Metternich had a central role in the diplomacy of the Concert of Europe from 1815 to 1822. During this time, Tsar Alexander I commanded the dominant Russian Army,[52] Viscount Castlereagh negotiated for Britain while Frederick William III, Chancellor Hardenberg, and Foreign Minister Christian Günther von Bernstorff (1818-1832) represented Prussia.[53] Bernstorff has been called the first modern Prussian Foreign Minister by some historians.[54] But Prussia was the weakest of the Great Powers of Europe.

In 1818, France was restored as a Great Power in the Concert of Europe, making it a Quintuple Alliance, at the Congress of Aix-la-Chapelle (Aachen). France had a larger standing army than Austria or Prussia.[55] France, Russia, Austria, and Prussia were interested in maintaining the conservative order in Europe. Then, in January 1820, a liberal revolt broke out against King Ferdinand VII of Spain. The spirit of revolution quickly spread across southern Europe. Soon, in July, a revolt broke out in the Kingdom of the Two Sicilies. Consequently, the Great Powers met at the Congress of Troppau to discuss the spread of revolution. They issued the Protocol of Troppau in November 1820. In this document, Austria, Russia, and Prussia reaffirmed the principle of intervention by the Great Powers if revolution in one state posed a threat to others. Two months later, in January 1821, the Great Powers at the Congress of Laibach authorized Austria to put down the liberal rebellion in the Kingdom of the Two Sicilies. Then, in 1822, the Congress of Verona, attended by Frederick William III, Hardenberg, and Bernstorff, considered the rebellion in Spain. France, with the diplomatic support of Russia, invaded and crushed the liberal rebellion in Spain.[56] Austria and Britain opposed the action. But, by this time, Metternich was conducting the foreign policy of a financially and military weakened state.[57] The Concert was quickly falling apart. Even so, the Great Powers handled the issues of Greek independence at the London Conference

---

52.    Russian foreign policy is discussed in Alan Palmer, *Alexander I: Tsar of War and Peace* (London: Weidenfeld and Nicolson, 1974); Janet M. Hartley, *Alexander I* (London: Longman, 1994); Patricia Kennedy Grimsted, *The Foreign Ministers of Alexander I: Political Attitudes and the Conduct of Russian Diplomacy, 1801-1825* (Berkeley: University of California Press, 1969); and W. Bruce Lincoln, *Nicholas I: Emperor and Autocrat of All the Russias* (London: Allen Lane, 1978).

53.    Baack, 41.

54.    Ibid., 98.

55.    Roger Bullen, "France and Europe, 1815-1848: The Problems of Defeat and Recovery," in *Europe's Balance of Power, 1815-1818*, ed. Alan Sked (London: Macmillan, 1979), 129.

56.    Roy Bridge, "Allied Diplomacy in Peacetime: The Failure of the Congress 'System', 1815-1823," in *Europe's Balance of Power, 1815-1818*, ed. Alan Sked (London: Macmillan, 1979), 44-52.

57.    Sked, "The Metternich System, 1815-1848," 107-8.

in 1830,[58] and Belgian independence at the London Conference in 1831.[59] The cornerstone to Metternich's foreign policy was a strong alliance with the conservative powers of Russia and Prussia.

In the meantime, Prussia pursued an economic policy that gradually increased its influence in the German Confederation. Karl Georg Maassen, the Prussian Director-General of Customs, used the Customs Law of 1818 to rid the Prussian state of internal import taxes and to implement low tariffs at Prussian external borders to encourage trade. Hesse-Kassel joined the Prussian Customs Union in 1828, followed by a merger of the Prussian Customs Union and South German Customs Union as the Prusso-German Customs Union Zollervein) in 1833-34.[60] Baden and Nassau joined the Customs Union in 1836. All of Germany except Brunswick, Hanover, Oldenburg, Holstein, Austria, and the Hanseatic cities were connected to the Zollervein. Many viewed this economic union as a step towards political union under Prussian leadership.[61] In addition to the Customs Union, the building of railroads contributed to the economic rise of Germany. The first German railroad was built in 1835. The Potsdam to Berlin railroad was completed in 1838, Berlin to Anhalt in 1841, Berlin to Stettin in 1842, Berlin to Frankfurt-on-the-Oder in 1842, Berlin to Hamburg in 1846, and Berlin to Cologne in 1848.[62]

## Revolutions of 1848 and Frankfurt Parliament

In 1840, Frederick William IV (1840-61) became the King of Prussia.[63] He was a romanticist, deeply inspired by poetic and mystical ideas. The monarch sought greater political freedom and stronger national unity in Prussia. He was interested in obtaining these objectives through the rule of the estates, not through constitutionalism. In 1841 he gave the provincial assemblies the right to elect commit-

---

58.    The Greek Question is investigated in Douglas Dakin, *The Greek Struggle for Independence, 1821-1833* (Berkeley: University of California Press, 1973).

59.    See J.S. Fishman, *Diplomacy and Revolution: The London Conference of 1830 and the Belgian Revolt* (Amsterdam, CHEV, 1988) and J.A. Betley, *Belgium and Poland in International Relations, 1830-1831* (The Hague: Mouton, 1960).

60.    Brendan Simms, *The Struggle for Mastery in Germany, 1779-1850* (New York: St. Martin's Press, 1998), 111-12. See also David T. Murphy, "Prussian Aims for the Zollervein, 1828-1833," *The Historian* 53 (1991).

61.    Holborn, *A History of Modern Germany*, 2:462.

62.    Ibid., 3:11.

63.    Frederick William IV's foreign policy is examined in Winfried Baumgart, "Zur Aussenpolitik Friedrich Wilhelms IV, 1840-1858," *Jahrbuch für die Geschichte Mittel-und Ostdeutschland* 39 (1987).

tees to meet in Berlin and discuss legislation for Prussia. But, Frederick William IV informed the committees in 1842 that they were not a popular assembly. Even so, the King was forced to agree to the summoning of the United Landtag (combined provincial assemblies) in an attempt to acquire funding for financial difficulties in 1847. He, nevertheless, informed the United Landtag that it had no power concerning legislation, the budget, and it could not hold regular meetings. The Prussian liberals were very upset at the situation.

In February 1848, revolution broke out in France and spread across Europe. The Habsburgs became busy with revolts by the Hungarians, Czechs, Croats, Venetians, and Lombards. By the end of July Austria temporarily ceased to be a factor in international politics. In the meantime, the German states of Württemberg, Saxony, Hanover, Bavaria, and Prussia experienced uprisings. The instigators called for liberal reforms and the unification of Germany. Revolt broke out in Berlin, the fourth largest city in Europe, with a population of 400,000, in March 1848.[64] The demonstrators erected barricades while the Prussian Army attempted to clear the streets. Frederick William IV, however, agreed to make concessions to the liberals instead of killing his people. He agreed to liberal reforms, including parliamentary elections, a constitution, and the freedom of the press. Furthermore, the King announced his willingness to work towards giving a united Germany a constitution.

In March 1848, liberal nationalists agreed to convene a German National Assembly (Nationalversammlung) at Frankfurt-on-the-Main. Eight hundred and thirty-one deputies from the German states met at the Frankfurt Parliament in May 1848.[65] The parliament was predominately a middle-class body, consisting of lawyers, professors, and businessmen. They discussed the possibility of German unification, a liberal German constitution, and the issue of a grossdeutsch or kleindeutsch solution to German unification. Those individuals who favored a grossdeutsch solution to German unification wanted the Habsburgs to accept the German imperial crown. Those representatives that sought to exclude the Habsburgs and Austria from a unified Germany argued that the Habsburgs would oppose a liberal constitution, and that much of the Habsburg Empire was inhabited by non-Germans. The majority of the representatives supported a kleindeutsch solution to the German Question. In March 1849, the German National Assembly created the Frankfurt Constitution. The constitution created a federal

64.    David E. Barclay, "Revolution and Counter-Revolution in Prussia, 1840-50," in *Modern Prussian History, 1830-1947*, ed. Philip G. Dwyer (London: Pearson Education, 2001), 69.

65.    For the history of the German National Assembly, see Frank Eyck, *The Frankfurt Parliament, 1848-1849* (New York: St. Martin's Press, 1968).

state under a hereditary German Emperor, ministers responsible to the parliament, and a two-house parliament of the Upper House (Staatenhaus) and Lower House (Volkshaus). The federal government would have complete control over foreign policy, the army, and the regulation of economic issues. Next, the Frankfurt Parliament elected Frederick William IV as the German Emperor. But, the Prussian monarch rejected the offer. He declared that a popular elected assembly did not have the authority to grant royal titles. Afterwards, the Frankfurt Assembly quickly melted away.

The Habsburg Empire recovered from the revolts of 1848-49.[66] Prince Alfred Windischgrätz crushed the Czech revolutionary movement in Prague in June 1848. General Joseph Radetzky defeated the Piedmontese Army at the Battle of Custozza and restored Habsburg control over Lombardy in July. Windischgrätz regained control of Vienna in October. Two months later, in December, Francis Joseph I (1848-1916) became the new ruler of the Habsburg Empire. In March 1849, Radetzky decisively defeated the Piedmontese Army at the Battle of Novara. The Habsburg Army then regained control of Venetia in August. And, finally, the Habsburg Army with the aid of Russia crushed the Hungarian revolt in August 1849. Now, with Prince Felix Schwarzenberg as the leading Austrian minister, the Habsburg Monarchy sought to restore Austria's position in Germany.

The reconquest of Vienna by Windischgrätz encouraged Frederick William IV to regain control of Prussia. While the Frankfurt Parliament was in session, the Prussian aristocrats and army regained control of Berlin. In November 1848, Count Friedrich Wilhelm von Brandenburg, the King's uncle, took over the position as Minister-President of Prussia. He was aided by Baron Otto von Manteuffel, the Prussian Minister of the Interior. General Friedrich von Wrangel deployed 13,000 troops to Berlin.[67] In December, Frederick William IV dissolved the Prussian National Assembly that was sitting in Berlin and debating a constitution for Prussia. The assembly had proposed that army officers take an oath of loyalty to the constitution, not the monarch, and that titles and privileges of nobility be abolished. Moreover, the assembly wanted to strike the words "by the grace of God" from the royal title.[68] Frederick William IV and his conservative advisers viewed this as a direct attack upon the monarchy. As a consequence,

---

66.   See Alan Sked, *The Survival of the Habsburg Empire: Radetzky, the Imperial Army, and the Class War, 1848* (London: Longman, 1979) and A.J.P. Taylor, *The Italian Problem in European Diplomacy, 1847-1849* (Manchester: Manchester University Press, 1934).

67.   Barclay, "Revolution and Counter-Revolution in Prussia, 1840-50," 81.

68.   Jonathan Sperber, *The European Revolutions, 1848-1851* (Cambridge: Cambridge University Press, 1994), 218.

the King issued his own constitution for Prussia by royal decree.[69] The constitution established a two-house parliament. The Upper House (Herrenhaus) consisted of the Junker nobility and the Lower House (Landtag) was elected by universal manhood suffrage. The Landtag was given power to vote new laws and taxes. However, the monarch retained an absolute veto over all legislation. He also kept the authority to suspend civil liberties and rule by royal decree.

At this point, Frederick William IV aimed at creating a unified Germany himself. The King, under the direction of General Joseph Maria von Radowitz in foreign affairs from 1849 to 1850,[70] wanted to create a larger German confederation to include the German states and the whole of the Austrian lands, German and non-German, thus creating a great Middle European bloc with immense economic possibilities.[71] This large empire, the so-called Erfurt Union, was to be divided into two parts for administrative purposes. One part would be an inner confederation (Prussian Union) made up of non-Habsburg Germany, under the leadership of Prussia. The other part, the Habsburg Monarchy, would remain intact. By August 1849, Prussia, Hanover, Saxony, Hesse-Darmstadt, Mecklenburg, Baden, Brunswick and several other territories agreed to discuss the Prussian Union. But, by this time, the Habsburg Empire had crushed the rebellions within its borders and now sought to restore control over Germany. In February 1850, Austria engineered the League of the Four Kings (Bavaria, Württemberg, Saxony, and Hanover) against Prussia. This situation caused Frederick William IV to hesitate. As a result, Prince Schwarzenberg convened a meeting at Frankfurt-on-the-Main, without inviting Prussia, and declared the revival of the Plenary Council of the Federal Diet of the German Confederation in May 1850. Austria, Bavaria, and Württemberg formed an alliance aimed at forcing Prussia to submit to the will of the Habsburg Empire. Radowitz, the Prussian Foreign Minister (1850), proposed mobilizing the Prussian Army. However, Brandenburg and Manteuffel advised Frederick William IV to dismiss Radowitz and call off the attempt to form a Prussian Union. The final action came after an Austrian ultimatum backed by Tsar Nicholas I of Russia. Austrian Emperor Francis Joseph I had marched an army to the Prussian frontier and was ready to wage war.[72]

---

69.    Roger Price, *The Revolutions of 1848* (Atlantic Highlands: Humanities Press International, 1988), 92.

70.    See Warren B. Morris, *The Road to Olmütz: The Career of Joseph Maria von Radowitz* (New York: Revisionist Press, 1976).

71.    Barclay, "Revolution and Counter-Revolution in Prussia, 1840-50," 84.

72.    Geoffrey Wawro, *The Austro-Prussian War: Austria's War with Prussia and Italy in 1866* (Cambridge: Cambridge University Press, 1996), 38.

Prussia backed down. Consequently, Manteuffel, the new Prussian Minister-President and Foreign Minister (1850-58), and Prince Schwarzenberg signed the Punctation of Olmütz in November 1850. In the summer of 1851 Austria resumed its leadership over the Federal Diet in Frankfurt-on-the-Main and the German Confederation.

## Crimean War and the Italian Wars of Liberation

The Habsburg Empire controlled Germany and Italy in the 1850s. However, war and revolution threatened Austria's role in Italy as well as the political stability of Europe during this time. The outbreak of the Crimean War (1853-56) resulted in the temporary breakup of the Concert of Europe. Britain, France, the Ottoman Empire, and Sardinia-Piedmont fought Russian forces in the Crimea and the Black Sea area. Austria and Prussia declared neutrality during the conflict. However, the Habsburg occupation of the Danubian Principalities of Moldavia and Wallachia in 1854 caused friction with the Russian Empire.[73] The war left Russia a weakened state.[74] But, the conflict also resulted in the diplomatic isolation of Austria. Norman Rich has written:

> Austria was isolated. During the Crimean War both sides had confidently anticipated Austrian backing: Russia had expected Austria to support the 1815 peace settlement against France and to repay a debt of gratitude for recent military and diplomatic aid [in Hungary]; Britain and France had been certain Austria would recognize the necessity of halting Russian expansion in southeastern Europe, where vital Austrian interests were at stake. Austria's neutrality antagonized all the belligerents, with the result that until 1879 Austria was without friends among the great powers.[75]

In 1858, Napoleon III of France sought an alliance with Sardinia-Piedmont in an attempt to liberate Italy from Habsburg control. In July, the French Emperor secretly met with Count Camillo di Cavour, the Prime Minister of Sardinia-Pied-

---

73.    For the Crimean War, see David M. Goldfrank, *The Origins of the Crimean War* (London: Longman, 1994) and Winfried Baumgart, *The Crimean War, 1853-1856* (London: Arnold, 1999). Austrian policy is the focus of Paul W. Schroeder, *Austria, Great Britain, and the Crimean War: The Destruction of the European Concert* (Ithaca: Cornell University Press, 1972). Prussian neutrality is discussed in Emanuel Halicz, *Danish Neutrality during the Crimean War (1853-1856): Denmark between the Hammer and Anvil*, trans. Jane Cave (Odense: Odense University Press, 1977).

74.    John Shelton Curtiss, *Russia's Crimean War* (Durham: Duke University Press, 1979), 526-29.

75.    Norman Rich, *Great Power Diplomacy, 1814-1914* (New York: McGraw-Hill, 1992), 121.

mont, at Plombières. The two leaders made an alliance against Austria in January 1859. Napoleon III and Cavour agreed to force Austria out of northern Italy. Afterwards, the House of Savoy would rule over Upper Italy, and France would acquire Nice and Savoy.[76] Thus, in April 1859, Cavour provoked Austria to launch an attack against Sardinia-Piedmont.[77] Napoleon III had the task of keeping Austria diplomatically isolated. He acquired benevolent neutrality from Russia by way of a treaty. The neutral powers of Britain, Prussia, and Russia condemned the Austrian attack against Sardinia-Piedmont. Shortly thereafter, in May, revolts engineered by the National Society broke out in Modena, Tuscany, and Parma against Habsburg control. The Franco-Piedmontese armies halted the Austrian advance into Piedmont, defeating the Habsburg forces at the Battles of Montebello and Palestro (May 1859), and forced the enemy to retreat into Lombardy. Then, in June, Franco-Piedmontese troops defeated the Austrian forces at the Battle of Magenta, compelling the Austrians to withdraw from Lombardy. At the same time, the Papal legations of Ravenna, Ferrara, and Bologna rose in rebellion. The Franco-Piedmontese armies then defeated the Austrians in the Battle of Solferino (June 1859). Venetia was open to a Franco-Piedmont invasion. However, at this point, Prussia and Russia pressured Napoleon III to come to terms with the Austrian Empire. Moreover, Napoleon III did not want to unite northern and central Italy under the leadership of Victor Emmanuel II of Sardinia-Piedmont, which would become a threat to French interests. Therefore, Napoleon III and Francis Joseph I agreed to an armistice in the Convention of Villafranca in July 1859. Piedmont gained most of Lombardy in the Peace of Zürich (November 1859). The rulers of the Italian states were supposed to be restored to their thrones. But, the Italian states of Parma, Modena, Tuscany, and Romagna refused to accept their former rulers and declared their union with Piedmont in March 1860. Cavour gained Napoleon III's acceptance of Piedmont's control of most of north Italy by ceding Savoy and Nice to France. This was followed by Giuseppe Garibaldi's conquest of the Kingdom of the Two Sicilies and Piedmont's annexation of Naples, Sicily, the Marches, and Umbria in 1860. The Kingdom of Italy was proclaimed by the first Italian Parliament, with

---

76.   C.J. Bartlett, *Peace, War and the European Powers, 1814-1914* (New York: St. Martin's Press, 1996), 73.

77.   The Italian Wars of Independence are discussed in Frank J. Coppa, *The Origins of the Italian Wars of Independence* (London: Longman, 1992); Harry Hearder, *Cavour* (London: Longman, 1994); Arnold Blumberg, *A Carefully Planned Accident: The Italian War of 1859* (Selinsgrove: Susquehanna University Press, 1990); Charles W. Hallberg, *Franz Joseph and Napoleon III, 1852-1864: A Study of Austro-French Relations* (New York: Bookman Associates, 1955); and Patrick Turnbull, *Solferino: The Birth of a Nation* (New York: St. Martin's Press, 1985).

Victor Emmanuel II as the monarch and a government based on the Piedmontese constitution of 1848. The power of Austria in Italy was gravely wounded in the Italian War of 1859. The Habsburgs were left with control of only Venetia. Moreover, the Austrian government was disorganized and in financial ruin. Austria also remained without an ally.

## Constitutional Crisis in Prussia

In 1858, Frederick William IV of Prussia was declared insane. His brother, William, served as Prince-Regent until the monarch's death. William wanted to get firm control of the army and use the military as a tool to enhance the power of Prussia. There had been no major reorganization of the army for fifty years. Without reform Prussia would not be able to maintain the status of a Great Power. The Prince-Regent, with the advice of General Edwin von Manteuffel, began exercising royal command over the Prussian Army through a Royal Military Cabinet in 1858. Manteuffel was the head of the Royal Military Cabinet. In 1859, the Prince-Regent selected General Albrecht von Roon as the Minister of War. Both General Roon and General Helmuth von Moltke, the Chief of the General Staff (1857-87), had the task of reforming the army in light of the increasing international tension in Europe. Prince William wanted to build a truly professional army, and he believed in his right, as head of the army, to make military reforms and secure the funding necessary to accomplish this goal. The Prince-Regent wanted to increase the size of the professional Prussian Army from 50,000 to 110,000. He also wanted to cut the size of the Landwehr (National Guard), place the Landwehr under the command of Prussian Army officers, as well as enforce the three-year term of service in the Landwehr. Prince William wanted the Landwehr to serve as an army reserve.[78] The Prince-Regent and the conservatives viewed the Landwehr as a dangerous democratic institution. The Landwehr had the makings of a parliamentary army. Nonetheless, the liberal majority in the Landtag challenged Prince William's rights concerning the army and the raising of taxes to fund army reform. The Prussian Parliament was willing to increase the grant for the Prussian Army, but the liberal majority wanted to keep the Landwehr as well as reduce the period of military service from three to two years. In 1860, the Prussian Parliament authorized a one year grant for the army. Meanwhile, the liberals organized into the German Progressive Party and became stronger opposition to Prince William's army reform efforts. In Septem-

---

78.    Kitchen, *A Military History of Germany*, 98; William Carr, *The Origins of the Wars of German Unification* (London: Longman, 1991), 51-52.

ber 1862, the Landtag voted 308 to 11 not to grant the monarchy further funds for army reform.[79] A stalemate developed in the attempt to pass army reform. Then, under the suggestion of General Roon, King William I (1861-88) summoned Otto von Bismarck-Schönhausen to become the Minister-President of Prussia and gain army reform through the Landtag in September 1862.

## Development of the Prussian Foreign Ministry

Although most of the European Great Powers possessed some form of foreign ministry as early as the seventeenth century,[80] the relatively late rise of Prussia and its autocratic nature delayed the establishment of the Prussian Foreign Ministry. Prussian rulers, especially the Elector Frederick William I (1640-88), King Frederick William I (1713-40) and King Frederick II (1740-86), preferred to manage their own diplomatic affairs with the assistance of a small staff. They treated foreign policy as a royal monopoly.

Elector Frederick William was instrumental in the rise of Brandenburg-Prussia as a Great Power. He controlled foreign policy decisions and ruled through a Privy Council (Geheimer Rat). The Privy Council considered foreign policy, territorial defense, economic and financial questions, and other issues of importance.[81] But, as Paul Gordon Lauren has pointed out, "this cumbersome process of *in plenum* discussions often resulted in delayed decisions, inefficiency, lack of secrecy, and the failure to develop specialized competence or permanence among the crown's servants."[82] In the 1640s, during the Thirty Years' War (1618-48), the Great Elector discussed important foreign policy issues with a small group of the Privy Council.[83] Privy Councilors were used to carry out the instructions of the Elector. During the first few years of his rule, several Privy Councilors greatly influenced foreign policy. These men were Konrad von Burgsdorff, Otto von Schwerin, Joachim Friedrich von Blumenthal, and George Friedrich von Waldeck.[84] In 1651, Frederick William reorganized the Privy Council and created an inner council or quasi-cabinet round himself. Within twenty years this inner council became the most important body.

---

79.   Kitchen, *A Military History of Germany*, 107. For the Prussian Army controversy of 1860-62, see Gerhard Ritter, *The Sword and the Sceptre: the Problem of Militarism in Germany*, 4 vols., (Coral Gables, FL: University of Miami Press, 1969-73), 1:121-60.

80.   Scott, *The Birth of a Great Power System, 1740-1815*, 133-37.

81.   Paul Gordon Lauren, *Diplomats and Bureaucrats: The First Institutional Responses to Twentieth-Century Diplomacy in France and Germany* (Stanford: Hoover Institution Press, 1976), 13-14.

82.   Ibid., 14.

83.   Dorwart, 46.

84.   Derek McKay, *The Great Elector*, 26, 64-67, 95.

He assigned the title of State Secretary (Geheimer Etatssekretarius) to the official responsible for external relations.[85] The Great Elector reserved foreign policy for private discussions with his favored ministers. But, after 1657, Frederick William was truly his own foreign minister.[86]

Elector Frederick III (later King Frederick I) (1688-1713) ruled Brandenburg-Prussia through various ministries. Frederick was less active in the administration of government than the Great Elector. He kept his father's councilors, including Paul von Fuchs, who influenced foreign policy.[87] Eberhard von Danckelmann, however, dominated Frederick's government from 1688 to 1697. As such, Danckelmann influenced Frederick's decision to side with the Grand Alliance against Louis XIV in the Nine Years' War (1688-97). Danckelmann was dismissed for the failed negotiations at the Peace of Rijswijk (1697) as well as his opposition to Frederick's quest for kingship.[88] Afterwards, Frederick was determined to be his own first minister. But, according to the historians Linda Frey and Marsha Frey, he "lacked the will, the stamina, the drive to direct the ministry and that task gradually fell to Wartenberg."[89] Count Johann Casimir Kolbe von Wartenberg was the dominant member of the newly created State Conference (Staatsconferenz). He had personal access to Frederick. Frederick now governed Brandenburg-Prussia from his own suite of offices within the royal residence, the so-called Cabinet (Kabinett).[90] He ceased presiding over the Privy Council and relegated all important issues to the State Conference. The State Conference included Fuchs and Heinrich Rüdiger von Ilgen who influenced foreign affairs. Wartenberg and Ilgen were the dominant officials in the formulation of foreign policy and the conduct of diplomatic negotiations after 1699.[91] As such, they advised the direction of Frederick's foreign policy that led to Brandenburg-Prussia's membership in the Grand Alliance against Louis XIV in the War of the Spanish Succession (1701-14) and the achievement of kingship for Frederick (1701). After the fall of Wartenberg in 1710, the Crown Prince and Ilgen were the main influences in the formulation of foreign policy.[92] This included the final

---

85.  Heinz Sasse, "Zur Geschichte des Auswärtigen Amts." *Mitteilungsblatt der Vereinigung der Angestellten des Auswärtigen Dienstes* 5 (May 1960), 107.

86.  McKay, 69; See also Schevill, 375.

87.  Frey and Frey, 71.

88.  Ibid., 74.

89.  Ibid., 85-86.

90.  Rodney Gothelf, "Frederick William I and the Beginnings of Prussian Absolutism, 1713-1740," in *The Rise of Prussia, 1700-1830*, ed. Philip G. Dwyer (London: Longman, 2000), 48.

91.  Frey and Frey, 72, 85-86, 145.

92.  Ibid., 207, 242.

years of the War of the Spanish Succession and Brandenburg-Prussia's involvement in the Great Northern War (1700-21). Ilgen served Frederick I and his son, Frederick William I, as the Director of Foreign Affairs from 1711 to 1728.

In 1713, King Frederick William I created a collegial structure when he added Baron Marquard Ludwig Printz and Count Christoph zu Dhona to the Department of Foreign Affairs. Nevertheless, Printz and Dhona were not equal members to Ilgen in the department.[93] Reinhold August Dorwart believed that, "the department for foreign affairs under Ilgen from 1713 to 1728 was more like a modern ministry, with a single, responsible head than a college with members of equal rank, all equally responsible."[94] Even so, in 1728, Frederick William I had Ilgen, who was retiring, submit his ideas for a real college of foreign affairs for Prussia. Following Ilgen's advice, the King established what unofficially became known as the Auswärtiges Amt (Department of External Affairs) in December 1728.[95] It became officially known as the Kabinettsministerium (Department of Foreign Affairs) in 1733.[96] Frederick William I established the department with two divisions within it. The department was headed by Count Adrian Bernhard von Borck, Baron Friedrich Ernst zu Inn und Knyphausen, and Ludwig Otto von Plotho as ministers. All three men had the title of Kabinettsminister.[97] Wilhelm Heinrich von Thulemeier had the rank of secretary. The collegial setup operated on the assumption that two or more ministers, under the direct supervision of Frederick William I, should together discuss foreign policy, meet diplomats, correspond with Prussia's own representatives in other capitals and conduct negotiations.[98] In foreign affairs, Frederick William I took advice from the Kabinettsministerium together with the Secret Chancery (Geheime Kanzlei) and the Cabinet. But day-to-day responsibility for Prussia's foreign policy was exercised by the Kabinettsministerium under the King's overall direction.[99] In 1730, Hein-

---

93.    Dorwart, 46-49.

94.    Ibid., 49.

95.    Scott, "Prussia's Emergence as a European Great Power, 1740-1763," 158; Scott, *The Birth of a Great Power System, 1740-1815,* 135; H.M. Scott, "Prussia's Royal Foreign Minister: Frederick the Great and the Administration of Prussian Diplomacy," in *Royal and Republican Sovereignty in Early Modern Europe: Essays in Memory of Ragnhild Hatton,* eds. Robert Oresko, G.C. Gibbs, and H.M. Scott (Cambridge: Cambridge University Press, 1997), 502-3.

96.    R. Koser, "Die Gründung des Auswärtigen Amts durch König Friedrich Wilhelm I. Im Jahre 1728," *Forschungen zur Brandenburgischen und Preussischen Geschichte* 2 (1889), 169-70.

97.    Lauren, 17.

98.    Scott, "Prussia's Emergence as a European Great Power, 1740-1763," 158; Scott, *The Birth of a Great Power System, 1740-1815,* 135; H.M. Scott, "Prussia's Royal Foreign Minister: Frederick the Great and the Administration of Prussian Diplomacy," 502-3.

99.    See note above.

rich von Podewils took the place of Knyphausen in the Kabinettsministerium, and in 1731, Thulemeier became a minister.[100] Commenting on the role of the three ministers, one historian has stated:

> The conduct of foreign policy…after 1728, was not entrusted to anyone as it had been to Ilgen before, but rather the King now conducted it himself from the Cabinet. Frederick William I was too guileless and ingenuous, too unsuspicious of the artful tricks of diplomacy to be a very successful foreign minister himself. It was his son who rose to fame as a master of diplomacy, with this same organization. The Kabinettsministerium continued its existence after Frederick William I as one of the three supreme organs of administration. When the order of rank among state offices was determined by Frederick William I it was placed above the General Directory (Generaldirektorium) and the Ministry of Justice.[101]

Frederick II of Prussia (1740-86) treated foreign policy as a royal monopoly. He acted as his own foreign minister.[102] In the first few weeks of his reign the King downgraded the role of the Kabinettsminister in foreign policy.[103] According to Hamish Scott:

> Frederick took over complete and direct responsibility for Prussian foreign policy, which he retained until the very end of his life. The experienced officials in the Kabinettsministerium and especially the leading adviser, Heinrich von Podewils, found their status and responsibilities downgraded to that of mere secretaries. They were mostly excluded from the formulation of policy, at least towards the major states, and while they continued to hold audiences with foreign diplomats, these became largely formal in nature: their own ignorance of Prussian policy meant that there was nothing to discuss. Policy was instead drawn up and executed by the King himself, who conducted the bulk of correspondence with Prussia's own diplomats and also negotiated personally with foreign representatives in Berlin.[104]

Frederick II alone made the decision to invade Silesia in 1740.[105]

---

100. Dorwart, 50-51; Scott, "Prussia's Royal Foreign Minister," 503.
101. Dorwat, 51-52.
102. Scott, "Prussia's Royal Foreign Minister," 500; Simms, *The Impact of Napoleon*, 39; Walter L. Dorn, "The Prussian Bureaucracy in the Eighteenth Century," in *Frederick the Great: A Profile*, ed. Peter Paret (New York: Hill and Wang, 1972), 65; Scott, *The Birth of a Great Powers System, 1740-1815*, 51.
103. Scott, *The Birth of a Great Power System, 1740-1815*, 51.
104. Scott, "Prussia's Emergence as a European Great Power, 1740-1763," 158-59.
105. Scott, *The Birth of a Great Power System, 1740-1815*, 51.

When Frederick the Great began his rule Prussia had three ministers in the Department of Foreign Affairs, including Heinrich von Podewils, Adrian Bernhard von Borck, and Wilhelm Heinrich von Thulemeier. Frederick II was in complete charge of foreign affairs that led to the two Silesian Wars (1740-42, 1744-45), Seven Years' War (1756-63), First Partition of Poland (1772), and War of the Bavarian Succession (1778-79). Thulemeier died in 1740 and was not replaced. Borck retired from the Kabinettsministerium in 1741, and was substituted by his nephew, Caspar Wilhelm von Borck. Baron Alexis von Mardeveld replaced the younger Borck in 1747. Then, in 1748, Count Karl Wilhelm Finck von Finckenstein supplanted Mardeveld in the Kabinettsministerium. Podewils was Frederick II's closest confidant concerning foreign affairs until his death in 1760. Even so, Podewils influence on the formulation of foreign policy was restricted. He, according to one historian, "had little influence upon Prussia's policy and was often left in ignorance by the secretive king."[106] Podewils was under strict orders from Frederick the Great. Hamish Scott has stressed that:

> Podewils...was to liaise with the diplomatic corps in the capital and could listen to anything a foreign representative wanted to say to him. But he must say nothing in reply without explicit orders from the king. The minister, in other words, was to be his royal master's ears and mouthpiece, but he was to have no share in the formulation of Prussian policy and would frequently remain ignorant of Frederick's real intentions.[107]

After the death of Podewils, Finckenstein was the sole Kabinettsminister. Count Ewald Friedrich von Hertzberg became the second Kabinettsminister towards the end of the Seven Years' War.[108] After 1763, Frederick II spent most of his time at Potsdam, out of contact from the government in Berlin. Few individuals, including Hertzberg and Finckenstein, had access to the monarch.[109] Both Hertzberg and Finckenstein would serve in the Kabinettsministerium beyond the reign of Frederick the Great.

In theory, the Prussian monarch was in full control of foreign affairs with the assistance of the Cabinet and Kabinettsministerium.[110] But, with the expanding scope of international relations in the French Revolutionary Wars (1792-1802),

---

106. Scott, "Prussia's Royal Foreign Minister," 508.
107. Ibid.
108. Hubatsch, 43, 223, 226-27.
109. Scott, "1763-1786: The Second Reign of Frederick the Great?," in *The Rise of Prussia, 1700-1830*. ed. Philip G. Dwyer (London: Longman, 2000), 182.
110. Simms, *The Impact of Napoleon*, 47.

Second Partition of Poland (1793), Third Partition of Poland (1795), and Napoleonic Wars (1803-15), Prussian foreign policy had expanded beyond the control of one man, the monarch. Instead, Count Hertzberg (1763-91), Count Finckenstein (1749-1800), Philip Karl von Alvensleben (1791-1802), and Count Heinrich Christian Kurt von Haugwitz (1792-1806) greatly influenced Prussian foreign policy during the reign of Frederick William II (1786-97).[111] In the early reign of Frederick William III (1797-1840), Cabinet secretaries Karl Friedrich Beyme, Councilor for the Internal Administration of Prussia, and Johann Wilhelm Lombard, Councilor for Foreign Affairs, had great influence over foreign affairs. Members of the Kabinettsministerium included Finckenstein, Alvensleben, and Haugwitz, along with newcomers Friedrich Wilhelm von der Schulenburg-Kehnert (1798-1802) and Karl August von Hardenberg (1803-6).[112]

Haugwitz and Hardenberg became Frederick William III's leading foreign policy advisers in 1802 and 1803.[113] But, after the Prussian catastrophe at Jena and Auerstädt (1806) at the hands of Napoleon, Frederick William III put his faith in Baron Heinrich Friedrich Karl von Stein as his Chief Minister (1807-8) and the Prussian Reform Movement. In this reform movement, Baron Stein encouraged the monarch to create ministries. He wanted the King to suppress the political role of the Cabinet secretaries and recognize the heads of ministries as the government's chief executives. He wanted the monarch to create a council of ministers and use this council to reach state decisions. He achieved his goal with the creation of five ministries in 1807, including the Ministry of Foreign Affairs (Ministerium der Auswärtigen Angelegenheiten) in Berlin.[114] Frederick William III chose Count August Friedrich Ferdinand Goltz to serve as the first Prussian Foreign Minister from 1808 to 1814. In 1810, Frederick William III divided the ministry into two sections. He created the Political and Commercial Divisions.[115] The Political Division was given the task of general administration of all political matters between Prussia and other states. The Commercial Division managed internal administrative matters, commercial and financial issues, consulates, boundaries, passports, and all other questions "not pertaining to high political affairs."[116] Then, in 1814, Frederick William III appointed Prince Karl August von Hardenberg, who was already the Prussian State Chancellor (1810-

---

111.   Ibid., 48-49.
112.   Ibid., 48-50.
113.   Scott, *The Birth of a Great Power System, 1740-1815*, 317-18.
114.   Holborn, *A History of Modern Germany*, 2:395-99.
115.   Lauren, 19.
116.   Sasse, 112.

22), as the Foreign Minister (1814-18). Hardenberg and the Foreign Ministry handled diplomatic affairs. Count Christian Günther von Bernstorff became the Foreign Minister in 1818, but Hardenberg controlled most diplomatic issues until 1822. Lawrence J. Baack has stated:

> Bernstorff did not assume substantial control over the formulation of Prussian foreign policy immediately after his appointment. Although he was granted the right to report directly to the King and was excused from attending the meetings of the Staatsministerium, in reality he was treated only slightly differently than the other ministers who served under Hardenberg's "Chancellor-system." Hardenberg retained control over the formulation of high policy, and,...Bernstorff turned to him frequently for instructions.[117]

Nevertheless, with the death of Hardenberg, Bernstorff became Frederick William III's primary adviser for foreign policy when the chancellor's duties were split between Karl Friedrich Heinrich von Wylich und Lottum and Bernstorff. Bernstorff received the additional titles of Geheimer Staats-und Kabinettsminister and Kabinettsminister. The King, however, had a strong influence over Prussian foreign policy.[118] In fact, the historian Alan Palmer has pointed out that "throughout most of the half-century which followed Waterloo the Berlin Foreign Ministry was a Cinderella in the Prussian bureaucracy, petted now and again by the King but kept firmly subordinate by the officer corps and the General Staff."[119] Moreover, according to Hajo Holborn, the Prussian Diplomatic Service did not attract outstanding talented men.[120]

In 1819, Bernstorff acquired a headquarters for the Prussian Foreign Ministry on the Wilhelmstrasse. Frederick William III had purchased the residence at Number 76 from the Russian government.[121] Tsar Alexander I had used it to house his ambassador to Prussia.[122] Like its French equivalent, the Quai d'Orsay, the Austrian known as the Ballhausplatz, and the British referred to as Whitehall, the newly created Prussian Foreign Ministry became known by the name of the

---

117.  Baack, 99.
118.  Ibid.
119.  Alan Palmer, *The Chancelleries of Europe* (London: George Allen and Unwin, 1983), 57.
120.  Hajo Holborn, "Diplomats and Diplomacy in the Early Weimar Republic," in *The Diplomats, 1919-1939*, eds. Gordon A. Craig and Felix Gilbert (Princeton: Princeton University Press, 1953), 123.
121.  Baack, 98.
122.  Prince Bernhard von Bülow, *Memoirs of Prince von Bülow*, trans. F.A. Voight and Geoffrey Dunlap, 4 vols. (Boston: Little, Brown and Company, 1931-32), 4:304-5; Lamar Cecil, *The German Diplomatic Service, 1871-1914* (Princeton: Princeton University Press, 1976), 3.

"Wilhelmstrasse" because of its physical presence on that particular street.[123] Since 1810 the staff of the Wilhelmstrasse had been divided into two divisions. There was a Political Section and an Administrative/Commercial Section.[124] Bernstorff supervised the entire Foreign Ministry. In 1824, Bernstorff appointed Moritz Haubold von Schönberg to manage the Administrative/Commercial Section while he directed the entire Foreign Ministry and the Political Section himself.[125] The ministry was staffed by thirty-eight officials who were kept very busy.[126] In 1831, the ailing Bernstorff again reorganized the Foreign Ministry. As Foreign Minister, he retained overall responsibility for the Foreign Ministry, while the State Secretary for Foreign Affairs, Johann Peter Friedrich von Ancillon, was responsible for the Political Section and Johan Albert Friedrich Eichhorn supervised the Commercial Section.[127] In 1832, Bernstorff resigned and was replaced by Ancillon (1832-37).[128]

King Frederick William IV (1840-61) exerted strong influence over foreign policy. In the view of Otto von Bismarck, the King controlled policy by appointing very few foreign policy experts to key positions in the Foreign Ministry, and then avoiding the advice that was offered.[129] The historian David E. Barclay argues that the King tended to treat his ministers as "instruments" of his own will.[130]

During the reign of Frederick William IV, the Prussian government was very unstable. There was a high turnover-rate during the first five years of the reign. The King appointed a succession of Foreign Ministers, Finance Ministers, and Interior Ministers from 1840 to 1844. Baron Heinrich Wilhelm Werther, who had taken over from Ancillon, was replaced by Count Mortimer Maltzan in 1841. Baron Heinrich von Bülow served as Prussian Foreign Minister from 1842

123. Paul Seabury, *The Wilhelmstrasse: A Study of German Diplomats under the Nazi Regime* (Berkeley: University of California Press, 1954), 1.
124. Baack, 100.
125. Ibid.
126. Ibid., 102.
127. Ibid., 279-80.
128. Ibid., 277, 295, 324, 326; Palmer, *The Chancelleries of Europe*, 58. Ancillon was the minister who turned down the young Otto von Bismarck-Schönhausen for a diplomatic position, stating that he was too rustic and unsophisticated to master the fine art of European diplomacy (Otto Pflanze, *Bismarck and the Development of Germany*, 3 vols. [Princeton: Princeton University Press, 1990], 1:43).
129. Prince Otto von Bismarck, *Bismarck: The Memoirs*, 2 vols., trans. A.J. Butler (New York: Howard Fertig, 1966), 1:308-9.
130. David E. Barclay, *Frederick William IV and the Prussian Monarchy, 1840-1861* (Oxford: Clarendon Press, 1995), 57.

till his death in 1845.[131] Baron Karl Ernst Wilhelm von Canitz und Dallwitz became the Foreign Minister in 1845.[132] The turmoil of 1848-49 led to a succession of Foreign Ministers, including Count Adolf Heinrich von Arnim-Boitzenburg (1848), Baron Heinrich Alexander von Arnim-Suckow (1848), Baron Alexander von Schleinitz (1848), Rudolf von Auerswald (1848), Count August Hermann von Dönhoff (1848), Count Friedrich Wilhelm von Brandenburg (1848), Franz August Eichmann (1848-49), Count Heinrich Friedrich von Arnim-Heinrichsdorff (1849-50), General Joseph Maria von Radowitz (1850), and Baron Otto Theodor von Manteuffel (1850-58).[133] Baron Alexander von Schleinitz served Prince-Regent William from 1858 to 1861. Then, as the Prussian monarch, William I (1861-88) was served by Count Albrecht von Bernstorff (1861-62) as the Foreign Minister.[134]

---

131.  Bülow, 4:321-22.

132.  Ibid., 58-59, 71.

133.  Ibid, 145; Bismarck, 1:83; Carr, *The Origins of the Wars of German Unification*, 57; Koch, 244-45; A.J.P. Taylor, *The Struggle for Mastery in Europe, 1848-1918* (Oxford: Clarendon Press, 1954), 41, 107; Friedrich von Holstein, *The Holstein Papers: The Memoirs, Diaries and Correspondence of Friedrich von Holstein, 1837-1909*, 4 vols. eds. Norman Rich and M.H. Fisher (Cambridge: Cambridge University Press, 1955-63), 1:4, 1:22, 1:94, 2:10.

134.  Holstein, 1:31; Bülow, 4:97; Taylor, 107, 129; Carr, *The Origins of the Wars of German Unification*, 114.

# 2

# *Bismarck, Foreign Policy, and the Wilhelmstrasse*

## Bismarck and German Unification

Otto von Bismarck was a Junker, an ultra-conservative, who had served in Prussia's United Landtag in 1847 and was elected to the Lower House of the Prussian Parliament in 1849. Frederick William IV appointed him to represent Prussia at the Federal Diet in Frankfurt-on-the-Main in 1851.[1] Bismarck went to Frankfurt as a strong supporter of Prussian cooperation with Austria in German affairs. But he quickly realized that Austria would never treat Prussia as an equal power. He soon became the leading opponent of the Habsburg's role in Germany. In March 1859, Prince-Regent William sent Bismarck to St. Petersburg to represent Prussia in Russia.[2] Three years later, in May 1862, Bismarck became the Prussian Ambassador to France.[3] He was then recalled to Berlin and appointed Minister-President in September 1862.[4]

The alliance between William I and Bismarck was uneasy. Otto von Bismarck would serve as Prussian Minister-President (1862-72, 1873-90) and Foreign Minister (1862-90).[5] The King wanted to enforce his rights to control the army and military issues. Bismarck, against the wishes of the monarch, sought to carry

---

1.   Prince Otto von Bismarck, *Bismarck: The Memoirs*, 2 vols., trans. A.J. Butler (New York: Howard Fertig, 1966), 1:86.
2.   Ibid., 1:234.
3.   Ibid., 1:276.
4.   Ibid, 1:294. Otto von Bismarck is examined in W.N. Medlicott, *Bismarck and Modern Germany* (London: English University Press, 1965); Erich Eyck, *Bismarck and the German Empire* (London: George Allen and Unwin, 1950); A.J.P. Taylor, *Bismarck: The Man and the Statesman* (London: Hamish Hamilton, 1955); Edward Crankshaw, *Bismarck* (New York: Viking, 1981); George O. Kent, *Bismarck and His Times* (Carbondale: Southern Illinois University Press, 1978); Alan Palmer, *Bismarck* (New York: Scribners, 1976); and Lothar Gall, *Bismarck: The White Revolutionary*, 2 vols., trans. J.A. Underwood (London: George Allen and Unwin, 1986).
5.   Otto von Bismarck was made a Count in 1865, and then a Prince in 1871.

out an adventurous foreign policy. Bismarck's main task, however, was to gain army reform. In this endeavor, the Minister-President noted that the Prussian constitution stated that the government budget must be agreed upon by the Chamber of Deputies, the Upper House, and the King. Bismarck stressed that if one of the three rejected the government budget there would be a governmental crisis not addressed in the constitution, and therefore, the government must collect the existing taxes and spend them until an agreement was reached between the three bodies. In his first address to the Chamber of Deputies, Bismarck stated his intentions concerning government and foreign policy. He stated that:

> Germany does not look at Prussia's liberalism but at her power–Prussia must keep her power together for the auspicious moment, which already has been missed a few times; the Prussian boundaries are not favorable for the formation of a healthy state. The great questions of the age are not settled by speeches and majority votes–this was the error of 1848-49–but by iron and blood.[6]

Then, "Bismarck announced," as Martin Kitchen has stated, "that if the Landtag refused to grant the funds which the government needed in order to govern effectively then he would simply collect the money regardless."[7] Bismarck would carry on the constitutional struggle with the Landtag for the next four years. In the meantime, the Prussian Army reorganized, grew in size, and updated its equipment. The Prussian Army increased from 100,000 troops in 1859 to 300,000 in 1866.[8] At the same time, Bismarck demanded that Austria recognize Prussia as its equal in the German Confederation. Prussia had economic and military might.

Bismarck pursued an aggressive foreign policy. In February 1863, the Minister-President sent General-Count Gustav von Alvensleben to St. Petersburg to assure Tsar Alexander II of Prussian support against the Polish rebellion in 1863. As a consequence, Prussia and Russia agreed to the Alvensleben Convention that provided for Prusso-Russian military cooperation against the Polish rebels.[9] Bismarck deployed half the Prussian Army to the Polish frontier. The Prussian action prevented Austria, Britain, and France from actively supporting the Polish

---

6.   Hajo Holborn, *A History of Germany*, 3 vols. (New York: Alfred A. Knopf, 1959-69), 2:162.
7.   Martin Kitchen, *A Military History of Germany from the Eighteenth Century to the Present Day* (London: Weidenfeld and Nicolson, 1975), 108.
8.   Geoffrey Wawro, *The Austro-Prussian War: Austria's War with Prussia and Italy in 1866* (Cambridge: Cambridge University Press, 1996), 16.
9.   Bismarck, *Memoirs*, 1:338-48.

rebels. As such, the rebellion was crushed by March 1864. Prussian action won Russian support for Bismarck's policies in the 1860s.[10]

While dealing with the Polish uprising, Bismarck was confronted by the Schleswig (Slesvig)-Holstein Question.[11] In March 1863, King Frederick VII of Denmark issued a royal proclamation that announced the Danish annexation of the Duchy of Schleswig. This was a clear violation of the London Protocol of 1852 in which the Great Powers guaranteed the inseparability of the Duchy of Schleswig and the Duchy of Holstein. The Danish king also handed Holstein, a member of the German Confederation, a new charter. Consequently, in July, the Federal Diet of the German Confederation responded by demanding that the two duchies be taken from Denmark and handed over to the German Duke Frederick of Augustenburg. Three months later, in October, the Federal Diet at Frankfurt voted for action and instructed Saxony and Hanover to furnish military forces for the conflict. Nevertheless, Frederick VII died a few weeks later, and Christian IX became the new ruler of Denmark. Twelve thousand Hanoverian and Saxon forces entered Holstein in December 1863.[12] At this point, in January 1864, Bismarck acquired an alliance with Austria, and then demanded that Denmark repeal the constitution. An Austro-Prussian army quickly moved from Hamburg and Lübeck into Holstein. Then, on 1 February, 57,000 Austro-Prussian forces under the command of General Frederick von Wrangel invaded Schleswig.[13] The allied army greatly outnumbered the Danish forces. Moreover, the Prussians were equipped with breech-loading Dreyse needle guns.[14] The international situation was favorable for the Austro-Prussian war against Denmark. With the collapse of the Concert of Europe during the Crimean War, Britain, France, and Russia could offer little opposition to Austria and Prussia.[15] As such, the Austro-Prussian armies quickly captured all of Schleswig except the fortifications at Dybbøl (Düppel) in eastern Schleswig. Dybbøl was one of the strongest fortifications in Europe at the time. But, in April, Austro-Prussian forces took the fortifications at Dyb-

---

10.    Norman Rich, *Great Power Diplomacy, 1814-1914* (New York: McGraw-Hill, 1992), 192.

11.    The Schleswig-Holstein Question is discussed in detail in Lawrence D. Steefel, *The Schleswig-Holstein Question* (Cambridge, MA: Harvard University Press, 1932) and William Carr, *Schleswig-Holstein, 1815-1848: A Study in National Conflict* (Manchester: Manchester University Press, 1963).

12.    Dennis Showalter, *The Wars of German Unification* (London: Arnold, 2004), 121.

13.    William Carr, *The Origins of the Wars of German Unification* (London: Longman, 1991), 84.

14.    Dennis Showalter, "The Prusso-German RMA, 1840-1871," in *The Dynamics of Military Revolution, 1300-2050*, eds. MacGregor Knox and Williamson Murray (Cambridge: Cambridge University Press, 2001), 97-98; Showalter, *The Wars of German Unification*, 140-41.

15.    Carr, *The Origins of the Wars of German Unification*, 78-79.

bøl,[16] and then the allies invaded Denmark. By June the allies had crushed the Danes. Christian IX was forced to give up the Duchies of Schleswig, Holstein, and Lauenburg to Austria and Prussia in the Peace of Vienna in October 1864. The Second Schleswig-Holstein War (1864) had resulted in a complete victory for Prussia and Austria. Bismarck soon took advantage of Austrian troubles with the Hungarians to achieve an advantage in Schleswig-Holstein. In 1860, Emperor Francis Joseph I had issued the October Diploma. This set up a federal constitution with an Imperial Diet for the Habsburg Empire. The Hungarians opposed this settlement and demanded the restoration of their own constitution. Then, in 1861, the Habsburg Emperor issued a new constitution, the February Patent, which set up a bicameral parliament with an electoral system designed to give the German middle class great influence over politics. Once again, the Hungarians demanded their own constitution. By 1865 Francis Joseph I was in the midst of tense relations with the Hungarians.[17] As a result, the Prussian Minister-President had the upper hand in negotiating the Convention of Gastein with Austria in August 1865.[18] In this agreement, Austria and Prussia accepted joint sovereignty over Schleswig-Holstein. But, Bismarck ensured that Prussia would administer the northern Duchy of Schleswig while Austria would control the southern Duchy of Holstein. It was agreed that the Duchy of Lauenburg would go to Prussia in exchange for 2.5 million Danish talers. Bismarck had set up a situation whereby Prussia had the advantage. The historian Norman Rich has stated:

> Austria's authority in Holstein was seriously compromised from the start. To ensure Prussia's access to Schleswig, Prussia was given the right to maintain permanent highway, railroad, and communication links through Holstein; Prussia was to be allowed to build a canal through Holstein connecting the Baltic and North seas; Austria and Prussia together were to recommend to the diet of the German Confederation the creation of a German fleet, based on the Holstein harbor of Kiel, which was to be under Prussian command. Both duchies were to become members of the Prussian-dominated German Customs Union, from which Austria was still excluded.[19]

---

16.   Gordon A. Craig, *The Politics of the Prussian Army, 1640-1945* (Oxford: Clarendon Press, 1955), 190.

17.   See A.J.P. Taylor, *The Habsburg Monarchy, 1809-1918: A History of the Austrian Empire and Austria-Hungary* (London: Hamish Hamilton, 1948); C.A. Macartney, *The Habsburg Empire, 1790-1918* (London: Weidenfeld and Nicolson, 1968); and C.A. Macartney, *A Short History of Hungary* (Edinburgh: Edinburgh University Press, 1962).

18.   Otto Pflanze, *Bismarck and the Development of Germany*, 3 vols. (Princeton: Princeton University Press, 1990), 1:258-64.

19.   Rich, *Great Power Diplomacy, 1814-1914*, 198.

As such, Austro-Prussian relations quickly deteriorated.

Bismarck sought Prussian control of both Schleswig and Holstein.[20] According to Geoffrey Wawro, the Prussian Minister-President had plotted throughout the Schleswig-Holstein War to annex the two duchies to Prussia in order to "round out Prussia's northern frontier and give it control of the Baltic Sea."[21] He also wanted Austrian recognition of Prussian dominance in northern Germany. There was always the possibility of war between Prussia and Austria. As a precaution, the Minister-President looked to diplomatically isolate Austria, especially from France and Russia. Bismarck believed that he had the support of Russia because of the Convention of Alvensleben, and Russian concerns over the possible growth of Austrian power. Britain was a minor concern. However, Bismarck had to deal with Napoleon III of France.[22] France would consider any political changes in Germany as a threat to French security. Even so, the French Emperor was looking for a diplomatic success for himself. He needed a success after the Austro-Prussian victory against Denmark as well as French difficulties in Mexico.[23]

In October 1865, Bismarck visited Napoleon III at the resort of Biarritz. He found the Emperor intrigued by the possibility of a German war. The Prussian Minister-President believed that France would remain neutral in a Prussian war against Austria. France had recently fought Austria in Italy in the late 1850s. Besides, Bismarck hinted that France could possibly acquire Belgium or Luxembourg as territorial compensation for any possible Prussian gains in an Austro-Prussian war.[24] In the meantime, Prussian General Helmuth von Moltke began making a detailed plan for war against Austria.[25] Then, in April 1866, Bismarck negotiated an alliance with Italy. The Minister-President agreed to help Italy obtain Venetia for joining a war against Austria.

Two months later, on 1 June 1866, Austria, ready to take a stand against Prussia, placed a motion before the Federal Diet of the German Confederation. Austria wanted the Federal Diet to determine the final status of Schleswig-Holstein. Austria had abandoned the Prussian alliance and Gastein Convention, and sought to reestablish a partnership with the Federal Diet. Bismarck responded to

---

20.   *APP*, 3:133.

21.   Wawro, *The Austro-Prussian War*, 42.

22.   For French foreign policy, see William E. Echard, *Napoleon III and the Concert of Europe* (Baton Rouge: Louisiana State University Press, 1983).

23.   See Nancy Nichols Barker, *The French Experience in Mexico, 1821-1861* (Chapel Hill: University of North Carolina Press, 1979).

24.   Carr, *The Origins of the Wars of German Unification*, 126; James F. McMillan, *Napoleon III* (London: Longman, 1991), 101.

25.   Martin Kitchen, *A Military History of Germany*, 116.

this action by declaring that Austria had violated its treaty commitments to Prussia. Consequently, Prussian forces entered Holstein to defend Prussia from an attack from the north on 8 June. The Austrian government responded by requesting and gaining support from the Federal Diet to mobilize all federal forces to protect the German Confederation on 14 June.[26] Austria wanted the German Confederation to punish Prussia for the invasion of Holstein.[27] Bavaria, Württemberg, Saxony, Hanover, Hesse-Darmstadt, Hesse-Kassel, Nassau, and the City of Frankfurt supported the Austrian cause. The Thuringian states, except for Saxony-Meiningen, along with Oldenburg, the two Mecklenburgs, Anhalt, Hamburg, Bremen, and Lübeck sided with Prussia.[28] The Prussian delegate at the Federal Diet denounced the Austrian action in the German Confederation, claiming that it violated the constitution of the German Confederation and was a declaration of war against Prussia.

Prussia had the most modern army in the world. The new Prussian Army was far more superior to the Austrian Army. The Prussians had outstanding leadership with General Helmuth von Moltke and his General Staff.[29] In 1866, William I authorized Moltke to issue orders to all military commanders in the king's name. The Prussian Army was highly organized. The infantry was fully equipped with the highly-accurate, breech-loading Dreyse needle gun compared to the Austrians who were armed with muzzle-loading rifles. Moreover, the Army had a high degree of mobility and speed because of the German road, railway, and telegraph networks.[30] On 16 June 1866, a Prussian army, commanded by General Eduard Vogel von Falkenstein, invaded Hanover, Saxony, and Hesse-Kassel, beginning the Seven Weeks' War (1866). Falkenstein successfully overran the three states within a few days. Several days later, the Prussian army attacked Austria from the north while Italy attacked Austria from the south. The rapid defeat of Saxony had placed Austria on the defensive against the advancing Prussians. Three Prussian armies led by Crown Prince Frederick William, Prince Frederick Charles, and General Karl Herwath von Bittenfeld moved into Bohemia. The

---

26.   Ibid., 133.
27.   Wawro, *The Austro-Prussian War*, 44.
28.   Holborn, *A History of Modern Germany*, 2:182.
29.   See Arden Bucholz, *Moltke, Schlieffen, and Prussian War Planning* (New York: Berg, 1991); Arden Bucholz, *Moltke and the German Wars, 1864-1871* (London: Palgrave, 2001); and Trevor N. Dupuy, *A Genius for War: The German Army and General Staff, 1807-1945* (Fairfax, Va: Hero, 1984).
30.   Wawro, *The Austro-Prussian War*, 13-25; See also Dennis Showalter, *Railroads and Rifles: Soldiers, Technology, and the Unification of Germany* (Hamden, CT: Archon, 1975) and Showalter, "The Prusso-German RMA, 1840-1871."

Prussian forces consisted of 280,000 troops with 900 guns.[31] On 3 July, the Prussian armies attacked and defeated the Austrians at the Battle of Königgrätz (Sadowa) in Bohemia.[32] In this decisive battle the Prussians had only 9,000 casualties compared to Austria's 64,000.[33] Two weeks later, on 18 July, the Prussians were within twelve miles of Vienna. At this point, Napoleon III threatened to intervene in the war on the side of Austria. Bismarck, therefore, convinced King William I to agree to an armistice on 22 July. Four days later, the Prussians and Austrians signed the preliminary peace settlement at Nikolsburg. The Austro-Prussian War was a short and decisive conflict. The final peace settlement that ended the Seven Weeks' War came in the Peace of Prague in August 1866. The peace treaty included the exclusion of Austria from German affairs. The German Confederation was dissolved, and Prussia soon concluded a treaty of federation with the North German states that had fought on the Prussian side. Austria agreed to pay forty million Prussian talers as a war indemnity to Prussia as well as surrendered Venetia to Italy. In addition to this settlement, Bismarck took the opportunity to annex Schleswig-Holstein, Hanover, Hesse-Kassel, Hesse-Homburg, Nassau, and the City of Frankfurt to Prussia. These actions linked up Prussia's western and eastern territories. Prussia was dominant in northern and central Germany. Furthermore, Bismarck secured military alliances with the south German states of Württemberg, Bavaria, and Baden.

The North German Confederation (Norddeutscher Bund) under Prussian leadership was created in July 1867. The Confederation consisted of the King of Prussia as the President (Präsidium), a North German Constitution, Federal Chancellor (Bundeskanzler), Bundesrat (Federal Chamber), and Reichstag (Parliament). The Bundesrat met in Berlin. It was given exclusive control of defense, foreign, and economic policy. Otto von Bismarck served as the Federal Chancellor, and continued his posts at Prussian Minister-President and Foreign Minister. Immediately after the creation of the North German Confederation, Bismarck renewed and expanded the Prusso-German Customs Union to include the North German states, as well as the South German states of Bavaria, Württemberg, Baden, and Hesse-Darmstadt.

---

31.   Carr, *The Origins of the Wars of German Unification*, 137.

32.   The Austro-Prussian War receives treatment in Gordon A. Craig, *The Battle of Königgrätz: Prussia's Victory over Austria, 1866* (Philadelphia: J.B. Lippincott, 1964) and Geoffrey Wawro, *The Austro-Prussian War: Austria's War with Prussia and Italy in 1866* (Cambridge: Cambridge University Press, 1996).

33.   Jeremy Black, *Western Warfare, 1775-1882* (Bloomington: Indiana University Press, 2001), 134.

After the Austro-Prussian War, relations between the North German Confederation and Napoleon III of France rapidly deteriorated. The French Emperor was full of himself after the successes of the Crimean War, War of 1859, and acquisition of Nice and Savoy in 1860. Napoleon III was demanding a return to the French borders of 1814 in the Rhineland (the Saarland, Landau, and parts of the Palatinate), Belgium, or Luxembourg as the price for French neutrality in the Seven Weeks' War and as territorial compensation for Prussian expansionism. Bismarck, on the other hand, continued to oppose French demands.[34] After a while, a war over Luxembourg became a possibility.[35] The other Great Powers immediately stepped in and mediated a settlement at an international congress in London. In May 1867, the Federal Chancellor agreed to the Treaty of London as a way to avoid a conflict. In this treaty, Luxembourg became independent and neutral, and this status would be guaranteed by the Great Powers.[36] The treaty prevented Napoleon III from acquiring Luxembourg. As such, the Treaty of London was a complete international humiliation for Napoleon III.[37] The French Emperor needed a foreign policy success. The Luxembourg Crisis and the collapse of French power in Mexico had both tarnished the image of the Second Empire.[38] Therefore, Napoleon III knew that he must deal with Prussia and the threat to the security of France. As a result, he set out to negotiate alliances with Austria-Hungary and Italy against Prussia's North German Confederation.[39]

In the meantime, in September 1868, a liberal revolution broke out in Spain. As a result, the Spanish forced Queen Isabella II (1833-68) off the throne in Madrid. She fled to France. The newly established Provisional Government of Marshal Francisco Serrano y Domínguez and General Juan Prim y Prats had the primary concern of finding a ruler for a constitutional monarchy.[40] They passed over the Duke Antoine of Montpensier, the French brother-in-law to Queen Isabella II. The position was then offered and declined by the Duke Amadeo of Aosta, Prince Ferdinand of Saxe-Coburg, Duke Thomas of Genoa, and General Baldomero Espartero.[41]

---

34.　E. Ann Pottinger, *Napoleon III and the German Crisis, 1865-1866* (Cambridge, MA: Harvard University Press, 1966), 183.

35.　McMillan, 111-13.

36.　Rich, *Great Power Diplomacy, 1814-1914*, 207.

37.　Roger Price, *Napoleon III and the Second Empire* (London: Routledge, 1997), 59.

38.　French forces withdrew from Mexico and Archduke Maximilian was executed in 1867.

39.　The weakness of the Habsburgs led to self-rule for Hungary within the Austrian Empire, which renamed itself the Dual Monarchy of Austria-Hungary in 1867. See Taylor, *The Habsburg Monarchy, 1809-1918*, 130-40.

40.　Raymond Carr, *Spain, 1808-1939* (Oxford: Clarendon Press, 1966), 299-304.

41.　Carr, *The Origins of the Wars of German Unification*, 183.

Finally, the offer was made to Prince Leopold von Hohenzollern-Sigmaringen in February 1870.[42] He was a Catholic cousin of King William I of Prussia. In March 1870, Chancellor Bismarck began to support the cause of the Hohenzollern candidacy for the Spanish throne.[43]

Prince Leopold accepted the offer of the Spanish throne in June 1870. The French immediately objected to the Hohenzollern candidate. On 6 July, Duke Antoine Agénor of Gramont, the French Foreign Minister, delivered a speech to the French National Assembly that indicated that France would go to war unless the Prussian government withdrew the candidacy.[44] The Prussian government responded by disclaiming all knowledge of the affair, and insisting that it was a Hohenzollern family issue. The French began implementing their war plans. Meanwhile, Napoleon III and Gramont sent Count Vincent Benedetti, the French Ambassador to Berlin, to visit King William I at the resort spa at Bad Ems, near Coblenz, on 9 July. Benedetti was instructed to ask William I to order Leopold to withdraw his candidacy to the Spanish throne. William I refused, but he sent a trusted envoy to advise Leopold to scrap his candidacy. On 12 July, the candidacy of Leopold of Hohenzollern-Sigmaringen was withdrawn. This action was a significant diplomatic victory for Napoleon III. However, the following day, Gramont had Benedetti demand that William I write a letter in which he apologized for the situation and guaranteed that Leopold would not accept the candidacy.[45] The historian A.J.P. Taylor believes that "this demand was made with the deliberate intention of provoking war or else of inflicting on Prussia a humiliation equivalent to a military defeat."[46] The Prussian King rejected this demand. Afterwards, the monarch sent a report of the meeting to his Chancellor. Bismarck, after checking with

---

42.    Pflanze, 1:453.

43.    The Hohenzollern Candidacy and origins of the Franco-Prussian War are examined in Robert Howard Lord, *The Origins of the War of 1870: New Documents from the German Archives* (Cambridge, MA: Harvard University Press, 1924); Georges Bonnin (ed.), *Bismarck and the Hohenzollern Candidature for the Spanish Throne: The Documents in the German Diplomatic Archives* (London: Chatto and Windus, n.d.); Lawrence D. Steefel, *Bismarck, the Hohenzollern Candidacy, and the Origins of the Franco-German War of 1870* (Cambridge, MA: Harvard University Press, 1962). The most recent study is David Wetzel, *A Duel of Giants: Bismarck, Napoleon III, and the Origins of the Franco-Prussian War* (Madison: University of Wisconsin Press, 2001).

44.    McMillan, 156; Friedrich von Holstein, *The Holstein Papers: The Memoirs, Diaries and Correspondence of Friedrich von Holstein, 1837-1909*, 4 vols., eds. Norman Rich and M.H. Fisher (Cambridge: Cambridge University Press, 1955-63), 1:40-41.

45.    Carr, *The Origins of the Wars of German Unification*, 192.

46.    A.J.P. Taylor, *The Struggle for Mastery in Europe, 1848-1918* (Oxford: Clarendon Press, 1954), 205.

General Helmuth von Moltke and General Albrecht von Roon (the Prussian Minister for War) on the status of the Prussian Army, then edited the Ems telegram for publication in the Berlin newspapers that evening. The published telegram depicted the French as insulting German pride, and William I's response as defying French demands (instead of backing down from the Hohenzollern candidacy).[47] The story was quickly published in French newspapers. On 15 July, the Second Empire voted to declare war against the North German Confederation.

Napoleon III was determined to launch a war against the Prussian threat. Both sides quickly mobilized for war. On the one side, Napoleon III expected the active support of Austria and Italy, as well as the neutrality of the South German states.[48] He did not realize that Austria, Italy, and the South German states could not be counted on. On the other side, Bismarck relied on the armed support of the South German states and the support of Russia.[49] Bismarck counted on the military alliances of 1866 with Baden, Bavaria, Hesse-Darmstadt, and Württemberg.[50] Tsar Alexander II was too weak diplomatically and militarily to oppose Prussia.[51] Britain would remain neutral.[52] On 16 and 17 July, Baden, Württemberg, and Bavaria began to mobilize for war.[53] The French Ambassador to Berlin delivered the declaration of war to Bismarck on 19 July. By 31 July, General Moltke and the General Staff had 1,183,000 troops from the North German Confederation and South German states mobilized.[54] This figure included 462,000 men concentrated on the frontier west of the Rhine River.[55] The First Army was led by General Karl von Steinmetz, the Second Army by Prince Frederick Charles, and the Third Army by Crown Prince Frederick William. Meanwhile, the French mobilization effort was chaotic. The French lacked a General Staff.[56] Napoleon III took command of the

---

47.   Carr, *The Origins of the Wars of German Unification*, 196-97.

48.   Ibid., 160.

49.   Pflanze, 1:434-38.

50.   Gordon A. Craig, *Germany 1866-1945* (Oxford: Oxford University Press, 1978), 27. The four South German states signed Treaties of Accession to the North German Confederation in November 1870 (see Holborn, *A History of Modern Germany*, 2:224-25).

51.   Werner E. Mosse, *The European Powers and the German Question, 1848-1871: With Special Reference to England and Russia* (Cambridge: Cambridge University Press, 1958), 365.

52.   See Richard Millman, *British Foreign Policy and the Coming of the Franco-Prussian War* (Oxford: Clarendon Press, 1965).

53.   Carr, *The Origins of the Wars of German Unification*, 205.

54.   Stephen Badsey, *The Franco-Prussian War, 1870-1871* (Botley: Osprey, 2003), 35. Gordon Craig believes the figure to be 1,830,000 (Craig, *Germany 1866-1945*, 28).

55.   Badsey, 35; Craig, *Germany 1866-1945*, 28.

56.   For an outstanding study of the French Army, see Richard Holmes, *The Road to Sedan: The French Army, 1866-1870* (London: Royal Historical Society, 1984).

French Army himself. Napoleon III had no more than 280,000 troops on the eastern frontier of France.[57] But, on 2 August, the French advanced and captured Saarbrücken.[58] Then, on 4 August, the Germans counterattacked and forced the French to fall back in the Battle of Wissembourg (Weissemburg), followed by the Battles of Spicheren and Wörth on 6 August. The German armies advanced on a wide front, forcing the French to continue their retreat after the Battles of Borny on 15 August; Mars-la-Tour on 16 August; and Gravelotte-St. Privat on 18 August. Finally, Moltke cornered the French Army and defeated Napoleon III at the Battle of Sedan on 1 September 1870. Napoleon III surrendered to the Germans the very next day. As a consequence, the French Second Empire toppled in a popular uprising in Paris two days later. General Louis Jules Trochu, Jules Favre, and Léon Gambetta quickly established a Provisional Government and prepared to defend the capital. Two weeks later, on 19 September, German forces advanced and began the siege of Paris. King William I established his headquarters at Versailles while General Moltke attempted to starve Paris into submission. In the meantime the German Army captured Strasbourg (September), Metz (October), and launched a large-scale military operation in the Loire and Sarthe Valleys. The German forces were victorious in the Battles of Orléans in December, followed by St. Quentin, Le Mans, and Belfort in January 1871.

While the German Army besieged Paris the Second Reich was established. On 18 January, William I was proclaimed German Emperor (Kaiser) in the Hall of Mirrors at the Palace of Versailles. On 27 January, General Trochu, with the city of Paris on the verge of starvation, agreed to an armistice. The city of Paris soon capitulated and agreed to a preliminary peace agreement, the Convention of Versailles, on 26 February. A few days later, on 1 March, German forces marched in triumph through Paris. The spring of 1871 was a busy time for Bismarck. Bismarck was the Imperial Chancellor (Reichskanzler) of Germany. He negotiated both the peace terms for the Franco-Prussian War and the government setup of the Second Reich. In April the constitution of the North German Confederation was remodeled and adopted by a new German Reichstag in Berlin. Germany included twenty-five states, including four kingdoms (Prussia, Saxony, Bavaria, and Württemberg), five grand duchies, thirteen duchies and principalities, and three free cities (Bremen, Hamburg, and Lübeck). Eventually, after the delay of

---

57.   Badsey, 36.
58.   The military operations of the Franco-Prussian War are treated in Michael Howard, *The Franco-Prussian War: The German Invasion of France, 1870-1871* (London: Ruper Hart-Davis, 1961) and Geoffrey Wawro, *The Franco-Prussian War: The German Conquest of France in 1870-1871* (Cambridge: Cambridge University Press, 2003).

the Paris Commune, the French Third Republic and the government of Adolphe Thiers accepted the final terms of the Peace of Frankfurt in May 1871. In the peace treaty, France agreed to hand over Alsace and part of Lorraine to Germany. The Third Republic also agreed to pay a war indemnity of five billion francs, and allow a German army of 30,000 men to occupy Paris until the indemnity was paid in full.[59]

## Bismarck's Foreign Policy, 1871-1888

Otto von Bismarck's foreign policy from 1862 to 1871 had the goal of expanding Prussian power. He created a unified Germany under Prussian leadership. In 1871, Bismarck claimed that Germany had reached saturation point, meaning that the Second Reich had no further plans to expand. During the next nineteen years, from 1871 to 1890, Bismarck sought to stabilize the European international system so Germany could consolidate its power and position in Europe. Thus, Bismarck set out to establish a system of complex European alliances in order to maintain the new balance of power in Europe and secure the Second Reich's position against the possible revenge motives of Austria-Hungary and France for their humiliations in 1866 and 1870-71. George O. Kent has written:

> The attitude of the powers toward Germany in the aftermath of the Franco-Prussian War was restrained and suspicious. France, thinking of revenge, looked to Russia and Austria as possible allies in case of future war with Germany. Austria, still smarting from her defeat at Königgrätz, was jealous of Germany's newly acquired big power status and kept her reserve toward Germany. Russia, though worried about the revolutionary developments in France, was disturbed by Prussia's vastly increased power and by the emergence of a unified Germany. Britain alone seemed unconcerned.[60]

In 1871, the Great Powers of Europe faced each other in isolation. There were no alliances between the Great Powers or with smaller powers. Imanuel Geiss stresses that "Germany, France, Britain, Austria-Hungary, Italy—all lived in a kind of diplomatic anarchy."[61] After the creation of the Second Reich, Bismarck's main goal was to manipulate the European system to keep France diplomatically isolated. The Imperial Chancellor worried about the French desire to reacquire Alsace-Lor-

---

59.  Craig, *Germany 1866-1945*, 33; Badsey, 83.
60.  George O. Kent, *Bismarck and His Times* (Carbondale: Southern Illinois University Press, 1978), 104.
61.  Imanuel Geiss, *German Foreign Policy, 1871-1914* (London: Routledge and Kegan Paul, 1976), 17.

raine. Bismarck wanted to block all French attempts to acquire an alliance system in Europe. As such, Bismarck supported the Third Republic. The Chancellor worked to prevent the restoration of a Bourbon monarchy in France because he believed that Austria and Russia would not ally with a revolutionary regime.

Bismarck sought to protect the new balance of power in Europe. His first move was an attempt to revive the Holy Alliance of 1815. This alliance had been a league of the conservative powers of Prussia, Austria, and Russia. It was weakened during the revolutions of 1848 and destroyed in the Crimean War. The German Chancellor wanted a new Holy Alliance to protect the international and domestic status quo. He wanted to avoid war at all costs. A war could only upset the social, political, and international status quo. The making of the alliance began at a meeting at Ischl in August 1871. About one year later, in September 1872, Emperor William I of Germany, Tsar Alexander II of Russia, and Emperor Francis Joseph I of Austria-Hungary met in Berlin. The making of the alliance advanced with a Russo-German military agreement in May 1873, followed by the Austro-Russian Schönbrunn Convention in June. The three Great Powers negotiated and created the defensive alliance of the Three Emperor's League (Dreikaiserbund) in October 1873.[62] The League had the aim of combating "any revolutions from whatever side they may come."[63] But the flaw of the Three Emperor's League was the suspicion between Austria-Hungary and Russia, especially concerning the Eastern Question. A.J.P. Taylor has called the alliance "a fair-weather system." He stresses that "a new conflict between France and Germany, a new twist of the Eastern Question, would destroy it."[64]

Republican France quickly recovered from the military defeat of 1870-71. The Third Republic paid off the war indemnity faster than expected, which resulted in the withdrawal of German forces from France in September 1873.[65] The French sought to reorganize and restore their military strength, as well as break out of diplomatic isolation. However, the political and military recovery of France made the German General Staff anxious. In the spring of 1875, General Helmuth von Moltke, the German Army, and the German Press suggested that the Second Reich might launch a preventive war against France before the French Army was fully recovered from the Franco-Prussian War.[66] Historians believe that Bismarck was

---

62.    *GP*, 1:206-7; Pflanze, 2:259-60; C.J. Bartlett, *Peace, War and the European Powers, 1814-1914* (New York: St. Martin's Press, 1996), 99-100.
63.    As quoted in Geiss, German Foreign Policy, 1871-1914, 29.
64.    Taylor, *The Struggle for Mastery in Europe, 1848-1918*, 221.
65.    Ibid., 223; Geiss, *German Foreign Policy, 1871-1914*, 28.
66.    Kent, *Bismarck and His Times*, 106-7; Pflanze, 2:268-69.

not interested in waging war. But, the Imperial Chancellor was willing to try to isolate and bully France out of rebuilding its army. On 8 April 1875, Bismarck had a front-page article under the headline "Is War in Sight?" appear in the Berlin *Post*. The article hinted that Germany may need to resort to a preventive war against France.[67] A similar article was published in the *Norddeutsche Allgemeine Zeitung*. The two articles created a sensation in Europe.[68] The French quickly appealed to Britain and Russia for support. Britain and Russia, seeing France as a victim of German militarism, soon responded and convinced Germany to back down.[69] Bismarck was completely outmaneuvered. The War-in-Sight Crisis resulted in Bismarck realizing Germany's isolation, despite the Three Emperor's League, and beating a hasty diplomatic retreat.[70] The historian Otto Pflanze calls the War-in-Sight Crisis the greatest diplomatic defeat in Bismarck's career.[71]

The Balkan Crisis of 1875-1878 would soon breakup the Three Emperor's League.[72] In July 1875, the South Slavs of Bosnia and Herzegovina revolted against the Ottoman Turks. The revolt was secretly supported by Serbia, Montenegro, and Panslavic groups in Russia. Russian Panslavs wanted Russia to take the lead in the South Slav fight for liberation from the Ottoman Empire.[73] Tsar Alexander II was not interested in supporting the South Slav movement. At first Bismarck welcomed the uprising in the Balkans. It diverted attention away from humiliating War-in-Sight Crisis.[74] In fact, Bismarck, Russian Foreign Minister Prince Alexander Gorchakov, and Austro-Hungarian Foreign Minister Count Julius von Andrássy met in Berlin to discuss the crisis in May 1876. In the Berlin Memorandum, the Three Emperor's League called for a two-month truce in the Balkans. But, in May 1876, the South Slav revolt against Turkish rule had spread to Bulgaria. Believing that the Ottoman Empire was disintegrating, Serbia declared war against the Sultan in June, followed by Montenegro in July 1876. Tsar Alexander II, who wanted to avoid a Balkan war, could not control the Russian Panslavs, Serbs, or Montenegrins. He had lost control of the situation in the

67.     Holstein, 1:94; F.R. Bridge and Roger Bullen, *The Great Powers and the European States System, 1814-1914*, 2 ed. (London: Longman, 2005), 196.
68.     Kent, *Bismarck and His Times*, 107.
69.     Holborn, *A History of Modern Germany*, 2:238.
70.     Bismarck, *Memoirs*, 2:252-54.
71.     Pflanze, 2:272.
72.     For background to the Eastern Question, see M.S. Anderson, *The Eastern Question, 1774-1923: A Study in International Relations* (New York: St. Martin's Press, 1966).
73.     Barbara Jelavich, *A Century of Russian Foreign Policy, 1814-1914* (Philadelphia: Lippincott, 1964), 174.
74.     Pflanze, 2:418.

Balkans.[75] On 8 July, Andrássy and Gorchakov attempted to coordinate their conflicting interests in the Balkans in a secret agreement at a meeting at Reichstadt in Bohemia.[76] They sought to avoid an Austro-Russian war over the Balkans.[77] Bismarck, observing the crisis from a distance, also dreaded being pulled into a conflict in the Balkans concerning Austro-Russian interests.[78] In December 1876, Bismarck declared that Germany had no interest in the Eastern Question "that was worth the healthy bones of a Pomeranian musketeer."[79] His only concern was to keep Austria-Hungary and Russia on good terms. But, as Otto Pflanze has pointed out, "Bismarck had already begun to think of Austria as the more valued ally."[80]

The Russian Panslavs strongly supported the Balkan rebellions of fellow Eastern Orthodox Christians against the Muslim Turks.[81] Russian General M.G. Cherniaev took charge of the Serbian Army and thousands of Russian volunteers joined the forces against the Turks. Russian Panslavs urged St. Petersburg to take control of the Balkans and place all South Slavs under the protection of Russia.[82] But, in the meantime, the Ottoman Army crushed the Serbian forces at the Battle of Alexinatz in September 1876.[83] Tsar Alexander II was now forced to act in support of the Orthodox Christians in the Balkans. Alexander II requested German support to ensure Austro-Hungarian neutrality in a Balkan war as pay back for Russian support in 1866 and 1870.[84] However, Bismarck refused to chose sides. The Imperial Chancellor wanted an Austro-Russian agreement in the Balkans.[85] As such, diplomatic activity shifted away from Berlin.[86] Gorchakov was forced to negotiate with Andrássy. Consequently, in January 1877, St. Petersburg

75.    W.E. Mosse, *Alexander II and the Modernization of Russia* (London: English Universities Press, 1958), 147-55.

76.    Geiss, *German Foreign Policy, 1871-1914*, 31; F.R. Bridge, *From Sadowa to Sarajevo: The Foreign Policy of Austria-Hungary, 1866-1914* (London: Routledge and Kegan Paul, 1972), 77.

77.    Bridge and Bullen, 202; A.L. Macfie, *The Eastern Question, 1774-1923*, rev. ed. (London: Longman), 38-39.

78.    Taylor, *The Struggle for Mastery in Europe, 1848-1918*, 229.

79.    Taylor, *Bismarck*, 167.

80.    Pflanze, 2:491-92.

81.    For Russian foreign policy, see Hugh Seton-Watson, *The Russian Empire, 1801-1917* (Oxford: Clarendon Press, 1967) and Dietrich Geyer, *Russian Imperialism: The Interaction of Domestic and Foreign Policy, 1860-1914* (Leamington Spa: Berg, 1987).

82.    Pflanze, 2:421.

83.    Kent, *Bismarck and His Times*, 110.

84.    Pflanze, 2:423.

85.    Taylor, *The Struggle for Mastery in Europe, 1848-1918*, 238-39.

86.    Palmer, *Bismarck*, 193.

confirmed the Reichstadt Agreement with the Austro-Hungarian Empire at the Budapest Convention. The Austro-Russian Military Convention called for the benevolent neutrality of Vienna in a Russo-Turkish conflict. Russia would be allowed to retake Bessarabia. In return, the Russians would allow the Dual Monarchy of Austria-Hungary, at a moment of its own choosing, to occupy the Turkish provinces of Bosnia and Herzegovina.[87] This was a great diplomatic success for Russia. As A.J.P. Taylor has commented, "the Russians were free to destroy the Turkish empire without interference if they were strong enough to do so and did it quickly."[88]

In April 1877, the Russian Empire declared war against the Ottoman Turks. Russia sought to occupy Constantinople and the Straits. One Russian army of 172,000 men crossed the Danube River in June.[89] It quickly advanced through the Balkans while another Russian army moved forward on the Caucasus front. The Russians captured Kars in November, and then failed to take Erzerum. On the western front, the Turks blocked the Russian offensive at the fortress-city of Plevna in the Balkan mountains of Bulgaria for five months. By December 1877, the Russian forces had defeated the Turks at Plevna,[90] and then moved forward to occupy Adrianople in January 1878. But they were too exhausted to take Constantinople. The Sultan asked for an armistice with Russian troops camped outside Constantinople on 31 January 1878. The Peace of San Stefano was signed in March 1878. The harsh peace agreement was dictated by the Russian High Command. It included war reparations from the Ottoman Empire. Moreover, the treaty called for the creation of an autonomous Greater Bulgarian state. Greater Bulgaria would stretch from the Black Sea to Albania, and from the Danube River to the Aegean Sea. Greater Bulgaria would become a Russian satellite state with the presence of Russian troops for two years. Russia gained Kars, Batum, and Bessarabia. The treaty also gave independence and additional territory to Serbia, Montenegro, and Rumania. Bosnia and Herzegovina were to become autonomous.[91]

Austria-Hungary, Britain, and France immediately protested the increase of Russian power in Southeast Europe and the Mediterranean Region. The leadership in Vienna were upset that the Treaty of San Stefano failed to mention Aus-

87.   Macfie, 40; Pflanze, 2:430.
88.   Taylor, *The Struggle for Mastery in Europe, 1848-1918*, 243.
89.   William C. Fuller, Jr., *Strategy and Power in Russia, 1600-1914* (New York: Free Press, 1992), 318.
90.   See Rupert Furneaux, *The Breakfast War* (New York: Thomas Y. Crowell, 1958) for an account of the siege of Plevna.
91.   Macfie, 42.

tro-Hungarian rights in Bosnia and Herzegovina. Britain wanted to maintain the Ottoman Empire and opposed the idea of Russian expansion towards the Mediterranean Sea.[92] Three days after the signing of the Treaty of San Stefano, Count Andrássy, after consultation with St. Petersburg and Berlin, called for the Great Powers to attend a diplomatic conference in Berlin to discuss a revision of the peace settlement. The government of St. Petersburg had no choice. The Tsar's military was too weak to oppose the Great Powers. Russia had to accept the invitation or face a possible war against a European coalition.

Why was Berlin selected as the site for the meeting? According to the historian Otto Pflanze:

> That Berlin was selected as the site for the international congress that concluded the Balkans crisis was symbolic of the position to which Bismarck's diplomacy had elevated the Prussian capital in merely fifteen years. The last previous European congress had been held at Paris in 1856 to conclude the Crimean War. On that occasion the choice of Paris had been looked upon as a recognition of the new prestige of France under Napoleon III. To go to Berlin—a difficult question for the French government—was to recognize the change wrought by German victories over Austria and France. But it was also proof that the war-in-sight crisis of 1875 had been a passing episode in European politics. The neutral course that Bismarck had steered since the fall of that year in the eastern question had left him the only statesman in Europe who, despite British distrust and Russian dissatisfaction, was presumed to have the authority and relative impartiality capable of presiding over a congress to resolve the Balkans crisis and preserve Europe's peace.[93]

The Congress of Berlin opened at the ballroom of the former Radziwill Palace on 13 June 1878. It was one of the major diplomatic meetings of the nineteenth century.[94] The Great Powers were represented by their chief ministers. The Dual Monarchy was represented by Foreign Minister Andrássy, Britain by Prime Minister Benjamin Disraeli and Foreign Secretary Lord Salisbury, France by Ambassador William Henry Waddington, Russia by Foreign Minister Gorchakov and Count Peter Shuvalov, and Italy by Foreign Minister Count Luigi Corti. Prince Otto von Bismarck played host to the congress. He served as president in accor-

---

92.   British policy is examined in Richard Millman, *Britain and the Eastern Question, 1875-1878* (Oxford: Clarendon Press, 1979).

93.   Pflanze, 2:434.

94.   For the Congress of Berlin and its aftermath, see W.N. Medlicott, *The Congress of Berlin and After: A Diplomatic History of the Near Eastern Settlement, 1878-1880* (London: Methuen, 1938) and W.N. Medlicott, *Bismarck, Gladstone, and the Concert of Europe* (London: Athlone Press, 1956).

dance with diplomatic custom. Bismarck was assisted by Foreign Secretary Bernhard Ernst von Bülow, and Prince Chlodwig zu Hohenlohe-Schillingsfürst, the German Ambassador to France. Others included Joseph Maria von Radowitz, Dr. Klemens August Busch, Lothar Bucher, Herbert von Bismarck, and Friedrich von Holstein of the German Foreign Office.[95]

Bismarck dominated the congress, established the agenda, and set the pace of the negotiations.[96] His role would be to facilitate a compromise settlement.[97] Bismarck and Germany had no direct interests in the Balkans. He knew, however, that the crisis could result in a European war that could destroy the German gains of 1870-1871. He did not like having to chose between Austria-Hungary and Russia.[98] But, he chose to support Austria-Hungary.[99] On 13 July 1878, the Great Powers agreed to the Treaty of Berlin. Commenting on Bismarck's role in the treaty, Imanuel Geiss has stated:

> The Berlin Congress of 1878, seen superficially, was the brilliant climax of Bismarck's career as a European statesman and confirmed Germany's central position in European affairs. Bismarck's mediating role as "honest broker," as he formulated it himself in a speech in the Reichstag…stressed the importance of the new German empire. The Congress was, indeed, a short-term success.[100]

George O. Kent argues that Bismarck was more of an umpire than an honest broker.[101] The Chancellor's main goals were to maintain the peace and come up with an agreement that was palatable to the Russians.

The final peace settlement divided the Greater Bulgaria created in the Treaty of San Stefano into three parts, including Bulgaria under Russian protection, Eastern Rumelia under Turkish administration, and Macedonia and the coast of Thracia were left to the Ottomans. Serbia, Montenegro, and Rumania gained their independence from the Turks. Rumania was forced to give up Bessarabia to Russia while receiving the Dobruja area south of the Danube River from the Ottoman Empire. As for the Great Powers, the Dual Monarchy acquired the right to occupy Bosnia

---

95. Norman Rich, *Friedrich von Holstein: Politics and Diplomacy in the Era of Bismarck and Wilhelm II*, 2 vols. (Cambridge: Cambridge University Press, 1965), 1:101-2. Radowitz was the son of the late General Joseph Maria von Radowitz (1797-1853), the former Prussian Foreign Minister.
96. Pflanze, 2:437.
97. John Lowe, *The Great Powers, Imperialism, and the German Problem, 1865-1925* (London: Routledge, 1994), 50-51.
98. Geiss, *German Foreign Policy, 1871-1914*, 31.
99. Ibid., 32.
100. Ibid.
101. Kent, *Bismarck and His Times*, 111-12.

and Herzegovina and to station troops in the Turkish district of Novi Pazar, located between Serbia and Montenegro. Russia acquired Ardahan, Batum, and Kars on the eastern side of the Black Sea. Britain was allowed to occupy the island of Cyprus. The Treaty of Berlin gave permission for France to occupy Tunis in North Africa. Germany and Italy acquired no territory. Bismarck was successful in maintaining peace in Europe, especially between Russia and Austria-Hungary, at the Congress of Berlin.[102] But, Bismarck had supported the Habsburg Empire. Russia viewed the Treaty of Berlin, despite its gains in Bulgaria, Bessarabia, and Asia Minor, as a great defeat.[103] Gorchakov and the Russians blamed Bismarck for this disaster.[104] Russia was now militarily weak and diplomatically isolated.[105] The Three Emperor's League was considered dead for all practical purposes.

After the Congress of Berlin, the Tsarist government of St. Petersburg became anti-German. Russia became extremely hostile towards Germany.[106] In August 1879, Tsar Alexander II complained to the German Emperor about Bismarck and the abandonment of Russian interests at the Congress of Berlin. Alexander II warned William I about the consequences of Bismarck's actions.[107] As a result, the Imperial Chancellor decided, with great reluctance, to commit Germany to the defense of Austria-Hungary. William I held out against an Austro-Hungarian alliance, preferring a tie with Russia, until Bismarck forced his hand by threatening his resignation and that of all of the Prussian ministers.[108] The Dual Alliance between Germany and Austria-Hungary was established in October 1879.[109] One historian has stated that "Russian resentment over Germany's blocking Russia's advance in the Balkans drove Germany and Austria-Hungary together and provoked the for-

---

102.   Rich, *Great Power Diplomacy, 1814-1914*, 227.

103.   For Russia's reaction to the treaty, see B.H. Sumner, *Russia and the Balkans, 1870-1880* (Oxford: Oxford University Press, 1937).

104.   Jelavich, *A Century of Russian Foreign Policy, 1814-1914*, 185.

105.   Charles Jelavich, *Tsarist Russia and Balkan Nationalism: Russian Influence in the Internal Affairs of Bulgaria and Serbia, 1879-1886* (Berkeley: University of California Press, 1962), 13-18.

106.   Pflanze, 2:495-500. See also Bruce Waller, "Bismarck and Gorchakov in 1879: 'The Two Chancellors' War'," in *Studies in International History*, ed. Kenneth Bourne and D.C. Watt (Hamden, CT: Archon, 1967) and Bruce Waller, *Bismarck at the Crossroads: The Reorientation of German Foreign Policy after the Congress of Berlin, 1878-1880* (London: Athlone Press, 1974).

107.   Geiss, *German Foreign Policy, 1871-1914*, 35; Pflanze, 2:500-7.

108.   Pflanze, 2:507; Kent, *Bismarck and His Times*, 113-14.

109.   Relations between Germany and Austria-Hungary and the making of the Dual Alliance are discussed in Nicholas der Bagdasarian, *The Austro-German Rapprochement, 1870-1879: From the Battle of Sedan to the Dual Alliance* (London: Associated University Presses, 1976). For Austro-Hungarian foreign policy, see F.R. Bridge, *The Habsburg Monarchy among the Great Powers, 1815-1918* (New York: Berg, 1990).

mation of the Dual Alliance."[110] Bismarck created the secret defensive alliance with the Dual Monarchy against an attack by Russia. He believed that Russia would not attack both Germany and the Austro-Hungarian Empire. The Dual Alliance would form the cornerstone of Bismarck's alliance system and last until 1918.

In spite of the Dual Alliance, Bismarck was not committed exclusively to Austria-Hungary. Bismarck still hoped that Russia would renew good relations with Germany and reestablish the Three Emperor's League. As Hajo Holborn has pointed out, "Bismarck expected that the alliance with Austria-Hungary would sober Russia and induce her to seek a reconciliation and the restoration of the Three Emperor's League."[111] Bismarck wanted a renewal of the Dreikaiserbund to deter revolutionary forces in Europe. This was not difficult. In late 1879, St. Petersburg offered to renew the Three Emperor's League.[112] The Russians sought security in the Balkans and Near East. The Russians again suggested reviving the League in January 1880.[113] But the Dual Monarchy objected.[114] During the continuing negotiations Alexander II was assassinated by anarchists in St. Petersburg in March 1881. Afterwards, his son, Alexander III, established a reactionary government in Russia. The new Russian ruler wanted to complete what his father had started and strongly desired to recreate the conservative alliance of Russia, Germany, and Austria-Hungary.[115] As such, Bismarck convinced Vienna to accept, albeit reluctantly, the new alliance.[116] Thus, in June 1881, Germany, Russia, and Austria-Hungary secretly created the Second Three Emperor's League. They agreed for the pact to last three years. The alliance was both a conservative partnership and a pact of practical partnership in the Near East. Historians, nevertheless, differ on the importance of the Second Three Emperor's League. Otto Pflanze believes that it was a "formal alliance between governments rather than an agreement by monarchs to consult in time of crisis."[117] He writes:

---

110. Geiss, *German Foreign Policy, 1871-1914*, 35.
111. Holborn, *A History of Modern Germany*, 2:242.
112. Pflanze, 3:79-80.
113. Taylor, *The Struggle for Mastery in Europe, 1848-1918*, 267.
114. Pflanze, 3:84-90.
115. Jelavich, *A Century of Russian Foreign Policy, 1814-1914*, 189.
116. Rich, *Great Power Diplomacy, 1814-1914*, 228-29.
117. Pflanze, 3:90.

The alliance, whose exact terms remained secret until 1919, provided that, if one of the three powers should find itself at war with a fourth, its allies would maintain benevolent neutrality and seek to localize the conflict. This stipulation should apply in the case of war with Turkey only if the three powers had agreed in advance concerning the results of the war. Russia agreed to respect the "new position" gained by Austria-Hungary in the Treaty of Berlin, while all three governments guaranteed the closure of the Straits to warships. They agreed to take into account their respective interests on the Balkan Peninsula and to reach accord on all new modifications in the territorial status of European Turkey. To facilitate that accord the three powers approved a list of specific agreements: Austria could annex Bosnia and Herzegovina whenever she found it "opportune"; Austria could garrison, but not administer or annex the Sanjak of Novi-Bazar in accord with prior agreements; the three powers would discourage the Sublime Porte from invading Eastern Rumelia; they were not opposed to the union of Bulgaria and Eastern Rumelia, if the "force of circumstances" made that necessary, but they would deter Bulgaria from aggression against Macedonia and other Turkish possessions.[118]

On the other hand, Imanuel Geiss dismisses the importance of the League and stresses that "the Treaty of 1881 was not an alliance, but contained only the agreement to remain neutral in the case of an attack by a fourth power and to try and settle all problems concerning the Balkans and Turkey."[119] Despite this debate, the Three Emperor's League was important for Germany because Bismarck would not have to chose between Austria-Hungary and Russia in the immediate future. Moreover, Bismarck had acquired a formal guarantee that Germany would not have to face a war on two fronts in the event of war with France. In addition, the alliance was important for Russia. It had broken out of the diplomatic isolation that had resulted from the Congress of Berlin.[120]

Then, in 1880-81, Italy became a possible German ally. Italy sought an alliance with Germany and the Dual Monarchy before and after the French had established a protectorate over Tunisia in North Africa in May 1881. Italian commercial and cultural interests in Tunisia were long-standing. Tunisia was part of the Ottoman Empire. But, both Italy and France sought the annexation of Tunisia.[121] French annexation of Tunisia (in the form of creating a protectorate) resulted in Italy seeking an alliance with Berlin and Vienna. Bismarck, despite the reluctance of the Dual

---

118.   Ibid.
119.   Geiss, *German Foreign Policy, 1871-1914*, 40.
120.   Kent, *Bismarck and His Times*, 115.
121.   C.J. Lowe and F. Marzari, *Italian Foreign Policy, 1870-1940* (London: Routledge and Kegan Paul, 1975), 21-25.

Monarchy, achieved the Triple Alliance of Germany, Austria-Hungary, and Italy in May 1882.[122] Germany and Austria-Hungary promised the Italians support against France, and Italy agreed to reciprocate in case of a Franco-German conflict. Rumania secretly joined the alliance in October 1883. The Rumanians sought protection against Russian aggression in the Balkans.[123]

Up until this point, Bismarck stayed out of the scramble for overseas colonies. The " Scramble for Africa" had begun in earnest in 1880. France had established a protectorate in Tunisia in 1881, and began colonial expansion from the Congo to Central Africa in 1882. Britain occupied Egypt in 1882. Belgium established the Congo Free State. Then, in May 1884, the Imperial Chancellor made a bid for colonies.[124] At that time, he suggested to the British that Berlin would support the British position in Egypt and elsewhere if London gave the strategic island of Heligoland, located in the North Sea, to Germany, and recognized German claims to several overseas territories.[125] The British government was not interested in the proposal. Even so, the Gladstone government (1880-85) changed its tune when Germany entered a temporary partnership with the French ministry of Jules Ferry on colonial issues. Britain was already competing against France and Russia for empire. It could not afford to antagonize Germany over colonies. The timing was just right. Bismarck supported France against British interests in Egypt and elsewhere. In the meantime, Russian forces advanced towards British interests in Persia and Afghanistan. In 1884-85, the Great Powers met at the Berlin Conference. At this meeting the Great Powers partitioned Africa among the imperial powers. Bismarck continued to support France against Britain. As a result, Bismarck's diplomacy at the Berlin Conference had gained the Great Power's acceptance of German claims to Southwest Africa (Namibia), the Cameroons, Togoland, German East Africa (Tanzania), and the northern part of New Guinea in the Pacific Ocean.[126] But, Franco-German colonial cooperation ended with the fall of the Ferry ministry in March 1885. Bismarck, nevertheless, had acquired a colonial empire for Germany.

In 1884, the Eastern Powers renewed the Second Three Emperor's League for another three years. The key to maintaining the Dreikaiserbund was keeping the peace in the Balkans. However, this peace would soon be shattered. In 1878, Russia

---

122.  Kent, *Bismarck and His Times*, 115; Pflanze, 3:92-94.

123.  Keith Hitchins, *Rumania, 1866-1947* (Oxford: Clarendon Press, 1994), 137-38, 140-42, 144-46, 152.

124.  See Pflanze, 3:119-42.

125.  Bismarck's quest for colonies is examined in A.J.P. Taylor, *Germany's First Bid for Colonies, 1884-1885: A Move in Bismarck's European Policy* (New York: W.W. Norton, 1970).

126.  Rich, *Great Power Diplomacy, 1814-1914*, 236.

had established control over Bulgaria. It had become an important, albeit shaky, Russian satellite. The Bulgarians were ruled by the anti-Russian Alexander of Battenberg and the Bulgarians sought independence from Russia. In September 1885, a revolt broke out against Turkish rule in Eastern Rumelia. These revolutionaries demanded the union of Eastern Rumelia and Bulgaria. Russian Panslavs supported the union, but the government of St. Petersburg opposed the creation of a Greater Bulgaria. The creation of a Greater Bulgaria would destroy the key provisions of the Treaty of Berlin and upset the balance of power in Southeast Europe.[127] The Tsar had little control over the situation. Two months later, in November, King Milan IV, the ruler of Austria-Hungary's satellite state of Serbia, demanded compensation for the unification of Bulgaria, declared war, and then invaded Bulgaria.[128] The Bulgarians defeated the Serbs at the Battle of Slivntsa, and then prepared to invade Serbia. Vienna and St. Petersburg were shocked at this outcome.[129] Count Gustav von Kálnoky, the Austro-Hungarian Foreign Minister, then handed the Bulgarians an ultimatum to stop the war or face the army of the Dual Monarchy. Alexander of Battenberg quickly backed down.[130] The Austro-Hungarian threats saved Serbia from complete annihilation.[131]

The Great Powers agreed to a compromise solution regarding Bulgaria in April 1886. At that time, Britain, Austria-Hungary, and Russia approved the "personal union" of Bulgaria and Eastern Rumelia under the Prince of Bulgaria. Russia had lost prestige and influence in the Balkans, and now faced an anti-Russian Greater Bulgaria. With the loss of the Bulgarian connection, St. Petersburg would shift its support to Serbia in the future.[132]

The South Slav situation was becoming a major problem for Austria-Hungary and Russia in the Balkans. It threatened the survival of the Three Emperor's League and peace in the Balkans. In November 1886, Bismarck, seeking to avoid war, suggested that the two Great Powers split the Balkans into two parts. Russia should take Bulgaria and Austria-Hungary should occupy Serbia.[133] The Imperial Chancellor stayed neutral, refusing to assist either side. He avoided committing Germany to the Dual Monarchy or Russia

---

127. Taylor, *The Struggle for Mastery in Europe, 1848-1918*, 305.
128. Ibid.
129. Jelavich, *A Century of Russian Foreign Policy, 1814-1914*, 201-10; Barbara Jelavich, *Russia's Balkan Entanglements, 1806-1914* (Cambridge: Cambridge University Press, 1991), 178-96.
130. Jelavich, *Tsarist Russia and Balkan Nationalism*, 231-32.
131. Bismarck warned Austria-Hungary not to attack Bulgaria, stating that such an attack would violate agreements concerning the Three Emperor's League (Pflanze, 3:222).
132. Jelavich, *Tsarist Russia and Balkan Nationalism*, 237-84.
133. Pflanze, 3:221-222; Kent, *Bismarck and His Times*, 116-17.

in the Balkans crisis.[134] As such, Russia, becoming hostile to both Austria-Hungary and Germany, backed away from negotiations to renew the Second Three Emperor's League in 1886.

In 1887, Bismarck sought to establish a complicated set of alliances to provide security for Germany. He needed to renew the Triple Alliance, preserve the status quo in the Balkans and Mediterranean Region, and improve German relations with Russia. He had to avoid the creation of a Franco-Russian alliance and the possibility of a two-front war.[135] During the course of the year, the Great Powers negotiated several agreements that assisted Bismarck in his goals. The first agreement occurred when Britain and Italy accepted the First Mediterranean Agreement in February. This agreement called for the maintenance of the status quo in the Mediterranean, Adriatic, Aegean, and Black Sea. The signatories agreed to defend Egypt and Constantinople. Austria-Hungary and Spain adhered to the agreement in March and May 1887.[136] Bismarck supported the agreement since it strengthened Austria-Hungary against Russia without involving Germany.[137] Then, in February 1887, Berlin, Vienna, and Rome renewed the Triple Alliance.[138] Several months later, in June 1887, Bismarck succeeded in acquiring a three-year agreement with Russia in the Reinsurance Treaty.[139] The German Chancellor promised to support Russia in Bulgaria.[140] It also called for the two powers to remain neutral should one of the powers wage war against a third power.[141] The treatyreduced the chances of a Franco-Russian alliance against Germany.The complex system of alliances was finalized when Britain, Austria-Hungary, and Italy signed the Second Mediterranean Agreement in December 1887. This agreement called for the allies to defend the status quo in the Near

---

134. Geiss, *German Foreign Policy, 1871-1914*, 53-54.

135. See George F. Kennan, *The Decline of Bismarck's European Order: Franco-Russian Relations, 1875-1890* (Princeton: Princeton University Press, 1979).

136. C.J. Lowe, *The Reluctant Imperialists: British Foreign Policy, 1878-1902*, 2 vols. (London: Routledge and Kegan Paul, 1967), 1:94-120; Lowe, *The Great Powers, Imperialism, and the German Problem, 1865-1925*, 66-67; C.J. Bartlett, *Defence and Diplomacy: Britain and the Great Powers, 1815-1914* (Manchester: Manchester University Press, 1993), 85; C.J. Lowe, *Salisbury and the Mediterranean, 1886-1896* (London: Routledge and Kegan Paul, 1965).

137. Pflanze, 3:243-48.

138. Medlicott, *Bismarck and Modern Germany*, 166.

139. Pflanze, 3:248-53.

140. Jelavich, *A Century of Russian Foreign Policy, 1814-1914*, 211.

141. Rich, *Great Power Diplomacy, 1814-1914*, 244-45.

East, including Bulgaria and the Turkish Straits.[142] The alliance system was set. Commenting on the alliance system, Norman Rich has written:

> The alliances fostered by Bismarck…did not divide the powers into two hostile camps. Instead, they brought them all into an interlocking network in which no single state, including Germany, could be assured of support in a war of aggression. On the contrary, an aggressive power would be confronted by an overwhelming defensive coalition, based either upon actual alliance treaties or upon natural alliances that could be expected to form. Because the system would come into operation against any effort to upset the status quo, it served as a deterrent to chauvinist agitators in every country.[143]

Nevertheless, Imanuel Geiss believes that "the Reinsurance Treaty with Russia and the Mediterranean Entente, so highly praised as the summit of Bismarck's statesmanship, were nothing more than desperate stop-gap measures to prolong and safeguard Bismarck's concept of conservative foreign policy."[144] Friedrich von Holstein, the Senior Counselor (Vortragender Rat) in the Political Division of the Foreign Office since 1886, adds that "Prince Bismarck eagerly indulged in his treaty-spinning in every direction. The more tangled the mesh, the more difficult it was to find one's way about in it *without* Prince Bismarck."[145]

## Bismarck and the Wilhelmstrasse

In 1862, King William I appointed Otto von Bismarck as Minister-President and Foreign Minister of Prussia. His office was located at Number 74 on the Wilhelmstrasse in Berlin.[146] As the Foreign Minister, Bismarck controlled the Foreign Ministry and Diplomatic Service at Number 76 on the Wilhelmstrasse. Moreover, he found himself in complete charge of diplomatic affairs since the King had little interest in managing such matters. The heart of the Foreign Ministry was Division (Abteilung) I, the Political Division. The ministry also consisted of Division II, the Central Bureau, and the Chiffrierbureau

---

142.  Lowe, *The Great Powers, Imperialism, and the German Problem, 1865-1925*, 67; Bridge and Bullen, 237-39; Lowe, *The Reluctant Imperialists*, 1:94-120.
143.  Rich, *Great Power Diplomacy, 1814-1914*, 245-46.
144.  Geiss, *German Foreign Policy, 1871-1914*, 54-55.
145.  Holstein, 1:127.
146.  Pflanze, 2:139.

which had their own directors. Division II took care of commercial and legal matters, the Central Bureau was responsible for distributing incoming correspondence and maintaining the archives, and the Chiffrierbureau handled the coding and ciphering of messages.[147] In addition, Bismarck controlled the Diplomatic Service. Prussia had ambassadorships in Paris, London, St. Petersburg, and Vienna, as well as ministries in Brussels, Copenhagen, The Hague, Lisbon, Stockholm, Bern, and Athens.[148] Taking charge of the Foreign Ministry, Bismarck discovered his diplomatic staff and representatives abroad consisted of mediocre personnel who were "disorganized, undisciplined, and destitute of either uniform method or clear channels of communication."[149] Bismarck set out to correct this situation by establishing and insisting upon strict discipline within the Foreign Ministry: he demanded complete subordination of his staff and diplomats to himself.[150] Moreover, the Foreign Minister educated the Foreign Ministry and Prussia's representatives abroad concerning his specific way of handling foreign affairs. Gordon A. Craig has described Bismarck's relationship with his staff in the Foreign Ministry and diplomats in the Diplomatic Service:

> Bismarck chose his aides with care and with an eye to their intelligence, their technical skills, and their judgement; he protected their rights against attacks from outsiders and always sought to improve the material conditions in which they had to work; and he always regarded them as the principal instruments by which his foreign policy was executed. But it was always *his* policy, and they were always *only* instruments....[151]

---

147. Craig, *Germany 1866-1945*, 135; Kurt Doss, "The History of the German Foreign Office," in *The Times Survey of Foreign Ministries of the World*, ed. Zara Steiner (London: Times Books, 1982), 229.

148. Cecil, *The German Diplomatic Service, 1871-1914*, 14-15.

149. Gordon A. Craig, "Bismarck and His Ambassadors: The Problem of Discipline," *Foreign Service Journal* 33 (June 1956); reprinted in *War, Politics, and Diplomacy: Selected Essays*, ed. Gordon A. Craig (London: Weidenfeld and Nicolson, 1966), 181.

150. Bismarck, *Memoirs*, 1:237.

151. Craig, *Germany 1866-1945*, 137.

With Bismarck in firm control, the Wilhelmstrasse gradually became more efficient, which resulted in raising the ministry's prestige, and acted as a catalyst for drawing higher caliber applicants wanting to enter the foreign service. Kurt Doss has pointed out that the political counselors of Division I came from diplomatic careers whereas the other leading ministry officials came from legal-administrative backgrounds.[152] Such efficiency, as well as Bismarck's successful foreign policy which led to the creation of the Second Reich, made the Foreign Ministry and Diplomatic Service an important part of the Prussian, and later, German government.[153] Craig stresses that "any of the major Powers would have been glad to be served by the Bismarckian diplomatists of the 1870s and 1880s."[154] Hajo Holborn called Bismarck "the real father of the German Diplomatic Service."[155]

From its early beginnings, the Prussian Foreign Ministry had to compete against the Prussian military tradition to recruit qualified aristocrats for service as civil servants and diplomats. Prussia's militaristic history, especially under Frederick the Great, meant that most talented Prussians preferred to serve the King in his prestigious military.[156] In fact, the Foreign Ministry became staffed by incompetent diplomats both in Berlin and serving abroad. According to Bismarck, many of the diplomats abroad held their positions just because they could communicate in the French language. They had little knowledge of politics.[157] The Foreign Ministry became known for its corrupt practices and inadequate proficiency in handling foreign affairs.[158]

---

152.  Doss, 229.

153.  Ibid.; Craig, "Bismarck and His Ambassadors," 181.

154.  Craig, *Germany 1866-1945*, 136.

155.  Hajo Holborn, "Diplomats and Diplomacy in the Early Weimar Republic," in *The Diplomats, 1919-1939*, eds. Gordon A. Craig and Felix Gilbert (Princeton: Princeton University Press, 1953), 124. A good description of the German Foreign Office and Diplomatic Service during the Bismarck era is contained in Joseph Maria von Radowitz, *Aufzeichnungen und Erinnerungen aus dem Leben des Botschafters Joseph Maria von Radowitz*, 2 vols., ed. Hajo Holborn (Stuttgart: Deutsche Verlags-Anstalt, 1925).

156.  Gordon A. Craig, *From Bismarck to Adenauer: Aspects of German Statecraft* (Baltimore: Johns Hopkins Press, 1958), 4.

157.  Bismarck, *Memoirs*, 1:4-5. Political reports from Prussian diplomats were written in French until Otto von Bismarck took office (Prince Bernhard von Bülow, *Memoirs of Prince von Bülow*, trans. F.A. Voight and Geoffrey Dunlap, 4 vols. [Boston: Little, Brown and Company, 1931-32], 4:297).

158.  Bismarck, 1:237.

Bismarck's success in war and diplomacy resulted in unifying the German states as the North German Confederation in 1867. As the newly appointed Federal Chancellor, Bismarck needed the services of his by now well-established, professionally-trained Prussian Foreign Ministry to administer the much expanded scope of German relations with other Great and Minor Powers. For several years Bismarck urged William I and the Reichstag to allow the Foreign Ministry to become the supreme federal office for foreign affairs.[159] The Chancellor finally succeeded in this task by way of his great influence and status within the North German Confederation. Thus, on 4 January 1870, William I gave the Prussian Foreign Ministry the official title of Foreign Office of the North German Confederation (Auswärtiges Amt des Norddeutschen Bundes).[160] It became the Foreign Office (Auswärtiges Amt) with the function of assisting the Federal Chancellor in diplomatic matters, instead of gaining status as a ministry. This new organization was almost totally created from the old Prussian Foreign Ministry. It took over the ministry's buildings and staff at the Wilhelmstrasse.[161] The Foreign Office, although subordinate to the Chancellor, was headed by the State Secretary for Foreign Affairs (Staatssekretär des Auswärtigen) or Foreign Secretary. Karl Hermann von Thile (1862-72),[162] Hermann von Balan (1872-73),[163] Bernhard Ernst von Bülow (1873-79),[164] Prince Chlodwig zu Hohenlohe-Schillingsfürst (1880),[165] Count Friedrich Wilhelm zu Limburg-Stirum (1880-81),[166] Count Paul von Hatzfeldt-

159.   Doss, 226-27; Paul Seabury, *The Wilhelmstrasse: A Study of German Diplomats under the Nazi Regime* (Berkeley: University of California Press, 1954), 5.

160.   Doss, 227.

161.   Despite the domination of Prussian foreign policy and diplomats in the newly created North German Foreign Office, the Wilhelmstrasse maintained a Prussian section in the office solely for the purpose of managing the foreign affairs of Prussia.

162.   Holstein, 1:49, 3:34. Thile had served as the Prussian Minister to the Holy See (1855-57) and Minister to Vienna (1857-59).

163.   Ibid., 1:74. Balan was the Prussian/German Minister in Brussels (1868-74), and served as the acting State Secretary from 1872 to 1873.

164.   Ibid., 1:60; Bülow, 4:285, 4:298. Bülow had served as the Minister to the Federal Diet in Frankfurt for Holstein and Lauenburg (1851-62), Minister of State in Mecklenburg-Strelitz (1862-68), and Minister for Mecklenburg-Strelitz in Berlin (1868-73) before becoming German Foreign Secretary.

165.   Holstein, 1:37, 2:61, 3:38. Prince zu Hohenlohe-Schillingsfürst had previously served as the Bavarian Minister-President (1866-70), and was the German Ambassador to Paris from 1874 to 1885. He temporarily acted as the State Secretary for Foreign Affairs in 1880.

166.   Ibid., 1:61, 2:39, 3:49. Count zu Limburg-Stirum had served as the Prussian Minister in Weimar (1875-80) and was serving as a Member of the Prussian Chamber of Deputies (1871-1905) when he acted as the interim Foreign Secretary for Germany in 1880 to 1881.

Wildenberg (1881-85),[167] and Herbert von Bismarck-Schönhausen (1885-1890)[168] all served Bismarck as the State Secretary for Foreign Affairs.[169] The Foreign Secretary was responsible for directing Division I (the Political Division) at the Wilhelmstrasse.[170]

With the creation of the Second Reich in 1871, the Foreign Office gained additional responsibilities and personnel. The Foreign Office was transferred to the new empire simply by omitting the words "of the North German Confederation."[171] Thus, as Norman Rich has written, the Foreign Office "was simply an expansion of the Prussian Foreign Ministry. There was no organic division between them."[172] Now, however, the German Foreign Office required additional space to house an expanded staff after the establishment of the German Empire. Bismarck, the Imperial Chancellor and Prussian Foreign Minister, acquired the additional space on the Wilhelmstrasse at Number 77 in 1874 and Number 75 in 1877.[173] But the requirements of the Second Reich also determined some reorganization in the Foreign Office. In 1879, the Personnel Section was separated from Division II (Legal and Commercial) and established as a separate division.[174] Two years later, in 1881, Bismarck created the position of Under State Secretary for Foreign Affairs.[175] Bismarck wanted the position to handle all non-political affairs of the Wilhelmstrasse. As such, the Under State Secretary was chosen on the basis of his administrative skill or his competence in non-political fields.[176] Dr. Klemens August Busch served as Bismarck's first Under State Secretary

---

167.  Ibid., 2:1, 3:13. Count von Hatzfeldt-Wildenburg had served as Secretary in Paris (1860-66), Secretary of the Legation at The Hague (1866-68), a Counselor in the Political Division of the Foreign Office (1868-74), part of Chancellor Bismarck's personal Foreign Office staff (1870-71), Head of the French Section in the Foreign Office (1872-74), Minister in Madrid (1874-78), and German Ambassador to Constantinople (1879-81) before becoming the State Secretary for Foreign Affairs.

168.  Ibid., 2:22, 3:26. Count Bismarck began serving his father, Otto von Bismarck, in the Foreign Office in January 1874. He was attached to several Legations but served mostly as a private secretary to his father. He was First Secretary in the German Embassy in London (1882-84), Acting First Secretary in St. Petersburg in 1884, Minister at The Hague (1884-85), and Under State Secretary in the Foreign Office (1885-86).

169.  Pflanze, 3:37-38.

170.  Holstein, 1:201.

171.  Doss, 227; Pflanze, 2:137.

172.  Holstein, 1:200.

173.  Lamar Cecil, *The German Diplomatic Service, 1871-1914* (Princeton: Princeton University Press, 1976), 3-4; Seabury, *The Wilhelmstrasse*, 3.

174.  Doss, 229; Holstein, 1:201.

175.  Holstein, 1:200.

176.  Craig, *Germany 1866-1945*, 135.

from 1881 to 1885.[177] The Imperial Chancellor's son, Herbert von Bismarck, served as the Under State Secretary for a short time in 1885 and 1886 before he was quickly promoted to Foreign Secretary.[178] The new official, according to Kurt Doss, "was supposed to relieve the State Secretary of all his non-political responsibilities, but in practice he was almost completely absorbed in the work of the Political Division."[179] As a consequence, the State Secretary was still instrumental in making all important decisions in non-political matters.[180] Gordon A. Craig, however, reminds us that "the heart of the Foreign Ministry was the Political Division."[181] This division was in charge of the general problems of foreign policy, press affairs (until 1915), colonial affairs, and, after 1895, the Personnel Section of the Diplomatic Service. It was staffed by four to six Counselors and a roughly equal number of Assistants.[182] Heads of all the other Foreign Office divisions were required to submit all matters regarding foreign policy to the Political Division for coordination. Therefore, the Political Division sometimes became involved in questions of foreign loans or railroad construction which normally would have been handled by other divisions.[183] Meanwhile, in 1885, Division II was divided into Division II (Economic Policy and Consular Service) and Division III (Legal Affairs).[184] Count Maximilian von Berchem, the new Under State Secretary (1886-90),[185] was put in charge of Division II.[186] In 1890, Colonial Affairs was separated from Division I and made a separate division.[187] Bismarck, who was not

177.  Holstein, 1:63; Rich, *Friedrich von Holstein*, 1:117. Dr. Busch had previously served Prussia as Dragoman in Constantinople (1861-72) and Germany as Consul in St. Petersburg (1872-74), Counselor in the Political Division of the Foreign Office (1874-79), Consul-General in Budapest (1879-80), and temporary Head of the Political Division in the Foreign Office (1880-81) before becoming the first Under State Secretary in 1881 (Holstein, 1:63, 3:48).

178.  Holstein, 1:68; Rich, *Friedrich von Holstein*, 1:165-68.

179.  Doss, 229.

180.  Holstein, 1:200.

181.  Craig, *Germany 1866-1945*, 135.

182.  Holstein, 1:201; Ludwig Biewer, "The History of the German Foreign Office: An Overview," (Berlin: Auswärtiges Amt, ca. 2005), 3.

183.  Holstein, 1:201.

184.  Doss, 229; Holstein, 1:201, 2:22. The Consular Service was separated from Division II and placed under the Personnel Division in 1903 (Holstein, 1:201).

185.  Holstein, 1:129, 2:11, 3:108. Count von Berchem had served Germany as the First Secretary in St. Petersburg (1875-78), First Secretary in Vienna (1878-83), Chargé d'Affaires in Stockholm (1884), and Director of the Economic Policy Division of the Foreign Office (1885-86) before becoming the Under State Secretary in 1886.

186.  Rich, *Friedrich von Holstein*, 1:166.

187.  Doss, 229; Holstein, 1:201. The Colonial Affairs Division was removed from the Foreign Office and established as a new imperial office in 1907.

only Reich Chancellor, but still held the position of Prussian Foreign Minister, ensured that the Auswärtiges Amt was totally subordinate to him.[188]

Article XI of the Imperial Constitution of 1871 declared that the German Emperor would represent Germany in foreign relations, conclude international treaties, and accredit and receive envoys. Moreover, the Constitution extended to the Kaiser the same general appointive power that he enjoyed in Prussia (Article XVIII).[189] As German Emperor, William I appointed the Imperial Chancellor, Bismarck, who was responsible only to him, to direct German foreign and domestic policies. William I solved the problem of the relationship between Prussia and the German Empire by uniting the positions of Imperial Chancellor and that of the Prussian Foreign Minister with the appointment of Bismarck to both. This gave Bismarck control over the whole German Empire and its foreign affairs, since William I, and later, Frederick III, preferred to leave much of the diplomatic affairs of Germany to the Iron Chancellor.[190] The role of the Foreign Office was to serve the Chancellor and his handling of foreign affairs without question. The Foreign Office served Bismarck as a bureaucratic technical apparatus. It was not allowed to contribute in the formulation of foreign policy!

The autocratic Bismarck ruled over the new German Foreign Office with complete authority. He continued to demand strict discipline and complete subordination of his diplomats in Berlin and abroad.[191] This included the expanded scope of the Diplomatic Service, including new ambassadorships in Constantinople (1874), Rome (1876), and Madrid (1888), along with ministries in Belgrade (1880), Bucharest (1881), and Luxembourg (1890).[192] Bismarck operated under the belief that he was the only one who could effectively formulate and exercise German foreign policy. He, according to the historian Lamar Cecil, had a very low opinion of his diplomats.[193] One Foreign Office official heard Bismarck complain that "German diplomats were mostly enthusiasts for some other country."[194] A historian has stated, "to Bismarck, many diplomats were no more than liveried letter carriers who consumed stately dinners and purveyed malicious gossip."[195] Friedrich von Holstein, a Foreign Office official under the Iron Chancellor, heard Bismarck once state: "Provided an Ambassador can obey that's all he

188.  Holstein, 1:200.
189.  Cecil, *The German Diplomatic Service, 1871-1914*, 190.
190.  Ibid.
191.  Ibid., 226-56; Craig, "Bismarck and His Ambassadors," 187.
192.  Cecil, *The German Diplomatic Service, 1871-1914*, 14-15.
193.  Ibid., 235.
194.  Bülow, 2:128.
195.  Cecil, *The German Diplomatic Service, 1871-1914*, 235.

needs."[196] Other than the Foreign Secretary, diplomats at the Wilhelmstrasse had no access to Bismarck.[197] Lamar Cecil has analyzed the situation:

> Bismarck was self-confident, overbearing, and hypercritical by nature, and he was therefore inclined to manage the Wilhelmstrasse dictatorially, both because his estimation of his own talents was boundless and because he had scant regard for a great many of his diplomatic servants.[198]

Bernhard Ernst von Bülow, the State Secretary for Foreign Affairs (1873-79), admitted that Bismarck "did not consider the Foreign Office an arena for discussion [on foreign policy] but rather the instrument for carrying out Bismarck's instructions to the letter."[199] In fact, when it came to diplomatic reports, the Chancellor insisted on two things. First, the reports needed to be concise and accurate, and, secondly, that the diplomat report only the facts and include no speculation. The Chancellor wanted to make his own analysis.[200] Bismarck, himself, wrote about diplomats and diplomatic reports in his memoirs:

> It is especially to be wished that we [Germany] should be represented at every friendly Court by diplomatists who, without encroaching on the general policy of their own country, should as far as possible foster the relations of both interested states, suppress as far as possible ill-humour and gossip, bridle their desire to be witty, and rather bring forward the practical side of the matter. I have often not shown dispatches from our representatives at German Courts in the highest quarters, because they had a tendency to be piquant, or to relate and give importance to annoying expressions or occurrences, rather than to foster and improve the relations between the two Courts, so long as the latter, as in Germany is always the case, was the task of our policy. When I was in St. Petersburg and Paris I always considered myself justified in suppressing things which would merely have caused useless ill-feeling at home, or were only adapted for satirical representations; and when I was minister I did not lay dispatches of this kind before those who filled the highest place in the state. In the position of an ambassador at the Court of a Great Power there is no obligation to report mechanically all the foolish talk and spiteful things that arise at the ambassador's place of residence. A man who looks only at the formal part of the course of business will certainly consider it the most correct thing

---

196.  Holstein, Diary entry for 11 February 1884, 2:78.
197.  Cecil, *The German Diplomatic Service, 1871-1914*, 227.
198.  Ibid., 226.
199.  As quoted in Paul M. Kennedy, *The Rise of the Anglo-German Antagonism 1860-1914* (London: George Allen and Unwin, 1980), 140.
200.  Craig, "Bismarck and His Ambassadors," 184-85.

that the ambassador shall report all that he hears without reserve and leave it to the minister to decide what is to be passed over and what is to be emphasised. Whether such a method is practically useful depends on the personality of the minister.[201]

Bismarck insisted upon complete subordination of his Foreign Office officials and diplomats to his foreign policy. He would not put up with any challenges to his authority. He declared that, "I…am His Majesty's sole adviser on Foreign Affairs."[202] Few had the nerve to oppose his diplomatic instructions. Kurt Doss has stated that, "those who ignored his warnings had the implacable fury of the Chancellor to fear."[203] In 1872, Bismarck fired Karl Hermann von Thile, the State Secretary for Foreign Affairs, after he had attempted to influence foreign policy.[204] As Alan Palmer has written, "the Chancellor regarded the State Secretary as an administrative official, not a person of political or executive rank."[205] Then, in 1874, Count Harry von Arnim, the German Ambassador to Paris (1871-74), opposed Bismarck's anti-Bourbon policy with France and worked to restore the Bourbons to the French throne. Bismarck made an example out of Arnim by having him charged with treason and convicted in court for disregarding his diplomatic instructions.[206] This lesson was remembered by diplomats in the Foreign Office for many years. The Arnim case gave proof how severe the Chancellor could act even against the highly privileged members of the Wilhelmstrasse should they put up any resistance to his policies. The Chancellor brought fear to even his most experienced counselors in the Political Division. Johann Maria von Radowitz, one of Bismarck's most talented subordinates, stated that "to oppose Bismarck of the 1870's and the 1880's in any matter would have been unthinkable to me!"[207] Gordon Craig described the situation as such: "it is not too much to say that the atmosphere in the Foreign Ministry came to resemble that of an oriental court ruled by a cruel and capricious tyrant."[208]

---

201.  Bismarck, *Memoirs*, 2:247-49.

202.  Bülow, 2:197.

203.  Doss, 228.

204.  George O. Kent, *Arnim and Bismarck* (Oxford: Oxford University Press, 1968), 89.

205.  Alan Palmer, *The Chancelleries of Europe* (London: George Allen and Unwin, 1983), 146.

206.  Ibid.; Bismarck, *Memoirs*, 2:177-84; Holstein, 1:95-96; Craig, *Germany 1866-1945*, 105-6; Norman Rich, *Friedrich von Holstein: Politics and Diplomacy in the Era of Bismarck and Wilhelm II*, 2 vols. (Cambridge: Cambridge University Press, 1965), 1:71-86; Norman Rich, "Holstein and the Arnim Affair," *Journal of Modern History* 28 (March 1956), 35-54. See also Kent's study concerning Bismarck and Arnim.

207.  As quoted in Craig, "Bismarck and His Ambassadors," 190.

208.  Craig, *Germany 1866-1945*, 138.

In firm control of foreign policy, Bismarck dominated the operations of the Wilhelmstrasse. From 1862 to 1890, the Chancellor presided over the daily business of the foreign service, putting his own personal stamp, one rooted in a thorough and professional knowledge of diplomacy, on its administration. Commenting on Bismarck's management of the Wilhelmstrasse, one historian of the Foreign Office has written:

> He would provide them [Foreign Office personnel] with orders and their role would be to carry out his directives to the letter. The result was a system in which both the design of policy and the discipline of the diplomatic service depended on a single indispensable figure. Bismarck encountered no opposition from his subalterns in the Foreign Office, for German diplomats understood that their role was implemental, not consultive.[209]

The Chancellor tended to be an extremely overbearing manager of the Foreign Office. This was evident in the thirty-two volumes of instructions he issued to his staff covering such matters as the size of blotting paper, the use of abbreviations, the color of ink, the pagination of lengthy reports, and the use of covers.[210] He allowed no one, with the exception of the Foreign Secretary, access to him.[211] From 1886 to 1890 this Foreign Secretary was Bismarck's own son, Herbert, whom the Chancellor groomed through rapid promotions with the hope of making him his successor.[212] The autocratic operations of the Foreign Office made a lasting impression on the young grandson of William I, the future Emperor William II, who worked in the Foreign Office under Herbert von Bismarck in 1886

---

209.  Cecil, *The German Diplomatic Service, 1871-1914*, 321.

210.  J.C.G. Röhl, *Germany without Bismarck: The Crisis of Government in the Second Reich, 1890-1900* (London: B.T. Batsford, 1967), 22; Holstein, Diary entry for 7 March 1885, 2:172.

211.  William II, *My Early Life* (New York: George H. Doran, 1926; reprint, New York: AMS, 1971), 210.

212.  Herbert joined the Foreign Office in 1874. He was attached to several Legations but was principally employed as a private secretary to his father. He served as the First Secretary in the German Embassy in London in 1882 to 1884, and then as the Acting First Secretary at the German Embassy in St. Petersburg in January 1884. Then, in May 1884, Herbert von Bismarck was appointed as the German Minister to The Hague. Herbert was sent to Britain as a Special Minister of the German Foreign Office in March 1885. Upon his return, he was promoted to the Under State Secretary for Foreign Affairs in Berlin in May 1885 (Rich, *Friedrich von Holstein*, 1:164-68 and Holstein, 2:22). See Louis L. Snyder, *Diplomacy in Iron: The Life of Herbert von Bismarck* (Malabar, FL: Krieger, 1985), 71-72. Holstein once made the comment to another diplomat: "Bismarck is a Wallenstein. His ambition is to found a Bismarck dynasty" (Karl Friedrich Nowak, *Germany's Road to Ruin*. trans. E.W. Dickes, [London: Longmans, 1932], 23).

and 1887, as particularly different than that of the German General Staff.[213] He wrote in his memoirs:

> The Foreign Office was conducted with the strictest discipline by Count Herbert, whose rudeness toward his employees particularly struck me. The gentlemen there simply flew when they were summoned or dismissed by the Count, so much so that a joking saying arose at the time that "their coat tails stood straight out behind them." The foreign policy was conducted by Prince Bismarck alone, after consultation with Count Herbert, who passed on the commands of the Chancellor and had them transformed into instructions. Hence the Foreign Office was nothing but an office of the great Chancellor, where work was done according to his directions. Able men, with independent ideas, were not schooled and trained there.[214]

The young diplomat, Bernhard von Bülow, the son of one of Bismarck's previous State Secretaries, and later to become not only a Foreign Secretary himself, but Imperial Chancellor, also noted the strict discipline of the Foreign Office under the two Bismarcks. He made the following observation of Herbert's operation of the Wilhelmstrasse:

> Herbert Bismarck had trained the messengers [in the Foreign Office]. He had kept them in such a permanent state of tension and fear that when he rang his bell they would dash into his room like a trout when it leaps over an obstruction.[215]

With this intense effort, the Chancellor eventually turned his foreign service into one of the most orderly and efficient in existence by improving its quality of personnel, technical expertise, and performance.[216] Even Harold Nicolson has admitted that from the standpoint of talent and efficiency Bismarck's foreign service compared favorably with any in Europe.[217]

In spite of Bismarck's autocratic rule of the Wilhelmstrasse, German aristocrats, especially Prussians, strongly desired a position at the Foreign Office or service as a diplomat abroad. Taking their tradition from the Prussian Foreign Ministry, German aristocrats sought to serve the Second Reich in the highly

---

213.  William II, *My Early Life*, 210.
214.  William II, *The Kaiser's Memoirs: Wilhelm II Emperor of Germany 1888-1918*, trans. Thomas R. Ybarra (New York: Harper and Brothers, 1922; reprint, New York: Howard Fertig, 1976), 6.
215.  Bülow, 1:8.
216.  Craig, *Aspects of German Statecraft*, 5.
217.  Harold Nicolson, *Diplomacy*, 2d ed., (Oxford: Oxford University Press, 1950), 148-49.

rationalized, professionally-trained bureaucracy of the Foreign Office. Under Bismarck, as Paul Seabury has commented, "the prestige of this bureaucracy as a whole was enormous."[218] But to acquire a post and experience career advancement one needed to come from noble lineage.[219] The Wilhelmstrasse, as Albert Ballin, one of Germany's leading bourgeois businessmen in the late nineteenth century, observed, was a "club into which one had to be admitted by and through birth."[220] In fact, as one historian has noted, sixty-eight percent of the diplomats working in the Foreign Office bore titles of nobility, while eighty-seven percent of the diplomats abroad were of noble lineage.[221] The German Emperor and Imperial Chancellor favored nobles since it was highly likely that these individuals would be conservatives and support the German monarchy.[222] It was true, however, that bourgeois applicants, especially those with considerable wealth, could acquire a position in the Foreign Office. Candidates for the Foreign Office were more likely, however, to be accepted if they held the patronage of the Emperor, Chancellor, or important Wilhelmstrasse officials; came from Prussian military families; or possessed law degrees and had belonged to certain university fraternities.[223] But, to gain advancement, an individual normally had to have noble birth, wealth, sociability, a well-born German wife which was acceptable to the Foreign Office leadership, as well as some ability for negotiation.[224] Conceit and back stabbing were prevalent. Moreover, some diplomats from old aristocratic families were intolerant of their colleagues whose titles were recent, considering them in all respects, except nomenclature, to be indistinguishable from the bourgeoisie.[225] On top of all this, the German government paid very low wages to officials and diplomats who worked in the foreign service.[226]

As already alluded to, the Chancellor appointed a State Secretary for Foreign Affairs to manage the every day routine administrative affairs of the Foreign Office. Bismarck created this Imperial position with the intention that it

---

218. Seabury, *The Wilhelmstrasse*, 5

219. Cecil, *The German Diplomatic Service, 1871-1914*, 328.

220. Lamar Cecil, *Albert Ballin: Business and Politics in Imperial Germany, 1888-1918* (Princeton: Princeton University Press, 1967), 123.

221. Cecil, *The German Diplomatic Service, 1871-1914*, 66.

222. Ibid., 72.

223. Ibid., 23, 27. For instance, Foreign Secretary Bernhard Ernst von Bülow was the nephew of former Prussian Foreign Minister Count Bernstorff. Bülow's own son climbed up the career ladder to not only become Foreign Secretary, but Imperial Chancellor (Bülow, 4:304-6).

224. Cecil, *The German Diplomatic Service, 1871-1914*, 188.

225. Ibid.

226. Ibid., 44.

should be held by a civil servant.[227] With the exception of Herbert von Bismarck, no Foreign Secretary exerted much influence on the formulation of German foreign policy. Lamar Cecil, in his study of the German Diplomatic Service from 1871 to 1914, wrote:

> Of all posts, none was so scrupulously avoided as the state secretaryship, and a long file of Foreign Office dignitaries—among them Alvensleben, Hatzfeldt, Hohenlohe, Holstein, Jagow, Monts, Radowitz, and Werthern—at one time or another declined the post or resisted its being thrust upon them. Bismarck himself admitted that it was a thankless job. The state secretary was allowed considerable latitude in administration, but in diplomatic matters he was only the chancellor's spokesman.[228]

The German Foreign Office, because of Bismarck's influence and its constitutional position, was incapable of formulating its own foreign policies. Even so, from 1886 onwards, Friedrich von Holstein, the Senior Counselor in the Political Division, who had supported Bismarck during the Arnim crisis,[229] quietly challenged the Chancellor with presenting his own foreign policy initiatives. Unaware of the entire scheme of Bismarck's diplomatic system, especially since the Chancellor did not confide in him, Holstein believed that Bismarck's diplomatic system, which was based upon the Triple Alliance (Germany, Austria-Hungary, and Italy) as well as the Reinsurance Treaty with Russia, was too complex and "governed by emotion and therefore unsound."[230] Thus, in the late 1880s, when Bismarck was experiencing political difficulties in his office as Chancellor, Holstein used the opportunity to lead a movement within the Foreign Office against his master.[231] Bismarck fought back, reproaching Holstein for corresponding directly with the German Emperor on diplomatic matters: the Chancellor had always forbidden any Foreign Office official other than himself from direct contact with the Emperor.[232] According to the Emperor, Bismarck warned him away from

---

227.  Holstein, 1:200.
228.  Cecil, *The German Diplomatic Service, 1871-1914*, 154-55.
229.  Ibid., 1:95-96. Many in the Foreign Office viewed Holstein with respect. In 1876, Foreign Secretary Bülow told his son, the future German Chancellor, that, "Holstein really possesses a first-class political head, a very strong political intellect" (Bülow, 4:394).
230.  Holstein, 1:116.
231.  Bülow, 2:126; Rich, *Friedrich von Holstein*, 1:280-83.
232.  Otto von Bismarck to Friedrich von Holstein memorandum, in Holstein, 3:296; Doss, 231.

Holstein, calling the young diplomat "dangerous."[233] Holstein, however, remained at his post, outlasting the Bismarck era.

233. William II, *The Kaiser's Memoirs*, 5.

# 3

# *Emperor William II and the Foreign Office 1888-1918*

## William II and the Iron Chancellor

William II became the German Emperor in 1888. He succeeded his father Frederick III (1888), who ruled Germany for a mere ninety-nine days, and his grandfather William I (1861-88). William I was almost ninety-one years old when he died in March 1888. Frederick III was fifty-six years old, but died from throat cancer in June 1888. Prince William was not expected to be the ruler of Germany at such a young age. Kaiser William II was only twenty-nine years old.[1] He had attended the University of Bonn, served in the First Foot Guards and Guard Hussars at Potsdam, acted as a diplomat, and worked in the German Foreign Office.[2]

The Emperor possessed a keen interest in foreign relations.[3] This attraction was aroused by the fact that he was related to most of the monarchs in Europe, with Queen Victoria I of Britain as his grandmother. His mother, Princess Victoria, was the daughter of Queen Victoria. It was further stimulated when Emperor William I sent Prince William as a diplomatic representative to the court of Tsar Alexander III in 1884. The occasion was the coming-of-age ceremonies for Crown Prince Nicholas.[4] It was during this trip that Prince William met and became a confidant of Count Herbert von Bismarck, the son of Chancellor Otto

---

1.  See J. Alden Nichols, *The Year of the Three Kaisers: Bismarck and the German Succession, 1887-1888* (Urbana: University of Illinois Press, 1987).

2.  Lamar Cecil, *Wilhelm II*, 2 vols. (Chapel Hill: University of North Carolina Press, 1989-96), 1: 37-85.

3.  John C.G. Röhl, *Wilhelm II: The Kaiser's Personal Monarchy, 1888-1900*, trans. Sheila de Bellaigue (Cambridge: Cambridge University Press, 2004), 139.

4.  Cecil, *Wilhelm II*, 1:80-81; Otto Pflanze, *Bismarck and the Development of Germany*, 3 vols. (Princeton: Princeton University Press, 1990), 3:293.

von Bismarck. Herbert von Bismarck was serving in the German diplomatic corps as the First Secretary to the German Embassy at St. Petersburg. Herbert von Bismarck took Prince William under his wing.[5] After this assignment, the Imperial Chancellor sent Prince William to Vienna, where he discussed Balkan affairs with Emperor Francis Joseph I of Austria-Hungary and King Milan IV of Serbia.[6] This was followed by a diplomatic mission to St. Petersburg in 1886.[7] Upon his return to Germany, William I, at the suggestion of the Imperial Chancellor, assigned his grandson to the German Foreign Office under the tutelage of State Secretary Herbert von Bismarck to learn something about the formulation of foreign policy.[8] Starting in the autumn of 1886, Prince William worked once or twice a week at the Wilhelmstrasse. He still had to carry out all of his military duties at Potsdam. On the days that William worked at the Foreign Office Herbert von Bismarck took time to show William key diplomatic documents, and gave him instruction concerning European politics.[9] In his memoirs, William wrote of his relationship with the young Bismarck: "Herbert von Bismarck was my instructor with regard to diplomatic events of former times, the general questions of the day in foreign politics, as well as foreign statesmen and diplomats, particularly the Ambassadors in Berlin."[10] William noted "Count Herbert's passion for work, his inexhaustible energy, and his political knowledge were amazing; while he did not possess his father's genius, he was undoubtedly his most gifted and important pupil."[11] William responded with enthusiasm at first, but slowly lost interest in studying the diplomatic documents.[12] In addition to this training, Prince William received instruction concerning colonial and non-European matters from Ludwig Raschdau, a young official in the trade section of the German Foreign Office.[13] While at the Wilhelmstrasse, Prince William witnessed the absolute control that the Imperial Chancellor had over foreign policy. He made the critical statement in his memoirs:

---

5.    Cecil, *Wilhelm II*, 1:64.
6.    Ibid., 1:82; William II, *My Early Life* (New York: George H. Doran, 1926; reprint, New York: AMS, 1972), 209.
7.    Cecil, *Wilhelm II*, 1:85.
8.    Ibid.; William II, *My Early Life*, 209.
9.    William II, *My Early Life*, 209-10.
10.   Ibid., 210.
11.   Ibid., 212.
12.   Cecil, *Wilhelm II*, 1:86.
13.   William II, *My Early Life*, 210.

Foreign policy was conducted by the Prince [Otto von Bismarck] alone, who took counsel with no one but his son; the latter passed the Chancellor's orders on and had them cast into the form of instructions. The Foreign Office was thus merely a branch office of the great Chancellor's; it was no school for men of independence, happy in the exercise of their responsibility, and was thus in sharp contrast with the General Staff under Moltke. On the General Staff, the younger generation were painstakingly trained on tried and proven principles, and were brought up to think and act for themselves. In the Foreign Office, on the other hand, they were only the executive organs of a single will: they could offer no independent assistance because they were taught nothing, or not enough, of the great interrelationships of the questions with which it fell to them to deal. The Prince bulked there like a huge granite boulder in a field; roll it away and you find beneath it but vermin and withered roots.[14]

However, Prince William, like many others, "revered and idolized the Chancellor."[15] William enjoyed his time at the Wilhelmstrasse. He once bragged to his grandmother, Queen Victoria of Britain, that he learned "how to do politics and how to manage to steer the ship of state between the shoals and intricate channels of treaties, foreign susceptibilities etc. It is vastly interesting and gives one a much broader horizon for judging people or nations in their actions."[16] Nevertheless, Friedrich von Holstein, the Senior Counselor in the Political Division at the German Foreign Office, was not impressed by Prince William's rare attendance and superficial training at the Wilhelmstrasse.[17] Prince William's training at the Foreign Office ended in the spring of 1887. However, this training was resumed in November 1887, once Emperor William I was convinced that Crown Prince Frederick was doomed to die from cancer. The Imperial Chancellor was given the responsibility to train Prince William in foreign affairs.[18] It was during this time that it became evident that Prince William wanted to control German affairs himself once he became the ruler.[19] Then, after the deaths of his grandfather and father in 1888, Emperor William II gradually worked to assume control over the German Empire.[20]

---

14.   Ibid.
15.   William II, *The Kaiser's Memoirs: Wilhelm II, Emperor of Germany, 1888-1918*, trans. Thomas R. Ybarra (New York: Harper and Brothers, 1922; reprint, New York: Howard Fertig, 1976), 1.
16.   As quoted in Cecil, *Wilhelm II*, 1:86.
17.   Friedrich von Holstein, *The Holstein Papers: The Memoirs, Diaries and Correspondence of Friedrich von Holstein, 1837-1909*, 4 vols., ed. Norman Rich and M.H. Fisher (Cambridge: Cambridge University Press, 1955-63), 2:355.
18.   Cecil, *Wilhelm II*, 1:97.
19.   Ibid., 126.
20.   Lamar Cecil, *The German Diplomatic Service 1871-1914* (Princeton: Princeton University Press, 1976), 212.

In 1887, the Imperial Chancellor had established his system of diplomatic alliances. He acquired the Mediterranean Agreements with Great Britain, Austria-Hungary, and Italy; renewed the Triple Alliance with Austria-Hungary and Italy; and obtained the secret Reinsurance Treaty with Russia.[21] He expected these agreements to keep France diplomatically isolated and maintain the peace in Europe. But, Russo-German relations became more tense in 1887. First, there was the issue of Russian support for the Pan-Slav movement. Then, there was St. Petersburg's ban against foreigners, including Germans, from buying land in Russia's western provinces.[22] Next, Bismarck retaliated by ordering the German National Bank (Reichsbank) to stop accepting Russian state bonds as collateral for loans, the so-called Lombardverbot. As a consequence, the Russians left the German financial market, and joined the French.[23] At the same time, the German General Staff was advocating a preventive war against Russia. General Moltke pleaded to launch a surprise attack against Russia in the winter.[24] In the meantime, anti-German sentiment in Russia put pressure on Tsar Alexander III to establish closer relations with Paris. But, anti-German sentiment did not lead to an immediate reorientation of Russian foreign policy. Bismarck, nevertheless, knew he needed to act. Beginning in November 1887, to counter the possibility of a Franco-Russian alliance, the Imperial Chancellor attempted to improve Germany's relations with Great Britain.[25] In January 1889, Bismarck approached the British government for an Anglo-German defensive alliance.[26] He received a reply in March, when Lord Salisbury, the British Prime Minister (1886-92), informed Herbert von Bismarck that Britain "wished to leave the matter on the table for the time being without saying yes or no."[27] Salisbury wanted to avoid offending Britain's imperial rivals of France and Russia. Even so, the British Prime Minister wanted to remain on good terms with Germany, so he invited William II to visit England, where the Kaiser quickly became an Anglophile.[28]

---

21.  See chapter 2.

22.  Imanuel Geiss, *German Foreign Policy 1871-1914* (London: Routledge and Kegan Paul, 1976), 56.

23.  Norman Rich, *Great Power Diplomacy 1814-1914* (New York: McGraw-Hill, 1992), 248.

24.  Geiss, *German Foreign Policy, 1871-1914*, 56.

25.  Ibid., 57.

26.  Paul Kennedy, *The Rise of the Anglo-German Antagonism, 1860-1914* (London: George Allen and Unwin, 1980), 190-91.

27.  Muriel E. Chamberlain, *"Pax Britannica"?: British Foreign Policy, 1789-1914* (London: Longman, 1988), 155; Rich, *Great Power Diplomacy 1814-1914*, 249.

28.  Kennedy, *The Rise of the Anglo-German Antagonism, 1860-1914*, 206.

After ascending to the throne in 1888, Emperor William II gradually confronted Bismarck's domestic and foreign policies. The Chancellor fought back, attempting to control the young ruler and Germany. The Kaiser had supreme decision-making authority according to the Imperial Constitution of 1871. He broke off his close relationship with Herbert von Bismarck. He surrounded himself with a group of relatives and friends who were hostile to the Bismarcks.[29] The Kaiser placed his confidence in General Count Alfred von Waldersee, the Chief of the General Staff (1888-91).[30] The initial confrontation between William II and Otto von Bismarck occurred over the issue of strikes in the Rhineland in May 1889.[31] Chancellor Bismarck slowly realized that he was not the leading servant of the state anymore. In a last attempt to regain political power, Bismarck sought to create a constitutional crisis over the renewal of the Anti-Socialist Law.[32] The Kaiser did not support his Chancellor or the Conservatives against the Social Democrats in this legislation. Bismarck had failed over domestic issues, and resigned from office in March 1890.[33]

William II was rid of the Iron Chancellor. The Kaiser was now in control of Germany. But the German Emperor needed a foreign relations expert. As such, he sought the services of Herbert von Bismarck. He did not want him to serve as Chancellor, but as State Secretary for Foreign Affairs. The Kaiser sent his friend and diplomat Count Philipp zu Eulenburg-Hertefeld, Adjutant Count Karl von Wedel, General Wilhelm von Hahnke, and Privy Councilor Hermann von Lucanus to encourage Herbert von Bismarck to remain in office. The Iron Chancellor's son, however, refused the position out of loyalty to his father.[34]

## William II and Foreign Policy, 1890-1896

With the dismissal of Chancellor Bismarck, Berlin experienced a "crisis in government" because there was no single person who could manage the Empire.[35] One historian has stated that "the appointment of an unpolitical General [Georg

---

29.    Cecil, *Wilhelm II*, 1:143-44.

30.    Ibid., 1:140.

31.    Ibid., 1:136-37.

32.    Ibid., 1:159-67; Pflanze, 3:337-73.

33.    Lynn Abrams, *Bismarck and the German Empire, 1871-1918* (London: Routledge, 1995), 41-42.

34.    William II, *The Kaiser's Memoirs*, 12-13; William II, *My Early Life*, 212; Louis L. Snyder, *Diplomacy in Iron: The Life of Herbert von Bismarck* (Malabar: Robert E. Krieger, 1985), 131-35; Röhl, *Wilhelm II*, 324-25.

35.    This is the argument of J.C.G. Röhl, *Germany without Bismarck: The Crisis of Government in the Second Reich, 1890-1900* (London: B.T. Batsford, 1967).

Leo von Caprivi] to one of the most powerful posts in Europe inevitably created a power-vacuum in Berlin."[36] There was nobody who could replace Bismarck. During the early nineties Berlin's complex constitutional government was ruled by an oligarchy composed of the Kaiser, Chancellor, cabinet chiefs, Prussian ministers, state secretaries, Friedrich von Holstein, and the Kaiser's close friend, Count Philipp zu Eulenburg-Hertefeld.[37] William II, however, wanted to assume full control of the government, including the direction of German foreign policy.[38] For several years, nonetheless, there was much confusion and disunity in the German government.[39] During this time William II worked to assert his constitutional rights concerning the control of foreign relations.

Since Herbert von Bismarck declined the offer to remain as Foreign Secretary, William II lacked a leading diplomatic adviser of high quality to assist him in directing German foreign policy. The Iron Chancellor had maintained complete control over foreign relations and failed to train anyone, other than Herbert, to follow in his footsteps and appreciate Germany's complex system of alliances.[40] With both Bismarcks gone, Germany lacked a Chancellor or State Secretary capable of providing the Kaiser with sound diplomatic advice.

From the beginning of his reign, the Kaiser believed he could be his own Foreign Minister. He thought he could manage diplomatic affairs through his own personal relations with other monarchs.[41] To lessen the chance of any ministerial challenge to his authority, William II appointed men to high positions who lacked experience in diplomacy. In most respects this made the Foreign Office the direct servant of the Kaiser. Meanwhile, the German Emperor maneuvered to acquire and consolidate his political power in the early nineties.

---

36.   Ibid., 64.
37.   Ibid., 271. Eulenburg served as the Secretary of the German Embassy in Paris (1881), Secretary of the Legation in Munich (1881-88), Minister in Oldenburg (1888-90), Minister in Stuttgart (1890-91), Minister in Munich (1891-94), and German Ambassador to Vienna (1894-1901). He served frequently as the German Foreign Office representative in Kaiser William II's retinue (Holstein, 1:176, 2:330, 3:163). The relationship between William II and Eulenburg is examined in John C.G. Röhl, *The Kaiser and His Court: Wilhelm II and the Government of Germany* (Cambridge: Cambridge University Press, 1994), 28.
38.   J. Alden Nichols, *Germany after Bismarck: The Caprivi Era, 1890-1894* (Cambridge, MA: Harvard University Press, 1958), 37-38; Cecil, *The German Diplomatic Service*, 261.
39.   Röhl, *Germany without Bismarck*, 185.
40.   William II, *The Kaiser's Memoirs*, 6, 75-76.
41.   Cecil, *The German Diplomatic Service*, 211; Prince Bernhard von Bülow, *Memoirs of Prince von Bülow*, trans. F.A. Voight and Geoffrey Dunlap, 4 vols. (Boston: Little, Brown and Company, 1931-32), 1:80, 2:62, 2:397; Röhl, *Wilhelm II*, 732. See Konrad Canis, *Von Bismarck zur Weltpolitik: Deutsche Aussenpolitik 1890 bis 1902* (Berlin: Akademie-Verlag, 1999).

In March 1890, William II appointed the fifty-nine-year old General Georg Leo von Caprivi as the new Imperial Chancellor, Prussian Minister-President, and Prussian Foreign Minister. General Caprivi had been Chief of Staff of the 10th Army Corps (1870-71), Section Chief in the War Ministry (1871-83), Head of the Admiralty (1883-88), and the Commanding General of the 10th Army Corps in Hanover (1889-90).[42] Caprivi possessed a poor background in foreign affairs.[43] He wanted, however, to maintain Bismarck's policy of concentrating on Central Europe, a policy referred to as Mittleuropa.[44] Caprivi sought to prop up his inexperience in foreign affairs with the appointment of Count Friedrich Johann von Alvensleben, the German Minister to Brussels, as the State Secretary for Foreign Affairs.[45] Alvensleben, however, declined the offer.[46] As a result, the Kaiser insisted upon appointing Baron Adolf Hermann Marschall von Bieberstein as the Foreign Secretary. Marschall had previously served as the Minister representing the Grand Duchy of Baden at the Federal Council in Berlin from 1883 to 1890. He lacked adequate training and experience in foreign affairs.[47] In this way the Emperor had positioned himself to have great influence over the formulation and conduct of German foreign policy. In fact, many high ranking individuals in Berlin, including Bernhard von Bülow, assumed that the Kaiser, not Caprivi or Marschall, would set the tone for Germany's foreign policy.[48] Lamar Cecil has commented on this situation, "the young monarch, in his own opinion, had the training for diplomacy that both Caprivi and Marschall lacked and he therefore was determined to manage Germany's relations with the other powers himself."[49] Marschall was known to have complained that William II

---

42.    Nichols, *Germany after Bismarck*, 29; Holstein, 1:92, 2:36, 3:124.

43.    Cecil, *Wilhelm II*, 1:171; Cecil, *The German Diplomatic Service*, 258; Nichols, *Germany after Bismarck*, 54.

44.    Geiss, *German Foreign Policy, 1871-1914*, 64-66.

45.    Holstein, 1:150, 2:136, 3:332. Count von Alvensleben had served as German Minister at The Hague (1882-84), Minister in Washington, D.C. (1884-86), and served as Minister to Brussels (1886-1901). He was later appointed as the German Ambassador to St. Petersburg (1901-5).

46.    Otto von Bismarck, *New Chapters of Bismarck's Autobiography*, trans. Bernard Miall (London: Hodder and Stoughton, 1920), 209-12; Nichols, *Germany after Bismarck*, 51; Rich, *Friedrich von Holstein*, 1:290.

47.    Bismarck, *Autobiography*, 62-63; Holstein, 1:60, 2:368, 3:333; Geiss, *German Foreign Policy, 1871-1914*, 64; Cecil, *Wilhelm II*, 1:216; Snyder, *Diplomacy in Iron*, 136, 154; Rich, *Friedrich von Holstein*, 1:289-92; Röhl, *Wilhelm II*, 326-28. Lamar Cecil argues that William II picked Marschall as a temporary Foreign Secretary, believing that he could convince Herbert von Bismarck to assume the position in the near future (Cecil, *Wilhelm II*, 1:172-73).

48.    Cecil, *Wilhelm II*, 1:175; Cecil, *The German Diplomatic Service*, 261.

49.    Cecil, *The German Diplomatic Service*, 211.

always interfered in the making of foreign policy.[50] Fully aware of his own short-comings, Caprivi became dependent upon the diplomatic experts in the Foreign Office.[51] While accomplishing one of his first foreign policy tasks, the Chancellor met Holstein, the Senior Counselor of the Political Division, who was acting as temporary head of the Foreign Office since the position of State Secretary was still vacant after the resignation of Herbert von Bismarck. This diplomat had built up much personal power and influence within the Foreign Office during the last half of the Bismarck era.[52] Bülow described him as a man with "extensive personal connections, wide experience, quickness of perception and…whose decision, cunning, and ruthlessness had set him in a position of high authority,"[53] while Count Eulenburg found Holstein possessed "infinite craftiness" and a "subtle intelligence".[54] During their conversation Holstein impressed Caprivi with his knowledge of the Foreign Office's filing system and understanding of world affairs. Caprivi, knowing his own inexperience in foreign affairs, came to realize that he could use this expert to assist him in matters of foreign policy.[55] Thus, Holstein was able to gain much influence over the formulation of German foreign policy during the Caprivi period.[56] Caprivi soon became aware that Holstein was gaining too much influence and was carrying on diplomatic correspondence behind his back, but "it was impossible to get along without him."[57]

Since the beginning of his reign William II was suspicious of Alexander III and Russia. In his memoirs, the Kaiser claims that he was unaware of Bismarck's Reinsurance Treaty between Germany and Russia until 1890.[58] He, himself, was anti-Russian and for the first few years of his reign believed that war was inevitable with Russia.[59] Caprivi was not so sure. Friedrich von Holstein was also anti-

50.   Wolfgang J. Mommsen, *Grossmachtstellung und Weltpolitik, 1870-1914: Die Aussenpolitik des Deutschen Reiches* (Frankfurt-am-Main: Propyläen, 1993), 130.

51.    William II, *The Kaiser's Memoirs*, 51; Gordon A. Craig, *Germany 1866-1945* (Oxford: Oxford University Press, 1978), 230-31; Gordon A. Craig, *From Bismarck to Adenauer: Aspects of German Statecraft* (Baltimore: Johns Hopkins Press, 1958), 32; Cecil, *The German Diplomatic Service*, 261.

52.   Bülow, 2:125-26; Norman Rich, *Friedrich von Holstein: Politics and Diplomacy in the Era of Bismarck and Wilhelm II*, 2 vols. (Cambridge: Cambridge University Press, 1965), 1:310.

53.   Bülow, 2:522.

54.   As quoted in Johannes Haller, *Philip Eulenburg: The Kaiser's Friend*, trans. Ethel Colburn Mayne, 2 vols. (New York: Alfred A. Knopf, 1930), 2:294.

55.   Röhl, *Wilhelm II*, 338; Cecil, *Wilhelm II*, 1:171-72.

56.   Craig, *Germany 1866-1945*, 231-33.

57.   Nichols, *Germany after Bismarck*, 324.

58.   William II, *The Kaiser's Memoirs*, 28-29.

59.   Pflanze, 3:312; Geiss, *German Foreign Policy, 1871-1914*, 66-67; Cecil, *Wilhelm II*, 1:188.

Russian. He had tried to prevent Bismarck's Reinsurance Treaty with Russia in 1887.[60] Now, with both Otto von Bismarck and Herbert von Bismarck out of office, Holstein and others in the Auswärtiges Amt strongly recommended to Caprivi that Germany not renew the Reinsurance Treaty in 1890.[61] Holstein and the others stressed that the treaty was incompatible with the Triple Alliance and could entangle Germany in a war started by Russia that had nothing to do with German interests.[62] The Chancellor took the advice of the foreign policy experts. As Imanuel Geiss has stated, "Caprivi, with his straightforward honesty, did not want to continue Bismarck's policy of juggling with five balls at the same time."[63] In addition to the Chancellor and the Foreign Office, the Kaiser's close associate, Count Philipp zu Eulenburg-Hertefeld, and General Lothar von Schweinitz, the German envoy at St. Petersburg, urged William II not to renew the treaty.[64] German leadership wanted to drop the treaty that conflicted with Germany's other commitments. Consequently, the German government refused to renew the Reinsurance Treaty in 1890.[65] Instead, Caprivi concentrated on a New Course (Neue Kurs) policy, a reliance on the Triple Alliance of Germany, Austria-Hungary, and Italy, along with links to Great Britain.[66] As such, Berlin renewed the Triple Alliance in May 1891 and made public the Mediterranean Entente of 1887.[67] The First and Second Mediterranean Agreements of 1887 were seen as checks on Russian expansion in the Near East and Mediterranean Region.[68] William II and Caprivi worked hard to gain a closer relationship with Prime Minister Salisbury of Great Britain.[69] As John Lowe has argued, "the main object of German foreign policy in the early 1890s…was to persuade or cajole Britain into joining the Triple Alliance, as a means of bolstering Germany's security in Europe."[70] As such, Germany gained the Heligoland-Zanzibar Agreement with

---

60.    Rich, *Friedrich von Holstein*, 1:210-11.

61.    Holstein, 1:129-30; Geiss, *German Foreign Policy, 1871-1914*, 67; Nichols, *Germany after Bismarck*, 54; Rich, *Friedrich von Holstein*, 1:311-12; Röhl, *Wilhelm II*, 338.

62.    Pflanze, 3:387; Geiss, *German Foreign Policy, 1871-1914*, 67; Cecil, *Wilhelm II*, 1:189.

63.    Geiss, *German Foreign Policy, 1871-1914*, 67.

64.    Cecil, *Wilhelm II*, 1:189.

65.    Klaus Hildebrand, *Das vergangene Reich: Deutsche Aussenpolitik von Bismarck bis Hitler, 1871-1945* (Stuttgart: Deutches Verlags-Anstalt, 1995), 118, 155.

66.    F.R. Bridge and Roger Bullen, *The Great Powers and the European States System, 1814-1914*, 2 ed. (London: Longman, 2005), 242.

67.    Nichols, *Germany after Bismarck*, 113-226.

68.    John Lowe, *The Great Powers, Imperialism, and the German Problem, 1865-1925* (London: Routledge, 1994), 66.

69.    Ibid., 268-87; Rich, *Great Power Diplomacy 1814-1914*, 254-60.

70.    Lowe, *The Great Powers, Imperialism, and the German Problem, 1865-1925*, 100-1.

Great Britain in July 1890. In this treaty Germany acquired the strategic island of Heligoland in the North Sea in exchange for considerable concessions in German East Africa (Tanganyika), the strategic island of Zanzibar, and other islands off the coast of East Africa. Britain had held Heligoland since the Napoleonic Wars.[71] Then, in July 1891, William II visited England, hoping for Britain to join the Triple Alliance.[72] As a result of Germany's actions, Alexander III and Russia were now diplomatically isolated. The Tsar soon ended this isolation with a rapprochement with Republican France. St. Petersburg and Paris agreed to a Military Convention in 1892, and established the Franco-Russian Dual Alliance in 1894.[73] The Iron Chancellor's web of diplomatic alliances that was meant to safeguard Germany was beginning to unravel.

William II listened to advice coming from Holstein and the Foreign Office, but the Kaiser believed that they were incompetent in matters of foreign relations.[74] Holstein, himself, admitted the difficulty that the Auswärtiges Amt had in continuing Bismarck's foreign policy: "the more tangled the mesh, the more difficult it was to find one's way about it without Prince Bismarck."[75] The Kaiser sincerely believed he did not need the Wilhelmstrasse. Moreover, the Kaiser greatly disliked most diplomats, with the exception of Philipp zu Eulenburg-Hertefeld, Bernhard von Bülow, Heinrich Leonard von Tschirschky und Bögendorff, and Alfred von Kiderlen-Wächter.[76] Holstein heard him once exclaim: "After the French, the people I hate most are diplomats and deputies."[77] Holstein wrote in his memoirs that "the Kaiser's dislike of the Foreign Ministry is almost pathological and recognized as such by the people concerned."[78] Commenting on the Kaiser's opinion of the Foreign Office, Lamar Cecil stated:

> William's language respecting the Foreign Office was often abusive. Its offi-
> cials were "swine"; it lacked both keenness and confidence; it was the depart-

---

71.   Kennedy, *The Rise of Anglo-German Antagonism, 1860-1914*, 205; Geiss, *German Foreign Policy, 1871-1914*, 68; Hajo Holborn, *A History of Modern Germany*, 3 vols. (New York: Alfred A. Knopf, 1959-69), 3:304; Chamberlain, 153; C.J. Lowe, *The Reluctant Imperialists: British Foreign Policy, 1878-1902*, 2 vols. (London: Routledge and Kegan Paul, 1967), 1:121-37.

72.   Bridge and Bullen, 243-44.

73.   See George F. Kennan, *The Decline of Bismarck's European Order: Franco-Russian Relations, 1875-1890* (Princeton: Princeton University Press, 1979) and George F. Kennan, *The Fateful Alliance: France, Russia, and the Coming of the First World War* (New York: Pantheon, 1984).

74.   William II, *My Early Life*, 210: William II, *The Kaiser's Memoirs*, 75-76.

75.   Holstein, 1:127.

76.   Cecil, *The German Diplomatic Service*, 213. See also Holstein, 4:289-96.

77.   Holstein, Diary entry for 11 November 1888, 2:382.

78.   Ibid., 1:173.

ment of the government for which he had the least respect; it did nothing but raise objections. "I will tell you something," he declared in 1912 to Wilhelm von Stumm, the Director of the Political Division, "You diplomats are full of shit and the whole Wilhelmstrasse stinks."[79]

Under Holstein, who was at the height of his power when he acquired firm control of management at the Auswärtiges Amt during 1890 to 1897, the Wilhelmstrasse gained some independence from the Chancellor in its operations. Within the Foreign Office Holstein's authority was virtually uncontested, especially after the resignation of Maximilian von Berchem as Under State Secretary for Foreign Affairs in July 1890.[80] Holstein was instrumental in getting Berchem replaced by the insignificant Baron Wolfram von Rotenhan, the former First Secretary in the German Embassy in Paris and Minister to Argentina.[81] The Senior Counselor of the Political Division controlled the formulation of foreign policy inputs as well as the administration of the Diplomatic Service.[82] His importance to the Wilhelmstrasse as an administrator and foreign relations adviser was greatly respected by diplomats because he was the only one in the inner circle of the Foreign Office who had been in the foreign service under Bismarck.[83] He had, as John C.G. Röhl has pointed out, dismissed and replaced the ambassadors with affiliations to Bismarck with his own people.[84] From 1890 to 1893, Holstein was responsible for replacing Hans Lothar Schweinitz with General Bernhard von Werder in St. Petersburg, Eberhard zu Solms-Sonnenwalde with Bernhard von Bülow in Rome, Prince Heinrich Reuss with Philipp zu Eulenburg-Hertefeld in Vienna, Joseph Maria von Radowitz with Hugo Leszczye von Radolin-Radolinski in Constantinople, Ferdinand von Stumm with Radowitz in Madrid, and Kurt von Schlözer with Otto von Bülow at the Vatican. Only two of Bismarck's diplomats retained their positions: Paul von Hatzfeldt-Wildenburg in London and Georg Herbert zu Münster in Paris.[85] Holstein also staffed the Political Division with his own supporters, such as Dr. Rudolf Lindau, Ludwig von Raschdau, Alfred von Kiderlen-Wächter, and Friedrich von Pourtalès.[86] Commenting on

---

79.    As quoted in Cecil, *The German Diplomatic Service*, 212.

80.    Rich, *Friedrich von Holstein*, 1:299.

81.    Ibid., 1:299-300; Craig, *Germany 1866-1945*, 233; Holstein, 2:174, 3:114, 3:120.

82.    Koppel S. Pinson, *Modern Germany: Its History and Civilization*, 2 ed. (New York: Macmillan, 1966), 303.

83.    Geiss, *German Foreign Policy, 1871-1914*, 64.

84.    Röhl, *The Kaiser and His Court*, 159.

85.    Rich, *Friedrich von Holstein*, 1:403-4; Craig, *Germany 1866-1945*, 233-34.

86.    Rich, *Friedrich von Holstein*, 1:300.

Holstein's influence with the Chancellor and Foreign Secretary, Bernhard von Bülow has stated: " Caprivi and Marschall, who lacked all knowledge of diplomatic routine and all insight into the international game, even as far as languages went, clung to Holstein like drowning men."[87]

After the termination of the Reinsurance Treaty, the Caprivi government focused on bolstering the Triple Alliance with Austria-Hungary and Italy. Moreover, Germany created commercial treaties with various countries during the economic depression of the early 1890s. Germany concluded treaties with Austria-Hungary, Italy, and Belgium in December 1891.[88] These agreements were followed by trade treaties with Rumania in December 1893 and Russia in March 1894.[89] The commercial treaties lowered German tariffs to facilitate the import of agrarian produce in return for more favorable terms for German industrial exports. In addition to these commercial treaties, Germany focused on improving relations with Great Britain. One historian has described Anglo-German relations as a "love-hate relationship" using Africa as the main arena for their diplomatic maneuvering. Berlin was able to offer colonial concessions in the Heligoland-Zanzibar Agreement of 1890, and the Germans exploited British difficulties in the Far East and Africa to put pressure on London to join the Triple Alliance.[90] As Norman Rich has stated, "the Germans were lulled into a false sense of the strength and security of their own position, confident that the British would someday be compelled to enter into an alliance with Germany on Germany's terms."[91] The Kaiser felt confident of improved Anglo-German relations during the temporary Anglo-French crisis over Siam in 1893. But British Prime Minister Gladstone (1892-94) was not interested in an Anglo-German alliance.[92] As a consequence, William II refused to back Britain in the Anglo-French quarrel over the Anglo-Congolese Treaty of May 1894.[93] He even offered to cooperate with the French in resisting the treaty. A.J.P. Taylor believed that the Kaiser was trying to force Archibald Primrose, the Earl of Rosebery, the new British Prime Minister (1894-95), to join the Triple Alliance.[94] But the result was that London

87.    Bülow, 2:126.

88.    Nichols, *Germany after Bismarck*, 138-53; Craig, *Germany 1866-1945*, 253.

89.    Nichols, *Germany after Bismarck*, 291-98, 303-7.

90.    Lowe, *The Great Powers, Imperialism, and the German Problem, 1865-1925*, 100.

91.    Rich, *Great Power Diplomacy, 1814-1914*, 262.

92.    Ibid., 257-58.

93.    Gordon Martel, *Imperial Diplomacy: Rosebery and the Failure of Foreign Policy* (Kingston: McGill-Queen's University Press, 1986), 208.

94.    A.J.P. Taylor, *The Struggle for Mastery in Europe, 1848-1918* (Oxford: Clarendon Press, 1954), 349-51.

had to abandon the Anglo-Congolese Treaty. The British were humiliated, and London warned Berlin that Britain may reconsider its international position if Germany kept supporting France in colonial issues.[95]

In October 1894, William II dismissed Caprivi and replaced him with an experienced diplomat, Prince Chlodwig zu Hohenlohe-Schillingsfürst, as Imperial Chancellor, Prussian Minister-President, and Prussian Foreign Minister.[96] Prince Hohenlohe was seventy-five years old and in poor health. He had served as the Bavarian Minister-President (1866-70), German Ambassador to France (1874-85), temporary State Secretary for Foreign Affairs (1880), and later as Governor of Alsace-Lorraine (1885-94).[97] The Kaiser bought control over Hohenlohe by doubling his salary as Chancellor.[98] William II had selected Hohenlohe as Chancellor so that he, himself, could establish his "personal rule" over Germany. He now, according to John C.G. Röhl, "controlled the foreign policy of the German Reich to an even greater extent than he had been able to do in Caprivi's time."[99] Wolfgang J. Mommsen has stressed that German foreign policy during Hohenlohe's chancellorship was dominated by the "uncontrolled personal rule" of the Kaiser.[100] Moreover, "he now determined the guidelines of foreign policy himself in characteristically impetuous and emotional fashion, often after discussing them with this or that favourite, Flügeladjutant, naval officers, ambassador or other visitor to the court, and expected his orders to be carried out by the Reich Chancellor and the Foreign Office."[101]

At this time, Germany adopted a Free Hand (Freie Hand) foreign policy. The Kaiser did not want to continue driving France and Russia together by opposing them at every turn, while attempting to associate Germany with the unreliable Great Britain. Instead, he sought to exploit the differences between the British Empire on one hand, and the French and Russian Empires on the other, for the benefit of Germany. The Kaiser was determined to improve relations with Russia.[102] In this way, William II began to cooperate with Tsar Nicholas II in the Far

---

95.   Ibid., 351; Martel, 213; Lowe, *The Great Powers, Imperialism, and the German Problem, 1865-1925*, 102.

96.   Prince Chlodwig zu Hohenlohe-Schillingsfürst, *Memoirs of Prince Chlodwig of Hohenlohe-Schillingsfürst*, 2 vols., ed. Friedrich Curtius, trans. George W. Chrystal (London: Macmillan, 1906), 2:473.

97.   Holstein, 1:37, 2:61, 3:38.

98.   Geiss, *German Foreign Policy 1871-1914*, 69.

99.   Röhl, *Wilhelm II*, 732.

100.  Mommsen, *Grossmachtstellung und Weltpolitik, 1870-1914*, 123. See also Canis, 14.

101.  Röhl, 732.

102.  Bridge and Bullen, 250-51.

East.[103] The "Triplice Powers" of Germany, Russia, and France opposed the growing power of Japan. Berlin joined St. Petersburg and Paris in protesting the Peace of Shimonoseki, which ended the Sino-Japanese War of 1894-95.[104] In May 1895, the Triplice opposition forced Japan to drop plans for further territorial expansion into China, including Port Arthur.[105] The Kaiser also sent Rear Admiral Alfred von Tirpitz to command the German Far East Squadron with the task of demonstrating German naval power in Chinese waters.[106] Meanwhile, the Kaiser continued to pressure Britain into joining the Triple Alliance. The method that the Kaiser used was to take advantage of British troubles overseas and demonstrate to London that an alliance with Germany had advantages. But this method only caused friction between Berlin and London. For instance, in January 1896, the Kaiser miscalculated the situation after the Jameson Raid and announced his support for the Boers in their struggle against the British in South Africa in the Krüger Telegram. The Kaiser recognized the independence of the Transvaal, greatly upsetting the British.[107] John Lowe has argued that the Kaiser either hoped to blackmail Britain into joining the Triple Alliance, or sought territorial compensation for any British gains in the Transvaal, possibly in Mozambique and/or Samoa.[108] However, as Norman Rich has stated, "No single incident in the years before 1914 did more to inflame British public opinion against Germany or make the British conscious of a German menace."[109] Then,

103.   Russian foreign policy under Nicholas II is examined in Hugh Seton-Watson, *The Russian Empire, 1801-1917* (Oxford: Clarendon Press, 1967); Dominic Lieven, *Nicholas II: Twilight of the Empire* (New York: St. Martin's Press, 1993); Dietrich Geyer, *Russian Imperialism: The Interaction of Domestic and Foreign Policy, 1860-1914*, trans. Bruce Little (Leamington Spa: Berg, 1987); Ian Nish, *The Origins of the Russo-Japanese War* (London: Longman, 1985); and William L. Langer, *The Diplomacy of Imperialism, 1890-1902*, 2 vols. (New York: Alfred A. Knopf, 1935).

104.   See S.C.M. Paine, *The Sino-Japanese War of 1894-1895: Perceptions, Power and Primacy* (Cambridge: Cambridge University Press, 2003).

105.   Ian H. Nish, *The Anglo-Japanese Alliance: The Diplomacy of Two Island Empires, 1894-1907* (London: Athlone Press, 1966), 23-45; Langer, 1:167-94; Peter Wesley-Smith, *Unequal Treaty, 1898-1997: China, Great Britain and Hong Kong's New Territories* (Oxford: Oxford University Press, 1980), 21-24; Bridge and Bullen, 253-54.

106.   Lawrence Sondhaus, *Preparing for Weltpolitik: German Sea Power before the Tirpitz Era* (Annapolis: Naval Institute Press, 1997), 215.

107.   Holstein, 1:169-70, 1:185; Iain R. Smith, *The Origins of the South African War, 1899-1902* (London: Longman, 1996), 105-11; Cecil, *Wilhelm II*, 1:286-90. See also A.N. Porter, *The Origins of the South African War: Joseph Chamberlain and the Diplomacy of Imperialism, 1895-1899* (Manchester: Manchester University Press, 1980).

108.   Lowe, *The Great Powers, Imperialism, and the German Problem, 1865-1925*, 106.

109.   Rich, *Great Power Diplomacy, 1814-1914*, 289.

in March 1896, William II, still hoping for a British alliance, warned London of the Franco-Russian plans to move eastward from Abyssinia into the Upper Nile Region. This move would threaten British plans in Africa. The Kaiser expected the Franco-Russian forces to trounce the Anglo-Egyptian army sent up the Nile River to Dongola. William II believed that Britain would need to join the Triple Alliance to counter this threat to the British Empire. In fact, the Kaiser stated, "the English will yet come to us crawling on their knees if only we let them struggle long enough."[110] He was wrong about the Dongola Expedition and the British desire for a German alliance. But, in March 1896, Lord Salisbury, the British Prime Minister (1895-1902), informed Berlin that Britain could not sign a treaty of alliance, but Britain must lean towards the Triple Alliance of Germany, Italy, and Austria-Hungary because the primary threat to the British Empire was still France and Russia.[111]

Meanwhile, back in Berlin, the Kaiser treated Chancellor Hohenlohe and State Secretary Marschall with little respect. He had a habit of bypassing the Imperial Chancellor and the Foreign Office on important issues. William II corresponded directly with German ambassadors abroad. He was beginning to push his agenda of Weltpolitik (the quest for World Power status) and the construction of a large Germany navy.[112] At the Foreign Office, Friedrich von Holstein, the Senior Counselor in the Political Division, was very concerned with the Kaiser's actions. He believed that William II's meddling in foreign affairs might lead to war. Holstein was the main opposition to the Kaiser's diplomatic activities,[113] especially since Hohenlohe and Marschall allowed him to continue his control over the Auswärtiges Amt. The reason for this might be that Hohenlohe and Holstein were old friends. Holstein had served under Hohenlohe at the German Embassy in Paris during the 1870s. Another reason might be because of the Chancellor's "senility and diffident, conciliatory nature".[114] But, the Chancellor treated the powerful Holstein with extreme caution.[115] Moreover, the Kaiser, backed by Count Eulenburg, kept Holstein at a distance.[116] Even Hohenlohe's confidence in Holstein was not as high as the foreign relations adviser desired.[117]

---

110.  As quoted in Rich, *Great Power Diplomacy, 1814-1914*, 274.

111.  J.A.S. Grenville, *Lord Salisbury and Foreign Policy: The Close of the Nineteenth Century* (London: Athlone Press, 1964), 98; Chamberlain, 153-54.

112.  Röhl, *Germany without Bismarck*, 160-62; Röhl, *Wilhelm II*, 153-58.

113.  Röhl, *Germany without Bismarck*, 161, 173, 178-79.

114.  Ibid., 175; Cecil, *Wilhelm II*, 1:216, 258.

115.  Cecil, *The German Diplomatic Service, 1871-1914*, 273, 275.

116.  Cecil, *Wilhelm II*, 1:217.

117.  Bülow, 2:126.

In fact, in 1897, Hohenlohe warned his new Foreign Secretary, Bernhard von Bülow, that "all doubtful and bad advice emanates in the main from Holstein."[118]

## William II, the Foreign Office, and Weltpolitik, 1897-1909

During the Hohenlohe chancellorship, the Kaiser's political power increased to a point where he was able to end the ministerial rule of Germany and create his own authoritarian government. Many leading Germans looked to William II to restore unity to the Berlin government and the Second Reich. The Kaiser overcame ministerial opposition to his autocratic rule by dismissing ministers who opposed him and replacing them with more reliable men.[119] The personal rule of William II, according to Imanuel Geiss, meant that he "could influence German foreign policy even more directly than before."[120] As such, the Kaiser pursued a policy of Weltpolitik, the quest to become a World Power like Great Britain, Russia, and France. This policy was the result of William II's personal ambitions; the strength of German steel, chemical, and electrical industries; a dramatic increase in German exports; the rise of German population; and the German ruling class desire to follow up economic growth with a corresponding growth of military power. These factors made further German expansion and, according to Geiss, "the building of a strong German fleet plausible and possible, to protect German commerce and colonies overseas."[121]

One of the Kaiser's first actions in pursuing Weltpolitik was to appoint Johannes von Miquel as the Vice-President of the Prussian Ministry. He then appointed Rear Admiral Alfred von Tirpitz as the State Secretary for the Imperial Navy Office, and then dismissed Marschall and appointed Count Bernhard von Bülow as his new Foreign Secretary in June 1897.[122] Bülow, the son of former State Secretary Bernhard Ernst von Bülow, had previously served as an Attaché in the Foreign Office (1873-74), Attaché at the German Ministry in Rome (1874-75), Secretary at the Legation in St. Petersburg (1875-76), Secretary at the Embassy in Vienna (1876), Minister in Athens (1876-78), First Secretary at the Embassy in Paris (1878-84), First Secretary at the Embassy in St. Petersburg (1884-88), Minister in Bucharest (1888-94), and Ambassador in Rome (1894-

118.  Ibid., 1:126-27.
119.  Röhl, *Germany without Bismarck*, 147, 259, 273, 276.
120.  Geiss, *German Foreign Policy, 1871-1914*, 76.
121.  Ibid.
122.  Röhl, *Germany without Bismarck*, 229-40; Bülow, 1:196. The Kaiser appointed Marschall as the German Ambassador to the Ottoman Empire (Cecil, *Wilhelm II*, 257).

97).[123] The Kaiser was ready to launch his new policy with Bülow carrying out the diplomacy of Weltpolitik, Miquel handling the domestic issues, and Tirpitz carrying out the modernization and expansion of the German Navy. These men pressed for a spectacular foreign policy and naval program to restore the popularity of the Kaiser in Germany, and strengthen the Kaiser's position vis-a-vis the German Reichstag.[124] Hohenlohe, the Imperial Chancellor and Prussian Foreign Minister, now in his late seventies, was reluctant to oppose William II on the issue of Weltpolitik.[125] Thus, William II, by taking control of the government and appointing loyal men to key positions, essentially became his own Chancellor and Foreign Minister during this period.[126] Imanuel Geiss, a leading German historian, has argued that at this point, the Kaiser, without parliamentary interference, exercised a considerable amount of influence on the formulation and execution of German foreign policy because of his strong will to rule besides the cringing subservience of many German ministers, ambassadors, generals, and politicians.[127] Another historian, Paul Kennedy, wrote:

> Wilhelm…was…at the centre of the governmental decision-making process, and all chains of authority terminated with him. Ministers were his men, and not senior politicians from the party or parties which had acquired the largest number of seats in the Reichstag; indeed, ministers could not be members of that institution. The entire conduct of foreign policy was in the hands of the Kaiser, and by delegation in those of the Chancellor and the Auswärtiges Amt.[128]

With Bülow serving as Foreign Secretary, the Wilhelmstrasse underwent few changes in personnel in 1897. Bülow kept the powerful Friedrich von Holstein as the Senior Counselor in the Political Division.[129] He was fully aware of Holstein's "dominating personality in the Foreign Office ever since the last years of the Bismarckian era."[130] But, he replaced Wolfram von Rotenhan with Baron Oswald von Richthofen as the Under State Secretary for Foreign Affairs.[131] Rich-

123.   Holstein, 1:99, 2:47, 3:54; Bülow, 4:298, 4:330-41, 4:369-92; 4:414-435.
124.   V.R. Berghahn, *Germany and the Approach of War in 1914* (London: Macmillan, 1973), 43; Röhl, *Germany without Bismarck*, 252, 259.
125.   Röhl, *Germany without Bismarck*, 178.
126.   Ibid., 278-79; Cecil, *Wilhelm II*, 1:259-60.
127.   Geiss, *German Foreign Policy, 1871-1914*, 63.
128.   Kennedy, *The Rise of the Anglo-German Antagonism, 1860-1914*, 403.
129.   Rich, *Friedrich von Holstein*, 2:552.
130.   Bülow, 1:7.
131.   Ibid., 1:28, 1:252.

thofen had served as a Permanent Assistant (Hilfsarbeiter) in the Political Division (1877-96) and the Director of the Colonial Division since 1896.[132] Richthofen would serve Bülow well until his untimely death in 1906. The Foreign Secretary viewed Richthofen in high esteem. In his memoirs he wrote:

> Baron von Richthofen, who until his too-early death supported me with uncommon industry, never-failing loyalty, far-seeing vision, and great conscientiousness in things great and small alike. Oswald, Baron von Richthofen, son of a diplomat, brought up in a diplomat's home, well acquainted with life abroad from his youth up, a fine linguist, added to his knowledge of the world and its ways the traditional excellent qualities of the good type of Prussian official. He had always been interested in economic questions, and, in particular, he had a more thorough knowledge of the commercial relations between the great trading countries and with the financial conditions of the Great Powers than the majority of the members of the diplomatic service.[133]

In November 1897, Germany opened its policy of Weltpolitik with the seizure of Tsingtao and Kiaochow on the Shantung Peninsula of northern China. The Kaiser ordered the German Far Eastern Squadron under Rear Admiral Otto von Diederichs to take the region after murder of two German missionaries in Shangtung. Consequently, German military and naval power forced China to agree to a ninety-nine year lease of the Bay of Kiaochow in March 1898. The Wilhelmstrasse, according to Friedrich von Holstein, had no hand in the action.[134] The Kaiser used the murders as an excuse for the seizure of the region, but the real reason for the action was the fact that the Kaiser wanted a port which could serve as a permanent headquarters for the German naval squadron in the Far East and as a coaling station for German ships on duty in the Pacific. Moreover, Tirpitz considered Kiaochow a suitable naval base for protecting German trade in China.[135] The taking of the Bay of Kiaochow increased tension in the Far East where the interests of Britain, Russia, France, and Japan were clashing. Russia responded by making an agreement with China for control of the Liaotung Peninsula, including Port Arthur, and permission to build the South Manchurian Railway. France acquired its own

---

132.  Holstein, 1:114, 2:133, 3:655.
133.  Bülow, 1:252.
134.  Holstein, 1:180-81.
135.  David Gillard, *The Struggle for Asia, 1828-1914: A Study in British and Russian Imperialism* (London: Methuen, 1977), 163; Langer, 2:448-54; Cecil, *Wilhelm II*, 1:319-21; Rich, *Great Power Diplomacy, 1814-1914*, 320-21.

treaty and took control of Kwang-Chow in southeastern China, while Britain took the Kowloon Peninsula on the Chinese mainland opposite Hong Kong, along with Weihaiwei, a harbor city on the northeastern shore of the Shantung Peninsula across from Port Arthur.[136]

In the meantime, during the spring of 1898, Prime Minister Salisbury of Britain began talking about closer relations, possibly an alliance, with Germany. Britain viewed France and Russia as the major enemies to the British Empire. A German alliance could block Russian expansionism in the Far East and elsewhere. British proposals for an alliance would continue for about four years.[137] Berlin turned down the first offer in 1898.[138] German public opinion was anti-British at this time. William II followed up the seizure of Kiaochow by establishing the German Battle Fleet in the late 1890s. The creation of the German Battle Fleet was the whim of the Kaiser and Admiral Alfred von Tirpitz. Tirpitz called for the building of a fleet of nineteen high sea battleships and eight coastal battleships, with twelve large cruisers, thirty small cruisers, and twelve divisions of torpedo boats. In March 1898, the German Reichstag passed the First Naval Law, which funded the creation of the German Battle Fleet.[139] This law increased the size of the existing German Navy by seven battleships, two heavy cruisers, and seven light cruisers.[140] It also increased British suspicion of Germany. Then, in August 1898, Berlin and London disagreed over the provisions of the Anglo-German Treaty concerning loans to the Portuguese government and the use of the Portugese colony of Mozambique as security for these loans.[141] At the same time, William II upset Whitehall by visiting Constantinople and building closer relations with the Turkish Sultan, including the

---

136.  Lowe, *The Great Powers, Imperialism, and the German Problem, 1865-1925*, 115; Gillard, 165.
137.  Holstein, 1:181.
138.  Geiss, *German Foreign Policy, 1871-1914*, 87; Röhl, *Germany without Bismarck*, 245; Craig, *Germany 1866-1945*, 311; C.J. Bartlett, *Peace, War and the European Powers, 1814-1914* (New York: St. Martin's Press, 1996), 132-35; Bridge and Bullen, 257; Lowe, *The Great Powers, Imperialism, and the German Problem, 1865-1925*, 116.
139.  Lawrence Sondhaus, *Naval Warfare, 1815-1914* (London: Routledge, 2001), 179-80. See also Jonathan Steinberg, *Yesterday's Deterrent: Tirpitz and the Birth of the German Battle Fleet* (New York: Macmillan, 1965) and Robert K. Massie, *Dreadnought: Britain, Germany, and the Coming of the Great War* (New York: Random House, 1991).
140.  Holborn, *A History of Modern Germany*, 3:308.
141.  Geiss, *German Foreign Policy, 1871-1914*, 88-89; Rich, *Great Power Diplomacy, 1814-1914*, 297, 384; Holstein, 1:163.

proposal of a Baghdad Railway.[142] The Kaiser continued his policy of Weltpolitik by purchasing the Mariana and Caroline Islands in the Pacific from Spain.[143]

William II's plans for making Germany a world power were challenged by Tsar Nicholas II of Russia's proposal for disarmament conference. From May to August 1899, the First Hague Conference considered the issues of disarmament and compulsory arbitration. German diplomats opposed and voted down most proposals at the conference, since the proposals were in direct conflict with the policy of Weltpolitik.[144] Then, in October 1899, the Germans quarreled over control of the Samoan Islands with Britain. London backed down in an attempt to maintain good relations with Berlin, especially while the British were tied down with the Boer War (1899-1902) in South Africa. As a consequence, Germany acquired control of Upolu and Savaii in the Samoan Islands.[145] The Kaiser was seeking to create a German Empire abroad.

When the Anglo-Boer War broke out in October 1899, the Kaiser pursued a policy of strict neutrality. The Boer War would tie Britain down for some time.[146] In November, Berlin rejected the British offer of an Anglo-German alliance.[147] Germany also turned down the Franco-Russian proposal for a continental league against Britain.[148] A few months later, beginning in June 1900, Germany, Britain, the United States, and other European powers worked together for fifty-five days to put down the anti-foreign Boxer Rebellion that broke out in China.[149] The Kaiser deployed additional troops to China under

142.    Langer, 2:629-50; Holborn, *A History of Modern Germany*, 3:314-16; Bartlett, *Peace, War and the European Powers, 1814-1914*, 137. See also John B. Wolf, *The Diplomatic History of the Baghdad Railway* (Columbus, MO: University of Missouri Press, 1936).

143.    Holborn, *A History of Modern Germany*, 3:307.

144.    David Stevenson, *Armaments and the Coming of War: Europe, 1904-1914* (Oxford: Clarendon Press, 1996), 105-6; Geiss, *German Foreign Policy, 1871-1914*, 90-92; Bartlett, *Peace, War and the European Powers, 1814-1914*, 136-37. For the First Hague Conference, see T.K. Ford, "The Genesis of the First Hague Peace Conference," *Political Science Quarterly* 51 (1935), 354-81; D.L. Morrill, "Nicholas II and the Call for the First Hague Conference," *Journal of Modern History* 46 (1974), 296-313; Calvin DeArmond Davis, *The United States and the First Hague Peace Conference* (Ithaca: Cornell University Press, 1962).

145.    Craig, *Germany 1866-1945*, 311; Lowe, *The Great Powers, Imperialism, and the German Problem, 1865-1925*, 106; Taylor, *The Struggle for Mastery in Europe, 1848-1918*, 389; Geiss, *German Foreign Policy, 1871-1914*, 90; Cecil, *Wilhelm II*, 1:324-26; Gillard, 163.

146.    Cecil, *Wilhelm II*, 1:326. See also Bill Nasson, *The South African War, 1899-1902* (London: Arnold, 1999) and Denis Judd and Keith Surridge, *The Boer War* (New York: Palgrave, 2002).

147.    Holstein, 1:181; Bridge and Bullen, 258.

148.    Bridge and Bullen, 258.

149.    Langer, 2:677-710. See also Peter Fleming, *The Siege at Peking: The Boxer Rebellion* (New York: Dorset Press, 1990).

the command of Field Marshal Count Alfred von Waldersee, but they arrived six weeks after the revolt was ended.[150] A few months later, in October 1900, Berlin and London agreed to the China (or Yangtse) Agreement. The agreement called for Anglo-German cooperation in safeguarding the Open Door in China and the integrity of the Chinese Empire.[151] In the meantime, the German Reichstag passed the Second Naval Law in June 1900. The law called for Germany to increase the Battle Fleet to thirty-eight battleships, fourteen large cruisers, and thirty-eight small cruisers by 1917.[152]

In October 1900, the Kaiser picked Foreign Secretary Bülow to become the new Imperial Chancellor and Prussian Foreign Minister.[153] Bülow had experienced a rapid advancement in the foreign service because of the patronage of Bismarck and Holstein.[154] Philipp zu Eulenburg-Hertefeld, a close friend of the Kaiser's, was responsible for Bülow's appointment as Chancellor.[155] The Kaiser declared that Bülow would become "my Bismarck."[156] One diplomatic historian has pointed out that, "no Chancellor except Bismarck, had as varied and thorough a training in foreign affairs."[157] Chancellor Bülow offered the post of Foreign Secretary to Friedrich von Holstein. But Holstein turned down the offer. He remained the Senior Counselor in the Political Division. The gesture, nonetheless, won Holstein's gratitude and loyalty.[158] Baron Oswald von Richthofen became the new Foreign Secretary and Otto von Mühlberg became the new Under State Secretary for Foreign Affairs at the Wilhelmstrasse.[159] Mühlberg had previously been a Counselor in the Political Division at the Foreign Office from

---

150.    Holborn, *A History of Modern Germany*, 3:310. See also Annika Mombauer, "Wilhelm, Waldersee, and the Boxer Rebellion," in *The Kaiser: New Research on Wilhelm II's Role in Imperial Germany*, ed. Annika Mombauer and Wilhelm Deist (Cambridge: Cambridge University Press, 2003) and Sabine Dabringhaus, "An Army on Vacation?: The German War in China, 1900-1901," in *Anticipating Total War: The German and American Experiences, 1871-1914*, eds. Manfred F. Boemke, Roger Chickering, and Stig Förster (Cambridge: Cambridge University Press, 1999).

151.    Taylor, *The Struggle for Mastery in Europe, 1848-1918*, 392-93; Bridge and Bullen, 258.

152.    Sondhaus, *Naval Warfare, 1815-1914*, 180; Holborn, *A History of Modern Germany*, 3:308.

153.    Bülow, 1:444.

154.    Holborn, *A History of Modern Germany*, 3:325.

155.    Bülow, 1:458; Imanuel Geiss, ed., *July 1914, The Outbreak of the First World War: Selected Documents* (New York: Charles Scribner's Sons, 1957), 23-24.

156.    Geiss, *July 1914*, 23-24; Rich, *Friedrich von Holstein*, 2:501.

157.    Craig, *Aspects of German Statecraft*, 46.

158.    Rich, *Friedrich von Holstein*, 2:552.

159.    Ibid., 2:625.

1885 to 1900.[160] Bülow acquired the promotion for Richthofen despite the Kaiser's objection. According to Katharine A. Lerman, William II's:

> reluctance to accept Richthofen as Foreign Secretary in 1900 stemmed from his perception of him as colourless and uninspiring, qualities he could tolerate in higher civil servants who headed departments with which he had little contact, but not at the Foreign Office which he visited frequently.[161]

During his nine years as Chancellor, Bernhard von Bülow spent an inordinate amount of time cultivating a close friendship with William II.[162] Bülow tried, and succeeded to convince the Kaiser, that he was indispensable. He would flatter William II in an attempt to manipulate him.[163] But, despite being the Imperial Chancellor and Prussian Foreign Minister, Bülow found himself not in control of German foreign policy. The Kaiser still acted as his own Foreign Minister.[164] In his memoirs, Bülow complained that the Kaiser had:

> A manifest tendency…to handle personally and *sou modo*, in accordance with his own whims and impressions, our future relationships…[and demonstrated] the wish to be his own Foreign Minister and attempt to shoulder a burden for which he was in no way equal.[165]

Philipp zu Eulenburg-Hertefeld, wrote of the situation:

> The Emperor often messed up our difficult foreign relations by his interference. In that respect I grant he *was* a football—but the football of his own character, his sudden"inspirations," his conviction that he must instantly realize some "brilliant idea, before it loses all its grit in that confounded Foreign Office melting-pot." That the unfortunate Foreign Office had to toil for months at mending his broken crockery was what never occurred to him.[166]

---

160.  Holstein, 3:514.
161.  Katharine A. Lerman, "The Kaiser's Elite? Wilhelm II and the Berlin Administration, 1890-1914," in *The Kaiser: New Research on Wilhelm II's Role in Imperial Germany*, ed. Annika Mombauer and Wilhelm Deist (Cambridge: Cambridge University Press, 2003), 80.
162.  Ibid., 79.
163.  Cecil, *Wilhelm II*, 2:71.
164.  Ibid.
165.  Bülow, 2:320.
166.  As quoted in Haller, 2:301.

Nonetheless, Chancellor Bülow along with the diplomats at the Wilhelmstrasse knew that if they wanted to remain in their positions they had to carry out the Kaiser's policy. The Kaiser controlled the careers of Bülow and the diplomats, and he expected them to align their views with his own as best as they could.[167] On more than one occasion, William II called the staff of the Foreign Office a bunch of swine.[168] Bülow, himself, would avoid arguing with William II over foreign policy issues, including the naval buildup, in spite of Foreign Office objections to the Kaiser's actions, because he realized that his position as Chancellor depended upon the continued support of his master. Bülow remembered that it was William II who had dismissed Bismarck.[169]

Operating from the background, Friedrich von Holstein served the Kaiser as an important diplomatic adviser in the Foreign Office. But, as the publication of *The Holstein Papers* have revealed, much of Holstein's advice to the Kaiser went unheeded.[170] Historians have traditionally given Holstein credit for being the "evil genius" behind German foreign policy during 1890 to 1906.[171] But Holstein, according to his most recent biographer, Norman Rich, was nothing more than a hard working civil servant who created a powerful hold over the administration of the Foreign Office.[172] Foreign Secretary Heinrich Leonard von Tschirschky und Bögendorff, who served in that capacity from 1906 to 1907, remarked of Holstein that:

> [He] was unquestionably a marvelous worker. You could bring a pile of files in the morning, which any other man would require a week to work through. Holstein would have them finished by night, and, with it all, his work was excellent and minutely exact.[173]

---

167.  Cecil, *The German Diplomatic Service, 1871-1914,* 214, 220.
168.  Friedrich von Holstein to Bernhard von Bülow, 25 June 1904, Holstein, 4:290.
169.  Holborn, *A History of Modern Germany,* 3:326; Kurt Doss, "The History of the German Foreign Office," in *The Times Survey of Foreign Ministries of the World,* ed. Zara Steiner (London: Times Books, 1982), 232; Ernest May, *Imperial Democracy: The Emergence of America as a Great Power* (New York: Harcourt, Brace and World, 1961), 197-98.
170.  See Holstein.
171.  For example, see Edward F. Willis, *Prince Lichnowsky Ambassador of Peace: A Study of Prewar Diplomacy, 1912-1914* (Berkeley: University of California Press, 1942) and Eugene N. Anderson, *The First Moroccan Crisis, 1904-1906* (Chicago: University of Chicago Press, 1930; reprint, New York: Archon, 1966).
172.  See Norman Rich, *Friedrich von Holstein: Politics and Diplomacy in the Era of Bismarck and Wilhelm II,* 2 vols. (Cambridge: Cambridge University Press, 1965).
173.  As quoted in Willis, 28.

In spite of his importance in the Foreign Office, Holstein refused to accept a higher position, such as State Secretary.[174] As the Senior Counselor in the Political Division he lacked direct access to the Kaiser. The Kaiser, who disliked Holstein, met him only once, in November 1904.[175] William II, however, recognized Holstein for his "great shrewdness, seconded by a phenomenal memory and a certain talent for political combinations."[176] But, did William II take Holstein seriously? Since he served as an intermediary between the Kaiser and Holstein,[177] what Eulenburg stated about the influence of Holstein on German policy is of vital importance:

> Neither Caprivi nor Hohenlohe nor Bülow ever promulgated an edict on even the most insignificant political matter without Holstein's putting in his oar; in some instances he drew up the document with his own hand. All these edicts, however,…were modified by reason of *the Emperor's very frequent interference* in foreign policy. And this because of His Majesty's direct telegraphic communication in cipher with the Royal colleagues, or the despatch of A.D.C.s with private letters to a sovereign, or brusque marginalia and commands on the reports from the German Ambassadors and Ministers, etc. This caused perpetual changes in the political temper of the Foreign Office.
>
> In such circumstances there could be no such thing as independent action on the part of Holstein, or the Imperial Chancellor, or the Secretary of State. For the Imperial interventions would soon be made to chime in with the policy of the [Foreign] Office—that is to say, would be remodeled, brought into conformity so far as might be, and then receive official countenance.[178]

With little influence over the actual conduct of foreign policy, Holstein and the once highly disciplined diplomats in the Foreign Office became difficult to manage. Diplomats, including Holstein, would not cooperate with Bülow or his Foreign Secretary, Oswald von Richthofen (1900-6), which resulted in the ineffectiveness of the Foreign Office as an organization. The Chancellor complained: "the Political Division of the Foreign Office became afflicted with petty jealousies and disputes. Most of them arose from Privy Councillor von Holstein's inability

---

174.  Holstein, 1:150.
175.  William II, *The Kaiser's Memoirs*, 99-101; Cecil, *The German Diplomatic Service*, 294; Alan Palmer, *The Chancelleries of Europe* (London: George Allen and Unwin, 1983), 179.
176.  William II, *The Kaiser's Memoirs*, 98.
177.  Count Philipp zu Eulenburg-Hertefeld resigned from the Diplomatic Service in 1902. After his resignation, Eulenburg met with the Kaiser on rare occasions (Cecil, *Wilhelm II*, 2:27).
178.  As quoted in Haller, 2:297-98.

to work with anybody else."[179] One historian of the German diplomatic service, Edward Willis, has commented:

> It was a strange group, composed of men who had little in common except a driving ambition, unbridled by the discipline of tradition or by the restraint of decency. Everywhere the Nietzschean lust for power was apparent. Nor did Bülow have a sufficiently strong hand to control them. His was the subtle, scintillating mind, the smooth tongue, and the suave personality, but he was no Bismarck. He had the artistry without the art, the form without the substance, of greatness.[180]

Holstein, himself, opposed the Kaiser's aggressive actions in foreign relations which increased the tension between Germany and other states. He wrote in his memoirs, "the Foreign Ministry, year in year out, had to resist the Kaiser's sudden inspirations, and I was chiefly responsible for this censorship."[181] Such opposition did not make Holstein popular with either the Kaiser or Chancellor.[182] After the unexpected death of Richthofen,[183] the new Foreign Secretary, Heinrich Leonard von Tschirschky und Bögendorff (1906-7), found it especially difficult to get along with his unruly subordinate.[184] Tschirschky was a friend of the German Emperor.[185] Thus, Holstein became dispensable, and was used as a scapegoat and held responsible for the Kaiser's foreign policy disaster during the First Moroccan Crisis in 1906.[186] Shortly before his death in 1909, Holstein stated in his memoirs:

> Future historians will compile a long list of the Kaiser's sudden impulses in conversation, in writing, in telegrams, which collectively and singly have had

---

179.  Bülow, 2:185.
180.  Willis, 30.
181.  Holstein, 1:175.
182.  Ibid, 1:173; Bülow, 2:125-26.
183.  Richthofen died from a heart attack induced by stress and overwork (Lerman, "The Kaiser's Elite," 72).
184.  Palmer, *The Chancelleries of Europe*, 207; Holstein, 1:174; Bülow, 2:235-37. Tschirschky's previous diplomatic career included Secretary of the German Legation in Athens (1889-90), Secretary of the German Legation in Bern (1890-1892), First Secretary at the German Embassy at Constantinople (1893), First Secretary at the German Embassy in St. Petersburg (1894-1900), German Minister in Luxembourg (1900-2), and Prussian Minister in Hamburg (1902-6). He would later be the German Ambassador to Vienna (1907-16) (Holstein, 1:174, 4:131).
185.  Lerman, "The Kaiser's Elite," 75.
186.  Bülow, 2:237; Holstein, 1:194-95; Cecil, *The German Diplomatic Service, 1871-1914*, 299.

the effect of gradually diminishing the prestige of the Kaiser and the Reich, of wrecking diplomatic negotiations and even of provoking immediate danger of war.[187]

With the Wilhelmstrasse under his control, Kaiser William II continued to determine German foreign policy during the Bülow chancellorship. In 1901-2, the Kaiser still hoped to tie Britain with the Triple Alliance. But, Anglo-German negotiations were fruitless because of incompatible aims. Britain did not need a German alliance after the military victory in the Boer War. At best, Salisbury sought only a loose alliance with Germany. On the other hand, the Kaiser could not conceive of the possibility of an understanding between Britain, France, and Russia. He pushed for a full alliance with Britain on German terms.[188] Even so, as Holstein has noted, the chances for an alliance quickly disappeared by January 1902.[189] During that month the British broke away from "splendid isolation" and concluded an alliance with Japan, the growing Great Power in the Far East.[190] Whitehall took this action to contain the threat of Russian expansionism into China. Russian forces had moved into Manchuria and were poised to expand further into China.[191] Then, in June 1902, Italy, a member of Germany's Triple Alliance, reached an agreement with France, the so-called Prinetti-Barrère Agreement. This agreement promised Italian neutrality in the event of a Franco-German war. It added to the Franco-Italian Agreement of December 1900 that called for Rome's recognition of French claims to Morocco. In return, Italy obtained a financial loan from France and a free hand to expand into North Africa in Tripoli.[192] "The Triple Alliance," according to Imanuel Geiss, "was partially paralysed."[193]

In the meantime, the Wilhelmstrasse received news that Whitehall had begun talks with the Quai d'Orsay. Bülow and Holstein, however, did not believe that an agreement was possible between these two rivals.[194] The talks, nevertheless,

---

187. Holstein, 1:190.

188. Geiss, *German Foreign Policy, 1871-1914*, 94.

189. Holstein, 1:184.

190. Ian H. Nish, *The Anglo-Japanese Alliance: The Diplomacy of Two Island Empires, 1894-1907* (London: Athlone Press, 1966; reprint, Westport, CT: Greenwood Press, 1976), 204-28; George Monger, *The End of Isolation: British Foreign Policy, 1900-1907* (London: Thomas Nelson and Sons, 1963), 46-66.

191. Rich, *Great Power Diplomacy, 1814-1914*, 325.

192. Ibid., 392; C.J. Lowe and F. Marzari, *Italian Foreign Policy, 1870-1940* (London: Routledge and Kegan Paul, 1975), 82, 88.

193. Geiss, *German Foreign Policy, 1871-1914*, 98.

194. Rich, *Friedrich von Holstein*, 2:673.

led to Lord Lansdowne, the British Foreign Secretary, and Paul Cambon, the French Ambassador to London, concluding the Anglo-French Entente Cordiale in April 1904. The core of the treaty that concerned colonial issues was the agreement over Morocco and Egypt. The British cabinet of Arthur Balfour (1902-5) promised to support French aspirations in Morocco, and the French agreed to support British plans in Egypt.[195] This was another setback for Germany. Norman Rich has written:

> Although the Germans knew that Anglo-French negotiations were in progress, the actual conclusion of the entente came as a terrible shock, for they had come to regard Anglo-French antagonism as a permanent fixture on the international chessboard. Bülow might tell the Reichstag that Germany welcomed the entente as a contribution to peace, but behind this public appearance of confidence the Germans worried about the broader implications of the entente for the own international position.[196]

Germany's international situation improved when the Japanese launched a surprise attack against the Russians at Port Arthur in February 1904.[197] The Japanese damaged seven Russian ships in the initial attack and then established a blockade that kept most of the Russian Pacific Fleet at Port Arthur. Two months later, in April, the Japanese defeated the Russians at the Battle of the Yalu in the northern part of Korea. In August, the Japanese fleet destroyed the rest of the Russian fleet at the Battles of the Yellow Sea and Ulsan. They then captured Port Arthur in January 1905. The Russians suffered a major setback on land in the Battle of Mukden in February and March. Two months later, in May 1905, the Japanese fleet destroyed the Russian Baltic Fleet at the Battle of Tsushima in the Straits of Tsushima. Meanwhile, Tsar Nicholas II was hard pressed to deal with the Russian Revolution of 1905. Both Japan and Russia were weary of war. They

---

195.  Dwight E. Lee, *Europe's Crucial Years: The Diplomatic Background of World War I, 1902-1914* (Hanover, NH: University Press of New England, 1974), 49-80; C.J. Lowe and M.L. Dockrill, *The Mirage of Power*, 3 vols. (London: Routledge and Kegan Paul, 1972), 1:4-11; John F.V. Keiger, *France and the Origins of the First World War* (London: Macmillan, 1983), 19. For a complete discussion of the Anglo-French agreement, see P.J.V. Rolo, *Entente Cordiale: The Origins and Negotiations of the Anglo-French Agreements of 8 April 1904* (London: Macmillan, 1969) and Christopher Andrew, *Théophile Delcassé and the Making of the Entente Cordiale: A Reappraisal of French Foreign Policy, 1898-1905* (London: Macmillan, 1968).

196.  Rich, *Great Power Diplomacy, 1814-1914*, 394-95.

197.  For Japanese foreign policy, see Richard Storry, *Japan and the Decline of the West in Asia, 1894-1943* (London: Macmillan, 1979) and Ian Nish, *Japanese Foreign Policy, 1669-1942: Kasumigaseki to Miyakezaka* (London: Routledge and Kegan Paul, 1977).

sought and acquired the mediation of President Theodore Roosevelt of the United States in the Peace of Portsmouth that ended the Russo-Japanese War in August 1905.[198] The conflict gravely weakened Russia as well as the Franco-Russian Dual Alliance. France remained neutral throughout the Russo-Japanese War. As a consequence, William II hoped that the Russo-Japanese War gave Germany an opportunity to wean Russia away from France. Berlin stayed neutral in the war. Germany signed a commercial treaty with Russia in July, and the Kaiser even offered an alliance with Russia against Britain and Japan in October 1904. But Russia would not commit to an alliance without France.[199] This was yet another setback for Germany.

Berlin continued to look for ways to break up the Franco-Russian Dual Alliance. The Wilhelmstrasse wanted to diplomatically humiliate France, hoping to end both the Franco-Russian alliance and the Anglo-French Entente Cordiale, with the result of diplomatically isolating the French. Berlin was concerned about the growing encirclement of Germany. The opportunity came in 1905. In January, the Quai d'Orsay, in the midst of the Russo-Japanese War, made the bold move to establish a French protectorate over Morocco.[200] Italy, Britain, and Spain had already agreed to French aspirations in Morocco in treaties signed in 1900 and 1904.[201] Berlin, on the advice of Friedrich von Holstein, responded by attempting to block the French move, causing the so-called First Moroccan Crisis of 1905-6.[202] The Kaiser believed that if Germany could force France to back down, Britain and Russia would have second thoughts about close relations with Paris.[203] Russia was occupied in the conflict with Japan, and the Anglo-French relationship was not an alliance by any means. As such, William II sailed to and landed at Tangier in Morocco in March 1905. At Tangier, the Kaiser declared that Germany would preserve the independence of Morocco.[204] At this point, the

---

198.   The origins of the Russo-Japanese War are discussed in Ian Nish, *The Origins of the Russo-Japanese War* (London: Longman, 1985). The conflict itself is examined in Geoffrey Jukes, *The Russo-Japanese War, 1904-1905* (Botley: Osprey, 2002). The diplomacy is covered in John Albert White, *The Diplomacy of the Russo-Japanese War* (Princeton: Princeton University Press, 1964) and Raymond A. Esthus, *Double Eagle and Rising Sun: The Russians and Japanese at Portsmouth in 1905* (Durham, NC: Duke University Press, 1988).

199.   Cecil, *Wilhelm II*, 2:100; Geiss, *German Foreign Policy, 1871-1914*, 99-101.

200.   M.B. Hayne, *The French Foreign Office and the Origins of the First World War, 1898-1914* (Oxford: Clarendon Press, 1993), 116-43.

201.   Rich, *Great Power Diplomacy, 1814-1914*, 393, 396.

202.   See Eugene N. Anderson, *The First Moroccan Crisis, 1904-1906* (Chicago: University of Chicago Press, 1930; reprint, Hamden, CT: Archon Books, 1966).

203.   Craig, *Germany 1866-1945*, 318.

204.   Ibid., 181-95.

Wilhelmstrasse, under the advice of Holstein, called for an international conference to discuss the French move in Morocco.[205] The Wilhelmstrasse argued that
France had violated the Treaty of Madrid (1880) in which the Great Powers,
including France, guaranteed the sovereignty and territorial integrity of Morocco.
France would need the consent of the Great Powers to establish a protectorate
over Morocco.[206] Holstein expected the United States, Britain, Austria-Hungary,
Spain, Italy, and Russia to block French aspirations.[207] He assumed that they
would support an Open Door Policy in Morocco. Under pressure, French For-
eign Minister Théophile Delcassé, the architect of the Anglo-French Entente
Cordiale, resigned from office in June, and Paris agreed to an international con-
ference. Then, on 24 July 1905, about two months after the disastrous Battle of
Tsushima and less than two weeks before the international conference, Kaiser
William II and Tsar Nicholas II of Russia signed a defensive alliance in the
Treaty of Björkö.[208] This was a major diplomatic coup for Germany. But the tri-
umph was short-lived. The Kaiser had changed the draft treaty without Bülow's
knowledge from a global Russo-German alliance to one that applied to just
Europe. It would be insufficient in the case of an Anglo-German war abroad.[209]
The Chancellor was extremely frustrated with William II and his irresponsible
exercise of power in foreign affairs.[210] But, as one historian has pointed out, the
Björkö agreement, with its scope limited to Europe, was still better than no
Russo-German alliance at all.[211] Nevertheless, the Russian government refused to
endorse the Tsar's signature on the treaty.[212] Russia would remain an ally of
France.

The Great Powers convened the international conference regarding Morocco
at Algeciras in Spain in January 1906. Over the next two months it became
apparent that the other Great Powers would not support Germany's position
concerning Morocco. The Great Powers allowed France and Spain to establish

205.   Rich, *Friedrich von Holstein*, 2:700.
206.   Rich, *Great Power Diplomacy, 1814-1914*, 396-99.
207.   Rich, *Friedrich von Holstein* 2:701.
208.   Lieven, *Nicholas II*, 156-57; Cecil, *Wilhelm II*, 2:101-3. See also Roderick R. McLean,
       "Dreams of a German Empire: Wilhelm II and the Treaty of Björkö of 1905," in *The Kaiser:
       New Research on Wilhelm II's Role in Imperial Germany*, ed. Annika Mombauer and Wilhelm
       Deist (Cambridge: Cambridge University Press, 2003).
209.   McLean, "Dreams of a German Empire," 131-32.
210.   Christopher Clark, *Kaiser Wilhelm II* (Harlow: Pearson, 2000), 99-100, 141.
211.   Katharine A. Lerman, *The Chancellor as Courtier: Bernhard von Bülow and the Governance of
       Germany, 1900-1909* (Cambridge: Cambridge University Press, 1990), 128-29.
212.   Anderson, *The First Moroccan Crisis, 1904-1906*, 279-310; McLean, "Dreams of a German
       Empire," 135-40.

spheres of influence in Morocco.[213] As such, the Conference of Algeciras was a complete humiliation for Germany. The only Great Power to support Germany was Austria-Hungary.[214] "William II," according to Alan Palmer, "looked for a scapegoat for the Algeciras disaster and placed the blame for Germany's failure on Baron Holstein, who was prised from his sanctum in the Foreign Ministry within a few days of the conference's final session." But Palmer adds, "the immediate cause of his political demise was, however, an inability to work with Heinrich von Tschirschky, who had taken over as State Secretary in the Wilhelmstrasse on the sudden death of Richthofen in the third week of January."[215] Holstein was forced to resign from the Foreign Office in April.[216] The powerful Holstein noted in a letter to Bülow that the Kaiser "finds me inconvenient and now wants to make foreign policy himself, without contradiction from the professional bureaucracy. That is why he is using Morocco as an excuse to get rid of me."[217] Even so, Chancellor Bülow, and later Foreign Secretary Wilhelm von Schön (1907-10) and Under State Secretary Wilhelm Stemrich,[218] would visit Holstein's apartment and seek advice regarding foreign policy until his death in May 1909.[219]

The First Moroccan Crisis resulted in a tightening of the Anglo-French Entente Cordiale. Fearing German aggression, the French and British governments entered into military and naval talks aimed to convert their entente into an alliance.[220] In addition, Britain sought an agreement with Russia. In April 1906,

---

213.  John Albert White, *Transition to Global Rivalry: Alliance Diplomacy and the Quadruple Entente, 1895-1907* (Cambridge: Cambridge University Press, 1995), 186-203.

214.  Anderson, *The First Moroccan Crisis, 1904-1906*, 348-96.

215.  Palmer, *The Chancelleries of Europe*, 207.

216.  Rich, *Friedrich von Holstein*, 2:750-53.

217.  Ibid., 2:750.

218.  Schön replaced Tschirschky in November 1907. Schön had formerly served as the German Minister in Copenhagen (1900-5) and German Ambassador in St. Petersburg (1905-7) (Holstein, 1:172, 4:290). Chancellor Bülow had difficulties with both Tschirschky and Schön. He wrote in his memoirs: "Herr von Schön, like Tschirschky his predecessor, was primarily interested in never offending the Emperor rather than doing his duty, the only difference being that Tschirschky had been what the French call "*un rond de cuir*," that is to say an official automat who at least feels bound to spend his days on the high stool at his office desk, whereas "*le Baron de Schön*" was equally flighty and inadequate" (Bülow, 2:493-94). Stemrich had been the German Counsel-General in Constantinople (1905) and Minister in Teheran (1906-7).

219.  Holstein, 4:577-78; Rich, *Friedrich von Holstein*, 2:812, 2:817.

220.  Monger, 147-85; Samuel R. Williamson, Jr., *The Politics of Grand Strategy: Britain and France Prepare for War, 1904-1914* (Cambridge, MA: Harvard University Press, 1969), 59-88; John Gooch, *The Plans of War: The General Staff and British Military Strategy, c.1900-1916* (London: Routledge and Kegan Paul, 1974), 191, 280-81.

British Foreign Secretary Sir Edward Grey sent Sir Arthur Nicolson to negotiate an entente with St. Petersburg.[221] The British treaty with Russia was concluded in August 1907. The agreement covered colonial matters in Persia, Afghanistan, and Tibet.[222] But, the Anglo-Russian Agreement completed the formation of the Triple Entente, which aimed to contain Germany and its Weltpolitik. Berlin had suffered another major setback.

The British government of Prime Minister Henry Campbell-Bannerman (1905-8) continued to watch and be concerned about the buildup of the German Navy. The naval arms race between Germany and Britain was a major source of tension between the two Great Powers. The Dreadnought class of warship was introduced in 1905 to maintain the superiority of the British fleet. The Germans followed suit. As such, after 1906, the British sought a naval arms agreement with Germany because of the great cost of the naval arms race. At the Second Hague Peace Conference in 1907, Germany and Austria-Hungary refused to support the call for a naval arms agreement. Berlin did not want any restraints in the pursuit of Weltpolitik.[223]

Instead, Germany increased efforts towards modernizing and expanding the size of the German Navy. This led to British Prime Minister Herbert Asquith (1908-16) suggesting a bilateral naval arms limitation treaty in the summer of 1908. But Kaiser William II, Chancellor Bülow, and Admiral Tirpitz rejected all British initiatives that might lead to an agreement.[224] Foreign Secretary Wilhelm von Schön had no objections to the Kaiser's policy at this time, or ever. In fact, Lamar Cecil has stated about the State Secretary that:

> Schön had not even a trace of the mettle that, on rare occasions, had surfaced in Tschirschky's handling of diplomatic affairs. Schön's desire always to please applied not only to the Kaiser but everyone. Not for nothing was he known as "safe Schön."[225]

---

221.  British foreign policy leading to the outbreak of war in 1914 is examined in Zara S. Steiner and Keith Neilson, *Britain and the Origins of the First World War*, 2 ed. (New York: Palgrave, 2003).

222.  Gooch, 281-95; Kenneth Bourne, *The Foreign Policy of Victorian England, 1830-1902* (Oxford: Clarendon Press, 1970), 185-86; Harold Nicolson, *Sir Arthur Nicolson, Bart., First Lord Carnock: A Study in Old Diplomacy* (London: Constable, 1930), 232-57.

223.  Geiss, *German Foreign Policy, 1871-1914*, 108.

224.  Ibid., 108-9; Lowe and Dockrill, 1:31-37.

225.  Cecil, *Wilhelm II*, 122.

The international position of Germany was threatened by the Triple Entente. The Triple Alliance of Germany, Austria-Hungary, and Italy, the cornerstone of German diplomacy, was shaky. The only ally that Berlin could count on was Austria-Hungary. But Vienna and St. Petersburg were rivals in Southeast Europe. In 1897 Austria-Hungary and Russia had concluded an agreement that called for the maintenance of the status quo in the Balkan Peninsula.[226] The Austro-Russian Agreement of 1897 kept the rivalry between the two Great Powers at bay for the next decade. Then, in 1908, St. Petersburg sought a revision of the Straits Convention of 1841. The Great Powers agreement closed the Turkish Straits to all foreign warships during peacetime.[227] St. Petersburg now wanted an agreement that would allow Russian warships to pass through the Turkish Straits during peacetime. Vienna agreed to this proposal if Russia would support Austria-Hungary's annexation of the Ottoman Empire's Balkan provinces of Bosnia, Herzegovina, and the Sanjak of Novi Pazar. The Treaty of Berlin of 1878 had already allowed Austria-Hungary to occupy these territories. In the midst of the Austro-Russian negotiations the Young Turk revolution broke out in the Ottoman Empire. The Young Turks opposed the repressive regime of Sultan Abdul Hamid. They also challenged Austro-Hungarian occupation of Bosnia, Herzegovina, and the Sanjak of Novi Pazar. The Russians believed that the Young Turks would also oppose their quest to gain access through the Turkish Straits. As such, the Austro-Hungarian Foreign Minister Baron Alois Lexa von Aehrenthal and Russian Foreign Minister Alexander Petrovich Izvolsky signed an agreement at Buchlau in Moravia in September 1908. In this agreement Vienna would support Russian aspirations to revise the Straits Convention and St. Petersburg would support the Austro-Hungarian annexation of Bosnia and Herzegovina.[228]

---

226.  Rich, *Great Power Diplomacy, 1814-1914*, 335. In return, Austria-Hungary agreed to Russia's demand that the Turkish Straits be closed to foreign warships.

227.  For background to the Straits Question, see Philip E. Mosely, *Russian Diplomacy and the Opening of the Eastern Question in 1838 and 1839* (Cambridge, MA: Harvard University Press, 1930); Harold N. Ingle, *Nesselrode and the Russian Rapprochement with Britain, 1836-1844* (Berkeley: University of California Press, 1976); and John C.K. Daly, *Russian Seapower and "the Eastern Question", 1827-1841* (Annapolis: Naval Institute Press, 1991). For the Straits Question in the aftermath of the Crimean War, see W.E. Mosse, *The Rise and Fall of the Crimean System, 1866-1871: The Story of a Peace Settlement* (London: Macmillan, 1963) and Barbara Jelavich, *The Ottoman Empire, the Great Powers, and the Straits Question, 1870-1887* (Bloomington: Indiana University Press, 1973).

228.  Rich, *Great Power Diplomacy, 1814-1914*, 411.

Austria-Hungary surprised everyone, including Russia, in early October 1908. After the Buchlau Agreement, Vienna quickly took actions in the Balkans. Bulgaria, with the encouragement of Aehrenthal, declared independence from the Ottoman Empire on 5 October. The following day Austria-Hungary announced the annexation of Bosnia and Herzegovina, thus beginning the so-called Bosnian Crisis of 1908-9.[229] Both actions violated the Treaty of Berlin (1878). The Great Powers, including Britain, Germany, and Russia, all cried foul. The Serbian government was upset over the annexation of Bosnia and Herzegovina because of its own designs on the provinces. At this point, Izvolsky, to save face with the Great Powers and the South Slavs, declared that Aehrenthal had agreed at Buchlau for Russia and Austria-Hungary to call for an international conference to discuss and settle the Austro-Hungarian and Russian aims concerning Bosnia-Herzegovina and the Turkish Straits. They had not agreed to Vienna's immediate annexation of the provinces. As Norman Rich has written, "Izvolsky now stepped forward as the champion of the Serbs and demanded that the Austrians honor their commitment to submit the Bosnian Question to an international tribunal."[230] Vienna refused to submit to a conference, remembering what had happened to Germany and Austria-Hungary at the Algeciras Conference in 1906. Berlin supported Vienna's decision, needing to keep the one trustworthy ally it had. Chancellor Bülow even told Aehrenthal to remain firm against the British, French, and Russian demand for a conference.[231] The crisis was ended when Austria-Hungary signed an agreement with the Ottoman Empire in January 1909. In this agreement, Vienna agreed to give the Sultan monetary compensation for the annexation of Bosnia and Herzegovina. In March, the German threat of war convinced Russia, still weakened by the Russo-Japanese War, to backdown, especially in light that neither Britain nor France would support Russia in a conflict.[232] The Central Powers of Austria-Hungary and Germany had scored a major diplomatic triumph. Nonetheless, the victory tarnished the international reputation of the two Great Powers.

Kaiser William II's pursuit of Weltpolitik, the pursuit of colonies and the buildup of the German Navy since 1897, caused many problems for Germany.

---

229.    The Bosnian Crisis is the focus of Bernadotte E. Schmitt, *The Annexation of Bosnia, 1908-1908* (Cambridge: Cambridge University Press, 1937).

230.    Rich, *Great Power Diplomacy, 1814-1914*, 412.

231.    Geiss, *German Foreign Policy, 1871-1914*, 114. Bülow did not have the support of his Foreign Secretary, Wilhelm von Schön, who literally "took to his bed. When the storm abated and the foreign crisis seemed finally overcome, he reappeared on the scene" (Bülow, 3:35).

232.    Craig, *Germany 1866-1945*, 322.

The Second Reich was seen as aggressive and dangerous to international peace. Berlin was unable to build up a large, valuable colonial empire while maintaining a dominant position in Europe. "A foreign policy of bluster and a naval policy of expansion," according to Richard Langhorne, "were incompatibles, and so frightened other powers that they converted old agreements into anti-German coalitions or built up new ones."[233] Britain, France, and Russia had built up the Triple Entente to contain Germany. Germany's only true ally was Austria-Hungary. German diplomacy and Weltpolitik had failed. As one German historian has summed up the situation:

> After ten years, positive results were meagre, even negative: Germany's liberty of action was restricted by the Triple Entente. The acquisition of various scattered bases and territories was minimal and gained only at the price of hostility from all sides. Germany's strategic position was not in any way improved, because the German colonies and territories were almost impossible to defend in case of war. They were 'sitting ducks', were objects of prestige and more of a liability than an asset for Germany.[234]

## Germany and the Great War, 1909-1918

Eventually losing confidence in Bülow,[235] the Kaiser replaced him with Theobald von Bethmann Hollweg as the new Imperial Chancellor and Prussian Foreign Minister in 1909.[236] According to Bernard von Bülow, Bethmann Hollweg, who had previously headed both the Imperial and Prussian Interior Ministries, "knew nothing of foreign affairs."[237] Even Bethmann Hollweg admitted that he was "only little acquainted with the complicated machinery of foreign policy."[238]

233.  Richard Langhorne, *The Collapse of the Concert of Europe: International Politics, 1890-1914* (London: Macmillan, 1981), 49.

234.  Geiss, *German Foreign Policy, 1871-1914*, 84.

235.  See Peter Winzen, *Das Kaiserreich am Abgrund: Die Daily-Telegraph-Affäre und das Hale Interview von 1908* (Stuttgart: Franz Steiner Verlag, 2002), 19-91.

236.  Bethmann Hollweg's chancellorship is examined in Konrad H. Jarausch, *The Enigmatic Chancellor: Bethmann Hollweg and the Hubris of Imperial Germany* (New Haven: Yale University Press, 1973) and W. Gutsche, *Aufstieg und Fall eines kaiserlichen Reichskanzlers: Theobald von Bethmann Hollweg, 1856-1921* (Berlin: Akademie-Verlag, 1973).

237.  Bülow, 1:15. See also Bülow, 1:497-98, 3:176; Cecil, *The German Diplomatic Service, 1871-1914*, 308. Bethmann Hollweg had served as the Head of the Administration of Brandenburg (1899-1905), Prussian Minister of the Interior (1905-7), and State Secretary of the Reich Ministry of the Interior (1907-9) before becoming Imperial Chancellor in 1909 (Holstein, 4:453).

238.  As quoted in Jarausch, 109.

George Peabody Gooch, however, believed that William II chose Bethmann Hollweg as his Chancellor because "the Kaiser was less anxious for another trained diplomatist than for a trustworthy official with who he could work."[239] Lamar Cecil stressed that the Kaiser chose Bethmann Hollweg because William II "himself would continue...to direct German diplomacy."[240] Consequently, the Kaiser had the "weak-willed and compliant" Wilhelm von Schön stay on as State Secretary for Foreign Affairs.[241] Schön was "incapable of standing up to the Kaiser's desire to control diplomacy."[242] Wilhelm Stemrich, the Under State Secretary, also kept his position at the Wilhelmstrasse.[243]

From the beginning of his reign the Kaiser held a low opinion of the Wilhelmstrasse. William II directed his own foreign policy and put more stock in the advice of military and naval leaders than he did diplomats. Admiral Tirpitz possessed a high degree of influence over William II for over a decade. As the leading diplomat in the German Empire, albeit without experience, Bethmann Hollweg was responsible for advising the Kaiser on foreign relations. Konrad H. Jarausch believed that Bethmann Hollweg set out "with much enthusiasm to master the intricacies of *die Grosse Politik*."[244] He sought to reduce the friction between Germany and the other Great Powers.[245] But, according to Edward Willis, the Imperial Chancellor "lacked the personality" to challenge Weltpolitik and the naval program supported by William II and Admiral Tirpitz.[246] Bethmann Hollweg and Tirpitz competed over the conduct of German foreign policy.[247] The Kaiser, himself, was known to have said that "one Tirpitz is worth ten Bethmanns."[248]

In October 1910, Bethmann Hollweg selected the experienced diplomat, Alfred von Kiderlen-Wächter, as his new Foreign Secretary. Kiderlen-Wächter was an experienced diplomat, and had served as the Secretary of the German Embassy in St. Petersburg (1881-85), Secretary of the Embassy in Paris (1885-86), Secretary of the Embassy in Constantinople (1886-88), Counselor for Balkan and Near Eastern Affairs in the Political Division of the Foreign Office

---

239.  G.P. Gooch, *Before the War: Studies in Diplomacy*, 2 vols. (New York: Russell and Russell, 1938), 2:203.
240.  Cecil, *Wilhelm II*, 2:147.
241.  Jarausch, 111.
242.  Cecil, *Wilhelm II*, 2:147.
243.  Jarausch, 111.
244.  Ibid., 109-10.
245.  Ibid., 110.
246.  Willis, 156.
247.  Jarausch, 111, 162, 455.
248.  Bülow, 1:132.

(1888-94), Prussian Minister in Hamburg (1894-95), German Minister in Copenhagen (1895-99), Minister in Bucharest (1899-1910), and as temporary State Secretary for Foreign Affairs from November 1908 to March 1909.[249] The Kaiser reluctantly agreed to Kiderlen-Wächter's appointment.[250] However, diplomats at the Wilhelmstrasse held a high opinion of Kiderlen-Wächter and considered him "a man of superior ability..., a second Bismarck."[251] Bethmann Hollweg considered Kiderlen-Wächter as "perhaps the ablest diplomat that Germany had had of late."[252] His exceptional diplomatic experience and ability, however, made him arrogant and difficult to get along with. He possessed a ruthless and dominating manner, which he picked up from Bismarck and Holstein, thinking that "he could accomplish everything by beating his fist on the table."[253] As the State Secretary, Kiderlen-Wächter quickly restored strict discipline to the Foreign Office and maintained the support of most diplomats.[254] One exception to this support came from Prince Karl Max von Lichnowsky, the German Ambassador to Britain, who greatly disliked Kiderlen-Wächter and described him as "a disciple and intimate friend of Holstein's...was underhand, artful, sly and crafty, not without common sense and not without humour, but unmannerly, untidy, spiteful, malevolent and malicious."[255]

As the diplomatic expert within Bethmann Hollweg's cabinet, Kiderlen-Wächter exerted a great deal of influence and independence.[256] Kiderlen-Wächter managed the affairs of the Foreign Office with great secretiveness and refused to coordinate diplomatic issues with the Chancellor because he did not trust Bethmann Hollweg. The Wilhelmstrasse, including the new Under State Secretary, Dr. Arthur Zimmermann (1911-16),[257] supported Kiderlen-Wächter against the efforts of Bethmann Hollweg to discover what diplomatic efforts were under way in the foreign service.[258]

---

249.  Holstein, 1:161, 2:174, 3:83.

250.  William II, *The Kaiser's Memoirs*, 132; Jarausch, 111; Cecil, *Wilhelm II*, 2:148.

251.  Pinson, 303.

252.  Theobald von Bethmann Hollweg, *Reflections on the World War*, trans. George Young (London: Thornton Butterworth, 1920), 32; Geiss, *July 1914*, 37.

253.  Pinson, 304.

254.  Jarausch, 111; Cecil, *The German Diplomatic Service, 1871-1914*, 314.

255.  Prince Lichnowsky, *Heading for the Abyss: Reminiscences*, trans. Sefton Delmer (New York: Payson and Clarke, 1928), xxi. See also Willis, 30.

256.  See Claude C. Bolen, *Kiderlen-Wächter and German Foreign Policy* (Durham: Duke University Press, 1940) and Ralf Forsbach, *Alfred von Kiderlen-Wächter (1852-1912): Ein Diplomatenleben in Kaiserreich*, 2 vols. (Göttingen: Vandenhoeck and Ruprecht, 1997).

257.  Zimmermann was previously a Counselor in the Political Division of the Foreign Office from 1905 to 1910 (Holstein, 4:56).

258.  Cecil, *The German Diplomatic Service, 1871-1914*, 312-13.

The previous Chancellor, Bülow, now a diplomat serving the Wilhelmstrasse abroad and a close friend of Kiderlen-Wächter, believed that the Foreign Secretary was given too free a reign because the Chancellor was afraid of him.[259] In fact, the relationship between the two men became so distant that Gordon A. Craig described the situation:

> His [Kiderlen-Wächter] self-confidence and arrogance blinded him to the necessity of keeping Bethmann [Hollweg] fully informed of his intentions so that the unfortunate Chancellor was reduced to on one occasion to the extremity of getting his Foreign Secretary intoxicated in order to find out what was on his mind.[260]

For obvious reasons Bethmann Hollweg regretted his choice of Kiderlen-Wächter as State Secretary because of such extreme insubordination.[261] Nonetheless, the Kaiser, who remembered his objection to Kiderlen-Wächter's appointment, refused to assist Bethmann Hollweg in the power struggle against his Foreign Secretary.[262] The Kaiser placed little importance on the activities within the Foreign Office,[263] despite Kiderlen-Wächter being an out-spoken critic of Tirpitz's naval buildup.[264]

Kiderlen-Wächter was to play an important role in the Second Moroccan Crisis. In April and May 1911, Berlin protested the French deployment of troops to put down revolts against the Sultan of Morocco in Fez and Rabat. France was about to take the final step in setting up a protectorate in Morocco. At this point, Berlin declared that the French action had violated the Algeciras Agreement of 1906. The Kaiser realized that Germany would receive no international backing against France. He therefore sent the gunboat *Panther* to the southern seaport of Agadir in Morocco, which also violated the Algeciras Agreement. This action began the crisis. Some Germans wanted the Kaiser to establish a permanent colony in Morocco. However, the Kaiser and Kiderlen-Wächter used the Second Moroccan Crisis as a way to force a West African colony out of the French in return for consenting to their occupation of Morocco.[265] The German Foreign

259. Bülow, 2:464.
260. Craig, *Germany 1866-1945*, 327-28.
261. William II, *The Kaiser's Memoirs*, 132.
262. Cecil, *The German Diplomatic Service, 1871-1914*, 313.
263. Ibid., 212.
264. Pinson, 304; Harold Nicolson, *Sir Arthur Nicolson, Bart., First Lord Carnock: A Study in the Old Diplomacy* (London: Constable, 1930), 395.
265. Jarausch, 120-21.

Secretary negotiated with French Prime Minister Joseph Caillaux to accomplish this quest. In 15 July 1911, Kiderlen-Wächter demanded that Paris give up the French Congo (Brazzaville) as the price for Germany's acceptance of French control of Morocco.[266] Two days later, Caillaux rejected this demand. At this point, the Kaiser wanted Kiderlen-Wächter to backdown for fear that Britain might support France. The State Secretary, however, continued to practice brinkmanship, risking war, for the sole purpose of gaining a colonial concession.[267] A few days later, on 21 July, David Lloyd George, the British Chancellor of the Exchequer, announced that Britain would completely support France in face of the German threat.[268] Consequently, the Kaiser ordered a German withdrawal from Morocco. The crisis was finally ended with Franco-German agreements concerning Morocco and Equatorial Africa in November 1911. William II recognized the French position in Morocco, while Paris handed Germany some territory in the French Congo that connected the German Cameroons with the Congo and Ubanghi Rivers, giving the Germans outlets for the colony's exports.[269] The overall result of the Second Moroccan Crisis was increased frustration in Germany and a further consolidation of the Triple Entente.

In January 1912, Chancellor Bethmann Hollweg initiated naval arms talks between Germany and Britain.[270] The Chancellor and the Foreign Office were supporters of good Anglo-German relations and an end to the Naval Arms Race. David Lloyd George and Winston Churchill, the British First Lord of the Admiralty, welcomed the possibility of a naval treaty for economic reasons. The Kaiser supported the possibility of a naval agreement. The talks began with the arrival of Lord Richard Haldane, the British Minister of War, in Berlin in February. But the talks came to nothing because of the British demand for the Germans to reduce the construction of their naval fleet, combined with the German demand for British neutrality in any war involving Germany and a continental European power. The Kaiser and Admiral Tirpitz refused to slowdown the building of the German battlefleet.[271] In fact, William II became so angered at the Auswärtiges Amt for attempting to slow down the ship-building program that he told Wilhelm von Stumm of the Foreign Office that "you diplomats have filled your pants, the entire Wilhelmstrasse

266.  Geiss, *German Foreign Policy, 1871-1914*, 133.
267.  Jarausch, 122.
268.  Geiss, *German Foreign Policy, 1871-1914*, 134.
269.  Rich, *Great Power Diplomacy, 1814-1914*, 420.
270.  Jarausch, 112-13.
271.  Geiss, *German Foreign Policy, 1871-1914*, 137-38.

stinks of _ _ _ _."[272] Berlin soon passed another Naval Law that called for the fleet to increase to forty-one Dreadnoughts and twenty battle cruisers.[273] Foreign Secretary Kiderlen-Wächter responded to the situation by stating, "I am an opponent of Tirpitz because I am afraid his policies will bring us to war with England."[274] But, the State Secretary realized that Tirpitz was too influential with William II to redirect German policy.[275]

In September 1911, in the midst of the Second Moroccan Crisis, Germany's ally, Italy, invaded the Ottoman provinces of Tripolitania and Cyrenaica in North Africa. The Italians proclaimed the annexation of "Libya" in November. The war was ended by the Treaty of Lausanne in October 1912. However, Italian success against the Sublime Porte encouraged a new attack on the Ottoman Empire. Bulgaria, Serbia, Greece, and Montenegro formed the Balkan League that attacked the Ottomans and began the First Balkan War in October 1912.[276] The Balkan League quickly achieved success against the Turks. The Balkan allies reached the gates of Constantinople by mid-November. As a result, Serbia was fast becoming the dominant power in the Balkans.[277] Serbia, backed by St. Petersburg, was threatening to unite the South Slavs. It was seeking to gain access to the Adriatic Sea. But the Habsburg Monarchy opposed the rising power of Serbia. Vienna sought to block Belgrade's access to the sea by creating the independent state of Albania. Moreover, Austria-Hungary wanted to launch a preventive war against Serbia.[278] As a result, tension between Austria-Hungary and Russia was high. In November and December, the Kaiser and the Wilhelmstrasse both supported Austria-Hungary and tried to pull back the leash to prevent a war in the Balkans.[279] Berlin would not support Habsburg action against Serbia. At that time, in February 1913, the Kaiser was not willing to go to war in support of the Habsburgs over the Balkans.[280] Bethmann

---

272.   William II to Wilhelm von Stumm, 15 January 1912, cited in J.C.G. Röhl, "Admiral von Müller and the Approach of War, 1911-1914," *Historical Journal* 12 (1969), 657.

273.   Sondhaus, *Naval Warfare, 1815-1914*, 204; Michael Epkenhans, "Wilhelm II and 'His' Navy, 1888-1918," in *The Kaiser: New Research on Wilhelm's Role in Imperial Germany*, ed. Annika Mombauer and Wilhelm Deist (Cambridge: Cambridge University Press, 2003), 14.

274.   As quoted in Pinson, 304.

275.   Ibid.

276.   Richard C. Hall, *The Balkan Wars, 1912-1913: Prelude to the First Balkan War* (London: Routledge, 2000), 12-13.

277.   Hall, 22-68.

278.   Fritz Fischer, *War of Illusions: German Policies from 1911 to 1914* (London: Chatto and Windus, 1975), 154.

279.   Ibid., 153-59.

280.   Geiss, *German Foreign Policy, 1871-1914*, 140, 151. See also Ernst Christian Helmreich, *The Diplomacy of the Balkan Wars, 1912-1913* (Cambridge, MA: Harvard University Press, 1938).

Hollweg told Count Leopold Berchtold, the Austro-Hungarian Foreign Minister, that an Austrian attack against Serbia would result in a confrontation with Russia.[281] Germany was not prepared for war. Berlin successfully restrained Austria-Hungary from taking aggressive action for the remaining part of the First Balkan War, and the conflict was eventually concluded with the Treaty of London in May 1913. The Austro-German alliance was strained, and Serbia remained a threat to Austro-Hungarian interests.

The First Balkan War embarrassed Berlin. Germany was not prepared for war, and the conflict had weakened the position of Austria-Hungary in Southeast Europe. William II, Bethmann Hollweg, and other German leaders realized that they must stand up for Austria-Hungary. On 2 December 1912, Bethmann Hollweg addressed the German Reichstag and stressed that Germany must support Austria-Hungary if it was attacked by Russia. Germany "would also fight, in order to preserve our position in Europe and to defend our future and security."[282] About one week later, on 8 December, William II gathered his chief military and naval advisers, including Admiral Tirpitz and General Helmuth von Moltke, Chief of the General Staff (1906-14). The German leaders discussed German preparedness, the combat readiness of its possible enemies, and particular scenarios for war. According to Fritz Fischer, the Kaiser:

> was in favour of an immediate war against Russia and France. If Austria did not "adopt a firm stand against the foreign Slavs (the Serbs)" it was in danger of losing control over the Serbs in the Monarchy. If Russia then supported the Serbs and perhaps entered Galacia "war would be unavoidable for us". In this great war Germany could hope to gain Bulgaria, Rumania, also Albania and possibly even Turkey as allies.[283]

At this meeting, General Moltke, the nephew of the great soldier who had led the Prussian armies to victory in the nineteenth century, believed that conflict was unavoidable, and he pressed for a preventive war as soon as possible. The Schlieffen Plan, a war plan for fighting both France and Russia, would be the only plan considered. Admiral Tirpitz stressed that the German Navy would need another eighteen months before it was ready for war.[284] The Chancellor, himself, was not informed about the meeting until a week later.[285]

---

281. Geiss, *German Foreign Policy, 1871-1914*, 151.
282. Ibid., 141.
283. Fischer, *War of Illusions*, 161.
284. Geiss, *German Foreign Policy, 1871-1914*, 142-43, 148.
285. Rich, *Great Power Diplomacy, 1814-1914*, 428.

Bethmann Hollweg, Kiderlen-Wächter, and the Wilhelmstrasse were rapidly losing any influence they had with the Kaiser. Count Philipp zu Eulenburg-Hertefeld complained about the situation that the military "acquired more and more influence [with the Kaiser] as time went on. These men, with the everlasting Berlin ribaldry, systematically derided the Foreign Office."[286] Kurt Reizler, the Assistant to the Chancellor, noted that Bethmann Hollweg had "absolutely no talent for getting along with the military, for impressing them and for getting information from them."[287] This situation especially became acute when, in 1912, German Army leaders acquired more influence when the Kaiser recognized the failure of Weltpolitik and switched to a foreign policy focused on Central Europe (Mitteleuropa), which increased the importance of land warfare, to protect Germany's Great Power status.[288] Thus, Bethmann Hollweg and the Foreign Office held little influence with the German Emperor. One diplomat commented that, "as Bethmann was filled with a burning desire to stay in office—no Minister clung to office as he did—he yielded to the Kaiser in everything from the beginning."[289] The Kaiser kept Bethmann as his Chancellor for this reason.[290]

The sudden death of Kiderlen-Wächter from a stroke left the Foreign Office without a strong leader in December 1912.[291] After the experience of Kiderlen-Wächter, the Kaiser and Bethmann Hollweg wanted to avoid filling the position of State Secretary with another strong-willed diplomat. Dr. Arthur Zimmermann, the Under State Secretary for Foreign Affairs, who was more of an administrator than a diplomat,[292] declined the offer of promotion.[293] They finally settled on a diplomat with twenty years of experience. Gottlieb von Jagow had served as a Secretary to the German Embassy in Rome, a Counselor in the Political Division of the Foreign Office, Minister to Luxembourg, and Ambassador to Italy (1909-13).[294] He, too, was unwilling, but Jagow accepted the position after being persuaded by Bethmann Hollweg in January 1913.[295] Jagow has been described by Barbara Tuchman as "a puny rodent of a man whose Charlie Chap-

---

286. As quoted in Haller, 2:300.
287. As quoted in Jarausch, 151.
288. Berghahn, 112, 115.
289. Bülow, 1:697-98.
290. William II, *The Kaiser's Memoirs*, 132.
291. Lerman, "The Kaiser's Elite," 72.
292. Bülow, 3:178.
293. Z.A.B. Zeman, *A Diplomatic History of the First World War* (London: Weidenfeld and Nicolson, 1971), 84.
294. Bülow, 3:38-39, 3:176.
295. Cecil, *The German Diplomatic Service, 1871-1914*, 318.

lin mustache and un-Teutonic look of an anxious rabbit caused him to be regarded by everybody, including himself, as inadequate for his post."[296] But, Foreign Secretary Jagow worked closely with Bethmann Hollweg and the Kaiser, supported the Army,[297] and became a "most loyal associate and unflagging counselor."[298] As early as January 1913, however, Edward Goschen, the British Ambassador to Germany, warned the British Foreign Office that "Jagow for his part was not made of reinforced concrete: he feared that, should a sudden crisis occur, Bethmann Hollweg and Jagow would be swept away."[299] Commenting on Jagow's relationship with Bethmann Hollweg, William II wrote in his memoirs, "the Secretary of State for Foreign Affairs was, under him [Bethmann Hollweg], a mere helper, so much so that the Foreign Office was almost affiliated with the office of the Chancellor."[300]

The influence of the military was too strong even for a Chancellor and Foreign Secretary who worked together. Bethmann Hollweg and Jagow came to the conclusion that Germany must limit the expansion of its fleet or risk war with Britain. In vain they attempted to influence the Kaiser to change his program.[301] Both men discovered that they were not allowed to participate in any discussions of military planning,[302] since the Kaiser believed Bethmann Hollweg to be a "pacifist."[303] Even Sir Edward Grey, the British Foreign Secretary, realized that the Chancellor and German Foreign Office had no influence over German policy. He wrote in his memoirs:

> Now something that had always been an uncomfortable suspicion in the background came to the front and took more definite and ugly shape. There were forces other than Bethmann-Hollweg in the seat of authority in Germany. He was not master of the situation; in negotiating with him we were not negotiating with a principal. Yet he was the only authority with who we could negotiate at all.[304]

---

296. Barbara W. Tuchman, *The Zimmermann Telegram* (New York: Macmillan, 1958), 111. Harold Nicolson described Jagow "as the very soul of gentleness" (Nicolson, *Sir Arthur Nicolson*, 395).

297. Berghahn, 131; Cecil, *The German Diplomatic Service, 1871-1914*, 319; Nicolson, *Sir Arthur Nicolson*, 395.

298. Gerhard Ritter, *The Sword and the Scepter: The Problem of Militarism in Germany*, trans. Heinz Norden, 4 vols. (Coral Gable: University of Miami Press, 1970), 3:213.

299. As quoted in Nicolson, *Sir Arthur Nicolson,* 395-96.

300. William II, *The Kaiser's Memoirs*, 138.

301. Berghahn, 130-31.

302. Craig, *Germany 1866-1945*, 317.

303. William II, *The Kaiser's Memoirs*, 132-33.

304. Viscount Grey of Fallodon, *Twenty-Five Years, 1892-1916*, 2 vols. (New York: Frederick A. Stokes, 1925), 1:312-13.

The Kaiser under the influence of military leaders was the central figure concerning German foreign policy. He had acted as his own Foreign Minister more or less throughout his reign. On numerous occasions, especially involving Morocco and the Balkans, he had backed down when confronted with the possibility of war.[305] However, by mid-1913, William II came to the realization that Germany needed to support the weakened Habsburg Monarchy against the Serbian military threat and South Slav movement in order for Austria to maintain its Great Power status. He knew that it was of vital importance for Germany to support its ally since the Serbian threat, backed by the Tsar, could drastically change the balance of power in Southeast Europe.[306] William II feared the disintegration of his one faithful ally, Austria, and perceived Germany "cornered and desperate" against the decline of the Triple Alliance vis-a-vis the Triple Entente.[307] Any decision for action to defend the alliance was up to him.

The next crisis broke out in June 1913. Bulgaria, desiring a larger portion of the spoils from the first conflict, attacked Serbia and Greece, beginning the Second Balkan War. Rumania and the Ottoman Empire joined Serbia and Greece against the Bulgarians a month later. The alliance quickly defeated the Bulgarians.[308] Serbia remained the dominant South Slav power. Serbia had doubled its territory and population at the expense of the Ottoman Empire and Bulgaria in the First and Second Balkan Wars.[309] Belgrade controlled most of Macedonia and Montenegro. Serbia, the only remaining Russian ally in Southeast Europe, now competed with Austria-Hungary for the loyalty of the Serbs, Croats, Slovenes, and Bosnians who lived in the Habsburg Empire.[310]

Belgrade provoked another Balkan crisis when Serbian troops crossed into the newly independent state of Albania in September 1913. The Serbs wanted access to the Adriatic Sea. Albania, however, had gained its independence during the Balkan Wars, and this status was guaranteed by the Great Powers, including Austria-Hungary.[311] The Dual Monarchy quickly responded to Serbian aggression. General Francis Conrad von Hötzendorf, the Chief of the General Staff for the Austro-Hungarian Army, called for a decisive diplomatic or military action to eliminate the Serbian menace. He believed that:

---

305.  See L.C.F. Turner, *Origins of the First World War* (London: Edward Arnold, 1970).
306.  Ibid., 81, 85; Berghahn, 139-40.
307.  Berghahn, 167.
308.  Hall, 107-29.
309.  David Stevenson, *The First World War and International Politics* (New York: Oxford University Press, 1988), 14.
310.  Hall, 129.
311.  Ibid., 130.

Serbia should accept peaceful integration into the Habsburg Empire with a status similar to that of Bavaria or Saxony in the German Empire; or, if Serbia refused, Austria should go to war, annex part of Serbia, and divide the rest among its Balkan neighbors, thereby winning their gratitude and bringing them into Austria's diplomatic orbit.[312]

William II of Germany completely supported the Dual Monarchy. The Kaiser, who believed the other Great Powers would not act, told General Conrad von Hötzendorf, that Germany would support Austria-Hungary in a localized war against Serbia.[313] One historian has stated:

> The Kaiser, who had turned a blind eye to Austrian concern about Serbia earlier in the year, now made a typical turnabout and was all for war. "Now or never! We must finally have order and quiet down there!" If Serbia did not give way, Belgrade should be bombarded and occupied. "And of this you can be certain," he hold the Austrians, "that I stand by you and am ready to draw the sabre whenever your action makes it necessary."[314]

By October 1913 Berlin's assurances of support to Vienna encouraged the Austrians to issue an ultimatum to Belgrade. The Austro-Hungarian government demanded that the Serbs withdraw from Albania or face the consequences. Belgrade backed down, and withdrew its military troops from Albania.[315] William II had made the decision to support the Habsburg Monarchy to maintain its Great Power status.

The incident that prompted the Kaiser to take further action was the assassination of his close associate, Archduke Franz Ferdinand, the heir to the Austro-Hungarian throne, by a Bosnian terrorist supported by Serbia on 28 June 1914.[316] With emotions running high, William II favored an immediate Austrian action against Serbia.[317] On 5 July, the Kaiser met with Count Ladislaus Szögyény-Marich, the

---

312.  Rich, *Great Power Diplomacy, 1814-1914*, 431.

313.  Geiss, *July 1914*, 44-45.

314.  Rich, *Great Power Diplomacy, 1814-1914*, 431.

315.  Hall, 131; Geiss, *German Foreign Policy, 1871-1914*, 153.

316.  There are scores of studies recounting the origins of World War I. Some of these studies include Luigi Albertini, *The Origins of the War of 1914*, 3 vols. (London: Oxford University Press, 1953); Vladimir Dedijer, *The Road to Sarajevo* (New York: Simon and Schuster, 1966); A.J.P. Taylor, *War by Timetable: How the First World War Began* (London: MacDonald, 1969); James Joll, *The Origins of the First World War* (London: Longman, 1984); John H. Maurer, *The Outbreak of the First World War: Strategic Planning, Crisis Decision Making, and Deterrence Failure* (Westport, CT: Praeger, 1995); Richard F. Hamilton and Holger H. Herwig, eds., *The Origins of World War I* (Cambridge: Cambridge University Press, 2003).

317.  Maurer, 59; Heinrich von Tschirschky to Theobald von Bethmann Hollweg, 30 June 1914, in Geiss, *July 1914*, 64-65.

Austro-Hungarian Ambassador to Berlin. William II informed the ambassador that he "expected some serious step...towards Serbia" and, without consulting with Bethmann Hollweg, told Szögyény-Marich that Austria could "rely upon Germany's full support."[318] The Kaiser was under the assumption that any Austrian action could be localized in the Balkans since "Russia at the present time was in no way prepared for war, and would think twice before it appealed to arms."[319]

Later that same day, on 5 July, the Kaiser summoned those of his highest military and political advisers who were available at a moment's notice to a meeting in Potsdam. The German Army was represented by General Eric von Falkenhayn, the Prussian Minister of War, and General Moritz von Lyncker, the Chief of the Kaiser's Military Cabinet.[320] Bethmann Hollweg and Zimmermann, both with little knowledge of foreign relations, represented the diplomats at the meeting since Jagow was on leave away from Berlin.[321] At the Potsdam Conference the Kaiser insisted upon Germany supporting Austria-Hungary because its preservation was vital to German security.[322] He questioned his advisers about Germany's readiness for war, and discovered that they all believed the Second Reich to be prepared.[323] They, however, agreed that any war between Austria-Hungary and Serbia could be limited to the Balkan Region.[324] As for any Austrian action, the Kaiser told Bethmann Hollweg:

> It was not our business...to advise our ally what it must do in respect of the bloody deed at Sarajevo. Austria-Hungary must settle that for itself. We must abstain from any direct action or advice, as we must labour with every means to prevent the Austro-Serbian dispute developing into an international conflict. But the Emperor Francis Joseph must also be given to know that we would not desert Austria-Hungary in its hour of peril.[325]

318. Ladislaus Szögyény-Marich to Leopold Berchtold, 5 July 1914, in Geiss, *July 1914*, 76-77.
319. Ibid. See also Gooch, 2:270.
320. Geiss, *July 1914*, 71.
321. *GD*, 1:28; *The Disclosures from Germany: The Lichnowsky Memorandum and the Reply of Herr von Jagow*, ed. and trans. Munroe Smith (New York: American Association for International Conciliation, 1918), 175-77; Bethmann Hollweg, 119.
322. *GD*, 1:32-33.; Gooch, 2:270.
323. *The Disclosures from Germany*, 175-76; Geiss, *July 1914*, 71. As for the confidence of the German military, see Mark Hewitson, *Germany and the Causes of the First World War* (New York: Berg, 2004).
324. Jarausch, 161, 471; Geiss, *July 1914*, 71.
325. Bethmann Hollweg, 119.

The next day, on 6 July, the Imperial Chancellor relayed the Kaiser's decision, the so-called "blank check" to the Austro-Hungarian government.[326] He informed Szögyény-Marich that Germany would support the Habsburg Empire, and that the Kaiser considered "immediate action on our [Austria-Hungary] part as the best solution of our difficulties in the Balkans."[327]

Upon returning to Berlin, Foreign Secretary Jagow was informed of the Potsdam Conference and subsequent communications with Vienna.[328] He also found out that the Kaiser was permitting Vienna to formulate an ultimatum to Serbia without German collaboration. Jagow believed this to be folly, but by the time he was consulted and drawn into the situation, the Kaiser "had so committed himself that it was too late for any action on customary diplomatic lines, and there was nothing more to be done."[329]

The diplomats at the Ballhausplatz in Vienna were reluctant to collaborate with the Wilhelmstrasse concerning any plans for Austrian military action against Serbia. The Austrian Foreign Minister, Count Leopold Berchtold, feared a leak of Austrian intentions.[330] Meanwhile, both Bethmann Hollweg and Jagow, under the direction of the Kaiser, pushed the Austro-Hungarians to take military action soon in hope of localizing the conflict and achieving a fait accompli.[331] The Chancellor and Foreign Secretary did not expect the conflict to break out into a European war.[332] Jagow communicated to Lichnowsky, the German Ambassador in London, the thinking of the leadership in Berlin:

> Russia was not ready; there would probably be some fuss and noise, but the more firmly we took sides with Austria the more would Russia give way. As it was, Austria was accusing us of weakness, and therefore we dare not leave her in a lurch. Public opinion in Russia, on the other hand, was becoming more and more anti-German, so we must just risk it.[333]

On 9 July, Under State Secretary Zimmermann told a fellow diplomat that he believed "the present moment very opportune for Austria to undertake a revenge

326.   Stevenson, 16.
327.   Szögyény-Marich to Berchtold, 6 July 1914, in Geiss, *July 1914*, No. 8, 79. See also Bethmann telegram to Tschirschky, 6 July 1914, *OWW*, 78-79.
328.   *The Disclosures from Germany*, 175-77.
329.   Ibid., 199.
330.   Samuel R. Williamson, Jr., *Austria-Hungary and the Origins of the First World War* (New York: St. Martin's Press, 1991), 201.
331.   *GD*, 1:22; Berghahn, 189, 193; Bülow, 3:173.
332.   Turner, *Origins of the First World War*, 85; Bülow, 3:176; Jarausch, 160.
333.   As quoted in Lichnowsky, 73.

campaign against its southern neighbor," and that "war could successfully be localized."[334] On 18 July, Jagow informed Lichnowsky:

> [I]n the interest of localization we abstained from any influence on the preparation of the Austrian step toward Serbia. We hoped to be able to prevent the Serbian conflict from becoming a European question.[335]

The Foreign Secretary, on 19 July, placed a statement in a German newspaper in which he expressed his desire to localize any Austro-Serbian conflict. He wrote:

> In the utterances of the European press in regard to the existing tension between Austria-Hungary and Serbia it is increasingly recognised that Austria-Hungary's desire to clear up her relations with Serbia is justified. In this connection we share the hope expressed in more than one quarter that a serious crisis will be avoided by the Serbian Government giving way in time. In any event the solidarity of Europe, which made itself felt during the long Balkan crisis in maintaining peace among the great Powers, demands and requires that the settlement of differences which may arise between Austria-Hungary and Serbia should remain localised.[336]

In his own analysis of the situation, Bernhard von Bülow described the Chancellor and Jagow as "a pair of wilful little urchins playing with what seems an empty shell case, which is liable to explode at any minute."[337]

On 22 July, Foreign Minister Berchtold forwarded a copy of Austria's ultimatum to Serbia to the German Foreign Office. The ultimatum was to be delivered to Belgrade the following day.[338] Jagow found the terms of the document excessively severe,[339] and told Bethmann Hollweg so when he gave the Chancellor the copy of the ultimatum.[340] Bethmann Hollweg, too, believed "the ultimatum, after I saw it, to be too sharp."[341] Both Bethmann Hollweg and Jagow realized, nonetheless, that such a short notice before the ultimatum would be served to Belgrade left the German diplomats no time to express their opinions to the Ball-

---

334.  As quoted in Jarausch, 470.
335.  As quoted in ibid., 471.
336.  Jagow statement in the *North German Gazette* of 19 July 1914, in Geiss, *July 1914*, 142.
337.  Bülow, 3:176.
338.  Williamson, 201.
339.  *GD*, 1:33.
340.  Bethmann Hollweg, 122.
341.  As quoted in Jarausch, 162.

hausplatz.[342] Both the Chancellor and State Secretary hoped for serious negotiations between Belgrade and Vienna to begin after the sharp ultimatum.[343]

But, two days after the delivery of the forty-eight hour ultimatum, Belgrade began the process of mobilization that eventually engulfed the whole of Europe in war. The Austro-Hungarians began partial mobilization, declared war on Serbia, and began shelling Serbian territory on 28 July. St. Petersburg took note of this threat to its ally, and prepared to come to its defense. On 29 July, the Russian Ambassador to Vienna, N.N. Shebeko, informed Sergei D. Sazonov, the Russian Foreign Minister, that a European conflict could not be avoided since the Austro-Hungarians and Germans "had gone too far to retreat without serious damage to their prestige and to the stability of their alliance."[344] The very next day, on 30 July, the Russians began general mobilization. While the German government warned Moscow about such action, the Austrians initiated general mobilization on 31 July.

Within Germany, the military leadership pressured the Kaiser to act by mobilizing and initiating the Schlieffen Plan.[345] The Kaiser and his advisers had miscalculated the Russian reaction to a war in the Balkans.[346] They had believed that Russia would not intervene. Russian mobilization made it a necessity for Germany to mobilize and carry out its plans for fighting a war on two fronts, against Russia and France.[347] General Helmuth von Moltke, the Chief of the General Staff, was anxious and hasty to force Germany into war against Russia because the Schlieffen Plan required a rapid German mobilization to counter any Russian and French military moves.[348] The historian L.C.F. Turner believed that "Russian and Austrian general mobilization made a great war inevitable."[349] On 1 August, the Germans began mobilizing and declared war on Russia. Germany's ally, Italy, quickly declared neutrality in the coming war between the Central

---

342.   Bethmann Holweg, 122; Gooch, 2:271.

343.   Jarausch, 130.

344.   D.C.B. Lieven, *Russia and the Origins of the First World War* (London: Macmillan, 1983), 150-51.

345.   Lichnowsky, 72; Geiss, *July 1914*, 60.

346.   Turner, *Origins of the First World War*, 114.

347.   L.C.F. Turner, "The Russian Mobilization in 1914," in *Journal of Contemporary History* 3 (1968), 65. See also *Military Strategy and the Origins of the First World War*, ed. Steven E. Miller, Sean M. Lynn-Jones, and Stephen Van Evera, 2 ed. (Princeton: Princeton University Press, 1991).

348.   Ritter, 2:270-71; Lichnowsky, 72; Turner, *Origins of the First World War*, 77.

349.   Turner, *Origins of the First World War*, 109.

Powers of Germany and Austria-Hungary on one side and the Triple Entente of Britain, France, and Russia on the other.[350]

Bethmann Hollweg and Jagow had possessed no influence on the sequence of events because of the clout the military held over the Kaiser. A few days later, Bernard von Bülow visited Bethmann Hollweg in Berlin. He described his reception:

> Bethmann stood in the centre of the room. Shall I ever forget his face. There is a picture by some celebrated English painter, which shows the wretched scapegoat with a look of ineffable anguish in its eyes—such pain as I now saw in Bethmann's. For an instant neither of us spoke. At last I said to him: "Well, tell me, at least, how it all happened." He raised his long, thin arms to heaven and answered in a dull, exhausted voice: "Oh—if I only knew!"[351]

Speaking to the British Ambassador to Berlin, Jagow blamed the outbreak of war on "this d_ _ _ _d system of alliances."[352] Reflecting upon the crisis, Sir Edward Grey wrote in his memoirs:

> It is of no use to look to the action of Bethmann-Hollweg and Jagow [to discover who directed German foreign policy]—the men who, having nominal direction of German policy, folded their hands after the murder of the Archduke, and…never asked to see the terms of their Austrian Ally's ultimatum to Serbia before it was sent; the men who, after that ultimatum was sent and the Serbian reply received, expressed some criticism of the former and thought that the latter went further in the direction of conciliation than could have been expected; and who yet let things drift or spoke only in whispers at Vienna, when a decisive word was wanted. I believe that neither the Emperor or Bethmann-Hollweg nor Jagow planned or desired war. But the Emperor, in the critical moment after the Serbian reply, apparently withheld his influence, when it might have been decisive for peace…. Bethmann-Hollweg and Jagow had no influence. They were powerless, and they were the only Germans with whom other Governments, including our own, could deal.[353]

---

350.  Zeman, 7.
351.  Bülow, 3:145.
352.  Edward Goschen to Sir Arthur Nicolson, No. 510, *BDOW*, 11:283-85.
353.  Grey, 2:26-27.

At the beginning of the war, Berlin established the German Army High Command (Oberste Heeresleitung or OHL). The High Command was headed by William II, the Supreme Warlord, and the Chief of the General Staff of the German Army. From the start of the war the Kaiser told General Moltke that he would not interfere in military operations.[354] William II had given up operational leadership of the German Army, but, according to Holger Afflerbach, "kept open the option of intervening in the decision-making process."[355] Thus, under the leadership of General Moltke, the German Army followed a modified Schlieffen Plan,[356] and invaded Belgium and France with seven armies in August 1914.[357] German forces amounted to 1,600,000 men.[358] The French Army, however, halted the German advance at the First Battle of the Marne in September 1914.[359] For the next two months the Germans continuously engaged Anglo-French forces, with both sides racing northwards towards the English Channel, attempting to outflank each other. Before long the Germans became bogged down in trench warfare stretching from Switzerland to the English Channel.[360] As for the Eastern Front, Germany achieved success in the initial stages of the war in the east. Field Marshal Paul von Hindenburg and General Erich Ludendorff

354.  Cecil, *Wilhelm II*, 2:211-12.

355.  Holger Afflerbach, "Wilhelm II as Supreme Warlord in the First World War," in *The Kaiser: New Research on Wilhelm II's Role in Imperial Germany*, eds. Annika Mombauer and Wilhelm Deist (Cambridge: Cambridge University Press, 2003), 201.

356.  See Arden Bucholz, *Moltke, Schlieffen, and Prussian War Planning* (New York: Berg, 1991).

357.  There are numerous general studies on the First World War. Some recent treatments include Ian F.W. Beckett, *The Great War, 1914-1918* (London: Longman, 2001); John Keegan, *The First World War* (New York: Alfred Knopf, 1999); Spencer Tucker, *The Great War, 1914-1918* (Bloomington: Indiana University Press, 1998); and Martin Gilbert, *The First World War* (New York: Henry Holt, 1994). German aspects are the focus of Holger H. Herwig, *The First World War: Germany and Austria-Hungary, 1914-1918* (London: Arnold, 1998). The German Navy and the naval war is treated in Holger H. Herwig, *"Luxury" Fleet: The Imperial German Navy, 1888-1918* (Atlantic Highlands, NJ: Ashfield Press, 1987) and Richard Hough, *The Great War at Sea, 1914-1918* (Oxford: Oxford University Press, 1983). The German Air Force and air war is covered in John H. Morrow, Jr., *German Air Power in World War I* (Lincoln: University of Nebraska Press, 1982) and Peter Kilduff, *Germany's First Air Force, 1914-1918* (London: Arms and Armour Press, 1991).

358.  Roger Chickering, *Imperial Germany and the Great War, 1914-1918*, 2 ed. (Cambridge: Cambridge University Press, 2004), 23.

359.  Herwig, *The First World War*, 96-106. See also Robert B. Asprey, *The First Battle of the Marne* (Philadelphia: Lippincott, 1962).

360.  Michael J. Lyons, *World War I: A Short History*, 2 ed. (Upper Saddle River, NJ: Prentice Hall, 2000), 88-89. Lancelot L. Farrar, Jr., *The Short-War Illusion: German Policy, Strategy, and Domestic Affairs, August-December 1914* (Santa Barbara, CA: ABC-Clio, 1973) stresses the German assumption that the war would not last long. The belief was ended with the military stalemate on the Western Front in 1914.

defeated the Russians at the Battle of Tannenberg in August and Battle of Masurian Lakes in September.[361] To the south, Austria-Hungary carried out military campaigns against Serbia and the Russians on the Eastern Front that both failed.[362] However, the Central Powers gained the active support of the Ottoman Empire, especially in the Black Sea, in October 1914.[363]

In the autumn of 1914 the Kaiser replaced Moltke with General Erich von Falkenhayn as Chief of the General Staff. In 1915, German forces under Hindenburg and Ludendorff forced the Russians to retreat 250 miles, and the Kaiser's army occupied Poland, Lithuania, and Latvia. This success, combined with the staunch Turkish defense of Gallipoli, convinced Bulgaria to join the Central Powers in September 1915.[364] Meanwhile, on the Western Front, the British and French conducted offensive operations against the Germans near Arras in May and June 1915. Italy joined the Triple Entente against the Central Powers in the spring of 1915.[365] In the meantime, the German fleet of sixteen battleships was blocked by the British Royal Navy and mines from breaking out into the North Sea.[366] In fact, the Royal Navy penetrated the Heligoland Bight and sank three German light cruisers and one destroyer, as well as damaged two other light cruisers in late August 1914. In January 1915 a skirmish between cruisers off the Dogger Bank resulted in the loss of another German ship. Afterwards, the German fleet stayed at its home ports for the next sixteen months.[367] Consequently, both General Falkenhayn and Admiral Tirpitz urged the Kaiser to launch an all-out campaign of unrestricted submarine warfare (the sinking of ships without warning) against allied commerce. At the time Germany had only nine U-boats capable of operating as far away as the English coastline.[368] Chancellor Bethmann Hollweg and Foreign Secretary Jagow, however, convinced the Kaiser to avoid such an offensive, realizing that it would antagonize the United States, especially

---

361.   For the war on the Eastern Front, see Norman Stone, *The Eastern Front, 1914-1917* (London: Hodder and Stoughton, 1975) and Dennis Showalter, *Tannenberg: Clash of Empires* (Hamden, CT: Archon, 1991).

362.   Lyons, *World War I*, 102-6. Austro-German relations during the war are examined in Gerard E. Silberstein, *The Troubled Alliance: German-Austrian Relations, 1914-1917* (Lexington: University Press of Kentucky, 1970).

363.   Zeman, 60. Relations between the Central Powers and the Ottoman Empire are the focus of Frank G. Weber, *Eagles on the Crescent: Germany, Austria, and the Diplomacy of the Turkish Alliance, 1914-1918* (Ithaca: Cornell University Press, 1970).

364.   Lyons, *World War I*, 137.

365.   Zeman, 36-38.

366.   Chickering, 88.

367.   Craig, *Germany 1866-1945*, 342.

368.   Ibid., 369.

after the sinking of the Cunard liner *Lusitania* in May 1915.[369] Admiral Tirpitz was dismissed from his position as Secretary of State for his part in the failure of the German Navy in March 1916.[370] Bethmann Hollweg, not in favor with Falkenhayn, preferred to support the war strategy of Hindenburg and Ludendorff against the Russians.[371]

At the outbreak of conflict, the German Foreign Office strongly supported the Kaiser's war effort. The Kaiser, Bethmann Hollweg, and Jagow left Berlin to direct their affairs from the Military Headquarters (Grosse Hauptquartier) of the German High Command. William II remained at the Military Headquarters, which moved from Coblenz, Luxembourg, Mézières, Pless, Kreuznach, to Spa, for the duration of the war.[372] However, as Martin Kitchen has pointed out, "he exercised very little control over military planning and decision making."[373] The General Staff was in charge of military decisions and operations. William II quickly became a back row figure or "shadow Kaiser" (Schattenkaiser) that was kept poorly informed about the conduct of the war by his generals.[374] The Supreme Warlord became a symbolic figure and was not treated as the head of the German High Command.[375] Meanwhile, Arthur Zimmermann, the Under State Secretary, managed the activities of the Foreign Office in Berlin.[376] The "dispirited" Foreign Office did the bidding of the German High Command.[377] At the battlefront, Jagow, who was sickly, retiring, and unimpressive, found it impossible to hold his own in discussions with Falkenhayn and the Army High Command.[378] Before long the Chancellor and Foreign Secretary returned to Ber-

---

369.   Zeman, 111, 115; Doss, 233; Ritter, *The Sword and the Scepter*, 3:166, 3:175, 3:265; 3:268; Tuchman, 110-11, 114, 137-43.

370.   Craig, *Germany 1866-1945*, 343.

371.   Chickering, 64.

372.   Kitchen, 45; Afflerbach, 201.

373.   Ibid.; Wilhelm Deist, "Kaiser Wilhelm in the Context of His Military and Naval Entourage," in *Kaiser Wilhelm II: New Interpretations*, ed. J.C.G. Röhl and Nicolaus Sombart (Cambridge: Cambridge University Press, 1982), 185.

374.   Cecil, *Wilhelm II*, 2:212.

375.   Kitchen, 46.

376.   Zeman, 83.

377.   Jarausch, 230. German attempts to divide the Anglo-French-Russian entente are discussed in Lancelot L. Farrar, Jr., *Divide and Conquer: German Efforts to Conclude a Separate Peace, 1914-1918* (Boulder, CO: East European Quarterly, 1978). German war aims are examined in Hans W. Gatzke, *Germany's Drive to the West: A Study of Germany's Western War Aims during the First World War* (Baltimore: Johns Hopkins Press, 1950) and Fritz Fischer, *Germany's Aims in the First World War* (New York: W.W. Norton, 1967).

378.   Zeman, 115.

lin, and remained there for the duration of the war, except for periodic visits to Military Headquarters at the Front.[379] Even so, the Chancellor and the Foreign Office kept representatives at Military Headquarters at the German High Command. "Their important function of bridging the gap between the civilians and the military was to give them considerable political power," according to one historian.[380]

In 1916, Falkenhayn sought to launch a two-prong offensive against the British and French on the Western Front. He wanted to begin a campaign of unrestricted submarine warfare against Britain while carrying out a land offensive against France. He was denied his submarine campaign, but Germany and Britain fought the naval Battle of Jutland in May 1916. The German fleet imposed serious damage on the British Grand Fleet. However, Germany was unable to breakout into the North Sea.[381] As for a land offensive, the German Army had 2,350,000 troops, comprising 118 divisions, on the Western Front. This force, nonetheless, had to face an enemy of 3,470,000 men in 145 divisions.[382] In February, Falkenhayn began the Battle of Verdun by launching an offensive against the French in the Meuse River Valley.[383] In the midst of this battle, in June 1916, Germany had to divert some of its military to reinforce Austria-Hungary and the Eastern Front when the Russians launched the Brusilov Offensive. Rumania joined Russia and the allies against the Central Powers in August 1916.[384] Then, in July, the British launched an offensive at the Somme River.[385] As a result of the Russian, Rumanian, and British moves, the German offensive at Verdun stalled during the summer before it ended in late 1916. Germany lost about 373,000 men in the Battle of Verdun.[386] Another 500,000 Germans died stopping the Allied advance at the Battle of the Somme.[387]

---

379.    Kitchen, 45. See Gerhard Ritter's third volume of *The Sword and the Scepter* for an examination of Bethmann Hollweg as War Chancellor.

380.    Ibid.

381.    See V.E. Tarrant, *Jutland: The German Perspective: A New View of the Great Battle, 31 May 1916* (Annapolis: Naval Institute Press, 1995).

382.    Chickering, 66.

383.    Herwig, *The First World War*,183-198. See also Alistair Horne, *The Price of Glory: Verdun 1916* (New York: St. Martin's Press, 1963) and Robert T. Foley, *German Strategy and the Path to Verdun: Erich von Falkenhayn and the Development of Attrition, 1870-1916* (Cambridge: Cambridge University Press, 2004).

384.    Lyons, *World War I*, 164.

385.    Herwig, *The First World War*, 199-204.

386.    Beckett, 166.

387.    Chickering, 70.

As a consequence of this failure, the Kaiser, with the encouragement of Jagow and Zimmermann,[388] replaced Falkenhayn with Field Marshal Paul von Hindenburg and General Erich Ludendorff as supreme commanders of the German High Command on 29 August 1916.[389] William II took this step to support Hindenburg and Ludendorff in an offensive designed to achieve a decisive victory. In the fall of 1916, the German Army launched an offensive against Rumania in Southeast Europe. The Germans quickly captured Bucharest. At this point, the Central Powers offered to negotiate an end to the war. Bethmann Hollweg sought the meditation of President Woodrow Wilson of the United States.[390] But, General Ludendorff ensured that the peace offer would place Germany in a victorious stance. The Triple Entente replied that Bethmann Hollweg's proposal was just a ploy or diplomatic maneuver during wartime. Both the Kaiser and Chancellor were upset by the reply.[391] As a result, Hindenburg and Ludendorff became supporters of unrestricted submarine warfare.[392] They, along with Zimmermann, who was appointed Foreign Secretary in November,[393] convinced the Kaiser to accept the renewal of unrestricted submarine warfare in January 1917, knowing that Germany risked war with the United States.[394] The campaign began in February, and, with the sinking of American ships and the intercept of Foreign Secretary Zimmermann's telegram to Mexico offering to support a Mexican war against the Americans,[395] the United States declared war against Germany in April 1917.

The Allied Powers of Britain and France took the initiative on the Western Front in 1917. The British launched an offensive against the so-called Hindenburg Line near Arras in April. At the same time the French initiated an offensive, the so-called Nivelle Offensive, against the Germans in the Champagne district.

---

388.   Kitchen, 31.

389.   Zeman, 115; Craig, *Germany 1866-1945*, 373. For Hindenburg's wartime career, see John W. Wheeler-Bennett, *Hindenburg: The Wooden Titan* (New York: St. Martin's Press, 1967). For Hindenburg and Ludendorff's conduct of the war, see Robert B. Asprey, *The German High Command at War: Hindenburg and Ludendorff Conduct World War I* (New York: William Morrow, 1991).

390.   Zeman, 113.

391.   Jarausch, 250-54; Zeman, 118.

392.   Asprey, 290-91; Chickering, 75-76.

393.   Holstein, 4:56.

394.   Zeman, 116, 187; Chickering, 92; Matthew Stibbe, "Germany's 'Last Card': Wilhelm II and the Decision in Favour of Unrestricted Submarine Warfare in January 1917," in *The Kaiser: New Research on Wilhelm II's Role in Imperial Germany*, eds. Annika Mombauer and Wilhelm Deist (Cambridge: Cambridge University Press, 2003), 232-33.

395.   Asprey, 299-300; Zeman, 202-3. See also Tuchman's, *The Zimmermann Telegram*.

The Germans held back both offensives. Then, in July, the British attacked the German lines in Flanders in the Battle of Passchendaele. This offensive stalled after five months. Little ground was gained, one way or another, on the Western Front. On the Eastern Front, in July, the Russians launched the so-called Kerensky Offensive into Galacia against Habsburg forces. The arrival of German reinforcements stalled the Russian offensive, and then the Central Powers launched a counter-offensive against the Russians. The Russian Army collapsed. Soon the Bolshevik Revolution led to Russia seeking and gaining a peace settlement with the Central Powers.[396] In the meantime, to the south, on the Italian Front, the Austro-German forces broke two years of stalemate in the Alps. In October, the Austro-German armies overran Italian positions near Caporetto and forced the Italian Army to fall back.[397]

Hindenburg and Ludendorff were in full control of Germany. They believed that the Central Powers could achieve a military victory to end the war. The Kaiser, according to Gordon A. Craig, had permitted the establishment of a military dictatorship that made all the major political decisions until the end of the war.[398] The Kaiser had lost control of the German government and policy. Martin Kitchen has stated that "Hindenburg and Ludendorff had no patience for all this talk about constitutional rights and correct procedure. They regarded themselves as standing outside the provisions of the constitution."[399] The Kaiser had little influence over decision-making. William II, according to Lamar Cecil, "no longer played even the already nominal role he had previously."[400] In fact, at one point, writes Kitchen, "the Supreme Warlord went down on his knees before the generals and begged them to accept his suggestions."[401] The military controlled the appointment of officials. The Chancellor and Foreign Office had little influence over the progress and outcome of the war. Bethmann Hollweg, who sought a peaceful resolution to the war,[402] was replaced by Georg Michaelis as the new

---

396.   Zeman, 243-86. Russia agreed to pay war reparations and gave up extensive territory, including Finland, Estonia, Latvia, Lithuania, Poland, and the Ukraine in the Treaty of Brest-Litovsk in March 1918. See John W. Wheeler-Bennett, *Brest-Litovsk: The Forgotten Peace, March 1918* (London: Macmillan, 1963).

397.   Keegan, 343-50.

398.   Craig, *Aspects of German Statecraft*, xv. See also Martin Kitchen, *The Silent Dictatorship: The Politics of the German High Command under Hindenburg and Ludendorff, 1916-1918* (New York: Holmes and Meier, 1976).

399.   Kitchen, 47.

400.   Cecil, *Wilhelm II*, 2:238.

401.   Kitchen, 141.

402.   Asprey, 326.

Imperial Chancellor and Prussian Foreign Minister in July 1917.[403] One month later, Richard von Kühlmann replaced Zimmermann as State Secretary for Foreign Affairs.[404] Then, in November, Georg von Hertling became the Chancellor and Foreign Minister.[405]

In 1918, with Russia out of the war, Hindenburg and Ludendorff sought to achieve military victory on the Western Front before the arrival of American forces could tip the balance in favor of Britain and France. With the end of the Russian war, Germany transferred thirty-three divisions, amounting to about 500,000 troops, to the Western Front.[406] Hindenburg and Ludendorff sought to use these forces to launch one last offensive to win the war in the spring of 1918. Even so, as Roger Chickering has pointed out, Germany's 4,000,000 troops on the Western Front were still twenty percent short of the troop strength for the Allied and Associated Powers in the same area.[407] Moreover, the Germans had less artillery pieces, airplanes, trucks, and other equipment than the allied forces.[408] Thus, in the spring of 1918, Germany launched the so-called Ludendorff Offensives. The German Army initiated five consecutive assaults against Allied positions, including the Somme Offensive in March,[409] Lys Offensive in Flanders in April, Aisne Offensive in May, Noyon-Montdidier Offensive in June, and Champagne-Marne Offensive in July 1918. All five offensives broke down in face of Allied artillery and resistance.[410] The offensives had cost Germany 500,000 men, and the German Army could not achieve the desired breakthrough.[411] In the midst of these failures, Hindenburg and Ludendorff forced the Kaiser and Chancellor Hertling to rid the Wilhelmstrasse of Kühlmann. The Army High Command viewed Kühlmann as a "defector" because the Foreign Secretary called for peace talks.[412] Hindenburg and Ludendorff selected Rear Admiral Paul von Hintze as the new State Secretary for Foreign Affairs in July 1918.[413] Ludendorff called Hintze "a fine German, a good diplomat and sol-

---

403. Cecil, *Wilhelm II*, 2:252.
404. Zeman, 148.
405. Chickering, 163.
406. Ibid., 176.
407. Ibid.
408. Ibid., 176-77.
409. See Martin Middlebrook, *The Kaiser's Battle, 21 March 1918: The First Day of the German Spring Offensive* (London: Allen Lane, 1978).
410. Asprey, 382-99, 411-34; Herwig, *The First World War*, 392-432.
411. Chickering, 180.
412. Herwig, *The First World War*, 416.
413. Asprey, 432-33; Cecil, *Wilhelm II*, 2:271.

dier."[414] Hindenburg viewed him as "clever, cunning, cold, ruthless, but still likeable, a thorough Prussian."[415] He was just the right person to straighten out the Wilhelmstrasse.

In July, the Allied and Associated Powers, including the United States, began launching their offensives against German positions on the Western Front. The allies conducted the Aisne-Marne Offensive in July and August, Amiens Offensive in August and September, St.-Mihiel Offensive in September, and, finally, the Meuse-Argonne Offensive in September to November 1918. The German Army was in full retreat. For the first two months the Army High Command would not give the Chancellor or Foreign Secretary a true briefing of the deteriorating military position. But, in late September, General Ludendorff announced to the government that the war was lost, and that Berlin needed to negotiate an immediate armistice. Germany faced total defeat.

On 29 September 1918, Field Marshal Hindenburg, General Ludendorff, and Foreign Secretary Hintze briefed Kaiser William II about the collapse of the German Army and the impending defeat. Hintze suggested that there was only one way to peace, by creating a "revolution from above" in the Second Reich. He suggested the dissolution of the Reich and the creation of a democratic government. The new government could ask President Wilson of the United States to arrange an armistice and preside over peace negotiations based upon his Fourteen Points. William II accepted this proposal. On 3 October, the liberal Prince Maximilian of Baden was made the Chancellor and Foreign Minister of a new democratic government. Dr. Wilhelm Solf became the new State Secretary at the Wilhelmstrasse.[416] As such, these men immediately began negotiations for an armistice with the United States. Two days before the signing of the armistice on 11 November 1918, Kaiser William II abdicated his throne, ending the rule of the Hohenzollerns. Germany would have constitutional reform, but it was the byproduct of a military decision to seek an end to the First World War.

---

414.  As quoted in Kitchen, 206.
415.  As quoted in Asprey, 433.
416.  Asprey, 475; Hajo Holborn, "Diplomats and Diplomacy in the Early Weimar Republic," in *The Diplomats, 1919-1939*, eds. Gordon A. Craig and Felix Gilbert (Princeton: Princeton University Press, 1953), 129.

# 4

# *Weimar Republic and the Foreign Office*

## Revolution of 1918-1919

The German government under Prince Maximilian of Baden consisted of mid-dle-of-the road liberals, Catholic Center Party (Zentrum) members, and a member of the Social Democratic Party (SPD).[1] While negotiations for an armistice were under way, German sailors at Kiel, the headquarters of the German naval command, began a mutiny and established a sailors' council that led to a German revolution.[2] The establishment of workers' and soldiers' councils swiftly spread throughout Germany, including Wilhelmshaven, Bremen, Cologne, Brunswick, Hanover, Leipzig, Frankfurt, Düsseldorf, Lübeck, and Hamburg.[3] In Berlin, factory workers demonstrated for an immediate armistice and the abdication of William II. This forced the politico-military issue of abdication. As a result, the Kaiser abdicated his position as German Emperor and Chancellor Prince Maximilian of Baden resigned from office on 9 November 1918.[4] At the same time, Prince Maximilian asked the leader of the Social Democrats, Friedrich Ebert, to become the Reich Chancellor of a Provisional Government.[5] As such, Ebert promised to govern constitutionally and call for a National Assembly.[6]

---

1.  Martin Kitchen, *Europe Between the Wars: A Political History* (London: Longman, 1988), 156.
2.  See Daniel Horn, *The German Naval Mutinies of World War I* (New Brunswick: Rutgers University Press, 1969).
3.  Eberhard Kolb, *The Weimar Republic*, trans. P.S. Falla (London: Unwin Hyman, 1988), 7; Gordon A. Craig, *Germany 1866-1945* (Oxford: Oxford University Press, 1978), 399-400; Ruth Henig, *The Weimar Republic, 1919-1933* (London: Routledge, 1998), 8-9; Hajo Holborn, *A History of Modern Germany*, 3 vols. (New York: Alfred A. Knopf, 1959-69), 3:511-12.
4.  Kitchen, *Europe Between the Wars*, 158.
5.  Dietrich Orlow, *A History of Modern Germany: 1871 to Present*, 3 ed. (Englewood Cliffs, NJ: Prentice Hall, 1995), 121.
6.  Holborn, *A History of Modern Germany*, 3:515.

Later that same day, Philipp Scheidemann, the second-ranking member of the SPD, proclaimed the establishment of a German Republic at a mass demonstration in front of the Reichstag.[7] However, Germany was turning into chaos. Kurt Eisner, the left-wing chairman of the Independent Social Democratic Party (USPD), had taken control of Munich and declared the "Free State of Bavaria."[8] Factory workers, soldiers, and sailors in Berlin were demonstrating for an end to the war. Count Franz von Matuschka, Wilhelm August von Stumm and other right-wing officials from the German Foreign Office led several hundred soldiers to the Reich Chancellery on the Wilhelmstrasse and embarrassed Ebert by awkwardly declaring him as the Reich President, or dictator of Germany.[9] Moreover, the revolutionary left was on the offensive. Left-wing Marxist socialists sought to overthrow the forces of capitalism and establish a workers' state. In Berlin, Karl Liebknecht and Rosa Luxemburg of the Spartacus League (later called the German Communist Party) declared a new German Socialist Republic.[10] Chancellor Ebert responded to the revolutionary movements by uniting with independent socialists and creating a Council of People's Representatives (Rat der Volksbeauftragten) (CCP), consisting of leaders from the SPD and USPD.[11] The CCP leaders included Ebert, Scheidemann, and Otto Landsberg of the SPD along with Hugo Haase, Emil Barth, and Wilhelm Dittmann of the USPD.[12]

Ebert needed to stabilize the political situation in Germany. The Chancellor had to demobilize two million front-line troops and transport them back into Germany, as well as beef up the internal security of Germany to protect the new government.[13] Most of all, Ebert wanted elections to take place as soon as possible to elect a National Assembly (Nationalversammlung). The assembly would have the responsibility for writing a constitution for Germany. The elections were scheduled for 19 January 1919. In this endeavor the Chancellor had the full support of the German Army High Command, government officials, local civil servants, and industrialists.[14] But,

---

7.    Craig, *Germany 1866-1945*, 401-2.
8.    Ibid., 400-1; Holborn, *A History of Modern Germany*, 3:512-213; Orlow, 120; Henig, *The Weimar Republic, 1919-1933*, 9.
9.    Richard M. Watt, *The Kings Depart: The Tragedy of Germany, Versailles and the German Revolution* (New York: Simon and Schuster, 1968), 225.
10.   Orlow, 122; Henig, *The Weimar Republic, 1919-1933*, 9.
11.   A.J. Nicholls, *Weimar and the Rise of Hitler*, 2 ed. (New York: St. Martin's Press, 1979), 12.
12.   Holborn, *A History of Modern Germany*, 3:516.
13.   Orlow, 123.
14.   Gordon A. Craig, *The Politics of the Prussian Army, 1640-1945* (Oxford: Clarendon Press, 1955), 348; Harold J. Gordon, Jr., *The Reichswehr and the German Republic, 1919-1926* (Princeton: Princeton University Press, 1957), 6; Kitchen, *Europe Between the Wars*, 159.

political stability was hard to achieve. The USPD members of the Council of the People's Representatives resigned from the government at the end of 1918.[15] Then, from 5 to 12 January 1919, the German Communist Party (KPD) carried out the so-called "Spartacus Uprising" in an attempt to overthrow the government in Berlin. The uprising was crushed by the troops of the German Army and Free Corps (Freikorps) under the leadership of the High Command. Martin Kitchen has argued that, "the pact between Ebert and [General Wilhelm von] Groener [Chief of Staff of the High Command] halted the revolution in its tracks."[16] The Free Corps murdered both Liebknecht and Luxemburg. The elections then took place as scheduled on 19 January.

The outcome of the elections appeared to support Ebert's political course of action. The SPD gained 165 out of 421 seats in the National Assembly. The Center Party acquired 91 seats, the German Democratic Party (DDP) got 75 seats, the German National People's Party (DNVP) captured 44 seats, the USPD snatched 22 seats, and the German People's Party (DVP) reaped 19 seats.[17] The KDP refused to take part in the elections. As one historian has commented about the election results: "These results, whatever else they proved, hardly constituted a strong vote of confidence for Ebert's party, which won only 38 percent of the vote."[18]

## Establishment of the Weimar Republic

The National Assembly convened in the National Theater at the town of Weimar in Thuringia on 6 February 1919. Five days later, the assembly selected Friedrich Ebert as the first President of the new Reich. Philipp Scheidemann became the Prime Minister and formed a coalition cabinet from members of the Social Democratic, Catholic Centre, and German Democratic parties on 13 February.[19] Count Ulrich von Brockdorff-Rantzau, a professional diplomat without party affiliation, was the Foreign Minister.[20] He had previously served Germany as the Minister to Denmark.[21] Hugo Preuss, the Minister of the Interior, had the task

---

15.    Orlow, 124; Kolb, 16.

16.    Martin Kitchen, *A Military History of Germany from the Eighteenth Century to the Present Day* (London: Weidenfeld and Nicolson, 1975), 235.

17.    Kolb, 16-17; Henig, *The Weimar Republic, 1919-1933*, 12; Craig, *Germany 1866-1945*, 412-13; Kitchen, *Europe Between the Wars*, 162.

18.    Craig, *Germany 1866-1945*, 413.

19.    Kolb, 17-18.

20.    Holborn, *A History of Modern Germany*, 3:545.

21.    Klaus Schwabe, *Woodrow Wilson, Revolutionary Germany, and Peacemaking, 1918-1919: Missionary Diplomacy and the Realities of Power*, trans. Rita and Robert Kimber (Chapel Hill: University of North Carolina Press, 1985), 185.

of drafting a constitution for Germany. The Weimar Constitution was accepted by the National Assembly by a vote of 262 to 75 in July.[22] It was then signed by the President on 11 August 1919.[23]

The Weimar Constitution established parliamentary democracy for the new German Reich. The new state was not named the German Republic, but the German Reich. The constitution established the Reichsrat (Upper Chamber) and Reichstag (Lower Chamber). The individual states of Germany were represented in the Reichsrat. But, at the heart of the constitution was the Reichstag. Members were elected by universal suffrage for terms of office up to four years. The Reichstag enacted legislation, as well as controlled the German Armed Forces (Reichswehr) and government officials, including the Reich President and Foreign Minister. Even so, the President received extensive powers. The President was elected by the people and was therefore independent of the parliamentary majority. He held office for seven years. He had the power to conclude treaties and alliances. The President possessed supreme command over the Reichswehr. He appointed and dismissed government officials (including the Reich Chancellor and Foreign Minister), had the power to dissolve the Reichstag, and could intervene in the legislative process by ordering a referendum. Moreover, the President could proclaim a state of emergency under Article 48 of the Weimar Constitution and govern, without parliamentary approval, by decree for a limited time to preserve public security and order. The delegates of the National Assembly gave the President such powers with the Spartacus Uprising fresh in their minds.[24] But, the writing of a constitution was not the only thing on the agenda for the National Assembly. It still had to deal with a peace settlement to the First World War.

## Treaty of Versailles

On 18 January 1919, the leaders, diplomats, soldiers, and government officials of twenty-seven countries met in Paris for the peace conference that would negotiate the settlement of World War I.[25] The Paris Peace Conference was opened by French President Raymond Poincaré (1913-20). On the suggestion of President Woodrow Wilson of the United States (1913-21), French Prime Minister

---

22.    Henig, *The Weimar Republic, 1919-1933*, 12.

23.    Kolb, 18.

24.    Kolb, 18-19; Henig, *The Weimar Republic, 1919-1933*, 13-14; Orlow, 127-28; Nicholls, 24-27.

25.    Zara Steiner, *The Lights that Failed: European International History, 1919-1933* (Oxford: Oxford University Press, 2005), 16.

Georges Clemenceau (1917-20) was selected as the chairman of the conference. The Supreme War Council had already agreed that the United States, Britain, France, Italy, and Japan would play the leading parts in the peace conference. They made up the Council of Ten. Each country had two representatives. By mid-March the shape of the Council changed when Japan stopped attending the meetings. Now, the United States, Britain, France, and Italy, each represented by only one member, made up the Council of Four.[26] The Big Four were represented by President Wilson, British Prime Minister David Lloyd George (1916-22), Prime Minister Clemenceau, and Italian Prime Minister Victorio Orlando (1917-19). A few weeks later Italy would walk out of the talks leaving the decisions to the Big Three.[27] These men and the Paris Peace Conference would decide the fates of Germany, Austria-Hungary, the Ottoman Empire, as well as other issues.[28]

The Allied and Associated Powers held 148 meetings during the Paris Peace Conference to hammer out peace conditions for Germany.[29] Each member of the Big Three had their own national ambitions. The war had been devastating for France. As Zara Steiner has pointed out:

> France had suffered most in terms of her active male population; France had lost 1.3 million soldiers, over a quarter of all men aged between 18 and 27, and incurred 700,000 wounded. The ten northern and eastern departments of the country had provided, along with parts of Belgium, the main battlefields of the war in the west. Much of the industrial heartland of France had been devastated. Neither its allies nor chief enemy had been similarly affected. Germany had proved, once again, more powerful than France, which achieved victory only as a member of a coalition. France emerged from the fighting more damaged in human and material terms than its defeated enemy, and with much of its adult population suffering from a psychic shock that proved as deep and more long-lasting than the German preoccupation with defeat.[30]

---

26. Ibid., 17.
27. Ibid., 18.
28. See Alan Sharp, *The Versailles Settlement: Peacemaking in Paris, 1919* (London: Macmillan, 1991); Ruth Henig, *Versailles and After, 1919-1933*, 2 ed. (London: Routledge, 1995); Arthur S. Link, *Woodrow Wilson: Revolution, War, and Peace* (Arlington Heights, IL: 1979); Inga Floto, *Colonel House in Paris: A Study of American Policy at the Paris Peace Conference, 1919* (Princeton: Princeton University Press, 1973); Michael J. Dockrill and J. Douglas Goold, *Peace without Promise: Britain and the Peace Conferences, 1919-1923* (London: Batsford, 1981); and René Albrecht-Carrié, *Italy at the Paris Peace Conference* (New York: Columbia University Press, 1938).
29. Kolb, 25.
30. Steiner, *The Lights that Failed*, 20.

At the heart of French war aims were security concerns regarding Germany. Prime Minister Clemenceau wanted territorial changes. He sought to create a security buffer zone between France and Germany. French President Raymond Poincaré and Marshal Ferdinand Foch urged Clemenceau to go even further and claim the left bank of the Rhine River for France. Clemenceau also wanted Germany to pay significant financial penalties to both cripple German recovery and aid that of France.[31] Britain had lost more than 500,000 men on the Western Front.[32] Lloyd George sought a just and harsh peace settlement with Germany. He wanted to teach the Germans a lesson for starting the war. But the Prime Minister saw it as important to quickly restore the balance of power on the European continent in order to allow Britain to concentrate on imperial interests.[33] Lloyd George wanted the disarmament of Germany to be part of a general disarmament.[34] The First World War resulted in the British Empire reaching its greatest territorial extent, and forced the British government to concentrate on imperial and financial issues.[35] As such, Lloyd George, according to W.N. Medlicott, was "the sturdy opponent of extreme French demands over the German territorial settlement."[36] As for the United States, Wilson's main aim was the stabilization of Europe and the creation of the League of Nations as a collective security organization.[37] In the end, the United States and Britain prevented

31.     J. Néré, *The Foreign Policy of France from 1914 to 1945* (London: Routledge and Kegan Paul, 1975), 11-25, 51; Marshall M. Lee and Wolfgang Michalka, *German Foreign Policy, 1917-1933: Continuity or Break?* (Leamington Spa: Berg, 1987), 22; Robert McCrum, "French Rhineland Policy at the Paris Peace Conference, 1919," *The Historical Journal* 21 (1978), 623-48.

32.     Steiner, *The Lights that Failed*, 26.

33.     Ibid., 29.

34.     Lorna S. Jaffe, *The Decision to Disarm Germany: British Policy towards Postwar German Disarmament, 1914-1919* (Boston: Allen and Unwin, 1985), 214-16.

35.     C.J. Lowe and M.L. Dockrill, *The Mirage of Power*, 3 vols. (London: Routledge and Kegan Paul, 1972), 2:335-49; Alan Sharp, "Holding up the Flag of Britain...with Sustained Vigour and Brilliance or 'Sowing the Seeds of European Disaster'? Lloyd George and Balfour at the Paris Peace Conference," in *The Paris Peace Conference, 1919: Peace without Victory?*, eds. Michael Dockrill and John Fisher (Basingstoke: Palgrave, 2001), 35-50; Michael Howard, *The Continental Commitment: The Dilemma of British Defence Policy in the Era of the Two World Wars* (London: Maurice Temple Smith, 1972), 72-82.

36.     W.N. Medlicott, *British Foreign Policy since Versailles, 1919-1963*, 2 ed. (London: Methuen, 1968), 3. See also F.S. Northedge, *The Troubled Giant: Britain among the Great Powers, 1916-1939* (London: G. Bell and Sons, 1966), 91-124.

37.     Erik Goldstein, *The First World War Peace Settlements, 1919-1925* (London: Longman, 2002), 6-7; Floto, 130; Akira Iriye, *The Globalizing of America, 1913-1945*, vol. 3 in *The Cambridge History of American Foreign Relations* (Cambridge: Cambridge University Press, 1993), 58-64.

France from achieving its territorial aspirations in the Rhineland but at the cost of promising defensive alliances.[38]

Germany began preparations for the peace conference in October 1918. Dr. Wilhelm Solf, the Secretary of State for Foreign Affairs, recalled Count Johann Heinrich von Bernstorff from the German Embassy in Constantinople to Berlin and entrusted him with the preparations for the peace negotiations.[39] Bernstorff had been the former Ambassador to the United States.[40] Count Ulrich von Brockdorff-Rantzau, the new Foreign Minister, joined the process in December 1919.[41] He now spent the next three months at the German Foreign Office preparing for the talks. He had a staff of forty officials and 120 experts.[42] The Council of Four was in no hurry to invite a German delegation to Paris. In the meantime, Bernstorff and the German peace conference staff received no reliable information concerning the ongoing Paris Peace Conference. As late as mid-April 1919, the German Foreign Office believed that the Allied and Associated Powers would submit a preliminary peace treaty to Germany and that negotiations would soon commence. The Wilhelmstrasse dismissed all rumors that the Allied and Associated Powers would present a final treaty to be signed by Germany without discussion.[43]

In late April 1919, the Supreme War Council of the Allied and Associated Powers requested the presence of the German peace delegation at Versailles. Count Ulrich von Brockdorff-Rantzau headed the German delegation.[44] The other five chief delegates were Dr. Otto Landsberg, Robert Leinert, Johann Giesberts, Dr. Carl Melchior, and Dr. Walter Schücking.[45] General Hans von Seeckt represented the Ministry of War in the delegation.[46] Dr. Walter Simons, the

---

38.  Norman Rich, *Great Power Diplomacy since 1914* (Boston: McGraw-Hill, 2003), 143.

39.  Johann Heinrich von Bernstorff, *The Memoirs of Count Bernstorff* (London: Heinemann, 1936), 202-5.

40.  Keith L. Nelson, *Victors Divided: America and the Allies in Germany, 1918-1923* (Berkeley: University of California Press, 1975), 62.

41.  Klaus Schwabe, "Germany's Peace Aims and the Domestic and International Constraints," in *The Treaty of Versailles: A Reassessment after 75 Years*, eds. Manfred F. Boemeke, Gerald D. Feldman, and Elisabeth Glaser (Cambridge: Cambridge University Press, 1998), 43.

42.  Nelson, 62; John Hiden, *Germany and Europe, 1919-1939* (London: Longman, 1977), 7.

43.  Alma Luckau, *The German Delegation at the Paris Peace Conference* (New York: Columbia University Press, 1941), 43,

44.  Brockdorff-Rantzau's diplomatic career is examined in Leo Haupts, *Graf Brockdorff-Rantzau: Diplomat und Minister im Kaiserreich under Republik* (Göttingen: Muster-Schmidt Verlag, 1984).

45.  Luckau, 54.

46.  Holborn, *A History of Modern Germany*, 3:560.

Director of the Legal Division; Franz von Stockhammern, the Director of the Economic Division; and Dr. Edgar Haniel von Haimhausen all represented the German Foreign Office.[47] Hundreds of other experts contributed to the German delegation.[48] Foreign Minister Brockdorff-Rantzau wanted a peace of accommodation.[49] He was pursuing a peace strategy with the goal of preserving Germany's status and prestige as a Great Power. Brockdorff-Rantzau believed that Germany would be allowed to negotiate a peace settlement based upon President Wilson's Fourteen Points.[50] In fact, he had already outlined his thoughts concerning a peace treaty with the Allied and Associated Powers in a speech before the National Assembly in February 1919. According to Alma Luckau, the main points of his speech were:

> Germany should ask to be admitted to the League of Nations immediately after the conclusion of peace; she should accept obligatory arbitration and disarm, provided that the Allied nations and the future neighbors of the German Republic did likewise. As to the economic principles of President Wilson, economic equality should apply to Germany also, and Germany should not be forced to surrender her whole merchant fleet. Of course the German government would make reparation payments for the devastated territory, excluding actual war costs. Brockdorff-Rantzau also spoke about the chief problems which would arise in connection with the territorial readjustments. Admitting that Alsace-Lorraine had to be ceded to France, he asked for a plebiscite, so that the injustice done to the population of Alsace-Lorraine in 1871 would not be repeated. He protested against the French claims to the Saar territory and the Polish attempts to forestall the decisions of the Paris Peace Conference by using military force to settle the future frontiers of the new Polish state. He declared that Germany was willing to grant Poland access to the sea by internationalizing the Vistula and certain harbor zones along the Baltic Sea.[51]

These ideas were identical with the principles written down in the official instructions drafted by the Wilhelmstrasse in April 1919 for the use of German plenipotentiaries at the future peace negotiations. Brockdorff-Rantzau even hoped that

---

47.    Luckau, 58.
48.    Ibid.
49.    Schwabe, "Germany's Peace Aims and the Domestic and International Constraints," 43-44; Udo Wengst, *Graf Brockdorff-Rantzau und die aussenpolitischen Anfänge der Weimarer Republik* (Frankfurt-am-Main: Peter Lang Verlag, 1973), 15-17.
50.    Hiden, 7; Lee and Michalka, 19-21.
51.    Luckau, 55.

the Allied and Associated Powers would allow the union of Germany and Austria based on the principle of national self-determination.[52]

The German peace delegation, consisting of 180 individuals, left Berlin aboard special trains destined for Versailles on 28 April 1919.[53] Upon arrival, the delegates and experts set up their headquarters at the Hotel des Réservoirs. Dr. Simons, the Commissioner General of the delegation, had the task of creating special commissions to continue the preparatory work towards peace negotiations. The German delegation anticipated that peace talks could begin at any moment. Finally, on 5 May, the Allied and Associated Powers informed Brockdorff-Rantzau that the conditions of peace would be handed to him at the Trianon Palace Hotel in Versailles. The German delegates learned that they would not be given a chance to negotiate with the Allied and Associated Powers across a conference table. In fact, the German delegation learned that once they received the conditions of peace, Germany would have just fifteen days to submit comments.[54] Brockdorff-Rantzau would later receive an additional week.[55]

On 7 May, the German delegation led by Brockdorff-Rantzau met with the Allied and Associated Powers at the Trianon Palace Hotel. The chief delegates, members of the Foreign Office, and two interpreters took their places at a table confronting a semicircle of French, British, and American delegates. Prime Minister Clemenceau opened the session with an introductory speech. He expressed that:

> This is neither the time nor the place for superfluous words. You have before you the accredited plenipotentiaries of the great and lesser Powers, both Allied and Associated, that for four years have carried on without respite the merciless war which has been imposed upon them. The time has now come for a heavy reckoning of the accounts. You have asked for peace. We are prepared to offer you peace.[56]

The Secretary General of the Paris Peace Conference then handed a large folio volume containing 440 articles to the German delegation. At this point, Brock-

---

52.    Stanley Suval, *The Anschluss Question in the Weimar Era: A Study of Nationalism in Germany and Austria, 1918-1932* (Baltimore: Johns Hopkins University Press, 1974), 10-17; Gerhard Schulz, *Revolutions and Peace Treaties* (London: Methuen, 1972), 177-78.

53.    Nelson, 63; Luckau, 59.

54.    Henig, *The Weimar Republic, 1919-1933*, 18; Luckau, 62.

55.    Sharp, *The Versailles Settlement*, 37.

56.    Speech of Prime Minister Georges Clemenceau at the Trianon Palace, Versailles, 7 May 1919, Document 30, in Luckau, 223-24.

dorff-Rantzau gave his speech, while remaining seated.[57] The Foreign Minister did not want to appear as an accused man but rather to emphasize that Germany regarded the initial meeting as having the character of negotiations.[58] He stated:

> Gentlemen, we are deeply impressed with the great mission that has brought us here to give the world forthwith a lasting peace. We have no illusions as to the extent of our defeat and the degree of our powerlessness. We know that the strength of the German arms is broken. We know the intensity of the hatred which meets us, and we have heard the victors' passionate demand that as the vanquished we shall be made to pay, and as the guilty we shall be punished.[59]

But, Brockdorff-Rantzau went on to deny that Germany alone was responsible for the First World War. The speech, according to Dr. Simons, did not make a favorable impression upon the Allied and Associated Powers. After the speech, Clemenceau closed the first and last joint meeting of the Allied and German plenipotentiaries of peace. The formal ceremony lasted exactly one hour.[60]

Afterwards, the German delegates returned to the Hotel des Réservoirs. They started the enormous task of translating the conditions of peace from French and English into the German language. They had just one copy of the document that contained 80,000 words in 440 articles. Once they had a rough idea of the conditions of peace, the entire German delegation agreed that the terms could not be accepted without major revisions. As a consequence, the German delegation sent note after note to the Paris Peace Conference attacking one section after another of the preliminary peace agreement during the next three weeks. They then waited for the reply from the Allied and Associated plenipotentiaries. Finally, on 16 June, the Allied and Associated Powers gave their reply and demanded that Germany unconditionally sign the Versailles Treaty within seven days.[61]

The chief delegates and experts quickly left Versailles on a train headed for Weimar. They needed to communicate the terms of the peace settlement to the National Assembly. On 18 June, the chief delegates recommended that the National Assembly reject the Treaty of Versailles. The Scheidemann Cabinet and National Assembly was split over whether to accept or reject the peace set-

---

57. Sharp, 37.
58. Schwabe, *Woodrow Wilson, Revolutionary Germany, and Peacemaking, 1918-1919*, 331.
59. Speech of Count Ulrich von Brockdorff-Rantzau at the Trianon Palace Hotel, Versailles, 7 May 1919, Document 29 in Luckau, 220-23.
60. Luckau, 67.
61. Ibid., 69-90.

tlement. On 19 June, Philipp Scheidemann, the German Prime Minister, resigned from office, ending the first coalition cabinet of the German Republic. Brockdorff-Rantzau and Simons then resigned as leaders of the German delegation.[62] Thus, Germany was without a cabinet or peace delegation to negotiate the Treaty of Versailles, and the Allied and Associated Powers' deadline of 23 June was quickly approaching. Finally, on 22 June, a new cabinet was formed. The new Prime Minister, Gustav Bauer of the Social Democratic Party, created a coalition cabinet from the SPD, Center Party, and German Democratic Party. Hermann Müller-Franken of the SPD became the new Foreign Minister.[63] Without much choice, the Bauer Cabinet and the National Assembly accepted the Treaty of Versailles with only one reservation, the German war guilt clause, on 22 June.[64] Nevertheless, the President of the Paris Peace Conference replied that the Allied and Associated Powers expected Germany to accept the Treaty of Versailles without exception. This was an ultimatum that threatened to renew the war.[65] As such, the Bauer Cabinet, realizing Germany's inability to fend off an invasion, gained permission from the National Assembly to unconditionally accept the Treaty of Versailles.[66] It was signed by Hermann Müller-Franken and Johannes Bell, the Minister of Communications, in the Hall of Mirrors at Louis XIV's palace of Versailles, the same place where William I was crowned as the German Emperor in 1871, on 28 June 1919.[67] The treaty entered into force in January 1920.

The terms of the peace settlement, known in Germany as the Versailles Diktat, were very harsh. Ruth Henig has stated that, "on close inspection, the terms of the treaty were deemed to be so harsh that they generated bitter hostility and universal condemnation throughout Germany."[68] The peace agreement severely limited the size of the German military. Germany could have an army of just 100,000 men, serving twelve year contracts. Conscription would not be allowed. The men "were to be recruited for long periods of service to prevent a repetition of the trick Prussia had practiced on Napoleon of giving brief intensive training to the soldiers permitted by treaty, and then training another group until a substantial army had been built up."[69] The army was restricted to just 4,000 officers, serving twenty-five year

62.   Craig, *Germany 1866-1945*, 425-26.
63.   Kolb, 32.
64.   Luckau, 107-12; Holborn, *A History of Modern Germany*, 3:574-78.
65.   Sharp, *The Versailles Settlement*, 38.
66.   Luckau, 107-12.
67.   Sharp, *The Versailles Settlement*, 38; Kolb, 32.
68.   Henig, *The Weimar Republic, 1919-1933*, 18.
69.   Rich, *Great Power Diplomacy since 1914*, 57.

contracts.[70] The German General Staff and War Academy were abolished. As for equipment, the Treaty of Versailles forbid the Germans to possess tanks, heavy artillery, and poison gas. The German armaments industry was placed under the severest restraint with Allied control and inspections. In regards to the German Navy, it was to be little more than a coastguard. The Navy was reduced to six battleships, six light cruisers, twelve destroyers, and twelve torpedo boats.[71] It could have no more than 15,000 personnel.[72] Germany was not allowed submarines or naval aircraft. It was also forbidden to have an Air Force.

The peace conditions placed the blame for the war on Germany. Clause 231, the so-called War Guilt Clause, stated that:

> The Allied and Associated Governments affirm and Germany accepts the responsibility of Germany and her allies for causing all the loss and damage to which the Allied and Associated Governments and their nationals have been subjected as a consequence of the war imposed upon them by the aggression of Germany and her allies.[73]

As such, the Allied and Associated Powers required Germany to pay substantial war reparations. The final amount of the war reparations would be left up to a Reparations Commission, which would report to the Allied and Associated Powers on 1 May 1921.[74] But, in the meantime, Germany would have to pay twenty billion gold marks, as well as surrender most of its merchant and fishing fleets, all German-owned property abroad, and pay part of the reparations in coal shipments to France.[75] The Allied and Associated Powers demanded that the payments begin in August 1919 and reach the twenty-billion gold marks goal by 1 May 1921.[76] In addition to reparations, Germany was required to turn over certain "war criminals," such as the former German Emperor, to be placed on trial for war crimes.[77] Germany would also not be allowed to join the League of Nations in the near future.[78]

---

70.  Kitchen, *A Military History of Germany*, 239.

71.  Henig, *The Weimar Republic, 1919-1933*, 18.

72.  Henig, *Versailles and After, 1919-1933*, 19; Kolb, 30.

73.  Article 231 of the Treaty of Versailles, 28 June 1919, Document 9 in Goldstein, 111.

74.  Rich, *Great Powers Diplomacy since 1914*, 57.

75.  Ibid., 58.

76.  Craig, *Germany 1866-1945*, 437.

77.  See James F. Willis, *Prologue to Nuremberg: The Politics and Diplomacy of Punishing War Criminals of the First World War* (Westport, CT: Greenwood Press, 1982).

78.  Christoph M. Kimmich, *Germany and the League of Nations* (Chicago: University of Chicago Press, 1976), 22.

When it came to territorial matters, the terms included Germany giving up territory to the newly independent state of Poland. Germany was forced to give up parts of the provinces of West Prussia and Poznan to Poland. This loss of land created the Polish Corridor, allowing Poland access to the Baltic Sea. As a result East Prussia was separated from the rest of the German republic. The port of Danzig was made a Free City under the administration of the League of Nations. Moreover, the future of the German provinces of Allenstein and Marienwerder would be decided by a plebiscite. A plebiscite would also determine the future of the industrial region of Upper Silesia. Further to the north, Germany was forced to give up the city and seaport of Memel. In addition, Germany had to return Alsace and Lorraine to France, and hand over Eupen, Malmédy, and Moresnet to Belgium. The League of Nations gained administration and France got economic control over the coal-rich Saarland for fifteen years, followed by a plebiscite to determine the future of the territory. The left bank of the Rhine River would be occupied by Allied forces. The Allies would evacuate the Rhineland in three stages in 1925, 1930, and 1935 if Germany carried out the Treaty of Versailles to the letter. However, the left bank, as well as fifty kilometers of the right bank, of the Rhine River would be permanently demilitarized. In the north, a plebiscite would be held in Schleswig to determine how much of the province would be turned over to Denmark.[79] In the south, Germany and Austria would not be allowed to be joined.[80]

To add to these harsh terms, Germany's prewar overseas colonies were taken over and administered by the League of Nations in the form of mandates. The colonies were parceled out to members of the League. Britain took control of German East Africa (Tanganyika); Belgium received Ruanda-Urundi (Rwanda and Burundi); South Africa got South-West Africa (Namibia); along with Britain and France splitting the Cameroons and Togoland, with the majority of the lands going to France. Australia received most of the German Pacific islands south of the equator, except German Samoa and Nauru which went to New Zealand. The islands north of the equator went to Japan.[81]

The Treaty of Versailles was harsh. However, as Gerhard L. Weinberg has stated, "With her industrial, technical, and population resources largely intact,

---

79.    Rich, *Great Power Diplomacy since 1914*, 55-57; Goldstein, 11-14; Sally Marks, *The Illusion of Peace: International Relations in Europe, 1918-1933* (London: Macmillan, 1976), 62.

80.    Kolb, 30.

81.    Goldstein, 14.

Germany came out of defeat confirmed as still a major power on the continent."[82]

During the following months after the signing of the Treaty of Versailles, the Paris Peace Conference forced the other defeated states to sign peace settlements. Austria signed the Treaty of St. Germain in September 1919, Bulgaria agreed to the Treaty of Neuilly in November 1919, Hungary accepted the Treaty of Trianon in June 1920, and Turkey signed the Treaty of Sèvres in August 1920.[83]

In the end, however, the United States Senate failed to ratify the Treaty of Versailles and join the League of Nations. The United States, Germany, and Soviet Russia were not part of the League of Nations. The League Council would be dominated by France and Britain.[84] Moreover, British ratification of the Treaty of Versailles depended on American participation, leaving the French without security guarantees from either Britain or the United States.

## Limits of Foreign Policy, 1919-1923

In the early years the Weimar Republic faced considerable difficulties. It first had to prepare for and deal with the presentation of the conditions of peace in the Treaty of Versailles. Then Germany had to carry out the demands outlined in the peace settlement. These were not politically, economically, or socially stable years in Germany.[85] Friedrich Ebert served as the Reich President during the existence of nine coalition cabinets until his death in 1925. Reich Chancellor Scheidemann and Foreign Minister Brockdorff-Rantzau had pursued a very active foreign policy concerning the making of the Versailles treaty, relations with the United States and Bolshevik Russia, as well as entrance into the League of Nations.[86] But, the Weimar Republic and the Treaty of Versailles were not very popular. Ruth Henig has stated:

> the problems [the Weimar Republic] faced were very deep-seated. Important and influential sections of the population despised the new republic and all it stood for. Judges, army officers, aristocrats and professors took every opportu-

---

82.   Gerhard L. Weinberg, "The Defeat of Germany in 1918 and the European Balance of Power," *Central European History* 2 (September 1969), 260; reprinted in *Germany, Hitler, and World War II* (Cambridge: Cambridge University Press, 1995), 22.

83.   See Goldstein.

84.   See George W. Egerton, *Great Britain and the Creation of the League of Nations: Strategy, Politics, and International Organization, 1914-1919* (London: Scolar Press, 1979).

85.   Kolb, 34.

86.   Otto-Ernst Schuddekopf, "Germany Foreign Policy between Compiegne and Versailles," *Journal of Contemporary History* 4 (April 1969), 196.

Heins.

face     opposition

nity to belittle its political leaders and their attempts to bring political and economic stability to Germany. And since many former officials, bureaucrats and army officials retained their positions under the new regime, they had ample opportunity to undermine it, while professing their loyalty to the German state.[87]

In 1919-20, Reich Chancellor Gustav Bauer and his Social Democratic, Catholic Center, and German Democratic coalition government, including Foreign Minister Hermann Müller-Franken, faced serious problems. Müller-Franken was a member of the Social Democratic Party and the first parliamentarian to assume control of the Wilhelmstrasse.[88] He was not a professional diplomat. First, the Chancellor was faced with paying reparations. Secondly, Bauer sought to reduce the size of the Army and disarm the Free Corps in order to adhere to the restrictions of the Treaty of Versailles. In March 1920, Bauer was challenged by the attempted right-wing military putsch to place Wolfgang Kapp in the Chancellery.[89] General Hans von Seeckt, the Chief of the Truppenamt (Troop Bureau), the successor to the old position of Chief of the General Staff,[90] would not call out loyal German troops to protect the government.[91] As a result, the Bauer government fled Berlin. They first went to Dresden, and then to Stuttgart.[92] From there, the government successfully appealed to the workers by way of a general strike to defend the Weimar Republic. Afterward the collapse of the attempted putsch, Hermann Müller-Franken, the former Foreign Minister, established a coalition government of Social Democrat, Catholic Center, and German Democratic party leaders in Berlin on 27 March.[93] Dr. Adolf Köster temporarily served as the German Foreign Minister. The Weimar Republic, according to Hajo Holborn, lacked a clear foreign policy.[94]

Elections were held in Germany in June 1920. The results were a loss of power for the Social Democratic, Catholic Center, and German Democratic coa-

---

87. Henig, *The Weimar Republic, 1919-1933*, 25.
88. Hajo Holborn, "Diplomats and Diplomacy in the Early Weimar Republic," in *The Diplomats, 1919-1939*, eds. Gordon A. Craig and Felix Gilbert (Princeton: Princeton University Press, 1953), 148.
89. Kolb, 36-37; Kitchen, *A Military History of Germany*, 242-44.
90. Wilhelm Deist, "The Road to Ideological War: Germany, 1918-1945," in *The Making of Strategy: Rulers, States, and War*, ed. Williamson Murray, MacGregor Knox, and Alvin Berstein (Cambridge: Cambridge University Press, 1994), 362.
91. Craig, *The Politics of the Prussian Army, 1640-1945*, 377; Gordon, 90-143.
92. Henig, *The Weimar Republic, 1919-1933*, 26.
93. Craig, *Germany, 1866-1945*, 165.
94. Holborn, "Diplomats and Diplomacy in the Early Weimar Republic," 156.

lition. The SPD got 21.7 percent of the vote, while the Catholic Center got 13.6 percent and DDP received 8.8 percent of the vote. This meant that the coalition received just 44.1 percent of the entire vote. On the other hand, the Independent Social Democratic Party achieved 17.9 percent, German National People's Party reigned in 15.1 percent, and German People's Party gained 13.9 percent of the vote.[95] The end result was the formation of a weak minority coalition led by Reich Chancellor Konstantin Fehrenbach of the Catholic Center Party and members of the German Democratic and German Peoples parties.[96] Dr. Walter Simons, a distinguished jurist who lacked practical knowledge concerning the Wilhelmstrasse, became the Foreign Minister.[97]

Soon after the formation of the Fehrenbach Cabinet, the question of reparations became the primary problem in German politics and foreign policy. In July 1920, the Inter-Allied Commission of France, Britain, Belgium, and Italy, headed by Raymond Poincaré, met at the Spa Conference to discuss reparations. The German delegation led by Chancellor Fehrenbach, Foreign Minister Simons, and General Seeckt found the meeting difficult because the Allied representatives also placed arms reduction on the agenda.[98] In fact, Simons admitted that the German delegation went to Spa unprepared, without a definite plan on disarmament and without concrete proposals about reparations.[99] At the conference, the Inter-Allied Commission decided that France would receive fifty-two percent of the reparations payments. Britain would get twenty-two percent, Italy ten percent, and Belgium eight percent.[100] Tension over reparations increased between Germany and France. The Fehrenbach government insisted that France reduce the demand for gold marks and material from Germany.[101] Then, in January 1921, the Allied Supreme Council set the reparations payment at 226,000 billion gold marks to be paid off over the next forty-two years.[102] Why so much? One historian has stressed:

---

95.    Kolb, 194-95.

96.    Ibid., 39.

97.    Richard Debo, *Survival and Consolidation: The Foreign Policy of Soviet Russia, 1918-1921* (Montreal: McGill-Queen's University Press, 1992), 301.

98.    Craig, *Germany 1866-1945*, 438.

99.    Marc Trachtenberg, *Reparation in World Politics: France and European Economic Diplomacy, 1916-1923* (New York: Columbia University Press, 1980), 145.

100.   Lee and Michalka, 40.

101.   Ibid.

102.   E.J. Feuchtwanger, *From Weimar to Hitler: Germany, 1918-1933* (New York: St. Martin's Press, 1993), 93.

The main reason for the size of the reparations bill was that the immediate beneficiaries—Belgium and France, and also Britain—were in turn in debt to the United States, whose loans had played a large part in financing the European war. As long as the Americans insisted on full and speedy repayment of these war loans, the west Europeans were forced to attempt to recoup by insisting on reparations from Germany.[103]

Germany rejected the terms in March 1921.[104] Consequently, on 8 March, French forces occupied Düsseldorf, Duisburg, and Ruhrort, seized the customs offices, and began collecting reparations.[105] In the midst of this situation, Germany also lost two-thirds of Upper Silesia to Poland in a plebiscite.[106] The following month, in April, the Reparations Commission appeased the Fehrenbach government by drawing up a payment schedule and fixing the total claim at 132,000 billion gold marks.[107] The London Reparations Convention presented the plan to Berlin on 6 May, giving Germany a six-day ultimatum or they would occupy the entire Ruhr Region, the industrial heart of the Rhineland.[108] As a result, the Fehrenbach Cabinet resigned from office.[109]

On 10 May 1921, the Weimar Republic formed a new coalition cabinet. Joseph Wirth of the Catholic Center Party joined with members of the Social Democrats and German Democrats. The Reichstag quickly voted to accept the London Ultimatum.[110] The acceptance of the London Payments Plan marked the beginning of Germany's Policy of Fulfillment. This policy was the brainchild of Chancellor Wirth and Walther Rathenau, the Minister for Reconstruction. According to Dietrich Orlow, the purpose of the policy was "a deliberate and dangerous gamble." He writes:

> Its supporters hoped an honest and committed effort on the part of the Germans to pay their bills for a time would convince those on the Allied side with

103.   Detlev J.K. Peukert, *The Weimar Republic: The Crisis of Classical Modernity*, trans. Richard Deveson (New York: Hill and Wang, 1991), 53.

104.   Kolb, 41.

105.   Charles S. Maier, *Recasting Bourgeois Europe: Stabilization in France, Germany, and Italy in the Decade after World War I* (Princeton: Princeton University Press, 1975), 239.

106.   Kitchen, *Europe Between the Wars*, 50; Hiden, 50. Germany had lost Northern Schleswig to Denmark in a plebiscite in 1920, followed by keeping Allenstein and Marienwerder after a plebiscite in July 1921.

107.   Peukert, 53; Orlow, 137; Feuchtwanger, 93.

108.   Kolb, 42.

109.   Craig, *Germany 1866-1945*, 441.

110.   Lee and Michalka, 41.

a truly open mind that even with the best of intentions the reparations system was not workable.[111]

Chancellor Joseph Wirth chose Friedrich Rosen as his first Foreign Minister in May 1921. Rosen had previously served as the German Minister to The Hague. He was a professional diplomat and a scholar of Persian literature. But, as David Felix has written, "he had neither imagination nor a real understanding of foreign relations." Moreover, "he promised to be harmless, and Wirth, who had set the main direction in foreign policy by accepting the principle of fulfillment, expected to continue making the major decisions."[112] When the first Wirth Cabinet resigned after the League of Nations announced the partition of Upper Silesia in October 1922, the second Wirth Cabinet was formed with Wirth as Chancellor and Foreign Minister.[113] Rosen had been dropped from the Foreign Ministry because of his incompetence and resistance to Wirth's Policy of Fulfillment.[114]

By the end of 1921, Chancellor Wirth had to report to the Reparations Commission that Germany could not meet the payment schedule for the upcoming year. He was seeking a reduction in payments.[115] As the Policy of Fulfillment was the center of government concerns, Wirth talked Walther Rathenau into becoming the Foreign Minister in February 1922.[116] Viscount D'Abernon, the British Ambassador to Germany (1920-26), admired the talent of the Foreign Minister. He wrote in his memoirs: "Rathenau enjoyed immense prestige abroad;…he was eloquent in three languages, he was subtle. His arguments were ingenious, even when unsound."[117] As head of the Wilhelmstrasse, Rathenau, who Hajo Holborn has called, "a man of large vision and great diplomatic ability," continued the Policy of Fulfillment.[118] Wirth and Rathenau worked as a team to evade paying reparations as much as possible.[119] They found the task extremely difficult because the new French Prime Minister, Raymond Poincaré (1922-24), was not

---

111.  Orlow, 138.
112.  Felix, 65.
113.  Ibid., 103-4.
114.  Ibid., 104.
115.  Lee and Michalka, 42.
116.  Felix, 124-25; Craig, *Germany 1866-1945*, 441; Kolb, 43.
117.  Viscount (Edgar) D'Abernon, *The Diary of an Ambassador*, 3 vols. (New York: Doubleday and Doran, 1929-31), 1:42.
118.  Holborn, *A History of Modern Germany*, 3:594.
119.  Felix, 80.

interested in reducing the reparations payments. The French government demanded reparations payments to support French reconstruction.[120]

The Policy of Fulfillment was supplemented by the Weimar Republic's establishment of closer economic ties with Soviet Russia. The Red Army had been successful in their struggle for victory in the Russian Civil War (1918-21) and the Russo-Polish War (1920).[121] Moscow was breaking diplomatic isolation and acquiring treaties with other states.[122] German-Soviet negotiations had been proceeding for some time, especially over the issue of Poland. General Seeckt had the view that Poland was "the mortal enemy of Germany, the creature and ally of France, the thief of German soil, [and] the destroyer of German culture." Moreover, he stated: "Let no German hand be raised to save Poland from Bolshevism, and if the devil wants to take Poland we should help him."[123] The German Foreign Office was slow to accept the success of the Red Army over the White Army, especially after the defeat of Soviet Russia by Poland.[124] General Seeckt gradually convinced Baron Ago von Maltzan, the Deputy of Department IV (East Europe, Scandinavia, and East Asia) in the Foreign Office, on the practicability of a Russo-German rapprochement.[125] In April 1920, Germany and Soviet Russia agreed to establish prisoner-of-war exchange offices.[126] Then, in May 1921, after Germany

---

120.  Lee and Michalka, 43.

121.  For the Russian Civil War, see Geoffrey Swain, *The Origins of the Russian Civil War* (London: Longman, 1996); W. Bruce Lincoln, *Red Victory: A History of the Russian Civil War* (New York: Simon and Schuster, 1989); and Michael Kettle, *Russia and the Allies, 1917-1920*, 2 vols. (London: Andre Deutsch/Routledge, 1981-88). The Polish-Soviet War is explored in Norman Davies, *White Eagle, Red Star: The Polish-Soviet War, 1919-1920* (London: Macdonald, 1972). Soviet Russian foreign policy is thoroughly examined in Richard K. Debo, *Revolution and Survival: The Foreign Policy of Soviet Russia, 1917-1918* (Toronto: University of Toronto Press, 1979) and *Survival and Consolidation: The Foreign Policy of Soviet Russia, 1918-1921*.

122.  Timothy Edward O'Connor, *Diplomacy and Revolution: G.V. Chicherin and Soviet Foreign Affairs, 1918-1930* (Ames: Iowa State University Press, 1988), 64-76.

123.  As quoted in Debo, *Survival and Consolidation*, 298.

124.  Ibid., 289-310.

125.  Holborn, "Diplomats and Diplomacy in the Early Weimar Republic," 168. Maltzan had formerly served as the Chief of the Russian Division in the Foreign Office, and was now second in charge of Department IV, whose figurehead Chief was the political appointee Gustav Behrendt. Maltzan was the power concerning Russo-German relations in the Foreign Office (Herbert von Dirksen, *Moscow, Tokyo, London: Twenty Years of German Foreign Policy* [Norman: University of Oklahoma Press, 1952], 14, 19, 29; Debo, *Survival and Consolidation*, 291).

126.  David Felix, *Walther Rathenau and the Weimar Republic: The Politics of Reparations* (Baltimore: Johns Hopkins Press, 1971), 135.

received the London Ultimatum, Germany signed a provisional commercial agreement with the Soviet Russia.[127] The agreement was negotiated by Baron Maltzan, recently promoted to Chief of Department IV in the German Foreign Office.[128] As a result of improved relations, General Hans von Seeckt, the Chief of Staff of the Reichswehr, began military collaboration with Moscow. The military established the Company for the Promotion of Industrial Enterprises (Gesellschaft zur Förderung gewerblicher Unternehmungen) in Berlin. Then Germany established a Junkers aircraft factory near Moscow, and several joint firms for the manufacture of various kinds of military equipment and ammunition in Russia. In addition, the Red Army created several tank and flying schools, in which there were many German instructors, as well as German students. A secret German military mission was established in Moscow, which was visited by officers of the Truppenamt planning and coordination group.[129] In January 1922, Chancellor Wirth, Foreign Minister Rathenau, and Baron Maltzan discussed the possibility of further improvements in German-Soviet relations with a Russian delegation in Berlin.[130]

In April and May 1922, the representatives of thirty-four countries met at the Genoa Economic Conference in northwest Italy. This meeting was held to discuss the economic reconstruction of Central and East Europe and to explore ways to improve relations between Soviet Russia and the West.[131] The German delegation consisted of Chancellor Wirth, Foreign Minister Rathenau, State Secretary for Foreign Affairs Ernst von Simson (1922), Baron Maltzan, and the legal adviser to the Foreign Office, Friedrich Gaus.[132] At the conference France and

---

127.  R.H. Haigh, D.S. Morris, and A.R. Peters, *German-Soviet Relations in the Weimar Era: Friendship from Necessity* (Totowa: Barnes and Noble, 1985), 76; Gustav Hilger and Alfred G. Meyer, *The Incompatible Allies: A Memoir-History of German-Soviet Relations, 1918-1941* (New York: Macmillan, 1953), 65-76.

128.  Hilger and Meyer, 65-68.

129.  Hans W. Gatzke, "Russo-German Military Collaboration during the Weimar Republic," in *European Diplomacy between Two Wars, 1919-1939*, ed. Hans W. Gatzke (Chicago: Quadrangle, 1972), 41-43; Craig, *The Politics of the Prussian Army, 1640-1945*, 408-11; O'Connor, 78; T.N. Dupuy, *A Genius for War: The German Army and General Staff, 1807-1945* (Fairfax, VA: Hero, 1984), 215.

130.  Jon Jacobson, *When the Soviet Union Entered World Politics* (Berkeley: University of California Press, 1994), 91.

131.  See Carole Fink, *The Genoa Conference: European Diplomacy, 1921-1922* (Chapel Hill: University of North Carolina Press, 1984) and Carole Fink, Axel Frohn, and Jürgen Heideking, eds., *Genoa, Rapallo, and European Reconstruction in 1922* (Cambridge: Cambridge University Press, 1991).

132.  Peter Krüger, "A Rainy Day, April 16, 1922: The Rapallo Treaty and the Cloudy Perspective for Germany Foreign Policy," in *Genoa, Rapallo, and European Reconstruction in 1922*, eds. Carole Fink, Axel Frohn, and Jürgen Heideking (Cambridge: Cambridge University, 1991), 51.

Britain dashed the hopes of the German delegation by removing the question of revising reparation payments from the agenda.[133] The Reparations Commission had called for Germany to make cash payments of 720 million and payments in kind of 1,450 million gold marks in 1922.[134]

The Germans disrupted the Genoa Conference by signing the Treaty of Rapallo with Soviet Russia.[135] On 16 April, under the instructions of the Reich Chancellor, Maltzan met with Soviet delegates at Rapallo and signed the agreement.[136] According to the German historian Peter Krüger, the treaty came about because the Chancellor sought to pursue "a more active, powerful, and independent foreign policy."[137] Rathenau had doubts about a Russo-German treaty right up to the last minute.[138] Rathenau and Dr. Carl von Schubert, the Chief of Department III (Britain, the United States, and the Orient) in the Foreign Office, leaned towards improving Germany's position by working with Britain and France.[139] But Wirth was strongly influenced by Baron Maltzan and General Seeckt.[140] Herbert von Dirksen, the Chief of the Polish Affairs Division at the Foreign Office, gave Maltzan all the credit for the Treaty of Rapallo. In his memoirs he stated:

> That the German delegation resolved to conclude the treaty was solely due to Maltzan's energy and skill. He was not only the author of the political combination involved in this treaty, he was also the pilot who steered this frail boat through the shallow waters of his own delegation. First, he succeeded in winning over Chancellor Wirth, who was unprejudiced and politically minded. The main obstacle was, of course, Rathenau. He was a Westerner to the very core of his being, a refined and cultivated man who abhorred the Russian Method of ruling and terrorizing. He was at last persuaded…to give way.[141]

Viscount D'Abernon, the British Ambassador to Germany, found Maltzan as "perhaps the cleverest man who has worked in the Wilhelmstrasse since the war.

133. Fink, *The Genoa Conference*, 129, 132.
134. Feuchtwanger, 99; O'Connor, 91.
135. Hilger and Meyer, 76-83.
136. See Gerald Freund, *Unholy Alliance: Russian-German Relations from the Treaty of Brest-Litovsk to the Treaty of Berlin* (New York: Harcourt, Brace and Company, 1957).
137. Krüger, 55-57.
138. Ibid., 56.
139. Ibid., 52, 60.
140. Gordon A. Craig, *From Bismarck to Adenauer: Aspects of German Statecraft* (Baltimore: Johns Hopkins Press, 1958), 68.
141. Dirksen, 32.

In diplomacy and politics a pupil of Kiderlen-Wächter, who in turn was a pupil of Bismarck."[142] Maltzan and his followers, including former Foreign Minister Ulrich von Brockdorff-Rantzau and Herbert von Dirksen, believed that, "rapprochement with the Soviet Union might, at the very least, provide a counterweight to the power of the West, and, at best, might open possibilities of treaty revision, especially along the eastern frontiers."[143]

In the Treaty of Rapallo, Chancellor Wirth hoped to continue the secret collaboration between the German and Russian armies. The treaty also called for Germany and Soviet Russia to restore full diplomatic relations, mutual renunciation of compensation claims for war costs and damages, and establish most-favored nation treatment in trade.[144] Many in the Foreign Office believed that an agreement with Soviet Russia was a significant step towards improving Germany's standing in the international system.[145] However, as E.J. Feuchtwanger has stated, "the immediate effect of Rapallo was sensational and destroyed any chance there might have been of the Genoa Conference producing results." He adds that "France was more than ever convinced of German bad faith."[146] Rapallo was a major turning point for Germany. It put a stop to the progress made toward better Allied-German relations and ruined Germany's Policy of Fulfillment. Berlin developed closer ties with Moscow. Wirth sent Count Ulrich von Brockdorff-Rantzau to Moscow to serve as the German Ambassador to Russia (1922-28).[147] In July 1922, Germany and Russia agreed to a secret military agreement. This so-called "trade" agreement was ratified in February 1923.[148]

In the meantime, the Reparations Question continued to top the agenda of German domestic and foreign policy. At the same time, the Weimar Republic was under constant threats from right wing radicals. Right wing organizations, including the National Socialist German Worker's Party (NSDAP) or Nazi Party, were growing in importance.[149] In fact, right-wing terrorists murdered Foreign Minister Rathenau on 24 June 1922.[150] At that time, Chancellor Wirth assumed control over the Foreign Office with Baron Maltzan being the major

142.   D'Abernon, 2:42.
143.   Kimmich, 32.
144.   Haigh, *German-Soviet Relations in the Weimar Era*, 78-80; George F. Kennan, *Soviet Foreign Policy, 1917-1941* (Princeton: Princeton University Press, 1960), 47; Feuchtwanger, 99.
145.   Hilger and Meyer, 80.
146.   Feuchtwanger, 100.
147.   Holborn, "Diplomats and Diplomacy in the Early Weimar Republic," 171.
148.   O'Connor, 92.
149.   Feuchtwanger, 108-15.
150.   Felix, 168-69.

influence in foreign policy. Three weeks later, on 12 July, the Weimar Republic requested the Reparations Commission to suspend the payment of the reparations for the rest of the year. In addition, the Wirth government declared that Germany could not make cash payments in 1923 and 1924.[151] As tension mounted between Germany and the Allied Powers, the Wirth Cabinet fell in November 1922.

Dr. Wilhelm Cuno, who was not associated with any particular political party, became the German Chancellor in November 1922. The Cuno Cabinet consisted of a coalition of the Catholic Center, German Democratic, and German People's parties. Cuno, himself, was the Director of the Hamburg-America Shipping Line.[152] Friedrich von Rosenberg became the new Foreign Minister. Baron Maltzan was promoted to State Secretary for Foreign Affairs (1922-24) in December 1922.[153] Under Cuno, the Weimar Republic swiftly moved away from the Policy of Fulfillment. Germany began to negotiate for a postponement of reparation payments, except for the delivery of wood and coal, for three to four years.[154] But Germany was slow to provide shipments of coal, timber, and telegraph poles.[155] Therefore, in December 1922, the London Reparations Conference declared that Germany had violated the peace settlement. As such, France, under the leadership of Raymond Poincaré as the Prime Minister and Foreign Minister, was determined to press all of its rights under the Treaty of Versailles.[156] On 9 January 1923, French troops, backed by Belgium and Italy, moved into previously unoccupied parts of the Ruhr Region. France sent a group of engineers into the Ruhr, protected by five French and one Belgium military divisions, to take charge of the coal production and delivery.[157] The force of 60,000 men was increased to 100,000 troops during the course of 1923.[158] As Eberhard Kolb has pointed out:

> Poincaré was interested in reparations as such, he also wished to create a political basis for pushing Germany's frontier back to the Rhine and thus achieving

---

151. Feuchtwanger, 117.

152. Craig, *Germany 1866-1945*, 445.

153. Robert P. Grathwol, *Stresemann and the DNVP: Reconciliation or Revenge in German Foreign Policy, 1924-1928* (Lawrence: Regents Press of Kansas, 1980), 6.

154. Henig, *The Weimar Republic, 1919-1933*, 34.

155. Orlow, 138; Feuchtwanger, 119; Lee and Michalka, 44-45.

156. See Walter A. McDougall, *France's Rhineland Diplomacy, 1914-1924: The Last Bid for a Balance of Power in Europe* (Princeton: Princeton University Press, 1978).

157. Feuchtwanger, 119.

158. Kolb, 46.

the permanent weakening of Germany which, in his view, ought to have been effected in 1919. In this sense the occupation of the Ruhr was a deliberate act of revisionism on the part of France.[159]

Britain objected to this French move. Prime Minister Andrew Bonar Law (1922-23) and Foreign Secretary Lord Curzon (1919-24) feared that the French action would undermine the British policy of European reconciliation and pacification. Britain did not want to see France becoming the dominant power in Europe.[160]

Unable to take military action,[161] the Weimar Republic suspended all reparation payments to France and Belgium. There was a mighty surge of nationalist outrage in Germany. Berlin would now pursue a Policy of Obstruction.[162] The Cuno Cabinet called for the population of the Ruhr Region to pursue a policy of "passive resistance" against the occupation forces.[163] The German government encouraged and supported a general strike against the French and Belgians. Marshall M. Lee and Wolfgang Michalka have stressed that "passive resistance was intended to demonstrate that France's policy of forcing payment by seizing territorial hostages would not be worthwhile."[164] As a result of passive resistance, shipments of strategic materials from Germany to France quickly dropped off significantly. Chancellor Cuno supported the idle German workers in the Ruhr by indiscriminately printing and paying out thousands of millions of marks in currency.[165] As a consequence, the floodgates to uncontrolled inflation were open. Moreover, the rest of Germany had to pick up the tax burden of the Ruhr Region. The Weimar Republic was soon in deeper financial troubles, and Berlin responded by printing more and more marks. In December 1922, the German mark was worth 8,000 to one American dollar. It stood at 20,000 to a dollar in April, and 1,000,000 to a dollar by August.[166] Three months later, just before inflation was finally brought under control with the introduction of the Rentenmark, the dollar was worth 4.2 trillion marks![167] Meanwhile, in August 1923,

---

159. Ibid.
160. Jaffe, 217.
161. The Reichswehr, limited to an army of 100,000, faced a French military of 750,000 men (Deist, "The Road to Ideological War," 357).
162. The crisis is thoroughly examined in Alfred E. Cornebise, *The Weimar in Crisis: Cuno's Germany and the Ruhr Occupation* (Washington, D.C.: University Press of America, 1977).
163. S.A. Schuker, *The End of French Predominance in Europe: The Financial Crisis of 1924 and the Adoption of the Dawes Plan* (Chapel Hill: University of North Carolina Press, 1976), 25.
164. Lee and Michalka, 45.
165. Orlow, 138.
166. Kolb, 47.
167. Orlow, 139.

London declared the French-Belgian occupation of the Ruhr as illegal. But Poincaré would not back down until the Germans ended their Policy of Obstruction. The situation with the German mark and the occupation of the Ruhr Region resulted in the downfall of the Cuno Cabinet in August 1923.[168]

President Ebert appointed Gustav Stresemann of the German People's Party as the next German Chancellor.[169] Stresemann also served as the German Foreign Minister.[170] The so-called "Great Coalition" cabinet consisted of members from the Social Democratic, Catholic Center, and German Democratic parties. At this point, in September, the Weimar Republic abandoned the failed Policy of Obstruction, and resumed the payment of reparations.[171] However, the Stresemann Cabinet experienced great turmoil with numerous uprisings in the autumn of 1923. In October, the Communists attempted an uprising in Hamburg. Then, in November, Adolf Hitler and the Nazi Party attempted a putsch in Munich.[172] Many statesmen, including Poincaré, believed that Germany was about to break up. On 23 November 1923, Stresemann resigned as Chancellor when he was defeated in a vote of confidence.[173] At this time Berlin placed the new German currency, the Rentenmark, in circulation. It quickly became a major success. Meanwhile, Britain and the United States put the French franc under a lot of strain. Now Germany, the United States, Britain, and France agreed to a proposal, originally made by U.S. Secretary of State Charles Evans Hughes, that a committee of experts should be established to look into Germany's ability to pay reparations.[174] Britain, the United States, and world opinion, along with the crisis with the French franc, was forcing Prime Minister Poincaré to back off his heavy-handed policy in Germany. France could not afford to become diplomatically isolated from the other Great Powers. The door was opening for the Dawes Plan. The collapse of French policy in the Ruhr, according to Corelli Barnett, "marked a major shift in power from the victors towards Germany."[175]

168.  Feuchtwanger, 126.
169.  Henry Ashby Turner, Jr., *Stresemann and the Politics of the Weimar Republic* (Princeton: Princeton University Press, 1963), 110.
170.  Ibid., 114.
171.  Feuchtwanger, 127-28.
172.  Ibid., 132-35.
173.  Ibid., 142.
174.  Feuchtwanger, 137.
175.  Corelli Barnett, *The Collapse of British Power* (London: Methuen, 1972), 327.

## Reforms in the Foreign Office

"Between 1890 and 1914," according to Hajo Holborn, "the political influence of the German Foreign Office declined rapidly from the height that it had attained under Bismarck."[176] The German Foreign Office then lost what prestige and little influence over the formulation of foreign policy that it had left during the course of the First World War.[177] By 1918 the traditional Foreign Office had been overshadowed by its complete subordination to the German Army High Command.[178]

Before the conflict, the Wilhelmstrasse, largely manned by aristocrats, had functioned as a tight-knit organization under the control of the German Emperor and Chancellor. As Friedrich Payer, the Vice Chancellor, commented in 1918:

> Over the AA [Auswärtiges Amt] prevailed a spirit of exclusiveness; for outsiders it had the aura of a mystery, impenetrable to laymen. It was an enclosed organism inside the government, into which only selected people were allowed glimpses, and even these reluctantly and not more than was absolutely necessary.[179]

In spite of its limited influence, many officials used the diplomats as scapegoats and held them responsible for the conflict as well as the disastrous end to the war.[180] With an end to the conflict, Germany experienced many political changes. The Kaiser abdicated and fled to the Kingdom of the Netherlands. A revolution, followed by the establishment of the Weimar Republic, as well as the Allied and Associated Powers imposing the Versailles settlement upon Germany created a whole new political framework in which the Wilhelmstrasse needed to operate. From the ashes of defeat gradually emerged a revitalized German Foreign Office.

For several years numerous Chancellors and Foreign Secretaries had recognized the need to reform the Wilhelmstrasse.[181] They realized the necessity of

---

176.  Holborn, "Diplomats and Diplomacy in the Early Weimar Republic," 125.

177.  Ibid., 125-26.

178.  Hiden, 6-7.

179.  As quoted in Kurt Doss, "The History of the German Foreign Office," in *The Times Survey of Foreign Ministries of the World,* ed. Zara Steiner (London: Times Books, 1982), 232-33.

180.  Gordon A. Craig, "The Revolution in War and Diplomacy, 1914-1939," chap. in *War, Politics, and Diplomacy: Selected Essays* (London: Weidenfeld and Nicolson, 1966), 204.

181.  Paul Gordon Lauren, *Diplomats and Bureaucrats: The First Institutional Responses to Twentieth-Century Diplomacy in France and Germany* (Stanford: Hoover Institution Press, 1976), 118-23.

appointing qualified personnel, other than aristocrats, to important diplomatic positions. They understood the need to reorganize the Auswärtiges Amt for more efficient operations. However, the leadership failed to reform the Foreign Office because of their reluctance to dismiss the highly valued technical expertise of aristocratic diplomats. As the Kaiser explained in his memoirs:

> Every new Chancellor, especially if he himself did not come from the ranks of the foreign service, needed the Foreign Office in order to work himself into foreign affairs, and this took time. But once he had worked himself in he was under obligation to the officials, and he was reluctant to make extensive changes, burdened as he was by other matters and lacking detailed knowledge regarding the Foreign Office personnel, particularly as he still believed that he needed the advice of those who were "orientated."[182]

In 1918, during the demise of the Wilhelmstrasse, Richard von Kühlmann, the State Secretary for Foreign Affairs (1917-18), began the reforming process. He asked Friedrich Edmund Schüler, the Head of the Consular Division, to outline changes for the Foreign Office.[183] The Foreign Office, according to one historian, was "possibly the most difficult ministry to alter because of its aristocratic background and strongly nationalistic character."[184] Schüler, only three years short of retirement, worked toward the reorganization of the Wilhelmstrasse, which included both its personnel and organizational structures. Schüler, being promoted to Superintendent of the Personnel Division, came up with a plan by the summer of 1918.[185] The Foreign Office took no actions during the secretaryships of Rear Admiral Paul von Hintze (1918) and Dr. Wilhelm Solf (1918).

In December 1918, Count Ulrich von Brockdorff-Rantzau became the State Secretary for Foreign Affairs.[186] He replaced Dr. Solf who had served as Foreign Secretary for two months.[187] Brockdorff-Rantzau had served as the German Minister to Denmark during the First World War.[188] He was a professional diplomat,

---

182. William II, *The Kaiser's Memoirs: Wilhelm II, Emperor of Germany, 1888-1918*, trans. Thomas R. Ybarra (New York: Harper and Brothers, 1922; reprint, New York: Howard Fertig, 1976), 77.

183. Doss, "The History of the German Foreign Office," 235.

184. Donald M. McKale, *Curt Prüfer: German Diplomat from the Kaiser to Hitler* (Kent: Kent State University Press, 1987), 57.

185. Doss, "The History of the German Foreign Office," 236.

186. Feuchtwanger, 47-48.

187. Holborn, "Diplomats and Diplomacy in the Early Weimar Republic," 129, 132.

188. Ibid., 132.

and the Council of People's Representatives considered him "the finest horse in the stable of the professional German diplomats."[189]

By February 1919, Germany was developing into a republic. The German Republic transformed all imperial offices into constitutional ministries under Reich Ministers. The Reich Ministers were responsible to the Reichstag. At this time, the Foreign Office became a ministry. However, the leading officials at the Wilhelmstrasse decided to keep the name "Foreign Office" instead of using "Foreign Ministry" because of their respect for tradition.[190] Even so, the Reichstag gave the former imperial position of State Secretary for Foreign Affairs (Foreign Secretary) the status of Foreign Minister (Reichminister des Auswärtigen). Moreover, the previous Under State Secretary for Foreign Affairs was now renamed the State Secretary or Foreign Secretary (Staatssekretär).[191] The State Secretary was designated as the highest-ranking civil servant in the Foreign Office.[192]

In February 1919, Brockdorff-Rantzau became the first Foreign Minister of the German Republic.[193] His primary task was to prepare for the negotiations with the Allied and Associated Powers at the Paris Peace Conference. On 10 April 1919, Foreign Minister Brockdorff-Rantzau announced the so-called Schüler Reforms.[194] These changes regarded several major areas within the Foreign Office. First, the consular and diplomatic careers were combined in Department I for Personnel and Administration. The reforms gave consular personnel the status of diplomats. Moreover, the Foreign Office would accept men of influence who were not of noble lineage to fill key diplomatic positions at the Wilhelmstrasse and embassies. In other words, the Diplomatic Service would be opened up to men from the world of commerce, industry, politics, and science. Second, Brockdorff-Rantzau created the Office of the Minister. The staff of this office would assist the Foreign Minister. Third, he created a Central Office to replace the Political Division. Fourth, the Foreign Minister established three regional groups (Länderabteilungen) within the Central Office. The regional system consisted of Department II for West, South, and Southeast Europe; Department III for Britain, America, and the Orient; and Department IV for East Europe, Scandinavia, and East Asia. Fifth, he designated Legal Affairs as Depart-

---

189.  Ibid.
190.  Doss, "The History of the German Foreign Office," 237.
191.  Ibid.
192.  Lauren, 135.
193.  Holborn, "Diplomats and Diplomacy in the Early Weimar Republic," 133.
194.  Doss, "The History of the German Foreign Office," 237. See also Kurt Doss, *Das deutsche Auswärtiges Amt im Übergang vom Kaiserreich zur Weimarer Republik: Die Schüler Reform* (Dusseldorf: Droste, 1977).

ment V and Cultural Affairs as Department VI. And, finally, the Foreign Minister founded a department for foreign trade (Department X).[195] Moreover, the Foreign Minister and State Secretary would be assisted by experienced diplomats and bureaucrats taking up the positions of Chief or Director (Ministerial-direktor) and Deputy Director (Ministerialdirigent) of each of the new major departments in the Auswärtiges Amt.[196]

In August 1919, Edmund Schüler was promoted to Director of Personnel and Administration (Department I) to oversee the recruitment of men to fit the reforms.[197] He worked on creating regulations for the education of the new recruits, establishing a salary for attachés, organizing economic education for Foreign Office and Diplomatic Service personnel, and building up Department X for foreign trade.[198] Schüler established new admission requirements, including the passing of difficult foreign service and language examinations. He sought to break the hold the aristocracy had on diplomatic posts and political desks in the Foreign Office.[199] Schüler was responsible for placing trusted non-aristocratic men as Directors of all departments. He ensured that most of the leading officials in the Central Office came from the consular career field and had an understanding of economic policies.[200] He helped place individuals from outside the diplomatic field into important diplomatic posts abroad. He recruited Dr. Friedrich Sthamer, the former Mayor of Hamburg, as the German Ambassador to Britain (1920-29); Otto Landsberg, a former member of the Council of the People's Representatives, as Ambassador to Belgium (1920-23); Dr. Adolf Müller, a politician, as the German Minister to Switzerland (1920-33); Wilhelm Mayer-Kaufbeuren, a politician, as Ambassador to France (1920-23); and Walter Koch as Minister to Czechoslovakia (1921-35).[201]

The Weimar Constitution made the Foreign Office the sole agency for the administration of German foreign policy.[202] However, the constitution gave the

---

195.   McKale, 57-58; Doss, "The History of the German Foreign Office," 237-38, 240; Dirksen, 12; Lauren, 122-154; Peter Krüger, *Die Aussenpolitik der Republik von Weimar* (Darmstadt: Wissenschaftliche Buchgesellschaft, 1985), 27-29; Erich Kordt, *Nicht aus den Akten: Die Wilhelmstrasse in Frieden und Krieg* (Stuttgart: Deutsche Verlags-Anstalt, 1950), 32, 40.

196.   Reichsministerium des Innern, *Handbuch für das Deutsche Reich* (Berlin: Carl Heymanns Verlag, 1922), 58-59.

197.   Doss, "The History of the German Foreign Office," 236.

198.   Ibid., 238.

199.   McKale, 58.

200.   Doss, "The History of the German Foreign Office," 238.

201.   Ibid., 239; Holborn, "Diplomats and Diplomacy in the Early Weimar Republic," 152.

202.   Ernst von Weizsäcker testimony, 10 June 1948, AMT, OGL 17, Box 137, Folder 2, 8085; Gaines Post, Jr., *The Civil Military Fabric of Weimar Foreign Policy* (Princeton: Princeton University, 1973), 16.

Reich President decisive powers in treaty-making and the appointment of diplomatic officers. Under a republic, the Foreign Office's influence in foreign policy was also limited by the voice of the Chancellor and Parliament. In practice, the Chancellor could, at times, ignore the advice of the Foreign Minister. Moreover, the Wilhelmstrasse needed the popular support of the Reichsrat and the Reichstag. The Weimar Constitution included the creation of a Reichstag Committee for Foreign Affairs (Reichstag Ausschuss für Auswärtige Angelegenheiten). But, the division of the political parties made it difficult to form a foreign policy.[203] Therefore, in practice, according to Hajo Holborn, "meetings between the Minister of Foreign Affairs and leaders or foreign affairs experts of the parties forming the government assumed the functions for which the parliamentary committee had been created."[204] It was difficult for the Foreign Office to formulate and pursue an effective foreign policy. The Reichswehr and other federal ministries, such as the Ministry of Finance and Ministry of Economics, were influential in foreign affairs.[205] One good reason for this situation was because the new financial diplomacy "was over the heads of the old-time diplomats."[206]

In the first eighteen months the Schüler Reforms found political backing by Foreign Ministers Brockdroff-Rantzau (1919), Hermann Müller-Franken (1919-20), and Dr. Adolf Köster (1920).[207] When Dr. Walter Simons (1920-21) opposed the reforms, Schüler retired from the Foreign Office.[208] The next six Foreign Ministers over the following three years gave the Schüler Reforms varying degrees of political support. Moreover, the Foreign Secretaries of the Weimar period, Dr. Edgar Haniel von Haimhausen (1920-22), Ernst von Simson (1922), Baron Ago von Maltzan (1922-24), Dr. Carl von Schubert (1924-30), and Dr. Bernhard Wilhelm von Bülow (1930-36), all came from traditional diplomatic backgrounds.[209] Many diplomats resented the reform that gave officials in the consular departments of the embassies the status of diplomats.

To meet the needs of Schüler's reforms, the staff of the Auswärtiges Amt dramatically increased in size during the early 1920s. In fact, a janitor at the Wilhelmstrasse made the comment, "I don't know what is going on. The German Reich is growing smaller and smaller but the Foreign Office bigger and big-

203. Holborn, "Diplomats and Diplomacy in the Early Weimar Republic," 148-49; Lauren, 149.
204. Holborn, "Diplomats and Diplomacy in the Early Weimar Republic," 149.
205. Ibid., 149-50.
206. Ibid., 150.
207. Graham Ross, *The Great Powers and the Decline of the European States System, 1914-1945* (London: Longman, 1983), 147; Doss, "The History of the German Foreign Office," 237.
208. Doss, "The History of the German Foreign Office," 237.
209. Ibid., 240.

ger."[210] Prior to the outbreak of war in 1914 the Auswärtiges Amt consisted of a State Secretary, Under State Secretary, four Directors, three Assistant Directors, about twenty-eight Counselors, twenty-three permanent Assistants, and eighteen junior officers without established posts.[211] By 1923 the Foreign Office had a staff of 1,330, not including 701 individuals at a total of 112 missions abroad.[212] Commenting on the changes, Herbert von Dirksen, a diplomat in the Baltic Affairs Division, stated: "He [ Schüler] shattered the old historical structure dating from Bismarck and built up a new organization big enough to be the political brain of a victorious World Power."[213] Even so, by late 1920, the older career diplomats began to reverse some of the reforms. Fewer outsiders were being appointed to important diplomatic posts. After the retirement of Schüler only three more outsiders gained important diplomatic posts.[214] The practice was essentially abandoned in 1923. The few outsiders who had found positions in the foreign service had made no significant impact. In fact, as Christoph Kimmich has pointed out:

> Some had found the atmosphere not to their liking and had left; some had been sent abroad to serve in legations and embassies. Those who attained influential positions soon adapted themselves to the reigning outlook and the traditional procedures. By mid-1920 the professionals felt secure once again, and within the next three or four years the ministry returned to old hands.[215]

The old hands were aided in this endeavor with a new practice initiated by Foreign Secretary Carl von Schubert in 1924. At this time Schubert began naming veteran diplomats as Deputy Directors to the Chiefs of the Foreign Office departments.[216] Deputy Directors had the duty of meeting frequently with the

---

210. As quoted in Dirksen, 12.

211. Ludwig Biewer, "The History of the German Foreign Office: An Overview," (Berlin: Auswärtiges Amt, ca. 2005), 4.

212. Ibid., 6.

213. Dirksen, 12.

214. Dr. Otto Wiedfeldt, a board member of the Krupp works, was the German Ambassador to the United States (1922-24); Ulrich Rauscher, a politician, was Ambassador to Poland (1922-30); and Dr. Adolf Köster, the former Foreign Minister, served as Minister to Latvia (1923-28), and later Yugoslavia (1928-30). By the end of the Weimar Republic in 1933, only two outsiders were still at their diplomatic positions: Koch in Czechoslovakia and Müller in Switzerland (Doss, "The History of the German Foreign Office," 239; Holborn, "Diplomats and Diplomacy in the Early Weimar Republic," 152).

215. Kimmich, 30.

216. McKale, 88-89.

Foreign Minister and Secretary of State for Foreign Affairs. Many times the Deputy Directors failed to keep the Chiefs, who were Schüler's recruits, informed of the secret discussions with the Foreign Minister and Foreign Secretary. Herbert von Dirksen has stated that:

> The newly appointed "Directors" were entrusted with important political negotiations. They accompanied the Minister to conferences, they drafted the notes, negotiated with the Embassies, and had direct access to the Secretary of State and the Minister. They were often party to the most secret affairs and were not allowed to communicate them to their chiefs.[217]

The system of directors was very similar to the Political Department of the old Foreign Office during the days of Bismarck and Kaiser William II.

## Stresemann and the Primacy of Revision, 1923-1929

Wilhelm Marx of the Catholic Center Party formed a coalition government in November 1923. The Cabinet consisted of members of the Catholic Center, Bavarian People's, German Democratic, and German People's parties. At the insistence of the German Democratic and Center parties Gustav Stresemann remained in the Cabinet as the Foreign Minister.[218] The Weimar Republic wanted to maintain continuity in German foreign policy.[219] Stresemann would remain the Foreign Minister and the dominant personality for the coalition governments of Wilhelm Marx (1923-24), Hans Luther (1925-26), Wilhelm Marx (1926-28), and Hermann Müller-Franken (1928-30) until his death in October 1929.[220] Stresemann was the leader of the German People's Party which received only 9.2 percent of the votes in May 1924, 10.1 percent in July 1924, and 8.7 percent in May 1928.[221] During these elections the strongest political organizations were the Social Democratic Party, German National People's Party, Catholic Center Party, German Communist Party, and German People's Party.[222] The DNVP represented the growing right-wing nationalist movement in Germany. Moreover, with the death of Friedrich Ebert, Germany elected the right-wing retired Field Marshal Paul von Hindenburg as the Reich President in April 1925.[223]

---

217. Dirksen, 42.
218. Kolb, 57; Feuchtwanger, 143.
219. Turner, 154.
220. Henig, *The Weimar Republic, 1919-1933*, 40.
221. Kolb, 193-94.
222. Ibid.
223. Feutchwanger, 40, 168-69.

Foreign Minister Stresemann was a "coolly calculating realist, nationalist and power-politician."[224] He was no different than the other leading European statesmen of the era. The main objective of Stresemann's foreign policy was the restoration of Germany as a Great Power with equal rights. Stresemann sought to resolve the Reparations Question, put an end to the Franco-Belgian occupation of the Ruhr, and revise the Treaty of Versailles. Moreover, he wanted to recover the Saarland and get rid of restrictions regarding the German military. Stresemann also had the long-range goal of revising Germany's eastern frontiers. With these goals, the Foreign Minister pursued a Policy of Reconciliation with the West, believing that his foreign policy objectives could only be achieved by satisfying French security concerns and cooperating with the Western Powers. This foreign policy was supported by the political parties of the moderate left and middle. It was also supported by the Foreign Office and diplomats abroad.[225] But it was opposed by the German National People's Party, National Socialist German Worker's Party, German Communist Party, and the right wing of Stresemann's own German People's Party.[226]

Gustav Stresemann took charge of German foreign policy at the right time. There was a swing in the mood of international relations. European statesmen were looking to cooperate with Germany instead of allowing France to establish predominance over Central Europe. In Britain, the David Lloyd George government was replaced by that of Andrew Bonar Law (1922-23) and Stanley Baldwin (1923-24). In January 1924, Prime Minister James Ramsay Mac-Donald of the Labour Party took charge of the British government. Mac-Donald pursued a foreign policy aimed at the reconciliation of France and Germany, the strengthening of the League of Nations, and the establishment of diplomatic relations with the Soviet Union. Ten months later, in October 1924, Baldwin once again took over the reins of British government (1924-29). Baldwin and his cabinet maintained the foreign policy pursued by Mac-Donald, seeking a lasting peace in Europe.[227] In France, the governments of Georges Clemenceau (1917-20), Etienne-Alexandre Millerand (1920), Jean-Claude Georges Leygues (1920-21), Aristide Briand (1921-22) and Raymond Poincaré (1922-24) sought for the strictest execution of the Treaty of Versailles or the revision of the agreement to benefit France. French foreign policy was

---

224.  Kolb, 175.
225.  Post, *The Civil Military Fabric of Weimar Foreign Policy*, 59.
226.  Kolb, 175-76; Craig, *Germany 1866-1945*, 511.
227.  John Robert Ferris, *Men, Money, and Diplomacy: The Evolution of British Strategic Policy, 1919-1926* (Ithaca: Cornell University Press, 1989), 142-43; Northedge, 123-47.

designed to achieve and maintain maximum security for France against the German threat.[228] The elections of May 1924 led to the rise of the radical socialist government of Édouard Herriot in Paris. French foreign policy now focused on cooperation with Britain regarding the German Question as well as the development of diplomatic relations with the Soviet Union.[229] In Italy, the successive cabinets of Vittorio Orlando (1917-19), Francesco Saverio Nitti (1919-20), Giovanni Giolitti (1920-21), Ivanoe Bonomi (1921-22), and Luigi Facta (1922) were unable to deal with the economic and social problems of the time. There was a rising militant right, led by Benito Mussolini and the Partito Nazionale Fascista, that led the nationalist, anti-socialist, and anti-liberal forces of Italy. After the Fascist march on Rome in 1922, King Victor Emmanuel III of Italy (1900-46) invited Mussolini to form a government. Mussolini was well on his way to gaining dictatorial powers by 1925.[230] In foreign affairs, the Fascist dictator cooperated with London and Paris to organize European security.[231] In Soviet Russia, in 1921, Vladimir Lenin proclaimed the New Economic Policy. This led to the Soviet Union's experimentation with capitalism, as well as efforts to join the international community. The Soviet Union established commercial treaties with Britain and Germany in 1921, diplomatic relations with Germany in 1922, and diplomatic ties with Britain, France, and Italy in 1924.[232] And, finally, in the United States, President Woodrow Wilson was unable to obtain the ratification of the Treaty of Versailles. The world's leading economic power backed away from the League of Nations and collective security, preferring to follow the path of "independent internationalism." The Republican administrations of Warren G. Harding (1921-23) and Calvin Coolidge (1923-29) expanded American involvement in world affairs, preferring the pursuit of a foreign policy of economic expansion and the "open

228.   Néré, 26-62; Anthony Adamthwaite, *Grandeur and Misery: France's Bid for Power in Europe, 1914-1940* (London: Arnold, 1995), 64-109. See also Judith M. Hughes, *To the Maginot Line: The Politics of French Military Preparation in the 1920's* (Cambridge, MA: Harvard University Press, 1971).

229.   Adamthwaite, 102-4.

230.   Stanley G. Payne, *A History of Fascism, 1914-1945* (Madison: University of Wisconsin Press, 1995), 80-128.

231.   H. James Burgwyn, *Italian Foreign Policy in the Interwar Period, 1918-1940* (Westport, CT: Praeger, 1997), 17-34; C.J. Lowe and F. Marzari, *Italian Foreign Policy, 1870-1940* (London: Routledge and Kegan Paul, 1975), 183-210; RJ.B. Bosworth, *Mussolini* (London: Arnold, 2002), 100-217.

232.   O'Connor, 47-132; Jacobson, *When the Soviet Union Entered World Politics*, 81-151; Debo, *Survival and Consolidation*, 147-343.

door" principle.[233] As such, the United States was deeply interested in European economic issues.

In October 1923, Britain, the United States, Italy, and Germany called for a conference to examine and assess Germany's ability to pay reparations within the terms of the Treaty of Versailles. Consequently, in November, the Reparations Commission appointed the independent Dawes Committee, led by American banker Charles G. Dawes, to examine the Reparations Question. Prime Minister Poincaré of France accepted the proposal at that time. The security of France was dependent on the support of Britain and the United States.[234] The Dawes Committee presented its report to the Reparations Commission in April 1924. The Dawes Plan called for a five-year schedule in which Germany would begin by paying one billion marks a year, with this annual payment increasing to 2.5 billion marks a year. Berlin would also receive an international loan to boost the German economy and enable it to make reparations payments. German state property, and in particular, the railroads, were to serve as security for the loan. Furthermore, Germany would make the reparation payments to Parker Gilbert, an American Reparations Agent in Germany. The Dawes Plan was accepted by Germany and the other Great Powers at the London Reparations Conference in August 1924.[235] France promised to withdraw troops from the Ruhr within a year. The first troops left in November 1924, and the last forces pulled out of the Ruhr in July 1925.[236]

Since the signing of the Treaty of Versailles the Weimar Republic had not enforced the provisions concerning the disarmament of the Reichswehr. General Seeckt, according to one historian, "had turned the Reichswehr into a state within a state."[237] One after another German cabinets dragged their feet on this question of forcing the Reichswehr to disarm. The Reichswehr itself was stubbornly committed to a policy of treaty evasion.[238] Stresemann, himself, was in favor of a strong army to support his foreign policy. As a matter of policy, Stresemann and the Wilhelmstrasse supported the secret rearmament of the Reichswehr and military collaboration with the Soviet Union. In fact, Stresemann

---

233.  Warren I. Cohen, *Empire without Tears: America's Foreign Relations, 1921-1933* (Philadelphia: Temple University Press, 1987), 1-99; Arnold A. Offner, *The Origins of the Second World War: American Foreign Policy and World Politics, 1917-1941* (Malabar: Krieger, 1986), 44-70.

234.  Rich, *Great Power Diplomacy since 1914*, 150.

235.  Henig, *The Weimar Republic, 1919-1933*, 41; Kolb, 58-59; Néré, 56-57; Feuchtwanger, 146-50.

236.  Adamthwaite, 105; Kolb, 61.

237.  Feuchtwanger, 179.

238.  Ibid., 170.

promoted such activity while "denying, explaining away, or screening German disarmament violations" to Western leaders.[239] As such, the Inter-Allied Military Control Commission (IMCC) was unable to force Germany to disarm to the levels as specified in the treaty. The Allies, according to the treaty, were supposed to withdraw from the Rhineland in three stages, with the first stage (Cologne) taking place in 1925.[240] However, in December 1924, the French and British governments informed Berlin that the Allies would not withdraw from the Cologne area until the IMCC was satisfied that Germany had honored its disarmament obligations. Once satisfied, the Allies would withdraw from the Cologne area and the IMCC would pass further responsibility for German disarmament to the League of Nations.[241] This situation presented Stresemann with the problem of gaining Allied withdrawal from Cologne without full German disarmament. The German Foreign Minister realized that Germany would have to resolve the French security crisis in order to gain the evacuation. With this in mind, in January and February 1925, Stresemann proposed to Britain and then France a Rhineland pact in which Germany would accept the Versailles peace settlement in the West, renounce war with France, and agree to submit any disputes with Poland over the eastern borders to arbitration.[242] In return, the German Foreign Minister expected the Allied evacuation of Cologne. As Martin Kitchen has stated, " Stresemann's hope was that the French would see a Rhineland pact as a better guarantee of their security than the disarmament of Germany and the occupation of the Rhineland, particularly in the absence of an Anglo-French military alliance."[243] France, Britain, and Germany talked about the possibility of a pact during the spring and summer of 1925. Finally, in October, Stresemann met with British Foreign Secretary Austen Chamberlain, French Foreign Minister Aristide Briand, Italian Prime Minister and Foreign Minister Benito Mussolini, and Belgian Foreign Minister Emile Vandervelde at Locarno in Switzerland. Count Alexandre Skrzyński, the Polish Foreign Minister, and Édouard Beneš, the Czech Foreign Minister, attended the last few days of the Locarno meeting.[244]

239. Gatzke, *Stresemann and the Rearmament of Germany*, 61, 110.
240. The second stage was Coblenz in 1930, followed by the third (Mainz) in 1935.
241. Marks, *The Illusion of Peace*, 62; Lee and Michalka, 81.
242. Jon Jacobson, *Locarno Diplomacy: Germany and the West, 1925-1929* (Princeton: Princeton University Press, 1972), 4-5, 12-35.
243. Kitchen, *Europe between the Wars*, 58-59.
244. Marks, 62-66.

In the resulting treaties, initialed at Locarno, Gustav Stresemann agreed to settlements in the West and East. In the West, Berlin, Paris, and Brussels accepted the Franco-German and Belgo-German borders that were established in the Treaty of Versailles. Germany gave up hope of recovering Alsace-Lorraine, Eupen, Malmédy, and Moresnet. This pact was guaranteed by Britain and Italy. Germany also accepted the continuing demilitarization of the Rhineland. In return, the first phase of the Allied occupation of the Rhineland would be ended, and the Inter-Allied Military Control Commission would be dissolved once Germany was accepted as a member of the League of Nations. Germany was promised a permanent seat on the League Council. The Council would be responsible for ensuring the further disarmament of Germany. As for the East, Stresemann, despite French and British insistence, would not guarantee Germany's borders with Poland or Czechoslovakia. Berlin still sought to regain the Polish Corridor, Danzig, and Upper Silesia. Stresemann was also concerned about the status of the German minority in Czechoslovakia. But, the German Foreign Minister agreed to arbitration treaties with Poland and Czechoslovakia to resolve future disputes by peaceful means.[245] The German arbitration treaties with Poland and Czechoslovakia were not guaranteed by any Great Powers.[246] Therefore, France concluded treaties of mutual assistance with Poland and Czechoslovakia to compensate for the lack of any German guarantee of the eastern frontiers.[247] One historian has summed up the Treaties of Locarno:

> The three powers had their reasons to be satisfied with their work, but these were very different. The French believed that they had guaranteed their security. Britain believed that they had given the French sufficient reassurance so as not to be tempted to act as foolishly as they had done in 1923. Germany saw the way open to revision of the eastern frontiers, eventually by force if necessary.[248]

The Reichstag ratified the Treaties of Locarno, also known as the Locarno or Rhineland Pact, in November. The Great Powers formally signed the Locarno Pact at a London Conference in December 1925.

---

245.   Jacobson, *Locarno Diplomacy*, 35-67; Ross, 59-60.

246.   Kolb, 62.

247.   Piotr S. Wandycz, *The Twilight of French Eastern Alliances, 1926-1936: French-Czechoslovak-Polish Relations from Locarno to the Remilitarization of the Rhineland* (Princeton: Princeton University Press, 1988), 14.

248.   Kitchen, *Europe between the Wars*, 62.

By the Locarno Pact Germany had rejoined the circle of the leading Great Powers of Europe. In January 1926, Allied forces withdrew from the Cologne area, completing the Allied withdrawal from the first of three Rhineland occupation zones.[249] But the French, British, and Belgians increased their troop strength to 75,000 men in the Coblenz and Mainz occupation zones.[250] Stresemann protested this move by the Allies. Then, in February, France and Poland placed an obstacle towards Germany's entrance into the League of Nations with a seat on the permanent League Council. Poland, backed by France, demanded a permanent seat too.[251] Consequently, the Reichstag Foreign Affairs Committee became adamant that Germany would enter the League only on the condition that it alone be given a permanent seat.[252] Berlin threatened to withdraw its application for admission. At this time, Germany's entrance into the League of Nations, planned for March, was delayed.[253] Finally, in September 1926, after France and Poland had backed down, Germany was admitted into the League of Nations with a permanent seat on the League Council.[254] Summing up Stresemann's foreign policy, Christoph M. Kimmich has written:

> Germany's admission to the League culminated a strategy which Stresemann had inaugurated in 1923. The economic détente opened by the Dawes plan led to the political détente of the Locarno pact. In her accession to the League, Germany returned to a position of international influence; as a permanent member of the council, she achieved formal parity with the great powers. It was the first step in Stresemann's grand design. He had brought Germany into the concert of European powers, and in this setting he could begin to revise the peace settlement.[255]

After the Locarno Pact, the Soviet Union feared the consequences of improved relations between Germany and the West. Moscow saw the League of Nations as an imperialist alliance against the Soviet Union.[256] Soviet Commissar for Foreign Affairs Georgii V. Chicherin knew that he was fighting a losing battle in trying to

---

249.  Kolb, 63.
250.  Jacobson, *Locarno Diplomacy*, 77.
251.  Kimmich, 78-79; Feuchtwanger, 174. Brazil also demanded a seat on the permanent League Council.
252.  Kimmich, 80.
253.  Ibid., 84.
254.  Kolb, 62.
255.  Kimmich, 90-91.
256.  R.H. Haigh, D.S. Morris, and A.R. Peters, *Soviet Foreign Policy, the League of Nations, and Europe, 1917-1939* (London: Gower, 1986), 7.

stop German rapprochement with the West. He had traveled to Berlin and pleaded with Stresemann not to join the League of Nations.[257] The German-Soviet Commercial Treaty signed by German Ambassador Ulrich von Brock-dorff-Rantzau and Maxim M. Litvinov, the Deputy Commissar for Soviet Foreign Affairs, in October 1925 "went a long way towards placating Soviet fears of Locarno."[258] Even so, Chicherin sought a non-aggression and neutrality pact with Germany.[259] He believed that a pact would balance Germany's relations between the East and West. On the German side, Stresemann and the Foreign Office sought close Russo-German relations to balance German relations with the East and West.[260] Moreover, General Seeckt and the Reichswehr sought closer Russo-German relations. The Reichswehr viewed Poland as the enemy and the main military threat to Germany since the Poles, with French backing, would not peacefully return the lost German lands.[261] According to Gaines Post, Jr., "the Army considered the Corridor vital to German security, regaining it, legitimate grounds for war."[262] It was in the midst of the crisis over Germany's entrance into the League of Nations that Chicherin and Stresemann agreed to the Treaty of Berlin in April 1926.[263] The treaty was a nonaggression and neutrality agreement that also reaffirmed the Treaty of Rapallo (1922).[264] The Treaty of Berlin was a success for both Germany and the Soviet Union. Poland became isolated from French assistance in the advent of a Russo-Polish war, and German hopes for a revision of the eastern borders were kept alive. For Poland, the Treaty of Berlin was a complete disaster.

The Locarno Pact led to improved relations between Germany and the West. The Inter-Allied Military Control Commission was withdrawn from Germany in January 1927. In that same year, France, Britain, and Belgium reduced their occupation forces to 60,000 men.[265] France, however, began the construction of the Maginot Line to defend its eastern border.[266] A Franco-German commercial

---

257.  O'Connor, 105.

258.  Haigh, *German-Soviet Relations in the Weimar Era*, 118.

259.  O'Connor, 109.

260.  Post, *The Civil Military Fabric of Weimar Foreign Policy*, 42.

261.  See Robert M. Citino, *The Evolution of Blitzkrieg Tactics: Germany Defends Itself against Poland, 1918-1933* (New York: Greenwood Press, 1987).

262.  Ibid., 100, 132.

263.  For the background of the negotiations that led up to the treaty, see Harvey Leonard Dyck, *Weimar Germany and Soviet Russia, 1926-1933: A Study in Diplomatic Instability* (New York: Columbia University Press, 1966), 13-65.

264.  Ibid., 13; Haigh, *German-Soviet Relations in the Weimar Era*, 119-20.

265.  Kitchen, *Europe between the Wars*, 66.

266.  Hughes, *To the Maginot Line*, 187-229.

treaty was signed in August 1927.[267] French Foreign Minister Briand suggested to the United States and other countries that they should sign a pact renouncing war as an instrument of policy. France, Germany, Britain, the United States, and other countries signed the Kellogg-Briand Pact outlawing war in August 1928.[268] Close on the heels of this pact, in October, was the German request to the League of Nations for an early evacuation of the Rhineland to the League of Nations. France and Britain insisted that such an agreement would have to be tied to a final reparations settlement.[269] As such, a committee of experts drew up the Young Plan. The plan was accepted at the First Hague Conference in August 1929.[270] Improved relations with the West, however, had a negative impact on Russo-German ties. Joseph Stalin feared the creation of a German alliance with the West against the Soviet Union. The Soviet Union began to back away from Germany.[271] Herbert von Dirksen, the German Ambassador to Moscow (1928-33), noted this change in relations in his memoirs and blamed Stresemann's Locarno policy with the West for ruining the close German-Soviet friendship that began at Rapallo.[272] Unfortunately, Stresemann did not live long enough to witness the success of his foreign policy in the West and the decline of Russo-German relations in the East. He died in October 1929. Summing up the diplomatic career of Stresemann, Viscount D'Abernon, the British Ambassador to Berlin (1920-26), stated:

> Stresemann may claim to have raised Germany from the position of a stricken and disarmed foe into that of a diplomatic equal, entitled to full consideration as a Great Power and enjoying international guarantee for the protection of her frontiers. To have accomplished this in a few years of power without the support of armed force is a feat worthy of those who have written their names most memorably on the scroll of fame. Stresemann left Germany infinitely stronger than when he took the helm in 1923, and Europe incomparably more peaceful. This achievement is the more remarkable in that Stresemann was not, by temperament, a pacifist.[273]

---

267.  Kolb, 63.
268.  Rich, *Great Power Diplomacy since 1914*, 153-54.
269.  Kolb, 64.
270.  Ibid.
271.  O'Connor, 112,
272.  Dirksen, 83.
273.  D'Abernon, 3:20.

## Foreign Office under Stresemann

Gustav Stresemann was the dominant force behind German foreign policy. He also took firm control over the Wilhelmstrasse. He gained full control over the Foreign Office by reassigning Foreign Secretary Baron Ago von Maltzan in December 1924. He sent Maltzan to Washington, D.C. as the German Ambassador to the United States (1924-28).[274] In his place, the Foreign Minister appointed Dr. Carl von Schubert, the former Chief of Department III in the Foreign Office, as the new State Secretary for Foreign Affairs (1924-30).[275] Stresemann wanted an "official who would be easier to handle than the autocratic initiator of the Rapallo-policy."[276] Those diplomats who remained in Berlin and abroad quickly became loyal to the Foreign Minister.[277] Herbert von Dirksen, the Deputy Director of the Eastern Department (1925-28), made the following observation:

> Stresemann, a member of the lower middle-class in the eastern suburbs of Berlin, was, when he took office, not altogether free from suspicion and a sense of inferiority towards the nobility and the diplomats. But soon he became convinced of the loyalty and the devotion of the Foreign Office staff. A feeling of mutual trust, amounting to friendship, developed between him and his colleagues.[278]

During the Stresemann era, the Wilhelmstrasse emerged once again as a major contributor to the formulation of German foreign policy. Its newly found influence was a result of Stresemann's influence in the Reichstag, as well as the Weimar Republic's obvious need for an effective foreign policy formulated and carried out by an efficient, centralized agency with the aim of ridding Germany of the Versailles Diktat and restoring its Great Power status. Stresemann served as the head of this organization, the Foreign Office, and directed foreign policy. However, the Foreign Minister was too busy with his duties in the Reichstag to closely manage the administrative affairs of the Foreign Office.[279] Instead, "a mutual trust and respect," according to Gaines Post, Jr., "grew between Stresemann and the officials in the Wilhelmstrasse."[280] Ernst von Weizsäcker, a young

---

274.  Ibid., 2:42; Offner, 50-51.
275.  Feuchtwanger, 170.
276.  Dirksen, 41.
277.  Grathwol, 6.
278.  Dirksen, 45-46.
279.  Ibid., 42, 46.
280.  Post, *The Civil Military Fabric of Weimar Foreign Policy*, 18.

diplomat in the foreign service, noted that the Foreign Minister only spent mornings at the Foreign Office. In fact, Weizsäcker claimed that, "in the Foreign Office he [Stressemann] knew only a few of the officials; he was a stranger to the rank and file. He was ignorant of a great deal that went on there."[281] In addition to this, Dirksen has stated:

> The routine work of a complicated bureaucratic machine bored him, and he would have tried to evade it even if he could have spared the time for it. He was thoroughly unbureaucratic, and he could drive his subordinates to despair by his failure to keep appointments or draw up minutes of his conversations.[282]

Left alone much of the time, the Foreign Office, under the careful management of Foreign Secretary Schubert, once again became a close-knit, elite organization. Schubert, "a strange and very complicated man" has been portrayed by a fellow diplomat:

> [He had] an outspoken gift for foreign politics...combined with very painstaking and conscientious routine work. He was suspicious, secretive, and lacked the gift of taking things easily and confining himself to the really important matters. He made life a burden to his collaborators, but still more to himself. He was passionately devoted to his task and believed that everything would be on the rocks if he were out of his office. A Westerner by birth and career, he was a convinced advocate of the pro-British school in the German foreign service. But he was sufficiently far-sighted and politically minded to take into consideration the duty incumbent on the conduct of German foreign policy: to counter-balance the Western influences by a good understanding with Russia.[283]

Schubert reorganized the leadership of the departments within the Foreign Office. He placed career diplomats, instead of civil servants, to serve as directors of key positions. These new directors became vital to Foreign Office operations. As Dirksen explained:

---

281.  Ernst von Weizsäcker, *Memoirs of Ernst von Weizsäcker*, trans. John Andrews (London: Victor Gollancz, 1951), 68.
282.  Dirksen, 46.
283.  Ibid., 43. For further descriptions of Schubert, see D'Abernon, 3:27 and Jacobson, *Locarno Diplomacy*, 176-77.

The newly appointed 'Directors' were entrusted with important political negotiations. They accompanied the [Foreign] Minister to conferences, they drafted the notes, negotiated with the Embassies, and had direct access to the Secretary of State and the [Foreign] Minister. They were often party to the most secret affairs…. Schubert set up a so-called 'Bureau of Ministers' in which these highly confidential matters were concentrated, but he shrank from the decisive step of forming a new political department.[284]

The leading officials within the Auswärtiges Amt formed an inner circle that worked closely together over issues. Although staying away from much of the Wilhelmstrasse's bureaucratic activities, Stresemann was a close friend of this inner circle.[285] It was under his leadership that the Foreign Office became a very important asset to the Weimar Republic.

Foreign Minister Stresemann and the Wilhelmstrasse were the prime formulators of German foreign policy.[286] At first, however, the Foreign Minister experienced problems with General Hans von Seeckt, the Chief of Staff of the Reichswehr. Stresemann had inherited the dual policies concerning the West and the Soviet Union. Stresemann favored the pursuit of both policies and planned to steer a middle course between the West and Moscow, playing one off against the other, to gradually regain sovereignty and security for Germany.[287] He also insisted upon the Reichswehr subordinating itself to the goals of German foreign policy.[288] General Seeckt, on the other hand, disliked Stresemann's leanings towards the West, especially France, and objected to the Locarno Pact and plans for Germany to join the League of Nations.[289] But Seeckt was dismissed from his position after he allowed the eldest son of the German Crown Prince to participate in army maneuvers in uniform in 1926. Afterwards, the Reichswehr had less political influence, especially in foreign policy, in the Weimar Republic.[290]

In 1926, General Wilhelm Heye replaced Seeckt as Chief of Staff of the Reichswehr. Under new leadership, the Defense Ministry cooperated with Stresemann in the mutual aim of restoring German military power and Great Power status. The Defense Ministry changed its own independent policy after recognizing the need to work closely with the diplomats in pursuing a rapprochement

---

284. Dirksen, 42.
285. Ibid., 45.
286. Post, *The Civil Military Fabric of Weimar Foreign Policy*, 14, 23.
287. Craig, *Aspects of German Statecraft*, 82; Dirksen, 41; Grathwol, 5.
288. Hans W. Gatzke, *Stresemann and the Rearmament of Germany* (Baltimore: Johns Hopkins Press, 1954), 25; Post, *The Civil Military Fabric of Weimar Foreign Policy*, 136.
289. Gatzke, *Stresemann and the Rearmament of Germany*, 38.
290. Feuchtwanger, 179-80.

with France to provide Germany security against a possible Franco-Polish attack, especially since the military lacked sufficient resources to fight a two-front war.[291] In fact, the Wehrmacht subordinated and integrated its military planning with Stresemann's foreign policy to avoid discrediting Germany in the European diplomatic system. This allowed the Foreign Minister to play the middle ground between the Soviet Union and the West in an attempt to achieve his policy goals of the regaining full German sovereignty and security, as well as the revision of the Versailles Treaty. Close cooperation between the Foreign Office and Defense Ministry was evident in their joint planning, use of military attachés in diplomatic roles, use of diplomats in military operations, and campaign for revision of the military clauses in the Treaty of Versailles.[292]

## Foreign Policy under Curtius and Brüning, 1929-1932

The stabilization of the Weimar Republic came to an abrupt end in 1929 and 1930. The crash of the New York Stock Exchange began a world economic crisis in October 1929. In the meantime, President Paul von Hindenburg and Chancellor Hermann Müller-Franken needed to replace Stresemann with someone who could take control of German foreign policy. The death of Stresemann left the Wilhelmstrasse without a strong leader who would continue a policy of reconciliation with the West. Baron Constantin von Neurath, the German Ambassador to Rome, turned down President Hindenburg's offer to become Foreign Minister in 1929.[293] Instead, Julius Curtius assumed the position. Curtius, a member of the German People's Party, had been the Economics Minister for Germany from 1926 to 1929. He was a strong supporter for the revision of the Treaty of Versailles.[294] As Foreign Minister, Curtius had to concentrate on carrying out Stresemann's revisionist foreign policies. However, the new minister, according to one Foreign Office member, "lacked the authority and vision which had elevated Stresemann to the rank of a European statesman."[295] Sir Horace Rumbold, the British Ambassador to Berlin (1928-33), believed Curtius although "honest, straightforward, and meticulous when engaged in detailed

291.   Post, *The Civil Military Fabric of Weimar Foreign Policy*,

292.   Ibid., 129-30.

293.   John L. Heineman, *Hitler's First Foreign Minister: Constantin Freiherr von Neurath, Diplomat and Statesman* (Berkeley: University of California Press, 1979), 38.

294.   William G. Ratliff, *Faithful to the Fatherland: Julius Curtius and Weimar Foreign Policy* (New York: Peter Lang, 1990), 2, 13

295.   Dirksen, 86.

negotiations, had no sense of political mission. Thoughtful and conciliatory by nature, he was no great leader."[296]

The Weimar Republic continued to carry out Stresemann's foreign policy after his death. The Allied Powers withdrew from the Coblenz area of the Rhineland in November 1929.[297] The Reichstag ratified the Young Plan in March 1930. The Young Plan set the total reparations payment at 112,000 million Reichsmarks. Germany was required to pay about 2,000 million Reichsmarks a year for the next fifty years. With the acceptance of this agreement, the Allied Powers promised to withdraw from the Mainz area of the Rhineland by the end of June 1930.[298]

In March 1930, Chancellor Müller-Franken's coalition government collapsed. A new coalition was formed, led by Chancellor Heinrich Brüning of the Catholic Center Party. Curtius stayed on as the Reich Foreign Minister, but Brüning sought to exercise personal control over German foreign policy.[299] The Chancellor's main interest and ambitions lay in foreign policy.[300] One historian has argued that Brüning's main goal was the end of reparations payments.[301] Brüning, according to Gordon A. Craig, was a "headstrong and willful statesman who believed that action was always better than inaction, even if it was taken without reflection, and whose tactics in foreign affairs did not bring advantage to his country."[302] On the other hand, Ernst von Weizsäcker believed that Brüning was "the one who moved with the greatest assurance along the narrow path between German needs and foreign resistance. With his tough and yet courteous, ascetic yet generous, nature, he won confidence in international circles."[303]

In May, Foreign Minister Curtius, under the direction of Brüning, worked to enhance Germany's world image by joining in the promotion of European disarmament, an idea that grew out of the Kellogg-Briand Pact.[304] Curtius began to devote most of his attention to the League of Nations disarmament negotiations in Geneva. The Foreign Office, backed by the Reichswehr, sought a reduction of

---

296.  Sir Horace Rumbold to Marquess of Reading, 6 October 1931, *DBFP*, second series, 2:278-79.

297.  Steiner, *The Lights That Failed*, 846.

298.  Kolb, 64.

299.  Ratliff, 64.

300.  Wolfgang J. Helbich, "Between Stresemann and Hitler: The Foreign Policy of the Brüning Government," *World Politics* 12 (October 1959), 32.

301.  Ibid., 33.

302.  Craig, *Aspects of German Statecraft*, 85.

303.  Weizsäcker, 76.

304.  Ratliff, 72.

arms among France, Poland, Czechoslovakia, Belgium, Italy, and Germany.[305] In June, the Allied Powers withdrew from the Mainz Region, the last occupation zone in the Rhineland.[306]

At this point, Chancellor Brüning and his supporters believed the time was right for making new demands. But, the British government warned Berlin against forcing France into considering more concessions too soon. In July 1930, Lord Tyrell, the British Ambassador to France commented:

> If the Germans create the impression here that they do not appreciate the spirit of [the French withdrawal from the Rhineland] and merely use it as a peg on which to hang fresh demands, they will play into the hands of M. Briand's critics. The advice, therefore, to Germany is that in her own interest she had better go slow now and rest content for the present with what Stresemann's enlightened policy has already achieved for her.[307]

Now, however, Chancellor Brüning changed German foreign policy from conciliation to a more nationalistic policy. Germany's new policy was "a more strident, impatient diplomatic method."[308] The swing in German foreign policy reflected the growing right-wing leanings of Germany. Nationalist parties were gaining the support of the people. In the Reichstag election results of September 1930 the National Socialist German Worker's Party received the second largest percentage of the vote at 18.3 percent. The Social Democratic Party dropped from 29.8 to 24.5 percent in this election.[309] Moreover, in September, the League of Nations Preparatory Commission for the Disarmament Conference, which was heavily influenced by France, issued a draft convention that called for numerical limitations on troop strength, a quota on the number of active-duty troops, a limit on tenure of service, and a ceiling on equipment expenditures. This proposal was immediately opposed by Foreign Minister Curtius and the Weimar Republic.[310] The Commission's plan would provide Germany's neighbors with a permanent military advantage.[311] By the end of 1930, with little progress having been made

---

305.   Ibid., 73.

306.   Steiner, *The Lights That Failed*, 847.

307.   Lord Tyrell to Arthur Henderson, 3 July 1930, *DBFP*, second series, 1:479.

308.   Ratliff, 75.

309.   Kolb, 194-95.

310.   Ratliff, 73-74.

311.   John W. Wheeler-Bennett, *Disarmament and Security since Locarno, 1925-1931* (London: Allen and Unwin, 1932), 73, 99-100.

on the disarmament question, the League of Nations agreed to convene a new Disarmament Conference in 1932.

In June 1930, Dr. Bernhard Wilhelm von Bülow replaced Schubert as the State Secretary for Foreign Affairs.[312] Schubert was appointed German Ambassador to Rome. Bülow had previously served the Wilhelmstrasse in the League of Nations Department.[313] He was a nephew of the prewar Chancellor. One foreign diplomat described the State Secretary as "filled with zeal and devotion to duty as he was silent and discreet, a statesman worthy of the traditions of a Prussian family which has given Germany numerous and honorable servants."[314] Christoph M. Kimmich has described Bülow as a diplomat with "excellent qualifications: a critical turn of mind, a great knowledge of international affairs, a good grasp of the legal dimension of diplomacy, and experience and expertise."[315] Bülow believed that the time was right for Germany "to embark on a greater activity," and push for an end to the Versailles restrictions.[316]

At the Second Hague Conference, in January 1930, Foreign Minister Curtius held secret talks with Austrian Chancellor Johannes Schober regarding the union of Germany and Austria.[317] German annexation of Austria would be a direct violation of the Treaty of Versailles. Then, in February, Schober visited Berlin and indicated that Austria was in favor of an economic union with Germany. With the formation of the Brüning Cabinet in March, Berlin sought a more assertive foreign policy. Brüning was willing to ignore French warnings about closer Austro-German relations. In the summer and fall of 1930, the German Foreign Office moved toward creating an economic union with Austria. Such action was a direct violation of the Treaties of Versailles and St. Germain which prohibited the uniting of Germany and Austria.[318] But the Brüning and Schober governments scheduled negotiations for a customs union for early 1931. Kar Ritter, the Chief of the Economics Department at the Auswärtiges Amt, was responsible for drawing up the agreement for a customs union.[319]

---

312. Post, *The Civil-Military Fabric of Weimar Foreign Policy*, 268.

313. Dirksen, 42, 88.

314. André François-Poncet, *The Fateful Years: Memoirs of a French Ambassador in Berlin, 1931-1938*, trans. Jacques LeClercq (New York: Harcourt, Brace and Company, 1949), 30.

315. Kimmich, 42.

316. F.G. Stambrook, "The German-Austrian Customs Project of 1931: A Study of German Methods and Motives," *Journal of Central European Affairs* 21 (1961), 20; Heinrich Brüning, *Memoiren, 1918-1934* (Stuttgart: Deutsche Verlags-Anstalt, 1970), 264-70.

317. Ratliff, 80-81.

318. Ibid., 72, 78, 86.

319. Ibid., 125.

In March 1931, Foreign Minister Curtius traveled to Vienna for a meeting with Austrian Chancellor Otto Ender and now Vice-Chancellor and Foreign Minister Johannes Schober to negotiate a customs union. They hammered out a preliminary agreement on 5 March. They also decided to present the customs union as a *fait accompli* to the rest of Europe.[320] Sixteen days later, on 21 March, German and Austrian diplomats announced the creation of the Austro-German Customs Union in Paris, London, and Rome.[321] The French government immediately denounced the customs union. The unexpected joint announcement led to strong international protests, especially by France, "alarmed by what it considered the spectre of a reawakening German hegemony in Central Europe."[322] In April, France demanded that both Germany and Austria suspend the Customs Union until the League of Nations Council of Ministers had been consulted. In the midst of this crisis, Austria and Germany suffered a banking crisis. In May, the Austrian Credit-Anstalt, the largest Austrian bank, collapsed. Then the Weimar Republic announced that Germany would suspend reparations payments. As a result, a massive amount of foreign and German funds were withdrawn from German banks. By the middle of July all German banks were closed. The crisis resulted in President Herbert Hoover of the United States declaring a one-year moratorium on international reparations payments. He believed that the financial and economic collapse of Germany would have disastrous consequences for the United States and the international system.[323] Wolfgang J. Helbich called this a major success for Brüning's foreign policy. It was one more step towards the end of German reparations.[324] In the midst of the economic crisis, the International Court of Justice finally gave the ruling that the Austro-German Customs Union was in violation of the Geneva Protocol of 1922. Summing up the Customs Union crisis, André François-Poncet, the French Ambassador to Berlin, wrote in his memoirs:

> The result proved catastrophic. Both the great and smaller powers rose in a storm of unanimous reprobation. France reacted with particular force. Germany and Austria were compelled to stand as culprits in the dock before the Council of the League of Nations at Geneva, whence their case was referred for arbitration by the International Court at The Hague.[325]

---

320.  Ibid., 128-29.
321.  Ibid., 133-34.
322.  Franz von Papen, *Memoirs*, trans. Brian Connell (New York: E.P. Dutton, 1953), 175.
323.  See Edward W. Bennett, *Germany and the Diplomacy of the Financial Crisis, 1931* (Cambridge, MA: Harvard University Press, 1962).
324.  Helbich, 37.
325.  François-Poncet, 5.

Germany was forced to back down because of international pressure. Both Brüning and Curtius suffered a serious defeat, although Bülow and the Foreign Office
lost little prestige over the incident. In the aftermath of this incident Curtius
resigned as the head of the Wilhelmstrasse in October 1931,[326] leaving Brüning
to act as his own Foreign Minister.[327]

Serving as Chancellor and Foreign Minister, Heinrich Brüning had to reply
on the expertise of State Secretary Bernhard Wilhelm von Bülow and the
Auswärtiges Amt for carrying out foreign affairs.[328] The Foreign Secretary
worked close with Chancellor Brüning on foreign policy issues.[329] But, as one
observer has noted about the highly intelligent Bülow:

> His wide knowledge of international affairs in their most varied aspects were
> somewhat handicapped by a critical and analytical mind which prevented a
> positive and creative approach to political problems. His analysis of every situ-
> ation was so thorough that he always found weighty reasons for a policy of
> "wait and see."[330]

Reparations and disarmament were the two major issues on the agenda for 1932.
Brüning andBülow pressed for an international conference to settle the reparations issue once and for all. But the meeting scheduled for Lausanne in January
was postponed.[331] Even so, the Great Powers convened at Geneva to discuss disarmament at the Conference for the Reduction and Limitation of Armaments
(WorldDisarmament Conference) on 2 February 1932. It was the biggest international gathering since the Paris Peace Conference of 1919. The conference was
under the chairmanship of former British Foreign Secretary Arthur Henderson
(1929-31). At the conference, Britain and the United States called for all countries to reduce or get rid of offensive weapons. France and its East European
allies, along with Belgium, were not interested in general disarmament. They
feared German rearmament. In fact, France indicated that it would block all
attempts by Germany to gain concessions. Brüning, when he addressed the conference on 9 February, stressed that the conference's "greatest responsibility" was
to secure disarmament "on the basis of equal rights and equal security for all peo-

---

326.  Papen, 143; Marks, 121.
327.  Dirksen, 101; Post, *The Civil-Military Fabric of Weimar Foreign Policy*, 266.
328.  Erich Eyck, *A History of the Weimar Republic*, trans. Harlan P. Hanson and Robert G.L.
      Waite, 2 vols. (Cambridge, MA: Harvard University Press, 1962-63), 2:331-32.
329.  Dirksen, 101.
330.  Ibid., 102. See also François-Poncet, 175.
331.  Feuchtwanger, 273.

ples."[332] Just over a week later, on 18 February, Rudolf Nadolny, the head of the German delegation, urged the conference to have the disarmament standards set by the Treaty of Versailles apply equally to all nations. He urged for certain offensive weapons, such as tanks, aircraft, and heavy artillery, to be banned, and all other armaments to be reduced.[333] The general debate at the conference was over by the end of February. The talks then became bogged down with political negotiations and a recess for the political elections in France and Germany. In April, President Paul von Hindenburg received 53 percent of the votes in his bid for reelection. He defeated Adolf Hitler of the National Socialists (36.8 percent of the vote) and Ernst Thälmann of the Communist Party (10.2 percent).[334] At this point, General Wilhelm Groener, the Reich Minister of Interior and Minister of Defense convinced Hindenburg and Brüning to ban Nazi paramilitary organizations, namely the Sturmabteilung (SA) and Schutzstaffel (SS).[335] Consequently the National Socialists and other rightist forces increased their opposition to the Brüning Cabinet. General Kurt von Schleicher, the head of the Defense Department's Ministeramt, or political bureau, conspired with the National Socialists against Chancellor Brüning and General Groener. Schleicher was able to drum up support from the German officer corps to force Groener's resignation on 12 May. Three weeks later, on 30 May 1932, President Hindenburg forced Brüning to tender his resignation as Reich Chancellor and Foreign Minister. President Hindenburg appointed Franz von Papen of the Catholic Center Party as the new Reich Chancellor of a presidential government and General Schleicher as the Minister of Defense.[336] Although, the Wilhelmstrasse, according to Ernst von Weizsäcker, regretted the departure of Brüning,[337] the change meant the appointment of one of their own, Baron Constantin von Neurath, as the new Foreign Minister.[338]

332.  Conference for the Reduction and Limitation of Armaments, *Records of the Conference for the Reduction and Limitation of Armaments, Series A, Verbatim Records of Plenary Meetings,* (Geneva: Conference for the Reduction and Limitation of Armaments, 1932-34), 1:67-70.

333.  Kimmich, 161. See also Edward W. Bennett, *German Rearmament and the West, 1932-1933* (Princeton: Princeton University Press, 1979).

334.  Kolb, 117.

335.  Craig, *Germany, 1866-1945*, 559.

336.  Marks, 128.

337.  Weizsäcker, 76.

338.  Kolb, 118.

# 5

# *Neurath, the Foreign Office, and the Rise of Hitler*

## Constantin von Neurath as Foreign Minister

Baron Constantin von Neurath was born in Württemberg in 1873. As a member of an aristocratic Swabian family with a long history of service to the kings of Württemberg, he broke with family tradition and entered Kaiser William II's consulate service in Berlin in 1901. He served abroad in London from 1903 to 1908 in the German Consulate before transferring to the German Diplomatic Service in 1913. In 1919, the Weimar Republic appointed Neurath as Minister to Denmark. He later served as Ambassador to Italy and managed German-Italian relations with the Fascist government of Benito Mussolini from 1922 to 1930. President Paul von Hindenburg, a close friend, was instrumental in acquiring Neurath's appointment as Ambassador to Britain from 1930 to 1932.[1] Hindenburg, however, preferred Neurath to become Foreign Minister. Both the President and former Chancellor Heinrich Brüning had asked him several times during 1931 and 1932 to accept such an appointment,[2] but Neurath, who enjoyed living in London, declined because of his conservative based distaste for serving in a parliamentary government cabinet. Neurath, who was not affiliated with any political parties, strongly disliked all political parties and parliaments, preferring a more autocratic type of government like that which existed under the

---

1.  John Louis Heineman, "Constantin Freiherr von Neurath as Foreign Minister, 1932-1935: A Study of a Conservative Civil Servant and Germany's Foreign Policy," (Ph.D. thesis, Cornell University, 1965), 50-76; John L. Heineman, *Hitler's First Foreign Minister: Constantin Freiherr von Neurath, Diplomat and Statesman* (Berkeley: University of California Press, 1979), 7-32; Constantin von Neurath testimony, 22 June 1946, *TMWC*, 16:593-94.
2.  Neurath testimony, 22 June 1946, *TMWC* 16:599; Heineman, "Constantin Freiherr von Neurath as Foreign Minister, 1932-1935," 81-83.

Kaiser.[3] As Neurath, himself, told the International Military Tribunal in 1946 why he refused an appointment to Foreign Minister:

> In view of the party conditions in the Reichstag in those days, I saw no possibility for a stable foreign policy. I was not a member of any of the thirty or so parties, so that I would not have been able to [find]…support in the Reichstag of those days.[4]

Neurath insisted that he would only become Foreign Minister under a party-free presidential cabinet that showed the promise of restoring leadership and stability to Germany.[5]

In May 1932, while still in London, Neurath received another offer from Hindenburg to become Foreign Minister. Hindenburg, who saw Neurath as a prudent, moderate, and reliable diplomat,[6] appealed to his close friend to travel to Berlin and discuss the matter.[7] In Berlin, Neurath told the President that he would only serve as Foreign Minister under a strong presidential cabinet that allowed him to formulate and conduct foreign policy without any interference.[8] On 2 June 1932, Hindenburg agreed to these terms and appointed Neurath as Foreign Minister in the newly formed cabinet, despite Chancellor Franz von Papen and Defense Minister General Kurt von Schleicher's support for the diplomats Rudolf Nadolny or Ulrich von Hassell.[9]

The State Secretary for Foreign Affairs, Dr. Bernhard Wilhelm von Bülow, and the leading members of the Auswärtiges Amt supported the appointment of Neurath over the other candidates.[10] They desired a Foreign Minister who would

---

3.    Curt Prüfer affidavit, 16 April 1946, *TMWC*, 16:600-1, 40:450-60; Heineman, "Constantin Freiherr von Neurath as Foreign Minister, 1932-1935," 50-52, 85.

4.    Neurath testimony, 22 June 1946, *TMWC*, 16:599.

5.    Heineman, "Constantin Freiherr von Neurath as Foreign Minister, 1932-1935," 85; Heineman, *Hitler's First Foreign Minister*, 40.

6.    Gerhard Köpke testimony, 26 June 1946, *TMWC*, 17:108.

7.    Paul von Hindenburg to Constantin von Neurath, 31 May 1932, *TMWC*, 40:460.

8.    Neurath testimony, 22 June 1946, *TMWC*, 16:600; Heineman, "Constantin Freiherr von Neurath as Foreign Minister, 1932-1935," 91; Heineman, *Hitler's First Foreign Minister*, 40, 45.

9.    Franz von Papen, *Memoirs*, trans. Brian Connell (New York: E.P. Dutton, 1953), 159; Neurath testimony, 22 June 1946, *TMWC*, 16:600; Köpke to Rümelin, 2 June 1932, *TMWC*, 40:461; Gerhard L. Weinberg, *The Foreign Policy of Hitler's Germany*, 2 vols. (Chicago: University of Chicago Press, 1970-80), 1:35-36.

10.    Köpke to Rümelin, 2 June 1932, *TMWC*, 40:461-65; Heineman, "Constantin Freiherr von Neurath as Foreign Minister, 1932-1935," 89; Heineman, *Hitler's First Foreign Minister*, 46.

continue the moderate foreign policy of Stresemann and Brüning. Neurath, as Ambassador to Britain, had represented Brüning's policy with the British and believed in continuing the former Chancellor's program.[11] Hans Dieckhoff, the Director of Department III (British-American) in the Foreign Office, believed Neurath to be a "man of high standards and an experienced diplomat."[12] Bülow, who many have viewed as "the most influential figure" in the Foreign Office during the early thirties,[13] believed Neurath's closeness and access to Hindenburg would strongly support the Wilhelmstrasse and its policy of gradual revision to the Versailles Treaty.[14] Bülow represented the peaceful policy of restoring Germany as a Great Power in Central Europe, including territorial revision in East Europe and the annexation of Austria.[15]

Neurath and Bülow held similar views concerning foreign relations. Bülow, however, served his superior not only as the administrator of the Foreign Office, but as the "intellectual father" of Neurath's foreign policy.[16] Both Bülow and Neurath advocated the continuation of Brüning's revisionist policy aimed at acquiring from the victors of World War I the acknowledgment of equal rights for Germany, an end of reparations, and territorial boundary changes in East Europe.[17] Neurath, who had been German Ambassador to Britain and Italy, and Bülow together desired improved German relations with Britain and Italy to gain leverage against France in negotiating revisions to the Treaty of Versailles.[18] They, along with Herbert von Dirksen and Rudolf Nadolny, promoted closer German relations with the Soviet Union to counterbalance any influence that

11.    Hans Dieckhoff testimony, 26 June 1946, *TMWC*, 17:121; Heineman, *Hitler's First Foreign Minister*, 57.

12.    Dieckhoff testimony, 26 June 1946, *TMWC*, 17:121.

13.    Marshall M. Lee and Wolfgang Michalka, *German Foreign Policy 1917-1933: Continuity or Break?* (Leamington Spa: Berg, 1987), 143; Hermann Rauschning, *Men of Chaos* (New York: G.P. Putnam's Sons, 1942), 172-76. For a character description of Bülow, see André François-Poncet, *The Fateful Years: Memoirs of a French Ambassador in Berlin, 1931-1938*, trans. Jacques LeClercq (New York: Harcourt, Brace and Company, 1949), 182.

14.    Rauschning, *Men of Chaos*, 179; Sir Horace Rumbold to Sir John Simon, British Foreign Secretary, 28 September 1932, *DBFP*, second series, 4:201; Heineman, "Constantin Freiherr von Neurath as Foreign Minister, 1932-1935," 102.

15.    Lee and Michalka, 145-46.

16.    Ibid., 143.

17.    Ibid., 136, 145; John Hiden, *Germany and Europe, 1919-1939* (London: Longman, 1977), 32; Klaus Hildebrand, *The Third Reich*, trans. P.S. Falla (London: George Allen and Unwin, 1984), 15; Heineman, "Constantin Freiherr von Neurath as Foreign Minister, 1932-1935," 136-42; Heineman, *Hitler's First Foreign Minister*, 57, 86.

18.    Lee and Michalka, 136, 138.

France held in East Europe.[19] Describing Neurath's foreign policy to the Nuremberg court, Hans Dieckhoff stated:

> It was the aim of Herr von Neurath to maintain good relations with all states and thereby to re-establish gradually Germany's status of equal rights which we had lost in 1919. This was the same policy that had been pursued by Stresemann and Brüning. Herr von Neurath was aware of the difficulties of Germany's position. His tendency was to exercise moderation.[20]

In his own words, Constantin von Neurath told the International Military Tribunal:

> It was my view that the solution of the various political problems could be achieved only by peaceful means and step by step. Complete equality for Germany in all fields, in the military field therefore as well, and also the restoration of sovereignty in the entire territory of the Reich and the elimination of any discrimination were prerequisite conditions. But to achieve this was primarily the first task of German foreign policy.[21]

But, in the case of lost German territories, Neurath strongly believed that Germany needed to rearm and threaten to use force in order to reacquire these lands if diplomacy ultimately failed.[22]

## From Papen to Hitler

Chancellor Franz von Papen had little support during his short time in office. President Paul von Hindenburg and General Kurt von Schleicher, the Minister of Defense, were the political power in the government. Schleicher had the support of the Reichswehr.[23] He also had a working agreement with Adolf Hitler and the National Socialists. They had driven Heinrich Brüning from the chancellorship. The ban on the Sturmabteilung and Schutzstaffel was lifted on 16 June

---

19.    Ibid., 146-47. Although Neurath and Bülow were for maintaining friendly relations with the Soviet Union, according to one source, Bülow "sought to keep German-Soviet dealings on a cool and noncommittal level," and Neurath held a "cool, self-assured reserve" regarding Russo-German relations (Gustav Hilger and Alfred G. Meyer, *The Incompatible Allies: A Memoir-History of German-Soviet Relations, 1918-1941* [New York: Macmillan, 1953], 250, 265).

20.    Dieckhoff testimony, 26 June 1946, *TMWC*, 17:122.

21.    Neurath testimony, 22 June 1946, *TMWC*, 16:604.

22.    Heineman, *Hitler's First Foreign Minister*, 87.

23.    E.J. Feuchtwanger, *From Weimar to Hitler: Germany, 1918-1933* (New York: St. Martin's Press, 1993), 280.

1932. Now, the Reichstag was dissolved and a new election was held on 31 July. The National Socialists promised not to oppose a nationalist presidential government.[24] In the Reichstag election, the Nationalist Socialists collected 37.3 percent of the vote, while the Social Democrats got 21.6 percent, the Communists 13.1 percent, and the Catholic Center Party 12.5 percent of the vote.[25] The NSDAP scored a remarkable success but did not gain an absolute majority. Immediately after the election, Adolf Hitler talked to General Schleicher and informed him that the National Socialists would not tolerate the Papen Cabinet. Hitler wanted to be appointed the head of the German government. But, Hindenburg kept Franz von Papen as the Reich Chancellor. Even so, the Reichstag defeated the Papen Cabinet with a vote of no confidence (512 to 42 votes).[26] Papen was supported by just the German National People's Party and German People's Party. Hindenburg and Papen immediately dissolved the Reichstag. In the Reichstag election of November 1932, the National Socialists received 33.1 percent of the vote. The Social Democrats acquired 20.4 percent, Communists 16.9 percent, Catholic Center 11.9 percent, and the German National People's Party got 8.3 percent of the vote.[27] Hitler pressed Hindenburg for the chancellorship. But, Hindenburg chose Schleicher to replace Papen as Reich Chancellor in a presidential government in December 1932.[28]

Hitler continued his fight for the chancellorship. He formed a coalition with Franz von Papen who sought to oust Schleicher from government. In the meantime, Chancellor Schleicher, who had inadequate support in the Reichstag, sought the dissolution of this newly elected body. President Hindenburg denied this request, forcing Schleicher to tender his resignation on 28 January 1933. Two days later, on 30 January, President Hindenburg appointed Adolf Hitler as the Reich Chancellor of a presidential government.[29] Franz von Papen became the Vice Chancellor. The new cabinet included General Werner von Blomberg as Minister of Defense, Wilhelm Frick as Minister of the Interior, Alfred Hugen-

---

24.   Eberhard Kolb, *The Weimar Republic*, trans. P.S. Falla (London: Unwin Hyman, 1988), 120.

25.   Ibid., 195.

26.   Ibid., 121.

27.   Feuchtwanger, 326.

28.   Kolb, 123.

29.   See Erich Eyck, *A History of the Weimar Republic*, trans. Harlan P. Hanson and Robert G.L. Waite, 2 vols. (Cambridge, MA: Harvard University Press, 1962-63), 2:448-87; William L. Shirer, *The Rise and Fall of the Third Reich: A History of Nazi Germany* (London: Secker and Warburg, 1959), 177-87; and Ian Kershaw, *Hitler*, 2 vols. (New York: W.W. Norton, 1998-2000), 1:413-23. For Joachim von Ribbentrop's role in Hitler's appointment as Chancellor, see Michael Bloch, *Ribbentrop* (New York: Crown, 1992), 22-33.

berg as Minister of Economics, Count Lutz Schwerin von Krosigk as Minister of Finance, and Hermann Göring as Minister without Portfolio. Hitler, Frick, and Göring were from the NSDAP.[30] The Hitler Cabinet, however, did not have a parliamentary majority. It was therefore decided to hold new Reichstag elections. In the buildup to the elections, Hindenburg issued a presidential decree on 4 February that made it possible to suppress the publication of Communist newspapers and political meetings. The National Socialists came down hard on the Communist Party. Then, on 27 February, the Reichstag building caught fire. The government immediately announced that the fire had been set by the Communists as a signal to launch the Bolshevik revolution. The following day, on 28 February, President Hindenburg, citing the Communist threat, issued an emergency decree authorizing the arrest of all members of the Communist Party and the suspension of civil liberties for the entire country. In the Reichstag election, on 5 March, the National Socialists obtained just 43.9 percent of the vote. Hitler's majority rule in the Reichstag relied upon a coalition with Alfred Hugenberg and the German National People's Party, which received 8 percent of the vote.[31] But, with the passing of the Enabling Act by the Reichstag, Hitler gained the power to rule by decree on 23 March 1933. Soon all political parties, except the Nazi Party, were illegal in Germany. By the end of the year the Nazi Party had achieved a monopoly on political power in Germany.[32]

## Lausanne and Geneva Conferences

The reparations conference that former Chancellor Heinrich Brüning sought convened at Lausanne, Switzerland, on 16 June 1932. The conference was under the chairmanship of British Prime Minister James Ramsay MacDonald (1929-35). Chancellor Franz von Papen went to the conference with plans to offer the French government under Prime Minister and Foreign Minister Édouard Herriot (1932) a military alliance against the Soviet Union. In return, Papen sought the cancellation of German reparations payments, the recognition of Germany's right to equality of treatment in military and security matters, and the retraction of Article 231 of the Treaty of Versailles (the war guilt clause).[33] Herriot responded by reminding the other delegates to the conference of Germany's eco-

---

30.    Feuchtwanger, 310, 326.

31.    Ibid., 313-34.

32.    Dietrich Orlow, *A History of Modern Germany: 1871 to Present*, 3 ed. (Englewood Cliffs, NJ: Prentice Hall, 1995), 190; A.J. Nicholls, *Weimar and the Rise of Hitler*, 2 ed. (New York: St. Martin's Press, 1979), 121.

33.    Feuchtwanger, 283.

nomic potential and the sacrifices being asked of France without compensation. The Italian government urged the Great Powers to cancel both the reparations and war debts. MacDonald, himself, pressed the idea of Germany paying a final lump-sum payment that would cancel out all German obligations under the Dawes and Young plans. The British Prime Minister encouraged Papen to demand further concessions, but this only angered Herriot. In the end, the Great Powers accepted the Lausanne Agreements on 9 July 1932. These agreements, a victory for former Chancellor Brüning and present Chancellor Papen, included an end to reparations payments.[34]

Meanwhile, the World Disarmament Conference in Geneva had bogged down over the definition of offensive and defensive weapons and on the methods of verification. The disarmament talks were stalled during the Lausanne Conference in June and early July. Afterwards, the German delegation, under the direction of General Schleicher, took a hard line approach in negotiations with the other Great Powers. Germany pressed Germany's claim to equal rights.[35] Then, on 12 July, the Papen Cabinet agreed to the Reichswehr's rearmament program regardless of what happened at Geneva. General Schleicher was eager to recruit members of the Sturmabteilung into the Reichswehr. The Defense Minister, ignoring the advice of Foreign Secretary Bülow, was ready for a showdown at the disarmament conference.[36] Two months later, on 6 September, Foreign Minister Neurath demanded the recognition of equal rights for Germany.[37] France and Britain rejected demands for armament equality, fearing that Germany would use military power to regain lost German lands in the East. Two weeks later, on 21 September, the German delegation withdrew from the disarmament conference.[38] This tactic resulted in the Versailles Powers recognizing equality of rights on security matters for Germany on 11 December 1932: a major triumph for the Foreign Office.[39] Germany was in the future to be treated on the same level as the

---

34.    Zara Steiner, *The Lights that Failed: European International History, 1919-1933* (Oxford: Oxford University Press, 2005), 685; Lee and Michalka, 131.

35.    Wilhelm Deist, "The Rearmament of the Wehrmacht," in *The Buildup of German Aggression*, vol. I in *Germany and the Second World War*, eds. W. Deist, M. Messerschmidt, H.-E. Volkmann, and W. Wette, trans. P.S. Falla, Dean S. McMurry, and Ewald Osers (Oxford: Clarendon Press, 1990), 395.

36.    Steiner, *The Lights that Failed*, 777-84.

37.    Neurath interview, 6 September 1932, *TMWC*, 40:481; Christoph M. Kimmich, *Germany and the League of Nations* (Chicago: University of Chicago Press, 1976), 151.

38.    Lee and Michalka, 132.

39.    Deist, "The Rearmament of the Wehrmacht," 395; Editor's note, *DGFP(C)*, 1:19-20; Kimmich, 169-72; Edward W. Bennett, *German Rearmament and the West, 1932-1933* (Princeton: Princeton University Press, 1979), 267.

other Great Powers since the declaration implied the elimination of all discriminatory provisions of the Versailles Treaty against Germany.[40] Commenting on this event, Hans Dieckhoff told the Nuremberg court in 1946 that the Foreign Office took the view that Germany now had "the indisputable right to rearm after all disarmament efforts had failed."[41] And yet, Neurath believed that rearmament would have to be slow so as not to disturb the security of its immediate neighbors.[42]

## Hitler and the Foreign Office

President Hindenburg appointed Adolf Hitler as Reich Chancellor in January 1933. Constantin von Neurath admitted that this action took him by surprise.[43] The President made Hitler's appointment as Chancellor on the conditions that Neurath was kept as Foreign Minister and there would be no changes in the Foreign Office or in the course of foreign policy.[44] Although Neurath at first refused to remain in office,[45] Hindenburg convinced the Foreign Minister to continue his work in guiding foreign affairs, and act as a counterbalance against any policy initiated by Hitler.[46] Hindenburg told his close friend that he wanted him to "secure the continuation of a peaceful foreign policy, and to prevent Hitler from taking the rash steps which were so possible in view of his impulsive nature, in one word, to act as a brake."[47] Neurath became convinced that he could, with Hindenburg's support, control foreign policy under the National Socialists and thus accepted the challenge.[48] Hermann Rauschning, a close friend and admirer of Hitler's political skill, wrote about Neurath's intentions:

> I am perfectly sure that he [Neurath] acted from the highest of motives: he was trying to train the Nazis and turn them into really serviceable partners in a

40.  Neurath testimony, 22 June 1946, *TMWC*, 16:606-7.
41.  Dieckhoff testimony, 26 June 1946, *TMWC*, 17:123-24. See also Heineman, *Hitler's First Foreign Minister*, 90.
42.  Heineman, *Hitler's First Foreign Minister*, 57.
43.  Ibid., 66.
44.  Ibid., 42; Rumbold to Simon, 4 February 1933, *DBFP*, second series, 4:406-8; Rauschning, *Men of Chaos*, 189; Neurath testimony, 22 June 1946, *TMWC*, 16:608; Prüfer affidavit, 16 April 1946, *TMWC*, 40:450-60.
45.  Heineman, "Constantin Freiherr von Neurath as Foreign Minister, 1932-1935," 221-22.
46.  Papen, 240; Simon to Basil C. Newton, 6 June 1932, *DBFP*, second series, 3:152-54; Karl Ritter affidavit, 28 May 1946, *TMWC*, 40:444; Manfred Zimmermann affidavit, 1 May 1946, *TMWC*, 40:437; Heineman, *Hitler's First Foreign Minister*, 65-66.
47.  Neurath testimony, 22 June 1946, *TMWC*, 16:608.
48.  Heineman, *Hitler's First Foreign Minister*, 67.

moderate nationalist regime.... He felt that it was his duty to make the best of the Nazis, and this could not mean getting rid of them quickly as possible. He regarded himself as the protector of a young and undisciplined element of which he flattered himself that he could form a politically serviceable one.[49]

The rise of Hitler, however, meant the introduction of new ideas to German foreign policy. Hitler had written manuscripts, including *Mein Kampf*, about his outlook on international relations as well as professed his ideas in numerous speeches.[50] Like the Foreign Office, Hitler wanted to be rid of the Treaty of Versailles and regain Great Power status for Germany. Hitler's ideas on the reacquisition of lost German territory, however, went beyond the position of the Wilhelmstrasse and advocated German expansion into East Europe, including the Soviet Union.[51] Moreover, he held strong anti-Bolshevik and anti-Semitic sentiments. In the mid-twenties, Hitler had written in *Mein Kampf*:

> Never forget that the rulers of present-day Russia are common blood-stained criminals; that they are the scum of humanity which, favored by circumstances, overran a great state in a tragic hour, slaughtered and wiped out thousands of her leading intelligentsia in wild blood lust, and now for almost ten years have been carrying on the most cruel and tyrannical regime of all time. Furthermore, do not forget that these rulers belong to a race [Jewish] which combines, in a rare mixture, bestial cruelty and an inconceivable gift for lying, and which today more than ever is conscious of a mission to impose its bloody oppression on the whole world. Do not forget that the international Jew who completely dominates Russia today regards Germany, not as an ally, but as a state destined to the same fate.[52]

Realizing that France would oppose any revision of the status quo, Hitler, who saw France as a "menace," wanted a German alliance with Britain and Italy to counter any French obstruction to a German attempt to regain Great

---

49.    Rauschning, *Men of Chaos*, 164.

50.    See Manfred Messerschmidt, "Foreign Policy and Preparation for War," in *The Buildup of German Aggression*, vol. I in *Germany and the Second World War*, eds. W. Deist, M. Messerschmidt, H.-E. Volkmann, and W. Wette, trans. P.S. Falla, Dean S. McMurry, and Ewald Osers (Oxford: Clarendon Press, 1990), 543-67.

51.    Adolf Hitler, *Mein Kampf*, trans. Ralph Manheim (Boston: Houghton Mifflin, 1943), 612; Adolf Hitler, *Hitler's Secret Book*, trans. Salvator Attanasio, intro. Telford Taylor (New York: Bramhall House, 1986), 44-52.

52.    Hitler, *Mein Kampf*, 660-61.

Power status, as well as to minimize the risk of war during this process.[53] He stated in *Mein Kampf*:

> England desires no Germany as a world power, but France wishes no power at all called Germany: quite an essential difference, after all! Today we are not fighting for a position as a world power: today we must struggle for the existence of our fatherland…. If we look about us for European allies from this standpoint, there remain only two states: England and Italy.[54]

In his second book, written in 1928 but never published during his lifetime, Hitler made further comments about his ideas concerning foreign policy:

> Germany decides to go over to [her future aim] a clear, far-sighted territorial policy. Thereby she abandons all attempts at world-industry and world-trade and instead concentrates all her strength in order, through the allotment of sufficient living space for the next hundred years to our people, also to prescribe a path of life. Since this territory can be only in the East, the obligation to be a naval power also recedes into the background. Germany tries anew to champion her interests through the formulation of a decisive power on land.
>
> This aim is equally in keeping with the highest national as well as folkish requirements. It likewise presupposes great military power means for its execution, but does not necessarily bring Germany into conflict with all European great powers. As surely as France here will remain Germany's enemy, just as little does the nature of such a political aim contain a reason for England, and especially for Italy, to maintain the enmity of the World War.[55]

Just as Neurath hesitated to serve under Hitler, the diplomats of the Auswärtiges Amt questioned the course of their careers and foreign policy in early 1933. Former Chancellor Brüning, nonetheless, influenced the members of the Wilhelmstrasse to stay at their posts. In his own words Brüning admitted:

> I advised Herr von Bülow strongly to remain in office, and to urge these others to do likewise, for they…together with moderate leaders in the Reich-

53.    Ibid., 612, 620, 624; Eberhard Jäckel, *Hitler's Weltanschauung: A Blueprint for Power*, trans. Herbert Arnold (Middletown, CT: Wesleyan University Press, 1972), 44; Geoffrey Stoakes, *Hitler and the Quest for World Domination: Nazi Ideology and Foreign Policy in the 1920s* (Leamington Spa: Berg, 1986), 226.
54.    Hitler, *Mein Kampf*, 620.
55.    Hitler, *Hitler's Secret Book*, 145.

swehr, alone would be in a position to frustrate any aggressive foreign or military policies of Hitler.[56]

Thus, Neurath and Bülow both stayed to manage the Foreign Office under Hitler's chancellorship and continue the moderate policy associated with Stresemann and Brüning. Writing in his memoirs, Herbert von Dirksen, the German Ambassador to Moscow, summed up the position of the diplomats stating:

> [W]e felt it to be our duty to assist in this process of normalization. We had been successful so far in our endeavors to train the newcomers in political leadership and to keep the ship of state on a straight course in spite of the storms which it had encountered. Thus, almost all the career diplomats as well as the other permanent officials remained in office. As to the constitutional and juristical implications of the new situation, the permanent officials were perfectly justified in placing their services at the disposal of the party which had gained power by constitutional and democratic elections.[57]

Besides, Neurath and Bülow were convinced that Hitler and the Nazi Party would not last long.[58]

Diplomats in the Foreign Office quickly came to believe that Hitler had intentions to peacefully pursue revisions to the Versailles Treaty.[59] In reply to the Soviet Union's concern over the rise of the anti-Bolshevik Hitler, Foreign Secretary Bülow told Ambassador Dirksen on 6 February 1933:

> I believe that they overestimate there [Moscow] the importance in terms of foreign policy of the change of government. When they have the responsibility the National Socialists are naturally different people and pursue a different policy than they proclaimed before. It was always like this, and it is the same with all parties. The persons of Neurath and also of Blomberg [the German War Minister] guarantee the continuity of the previous political relations.[60]

---

56.   As quoted in Paul Seabury, *The Wilhelmstrasse: A Study of German Diplomats under the Nazi Regime* (Berkeley: University of California Press, 1954), 28. See also John P. Fox, *Germany and the Far Eastern Crisis, 1931-1938: A Study in Diplomacy and Ideology* (Oxford: Clarendon Press, 1982), 25.

57.   Herbert von Dirksen, *Moscow, Tokyo, London: Twenty Years of German Foreign Policy* (Norman: University of Oklahoma Press, 1952), 107.

58.   Ibid., 170; Rauschning, *Men of Chaos*, 165.

59.   Neurath testimony, 25 June 1946, *TMWC*, 17:20; Dieckhoff testimony, 26 June 1946, *TMWC*, 17:123.

60.   Bernhard Wilhelm von Bülow to Herbert von Dirksen, 6 February 1933, *DGFP(C)*, 1:21. See also Bülow circular, 30 January 1933, *DGFP(C)*, 1:1.

While diplomats believed that Hitler would follow their lead in foreign affairs, Hitler continued to quietly profess his own policy intentions to close friends such as Joachim von Ribbentrop, a fairly new member of the Nazi Party who had impressed him with his knowledge of world affairs.[61] Ribbentrop was a champagne salesman who had lived in Britain, France, Canada, and the United States.[62] He was a strong advocate of close relations with Britain and France while being anti-Bolshevik.[63] In February 1933, Hitler related to Ribbentrop over dinner his inner most thoughts on policy:

> At this first discussion [on foreign affairs] Adolf Hitler told me that he wanted peace at all costs. One world war had been enough for Germany; it must not happen again. But he must achieve Germany's equality. The German nation was too strong to tolerate permanent discrimination. A revision of certain Versailles terms had to be brought about. Nor was it possible for Germany, surrounded as she was by States armed to the teeth, to remain undefended. Yet there was time for him to do all this gradually.
>
> What he wanted beyond all else, said Hitler, was a permanent and clear settlement with Britain. He also wanted friendship with Italy, and thought that the kinship of the National Socialist and fascist philosophies would provide the basis for this.
>
> Hitler's attitude to Soviet Russia was sharply antagonistic.... When discussing this subject his face became stern and his expression inexorable. It was clear to me even then that Hitler was fanatically resolved to destroy communism for good.[64]

On 7 April 1933, with the belief that the Wilhelmstrasse had complete control over the formulation and conduct of German foreign policy, Neurath briefed Hitler at the Reich Chancellery concerning Germany's situation in the international system.[65] The Foreign Minister stressed that the "demand for revision [of the Versailles Treaty] requires the employment of all possible energies." Neurath outlined the Foreign Office's main goal of reacquiring lost German territories in East Europe, and declared that "border revisions can be broached only when Germany

---

61.    Joachim von Ribbentrop testimony, 29 March 1946, *TMWC*, 10:232; DeWitt C. Poole, "Light on Nazi Foreign Policy," *Foreign Affairs* 25 (October 1946), 133.

62.    Joachim von Ribbentrop, *The Ribbentrop Memoirs*, trans. Oliver Watson, ed. A. von Ribbentrop, intro. Allan Bullock (London: Weidenfeld and Nicolson, 1954), 1-20; Paul Schwarz, *This Man Ribbentrop: His Life and Times* (New York: Julian Messner, 1943), 79.

63.    Ribbentrop, 28, 42; Schwarz, 75.

64.    Ribbentrop, 26-27.

65.    Bülow was the primary formulator of the policy presented by Neurath of Hitler on 7 April 1933.

has become strong militarily, politically, and financially." He emphasized that closer relations with Britain, Italy, and the Soviet Union were essential to revise territorial borders in face of strong opposition from Poland and France. The Foreign Minister declared that "an understanding between Germany and France is as good as impossible," and "an understanding with Poland is neither possible nor desirable." Additionally, Neurath briefed the Chancellor that "the Anschluss of Austria can not be actively promoted for the time being owing to Italy's opposition."[66]

The following month, on 17 May 1933, the Chancellor spoke to the Reichstag and addressed foreign policy issues.[67] Ernst Woermann, Head Counselor for International Law at the Wilhelmstrasse, and his colleagues were "deeply impressed" by Hitler's speech, and came to the conclusion that the Chancellor would follow the policy formulated by the Foreign Office.[68] In this speech Hitler stated:

> Germany does not want war. She has demonstrated her good will by disarming; let the other powers now demonstrate theirs by doing likewise.... France invokes her anxiety as to her security, yet France it is who remains armed whereas Germany has disarmed.... It has been declared desirable that Germany's military status be modified; Germany is willing. She has concurred in the proposed MacDonald Plan, but on condition that it establish a strict parallelism and true equality among the powers involved.... If a decision were to be imposed on Germany under pretext that it was a majority decision, then Germany would refuse to yield, preferring rather to resign from both the Disarmament Conference and the League of Nations....[69]

Despite agreeing to Hindenburg's terms in January 1933, Adolf Hitler greatly disliked career diplomats and the thought of allowing the Wilhelmstrasse to formulate and conduct foreign policy. Paul Otto Schmidt, who became Hitler's chief interpreter, stressed in his memoirs that " Hitler disliked the German Foreign Office and everyone connected with it."[70] But, the Chancellor realized that

---

66.   Conference of Ministers minutes, 7 April 1933, *DGFP(C)*, 1:256-60.

67.   Adolf Hitler, *The Speeches of Adolf Hitler, April 1922 to August 1939*, 2 vols., trans. and ed. Norman H. Baynes (London: Oxford University Press, 1942), 2:1041-58.

68.   Ernst Woermann testimony, 2 July 1948, AMT transcript, OGL 17, Box 140, Folder 2, 10855-856.

69.   As quoted in François-Poncet, 102.

70.   Dr. Paul Schmidt, *Hitler's Interpreter*, ed. RH.C. Steed (New York: Macmillan, 1951), 13. See also Adolf Hitler, *Hitler's Secret Conversations, 1941-1944,* trans. Norman Cameron and R.H. Stevens (New York: Octagon, 1972), 226; Dirksen, 109-10; Seabury, *The Wilhelmstrasse,* 31; Gordon A. Craig, *Germany 1866-1945* (Oxford: Oxford University Press, 1978), 698; William Carr, *Arms, Autarky and Aggression: A Study in German Foreign Policy, 1933-1939* (London: Edward Arnold, 1972), 29-30; Heineman, *Hitler's First Foreign Minister,* 134.

he needed to use the Wilhelmstrasse to pursue a "policy of concealment" in order to convince foreign governments that Germany's foreign policy would remain peaceful and not undergo any fundamental changes.[71] Besides, Hitler fully agreed with the Foreign Office's revisionist policy.[72] Until he consolidated his power base in the government, the Chancellor was therefore forced by circumstances to accept the influence of Neurath and the Wilhelmstrasse in foreign relations.[73] In his analysis of the situation, Gordon Craig has stated:

> He [Hitler] recognized his vulnerability and his need for time [to consolidate his power base] and therefore encouraged the democratic governments in their illusions lest they undertake to baulk his plans before he could do anything to prevent that. Indeed, he strengthened the impression that no fundamental change in German policy need be expected by retaining the Foreign Ministry staff and diplomatic personnel that had served his predecessors, keeping Baron von Neurath and Bernhard von Bülow in the posts of Foreign Minister and Secretary of State respectively and leaving the ambassadorial posts untouched.[74]

In fact, the Wilhelmstrasse experienced no major changes in leadership until a major reorganization in 1935 and 1936. Hitler kept the senior members of the Foreign Office, including the seven department directors, until he had taken full control of Germany.[75] In early 1936, when he arrived in Berlin on leave from his mission as Ambassador to Tokyo, Herbert von Dirksen discovered:

> In the Foreign Office…there were no signs of any radical changes. It was staffed by the same officials who had been in office before 1933, with Neurath

---

71.  Gordon A. Craig and Alexander L. George, *Force and Statecraft: Diplomatic Problems of Our Time* (New York: Oxford University Press, 1983), 96-99; Kimmich, 174; Weinberg, *The Foreign Policy of Hitler's Germany*, 1:35; Lee and Michalka, 140-41; Craig, *Germany 1866-1945*, 698.

72.  Hiden, 43; Hildebrand, *The Third Reich*, 15; Bennett, *German Rearmament and the West*, 508; A.J.P. Taylor, *The Origins of the Second World War* (London: Hamish Hamilton, 1961), 68.

73.  Ernst von Weizsäcker, *Memoirs of Ernst von Weizsäcker*, trans. John Andrews (London: Victor Gollancz, 1951), 109; Kimmich, 174; Weinberg, *The Foreign Policy of Hitler's Germany*, 1:25-26; Gordon A. Craig, "The German Foreign Office from Neurath to Ribbentrop," in *The Diplomats, 1919-1939*, ed. Gordon A. Craig and Felix Gilbert (Princeton: Princeton University Press, 1953), 409; Rumbold to Simon, 4 February 1933, *DBFP*, second series, 4:406-7.

74.  Craig, *Germany 1866-1945*, 677. See also Rumbold to Simon, 15 February 1933, *DBFP*, second series, 4:421; Heineman, *Hitler's First Foreign Minister*, 68.

75.  Seabury, *The Wilhelmstrasse*, 26; Dirksen, 108.

as Minister and Bülow as Secretary of State. The thinly veiled anti- Nazi senti-ments of the latter were common knowledge. There was not a single party "bigwig" among the higher ranks of officials. Membership in the party was a minor issue.[76]

Even so, the Chancellor had his diplomats closely watched by his party mem-bers.[77] The Nazi leadership distrusted the activities of the Wilhelmstrasse to the point of bugging their headquarters.[78]

Hitler's continued use of the Wilhelmstrasse reflected his need for putting forward a respectable image toward the other Great Powers. Hitler, himself, had never traveled outside of Germany or his native Austria, and had no knowledge of foreign languages.[79] Moreover, the National Socialists lacked party members with diplomatic experience and language skills to seriously challenge the author-ity of the Foreign Office.[80] One possibility, however, was Alfred Rosenberg who sought to replace Neurath as Foreign Minister. Rosenberg had published a book in 1927 on Germany's new course in foreign affairs.[81] But President Hindenburg insisted upon keeping Neurath as the Foreign Minister. As a consequence, Hitler created the Foreign Policy Office of the Nazi Party (Aussenpolitisches Amt [APA]) and named Rosenberg as its head in April 1933.[82] Even so, the APA failed to influence German foreign policy and Rosenberg never rose to a position of great influence. In fact, in 1933, Rosenberg embarrassed Hitler, who never for-gave him, with his inappropriate actions while representing Germany in Lon-don.[83] Another possibility was Joachim von Ribbentrop. Ribbentrop, with the support of Hitler, wanted to become State Secretary for Foreign Affairs. Never-theless, Vice Chancellor Franz von Papen refused to entertain any such notion

---

76.   Dirksen, 169.

77.   Weizsäcker, 89, 104.

78.   Sumner Welles, *The Time for Decision* (New York: Harper, 1944), 99.

79.   François-Poncet, 237; Heineman, *Hitler's First Foreign Minister*, 88.

80.   Seabury, *The Wilhelmstrasse*, 26, 31; Heineman, *Hitler's First Foreign Minister*, 89.

81.   See Alfred Rosenberg, *Der Zukunftsweg einer deutschen Aussenpolitik* (Munich: F. Eher Nachf, 1927).

82.   Zachary Shore, *What Hitler Knew: The Battle for Information in Nazi Foreign Policy* (Oxford: Oxford University Press, 2003), 12.

83.   Neurath interrogation testimony, 3 October 1945, *NCA*, supplement B, 1491; John P. Fox, "Alfred Rosenberg in London," *Contemporary Review* 213 (July 1968), 6-11; Leonidas E. Hill, "The Wilhelmstrasse in the Nazi Era," *Political Science Quarterly* 83 (December 1967), 553-54; Paul Seabury, "Ribbentrop and the German Foreign Office," *Political Science Quarterly* 66 (December 1951), 535; Seabury, *The Wilhelmstrasse*, 33-37; Rauschning, *Men of Chaos*, 190-91; Neurath memorandum, 11 May 1933, *DGFP(C)*, 1:404-6; Leopold von Hoesch to Ger-man Foreign Office, 15 May 1933, *DGFP(C)*, 1:432-34.

since the champagne salesman did not have any diplomatic experience.[84] Consequently, Hitler was forced to use the diplomats of the Auswärtiges Amt. The Chancellor, nonetheless, refused to become completely dependent upon the Wilhelmstrasse. He gradually began using not only Ribbentrop, but Hermann Göring, Rudolf Hess, and other amateur diplomats to bypass the control of the Wilhelmstrasse in conducting foreign relations.[85] Such practices, however, as Gordon Craig has pointed out, were not uncommon among the leadership of the other Great Powers, including Britain and France, in the conduct of international affairs.[86] The Weimar Republic, nonetheless, had refrained from such methods and left international relations in the hands of the professional diplomats. In his analyzation of Hitler's extensive use of amateur diplomacy after 1933, Ernst von Weizsäcker, who became Director of the newly reestablished Political Department in 1936, and later Foreign Secretary in 1938, commented:

> Amateurish and irregular reports were often preferred to the official ones. Decisions were taken without the Foreign Minister or the Foreign Office having had a say in the framing of them. The carrying out of the decisions was entrusted to the most various quarters…. The foreign service had been delegated to the level of a mere technical apparatus.[87]

---

84.    Papen, 373; Dirksen, 108. For details to Ribbentrop's challenge to the Foreign Office, see chapter 6.

85.    Seabury, *The Wilhelmstrasse*, 31-32; Craig, *Germany 1866-1945*, 698; Sir Ronald Graham to Sir Robert Vansittart, 26 July 1933, *DBFP*, second series, 5:448; Shore, 12-14.

86.    See Gordon A. Craig, "The Professional Diplomat and His Problems, 1919-1939," in *War, Politics, and Diplomacy: Selected Essays* (London: Weidenfeld and Nicolson, 1966), 207-19; Keith Feiling, *The Life of Neville Chamberlain* (Hamden, CT: Archon, 1970), 207. Craig called the use of amateur diplomats as "new diplomacy" which was "the practice of bypassing the Foreign Office, of failing to consult it or keep it informed in important matters" (Craig, "The Professional Diplomat and His Problems," 217).

87.    Weizsäcker, 106.

# 6

# *Hitler, Ribbentrop, and the Decline of the Foreign Office*

## Hitler Challenges the Wilhelmstrasse

Becoming Chancellor in January 1933, Adolf Hitler agreed to leave the formulation and conduct of foreign affairs in the hands of the Foreign Office. He declared that Germany would continue the peaceful policy pursued by Stresemann and Brüning. However, Hitler only acquiesced to the desires of President Hindenburg in order to buy himself time to consolidate his own power base in Germany. The Chancellor's behavior, according to William Carr, was calculated to lull both his own diplomats as well as Germany's foreign neighbors into a false sense of security.[1] Gordon Craig has written that Hitler thought that foreign relations "was too important to be left in the hands of professional diplomats."[2] Agreeing with this judgment, Klaus Hildebrand has professed that Hitler quietly took control of foreign policy in 1933.[3] In his study on German policy, Hildebrand has written:

> Already in the first few days after the "seizure of power," it became clear that Hitler was adhering to the aims drawn up in his Programme. In an address to the most senior officers of the Reichswehr, he expounded views thoroughly in line with his Programme set down in *Mein Kampf.*[4]

1.  William Carr, *Arms, Autarky and Aggression: A Study in German Foreign Policy, 1933-1939* (London: Edward Arnold, 1972), 29-30.
2.  Gordon A. Craig, "The Professional Diplomat and His Problems, 1919-1939," in *War, Politics, and Diplomacy: Selected Essays* (London: Weidenfeld and Nicolson, 1966), 207.
3.  Klaus Hildebrand, *The Third Reich*, trans. P.S. Falla (London: George Allen and Unwin, 1984), 15-16.
4.  Klaus Hildebrand, *The Foreign Policy of the Third Reich*, trans. Anthony Fothergill (Berkeley: University of California Press, 1973), 28.

During the first few months of the new government, the struggle for control of foreign affairs between Hitler and Foreign Minister Constantin von Neurath gradually became evident. Ernst von Weizsäcker, who was temporarily in Berlin during early 1933, witnessed the difficult time that Neurath had with Hitler's use of amateur diplomats as well as the transfer of responsibility for propaganda intended for foreign distribution from the Wilhelmstrasse to the newly established Propaganda Ministry, directed by the Nazi Joseph Goebbels.[5] During this period the Foreign Minister threatened to resign three times.[6] Hitler appeased Neurath for a short time because he knew that he had to treat Neurath, as Gerhard Köpke testified at Nuremberg, "carefully and politely" while he consolidated his power base.[7] It was of the utmost importance that during this consolidation of power that Hitler, while his own political strength was still weak, kept the support of Hindenburg as well as presented a non-threatening, favorable image of the Nazi regime to the outside world.[8] Nonetheless, as Weizsäcker told the Nuremberg court, when Hitler came to power "foreign policy was very soon split into the policy of the Foreign Office and the policy of the [Nazi] Party."[9]

Although Adolf Hitler gradually began to dominate German foreign policy this was not readily apparent since the objectives of Hitler and the Wilhelmstrasse were very similar. The success of Hitler's struggle with Neurath over policy was made much easier because of the Foreign Minister's "weak leadership" characteristics.[10] Neurath, a conservative civil servant who was "fascinated by authority" and preferred Germany to be in the hands of a strong leader without parliamen-

5.    Ernst von Weizsäcker testimony, 10 June 1948, AMT transcript, OGL 17, Box 137, Folder 2, 8086-87; Weizsäcker testimony, 8 June 1948, AMT transcript, OGL 17, Box 136, Folder 10, 7605; Minutes of the Conference of Department Heads, 24 May 1933, *DGFP(C)*, 1:483-85. As early as July 1933, Mussolini had complained that "there seemed to be six if not seven members of the German Government who acted from time to time as Foreign Minister. Hitler,… Neurath, Göring…, von Papen, Goebbels, and Rosenberg not to mention General Blomberg who was brought into all discussions of foreign affairs. This rendered dealing with the German Government a matter of considerable difficulty" (Sir Ronald Graham to Sir Robert Vansittart, 26 July 1933, *DBFP*, second series, 5:448).

6.    Ernst von Weizsäcker, *Memoirs of Ernst von Weizsäcker*, trans. John Andrews (London: Victor Gollancz, 1951), 86, 88.

7.    Gerhard Köpke testimony, 26 June 1946, *TMWC*, 17:108.

8.    John L. Heineman, *Hitler's First Foreign Minister: Constantin Freiherr von Neurath, Diplomat and Statesman* (Berkeley: University of California Press, 1979), 71.

9.    Ernst von Weizsäcker testimony, 7 June 1948, AMT transcript, OGL 17, Box 136, Folder 10, 7599.

10.   John P. Fox, *Germany and the Far Eastern Crisis, 1931-1938: A Study in Diplomacy and Ideology* (Oxford: Clarendon Press, 1982), 3, 6.

tary interference in foreign affairs, found it easy to fall under the influence of Hitler's style of government.[11] André François-Poncet, the French Ambassador to Germany (1931-38), found the Foreign Minister to be timid.[12] In his overall impression of Neurath, François-Poncet stated:

> He…was almost always good humored and simple, but with dignity…. [H]e was extremely polite, which made all relations with him easy and agreeable. His intelligence was in no way arresting, but he possessed intelligence, common sense and composure.[13]

Sir Eric Phipps, the British Ambassador to Berlin (1933-37), saw Neurath as lazy in managing foreign affairs, leaving the administration of the Wilhelmstrasse in the hands of Bernhard Wilhelm von Bülow, the Foreign Secretary.[14] Unfortunately, Bülow, who was strongly anti-Nazi,[15] had become so ill that Neurath had to consider replacing him with Weizsäcker in April 1933.[16] Neurath's personal characteristics of timidness and laziness, combined with his failure to build a personal relationship and join the inner circle of the Chancellor's advisers,[17] doomed the influence of the Foreign Office in any of Hitler's cabinet meetings. Hitler dominated the discussion of foreign policy issues. The diplomats at the Wilhelmstrasse realized that these traits, combined with Neurath's well-known lack of speaking skills, made the task of controlling the direction of foreign policy difficult. Weizsäcker wrote in his memoirs:

> His [Neurath's] chief failing was his inability to express himself in a conversation, particularly in a large circle of people. We in the Foreign Office found it difficult to imagine how he could possibly manage to get a word in edgeways when subject to Hitler's outpourings.[18]

11.   Marshall M. Lee and Wolfgang Michalka, *German Foreign Policy 1917-1933: Continuity or Break?* (Leamington Spa: Berg, 1987), 142; Heineman, *Hitler's First Foreign Minister*, 72.

12.   André François-Poncet, *The Fateful Years: Memoirs of a French Ambassador in Berlin, 1931-1938*, trans. Jacques LeClercq (New York: Harcourt, Brace and Company, 1949), 232.

13.   Ibid., 29.

14.   Hermann Rauschning, *Men of Chaos* (New York: G.P. Putnam's Sons, 1942), 175-76; Fox, *Germany and the Far Eastern Crisis, 1931-1938*, 25.

15.   François-Poncet, 182-83; Heineman, *Hitler's First Foreign Minister*, 131.

16.   Weizsäcker, 88.

17.   Köpke testimony, 26 June 1946, *TMWC*, 17:108; Constantin von Neurath testimony, 24 June 1946, *TMWC*, 16:638; Heineman, *Hitler's First Foreign Minister*, 73.

18.   Weizsäcker, 110.

Franz von Papen agreed with this judgment of Neurath. He commented:

> What he [Neurath] lacked was the ability to break into Hitler's long mono-
> logues and…get a word in. Neurath's standards of diplomatic politeness made
> him think it rather ill-mannered…[to interrupt].[19]

Nevertheless, Neurath stayed in office and faithfully served Germany as Hitler's
Foreign Minister in spite of his objections to the National Socialists and their
methods in politics. Neurath firmly believed that he could control Hitler's
involvement in foreign affairs with strong support from President Hindenburg.[20]

## Disarmament and the League of Nations

The question of disarmament was the first major diplomatic issue that arose after
Hitler took power. Neurath had broke off talks at the World Disarmament Conference in Geneva in September 1932. The Versailles Powers recognition of German equality prompted Germany, under the advice of Foreign Secretary Bülow,
to return to the disarmament talks in January 1933.[21] The Foreign Office negotiated with Britain, France, and Italy to uphold the Treaty of Versailles that called
for general disarmament.[22] After several months of talks, France would not agree
to disarmament, fearing future German aggression, especially after Hitler took
office.[23] Since the issue of general disarmament was not making progress, the
negotiators discussed arms limitations with an increase of German arms to a level
approximately equivalent to the other Great Powers. France, for instance, had a
peacetime army of 450,000 troops in 1933.[24] But the negotiators could not come
to a mutual agreement, and the talks resulted in a deadlock.[25] During the Disarmament Conference, Hitler allowed Neurath to manage the negotiations since

---

19.    Franz von Papen, *Memoirs*, trans. Brian Connell (New York: E.P. Dutton, 1953), 332.

20.    John Louis Heineman, "Constantin Freiherr von Neurath as Foreign Minister, 1932-1935:
       A Study of a Conservative Civil Servant and Germany's Foreign Policy," (Ph.D. thesis, Cor-
       nell University, 1965), 255.

21.    Editorial note, *DGFP(C)*, 1:18-20; Christoph M. Kimmich, *Germany and the League of
       Nations* (Chicago: University of Chicago Press, 1976), 163-64.

22.    Heineman, *Hitler's First Foreign Minister*, 90.

23.    Constantin von Neurath interrogation testimony, 3 October/12 November 1945, *NCA*, sup-
       plement B, 1488-89, 1503; Kimmich, 150.

24.    Robert J. Young, *In Command of France: French Foreign Policy and Military Planning, 1933-
       1940* (Cambridge, MA: Harvard University Press, 1978), 36-37.

25.    Neurath testimony, 22 June 1946, *TMWC*, 16:616; Neurath to Hitler, 19 June 1933,
       *TMWC*, 40: 469; Kimmich, 184; Gerhard L. Weinberg, *The Foreign Policy of Hitler's Ger-
       many*, 2 vols. (Chicago: University of Chicago Press, 1970-80), 1:160.

both men had the similar goals of German equality in political rights and military issues.[26] After returning from Geneva in September 1933, Neurath told Hitler of the deadlock. During his interrogation by Allied authorities at Nuremberg in 1945, Neurath recounted this discussion with the Reich Chancellor stating that:

> I pointed out to him [Hitler] how things were going [in Geneva], and that no agreement could be reached there. Then he decided to leave the conference. He said it was of no use in Geneva anymore.[27]

Hitler made the decision to abandon the World Disarmament Conference. Frustrated with the whole process, and considering that he viewed the organization as "worthless,"[28] Hitler also made the decision that Germany would withdraw from the League of Nations.[29] He wanted no part of an agreement with a League that would not recognize Germany's equality on military matters. The Chancellor's decisions were greatly influenced by General Werner von Blomberg, the Defense Minister, and Neurath, with the support of President Hindenburg, who strongly wanted German rearmament and the return of Germany to Great Power status.[30] On 13 October 1933, Hitler briefed a gathering of the Reich ministers that he had decided that Germany would "leave both the Disarmament Conference and the League of Nations, since the condition that we be recognized as a nation with equal rights is not fulfilled."[31] It was left to the Foreign Minister to communicate Hitler's decisions to the world shortly thereafter.[32] During the following months Germany began to rearm, according to Neurath, to meet defensive requirements.[33] In analyzing this cooperation between Hitler and Neurath, Gordon Craig has stated:

26.    Weinberg, *The Foreign Policy of Hitler's Germany*, 1:160; Kimmich, 175.
27.    Neurath interrogation testimony, 12 November 1945, *NCA*, supplement B, 1504. See also Weinberg, *The Foreign Policy of Hitler's Germany*, 1:164, 1:166.
28.    Adolf Hitler, *Hitler's Secret Book*, trans. Salvator Attanasio, intro. Telford Taylor (New York: Bramhall House, 1986), 112.
29.    Neurath interrogation testimony, 12 November 1945, *NCA*, supplement B, 1504.
30.    Dr. Bernhard Wilhelm von Bülow memorandum, 4 October 1933, *DGFP(C)*, 1:887; Kimmich, 175, 178, 186, 207.
31.    Conference of Ministers minutes, 13 October 1933, *DGFP(C)*, 1:922-26.
32.    Neurath announced Germany's withdrawal from the World Disarmament Conference on 14 October 1933 and from the League of Nations on 21 October 1933 (*NCA*, 2:1018, Kimmich, 190).
33.    Neurath testimony, 24 June 1946, *TMWC*, 16:621. See Wilhelm Deist, "The Rearmament of the Wehrmacht," in *The Buildup of German Aggression*, vol. I in *Germany and the Second World War*, eds. W. Deist, M. Messerschmidt, H.-E. Volkmann, and W. Wette, trans. P.S. Falla, Dean S. McMurry, and Ewald Osers (Oxford: Clarendon Press, 1990), 373-540; Wilhelm Deist, *The Wehrmacht and German Rearmament* (Toronto: University of Toronto Press, 1982).

[I]n this first marked sally of Nazi foreign policy, the Foreign Office and the Führer were at one. The diplomats had, indeed, every reason for satisfaction. They had, for the most part, been left free to follow to its logical end the line they had laid down in 1932; the cooperation between the Reichskanzlei [Chancellery] and the Wilhelmstrasse had at all times been amicable and effective;...and the result of the joint effort had been a diplomatic success, or at least a diplomatic sensation.[34]

## German-Polish Relations

While involved in disarmament talks with the West, Berlin engaged in secret communications with Warsaw regarding Danzig and the Polish Corridor. As early as April 1933, Marshal Joseph Pilsudski, the Dictator of Poland (1926-35), sought talks with Hitler to acquire a relaxation of tension between the two states over the lost German territories.[35] He feared Hitler's intentions and that "growing uneasiness" between Poland and Germany over the status of Danzig might erupt into a conflict.[36] Pilsudski sent a request to Hitler for the German Chancellor to meet personally Alfred Wysocki, the Polish Ambassador to Berlin. The Marshal of Poland realized that the Wilhelmstrasse, whose foreign policy was hostile to Poland, would object to any attempts by his government to improve relations with Germany.[37] Hitler was interested in such talks because former Chancellor Brüning as well as diplomats in Prague and Warsaw warned him, in April 1933, of the possibility of France, Poland, and Czechoslovakia launching a preventive war against Germany.[38] The Reich Chancellor was interested in blocking any foreign intervention into German affairs, breaching France's system of alliances in East Europe, as well as seeking improved relations with France.[39]

---

34.    Gordon A. Craig, "The German Foreign Office from Neurath to Ribbentrop," in *The Diplomats, 1919-1939*, ed. Gordon A. Craig and Felix Gilbert (Princeton: Princeton University Press, 1953), 415.

35.    Józef Lipski, *Diplomat in Berlin, 1933-1939: Papers and Memoirs of Józef Lipski, Ambassador of Poland*, ed. Wacław Jędrzejewicz (New York: Columbia University Press, 1968), 71.

36.    Neurath memorandum, 2 May 1933, *DGFP(C)*, 1:365-67; Józef Lipski to Józef Beck, *The Polish White Book: Official Documents concerning Polish-German and Polish-Soviet Relations, 1933-1939*, ed. Polish Government-in-Exile (New York: Farrar and Rinehart, 1940), 16.

37.    Lipski, 71.

38.    Ibid., 75; Hans Adolf von Moltke to Constantin von Neurath, 23 April 1933, *DGFP(C)*, 1:328-33; Walter Koch to Neurath, 25 April 1933, *DGFP(C)*, 1:343.

39.    Józef Lipski to Roman Debicki, 3 December 1933, *DB*, 107; William Carr, *Hitler: A Study in Personality and Politics* (London: Edward Arnold, 1978), 49; Klaus Hildebrand, "Hitler's Policy towards France until 1936," in *German Foreign Policy from Bismarck to Adenauer: The Limits of Statecraft*, trans. Louise Willmot (London: Unwin Hyman, 1989), 133-34.

Moreover, Hitler wanted to negotiate the return of lost German territory and seek Polish adherence to an anti-Bolshevik alliance against the Soviet Union.[40] The Chancellor therefore met with Ambassador Wysocki in Berlin on 2 May 1933. At this meeting, in the presence of Neurath, Wysocki presented Pilsudski's request for closer German-Polish relations. He also pressed Hitler and acquired an understanding over the status of Danzig and a promise that Germany would not take any aggressive measures against Poland.[41] Wysocki discovered later that Neurath, who had kept quiet during the meeting, had "serious misgivings" about the agreement.[42] Neurath, under the influence of Foreign Secretary Bülow and other diplomats, still supported a policy, centered on close German-Soviet relations, aimed against Poland.[43] Hitler's agreement with Wysocki, nevertheless, resulted in much improved relations between Germany and Poland.[44]

In late September 1933, while at the Disarmament Conference, the Polish Foreign Minister, Józef Beck, approached Neurath in Geneva about German-Polish relations. Beck told his counterpart that Pilsudski was willing to discuss with Hitler a settlement of outstanding issues between their respective countries.[45] Shortly thereafter, Marshal Pilsudski replaced Wysocki in Berlin with Józef Lipski in order to negotiate a more substantial agreement.[46] Adding incentive for obtaining better relations with Germany was the Polish government's fear of German intentions after it withdrew from the Disarmament Conference and the League of Nations.

Despite Hitler's interest in closer relations with Poland and opposition to improved German-Soviet ties, Foreign Minister Neurath and the Wilhelmstrasse continued to support the latter policy. The Foreign Office replaced Herbert von Dirksen, who was reassigned to Tokyo, with Rudolf Nadolny, who had previously headed the German delegation at the Geneva disarmament talks, as the new Ambassador to Moscow. On 13 November 1933, Neurath provided the following diplomatic instructions to Nadolny concerning his new assignment:

---

40.    Lipski to Beck, 25 January 1934, *DB*, 124.
41.    Neurath memorandum, 2 May 1933, *DGFP(C)*, 1:365-67; Alfred Wysocki to Józef Beck, 2 May 1933, *DB*, 79.
42.    Wysocki to Beck, 2 May 1933, *DB*, 79.
43.    Conference of Minister minutes, 7 April 1933, *DGFP(C)*, 1:256-60; Lee and Michalka, 147; Neurath to Rudolf Nadolny, 13 November 1933, *DGFP(C)*, 2:123; Craig, "The German Foreign Office from Neurath to Ribbentrop," 417.
44.    Moltke to Neurath, 20 May 1933, *DGFP(C)*, 1:470-71.
45.    Neurath memorandum, 25 September 1933, *DGFP(C)*, 1:840; Neurath memorandum, 26 September 1933, *DGFP(C)*, 1:842.
46.    Ambassador Lipski arrived in Berlin in October 1933. The ambassadorship had been vacant since July (Lipski, 94; François-Poncet, 110).

> Good German-Soviet relations are of essential importance to Germany. In Germany's relations with Poland they are of extreme importance. What must naturally be prevented…is the incorporation of the Soviet Union in any political front directed against Germany.[47]

Hitler secretly met with Lipski in direct opposition to the advice of the Wilhelmstrasse on 15 November 1933. Both the Chancellor and Polish Ambassador wished to avoid the interference and hostility of the Foreign Office.[48] They discussed the possibility of a nonaggression pact. Hitler was willing to declare that Germany had no intention of aggression against the Poles to settle their territorial differences, but he declined the opportunity to discuss a boundary settlement.[49] Faced with Hitler's decision to sign a nonaggression pact, which would seriously affect German-Soviet relations, the foreign service divided into the traditional East-West factions. Foreign Minister Neurath, who found it difficult to contradict the opinion of Hitler, Gerhard Köpke, the Director of Department II (West, South, and South-East Europe), and Hans Adolf von Moltke, the German Ambassador to Warsaw, accepted the Polish card as a way to improve not only German-Polish, but Franco-German relations. State Secretary Bülow and Ambassador Nadolny, on the other hand, argued against a rapprochement with Poland, preferring the Rapallo policy of closer German-Soviet ties.[50]

Because of the split in opinion at the Wilhelmstrasse, the subsequent negotiations between Germany and Poland were held in strict secrecy and bypassed many of the diplomats who would have normally been involved in the conduct of foreign relations.[51] For two months German and Polish diplomats passed each other draft nonaggression agreements until both sides were finally agreeable to the wording of the treaty.[52] In the process Neurath had managed to influence the Chancellor to accept a weaker version of the draft treaty to appease those diplo-

---

47.    Neurath to Nadolny, 13 November 1933, *DGFP(C)*, 2:123.
48.    Lipski, 98-99.
49.    Richard Meyer to Moltke, 15 November 1933, *DGFP(C)*, 2:128-29; Lipski, 97; Lipski to Beck, 30 November 1933, *DB*, 101.
50.    Richard Meyer memorandum, German Foreign Office Director of Department IV, 23 November 1933, *DGFP(C)*, 2:146; Lipski, 97; Lipski to Beck, 30 November 1933, *DB*, 103; Craig, "The German Foreign Office from Neurath to Ribbentrop," 417-18; Lipski to Dębicki, 3 December 1933, *DB*, 107.
51.    Lipski to Beck, 5 February 1934, *DB*, 126.
52.    Meyer memorandum, 23 November 1933, *DGFP(C)*, 2:146; Neurath to Moltke, 24 November 1933, *DGFP(C)*, 2:148-149; Moltke to Neurath, 28 November 1933, *DGFP(C)*, 2:155-57; Neurath memorandum, 9 January 1934, *DGFP(C)*, 2:312-14; Friedrich Gaus memorandum, German Foreign Office Director of Legal Department, 22 January 1934, *DGFP(C)*, 2:393-95.

mats in the Foreign Office who objected to close German-Polish relations.[53] Even so, Ambassador Nadolny continuously warned Neurath that the Soviet leadership was leaning toward a rapprochement with France if Germany failed to pursue closer German-Soviet relations.[54] The negotiations came to an end when Neurath and Lipski signed a nonaggression pact in Berlin on 26 January 1934, which was ratified in Warsaw a month later.[55] The agreement brought changes. It surprised the Soviet leader, Joseph Stalin, and brought a complete change in German-Soviet relations. George Kennan, a diplomat and historian, wrote that the pact "suddenly brought home to him [Stalin] how completely the Germans had cut loose from the old Rapallo concept."[56] The treaty led to the collapse of the Franco-Polish alliance.[57] Moreover, the treaty had the effect of greatly weakening the influence of Neurath and the Foreign Office with Hitler. The Chancellor found that the professional diplomats had represented an obstacle in his conduct of foreign relations. He had gained the upper advantage over the Foreign Minister and the now divided diplomatic corps. In the future he would avoid the use of the foreign service as much as possible by employing the services of amateur diplomats. Gordon Craig viewed the German-Polish agreement as the turning point as to who controlled the formulation and conduct of German foreign policy.[58] Such control was noted by the foreign diplomats in Berlin. On 27 December 1933, André François-Poncet, the French Ambassador, reported to Paris:

> Adolf Hitler, today, is truly in control of his people. He exercises a complete hold over them.... He maintains the balance between competing rivals; he judges over their quarrels; his authority is not in question.[59]

53.  Zygmunt J. Gasiorowski, "The German-Polish Nonaggression Pact of 1934," *Journal of Central European Affairs* 15 (April 1955), 14.

54.  Nadolny to Neurath, 5 January 1934, *DGFP(C)*, 2:301-4; Nadolny to Neurath, 9 January 1934, *DGFP(C)*, 2:318-22; Nadolny to Bülow, 23 January 1934, *DGFP(C)*, 2:408-10. After the German-Polish Nonaggression Pact, Nadolny continued his warnings of Soviet intentions to seek a rapprochement with France until his resignation in April 1934 (Nadolny to Neurath, 12 April 1934, *DGFP(C)*, 2:739-40. See also Lee and Michalka, 147-48).

55.  Lipski to Beck, 5 February 1934, *DB*, 126.

56.  George F. Kennan, *Russia and the West under Lenin and Stalin* (Boston: Little, Brown and Company, 1960), 300.

57.  William Evans Scott, *Alliance against Hitler: The Origins of the Franco-Soviet Pact* (Durham: Duke University Press, 1962), 188.

58.  Craig, "The German Foreign Office from Neurath to Ribbentrop," 415, 418.

59.  As quoted in Hildebrand, "Hitler's Policy towards France until 1936," 125.

After the interrogation of those involved in diplomatic affairs, including Neurath, Ribbentrop, Papen, and Göring, before the Nuremberg trials, DeWitt C. Poole, the Chief Interrogator and Special Representative of the U.S. Secretary of State, came to the conclusion that, " Hitler dominated every situation. Every decision setting the course of German external relations from 1933 on was made by Hitler personally, and it was he who set the exact timing of every important action."[60]

## Austrian Question

In control of foreign policy, Hitler now turned his efforts towards the issues of closer German-Italian relations and the Austrian Question. Hitler sought Italian support of German rearmament as well as an alliance.[61] However, the Chancellor realized that the acquisition of an alliance with Benito Mussolini would have to wait until the two leaders agreed upon the status of Austria.[62] Hitler wanted to annex his homeland.[63] Mussolini, on the other hand, feared German intentions towards the South Tyrol, largely populated by Germans. The Duce preferred for Austria to remain independent and serve as a buffer state between Germany and Italy.[64]

Conscious of the value of closer German-Italian relations, Foreign Minister Neurath and the Wilhelmstrasse advised the Chancellor not to take any aggressive action against Austria aimed at annexation. Foreign Secretary Bülow cautioned against pursuing a policy of pressuring Austria,[65] and Gerhard Köpke, the Director of Department II, believed the international climate was not right for a German attempt to annex Austria.[66] Neurath, himself, preferred closer Austro-German economic ties, not political union. Remembering the crisis over the Austro-German Customs Union in 1931, Neurath, nonetheless, was "resolved [not to] touch this hot iron again."[67]

Hitler largely ignored the Auswärtiges Amt concerning the Austrian Question. He viewed Austro-German relations as an internal German problem, not as

---

60.    DeWitt C. Poole, "Light on Nazi Foreign Policy," *Foreign Affairs* 25 (October 1946), 130.

61.    François-Poncet, 121-22. Hitler also counted on British support for German rearmament.

62.    Eberhard Jäckel, *Hitler's Weltanschauung: A Blueprint for Power*, trans. Herbert Arnold (Middletown, CT: Wesleyan University Press, 1972), 44; Christian Leitz, *Nazi Foreign Policy, 1933-1941: The Road to Global War* (London: Routledge, 2004), 9-19.

63.    Papen, 298-99.

64.    Denis Mack Smith, *Mussolini* (London: Weidenfeld and Nicolson, 1981), 96.

65.    Bülow to Neurath, 1 August 1933, *DGFP(C)*, 1:708-12.

66.    Köpke to Kurt Rieth, 22 March 1933, *DGFP(C)*, 1:193-95.

67.    Köpke testimony, 26 June 1946, *TMWC*, 17:112. See also Hans Dieckhoff testimony, 26 June 1946, *TMWC*, 17:123; Papen, 300.

an international issue.[68] He therefore bypassed the Wilhelmstrasse to a large extent, relying upon Hermann Göring and Franz von Papen to conduct much of his policy aimed towards the overthrow of the Austrian government,[69] headed by Chancellor Engelbert Dollfuss. Hitler pressured the Austrian government, despite the protests of Neurath, with German economic sanctions as well as support for the Austrian National Socialist Party's illegal activities against the Dollfuss regime.[70] With the aid of the Austrian Nazis, Hitler hoped to gain influence over Austria, and thus force a settlement in Germany's favor.[71]

Although he supported the Nazi Party's actions in Austria, Hitler was cautious in his diplomatic maneuvering so as not to offend, but to woo Mussolini. At a meeting with the Italian leader in Venice, which was arranged by Papen, not the Foreign Office, Hitler avoided any mention of his desire to annex Austria.[72] Instead, the Chancellor sought improved German-Italian relations as well as an understanding over Austria.[73]

In spite of such caution with Mussolini, Hitler conspired to take full charge of the German government. Shortly after returning from Venice, Hitler gave the orders to eliminate his political opposition. On the night of 30 June, Hitler had Ernst Röhm and other Sturmabteilung leaders murdered.[74] The purge made a deep impression upon Neurath, and placed him in fear of Hitler. On 11 July, during a meeting with Hitler, Hermann Rauschning noticed that the Foreign Minister was "anxiously servile" in his "manner towards the Reich Chancellor. This was something very different from the once much-contumned fawning of the former monarch. This was abject fear of the hangman."[75] On 19 July, fearing

---

68.    Eric Kordt testimony, 4 June 1948, AMT transcript, OGL 17, Box 136, Folder 7, 7364; Papen, 299; Jürgen Gehl, *Austria, Germany, and the Anschluss, 1931-1938* (London: Oxford University Press, 1963), 59.

69.    Ulrich von Hassell to Neurath, 29 March 1934, *DGFP(C)*, 2:690-91; Adolf Hitler to Papen, 26 July 1933, *DGFP(C)*, 2:252; Neurath to Bülow, 31 July 1933, *DGFP(C)*, 1:708; Conference of Ministers minutes, 26 May 1933, *DGFP(C)*, 1:487-90; Carr, *Hitler*, 49; Gehl, 59; Heineman, "Constantin Freiherr von Neurath as Foreign Minister, 1932-1935," 378; Roger Manvell and Heinrich Fränkel, *Göring* (New York: Simon and Schuster, 1962), 143.

70.    Papen, 300; Neurath testimony, 24 June 1946, *TMWC*, 16:630; Gehl, 96-97.

71.    Gehl, 96-97.

72.    Hassell to Neurath, 29 March 1934, *DGFP(C)*, 2:691; Neurath memorandum, 15 June 1934, *DGFP(C)*, 3:13-14. This was Hitler's first visit abroad other than Austria and the time served on the Western Front during the First World War (Poole, 132).

73.    Neurath memorandum, 15 June 1934, *DGFP(C)*, 3:10-11.

74.    William L. Shirer, *The Rise and Fall of the Third Reich: A History of Nazi Germany* (London: Secker and Warburg, 1959), 213-226.

75.    Hermann Rauschning, *Voice of Destruction* (New York: G.P. Putnam's Sons, 1940), 167.

for his own life and the safety of his family, Neurath asked President Hindenburg for permission to resign as Foreign Minister.[76] Hindenburg, however, convinced Neurath to remain at his post.[77] As long as Hindenburg was alive Neurath would have the President's strong support.[78]

Such violence that existed in Germany was also evident in Austria. On 25 July 1934, the Austrian National Socialists attempted a putsch against the Dollfuss government. Although it failed, Dollfuss was murdered in the attempt. The international community believed that Hitler was responsible for the incident. Hitler had supported the Austrian Nazis despite the advice of the Wilhelmstrasse. German diplomats were naturally upset at the turn of events. Paul Otto Schmidt told the Nuremberg Court that "the attempted Putsch in Austria and the murder of Dollfuss on 25 July 1934 seriously disturbed the career personnel of the Foreign Office because these events discredited Germany in the eyes of the world."[79] On 26 July, Hitler completely bypassed Neurath's control of relations with Austria by appointing Papen as German Ambassador to Vienna. Papen was to report directly to the Chancellor instead of Neurath on Austrian issues.[80] Within weeks, Hitler decided to back off from interference in Austria's internal affairs because of international pressure.[81] The international community saw Germany as an aggressive force about to upset the status quo. German diplomats recognized that Germany's aggressiveness during the summer of 1934 and quest to rearm had resulted in increased suspiciousness towards German intentions, and served as the catalyst that encouraged France to seek a rapprochement with both Italy and the Soviet Union.[82]

## Rise of the Führer

The death of President Hindenburg, on 2 August 1934, had a tremendous impact on the internal political situation of Germany. Hitler assumed sole leadership of Germany as Reich President, Reich Chancellor, and Führer of the

---

76. Heineman, "Constantin Freiherr von Neurath as Foreign Minister, 1932-1935," 257; Heineman, *Hitler's First Foreign Minister*, 80.
77. Heineman, *Hitler's First Foreign Minister*, 80.
78. Heineman, "Constantin Freiherr von Neurath as Foreign Minister, 1932-1935," 255.
79. Paul Otto Schmidt affidavit, 28 November 1945, *NCA*, 5:1101-102.
80. Hitler to Papen, 26 July 1934, *DGFP(C)*, 3:252-53.
81. Papen to Neurath, 4 November 1934, *DGFP(C)*, 3566, note 7.
82. William I. Shorrock, *From Ally to Enemy: The Enigma of Fascist Italy in French Diplomacy, 1920-1940* (Kent: Kent State University Press, 1988), 100; C.J. Lowe and F. Marzari, *Italian Foreign Policy, 1870-1940* (London: Routledge and Kegan Paul, 1975), 228; Schmidt affidavit, 28 November 1945, *NCA*, 5:1101-102.

Nazi Party. He gained the support of Reichswehr officers when they swore an oath of personal loyalty to the Führer.[83] The result was that Hitler, according to Norman Rich, held the "ultimate control of power and authority" in Germany.[84] The death of Hindenburg meant that Neurath had no support in the battle with Hitler for influence over the formulation and conduct of foreign policy. Neurath and the Foreign Office diplomats, fearing the consequences of opposing Hitler as well as still hoping to influence international relations, thus agreed to the Führer's demand that they swear allegiance to him.[85] The American Ambassador to Berlin, William E. Dodd, immediately noticed the change in the Foreign Minister. He wrote in his diary, "Neurath heiled Hitler…when supreme powers were taken on. I have never seen evidence that…[Neurath] ever resists the arbitrary conduct of the Führer."[86] With firm control over the German Reich, Hitler became his own Foreign Minister. Ernst Woermann, who was Head Counselor for International Law in the Foreign Office in 1934, stated at his trial at Nuremberg:

> In 1934, after Reich President von Hindenburg had died, Hitler decided foreign policy exclusively by himself, although it's a fact that there were many, and far too many, who did bother about foreign policy, too.[87]

In fact, Hitler wanted to rid himself of Neurath and the Wilhelmstrasse. The Führer became impatient with his professional diplomats. He commented to Hermann Rauschning:

> I told these Father Christmases at the Foreign Ministry that what they were up to was good enough for quiet times, when they can all go their sleepy way; but not good enough for creating a new Reich. They must take the trouble to learn more modern methods. Neurath is unimaginative. Shrewd as a peasant, but with no ideas.[88]

---

83.   Dietrich Orlow, *A History of Modern Germany: 1871 to Present*, 3 ed. (Englewood Cliffs, NJ: Prentice Hall, 1995), 190.

84.   Norman Rich, *Hitler's War Aims*, 2 vols. (New York: W.W. Norton, 1973-74), 1:76-77.

85.   William E. Dodd, *Ambassador Dodd's Diary, 1933-1938*, ed. William E. Dodd and Martha Dodd (New York: Harcourt, Brace and Company, 1941), 179-80; Heineman, "Constantin Freiherr von Neurath as Foreign Minister, 1932-1935," 257.

86.   Dodd, 139.

87.   Ernst Woermann testimony, 2 July 1948, AMT transcript, OGL 17, Box 140, Folder 5, 11036.

88.   Rauschning, *Voice of Destruction*, 275.

Hitler, nevertheless, retained Neurath and the professional diplomats of the Foreign Office. Even so, the Führer largely ignored the Wilhelmstrasse. He "practically stopped" cabinet meetings that included Neurath.[89] Instead, he preferred to employ his own amateur diplomats in the conduct of policy formulated by himself.[90] The rise of Hitler's personal diplomats, especially Joachim von Ribbentrop, eclipsed any influence that the Wilhelmstrasse had concerning the formulation of foreign policy.[91]

## Joachim von Ribbentrop

Ribbentrop was born in the Rhineland city of Wesel in 1893. His family had a long tradition of serving in the military. Growing up the son of a German Army officer, the young Ribbentrop lived in Alsace-Lorraine, and later, Switzerland. He studied and became fluent in the French and English languages. As a young man Ribbentrop traveled to England, Canada, and the United States. He returned to Germany to join the German Army in 1914, and served in Berlin, and later, Turkey. After the war, Ribbentrop married into the wealthy Henkell family, which specialized in the wine and spirits trade, in 1920. He prospered in this trade himself, making high society contacts not only in Germany, but throughout Britain and France. A vain and ambitious man, Ribbentrop turned to politics in the early thirties.[92]

Ribbentrop first met Hitler at Berchtesgaden in August 1932. Count Wolf Heinrich von Helldorf, a Sturmabteilung leader in Berlin, introduced Ribbentrop to the rising Nazi leader because Hitler needed someone who could read foreign newspapers to him.[93] Hitler quickly took a liking to Ribbentrop, who happened to hold similar views as the Nazi leader on world affairs. Besides being

---

89.    Weizsäcker testimony, 10 June 1948, AMT transcript, OGL 17, Box 137, Folder 2, 8087; Weizsäcker, 109.

90.    Schmidt, 13.

91.    Eric Kordt, *Nicht aus den Akten: Die Wilhelmstrasse in Frieden und Krieg, Erlebnisse, Begenungen und Eindrücke, 1928-1945* (Stuttgart: Union Deutsche Verlagsgesellschaft, 1950), 91-92.

92.    Joachim von Ribbentrop, *The Ribbentrop Memoirs*, trans. Oliver Watson, ed. A. von Ribbentrop, intro. Allan Bullock (London: Weidenfeld and Nicolson, 1954), 1-20; Joachim von Ribbentrop testimony, 28 March 1946, *TMWC*, 10:224-25; H.W. Koch, *Aspects of the Third Reich* (New York: St. Martin's Press, 1985), 194; Ribbentrop biological data, D-472, *NCA*, 7:59-69; John Weitz, *Hitler's Diplomat: The Life and Times of Joachim von Ribbentrop* (New York: Ticknor and Fields, 1992), 4-20; Michael Bloch, *Ribbentrop* (New York: Crown, 1992), 1-21.

93.    Joachim C. Fest, *The Face of the Third Reich: Portraits of the Nazi Leadership*, trans. Michael Bullock (New York: Pantheon, 1970), 177; Rauschning, *Men of Chaos*, 196.

a well-known anti-Bolshevik, Ribbentrop believed that Germany should seek closer ties with Britain and France. Ribbentrop's ties with the higher circles of Berlin society, as well as his accumulated knowledge of foreign affairs by way of his business trips also impressed Hitler.[94] Thus, Hitler began to use Ribbentrop as an adviser on international relations. At the same time, the ambitious Ribbentrop made the conscientious decision to attach himself to the rising Nazi leader, and played a key role in Hitler's rise to power in January 1933.[95]

Once Hitler became Chancellor, Ribbentrop believed the Nazi leader owed him an appointment to an official diplomatic position. But, Vice Chancellor Papen objected to Ribbentrop replacing Bülow as Foreign Secretary.[96] Ribbentrop bided his time waiting for Hitler to utilize him. It was during this interim period that Ribbentrop discovered a tactic that he would successfully employ with Hitler throughout his service to the Third Reich. As Gordon Craig has written:

> He [Ribbentrop] became the most constant attendant in the Chancellor's anteroom, where, by the simple expedient of making a fine art of hanging around, he managed to have frequent talks with Germany's new ruler. In the conversations…, he stumbled on the technique that was to be the foundation stone of his career. This was the gift of storing away in his memory pet ideas of the Führer and then introducing them on later occasions as ideas of his own—a procedure which could not help but persuade Hitler that Ribbentrop was a man of discernment and judgment.[97]

As already discussed, Hitler disliked professional diplomats and sought to bypass the Wilhelmstrasse in the formulation and conduct of foreign policy. Hitler and Göring, nonetheless, were highly impressed with Ribbentrop's credentials that included his knowledge of foreign languages and world affairs, personal connections abroad, party membership, and the fact that he was not a professional diplomat. Göring declared that Ribbentrop "seemed made to order."[98] In 1933, the Chancellor provided Ribbentrop money from the Nazi Party's treasury to establish an orga-

---

94.    Fest, *The Face of the Third Reich*, 177.

95.    Ribbentrop, 22-26; Ribbentrop testimony, 28 March 1946, *TMWC*, 10:231-32.

96.    Papen, 373; Heineman, "Constantin Freiherr von Neurath as Foreign Minister, 1932-1935," 273; *NCA*, supplement A, 470.

97.    Craig, "The German Foreign Office from Neurath to Ribbentrop," 420. See also Herbert von Dirksen, *Moscow, Tokyo, London: Twenty Years of German Foreign Policy* (Norman: University of Oklahoma Press, 1952), 170; Weizsäcker testimony, 7 June 1948, AMT transcript, OGL 17, Box 136, Folder 13, 7703.

98.    As quoted in Poole, 133. See also Heineman, "Constantin Freiherr von Neurath as Foreign Minister, 1932-1935," 326.

nization—the Bureau (Dienststelle) Ribbentrop—that would challenge the German Foreign Office for control over the conduct of foreign relations.[99] The Bureau Ribbentrop served as the personal foreign service of Hitler, falling under the direction of Hitler and Rudolf Hess.[100] Ribbentrop set up the Bureau across the street from the Foreign Office at Number 64 on the Wilhelmstrasse.[101] Initially it began with a small staff,[102] but the Bureau gradually increased to over 300 personnel,[103] a figure much larger than the number of staff at the Foreign Office.[104] It was staffed by men without diplomatic qualifications who sought a short cut to a career in foreign relations.[105] The Bureau, according to Eric Kordt, a professional diplomat at the Wilhelmstrasse, became an "exact replica of the Foreign Office" in organizational structure.[106]

Hitler began using Ribbentrop as a personal diplomat by sending him on unofficial visits to France in late 1933. Both men sought a better understanding between Germany and France concerning armament issues.[107] Ribbentrop had impressed upon Hitler that Germany needed closer relations with France, Britain, and Italy to acquire their acceptance of equal rights, rearmament, and a return to Great Power status for Germany.[108] With increasing control over foreign policy, Hitler made a direct challenge against the authority of the Foreign Office by appointing Ribbentrop as Special Commissioner for Disarmament Questions on 27 April 1934.[109] Despite Neurath's protests,[110] Hitler sent Ribbentrop on several trips to London, Paris, and Rome during April to November 1934,[111] hoping that his envoy could

---

99.    Paul Seabury, *The Wilhelmstrasse: A Study of German Diplomats under the Nazi Regime* (Berkeley: University of California Press, 1954), 52; Papen, 373-74; Leonidas E. Hill, "The Wilhelmstrasse in the Nazi Era," *Political Science Quarterly* 83 (December 1967), 556.

100.    Papen, 374.

101.    Heineman, "Constantin Freiherr von Neurath as Foreign Minister, 1932-1935," 275-76.

102.    Ibid.

103.    Kordt testimony, 4 June 1948, AMT transcript, OGL 17, Box 136, Folder 7, 7345.

104.    Papen, 374.

105.    Ibid.; Kordt testimony, 4 June 1948, AMT transcript, OGL 17, Box 136, Folder 7, 7345.

106.    Kordt testimony, 4 June 1948, AMT transcript, OGL 17, Box 136, Folder 7, 7346.

107.    Weinberg, *The Foreign Policy of Hitler's Germany*, 1:170.

108.    Ribbentrop, 33-35.

109.    Neurath to Hans Koester and Leopold von Hoesch, 18 April 1934, *DGFP(C)*, 2:751-52; Weinberg, *The Foreign Policy of Hitler's Germany*, 1:175.

110.    Sir Eric Phipps to Sir John Simon, the British Foreign Secretary, 25 April 1934, *DBFP*, second series, 6:657.

111.    Ribbentrop to Neurath, 16 November 1934, *DGFP(C)*, 3:638-41; Ribbentrop testimony, 29 March 1946, *TMWC*, 10:234-35; Heineman, "Constantin Freiherr von Neurath as Foreign Minister, 1932-1935," 274; Seabury, *The Wilhelmstrasse*, 53; François-Poncet, 128; Ribbentrop biographical data, D-472, *NCA*, 7:60.

make use of his special contacts and make some headway regarding the acceptance of German military equality.[112] Although his talks with British Foreign Secretary Sir John Simon (1931-35) and French Foreign Minister Louis Barthou (1934) failed to achieve any positive results,[113] this fact did not affect Ribbentrop's standing with Hitler.[114] This affair, nevertheless, was of the utmost importance for Neurath and the Foreign Office since it seriously curtailed their influence over the major foreign policy issue of rearmament.[115]

## German Rearmament

German rearmament and aggressiveness created instability in Europe in 1934. Fearing German intentions, the French government reacted by seeking rapprochement with Italy and the Soviet Union with the hope of creating an Eastern Locarno.[116] France supported the entrance of the Soviet Union into the League of Nations in September 1934.[117] Talks culminated in the Laval-Mussolini Accords on 7 January 1935. The French and Italians agreed to oppose any unilateral rearmament by Germany, as well as to support the continuation of Austrian independence.[118] Hitler had no immediate reaction to this challenge since the Saar Plebiscite was scheduled for 13 January. He wanted the return of the Saarland from French control.[119] After the successful reacquisition of this territory, Hitler planned his next move. On 25 February 1935, the Führer appointed Ribbentrop as the Commissioner for Foreign Policy Questions, and attached him to Rudolf Hess' staff.[120] Such an appointment as the top Nazi diplomat illustrated Ribbentrop's favor with Hitler.[121] But, having made no advancement in gaining acceptance of German military equality, Hitler was becoming frustrated. Then, in the first week of March, the MacDonald Cabinet criticized German

---

112.  Neurath memorandum, 10 March 1934, *DGFP(C)*, 2:584-85; Carr, *Hitler*, 51.
113.  Ribbentrop, 35-38.
114.  Ribbentrop memorandum, 10 May 1934, *DGFP(C)*, 2:805-9; Ribbentrop memorandum, 18 May 1934, *DGFP(C)*, 2:826-31.
115.  Hoesch to Neurath, 25 May 1934, *DGFP(C)*, 2:842-45; Hoesch to Neurath, 27 May 1934, *DGFP(C)*, 2:848-50.
116.  Anthony Adamthwaite, *Grandeur and Misery: France's Bid for Power in Europe, 1914-1940* (London: Arnold, 1995), 193.
117.  Scott, *Alliance against Hitler*, 136-37; R.H. Haigh, D.S. Morris, and A.R. Peters, *Soviet Foreign Policy, the League of Nations, and Europe,1917-1939* (London: Gower, 1986), 27.
118.  Shorrock, 110; Lowe and Marzari, 239; J. Néré, *The Foreign Policy of France from 1914 to 1945* (London: Routledge and Kegan Paul, 1975), 152.
119.  Department II German Foreign Office memorandum, 15 January 1935, *DGFP(C)*, 3:810.
120.  Heineman, *Hitler's First Foreign Minister*, 131.
121.  Kordt, *Nicht aus den Akten*, 88.

rearmament efforts and urged for British rearmament.[122] Hitler quickly reacted by taking steps in the unilateral rearmament of Germany.

On 9 March 1935, the Führer made the establishment of the German Luftwaffe (Air Force) public knowledge.[123] The Luftwaffe had about 2,500 aircraft of all types, of which 800 could be used in combat in the event of war, and a cadre of 20,000 officers and men.[124] One week later, on 16 March, the Führer declared the reintroduction of universal military conscription. He also announced that Germany would not respect the Versailles military clauses limiting it to 100,000 troops in the future.[125] In fact, the German Army already consisted of 180,000 men.[126] Hitler planned to build a peacetime military of thirty-six divisions consisting of 550,000 troops.[127] Both of these March announcements were planned by Hitler without the advice of the Foreign Office.[128] Shortly thereafter, General Werner von Blomberg, the War Minister, was appointed the Supreme Commander of the new Wehrmacht (combined Army, Air Force, and Navy).

International tension heightened with the announcements of the rearmament of Germany. As a British initiative, representatives from Britain, France, and Italy met at the Stresa Conference in Switzerland to discuss collective security issues on 11 April 1935.[129] Mussolini sought to create an alliance system, but Britain hesitated at this suggestion. Prime Minister Ramsay MacDonald and Foreign Secretary Sir John Simon refused to commit Britain to a European security agreement against Germany.[130] London already was stretched thin with worldwide commitments and wanted to avoid further obligations that might lead to action.[131] The

---

122. D.C. Watt, "The Anglo-German Naval Agreement of 1935: An Interim Judgment," *The Journal of Modern History* 28 (June 1956), 155-56; Neurath to Hoesch, Koester, and Hassell, 6 March 1935, *DGFP(C)*, 3:979.

123. Watt, "The Anglo-German Naval Agreement of 1935," 155-56; François-Poncet, 168; Scott, *Alliance against Hitler*, 227.

124. Deist, "The Rearmament of the Wehrmacht," 491. See also Louis L. Snyder, *Encyclopedia of the Third Reich* (New York: Paragon House, 1976), 217.

125. François-Poncet, 170; Neurath memorandum, 18 March 1935, *DGFP(C)*, 3:1015; Diest, *The Wehrmacht and German Rearmament*, 37.

126. Deist, *The Wehrmacht and German Rearmament*, 36.

127. Deist, "The Rearmament of the Wehrmacht," 422; Snyder, *Encyclopedia of the Third Reich*, 157.

128. Weinberg, *The Foreign Policy of Hitler's Germany*, 1:205.

129. A.R. Peters, *Anthony Eden at the Foreign Office, 1931-1938* (New York: St. Martin's Press, 1986), 96.

130. Ibid., 88-89.

131. Maurice Cowling, *The Impact of Hitler: British Politics and British Policy, 1933-1940* (Chicago: University of Chicago Press, 1975), 74.

British government knew that it had to rearm to defend interests in Europe and abroad. This would include a buildup of the Royal Navy and Air Force.[132] Instead of an alliance, Britain, Italy, and France agreed to create a common front, the so-called Stresa Front, against German unilateral rearmament.[133] The Stresa Front issued a statement that "spanked" Germany for repudiating its disarmament obligations.[134] Several weeks later, on 2 May, Pierre Laval, the French Foreign Minister (1934-36) gained a five-year Franco-Soviet Treaty of Mutual Assistance in case of German aggression.[135] Laval also assisted Stalin and the Soviet Union in backing up the Franco-Soviet treaty with a mutual assistance pact with Czechoslovakia on 16 May.[136] Six weeks later, on 28 June, France and Italy signed military accords to strengthen the Stresa Front. These accords outlined possible Franco-Italian military cooperation in case of German aggression against France, Austria, or Italy.[137] It seemed that the Great Powers of Europe were uniting in a common front against German designs to destroy the Versailles agreement. As Norman Rich has pointed out:

> Germany remained isolated and was now encircled by a formidable great-power coalition of Britain, France, Italy, and the Soviet Union, and by the lesser powers of Poland and the Little Entente.[138]

---

132.  Ibid., 70-71. See also Michael Howard, *The Continental Commitment: The Dilemma of British Defence Policy in the Era of Two World Wars* (London: Maurice Temple Smith, 1972) and Brian Bond, "The Continental Commitment in British Strategy in the 1930s," in *The Fascist Challenge and the Policy of Appeasement*, eds. Wolfgang J. Mommsen and Lothar Kettenacker (London: George Allen and Unwin, 1983).

133.  Weinberg, *The Foreign Policy of Hitler's Germany*, 1:207; Manfred Messerschmidt, "Foreign Policy and Preparation for War," in *The Buildup of German Aggression*, vol. I in *Germany and the Second World War*, eds. W. Deist, M. Messerschmidt, H.-E. Volkmann, and W.Wette, trans. P.S. Falla, Dean S. McMurry, and Ewald Osers (Oxford: Clarendon Press, 1990), 605-8; Norman Rich, *Great Power Diplomacy since 1914* (Boston: McGraw-Hill, 2003), 176-77.

134.  H. James Burgwyn, *Italian Foreign Policy in the Interwar Period, 1918-1940* (Westport, CT: Praeger, 1997), 112. Italian relations with the Soviet Union are related in J. Calvitt Clarke, *Russia and Italy Against Hitler: The Bolshevik-Fascist Rapprochement of the 1930s* (New York: Greenwood Press, 1991).

135.  Néré, 170, 322-25; Scott, *Alliance against Hitler*, 246.

136.  Geoffrey Roberts, *The Soviet Union and the Origins of the Second World War: Russo-German Relations and the Road to War, 1933-1941* (New York: St. Martin's Press, 1995), 18; Jiri Hochman, *The Soviet Union and the Failure of Collective Security, 1934-1938* (Ithaca: Cornell University Press, 1984), 52; Piotr S. Wandycz, *The Twilight of French Eastern Alliances, 1926-1936: French-Czechoslovak-Polish Relations from Locarno to the Remilitarization of the Rhineland* (Princeton: Princeton University Press, 1988), 399-400.

137.  Burgwyn, 114.

138.  Rich, *Great Power Diplomacy since 1914*, 177.

However, Hitler would break this front by negotiating and concluding a naval arms pact with Britain.[139]

From his earlier writings on foreign relations, Hitler had always believed that Germany should seek an arrangement with Britain over spheres of influence. He strongly desired close ties with Britain.[140] During the mid-thirties Hitler came to realize that he could only reach an accommodation with Britain if Germany recognized British supremacy on the high seas.[141] Thus, the Führer was willing to offer an arms limitation agreement to Britain that would place the German Navy in a much inferior status compared to the Royal Navy.[142] He thought that such an arrangement would encourage the British to support German military rearmament.[143] In April 1935, shortly after Germany's declaration to rearm, Hitler received indications from Sir John Simon that the British government was willing to negotiate a naval arms limitation agreement in order to avoid a naval arms race.[144] The following month, Sir Eric Phipps, the British Ambassador to Berlin, pressed Hitler for the initiation of naval arms talks in London.[145] Hitler decided to participate, and therefore appointed Ribbentrop as German Ambassador at Large to travel to London and negotiate an agreement.[146] Beginning the talks on 4 June, Ribbentrop submitted Hitler's proposal that Germany would build a fleet only thirty-five percent the size of the Royal Navy.[147] According to Paul Otto Schmidt, the German Foreign Office interpreter who accompanied him to London, Ribbentrop declared to Simon, "if the British Government does not immediately accept this condition, there is no point at all in continuing these negotiations. We must insist upon an immediate answer."[148] Such a tactic was

---

139.   Kimmich, 193; Weinberg, *The Foreign Policy of Hitler's Germany*, 1:214-15; Jäckel, 44.

140.   Ribbentrop testimony, 29 March 1946, *TMWC*, 10:235.

141.   Ibid.; Poole, 132.

142.   Weinberg, *The Foreign Policy of Hitler's Germany*, 1:214; Hildebrand, *The Foreign Policy of the Third Reich*, 38.

143.   Ribbentrop testimony, 29 March 1946, *TMWC*, 10:235; Hildebrand, *The Foreign Policy of the Third Reich*, 38-39; Weinberg, *The Foreign Policy of Hitler's Germany*, 1:214.

144.   Neurath memorandum, 9 April 1935, *DGFP(C)*, 4:28; Neurath testimony, 24 June 1946, 16:623; Weinberg, *The Foreign Policy of Hitler's Germany*, 1:210.

145.   Phipps to Neurath, 24 May 1935, *DGFP(C)*, 4:195-96.

146.   Ribbentrop testimony, 1 April 1946, *TMWC*, 10:235; Ribbentrop biographical data, D-472, *NCA*, 7:60.

147.   R.A.C. Parker, *Chamberlain and Appeasement: British Policy and the Coming of the Second World War* (New York: St. Martin's Press, 1993), 30-31.

148.   Schmidt, 33; Anglo-German Naval Talks memorandum, 4 June 1935, *DGFP(C)*, 4:253-62; Joachim C. Fest, *Hitler*, trans. Richard Winston and Clara Winston (London: Weidenfeld and Nicolson, 1973), 491-92.

shocking to the British Foreign Office, and even to the highly experienced Schmidt, but within a few days the British agreed to Hitler's demand, and Ribbentrop acquired his Anglo-German Naval Agreement on 18 June 1935.[149] Ribbentrop had broken up the Stresa Front.[150] Moreover, his success convinced Hitler that Ribbentrop was the obvious person to employ for implementing his ideas of a "general accommodation" with Britain.[151] Hitler hailed Ribbentrop as "greater than Bismarck" for his success in acquiring an agreement with Britain.[152]

## Remilitarization of the Rhineland

In spite of diplomatic success in Britain, Hitler discovered that the rearmament of Germany continued to bring together states that viewed the Third Reich as a threat to European political stability. France and the Soviet Union worked to create alliances against Germany to protect the status quo. As for Germany's return to Great Power status, there was only one more Versailles military restriction still in enforcement, the demilitarization of the Rhineland, which was reinforced by the Treaty of Locarno.[153] Hitler and the Wilhelmstrasse realized they would have to negotiate against French opposition to rid themselves of the Versailles and Locarno agreements in order to reacquire full sovereignty over the Rhineland, and thus regain Great Power status. But France was moving closer to ratifying the Franco-Soviet Mutual Assistance Pact. This pact, along with French and Soviet alliances with other European states, such as Czechoslovakia, threatened German security.[154] As such, Hitler's attempt to dissuade France from ratifying the Franco-Soviet agreement by reassuring Paris of Germany's peaceful intentions was failing.[155] In February 1936, Hitler confided to Ulrich von Hassell, the German Ambassador to Italy, his thoughts about using the possible ratification of the Franco-Soviet Pact as grounds for denouncing the Locarno Treaty, followed by the German military moving into the Rhineland zone.[156] He believed that the time was right for such action since the international community was busy protesting the Italian invasion of Abyssinia. Mussolini had launched an invasion of

149.  Anglo-German Naval Talks memorandum, 6 June 1935, *DGFP(C)*, 4:277-81; Dodd, 257; Carr, *Hitler*, 50; Ribbentrop biological data, D-472, *NCA*, 7:60.

150.  Messerschmidt, 602.

151.  Hildebrand, *The Third Reich*, 19; Weinberg, *The Foreign Policy of Hitler's Germany*, 1:214.

152.  As quoted in Fest, *Hitler*, 492.

153.  Heineman, *Hitler's First Foreign Minister*, 115.

154.  Hermann Göring testimony, 14 March 1946, *TMWC*, 9:285; Neurath testimony, 24 June 1946, *TMWC*, 16:625.

155.  Adolf Hitler and Bertrand de Jouvenel interview, 21 February 1936, *TMWC*, 40:506.

156.  Hassell memorandum, 14 February 1935, *DGFP(C)*, 4:1142-144.

Abyssinia in October 1935.[157] Hitler had determined, and Ribbentrop encouraged such thought, that neither Britain nor France would act militarily to oppose German reoccupation of the Rhineland.[158]

The French Chamber of Deputies ratified the Franco-Soviet agreement on 27 February 1936.[159] Hitler quickly made the decision to send the German military into the Rhineland.[160] On 2 March, General Blomberg ordered a division of German troops to move into the Rhineland on 7 March 1936.[161] Hitler informed Neurath of his decision on 5 March, stating that he took the view that the Franco-Soviet Pact was incompatible with the Treaty of Locarno and made it obsolete.[162] The threat of the French and Soviet alliance systems to Germany made it imperative that Hitler reoccupy the Rhineland with troops for defensive reasons.[163] Understanding Hitler's reasoning and the desirability for the reoccupation of the Rhineland, the Foreign Minister advised Hitler against taking such a bold move because of the possible international reaction. Even so, Neurath had also advised Hitler that Britain and France would not intervene militarily.[164] He, however, failed to contest Hitler's decision because of his fear of the Führer.[165] On the other hand, Göring, Ribbentrop, and Goebbels encouraged Hitler to remilitarize the Rhineland, and therefore, when German troops successfully

157.  See George W. Baer, *The Coming of the Italian-Ethiopian War* (Cambridge, MA: Harvard University Press, 1967).

158.  Hassell memorandum, 20 February 1935, *DGFP(C)*, 4:1165; James T. Emmerson, *The Rhineland Crisis, 7 March 1936: A Study in Multilateral Diplomacy* (London: Maurice Temple Smith, 1977), 82; Kordt, *Nicht aus den Akten*, 129-30; François-Poncet, 241.

159.  Jean-Baptiste Duroselle, *France and the Collapse of French Diplomacy, 1932-1939*, trans. E. Dop and Robert L. Miller (New York: Egnima, 2004), 114-16.

160.  Göring testimony, 14 March 1946, *TMWC*, 9:285; Emmerson, 72; Neurath testimony, 24 June 1946, *TMWC*, 16:626.

161.  Hitler to General Werner von Blomberg, 2 March 1936, *TMWC*, 34:644-47; Editor's note, *DGFP(C)*, 4:128.

162.  Neurath testimony, 24 June 1946, *TMWC*, 16:626; François-Poncet, 191-94; Dieckhoff testimony, 26 June 1946, *TMWC*, 17:124; Neurath interrogation testimony, 4 October 1945, *NCA*, supplement B, 1495; Neurath to Missions in Great Britain, France, Italy, and Belgium, 5 March 1936, *DGFP(C)*, 5:11-19; Conference of Ministers minutes, 6 March 1936, *DGFP(C)*, 5:26-28.

163.  Neurath testimony, 24 June 1946, *TMWC*, 16:627; Official Declaration of the German Government, 12 March 1936, *TMWC*, 40:509; Göring testimony, 14 March 1946, *TMWC*, 9:285.

164.  Hassell memorandum, 20 February 1936, *DGFP(C)*, 4:1164; Heineman, *Hitler's First Foreign Minister*, 114; Emmerson, 83; Neurath testimony, 25 June 1946, *TMWC*, 17:41-42.

165.  Emmerson, 83-84; Anthony Eden, *The Memoirs of Anthony Eden, Earl of Avon: Facing the Dictators* (Boston: Houghton Mifflin, 1962), 386.

moved into the Rhineland without any military reaction from the Versailles Powers on 7 March, their stock with the Führer dramatically increased while the Wilhelmstrasse only received his contempt.[166] In fact, Hitler sent Ribbentrop, instead of a diplomat from the Foreign Office, to defend the German action to the League of Nations Council in London on 10 March 1936.[167]

In regards to the decision to reoccupy the Rhineland, both Nazi Party members and professional diplomats of the Foreign Office agreed that Hitler made the decision himself on the spur of the moment. According to witnesses, this pattern of decision-making continued throughout the Third Reich. In 1945, Hermann Göring told his Nuremberg interrogators:

> Hitler's arbitrary decisions…were as unquestionable as a turn in the weather. We would talk one day about something…and Hitler would agree with us; then suddenly a day or so later Hitler would announce that he had decided something altogether different.[168]

Ernst von Weizsäcker, the German Ambassador to Sweden (1933-36), and later Director of the Political Department (1936-38) and Foreign Secretary (1938-43),[169] declared that "Hitler was not logical. He would pull his ideas out of the air, just like that, just as the moment inspired him."[170] As for Neurath's influence with Hitler, Weizsäcker stated during his Nuremberg trial, "Neurath saw little of Hitler—much too little, in view of Hitler's tendency to act on the spur of the moment. With Hitler, anyone who was not on the spot did not count."[171] "Decisions were made," so stated Weizsäcker, "without the Foreign Minister…. Sometimes they didn't even listen to him…."[172] Göring even admitted that the Foreign Office had no influence over the formulation of policy. He told the Nuremberg judges:

---

166. Hassell memorandum, 20 February 1936, *DGFP(C)*, 4:1165; Dirksen, 181; John W. Wheeler-Bennett, *The Nemesis of Power: The Germany Army in Politics* (London: Macmillan, 1954), 225; Emmerson, 238; Craig, "The German Foreign Office from Neurath to Ribbentrop," 426; Kordt, *Nicht aus den Akten*, 129-30; François-Poncet, 195-97.

167. François-Poncet, 198; Weinberg, *The Foreign Policy of Hitler's Germany*, 1:259; Schmidt, 41; Ribbentrop to British Government, undated, *DGFP(C)*, 5:283-86; Sir David Maxwell-Fyfe, 8 January 1946, *TMWC*, 4:559; *NCA*, 2:490; Göring testimony, 8 March 1946, *TMWC*, 9:7.

168. As quoted in Poole, 131.

169. Weizsäcker testimony, 7 June 1948, AMT transcript, OGL 17, Box 136, Folder 10, 7593-594.

170. Weizsäcker testimony, 8 June 1948, AMT transcript, OGL 17, Box 135, Folder 14, 7756.

171. Weizsäcker, 109.

172. Weizsäcker testimony, 10 June 1948, AMT transcript, OGL, 17, Box 137, Folder 2, 8086.

>As far as foreign policy was concerned, Hitler only consulted his colleagues more on the…purely technical side. The most important and far-reaching political decisions were taken by himself, and he then announced them to his collaborators and colleagues as ready-made conceptions. Only very few people were allowed to discuss them, myself for instance; and the technical execution of his decisions in the field of foreign policy, when it came to the framing the diplomatic notes, was done by the Foreign Office and its minister.[173]

## Reorganization of the Foreign Office

After the highly successful reoccupation of the Rhineland, the Führer sought to complete his plans for reforming the Wilhelmstrasse. He strongly disliked professional diplomats and wanted to replace the Foreign Office leadership with Nazi Party members. Hitler planned to take control of the foreign service by integrating Ribbentrop and members of the Bureau Ribbentrop into the Wilhelmstrasse. According to one observer:

>The Führer saw in the Foreign Office a body of ossified red-tape civil servants, more or less untouched by National Socialism. [H]e often made fun of the Foreign Office. He considered it to be the home of reaction and defeatism.[174]

As early as 1935, many foreign diplomats, including Ambassador Dodd, believed that Ribbentrop would soon become either the new Foreign Minister or State Secretary.[175] In October 1935, the Führer had proposed to Neurath that Ribbentrop should replace Bülow as Foreign Secretary. But, the Foreign Minister strongly objected to the appointment of an unqualified person, such as Ribbentrop, and threatened to resign.[176] After this refusal to bend to his wishes, Hitler demanded the reform of the Wilhelmstrasse, calling for the dismissal of such "scoundrels and traitors" as Bülow.[177] On 4 November 1935, Hitler told Neurath that, "the [Foreign Office] has refused to cooperate. It stands outside the party, refuses to understand the policies of the Führer, and continued to make difficulties everywhere."[178]

---

173.   Göring testimony, 14 March 1946, *TMWC*, 9:620.
174.   Fraulein Blank testimony, 23 March 1946, *TMWC*, 10:189.
175.   Dodd, 250; Heineman, "Constantin Freiherr von Neurath as Foreign Minister, 1932-1935," 278.
176.   Neurath to Hitler, 25 October 1935, *TMWC*, 40:470-71.
177.   As quoted in Heineman, *Hitler's First Foreign Minister*, 139.
178.   As quoted in ibid.

Fearing Hitler's wrath, Neurath and Bülow made extensive plans to reorganize the Wilhelmstrasse. They had already started this process by disbanding Department IV (East Europe, Scandinavia, and East Asia) and transferring its responsibilities to Departments II (West, South, and South-East Europe) and III (Britain, American, and the Orient) in September 1935.[179] Such action was driven by Hitler's threat to the Jewish Director of Department IV, Richard Meyer, who was granted a leave of absence by Neurath in response to the Nuremberg Laws of September 1935 that deprived Jews of their German citizenship.[180] When Gerhard Köpke, the Director of Department II, became seriously ill,[181] Neurath temporarily combined this department with Department III, headed by Hans Dieckhoff, in December 1935.[182] Thus, with the functions of the three main departments falling under the direction of Dieckhoff, the Foreign Minister and Bülow planned to reorganize the foreign service by reestablishing the Political Department, under the leadership of Dieckhoff, to replace Departments II and III.[183] This reorganization became effective on 15 May 1936.[184] Afterwards, the Auswärtiges Amt consisted of Department I (Personnel and Budget), Department II (Political), Department III (Commercial Politics), Department IV (Legal), and Department V (Cultural Politics).[185]

During this period of reorganization Neurath and the Foreign Office suffered considerable losses in diplomatic expertise. Not only did Richard Meyer retire, but Roland Köster, the German Ambassador to France died in December 1935.[186] Gerhard Köpke resigned because of his illness in early January 1936.[187] Three months later, in April, the Director of Personnel, Werner von Grünau, also became ill and resigned while the German Ambassador to Britain, Leopold von Hoesch, unexpectedly died in London.[188] Within several months Neurath had lost his top two advisers (Meyer and Köpke), his personnel director, and the

---

179.  Appendix B, *DGFP(C)*, 4:1242; Editor's note, *DGFP(C)*, 4:941.

180.  Heineman, *Hitler's First Foreign Minister*, 139; Editor's note, *DGFP(C)*, 4:941.

181.  Köpke had a Jewish grandmother (Donald M. McKale, *Curt Prüfer: German Diplomat from the Kaiser to Hitler* [Kent: Kent State University Press, 1987], 130).

182.  Appendix B, *DGFP(C)*, 4:1239.

183.  Ibid.

184.  Appendix A, *DGFP(C)*, 5:1177; Woermann testimony, 2 July 1948, AMT transcript, OGL 17, Box 140, Folder 2, 10848.

185.  Kurt Doss, "The History of the German Foreign Office," in *The Times Survey of Foreign Ministries of the World*, ed. Zara Steiner (London: Times Books, 1982), 242.

186.  Herbert von Dirksen to Otto von Ermannsdorff, 1 January 1936, *DGFP(C)*, 4:952; Editor's note, *DGFP(C)*, 4:941; Heineman, *Hitler's First Foreign Minister*, 141.

187.  Appendix B, *DGFP(C)*, 5:1239.

188.  Heineman, *Hitler's First Foreign Minister*, 141.

two most influential ambassadors in the foreign service. As if such losses were not enough, Foreign Secretary Bernhard Wilhelm von Bülow died of pneumonia on 21 June 1936.[189] The blows of fate had destroyed what little resistance to Hitler's policies that was left in the Foreign Office. Hans Dieckhoff was appointed as the temporary Foreign Secretary (1936-37) and Ernst von Weizsäcker assumed control of Department II (the Political Department). The pro- Nazi Curt Prüfer was appointed Director of Department I (Personnel and Budget). Other directors included Emil Wiehl (Department III), Dr. Friedrich Gaus (Department IV), and Dr. Friedrich Stieve (Department V).[190] Arriving in Berlin from his post in Stockholm, Weizsäcker noted the changes at the Wilhelmstrasse:

> On this occasion I found that in the Foreign Office the reins of government had slipped. Hitler had no great opinion of this office. Even then…he already called us a club of defeatists. He preferred information from laymen to that obtained from us. Decisions were taken without the Foreign Office or even the Foreign Minister being heard on the subject. Under normal conditions, an opinion is formed by the expert and is passed on to the top levels for decision. Instead of this, orders came to us out of a clear sky, from top to bottom, as an accomplished fact. Our Foreign Service had sunk to the level of a technical apparatus. It was really only a facade, the facade of a firm which had undergone considerable internal arrangements.[191]

## Hitler's Diplomacy

While the Wilhelmstrasse was undergoing drastic personnel and organizational changes, the Führer continued to employ Nazi diplomats in the conduct of his foreign policy. Hitler's primary focus was on gaining closer relations with Britain, Italy, and Japan. He sought to not only gain a free hand for German expansion into East Europe, but a bloc against the Soviet Union. He recognized the value of an understanding with Britain and Italy to protect any territorial acquisitions, while noting the benefit of closer German-Japanese relations aimed against the common enemy of the Soviet Union. Thus, the Führer's diplomacy was aimed at securing closer relations with all three countries from 1935 to 1937.[192] He used Joachim von Ribbentrop and his Bureau Ribbentrop to negotiate in Berlin and

---

189.   Dirksen, 169; Appendix A, *DGFP(C)*, 5:1177.
190.   Weizsäcker testimony, 7 June 1948, AMT transcript, OGL 17, Box 136, Folder 10, 7604; Weizsäcker, 104; Appendix A, *DGFP(D)*, 1:1178.
191.   Weizsäcker testimony, 7 June 1948, AMT transcript, OGL 17, Box 136, Folder 10, 7604.
192.   Ribbentrop testimony, 29 March 1946, *TMWC*, 10:235; Neurath testimony, 24 June 1946, *TMWC*, 16:639.

Tokyo, without the knowledge of the Wilhelmstrasse, for closer ties with Japan as early as the spring of 1935.[193] In November 1935, Hitler took a neutral stance in the ongoing war between Italy and Ethiopia.[194] The Ethiopian conflict brought the two dictatorships more closely together. He then employed Franz von Papen, the German Ambassador to Austria, to secretly negotiate the "Gentlemen's Agreement" with Austrian Chancellor Kurt von Schuschnigg during May to July 1936, which recognized Austrian independence, in order to improve German-Italian relations, especially considering Mussolini's fears of German intentions to expand southwards.[195] The Spanish Civil War was to establish a firm bond between Hitler and Mussolini. On 17 July 1936, General Francisco Franco began a revolt against the Popular Front government of the Second Spanish Republic in Madrid.[196] The revolt started in Spanish Morocco, and within a week both Germany and Italy backed Franco. Hitler, despite the advice of the Foreign Office,[197] promised aid to Franco, perhaps expecting a quick victory.[198] Germany initially provided Ju-52 transport planes, vital for taking the rebels from Morocco to Spain, and Italy gave Franco some bombers.[199] Hitler let Mussolini play the role of senior partner in their intervention during the Spanish Civil War (1936-39). The Auswärtiges Amt continued to object to the deployment of German troops and military weapons to Spain.[200] But, the Führer did not want the Popular Front regime to link Spain with the Franco-Soviet bloc.[201] The

---

193.   Dirksen, 142, 146, 153, 170-71; Editor's note, *DGFP(C)*, 4:948; Bülow memorandum, 9 June 1936, *DGFP(C)*, 5:603. The professional diplomats of the Wilhelmstrasse were traditionally in favor of closer ties with China (Dirksen, 184; Dirksen to Ermannsdorff, 16 January 1936, *DGFP(C)*, 4:948-52).

194.   Leitz, *Nazi Foreign Policy, 1933-1941*, 21.

195.   Weizsäcker, 108; Gentlemen's Agreeement Between Governments of Germany and Austria, 11 July 1936, *NMT*, 12:682-85; Papen, 370; Papen to Neurath, 4 May 1936, *DGFP(C)*, 5:499; Neurath memorandum, 13 May 1936, *DGFP(C)*, 5:537; Neurath to Papen, 13 June 1936, *DGFP(C)*, 5:621-22; Papen to Hitler, 12 January 1937, *DGFP(D)*, 1:366-74; Burgwyn, 139-43.

196.   Neurath interrogation testimony, 12 November 1945, *NCA*, supplement B, 1506; Hildebrand, *The Third Reich*, 165. See Michael Alpert, *A New International History of the Spanish Civil War*, 2 ed. (Basingstoke: Palgrave Macmillan, 2004) and Frances Lannon, *The Spanish Civil War, 1936-1939* (Botley: Osprey, 2002).

197.   Weizsäcker testimony, 7 June 1948, AMT transcript, OGL 17, Box 136, Folder 10, 7604; Weizsäcker, 107; Carr, *Hitler*, 52; Dieckhoff memorandum, 25 July 1936, *DGFP(D)*, 3:10-11; Shore, 81.

198.   Messerschmidt, 621.

199.   Rich, *Great Power Diplomacy since 1914*, 185; Lannon, 40.

200.   Dieckhoff memorandum, 22 August 1936, *DGFP(D)*, 3:50-52.

201.   Dr. Karl Schwendemann to Neurath, 23 July 1936, *DGFP(D)*, 3:5-7.

Soviet Union was supporting the Republican government while France and Britain were maintaining a policy of non-involvement.

With the death of Bülow in June 1936, Joachim von Ribbentrop made another bid to become Foreign Secretary. Although Hitler favored this appointment, Neurath, in a rare moment of defiance, objected to Ribbentrop's appointment by threatening to resign.[202] Realizing that Hitler could not be controlled, Neurath, who had much to gain with the champagne salesman out of Berlin, quickly suggested that the Führer appoint Ribbentrop as the new Ambassador to Britain.[203] He reminded Hitler of Ribbentrop's connections with Britain and his success with the Anglo-German Naval Agreement, as well as pointed out that Ribbentrop was the best possible choice as an ambassador who could acquire Hitler's long sought after Anglo-German understanding.[204] Agreeing with such logic, Hitler appointed Ribbentrop as Ambassador to Britain on 24 July 1936.[205] Neurath, however, really believed that this diplomatic assignment would destroy Ribbentrop's credibility. Neurath told Papen that Ribbentrop would "make a fool of himself" in London,[206] while Neurath told Italian Foreign Minister Galeazzo Ciano (1936-43) that "Ribbentrop will soon discover in London it is easier to have compliments paid to one as a representative of a brand of champagne than as a representative of the Government of the Reich."[207] But Hitler greatly upset Neurath by making Ribbentrop responsible directly to the Führer in Anglo-German affairs, thus bypassing the control of the Wilhelmstrasse.[208]

Hitler simultaneously worked for closer relations with Britain, Italy, and Japan during 1936 and 1937. His foreign policy centered on uniting Germany with these Great Powers in an anti-communist bloc that would help secure eastern expansion for the Third Reich.[209] To carry out such policy, the Führer primarily relied upon the services of Ribbentrop and his Bureau. But, Hitler also employed the traditional offices of the Wilhelmstrasse, without informing

---

202.  Kordt, *Nicht aus den Akten*, 148; Papen, 374; Gustave M. Gilbert, *Nuremberg Diary* (London: Eyre and Spottiswoode, 1948), 229-30; Neurath to Hitler, 27 July 1936, *TMWC*, 40:472-73.

203.  Papen, 375; Heineman, *Hitler's First Foreign Minister*, 141.

204.  Heineman, *Hitler's First Foreign Minister*, 141.

205.  Weizsäcker testimony, 7 June 1948, AMT transcript, OGL 17, Box 136, Folder 10, 7605.

206.  Papen, 375.

207.  Galeazzo Ciano, *Ciano's Diplomatic Papers: Being a Record of nearly 200 Conversations held during the Years 1936-1942*, ed. Malcolm Muggeridge, trans. Stuart Hood (London: Odhams, 1948), 60.

208.  Weizsäcker testimony, 7 June 1948, AMT transcript, OGL 17, Box 136, Folder 10, 7605; Neurath testimony, 24 June 1946, *TMWC*, 16:639.

209.  Ribbentrop, 75; Ribbentrop testimony, 29 March 1946, *TMWC*, 10:240; Hildebrand, *The Third Reich*, 25.

Neurath of the full extent of his plans or taking the Foreign Office's diplomatic advice, in seeking arrangements with Britain and Italy.[210] At the Nuremberg trial, Hans Dieckhoff told the court that Neurath and the Wilhelmstrasse, despite their lack of influence in the formulation of policy, continued to carry out the Führer's instructions believing that Germany would peacefully pursue its goals.[211]

Hitler kept Ribbentrop in Berlin following his personal diplomat's appointment to the ambassadorship to Britain. The Führer needed Ribbentrop to conclude talks for closer relations with Japan. Ribbentrop and his Bureau had been secretly negotiating for an understanding with Japan without Neurath's involvement since 1935.[212] These talks, nonetheless, had turned from the prospect of a military alliance toward an ideological agreement at the insistence of General Werner von Blomberg, the German Minister of Defense.[213] The idea of a German-Japanese pact against the common threat of the Communist International was introduced by Hans von Raumer, a key staff member of the Bureau Ribbentrop.[214] With the full support of Hitler, Ribbentrop sought an Anti-Comintern Pact with Japan, aimed, of course, against the Soviet Union.[215] Hitler sought closer relations with Japan to counter the Franco-Soviet threat to Germany.[216] Ribbentrop and Kintomo Mushakoji, the Japanese Ambassador to Germany, agreed to the initial terms of such a pact at the Bureau Ribbentrop on 23 October 1936.[217]

While using Ribbentrop for negotiations with Japan, the Führer employed his Foreign Minister and Hermann Göring in seeking a rapprochement with Italy.[218] In pursuing closer ties with Mussolini, Hitler had already recognized Austrian independence, provided military assistance to Franco's struggle in Spain, and had recognized Italy's annexation of Abyssinia.[219] In September 1936, the German

210.  Seabury, *The Wilhelmstrasse*, 55; Neurath testimony, 26 June 1946, *TMWC*, 17:101; Neurath testimony, 24 June 1946, *TMWC*, 16:638-39.

211.  Dieckhoff testimony, 26 June 1946, *TMWC*, 17:123.

212.  Dirksen, 170-71.

213.  Editor's note, *DGFP(C)*, 4:948.

214.  Dirksen, 171; Ribbentrop, 74. See also E.H. Carr, *Twilight of the Comintern, 1930-1935* (New York: Pantheon, 1982).

215.  Ribbentrop testimony, 29 March 1946, *TMWC*, 10:240; Editor's note, *DGFP(C)*, 4:948; Bülow memorandum, 9 June 1936, *DGFP(C)*, 5:603; Ribbentrop to Hitler, 16 August 1936, *DGFP(C)*, 5:899-900.

216.  Dirksen to Neurath, 10 March 1936, *DGFP(C)*, 5:86-87.

217.  Anti-Comintern Pact, 25 November 1936, *DGFP(C)*, 5:1138-140.

218.  See Elizabeth Wiskemann, *The Rome-Berlin Axis: A History of the Relations between Hitler and Mussolini* (London: Oxford University Press, 1949), 64-69.

219.  François-Poncet, 242-43.

leader sent his personal legal adviser, Hans Frank, as an unofficial envoy to Rome with an invitation for Ciano, the Italian Foreign Minister and son-in-law of the Duce, to visit Germany to negotiate and form an agreement for closer relations.[220] Ciano, a Germanophile,[221] traveled to Germany under Mussolini's directions in October 1936.[222] After a meeting with the Führer, where Hitler professed his strong desire for closer German-Italian relations and a common front against the communist threat, Ciano and Neurath signed a protocol at the Wilhelmstrasse, drawn up by the Foreign Office, that created the Rome-Berlin Axis on 23 October 1936, the same day that across the street Ribbentrop and Mushakoji were agreeing to the Anti-Comintern Pact.[223]

Having secured initial agreements with Japan and Italy, Hitler sent Ribbentrop to London. Upon his ambassador's departure, Hitler told Ribbentrop to "bring me back the British alliance."[224] Ribbentrop arrived in London with several members of his Bureau to present his diplomatic credentials on 30 October 1936.[225] The German Ambassador immediately sensed hostility from the British Foreign Office towards any suggestion of closer relations between the two countries.[226] Sir Robert Vansittart, the Permanent Undersecretary of State at the British Foreign Office, who was a Germanophobe, was at the center of British abhorrence of Ribbentrop's diplomatic mission.[227] From the start, the German Ambassador knew it would be "very difficult" to conclude a pact with Britain.[228] The British Foreign Office was committed to Austrian independence and the status quo in Central and East Europe.[229] Sir Anthony Eden, the British Foreign

---

220.  Wiskemann, 65. See Ray Moseley, *Mussolini's Shadow: The Double Life of Count Galeazzo Ciano* (New Haven: Yale University Press, 1999) for background on the Italian Foreign Minister.

221.  François-Poncet, 242.

222.  Ciano, *Ciano's Diplomatic Papers*, 52-60; Dodd, 359.

223.  Hildebrand, *The Third Reich*, 165; Weinberg, *The Foreign Policy of Hitler's Germany*, 1:337.

224.  As quoted in Hildebrand, *The Foreign Policy of the Third Reich*, 46.

225.  Martin Gilbert and Richard Gott, *The Appeasers* (Boston: Houghton Mifflin, 1963), 27; Eric Kordt testimony, 4 June 1948, AMT transcript, OGL 17, Box 136, Folder 7, 7347.

226.  Gilbert and Gott, 27.

227.  Ibid., 20; Ribbentrop testimony, 29 March 1946, *TMWC*, 10:238; Ribbentrop, 42, 44, 47, 57, 65; Ribbentrop interrogation testimony, 20 September 1945, *NCA*, supplement B, 1215; Ribbentrop to Neurath 6 February 1937, *DGFP(C)*, 6:378-79. See also Lord Vansittart, *Bones of Contention* (New York: Knopf, 1945) and *The Mist Procession* (London: Hutchinson, 1958).

228.  Ribbentrop testimony, 29 March 1946, *TMWC*, 10:239.

229.  John Charmley, *Chamberlain and the Lost Peace* (London: Hodder and Stoughton, 1989), 111.

Secretary (1935-38), himself, sought a Western Pact between Britain, Germany, Italy, France, and Belgium.[230] Eden was especially interested in improved relations with Italy.[231] Nevertheless, Ribbentrop spoke to British politicians of Hitler's desire for closer relations with Britain and the need to join together in the common struggle against communism.[232] Despite British diplomatic advice, King Edward VIII, Prime Minister Stanley Baldwin (1935-37), Lord Londonderry, and Lord Halifax told Ribbentrop of their sympathy for German concerns.[233]

Shortly after his arrival in London, Hitler recalled Ribbentrop to Berlin to officially sign the Anti-Comintern Pact with Japan on 25 November 1936.[234] Ribbentrop spent the next thirteen months traveling back and forth between Britain and Germany to attend to Hitler's diplomatic needs.[235] His unprofessional diplomatic behavior in London as well as his frequent absences offended many of the leading British politicians.[236] Wilhelmstrasse diplomats, however, recognized that Ribbentrop's motive for these frequent trips was to maintain his influence with Hitler.[237] Ernst Woermann, whom Neurath had appointed as the German Embassy Counselor in London, not only spied upon, but handled Ribbentrop's diplomatic affairs during these absences.[238] However, Reinhard Spitzy, Ribbentrop's personal secretary in London, has stated that the British believed "the Ambassador should spend most of his time carrying out his duties in London. They had little use for a 'part-time Ambassador'."[239] Even so, when in Britain, Ribbentrop made many mistakes, including living an extravagant life-

---

230.   Peters, 222.

231.   Ibid., 234-35.

232.   Gilbert and Gott, 28.

233.   Ibid., 22, 28; Woermann to Neurath, 20 November 1936, *DGFP(C)*, 6:89; Ribbentrop, 61; Ribbentrop interrogation testimony, 20 September 1945, *NCA*, supplement B, 1214; Anthony Cave Brown, *"C": The Secret Life of Sir Stewart Graham Menzies, Spymaster to Winston Churchill* (New York: Macmillan, 1987), 182-83.

234.   Dodd, 366; Ian Nish, *Japanese Foreign Policy, 1869-1942: Kasumigaseki to Miyakezaka* (London: Routledge and Kegan Paul, 1977), 228.

235.   Wolfgang Michalka, *Ribbentrop und die deutsche Weltpolitik, 1933-1940: Aussenpolitische Konzeptionen und Entscheidunsprozesse in Dritten Reich* (Munich: Wilhelm Fink, 1980), 112-13.

236.   Schmidt 51; Oliver Harvey, *The Diplomatic Diaries of Oliver Harvey, 1937-1940*, ed. John Harvey (London: Collins, 1970), 33, 41.

237.   Papen, 375; Schmidt, 51.

238.   Woermann testimony, 2 July 1948, AMT transcript, OGL 17, Box 140, Folder 2, 10848-872.

239.   Reinhard Spitzy, *How We Squandered the Reich*, trans. G.T. Waddington (Norwich: Michael Russell, 1997), 64.

style, speaking his mind in public, and giving the Nazi salute to the British King George VI.[240]

Fearing that the political instability of Europe might lead to war, the Baldwin Cabinet, despite the advice of the British Foreign Office, sought closer relations with Germany in order to obtain a security arrangement in West Europe to replace the Treaty of Locarno.[241] Ribbentrop found Lord Halifax, who was serving as the Acting Foreign Secretary during Sir Anthony Eden's illness, and Lord Derby, a leading British Conservative politician, desiring a "friendly understanding" between Britain and Germany to avoid any possibility of war.[242] In April 1937, the Baldwin government replaced the pessimistic Sir Eric Phipps with Sir Nevile Henderson, a Germanophile, as the British Ambassador to Berlin, with hopes of achieving an understanding with Hitler.[243] Now, beginning in May 1937, the actions of certain British statesmen began to give Hitler the impression that Britain's desire to avoid war would include allowing Germany a free hand in Central and East Europe. The British government bypassed its Foreign Office and sent an unofficial envoy to Berlin to sound out Hitler's intentions. On 4 May, Lord Lothian told Hitler during their conversation that "Britain had no primary interests in Eastern Europe."[244] At the same time, Henderson, after conversations with the Führer, began urging London to allow peaceful German expansion in Central and East Europe.[245] Shortly before becoming Prime Minister, Sir Neville Chamberlain, along with Baldwin and Eden pressed their desires for an Anglo-German rapprochement to General Blomberg during his London visit on 13 and 14 May 1937.[246] Ribbentrop noted, however, that these politicians would not discuss as to how an understanding could be achieved.[247] Chamberlain personally wanted closer ties with Germany and Italy while gradually

---

240.  Ibid., 66-69.
241.  W.N. Medlicott, *Britain and Germany: The Search for Agreement, 1930-1937* (London: Weidenfeld and Nicolson, 1969), 17-27; Keith Middlemas, *Diplomacy of Illusion: The British Government and Germany, 1937-1939* (London: Weidenfeld and Nicolson, 1972), 110-156. See also Gaines Post, Jr. *Dilemmas of Appeasement: British Deterrence and Defense, 1934-1937* (Ithaca: Cornell University Press, 1993).
242.  Ribbentrop to Hitler and Neurath, 14 February 1937, *DGFP(C)*, 6:414-22; Ribbentrop's Adjutant Thorner to Neurath, 8 March 1937, *DGFP(C)*, 6:516-19.
243.  Gilbert and Gott, 37; Sir Nevile Henderson, *Failure of a Mission, Berlin 1937-1939* (Toronto: Musson, 1940), 29. For background on Henderson, see Peter Neville, *Appeasing Hitler: The Diplomacy of Sir Nevile Henderson, 1937-1939* (New York: St. Martin's Press, 2000).
244.  J.R.M. Butler, *Lord Lothian, 1882-1940* (London: Macmillan, 1960), 337-45.
245.  Weinberg, *The Foreign Policy of Hitler's Germany*, 2:60.
246.  Woermann to Neurath, 18 May 1937, *DGFP(C)*, 6:758-64.
247.  Ribbentrop to Neurath, 21 May 1937, *DGFP(C)*, 6:777-82.

rearming Britain without financial ruin to defend its European and imperial interests.[248]

From Berlin, Henderson continued to appeal to Whitehall for a rapprochement with Germany. Henderson wanted to contain the German threat to British interests.[249] Reporting Hitler's position on international affairs, the British Ambassador suggested that the Chamberlain Cabinet (1937-40) support the German annexation of Austria and other Germanic peoples, eastward expansion, and the return of Germany's lost overseas colonies.[250] He argued that "Germany is now too powerful to be persuaded or compelled to enter into an Eastern Pact, that a certain German predominance eastward is inevitable…."[251] London considered such arguments, but preferred diplomatic efforts towards acquiring a Western European security pact to replace the Locarno agreement.[252] By November 1937, Foreign Secretary Eden began to regret his appointment of Henderson to Berlin, and directed him not to encourage Hitler into believing that Britain "would contemplate any settlement at the expense of the political independence of the nations of Eastern and Central Europe."[253]

By this time Hitler had made up his mind that it was highly unlikely that Britain would militarily intervene in any German attempts to incorporate German populated areas in Central or East Europe. He perceived Britain's failure to pressure Germany into a Western European security pact as proof of the Chamberlain government's lack of interest in European affairs.[254] But, in an effort to gain an understanding between the two countries that favored Germany, Hitler had Ribbentrop inform Eden of German-Italian negotiations for the admission of Italy into the Anti-Comintern Pact as a way to pressure Britain into making a decision to join the pact in October 1937. The Führer believed that Britain's admission into the pact would guarantee Germany a free hand in Eastern Europe.[255]

248. Middlemas, 52-58. See also Robert Paul Shay, Jr. *British Rearmament in the Thirties: Politics and Profit* (Princeton: Princeton University Press, 1977).

249. Ibid., 71.

250. Sir Nevile Henderson to Orme Sargent, 20 July 1937, *DBFP*, second series, 19:97-105.

251. Ibid.

252. Woermann to Neurath, 20 November 1936, *DGFP(C)*, 6:83-88; Woermann to Neurath, 22 February 1937, *DGFP(C)*, 6:467-68; Woermann to Neurath, 17 July 1937, *DGFP(C)*, 6:926-29.

253. Sir Anthony Eden to Henderson, 6 November 1937, *DBFP*, second series, 19:471-72.

254. Kurt von Kamphoevener memorandum, 5 November 1937, *DGFP(C)*, 6:1097-98.

255. Eden, 571-72; Weitz, 113; Michalka, *Ribbentrop und die deutsche Weltpolitik, 1933-1940*, 155.

The National Socialist hierarchy was well aware of Hitler's foreign policy plans for the annexation of Austria and the reacquisition of German territory lost in the Versailles agreement. Eastward expansion to provide living space (lebensraum) for the German race was a theme of Hitler's for over a decade. Göring had informed Ambassador Henderson on numerous occasions during the summer and autumn of 1937 that Germany had designs on regaining Danzig, Memel, and the Polish Corridor.[256] Thus, on 5 November 1937, when Hitler assembled his key staff in the Reich Chancellery to discuss his policy plans at the so-called Hossbach Conference, Nazi party members, such as Göring, were not surprised to hear the Führer's plans for aggressive action to conquer Austria and Czechoslovakia.[257] Nevertheless, Foreign Minister Neurath, as well as General Blomberg, were surprised by the unfolding of such plans. Neurath had been out of contact with Hitler for many months since the German leader had favored the counsel of Ribbentrop and his Bureau over the Wilhelmstrasse.[258] During the meeting Hitler, who was obviously confident of his own strength and the military weakness of the other Great Powers, insisted that Britain and France would not intervene during a German move against Austria and Czechoslovakia because of the German-Italian bloc.[259]

Having obtained the Axis agreement in 1936, the Führer had immediately started diplomatic talks towards acquiring a stronger bond with Italy in order to strengthen his control over affairs in Central Europe. Hitler understood that a German-Italian agreement would suffice as the necessary diplomatic tool to use in pursuit of his ambitions in Central and East Europe in case Ribbentrop could not achieve an Anglo-German understanding.[260] For his own reasons, Mussolini also sought closer Italo-German relations, to include the coordination of defense matters in the event of war against Britain and France.[261] Hitler therefore employed the diplomatic services of Göring, Ribbentrop, Raumer, as well as the Wilhelmstrasse to negotiate the Italian admission to the German-Japanese Anti-

256.  David Irving, *Göring: A Biography* (New York: William Morrow, 1989), 189-90.
257.  Colonel Friedrich Hossbach memorandum, 10 November 1937, *DGFP(D)*, 1:29-39; Henry Cord Meyer, *The Long Generation from Empire to Ruin, 1913-1945* (New York: Walker, 1973), 50.
258.  Weizsäcker, 109; Heineman, "Constantin Freiherr von Neurath as Foreign Minister, 1932-1935," 389; Neurath testimony, 24 June 1946, *TMWC*, 16:639-40.
259.  Hossbach memorandum, 10 November 1937, *DGFP(D)*, 1:38; Papen, 386, 388; Schmidt, 76.
260.  Stoakes, 228; Hildebrand, *The Third Reich*, 25.
261.  Hassell to Neurath, 5 March 1937, *DGFP(C)*, 6:503.

Comintern Pact.[262] In September 1937, Mussolini visited Berlin and displayed visible signs to the diplomatic community of Italian submission to Hitler's desires.[263] Shortly thereafter, in October, the German leader sent Ribbentrop to Rome to conclude the Anti-Comintern Pact with Italy.[264] The agreement was formally signed, without any German Foreign Office involvement, by Ribbentrop and Ciano in Berlin on 6 November 1937, the day after the Hossbach Conference.[265] On the significance of this agreement, André François-Poncet, the French Ambassador to Berlin, stated, "Britain and France, separated from Central Europe by a solid barrier, were now powerless directly to succor Austria or Czechoslovakia."[266] The Italian Foreign Minister, Ciano, viewed the pact with Germany as "ostensibly anti-Communist but in reality anti-British."[267]

Even so, Adolf Hitler still had hopes of an Anglo-German understanding. He continued to meet with important British statesmen, including the Duke of Windsor, the former King Edward VIII, to discuss the possibility of an arrangement in Eastern Europe.[268] The Chamberlain government, in spite of the British Foreign Office, wanted a settlement. The Prime Minister thus sent Lord Halifax, the Lord President of the Council, who had a keen interest in foreign policy, to Germany in an effort to gain an Anglo-German understanding so as to avoid the possibility of a European war.[269] Foreign Secretary Eden

---

262. Hassell to Neurath, 30 January 1937, *DGFP(C)*, 6:351-52; Johann von Plessen memorandum, 23 January 1937, *DGFP(D)*, 1:381; Plessen memorandum, 17 January 1937, *DGFP(D)*, 1:382-83; Hassell memorandum, 30 January 1937, *DGFP(D)*, 1:384-85; Hassell to Neurath, 30 January 1937, *DGFP(D)*, 1:386-87; Hassell to Neurath, 18 February 1937, *DGFP(C)*, 6:457-61; Hassell to Neurath, 25 May 1937, *DGFP(C)*, 6:790; Neurath to Hassell, 29 June 1937, *DGFP(C)*, 6:884-85; Neurath memorandum, 3 May 1937, *DGFP(C)*, 6:717-19; Neurath memorandum, 4 May 1937, *DGFP(C)*, 6:726-27; Neurath memorandum, 4 May 1937, *DGFP(C)*, 6:727-28; Hassell to Neurath, 5 August 1937, *DGFP(C)*, 6:998-99; Hassell memorandum, 24 March 1937, *DGFP(C)*, 6:594-95.

263. François-Poncet, 245; German-Italian Agreement Draft, *DGFP(C)*, 6:1073-74.

264. Hassell to Neurath, 20 October 1937, *DGFP(D)*, 1:16-18; Ciano, *Ciano's Diplomatic Papers*, 139; Hans-Georg von Mackensen memorandum, 6 October 1937, *DGFP(C)*, 6:1085.

265. Kordt testimony, 4 June 1948, AMT transcript, OGL 17, Box 136, Folder 8, 7416; Protocol, 6 November 1937, *DGFP(D)*, 1:26-27; François-Poncet, 245; Weizsäcker, 116; Ciano, *Ciano's Diplomatic Papers*, 140.

266. François-Poncet, 247.

267. As quoted in Weinberg, *The Foreign Policy of Hitler's Germany*, 2:117.

268. Mackensen memorandum, 17 September 1937, *DGFP(C)*, 6:1067-68.

269. Charmley, 14, 17-18; Lord Halifax, *Fullness of Days* (New York: Dodd, Mead and Company, 1957), 186.

and Permanent Undersecretary Vansittart were highly against the visit, but Chamberlain insisted.[270]

The Halifax diplomatic mission had the effect of confirming Hitler's notions that Germany could eventually expand eastwards without British intervention. At Berchtesgaden, on 19 November 1937, the Führer told Lord Halifax of his aims for "a close union between Austria and the Reich" as well as security for the Sudeten Germans.[271] Paul Otto Schmidt, the Wilhelmstrasse interpreter, recorded the conversation between Hitler and Halifax. According to Schmidt:

> Halifax admitted of his own accord that certain changes in the European system could probably not be avoided in the long run. The British did not believe that the status quo had to be maintained under all circumstances. Among the questions in which changes would probably be made sooner or later were Danzig, Austria, and Czechoslovakia. England was only interested in seeing that such changes were brought about by peaceful development.[272]

Lord Halifax made such comments, as he later explained to the British government, with the view that Hitler had no immediate plans to expand into Central or East Europe.[273]

While the Chamberlain Cabinet was warming up, albeit slowly, to an Anglo-German understanding, Joachim von Ribbentrop was becoming frustrated in his lack of success to quickly achieve Hitler's much wanted alliance. He had suffered the coldness of Sir Anthony Eden, Sir Robert Vansittart, and the diplomats of the British Foreign Office.[274] He had been ridiculed by the British Press.[275] He had no breakthrough in convincing Sir Winston Churchill of the mutual benefits of an Anglo-German agreement.[276] Ribbentrop, according to his personal secretary, had grown hostile to Britain.[277] The German Ambassador had come to the con-

---

270.   Richard Cockett, *Twilight of Truth: Chamberlain, Appeasement and the Manipulation of the Press* (New York: St. Martin's Press, 1989), 33, 36-37; Charmley, 13-14.
271.   Schmidt, 76.
272.   Neurath to German Embassies in Britain, Italy, France, and the United States, 22 November 1937, *DGFP(D)*, 1:69. See also Ian Colvin, *The Chamberlain Cabinet* (New York: Taplinger, 1971), 52.
273.   Harvey, 62.
274.   Ribbentrop, 65; Ribbentrop interrogation testimony, 20 September 1945, *NCA*, supplement B, 1215.
275.   Spitzy, 67.
276.   Winston C. Churchill, *The Second World War*, 6 vols. (Boston: Houghton Mifflin, 1948-53), 1:222-23; Martin Gilbert, *Churchill: A Life* (New York: Henry Holt, 1991), 581.
277.   Spitzy, 67.

clusion that his diplomatic mission was a failure.[278] He blamed his dismal performance on Hitler's ties to Mussolini and Franco as well as the German demand for the return of lost overseas colonies.[279] More importantly, Ribbentrop believed that "there was a very strong tendency of very important Englishmen who...in their internal policy, if not outwardly, [took] a very firm stand against Germany, thinking that one day...Germany would get too strong."[280]

In November 1937, Joachim von Ribbentrop prepared a report that included his estimation of Anglo-German relations. According to observers in the German Embassy in London Ribbentrop had clearly become hostile to Britain. He did not want an Anglo-German understanding for personal reasons.[281] After much hesitation Ribbentrop had the report delivered to Hitler during the first week of January 1938.[282] In the report, the Ambassador admitted his failed diplomatic mission. He informed Hitler that since Germany planned to expand into Central and East Europe the hope of an understanding with Britain was at an end. The future, and the likelihood of war between them, depended upon whether Britain would follow France in defense of its Eastern allies. London, according to Ribbentrop, would not consent to be dragged into a conflict if conditions were unfavorable for the British Empire. He told the Führer that "over a local problem in central Europe, even if it were to add considerably to Germany's strength, England would, in my opinion, not risk a struggle for the survival of her Empire."[283] Ribbentrop strongly suggested that Germany solidify its alliance with Italy and Japan so as to deter any British prospect of intervention against German designs in Central and East Europe.[284] He summed up his analyzation by stating that:

> The special problem as to whether France and thereby England would intervene if Germany should become involved in a conflict in Central Europe depends upon circumstances and the time when such a conflict were to break out and end upon military considerations....[285]

278. Ribbentrop interrogation testimony, 20 September 1945, *NCA*, supplement B, 1214-215.
279. Ibid., 1214; Ribbentrop testimony, 29 March 1946, *TMWC*, 10:238.
280. Ribbentrop interrogation testimony, 20 September 1945, *NCA*, supplement B, 1215-216.
281. Spitzy, 73.
282. Ibid., 143-44.
283. Ribbentrop to Hitler, 2 January 1938, *DGFP(D)*, 1:164.
284. Michalka, *Ribbentrop und die deutsche Weltpolitik, 1933-1940*, 247-48.
285. Ribbentrop to Hitler, 2 January 1938, *DGFP(D)*, 1:167.

Many contemporaries blamed Ribbentrop for Hitler's firm belief that Britain would not intervene in a local European conflict because of his advice. After all, Ribbentrop was considered by Hitler the expert on Britain, and, therefore, his opinions were of utmost significance.[286] Franz von Papen wrote in his memoirs, "Ribbentrop's opinion that the British Empire had passed its peak, and would no longer take military steps to restore the balance of power in Europe, formed the basis for Hitler's aggressive plans against Czechoslovakia and Poland."[287] But, Papen and others, such as Hermann Göring, Ernst von Weizsäcker, Eric Kordt, and Ernst Woermann, who have stated similar arguments, were unfair to Ribbentrop, whom they despised.[288] Hitler had formed his own evaluation based upon contacts with British statesmen that Britain was unlikely to intervene in German expansion towards the east. Ribbentrop knew Hitler's beliefs, since the two had had numerous chats on international affairs since the early thirties, and in his own typical way of endearing himself to the Führer, the ambassador had adopted and repeated Hitler's viewpoint. Ribbentrop's only influence during the late thirties concerning the question of whether the British would intervene in the event of German expansion was to reinforce the Führer's already formed opinion. The relationship between Hitler and Ribbentrop was best stated by Paul Otto Schmidt, who spent long hours with both men:

> His [Ribbentrop] relationship to Hitler was one of extreme dependency. If Hitler was displeased with him, Ribbentrop went sick and took to his bed like a hysterical woman. He was indeed nothing but his master's voice...."[289]

Hitler, himself, found Ribbentrop a "sturdy and obstinate man," despite his companion's disagreeable personality.[290] André François-Poncet, the French Ambassador to Berlin, nonetheless, best described the Hitler-Ribbentrop relationship in his memoirs:

> Typical of the perfect courtier, he [Ribbentrop] would hurl thunderbolts of flattery at Hitler without turning a hair. His method of keeping in favor

---

286.  Middlemas, 174-75; François-Poncet, 233.
287.  Papen, 376.
288.  Poole, 133; Kordt testimony, 4 June 1948, AMT transcript, OGL 17, Box 136, Folder 7, 7388; Weizsäcker testimony, 8 June 1948, AMT transcript, OGL 17, Box 136, Folder 13, 7719; Woermann testimony, 6 July 1948, AMT transcript, OGL 17, Box 140, Folder 7, 11128-129.
289.  Schmidt, 33. See also Fest, *The Face of the Third Reich*, 179.
290.  Hitler, *Hitler's Secret Conversations, 1941-1944*, 212.

was very simple. It consisted in listening religiously to his master's endless monologues and in committing to memory the ideas developed by Hitler. Also, more importantly, Ribbentrop noted the intentions to be divined behind these ideas. Then, after Hitler had forgotten ever discussing them with Ribbentrop, the courtier passed them off as his own, unfolding them with great warmth. Struck by this concordance, Hitler attributed to his collaborator a sureness of judgment and a trenchant foresight singularly in agreement with his own deepest thought. He [Ribbentrop] not only never contradicted his master or offered the slightest objection, he also systematically piled argument upon argument in agreement. He was more Hitlerian than Hitler. By clearing up the Führer's doubts and by dissipating the Führer's occasional hesitancies Ribbentrop excited the Führer's supreme audacity; he pushed and pulled him into ways toward which Hitler was all too dangerously inclined.[291]

Even Weizsäcker admitted to the Nuremberg court that "Ribbentrop had a special gift for approaching Hitler in an intuitive manner, listening for his opinion and then exceeding, and outdoing him in his own opinions."[292] Ribbentrop, however, was the favorite target among the Nazi Party elite as well as the Foreign Office to blame for all German foreign policy failures. Ribbentrop was considered an outsider by the Party elite because of his late involvement with Hitler, and the Wilhelmstrasse viewed him as an usurper of its traditional responsibilities for international affairs.[293]

The rise of Ribbentrop had completely eclipsed the little control over foreign affairs held by Constantin von Neurath. For some time Neurath had lived in fear of Hitler's wrath towards the Wilhelmstrasse.[294] He had lost in the struggle for influence with Ribbentrop and his Bureau.[295] Hitler had sent Hans Dieckhoff, the Foreign Secretary, away from Berlin to an unimportant post in the United States.[296] With the loss of many key diplomats at the top positions within the

---

291. François-Poncet, 232-33.
292. Weizsäcker testimony, 8 June 1948, AMT transcript, OGL 17, Box 136, Folder 3, 7703.
293. Koch, *Aspects of the Third Reich*, 194; Fest, *The Face of the Third Reich*, 179; Gilbert, *Nuremberg Diary*, 11.
294. Dodd, 424; Heineman, *Hitler's First Foreign Minister*, 156.
295. Hassell memorandum, 24 March 1937, *DGFP(C)*, 6:594-95; Neurath memorandum, 23 April 1937, *DGFP(C)*, 6:680-81; Mackensen memorandum, 5 October 1937, *DGFP(C)*, 6:1085; Mackensen memorandum, 6 October 1937, *DGFP(C)*, 6:1085-86; Mackensen memorandum, 16 October 1937, *DGFP(C)*, 6:1093; Neurath testimony, 24 June 1946, *TMWC*, 16:641.
296. Dieckhoff testimony, 26 June 1946, *TMWC*, 17:122. See Gerhard L. Weinberg, "Hitler's Image of the United States," in *World in the Balance: Behind the Scenes of World War II* (Hanover: University of New England, 1981), 59.

Wilhelmstrasse in less than a year, the Foreign Minister, despite the appointment of his son-in-law, Dr. Hans-Georg von Mackensen, a Nazi Party member, to the post of Foreign Secretary, admitted defeat to Hitler's absolute control over foreign policy.[297] After the Hossbach Conference, Neurath "was so deeply shaken that he decided once and for all," according to Harold Deutsch, "that he would have no truck with such a policy."[298] Commenting on the Hossbach Conference, Neurath told the Nuremberg court:

> Although the plans set forth by Hitler in that long speech had no concrete form, and various possibilities were envisaged, it was quite obvious to me that the whole tendency of his plans was of an aggressive nature. I was extremely upset at Hitler's speech, because it knocked the bottom out of the whole foreign policy which I had consistently pursued—the policy of employing only peaceful means.[299]

He thus sought an audience with the Führer to hand in his resignation. But, Hitler, who left Berlin for the Berghof at Berchtesgaden, refused to see his Foreign Minister.[300] Neurath, mentally and physically upset about the Hossbach Conference, was ordered to remain silent about Hitler's plans. He suffered a heart attack while waiting for the Führer to return to Berlin.[301] Hitler, finally, after over two months, agreed to see Neurath in order to allow him the opportunity to submit his retirement papers on 14 January 1938.[302] But, the Führer refused to allow Neurath to retire on his sixty-fifth birthday at the end of January 1938.[303]

---

297.  Weizsäcker, 110.

298.  Harold C. Deutsch, *Hitler and His Generals: The Hidden Crisis, January-June 1938* (Minneapolis: University of Minnesota Press, 1974), 70.

299.  Neurath testimony, 24 June 1946, *TMWC*, 16:640.

300.  Ibid., 16:640-41; Manfred Zimmerman affidavit, 1 May 1946, *TMWC*, 40:442; Heineman, *Hitler's First Foreign Minister*, 164.

301.  Baroness Theda von Ritter affidavit, 28 May 1946, *TMWC*, 40:444; Middlemas, 165; Neurath testimony, 26 June 1946, *TMWC*, 17:99; Deutsch, 71.

302.  Neurath testimony, 24 June 1946, *TMWC*, 16:638; Seabury, *The Wilhelmstrasse*, 41: Deutsch, 71.

303.  Heineman, *Hitler's First Foreign Minister*, 166.

# 7

# *Path to War 1938-1939*

## Hitler Takes Control of the Foreign Office

Since 1933 Adolf Hitler had acted as the prime formulator of German for-
eign policy. He had pursued closer relations with Britain, France, Austria,
Italy, Japan, and Poland with the aim of reestablishing Germany as a Great
Power in Central Europe as well as creating an anti-Soviet bloc. He accom-
plished a rapprochement with Poland and Austria, a pact with Italy and
Japan, and continued talks with Britain concerning a general understanding.
His main goals were a close union between Germany and his homeland of
Austria, the reacquisition of lost German territory, an understanding with
Britain concerning spheres of influence, and eastward expansion for the Ger-
man race. In developing a bloc that challenged the status quo, Hitler
employed his anti-communist sentiments to unite Germany with Italy and
Japan. Such diplomacy successfully placed Germany in a dominant position
in Central and Eastern Europe. The Berlin-Rome Axis, along with his per-
ception of British and French unwillingness to intervene militarily against
German actions, only encouraged Hitler to pursue his foreign policy goals.
To carry out his foreign policy the Führer had relied mainly upon amateur
diplomats, such as Joachim von Ribbentrop, while bypassing the German
Foreign Office. Having regained Great Power status and a strong diplomatic
position for Germany, Hitler decided to take control of the Wilhelmstrasse.
He would be his own Foreign Minister. The Führer, however, decided not to
officially appoint himself to the office, but to appoint the loyal and subservient Ribbentrop to this top position. Ribbentrop, fully reliant upon the
Führer's wishes, would serve his master not as a Foreign Minister, but as Hit-

ler's top diplomat. Hitler, himself, would remain the primary formulator of German foreign policy.[1]

In early 1938 Hitler decided to take direct control over the Auswärtiges Amt and the Wehrmacht. He dismissed General Werner von Blomberg, the War Minister, and General Werner von Fritsch, the Commander-in-Chief of the German Army, because of scandals, and took personal command of the German military.[2] He then appointed General Wilhelm Keitel as his Chief of the High Command of the Armed Forces (Chef des Oberkommando der Wehrmacht [OKW]) and General Walther von Brauchitsch as the new Commander-in-Chief of the German Army. At the same time, on 4 February 1938, Hitler informed Constantin von Neurath of his dismissal as Foreign Minister.[3] Ribbentrop would take his place.[4] The news surprised both Neurath and Ribbentrop, who happened to be in Berlin, absent from his diplomatic post in

---

1.    Wolfgang Michalka, "Conflicts within the German Leadership on the Objectives and Tactics of German Foreign Policy, 1933-1939," in *The Fascist Challenge and the Policy of Appeasement*, ed. Wolfgang Mommsen and Lothar Kettenacker (London: George Allen and Unwin, 1983), 48; Herbert von Dirksen, *Moscow, Tokyo, London: Twenty Years of German Foreign Policy* (Norman: University of Oklahoma Press, 1952), 186; Joachim C. Fest, *The Face of the Third Reich: Portraits of the Nazi Leadership*, trans. Michael Bullock (New York: Pantheon, 1970), 179; Ernst Woermann testimony, 2 July 1948, AMT transcript, OGL 17, Box 140, Folder 6, 11036, 11052; Gustav Adolf Steengracht von Moyland testimony, 23 June 1948, AMT transcript, OGL 17, Box 140, Folder 1, 9878; Eric Kordt testimony, 4 June 1948, AMT transcript, OGL 17, Box 136, Folder 8, 7400-1; John Weitz, *Hitler's Diplomat: The Life and Times of Joachim von Ribbentrop* (New York: Ticknor and Fields, 1992), 143.

2.    Franz von Papen, *Memoirs*, trans. Brian Connell (New York: E.P. Dutton, 1953), 407; André François-Poncet, *The Fateful Years: Memoirs of a French Ambassador in Berlin, 1931-1938*, trans. Jacques LeClercq (New York: Harcourt, Brace and Company, 1949), 226; Leonidas E. Hill, "The Wilhelmstrasse in the Nazi Era," *Political Science Quarterly* 83 (December 1967), 46; Order of the Führer and Reich Chancellor on the Command of the Wehrmacht, 4 February 1938, *Hitler's Third Reich: A Documentary History*, ed. Louis L. Snyder (Chicago: Nelson-Hall, 1981), 275.

3.    Constantin von Neurath testimony, 24 June 1946, *TMWC*, 16:641; Joachim C. Fest, *Hitler*, trans. Richard Winston and Clara Winston (London: Weidenfeld and Nicolson, 1973), 543; Paul Seabury, *The Wilhelmstrasse: A Study of German Diplomats under the Nazi Regime* (Berkeley: University of California Press, 1954), 45.

4.    François-Poncet, 227; Joachim von Ribbentrop testimony, 28 March 1946, *TMWC*, 10:241; Hitler's Decree, 4 February 1938, 1337-PS, *NCA*, 3:913.

London.[5] Simultaneous with these actions, Hitler shook up the Diplomatic Service by announcing the termination of the assignments of Franz von Papen, Ulrich von Hassell, and Herbert von Dirksen to their ambassadorial posts in Vienna, Rome, and Tokyo.[6] Neurath was told of his appointment to the newly created Secret Cabinet Council.[7] Dirksen was to be transferred to London as a replacement for Ribbentrop,[8] while Papen was to be of further use as an expert in Austro-German affairs,[9] and Hassell was retired because of his opposition to the anti-Comintern pacts.[10] Dr. Hans-Georg von Mackensen, the Foreign Secretary, was relieved of his post and transferred to the embassy in Rome.[11] The decision to appoint Ribbentrop as Foreign Minister was not easy for Hitler, since Hermann Göring, his close personal friend, showed interest in the post. But, the Führer obviously wanted no one of intellect and influence to be in a central position to interfere with his foreign policy.[12] Göring, according to Leonidas Hill, was more influential with Hitler over matters of foreign affairs than Ribbentrop during this period.[13]

### Ribbentrop and the Wilhelmstrasse

The sudden appointment of Ribbentrop as Foreign Minister astonished the Wilhelmstrasse and foreign diplomats in Berlin. The professional diplomats viewed the champagne salesman as unqualified to hold such a highly esteemed position. Ribbentrop lacked adequate diplomatic training and had very little experience in the foreign service. As André François-Poncet, the French Ambassador to Berlin,

5.  Joachim von Ribbentrop, *The Ribbentrop Memoirs*, trans. Oliver Watson, ed. A. von Ribbentrop, intro. Allan Bullock (London: Weidenfeld and Nicolson, 1954), 78; Ernst von Weizsäcker, *Memoirs of Ernst von Weizsäcker*, trans. John Andrews (London: Victor Gollancz, 1951), 119; Galeazzo Ciano, *Ciano's Hidden Diary, 1937-1938*, trans. Andreas Major, introd. Malcolm Muggeridge (New York: E.P. Dutton, 1953), diary entry for 7 February 1938, 71; Weitz, 151.

6.  Dirksen, 181; Papen, 406.

7.  John L. Heineman, *Hitler's First Foreign Minister: Constantin Freiherr von Neurath, Diplomat and Statesman* (Berkeley: University of California Press, 1979), 169.

8.  Dirksen, 186.

9.  Papen, 408-39. Papen served as the German Ambassador to Turkey form April 1939 to August 1944 (Louis L. Snyder, *Encyclopedia of the Third Reich* [New York: Paragon House, 1976], 266-67).

10.  Ulrich von Hassell, *The Von Hassell Diaries, 1938-1944*, introd. Allen W. Dulles (Garden City: Doubleday, 1947), 5.

11.  Weizsäcker, 118.

12.  Gustave M. Gilbert, *Nuremberg Diary* (London: Eyre and Spottiswoode, 1948), 138; David Irving, *Göring: A Biography* (New York: William Morrow, 1989), 203.

13.  Hill, "The Wilhelmstrasse in the Nazi Era," 557.

summed up Ribbentrop: "The new Minister for Foreign Affairs was neither prepared nor fitted for his office. Culturally and intellectually he was mediocre. His
ignorance of historical and diplomatic questions was prodigious."[14] One major
diplomatic shortcoming was Ribbentrop's lack of communicative skills. He,
according to Ernst von Weizsäcker, the Director of the Political Department,
"had no feeling for the most important means of diplomacy; that is, for diplomatic conversation."[15] More importantly, Weizsäcker noted that the new Foreign
Minister "did not possess the art of listening, certainly not with regard to German
professional diplomats anyway, nor with regard to foreign diplomats either."[16]
Confirming this view of Ribbentrop, François-Poncet declared:

> It was difficult to conduct a genuine conversation with him [Ribbentrop].
> Like the Führer he copied, he indulged in lengthy monologues; he never
> caught, let alone retained, the arguments of his interlocutor; he listened only
> to himself, repeating the lesson he had learned.[17]

Despite disliking the new Foreign Minister, there were members of the Wilhelmstrasse who viewed the appointment of Ribbentrop as an opportunity for the
Foreign Office to regain influence over the formulation and conduct of policy.[18]
Weizsäcker told the American Military Tribunal that "some of my colleagues
thought it was a good thing [the appointment of Ribbentrop] because in this way
the actual adviser of Hitler in foreign affairs would now also have the official
responsibility."[19] They believed that Ribbentrop could be manipulated into following their advice.[20] These diplomats, however, misjudged Ribbentrop's influence over Hitler's foreign policy. The new minister had no clout with Hitler, at
least compared to the significance of Hermann Göring, Rudolf Hess, and Heinrich Himmler.[21] In February 1938, Göring told Sir Nevile Henderson, the British Ambassador to Berlin (1937-39), that Ribbentrop had no influence in the
formulation of German foreign policy, adding that "there is only one person dic-

---

14.    François-Poncet, 233.
15.    Ernst von Weizsäcker testimony, 10 June 1948, AMT transcript, OGL 17, Box 137, Folder
       2, 8098.
16.    Weizsäcker testimony, 8 June 1948, AMT transcript, OGL 17, Box 136, Folder 13, 7701.
17.    François-Poncet, 233.
18.    Ibid.
19.    Weizsäcker testimony, 8 June 1948, AMT transcript, OGL 17, Box 136, Folder 13, 7692.
20.    Hill, "The Wilhelmstrasse in the Nazi Era," 564.
21.    Paul Seabury, "Ribbentrop and the German Foreign Office," *Political Science Quarterly* 66
       (December 1951), 539.

tating foreign policy in Germany, and that is Hitler himself."[22] Herbert von Dirksen saw Ribbentrop as "nothing but the Dictator's message boy...."[23] Even Ribbentrop, himself, realized his own personal shortcomings and told the French Ambassador, "the policy I follow is not mine but the Führers."[24] During his trial at Nuremberg, Ribbentrop told the court:

> It was clear to me from the very beginning, after I took over the ministry, that I would be working, so to speak, in the shadow of a titan and that I would have to impose on myself certain limitations, that is to say, that I would not be in a position, one might almost say, to conduct the foreign policy as it is done by other foreign ministers, who are responsible to a parliamentary system or a parliament. The commanding personality of the Führer naturally dominated the foreign policy.... He [Hitler] occupied himself with all details. It went like this more or less: I reported to him and forwarded to him important foreign policy reports through a liaison man, and Hitler in turn gave me definitive orders as to what views I should take in regard to problems of foreign policy....[25]

## Annexation of Austria

Having appointed his top Nazi diplomat as Foreign Minister during the first week of February 1938, Hitler quickly utilized Ribbentrop to assist him in the conduct of German policy towards Austria. The Austrian Chancellor, Kurt von Schuschnigg, had informed the Wilhelmstrasse about fears that Hitler's purge of his top generals and diplomats might represent a change in German policy towards Austria.[26] Wilhelm Keppler, a Nazi who Hitler used as an envoy to Austria after Papen's dismissal,[27] forwarded Schuschnigg's request for a meeting with Hitler to discuss the future of Austro-German relations.[28] Thus the two leaders and their respective foreign ministers met at Berchtesgaden on 12 February 1938. Franz von Papen, who was temporarily reinstated as German Ambassador to Austria, accompanied Hitler and Ribbentrop to provide them

---

22. As quoted in Irving, *Göring*, 203.
23. Dirksen, 186.
24. As quoted in Michalka, "Conflicts within the German Leadership on the Objectives and Tactics of German Foreign Policy, 1933-1939," 48.
25. Ribbentrop testimony, 29 March 1946, *TMWC*, 10:243.
26. Hans-Georg von Mackensen memorandum, 8 February 1938, *DGFP(D)*, 1:503-4.
27. *NMT*, 12:14; Gerhard L. Weinberg, *The Foreign Policy of Hitler's Germany*, 2 vols. (Chicago: University of Chicago Press, 1970-80), 2:278-79. Keppler was Hitler's expert on Austrian political and economic matters (Weitz, 149).
28. Wilhelm Keppler to Joachim von Ribbentrop, 7 February 1938, *DGFP(D)*, 1:500-2.

diplomatic advice, especially since the Foreign Minister was uninformed about Austro-German relations as well as being unsure of himself.[29] At this meeting Hitler browbeat Schuschnigg to accept his demands for a closer union between the two states. The Führer had Ribbentrop hand over his list of demands to the Austrian Foreign Minister, Guido Schmidt.[30] Ribbentrop, in his arrogant style of diplomacy, told Schmidt that "these demands that I now offer you are the final demands of the Führer and that he, Hitler, is not prepared to further discuss them."[31] Ribbentrop strongly advised the Austrians to accept Hitler's demands. Meanwhile, Hitler pressured Schuschnigg by declaring: "You will sign it [the protocol] and fulfill my demands in three days, or I will march into Austria."[32] These demands, actually drafted by Hitler and Ribbentrop earlier that day, on the basis of Keppler's advice, called for Schuschnigg to appoint National Socialists to key Austrian posts, including Arthur Seyss-Inquart to the post of Austrian Minister of Security and the Interior; meetings between the general staffs; an exchange of military officers; and the assimilation of the Austro-German economic system within a matter of days.[33] The pressure by both Hitler and Ribbentrop resulted in Schuschnigg and Schmidt agreeing to the demands.[34]

Throughout the following weeks Hitler pressured the Austrian government to meet the provisions of the Berchtesgaden Protocol. Although they found Ribbentrop useful at Berchtesgaden, Hitler and Göring kept Austro-German relations to themselves and limited the involvement of the Wilhelmstrasse.[35] Meanwhile, the British government, which was troubled by the Berchtesgaden Protocol, sought an understanding with Hitler.[36] Prime Minister Neville Chamberlain dismissed

29. Papen, 414; Weitz, 152.

30. Excerpt from General Alfred Jodl's diary (at the time a Colonel and the Chief of the National Defense Section in the High Command of the Armed Forces from 1935 to 1938), 1780-PS, *NCA*, 4:361; Alan Bullock, *Hitler and Stalin: Parallel Lives* (New York: Alfred A. Knopf, 1992), 564; Papen, 414; Weitz, 153.

31. Kurt von Schuschnigg affidavit, 13 November 1945, 2995-PS, *NCA*, 5:711.

32. As quoted in Bullock, *Hitler and Stalin*, 565.

33. Jürgen Gehl, *Austria, Germany, and the Anschluss, 1931-1938* (London: Oxford University Press, 1963), 173.

34. Adolf Hitler-Kurt von Schuschnigg meeting minutes, 12 February 1938, *NMT*, 12:714-16; Berchtesgaden Protocol, 12 February 1938, *DGFP(D)*, 1:515-17.

35. Kordt testimony, 4 June 1948, AMT transcript, OGL 17, Box 136, Folder 7, 7364; Hill, "The Wilhelmstrasse in the Nazi Era," 566; Ribbentrop testimony, 29 March 1946, *TMWC*, 10:244-49.

36. Ernst Woermann to Ribbentrop, 17 February 1938, *DGFP(D)*, 1:525; Weizsäcker memorandum, 28 February 1938, *DGFP(D)*, 1:227.

Sir Anthony Eden and Sir Robert Vansittart, and replaced the leadership of Whitehall with men, such as Lord Halifax and Sir Alexander Cadogan, who were advocates of an Anglo-German understanding.[37] With no immediate plans for action,[38] Hitler and the Wilhelmstrasse began to perceive that London understood the Führer's desire to expand into Central and Eastern Europe.[39] On 4 March 1938, in a conversation with the British Ambassador, Hitler gained the perception that Sir Nevile Henderson supported the German annexation of Austria.[40]

On 8 March 1938, Ribbentrop traveled to London to finish his business there as ambassador.[41] The following day, on 9 March, Schuschnigg announced that Austria would hold a plebiscite on the thirteenth in order to gain support for continued Austrian independence. This compelled Hitler to take action. He immediately sent Keppler to Vienna to delay or prevent the plebiscite.[42] For the next twenty-four hours the Führer was indecisive about what action to take.[43] Göring urged Hitler to mobilize the Wehrmacht and invade Austria.[44] The Führer weighed the diplomatic and military possibilities and made the sudden decision, about midnight on the ninth, in favor of military action, with the firm belief that neither Britain nor France would militarily intervene.[45]

The next day, on 10 March, Hitler gave Göring authority to conduct German operations during the Austrian crisis.[46] Göring, who held a high opinion of the former Foreign Minister,[47] recalled Neurath, who had happened to stay in Ber-

---

37. Woermann to Ribbentrop, 21 February 1938, *DGFP(D)*, 1:208-9; Oliver Harvey, *The Diplomatic Diaries of Oliver Harvey, 1937-1940*, ed. John Harvey (London: Collins, 1970), 64, 66; Richard Cockett, *Twilight of Truth: Chamberlain, Appeasement and the Manipulation of the Press* (New York: St. Martin's Press, 1989), 48; Lord Halifax, *Fullness of Days* (New York: Dodd, Mead and Company, 1957), 198; Martin Gilbert and Richard Gott, *The Appeasers* (Boston: Houghton Mifflin, 1963), 68-69.

38. Keppler memorandum, 28 February 1938, *DGFP(D)*, 1:548-49.

39. Weizsäcker to Ulrich von Hassell, 10 January 1938, *DGFP(D)*, 1:171-72.

40. Ribbentrop to Nevile Henderson, 4 March 1938, *DGFP(D)*, 1:248. Henderson denied this statement to Ribbentrop the following day, but Hitler had already formed his own perception of the conversation (Henderson to Ribbentrop, 5 March 1938, *DGFP(D)*, 1:249-50).

41. Reinhard Spitzy, *How We Squandered the Reich*, trans. G.T. Waddington (Norwich: Michael Russell, 1997), 178.

42. Weizsäcker to Ribbentrop, 9 March 1938, *DGFP(D)*, 1:562.

43. David Irving, *The War Path: Hitler's Germany, 1933-1939* (New York: Viking, 1978), 81.

44. Fest, *Hitler*, 545; Irving, *Göring*, 206.

45. Andreas Hillgruber, *Germany and the Two World Wars*, trans. William C. Kirby (Cambridge, MA: Harvard University Press, 1981), 64; Irving, *The War Path*, 81; Fest, *Hitler*, 546.

46. Irving, *Göring*, 210.

47. Gilbert, *Nuremberg Diary*, 304.

lin, to the Chancellery.[48] Acting independent of the Foreign Office, Neurath, advised the German leadership to oppose the plebiscite which might result in an international guarantee of Austrian independence. He favored mobilization to threaten Austria, but opposed an actual invasion.[49] Hitler and Göring, nonetheless, informed Neurath that they had already decided on the military option.[50] Meanwhile, the German leadership had drafted orders for Austrian Nazis to take to the streets and demonstrate against the Schuschnigg government, as well as an ultimatum to Schuschnigg to call off the plebiscite and resign in favor of Seyss-Inquart.[51] At the same time, they requested the opinions of the German Ambassadors in London and Paris as to the expected reaction from Britain and France.[52] Göring, who did not want the new Foreign Minister to interfere with the Austrian Question, demanded that Ribbentrop stay in London during the crisis to handle the reaction of the Chamberlain government.[53] Ribbentrop, after meeting with the Prime Minister, took his time in reporting to Hitler that Britain strongly desired to avoid war.[54] He stated:

> What now will England do if the Austrian question cannot be settled peacefully? Basically, I am convinced that England…will do nothing in regard to it at present, but that she would exert a moderating influence upon the other powers. I believe that the French would not go to war now over a German solution of the Austrian question, and neither would the allies of France….[55]

Curt Bräuer, the Counselor at the German Embassy in Paris, informed his government that, in his opinion, France would not intervene in Austria.[56] Thus, the international situation looked favorable for Hitler's invasion of Austria.

Receiving the ultimatum from Hitler, Schuschnigg bowed to German pressure and called off the plebiscite before resigning on 11 March 1938. Hitler had completely bypassed the Foreign Office during the entire affair. Ribbentrop had

---

48.   Neurath testimony, 24 June 1946, *TMWC*, 16:642; Irving, *The War Path*, 81.
49.   Weizsäcker testimony, 7 June 1948, AMT transcript, OGL 17, Box 136, Folder 13, 7700; Neurath testimony, 24 June 1946, *TMWC*, 16:643; Heineman, *Hitler's First Foreign Minister*, 171.
50.   Irving, *The War Path*, 82; Heineman, *Hitler's First Foreign Minister*, 172.
51.   Bullock, *Hitler and Stalin*, 566; Irving, *Göring*, 206; Heineman, *Hitler's First Foreign Minister*, 172.
52.   Irving, *The War Path*, 81.
53.   Woermann testimony, 2 July 1948, AMT transcript, OGL 17, Box 140, Folder 2, 10872.
54.   Spitzy, 182-86.
55.   Ribbentrop to Hitler, 10 March 1938, *DGFP(D)*, 1:263.
56.   Curt Bräuer memorandum, 11 March 1938, *DGFP(D)*, 1:570.

been kept in London unaware of Hitler's intentions,[57] while Weizsäcker, who was asked by the new Foreign Minister to become his State Secretary on 5 March,[58] was not informed of the impending military action until the eleventh.[59] During the afternoon of 11 March, while Ribbentrop was meeting with Chamberlain and Halifax at Downing Street, telegrams from the British Embassy in Vienna arrived informing the British Cabinet of Hitler's ultimatum. News of Hitler's actions came as a complete surprise to the German Foreign Minister.[60] Ribbentrop had received no instructions and was therefore in the embarrassing position of not being able to give a prepared statement.[61]

Despite Schuschnigg's adherence to his demands, Hitler gave the final order to invade Austria on the evening of 11 March.[62] Without prior coordination with Mussolini, the Führer presented the Fascist leader with a *fait accompli* concerning the status of Austria, which, according to Paul Otto Schmidt, was accepted in "good grace."[63] As Ray Moseley has written:

> Mussolini and Ciano were aware there was nothing they could do to prevent the German takeover of Austria, but they insisted that the Germans agree with them on the timing and method. In the event, the Germans did no such thing. Their march across the border caught the Italians as much by surprise as it did the rest of the world. The lack of consultation was to be repeated, humiliatingly for Mussolini and Ciano, frequently in the next few years.[64]

German forces moved into Austria on the twelfth. Both Göring and Neurath handled diplomatic matters with the foreign diplomats in Berlin, reassuring the British and French governments that Hitler had no intentions towards Czechoslovakia.[65] It

57.  Ribbentrop, 86; Spitzy, 180, 173, 176.

58.  Irving, *The War Path*, 78.

59.  Weizsäcker testimony, 8 June 1948, AMT transcript, OGL 17, Box 136, Folder 13, 7712.

60.  Woermann testimony, 2 July 1948, AMT transcript, OGL 17, Box 140, Folder 2, 10872.

61.  Ribbentrop memorandum, 11 March 1938, *DGFP(D)*, 1:273-75; Esmonde M. Robertson, *Hitler's Pre-War Policy and Military Plans, 1933-1939* (New York: Citadel Press, 1963), 118.

62.  Klaus Hildebrand, *The Foreign Policy of the Third Reich*, trans. Anthony Fothergill (Berkeley: University of California Press, 1973), 63; Robertson, *Hitler's Pre-War Policy and Military Plans, 1933-1939*, 115; Christopher Thorne, *The Approach of War, 1938-1939* (London: Macmillan, 1967), 46-47.

63.  Dr. Paul Schmidt, *Hitler's Interpreter*, ed. R.H.C. Steed (New York: Macmillan, 1951), 80. See also Ciano, *Ciano's Hidden Diary, 1937-1938*, 87; Hitler to Benito Mussolini, 11 March 1938, *DGFP(D)*, 1:573; R.J.B. Bosworth, *Mussolini* (London: Arnold, 2001), 331.

64.  Ray Moseley, *Mussolini's Shadow: The Double Life of Count Galeazzo Ciano* (New Haven: Yale University Press, 1999), 41.

65.  André François-Poncet to Yvon Delbos, 12 March 1938, *FYB*, 2-3; François-Poncet to Delbos, 12 March 1938, *FYB*, 3.

was not until the next day that Göring called Ribbentrop in London and informed him of the week's events.[66] The Foreign Minister, with a wounded ego, since he realized that Hitler had not counted on him during the crisis, at once left London for Austria.[67] He arrived in Vienna, after Hitler and Göring had already departed,[68] to sign the formal law making Austria a province of Germany.[69] With the annexation of Austria, Hitler acquired 6.5 million Germans for the Third Reich. He gained control over an economy with valuable supplies of raw materials, plus foreign exchange and gold reserves worth about four hundred million Reichsmarks.[70] Meanwhile, the only actions taken by Britain and France were Henderson and François-Poncet submitting their respective governments' formal protests to the takeover of Austria.[71] Great Britain lacked the military might on the European continent to make a difference, and France, following London's diplomatic leadership, could not afford to oppose Germany without active British involvement.[72]

## Hitler's Puppet

After the Austrian crisis, Ribbentrop returned to Berlin to take the reigns of the Foreign Office. Despite his dislike of professional diplomats, the new Foreign Minister avoided a mass reorganization of the Wilhelmstrasse and tried to gain the assistance of the foreign service in the conduct of Hitler's diplomacy by retaining most of the diplomatic staff.[73] Ribbentrop realized that he needed to maintain and trust the professional diplomatic corps to fill in for his own lack of diplomatic training and experience.[74] In the small reshuffle of personnel, Ribbentrop appointed Eric Kordt, who had acted as a Foreign Office liaison between the Bureau Ribbentrop and the Wilhelmstrasse (1933-36) and Ribbentrop's First Secretary at the German Embassy in London (1936-38), as the Head of the Foreign Office Secretariat or Bureau RAM.[75]

---

66. Transcripts of telephone calls from the German Air Ministry, 11-14 March 1938, 2949-PS, *NCA*, 5:642-54.
67. Weitz, 157-58.
68. Ibid.
69. Law concerning the union of Austria and Germany, 13 March 1938, 2307-PS, *NCA*, 4:997-98.
70. Norman Rich, *Great Power Diplomacy since 1914* (Boston: McGraw-Hill, 2003), 200.
71. Henderson to Neurath, 11 March 1938, *DGFP(D)*, 1:578; François-Poncet to Neurath, 11 March 1938, *DGFP(D)*, 1:578.
72. Anthony Adamthwaite, *Grandeur and Misery: France's Bid for Power in Europe, 1914-1940* (London: Arnold, 1995), 208-12.
73. Weizsäcker testimony, 10 June 1948, AMT transcript, OGL 17, Box 137, Folder 2, 8090.
74. Weitz, 155.
75. Seabury, *The Wilhelmstrasse*, 61; Lewis Namier, "Ernst von Weizsäcker," chap. in *In the Nazi Era* (London: Macmillan, 1952); Spitzy, 169.

At Kordt's suggestion, Ribbentrop selected Ernst von Weizsäcker, the former Director of the Political Department (1936-38), to become his Foreign Secretary.[76] The Foreign Minister replaced Weizsäcker with Ernst Woermann, Ribbentrop's former Counselor at the London Embassy (1936-38), as Director of the Political Department.[77] Moreover, Ribbentrop appointed the Nazi Wilhelm Keppler as a State Secretary for Special Duties while maintaining the Nazi Ernst Wilhelm Bohle as Head of the Auslandorganisation in the Foreign Office.[78] To replace himself in London, Ribbentrop appointed Herbert von Dirksen as German Ambassador to Britain.[79] The new Foreign Minister brought only a select few members of the Bureau Ribbentrop across the street to work at the Foreign Office: the Bureau was not disbanded until 1940.[80] The Auswärtiges Amt expanded to 2,665 employees in 1938.[81] But Ribbentrop insisted that members of the Foreign Office join the Nazi Party. Under pressure from the Foreign Minister the majority of the officials joined the Nazi Party from 1938 to 1940. By 1940, 71 out of 121 higher officials were party members. Eleven officials attempted to gain membership but had been refused.[82]

Trusting them to conduct the affairs of the Foreign Office in accordance to Hitler's policy, Ribbentrop was slow to discover that Kordt, Weizsäcker, and Woermann worked against the Nazi program. These men tried to keep Ribbentrop out of the management of the Foreign Office.[83] In fact, according to Kordt, Ribbentrop "had little help or unwilling help from the normal departments of the Foreign Office" in managing the ministry.[84] As for administering the Wilhelmstrasse, Weizsäcker stated at his trial that "at first Ribbentrop was in Berlin a great

---

76.   Weizsäcker, 122; Seabury, *The Wilhelmstrasse*, 61. Eric Kordt and the professional diplomatic corps had faith that Weizsäcker would regain control of foreign policy for the Wilhelmstrasse (Kordt testimony, 3 June 1948, AMT transcript, OGL 17, Box 136, Folder 6, 7335-336).

77.   Woermann testimony, 2 July 1948, AMT transcript, OGL 17, Box 140, Folder 2, 10848, 10873.

78.   Appendix B, *DGFP(D)*, 2:1031; Appendix D, *DGFP(D)*, 2:1044, 1052.

79.   Dirksen, 194, 196. See also C.E. Schorske, "Two German Ambassadors: Dirksen and Schulenburg," in *The Diplomats 1919-1939*, eds. Gordon A. Craig and Felix Gilbert (Princeton: Princeton University Press, 1953).

80.   Eric Kordt, *Nicht aus den Akten: Die Wilhelmstrasse in Frieden und Krieg, Erlebnisse, Begenungen und Eindrücke, 1928-1945* (Stuttgart: Union Deutsche Verlagsgesellschaft, 1950), 183-89; Woermann testimony, 6 July 1948, AMT transcript, OGL 17, Box 140, Folder 7, 11127.

81.   Donald M. McKale, *Curt Prüfer: German Diplomat from the Kaiser to Hitler* (Kent: Kent State University Press, 1987), 167.

82.   Kurt Doss, "The History of the German Foreign Office," in *The Times Survey of Foreign Ministries of the World*, ed. Zara Steiner (London: Times Books, 1982), 245.

83.   Kordt testimony, 3-4 June 1948, AMT transcript, OGL 17, Box 136, Folder 7, 7335-336, 7343.

84.   Ibid., 4 June 1948, Box 136, Folder 7, 7345.

deal and came to the Office fairly often. But his office hours were irregular. Like Hitler, he got up late in the morning and did not adapt himself readily to office routine."[85] One historian has noted that the Foreign Minister spent most of his time attending Hitler's cabinet meetings, thus missing the daily diplomatic meetings at the Wilhelmstrasse, in order to guard his position within the Führer's retinue as well as the Foreign Office's responsibility for the conduct of foreign policy versus the interference of Göring, Goebbels, Rosenberg, and Hess.[86] Slowly realizing the lack of assistance from Weizsäcker and the Wilhelmstrasse, Ribbentrop opted to rely upon the Bureau Ribbentrop to assist him with foreign affairs.[87] Because of the difficulty with the Foreign Office, Ribbentrop engaged in heated arguments with his subordinates and began to treat the professional diplomats with total distrust.[88] Commenting on the Foreign Minister, Wilhelm Keppler told the Nuremberg court:

> Ribbentrop's character changed completely when he became Foreign Minister. Within a very short time he got bossy; he showed a great need to demonstrate his prestige. He got into competency quarrels with almost all his colleagues, and it was characteristic of him that he treated his associates in a pretty inconsistent manner.[89]

André François-Poncet, the French Ambassador to Berlin, added:

> In the Wilhelmstrasse administration, which he [Ribbentrop] claimed to domineer as a subaltern dominates his platoon, he was cordially detested. He retorted by bullying his subordinates and inflicting upon his department all sorts of pretentious and worthless fellow Nazis. In his contacts with chiefs of diplomatic missions he behaved in arrogant, brutal, and peremptory fashion, fancying that language of this nature was best calculated to inspire foreigners with a lofty idea of the new Germany.[90]

---

85.   Weizsäcker, 126.
86.   Weitz, 163. See also Weizsäcker, 128; Ribbentrop, 80-81.
87.   Weizsäcker testimony, 10 June 1948, AMT transcript, OGL 17, Box 137, Folder 2, 8090; Kordt testimony, 4 June 1948, AMT transcript, OGL 17, Box 136, Folder 7, 7345; Woermann testimony, 6 July 1948, AMT transcript, OGL 17, Box 140, Folder 7, 11128.
88.   Woermann testimony, 6 July 1948, AMT transcript, OGL, Box 140, Folder 6, 11052-54.
89.   Wilhelm Keppler testimony, 16 July 1948, AMT transcript, OGL 17, Box 142, Folder 2, 12931-932.
90.   François-Poncet, 233.

For his position as Foreign Minister, Ribbentrop totally relied upon the patronage of Hitler. Ribbentrop, who more than anything wanted high status in the Third Reich, understood that it was necessary to cater to the Führer's every whim in order to maintain his ministerial position. He had no leverage with the other top Nazis like Hermann Göring. He was viewed by his Nazi associates as an interloper, by the Wehrmacht as "Hitler's puppet," and by professional diplomats as a parvenu.[91] Without friends in the Nazi Party or at the Wilhelmstrasse, Ribbentrop would have to rely upon the qualities of complete loyalty and subservience to Hitler to not only maintain his status as Foreign Minister, but to aid him in the battle for influence with the Führer. Although Hitler controlled foreign policy, Ribbentrop sought to be his master's main foreign relations adviser. He would use any tactic available to achieve this goal against his rivals. The method Ribbentrop practiced was to completely agree with Hitler's policy ideas and support these designs against any opposing arguments from the Nazi elite or the Wilhelmstrasse. Such a tactic not only demonstrated Ribbentrop's complete loyalty to his master, but displayed total faith in Hitler's foreign policy program which could only gain Hitler's confidence in his Foreign Minister. Commenting on Ribbentrop's total compliance towards the Führer's management of foreign affairs, Ernst Woermann told the American Military Tribunal that Hitler formulated foreign policy while Ribbentrop "followed in his wake."[92] In fact, Woermann went as far to state, "Ribbentrop knew, or at least he had an idea of Hitler's intentions and policies, and very often, though he may have had a better point of view, he yielded his own point of view in favor of Hitler's...."[93] During the trials of his former colleagues in 1948, Eric Kordt told the Nuremberg court:

> Hitler was in absolute control of the whole state machinery. Ribbentrop followed in the most slavish way Hitler's instructions. He [Ribbentrop] submitted the drafts of telegrams and instructions to him [Hitler] to have them corrected, even their wording. Any instruction or telegram which he expected to be put again before the eyes of Hitler he wanted more or less to have his blessing for it.[94]

Such dependency upon Hitler prompted Joachim Fest to call Ribbentrop "the despised shadow of Hitler."[95]

---

91. Weitz, 162.
92. Woermann testimony, 6 July 1948, AMT transcript, OGL 17, Box 140, Folder 6, 11052.
93. Woermann testimony, 2 July 1948, AMT transcript, OGL 17, Box 140, Folder 6, 11036.
94. Kordt testimony, 4 June 1948, AMT transcript, OGL 17, Box 140, Folder 8, 7400-1.
95. Fest, *The Face of the Third Reich*, 179.

## Sudetenland Question and the Munich Conference

Within weeks of the annexation of Austria, Hitler was applying pressure on Czechoslovakia to resolve the Sudetenland Question. There were about three million Germans living in the Sudetenland.[96] The Sudeten Germans were pressing for either autonomy from Czechoslovakia or unification with Germany.[97] Hitler's annexation of Austria resulted in increased tension between the Sudeten Germans and the Czech government. Konrad Henlein, the leader of the Sudeten German Party, had met with Hitler and Ribbentrop in March 1938, and received the promise of the Führer's support for all Sudeten German political demands against Czechoslovakia.[98] On 28 March, Hitler told Henlein that he was determined "to solve the Czechoslovak question in the near future."[99]

Hitler, however, began to develop plans for taking over all of Czechoslovakia. In order to safeguard such an action from British and French interference, the Führer saw the necessity of closer military relations with Italy. Thus, on 19 April 1938, Hitler had Ribbentrop propose to Galeazzo Ciano, the Italian Foreign Minister, the creation of a dual alliance against Britain.[100] Although the Italians did not jump at the suggestion, Hitler informed his key military leaders to begin planning Operation Green, the invasion of Czechoslovakia, on 21 April.[101]

Meanwhile, the tension between the Sudeten Germans and Prague was quickly mounting to a crisis situation. Mutual acts of violence between the Czechs and Sudeten Germans failed to overshadow the obvious threat of German military action against Czechoslovakia. As the crisis continued into May, Hitler sent Ribbentrop to Rome to acquire the much desired military alliance.[102] The German Foreign Minister, nonetheless, continued to encounter Ciano's opposition to such an arrangement.[103] Within days it became known that Prime Minister Chamberlain had declared that Britain would not militarily support Czechoslovakia in a crisis sit-

---

96.    Christian Leitz, *Nazi Foreign Policy, 1933-1941: The Road to Global War* (London: Routledge, 2004), 56.

97.    See Ronald M. Smelser, *The Sudeten Problem, 1933-1939: Volkstumpolitik and the Formulation of Nazi Foreign Policy* (Middletown: CT: Wesleyan University Press, 1975).

98.    Weitz, 165; Ribbentrop memorandum, 29 March 1938, 2788-PS, *NCA*, 5:422-24.

99.    As quoted in Weitz, 165.

100.    Leonidas E. Hill, ed., *Die Weizsäcker-Papiere* (Frankfurt-am-Main: Propylaeen, 1977), 126; Mario Toscano, *The Origins of the Pact of Steel*, (Baltimore: Johns Hopkins University Press, 1964), 5.

101.    Major Rudolf Schmundt (Hitler's Military Adjutant) memorandum, 22 April 1938, *DGFP(D)*, 2:239-40; Irving, *Göring*, 219.

102.    Ciano, *Ciano's Hidden Diary, 1937-1938*, 112.

103.    Ibid.; Moseley, 41.

uation.[104] Fearing a possible German military action, Edouard Beneš, the Czech President, initiated a partial mobilization of Czech forces on 20 May.[105] While secretly taking this action, Prague spread rumors of German troop movements near the Czech-German border.[106] These rumors greatly upset Hitler since they were untrue.[107] The World Press spread the false story as well as Britain's demand for Hitler to stop such troop movements on 21 and 22 May. Since no troop movements were discovered by British and French military attachés sent to discover the truth, the World Press reported that Hitler had ordered the termination of troop movements due to Chamberlain's warning.[108] It was then, humiliated by untrue stories spread by the World Press, that Hitler made the decision to settle the Czech Question with the use of force.[109] According to the Foreign Office interpreter, Paul Otto Schmidt, who served as Hitler's chief interpreter:

> On account of the alleged German troop concentrations the Czechs had carried out partial mobilisation on May 20th, and when Germany did nothing the World Press announced jubilantly that the German dictator had yielded. One had only to stand up to him, as the Czechs had done, they said, to make him see reason. Anyone deliberately planning to madden Hitler could have thought of no better method. Openly to accuse a dictator of weakness is the thing least likely to make him see reason—all the more so when, as in this case, the whole matter was pure invention.[110]

In Weizsäcker's analyzation of the situation:

> The World Press had committed an unpardonable psychological error...by spreading the story that Hitler had yielded to foreign pressure in the Czech question. Such an allegation Hitler could not endure—particularly as it was untrue. Hitler had embarked on no military enterprise, and could not therefore withdraw from one. But this unfortunate provocation by the Foreign Press now really set Hitler going. From then on he was emphatically in favour of settling the Czech question by force of arms....[111]

---

104.   Ernst Eisenlohr to Ribbentrop, 12 May 1938, *DGFP(D)*, 2:275.
105.   Weizsäcker, 134; Spitzy, 218.
106.   Ibid.; Dirksen, 197; Schmidt, 85-86; Weizsäcker to Ribbentrop, 20 May 1938, *DGFP(D)*, 2:296.
107.   Spitzy, 218.
108.   Hill, *Die Weizsäcker Papiere*, 144-45; Irving, *Göring*, 219.
109.   Operation Green directive, 20 May 1938, 388-PS, *NCA*, 3:311.
110.   Schmidt, 88. See also Sir Nevile Henderson, *Failure of a Mission, Berlin 1937-1939* (Toronto: Musson, 1940), 178.
111.   Weizsäcker, 135-36.

Set on destroying Czechoslovakia, the German leader immediately sounded out the Italian position. He acquired Mussolini's word that Italy was not interested in the fate of Czechoslovakia on 25 May.[112] The following day Hitler informe Göring of his decision to launch an invasion in the autumn.[113] Two days later, on 28 May, the Führer declared to his cabinet members, including Ribbentrop, at a Chancellery meeting that it was his "unshakable will that Czechoslovakia shall be wiped off the map."[114] Hitler was confident that a war against Czechoslovakia could be localized without British and French intervention.[115]

Knowing Hitler's thoughts about the Czech Question, the German Foreign Minister fully supported his master's dream of conquest. Ribbentrop pressed for war against Czechoslovakia, assuring the Führer that the West would not intervene.[116] In the meantime, in early July 1938, the British and French governments declared their willingness to defend the sovereignty of Czechoslovakia.[117] Sir Nevile Henderson, the British Ambassador in Berlin, had warned London of German military preparations to invade Czechoslovakia.[118] Hitler and Ribbentrop therefore renewed their efforts toward acquiring a military alliance with Italy.[119] Becoming confident of Mussolini's support, Hitler, aided by the constant verbal backing of Ribbentrop, was convinced that he could resolve the Czech Question with the use of arms without intervention by the West because of the Berlin-Rome Axis. Ribbentrop informed Weizsäcker of Hitler's intentions on 21 July.[120] Two weeks later, on 3 August, the Foreign Minister sent a telegram to his ambassadors abroad stating that the West would not intervene in a Czech-German conflict, and "Czechoslovakia presents no military problem for

---

112.  Ciano, *Ciano's Hidden Diary, 1937-1938*, 121.

113.  Irving, *Göring*, 220.

114.  Captain Fritz Wiedeman (Hitler's Aide) memorandum, 21 November 1945, 3037-PS, *NCA*, 5:743. See also Major Schmundt's papers, April to October 1938, *NCA*, 3:305, 311; Hitler's speech, 30 January 1939, *NCA*, 4:1101.

115.  Weizsäcker testimony, 8 June 1948, AMT transcript, OGL 17, Box 136, Folder 13, 7717; Kordt testimony, 4 June 1948, AMT transcript, OGL 17, Box 136, Folder 7, 7376.

116.  Weizsäcker testimony, 8 June 1948, AMT transcript, OGL 17, Box 136, Folder 13, 7717; Weizsäcker memorandum, 21 July 1938, *DGFP(D)*, 2:504; Weizsäcker memorandum, ca. 19 August 1938, *DGFP(D)*, 2:593-94; Weizsäcker memorandum, 30 August 1938, *DGFP(D)*, 2:662-63; Erich Kordt affidavit, 25 September 1947, AMT documents, OGL 17, Box 235, Folder 4, NG-3605, 2. See also Williamson Murray, *The Challenge in the European Balance of Powers, 1938-1939* (Princeton: Princeton University Press, 1984), 182.

117.  François-Poncet, 258-59.

118.  Henderson to William Strang, 28 July 1938, *DBFP*, third series, 2:21-22.

119.  Ciano, *Ciano's Hidden Diary, 1937-1938*, 135.

120.  Weizsäcker memorandum, 21 July 1938, NG-3716, *NMT*, 12:797-98.

the German Army and German Luftwaffe, for Czechoslovakia would be over-thrown at one blow."[121]

In mid-August Weizsäcker began to realize the seriousness of the situation. For the second time Ribbentrop had informed him of Hitler's intentions. According to the Foreign Secretary, on 19 August, Hitler told Ribbentrop that he:

> was firmly resolved to settle the Czech affair by force of arms. He described the middle of October as the latest possible date…. The other powers would certainly not make any move and, even if they did, we should accept their challenge and defeat them….[122]

When Weizsäcker disagreed with this view, stating that Britain and France would intervene in Eastern Europe, Ribbentrop became emotional and demanded the Foreign Secretary's complete trust in the Führer's judgment. Weizsäcker recounted the discussion in his memoirs:

> Ribbentrop explained to me that Hitler had never made a mistake…. I ought to have faith in his genius, just as he, Ribbentrop, had as a result of many year's experience. If I had not yet won through to this "blind faith"—he used these actual words—he could only wish most urgently, though in all friendli-ness, that I might soon do so.[123]

For the next few weeks the Foreign Secretary contemplated his predicament. Hitler and Ribbentrop were not interested in any opinions that were contrary to their own.[124] He was convinced that war would break out over the Czech Ques-tion. Thus, Weizsäcker, as well as Eric Kordt, used their diplomatic contacts to warn Britain and France of the Führer's intentions. They employed Theo Kordt, a Counselor at the German Embassy in London and trusted brother of Eric to inform Whitehall,[125] besides informing the British, French, and Italian Ambassa-dors in Berlin.[126] The Foreign Secretary and the Wilhelmstrasse were fully con-vinced that Hitler's intentions to resolve the Czech Question by use of force

---

121.  Ribbentrop to Embassies Abroad, 3 August 1938, *DGFP(D)*, 2:529-31.
122.  Weizsäcker memorandum, 19 August 1938, *DGFP(D)*, 2:593. See also Weizsäcker, 137.
123.  Weizsäcker, 137.
124.  Hitler and Ribbentrop refused to see Herbert von Dirksen in August and September 1938 although they knew that the German Ambassador to Britain carried warnings from Prime Minister Chamberlain (Dirksen, 207).
125.  Erich Kordt testimony, 4 June 1938, AMT transcript, OGL 17, Box 136, Folder 7, 7386.
126.  Weizsäcker, 146, 148.

would result in war since they firmly believed that Britain and France would militarily support the Czechs.[127]

In early September 1938, Czech President Beneš, facing the possibility of German military action, conceded to the demand for the political autonomy of the Sudetenland. Having acquired this concession, Henlein, the Sudeten German leader, backed by Hitler's promise, immediately broke off talks with the Czech government. Both Hitler and Henlein had hoped for the ultimate goal: the German annexation of the Sudetenland. Because of the deadlock in the Sudetenland talks rioting broke out in the region. The ongoing crisis seemed headed for further hostilities with a German invasion looming in the background.[128] As the Sudetenland situation deteriorated, the British government, informed by the Wilhelmstrasse of Hitler's intentions, sought to diplomatically resolve the Czech Question. In early September 1938, the British Prime Minister, Neville Chamberlain, proposed a meeting with Hitler. Both Göring, who held great influence with Hitler at the time, and Weizsäcker urged the Führer to accept.[129] Therefore, on 15 September, Chamberlain discussed the Czech Question with Hitler, without the presence of Ribbentrop, at Berchtesgaden.[130] At first, according to Schmidt who interpreted the conversation, the Führer came on strong to Chamberlain: "I shall not put up with this [the Czech affair] any longer. I shall settle this question in one way or another. I shall take matters into my own hands."[131] Calming down after a few minutes, Hitler took another approach with Chamberlain. He suggested that a plebiscite be held in the Sudetenland to determine the future of the region.[132] Acknowledging his preference for this method of resolving the Czech Question instead of German military action, Chamberlain told Hitler he would seek the approval of the British, French, and Czech governments for such a plan.[133] Perceiving that Chamberlain had bowed to his "demand," Hitler viewed the British Prime Minister as weak and willing to abandon the Czechs.[134]

One week later, on 22 September, Chamberlain returned to Germany with a reply to Hitler's proposal. Meeting at Godesberg, the British Prime Minister

---

127.  Weizsäcker testimony, 8 June 1948, AMT transcript, OGL 17, Box 136, Folder 13, 7717; Kordt affidavit, 25 September 1947, AMT documents, OGL 17, Box 235, Folder 4, NG-3605, 2; Weizsäcker, 148-49.
128.  Smelser, 234-42.
129.  Schmidt, 91.
130.  Ibid.
131.  Ibid., 92.
132.  Weizsäcker note, 16 September 1938, *DGFP(D)*, 2:810.
133.  Schmidt memorandum, 15 September 1938, *DGFP(D)*, 2:786-98.
134.  Weizsäcker, 150-51.

informed the Führer of British support for a plebiscite in the Sudetenland.[135] Hitler, nevertheless, had changed his mind. He now demanded German occupation of the Sudetenland by no later than 1 October 1938.[136] The next day Hitler again gave Chamberlain an ultimatum.[137] The likelihood of war was apparent to all present at the meeting. During a key moment at the conference both leaders were informed of the Czech initiation of general mobilization. Both leaders realized the crisis had taken a turn towards war.[138] Having missed an opportunity to diplomatically resolve the affair, Chamberlain returned to London to reconsider the British response.

On 26 September, three days after their meeting at Godesberg, Chamberlain sent an envoy, Sir Horace Wilson, to inform the Führer of the British position regarding the Czech Question. Wilson told Hitler that the Czech government would not give in to Hitler's demand for the Sudetenland and Britain, as well as France, would defend the sovereignty of Czechoslovakia.[139] In response, Hitler demanded the immediate German annexation of the Sudetenland. Schmidt, who served as the interpreter, related in his memoirs that Hitler told Wilson:

> And if they [the Czech government] choose to refuse I shall smash Czechoslovakia! If the Czechs have not accepted my demands by 2 p.m. on Wednesday September 28th I shall march into the Sudeten territory on October 1st with the German Army.[140]

Although his declared intentions were to annex the Sudetenland, Hitler desired to annex much more of Czechoslovakia to satisfy his appetite for eastwards expansion. Advice from the Wilhelmstrasse did not support either plan.[141] His close confident, Göring, and Neurath, who remained in Berlin as an adviser, both urged Hitler not to attack Czechoslovakia, but to negotiate a

---

135.  Schmidt, 96-97.
136.  François-Poncet, 263; Weizsäcker, 151.
137.  Schmidt, 100; Adolf Hitler to Neville Chamberlain, 23 September 1938, *DGFP(D)*, 2:889-91; Hitler to Chamberlain, ca. 23 September 1938, *DGFP(D)*, 2:908-10.
138.  Andor Hencke to Ribbentrop, 24 September 1938, *DGFP(D)*, 2:920; Schmidt, 101.
139.  Schmidt, 103, 105; Weitz, 182; Spitzy, 245-46.
140.  As quoted in Schmidt, 104.
141.  Weizsäcker testimony, 8 June 1948, AMT transcript, OGL 17, Box 136, Folder 13, 7717; Kordt testimony, 4 June 1948, AMT transcript, OGL 17, Box 136, Folder 7, 73888; Hassell, 38; Weizsäcker, 148-49; Hill, "The Wilhelmstrasse in the Nazi Era," 567.

settlement.[142] Hitler, nevertheless, was willing to risk war to achieve his goals, firmly believing that the West would not come to the aid of Czechoslovakia.[143] Only Ribbentrop supported Hitler's view of the situation.[144] Weizsäcker warned his superior of this false interpretation of the diplomatic situation, but to no avail.[145] Ribbentrop had "blind faith" in Hitler's judgment. According to Weizsäcker, Ribbentrop "moved around in dreams of war and victory...."[146]

With time running short, Weizsäcker, representing the professional diplomats of the Wilhelmstrasse, met with Göring and Neurath to discuss the crisis. The Foreign Secretary enlisted both men in a movement aimed at forcing Hitler into mediation.[147] In fact, Weizsäcker suggested that the three of them draft a compromise agreement and provide it to Mussolini for him to propose the settlement to Hitler.[148] Thus, without the knowledge of Ribbentrop, the Foreign Office, Göring, and Neurath drafted the compromise and forwarded it to Mussolini.[149] Meanwhile Göring tried to destroy Ribbentrop's influence with Hitler by accusing the Foreign Minister of "inciting war" and calling him a "criminal fool" in front of the Führer.[150]

---

142.   Paul Otto Schmidt testimony, 24 August 1948, AMT transcript, OGL 17, Box 146, Folder 19, 7831-835; Neurath testimony, 24 June 1946, *TMWC*, 16:646-47; Irving, *Göring*, 229; Heineman, *Hitler's First Foreign Minister*, 175-76, 181; Roger Manvell and Heinrich Fränkel, *Göring* (New York: Simon and Schuster, 1962), 200; Kordt testimony, 4 June 1948, AMT transcript, OGL 17, Box 136, Folder 7, 7388.

143.   Weizsäcker testimony, 8 June 1948, AMT transcript, OGL 17, Box 136, Folder 13, 7717; Ciano, *Ciano's Hidden Diary, 1937-1938*, 161; Kordt testimony, 4 June 1948, AMT transcript, OGL 17, Box 136, Folder 7, 7376.

144.   Kordt testimony, 4 June 1948, AMT transcript, OGL 17, Box 136, Folder 7, 7376; Weizsäcker, 152; Robertson, *Hitler's Pre-War Policy and Military Plans, 1933-1939*, 145; Hassell, 10; Ciano, *Ciano's Hidden Diary, 1937-1938*, 161; Weizsäcker testimony, 8 June 1948, AMT transcript, OGL 17, Box 136, Folder 13, 7712, 7717; Manvell and Fränkel, *Göring*, 201. Reinhard Spitzy, Ribbentrop's personal secretary, puts the Hitler-Ribbentrop relationship in a different light. According to Spitzy, Ribbentrop controlled all information concerning international affairs that went to the Führer. As such, the Foreign Minister shaped Hitler's views of foreign affairs (Spitzy, 221). He wrote in his memoirs, "the information which was served up to him [Hitler] and upon which he formed his own opinions was always sifted, monitored and modified by the Ribbentrops before it had a chance to reach him" (Spitzy, 222).

145.   Weizsäcker testimony, 8 June 1948, AMT transcript, OGL 17, Box 136, Folder 13, 7717.

146.   Ibid., 7718.

147.   Kordt testimony, 4 June 1938, AMT transcript, OGL 17, Box 136, Folder 7, 7388.

148.   Ibid.; Spitzy, 252-53.

149.   Weizsäcker, 154; Schmidt testimony, 24 August 1948, AMT transcript, OGL 17, Box 146, Folder 19, 17831-835; Schmidt, 111; Manvell and Fränkel, *Göring*, 201, Hill, "The Wilhelmstrasse and the Nazi Era," 567.

150.   Manvell and Fränkel, *Göring*, 200.

With time running out on Hitler's ultimatum, the British, French, and Italian governments worked to avoid a war. On 28 September 1938, the French Ambassador, André François-Poncet, met with Hitler and Ribbentrop at the Chancellery. He warned the Führer that war would result if Germany invaded Czechoslovakia. Schmidt, who witnessed the discussion conducted in the German language, recorded the event in his memoirs:

> From my corner of the room I closely watched the actors in this tense battle for peace. I observed Hitler's reactions how, very gradually, the balance tilted in favour of peace. He no longer flared up, and it was only with the greatest difficulty that he could find anything to say to the arguments which François-Poncet advanced with devastating French logic. He became very pensive. Ribbentrop tried to intervene once or twice—and not on the side of peace. François-Poncet, who fully realized the danger of even one false word in such a situation, called him sharply to order, with suppressed irritation.[151]

Shortly after this meeting, the Italian Ambassador, Bernardo Attolico, delivered the proposal of an immediate Great Powers meeting in Munich to mediate a peaceful resolution of the Czech Question.[152] The compromise suggestion came as a complete surprise to Ribbentrop, who strongly advocated the invasion of Czechoslovakia.[153] Fearing the loss of Italian support for his dreams of conquest in Eastern Europe Hitler took the proposal seriously.[154] Faced at the same time by pressure from his military leaders, including Göring, that Germany was not ready to fight a European war, Hitler accepted Neurath's advice to immediately meet with British, Italian, and French leaders in Munich.[155]

Hitler met with Mussolini, Chamberlain, and French Prime Minister Édouard Daladier (1938-40) in Munich on 29 September 1938. Hitler made all the important German decisions at the Munich Conference. The Führer consulted Ribbentrop, but he relied upon Weizsäcker for diplomatic assistance.[156] In the negotiations, Hitler agreed to a compromise that gave Germany the Sudeten-

---

151.  Schmidt, 106-7. See also François-Poncet, 266.
152.  François-Poncet, 267; Ciano, *Ciano's Hidden Diary, 1937-1938*, 165.
153.  Weizsäcker testimony, 7 June 1948, AMT transcript, OGL 17, Box 136, Folder 13, 7719, 7723.
154.  Count Lutz Schwerin von Krosigk affidavit, German Minister of Finance (1932-1945), 18 May 1946, *TMWC* 40:476; Weitz, 154.
155.  Manvell and Fränkel, *Göring*, 199, 201; Keith Middlemas, *Diplomacy of Illusion: The British Government and Germany, 1937-1939* (London: Weidenfeld and Nicolson, 1972), 400; Schmidt, 107; Ribbentrop to Missions Abroad, 28 September 1938, *DGFP(D)*, 2:994.
156.  Spitzy, 251.

land, and promised no further aggression against Czechoslovakia.[157] Hitler had allowed himself to be side-tracked from his dream of eastwards expansion into Czechoslovakia due to advice from Göring, Neurath, and the Wilhelmstrasse. He immediately regretted this decision.[158] Hitler perceived the British and French acceptance of the German annexation of the Sudetenland as a sure sign of weakness, believing that if he would have followed his own gut feeling, and Ribbentrop's advice, that all of Czechoslovakia would be his.[159] Upon returning to Berlin, Hitler was heard saying, "that fellow Chamberlain has spoiled my entry into Prague."[160] Ribbentrop, who was unable to influence Hitler towards an invasion of Czechoslovakia, criticized the Munich agreement. Reinhard Spitzy, Ribbentrop's personal secretary, overheard Hitler quietly telling his Foreign Minister: "Oh, don't take it all so seriously. That piece of paper [the Munich Protocol] is of no significance whatsoever."[161] Even in the Foreign Office, according to Ambassador Dirksen, "it was whispered…that the signing of the protocol meant no change in policy."[162] In fact, on 21 October 1938, Hitler gave orders for the Wehrmacht to prepare for a surprise attack on Czechoslovakia sometime in the near future.[163]

## Ribbentrop and the Foreign Office

The Führer's disappointment at Munich changed his view of Ribbentrop overnight. Ribbentrop had been the only adviser who urged Hitler to take action against Czechoslovakia. Göring, Neurath, and the others opposed such an adventure. Now, after the fact, Hitler viewed his Foreign Minister as the only person who had provided him sound advice. Ribbentrop would replace Göring and Neurath as his key diplomatic adviser.[164]

Ribbentrop, realizing his newly acquired importance, understood that the Wilhelmstrasse had betrayed him during the Sudetenland crisis. The Foreign

---

157.  Munich Protocol, 29 September 1938, *NMT*, 12:818-20.
158.  Weizsäcker testimony, 8 June 1948, AMT transcript, OGL 17, Box 136, Folder 13, 7729; William Carr, *Arms, Autarky and Aggression: A Study in German Foreign Policy, 1933-1939* (London: Edward Arnold, 1972), 102.
159.  Carr, *Arms, Autarky and Aggression*, 102; François-Poncet, 261.
160.  Dr. Hjalmar Schacht testimony, German Minister without Portfolio (1937-1943), 2 May 1946, *TMWC*, 12:531.
161.  Spitzy, 254.
162.  Dirksen, 211.
163.  Carr, *Arms, Autarky and Aggression*, 102.
164.  Weizsäcker, 157.

Minister had lost all trust of his professional diplomats.[165] He thus decided to separate himself from disloyal professional diplomats by concentrating his diplomatic activity to a small special staff that would bypass Weizsäcker and the traditional functions of the Foreign Office.[166] Besides establishing his special staff, consisting of former Bureau Ribbentrop members and faithful Foreign Office diplomats, Ribbentrop transferred large numbers of Bureau Ribbentrop members to the Wilhelmstrasse without enforcing entry requirements.[167] At the same time Ribbentrop moved his office from the ministry to the newly renovated Presidential Palace, which became the official residence of the Foreign Minister, and thereafter he rarely visited the Foreign Office.[168]

Ribbentrop was determined not to rely upon the professional diplomatic corps to conduct Hitler's foreign policy. The Foreign Minister would instead employ his hand-picked special staff and trusted members of the Bureau Ribbentrop for diplomatic advice.[169] Commenting on the effect that Ribbentrop's decision had on the Wilhelmstrasse, Ernst Woermann, the Director of the Political Department, told the Nuremberg court:

> [T]he normal duties of a Political Department were missing...to use the information received for the purpose of submitting suggestions and give advice to the Foreign Minister; but,...in the Fall...of 1938...Ribbentrop had specifically told me that he did not desire to receive any unsolicited advice. [Ribbentrop]...instituted his own personal working staff with which he discussed all important questions and particularly such questions, which, before this time, had belonged to the sphere of duties of the Political Department.[170]

165. Ibid., 159; Weizsäcker testimony, 10 June 1948, AMT transcript, OGL 17, Box 137, Folder 2, 8090, 8093.
166. Weizsäcker testimony, 10 June 1948, AMT transcript, OGL 17, Box 137, Folder 2, 8090-91; Kordt testimony, 4 June 1948, AMT transcript, OGL 17, Box 136, Folder 7, 7347.
167. Kordt testimony, 4 June 1948, AMT transcript, OGL 17, Box 136, Folder 7, 7341, 7346.
168. Ibid., 7553; Schmidt, 175; Albert Speer, *Spandau: The Secret Diaries*, trans. Richard and Clara Winston (New York: Macmillan, 1976), 142; Hans-Georg von Studnitz, *While Berlin Burns: The Diaries of Hans-Georg von Studnitz, 1943-1945*, trans. R.H. Stevens (London: Weidenfeld and Nicolson, 1964), 259; Weitz, 238.
169. Weizsäcker testimony, 10 June 1948, AMT transcript, OGL 17, Box 137, Folder 2, 8092; Woermann testimony, 6 July 1948, AMT transcript, OGL 17, Box 140, Folder 6, 11050.
170. Woermann testimony, 6 July 1948, AMT transcript, OGL 17, Box 140, Folder 6, 11039-40. Erich Kordt stated at the trial of his colleagues in Nuremberg in 1948: "Ribbentrop had...given an order that the foreign mission [embassy] should only report facts and abstain from commenting on them" (Kordt testimony, 4 June 1948, AMT transcript, OGL 17, Box 136, Folder 7, 7375).

In November 1938, Ribbentrop, according to Woermann, declared that the Political Department "was to be restricted to the handling of routine matters."[171] In fact, the Foreign Minister consulted Woermann on official business only five times from the autumn of 1938 to 1943, and then on matters of minor importance.[172] The consequence was that Ribbentrop came to rely upon the amateur abilities of current and former members of his Bureau for diplomatic advice. Commenting upon Bureau Ribbentrop methods, Woermann stated that Ribbentrop's confidants prepared their diplomatic advisory notes in a very unprofessional manner. They worked on "principles of speed and not of accuracy" when preparing reports.[173] And, from what he observed, these reports "played a pretty important part [in diplomatic affairs] because such notes as a rule contained whatever the authors believed Ribbentrop wanted to hear."[174] Summing up the situation within the Wilhelmstrasse, Ulrich von Hassell wrote in his diary on 20 December 1938:

> He [Ribbentrop] is no more inclined to listen to divergent views than his lord and master. The pace in the Foreign Office, it seems, borders on the unbearable; it is a frantic merry-go-round in which everybody's nerves are getting frayed. Even the highest officials—with the possible exception of Weizsäcker, and he to a limited extent—know nothing about the political objectives and general lines of policy.[175]

## Czech and Polish Questions

After Munich, Hitler's foreign policy aimed at acquiring a military alliance with Italy that would allow Germany the opportunity to resolve both the Czech and Polish Questions. Hitler, supported by Ribbentrop, decided to tackle the Czech situation first.[176] The Führer therefore pursued closer relations with Italy as Germany prepared to conquer Czechoslovakia.[177] On 21 October 1938, the German leader directed the Wehrmacht to make preparations for the "liquidation of the remainder of the Czech state at any time…."[178]

---

171. Woermann testimony, 6 July 1948, AMT transcript, OGL 17, Box 140, Folder 6, 11055.
172. Ibid., OGL 17, Box 140, Folder 6, 11056.
173. Ibid., OGL 17, Box 140, Folder 7, 11128.
174. Ibid.
175. Hassell, 26.
176. Ibid., 54.
177. Ibid., 16; Robertson, *Hitler's Pre-War Policy and Military Plans, 1933-1939*, 150.
178. Hitler directive, 21 October 1938, *DGFP(D)*, 4:99-100. See also Norman Rich, *Hitler's War Aims*, 2 vols. (New York: W.W. Norton, 1973-74), 1:111; Thorne, 93; Carr, *Arms, Autarky, and Aggression*, 102.

Meanwhile, Hitler sent Ribbentrop to meet with Józef Lipski, the Polish Ambassador to Germany, at Berchtesgaden on 24 October. In a wide-ranging set of proposals, the German Foreign Minister indicated to Lipski that Hitler was interested in obtaining a general settlement of German-Polish differences. After pointing out Poland's isolation from the West, largely achieved by the Berlin-Rome Axis, Ribbentrop suggested an extension of the German-Polish Nonaggression Pact of 1934 as well as Poland joining the Anti-Comintern Pact. Additionally, Ribbentrop proposed the return of the Free City of Danzig to Germany, an extraterritorial autobahn and railway through the Polish Corridor connecting Germany with Danzig and East Prussia, as well as a treaty confirming the German-Polish borders.[179] After these talks, in which Lipski gave no formal response, the German Foreign Minister traveled to Rome where he proposed a military alliance to Mussolini and Ciano on 28 October.[180]

Several weeks later, on 19 November, Lipski provided his government's reply to Ribbentrop concerning Hitler's proposals in Berlin. Warsaw flatly refused the German offers.[181] Upset that the Poles failed to accept Hitler's limited demands, Ribbentrop issued Lipski a veiled threat. According to the Polish Ambassador:

> Ribbentrop was discursive, reverting to the history of the last crisis, and repeating a statement already known to me that in the political constellation of that time France was actually isolated and that he was convinced that neither France nor England would move to the defense of Czechoslovakia. Ribbentrop quoted…this detail to me in order to stress that the Reich could absolutely count on Italy's military aid. Ribbentrop emphasized in his further deliberations Germany's military superiority at that time, remarking that at the present the situation has become even more favorable for the Reich.[182]

Shortly thereafter, on 24 November, Hitler directed his military to prepare for an occupation of Danzig.[183] Meanwhile, the German Army continued to plan for the invasion of Bohemia and Moravia.[184]

---

179.  Józef Lipski memorandum, 24 October 1938, *DB*, 453-54; Walther Hewel memorandum, 24 October 1938, *DGFP(D)*, 5:104-7.

180.  Galeazzo Ciano, *Ciano's Diplomatic Papers: Being a Record of nearly 200 Conversations held during the Years 1936-1942*, ed. Malcolm Muggeridge, trans. Stuart Hood (London: Odhams, 1948), 242-46; Ciano, *Ciano's Hidden Diary, 1937-1938*, 185; Schmidt memorandum, 28 October 1938, *DGFP(D)*, 4:515-20.

181.  Ribbentrop memorandum, 19 November 1938, *DGFP(D)*, 5:127-28.

182.  Lipski to Beck, 19 November 1938, *DB*, 466-67.

183.  General Wilhelm Keitel directive, 24 November 1938, 137-C, *NCA*, 6:949-50.

184.  Keitel directive, 17 December 1938, *DGFP(D)*, 4:185-86.

Hitler's diplomacy was unfolding in a manner that would provide Germany a military alliance with Italy while forcing the Czech state and Poland to come to terms with the Third Reich. At the beginning of the new year, Hans-Georg von Mackensen, the German Ambassador to Italy, reported Mussolini's great interest in forming a military alliance.[185] In the meantime, Hitler met with Slovak politicians who sought independence from Prague.[186] The Führer and Ribbentrop also met with the Polish Foreign Minister, Józef Beck, and Lipski at Berchtesgaden on 5 January 1939. Hitler personally resubmitted his proposals for a German-Polish settlement.[187] The following day, in Munich, Ribbentrop insisted that Beck accept Hitler's proposals, especially the reunion of Danzig with Germany and the construction of an extraterritorial road and railway system.[188] In late January, Ribbentrop traveled to Warsaw to seek Polish acceptance of Hitler's proposals, but failed to acquire the much desired settlement.[189]

Hitler increased the pressure on Prague. Although military plans were drawn up, the Führer continued to keep this fact from Ribbentrop and the Wilhelmstrasse.[190] Ribbentrop, his special staff, as well as the Foreign Office were under the assumption that Hitler was trying to force a crisis situation in order peacefully resolve the Czech Question by diplomatic means, similar to Munich.[191] Hitler employed Ribbentrop to discuss affairs with František Chvalkovský, the Czech Foreign Minister, in Berlin on 21 January 1939. Following Hitler's directive, Ribbentrop threatened the Czech that "unless there would be a change in Czechoslovakia, the situation might become catastrophical."[192]

Although unaware of actual military plans for the invasion of the Czech state, Weizsäcker and the Foreign Office received indications through their many contacts that Hitler was planning a crisis situation. On 13 February, the Foreign Secretary jotted down on paper that "Czechoslovakia will receive its death blow in approximately four weeks."[193] In fact, Hitler, who continued to distrust diplo-

---

185.   Mackensen memorandum, 3 January 1939, *DGFP(D)*, 4:545-46; Ribbentrop to Ciano, 9 January 1939, *DGFP(D)*, 4:550.

186.   Simon Newman, *March 1939: The British Guarantee to Poland* (Oxford: Clarendon Press, 1976), 90.

187.   Lipski, 482; Schmidt memorandum, 5 January 1939, *DGFP(D)*, 5:152-58.

188.   Ribbentrop memorandum, 19 January 1939, *DGFP(D)*, 5:159-61: Lipski, 482.

189.   Lipski, 485; Ribbentrop memorandum, 1 February 1939, *DGFP(D)*, 5:167-68.

190.   Woermann testimony, 6 July 1948, AMT transcript, OGL 17, Box 140, Folder 2, 11084; Weizsäcker testimony, 8 June 1948, AMT transcript, OGL 17, Box 136, Folder 13, 7715, 7731.

191.   Weizsäcker testimony, 8 June 1948, AMT transcript, OGL 17, Box 136, Folder 13, 7731.

192.   Schmidt memorandum, 21 January 1939, Staff Summary Analysis, IMT documents, OGL 17, Box 195, Folder 6, 2795-PS, 55.

193.   Leonidas E. Hill, "Three Crises, 1938-1939," *Journal of Contemporary History* 3 (January 1969), 124. See also Hill, *Die Weizsäcker Papiere*, 150-52.

mats, did not even inform Ribbentrop of the impending invasion until 11 March.[194] About the same time, Weizsäcker discovered the truth from Slovakian sources.[195] Hitler's intentions, however, became obvious. Robert Coulondre, the French Ambassador to Berlin, reported to Paris that German troops were on the move toward Czechoslovakia.[196]

As German forces made final preparations to pounce on Bohemia and Moravia, Hitler called Josef Tiso, the Slovak nationalist leader, and a delegation of pro-Nazi Slovaks to Berlin on 13 March. Hitler and Ribbentrop directed Tiso to proclaim Slovakia as an independent state, or Germany would be forced to invade Slovakia as well as the rest of Czechoslovakia.[197] Ribbentrop added that Germany would annex a part of Slovakia with the rest being divided among Hungary and Poland.[198] The German Foreign Minister even provided Tiso a draft of Slovakia's declaration of independence.[199] The very next day, on 14 March, Tiso had the Slovak Diet declare Slovakian independence from control of the Prague government.[200] At the same time Ribbentrop informed the Italian government of Hitler's decision to occupy Bohemia and Moravia.[201]

Fearing the disintegration of his state, Czech President Emil Hácha requested through the German Embassy in Prague a meeting with Hitler.[202] Hácha and Chvalkovský, the Czech Foreign Minister, arrived in Berlin late in the evening of 14 March. After midnight they met with Hitler, Ribbentrop, Göring, Weizsäcker, and others.[203] During the meeting Hitler browbeat Hácha to accept an ultimatum requiring his acceptance of peaceful German occupation of Bohemia and Moravia otherwise the Luftwaffe would bomb Prague.[204] Schmidt, the interpreter, described the situation in his memoirs: "Here was no intimate discussion between man and man. There were a number of people present, but Hácha,

---

194. Keitel to Ribbentrop, 11 March 1939, *DGFP(D)*, 4:234-35; Ribbentrop, 94.
195. Weizsäcker testimony, 8 June 1948, AMT transcript, OGL 17, Box 136, Folder 13, 7732; Weizsäcker, 175.
196. Robert Coulondre to Georges Bonnet, 13 March 1939, *FYB*, 67-68.
197. Crimes against Czechoslovakia Report, Czech Government, 3061-PS, *NCA*, 5:867; Hewel memorandum, 13 March 1939, 2802-PS, *NCA*, 5:443-47.
198. Weinberg, *The Foreign Policy of Hitler's Germany*, 2:471, n.21.
199. Ibid.
200. Newman, 91; Ribbentrop, 94; Günther Altenburg memorandum, 14 March 1939, *DGFP(D)*, 4:252-53.
201. Weizsäcker memorandum, 14 March 1939, *DGFP(D)*, 4:261.
202. Andor Henke to Ribbentrop, 13 March 1939, *DGFP(D)*, 4:249; Newman, 91.
203. Hewel memorandum, 15 March 1939, *DGFP(D)*, 4:263-69.
204. Ibid., 266-69; Lacroix to Bonnet, 15 March 1939, *FYB*, 86; German Crimes against Czechoslovakia Report, Czech Government, 3061-PS, *NCA*, 5:857; Weizsäcker, 176; Schmidt, 123-24.

Chvalkovský, and the rest, even Göring and Ribbentrop, were the audience, Hitler the speaker."[205] After a few dramatic moments, including Hácha passing out, the Czech President agreed to Hitler's terms and placed the fate of Czechoslovakia in the Führer's hands.[206] Within days the former Czechoslovakia became the Protectorate of Bohemia and Moravia, as well as the state of Slovakia, a satellite of Germany.[207]

With such a sudden change in the balance of power in Central Europe, the world viewed Hitler as a very dangerous menace. Many, especially in Eastern Europe, feared Hitler's next move. The Lithuanian government, realizing that Hitler might have designs on Memeland, a territory largely populated by Germans and annexed by Lithuania in 1923, sought support from Britain and France.[208] "The occupation of Prague," according to A.J.P. Taylor, "flung the people of Memel into ungovernable excitement...."[209] The West, however, declined to come to the aid of Lithuania.[210] Thus, on 20 March 1939, the Lithuanian Foreign Minister, Juosaz Urbsys, traveled to Berlin to meet with Ribbentrop regarding the Memeland Question. Ribbentrop, under the guidance of Hitler, browbeat his Lithuanian counterpart by telling him that:

> There were only two ways of solving the Memel problem. The one is the friendly cession of this territory to Germany. Otherwise revolts and shootings would occur and Hitler would then act with lightening speed. Future developments would be governed by the military and not by the politicians.[211]

Having received such a threat, the Lithuanian government agreed to cede Memeland to Germany on 22 March. German troops occupied the territory two weeks later.[212]

In spite of not taking any action to support Lithuania, London objected to German aggression in Eastern Europe. The invasion of Czechoslovakia, in the

---

205. Schmidt, 123.
206. Czech-German Declaration, 15 March 1939, *DGFP(D)*, 4:270; Schmidt, 124-25.
207. German-Slovak Protocol, 23 March 1939, IMT documents, OGL 17, Box 195, Folder 6, 2793-PS; Anita J. Prażmowska, *Eastern Europe and the Origins of the Second World War* (New York: St. Martin's Press, 2000), 83-84.
208. Alfred E. Senn, *The Great Powers, Lithuania, and the Vilna Question, 1920-1928* (Leiden: E.J. Brill, 1966), 107-21.
209. A.J.P. Taylor, *The Origins of the Second World War* (London: Hamish Hamilton, 1961), 209.
210. Julius P. Slavenas, "Lithuania, Klaipeda-Memel, and Hitler," *Baltic History* 3 (1974), 266.
211. Hewel memorandum, 20 March 1939, Staff Evidence Analysis, IMT documents, OGL 17, Box 196, Folder 3, 2956-PS.
212. Slavenas, 266; Reich decree, 23 March 1939, TC-53-A, *NCA*, 8:408.

eyes of British statesmen, upset the balance of power in Europe in a way that was unacceptable to European security. The British had understood the German desire to reunite lost German territories to the Third Reich, but the annexation of Bohemia and Moravia went beyond the concept of self-determination.[213] As the German Ambassador to London, Herbert von Dirksen, wrote in his memoirs:

> The average Englishman had understood the linking of the Sudetenland as a union of Germans with Germans. The incorporation, however, of seven millions of [a] foreign race was considered irreconcilable with the declared principles of National Socialism itself. It was regarded as unadulterated imperialism.[214]

After the annexation of the Czech state, the Chamberlain Cabinet found it extremely difficult to trust Hitler's stated intentions concerning the rest of East Europe.[215] As the British Ambassador, Sir Nevile Henderson, explained to Ulrich von Hassell, "Hitler had broken every promise made at Berchtesgaden, Godesberg, and Munich. All faith in him is destroyed. He [Henderson] believes that the seizure of Czechoslovakia was a great mistake from the German point of view."[216] In response to Hitler's aggression the British and French governments considered defensive alliances with Poland, Rumania, Greece, and the Soviet Union to encircle Germany and maintain the existing balance of power in Europe.[217] Leaving London, Dirksen traveled to Berlin to warn Hitler and Ribbentrop of the change in British policy towards Germany. He warned the Foreign Minister of British intentions to defend East Europe at the cost of war, but his superior was not interested in such views. According to Dirksen, "I came to the obvious conclusion that he [Ribbentrop] was imitating Hitler's methods in not wanting to listen to anything not in accordance with his views of world affairs."[218]

Living on the emotional high of successful annexations of Bohemia, Moravia, and Memeland, Hitler and Ribbentrop set upon the path to resolve the Polish Question by means of intimidation and diplomacy.[219] On 21 March 1939, the Foreign Minister met with the Polish Ambassador in Berlin. Ribbentrop insisted

213.   Sir Nevile Henderson to Lord Halifax, 28 March 1939, *BWBB*, 24.
214.   Dirksen, 217.
215.   Newman, 104.
216.   Hassell, 45.
217.   Theo Kordt to Ribbentrop, 22 March 1939, *DEPOW*, 295; Theo Kordt to Ribbentrop, 23 March 1939, *DEPOW*, 295-96.
218.   Dirksen, 216, 218.
219.   Hitler directive, 25 March 1939, *DGFP(D)*, 6:117-19.

that Warsaw accept Hitler's proposals.[220] Fearing the German threat, on 21 March, the Poles began partial mobilization of their armed forces to defend their homeland against German aggression.[221] Several days later, on 26 March, Lipski warned Ribbentrop that any German move toward Danzig would result in a German-Polish war.[222] The Poles, however, would guarantee the Free City of Danzig as well as offer far-reaching traffic concessions between Germany and East Prussia while still maintaining Polish sovereignty in the Corridor.[223] Ribbentrop, reveling in recent diplomatic successes, made known that this reply was totally unacceptable, and indirectly threatened Lipski by comparing the Polish attitude to that of the Czechs during the previous year.[224] The following day, on 27 March, Ribbentrop stressed to Lipski that "relations between the two countries were…deteriorating sharply."[225] By the twenty-ninth, the Foreign Minister believed that the climax of the German-Polish crisis had been reached, and the Poles would soon be forced to accept Hitler's demands.[226] But, on 31 March, London announced its guarantee to defend the sovereignty of Polish territory in the event of unprovoked aggression by Germany.[227] This revelation suddenly changed the diplomatic situation. Within days the British and Polish governments concluded a defensive arrangement, which was quickly followed by British guarantees to Rumania and Greece.[228]

Hitler took offense to this diplomatic activity. He looked for ways to isolate Poland so as to pressure Warsaw to concede to his demands. In the meantime, on 3 April, the Führer directed the Wehrmacht to draw up plans for a surprise invasion of the Polish Corridor and Danzig no later than 1 September 1939.[229] Hitler meant to retake lost German territory one way or another. On 4 April, Hitler, upset at Ribbentrop about Britain's unexpected reaction to the invasion of Prague, ordered Ribbentrop to avoid talks with the Polish government.[230] The next

---

220.  Lipski, 502; Ribbentrop memorandum, 21 March 1939, *DGFP(D)*, 6:70-72.
221.  Neville Chamberlain speech, 31 March 1939, *TMWC*, 41:109-10; Lipski, 508.
222.  Ribbentrop memorandum, 26 March 1939, *TMWC*, 41:110-14.
223.  Ribbentrop memorandum, 26 March 1939, *DGFP(D)*, 6:121-24.
224.  Weizsäcker to Moltke, 27 March 1939, *DGFP(D)*, 6:127.
225.  Ribbentrop, 102; Schmidt memorandum, 27 March 1939, *DGFP(D)*, 6:135-36.
226.  Martin Schliep to Hans-Adolf von Moltke, 29 March 1939, *DGFP(D)*, 6:155-56.
227.  Chamberlain speech, 31 March 1939, *TMWC*, 41:109-10; Chamberlain speech, 31 March 1939, *BWBB*, 48.
228.  Ciano, *Ciano's Diplomatic Papers*, 282; Theo Kordt to Ribbentrop, 13 April 1939, *DEPOW*, 309; Anglo-Polish Communique, 6 April 1939, *BWBB*, 49.
229.  Keitel directive, 3 April 1939, *DGFP(D)*, 6:186-87; Hitler directive, 11 April 1939, *DGFP(D)*, 6:223-28.
230.  Hassell, 54; Weinberg, *The Foreign Policy of Hitler's Germany*, 2:561.

day, however, the Foreign Minister, in an attempt to avoid a European war, had Weizsäcker inform the Polish government that Hitler would not repeat his demands, stressing that "the Polish Government had apparently not fully understood the significance of the offer."[231] Upset at the Foreign Minister's disobedience, on 6 April, Hitler ordered Ribbentrop to mind his own business demanding "the Polish question was to be reserved entirely to himself."[232] In fact, Weizsäcker stated at his Nuremberg trial that Ribbentrop and the Wilhelmstrasse had little to do with Poland between April and August 1939 because Hitler monopolized German-Polish relations.[233]

Hitler served notice on Britain and Poland regarding their pact. On 27 and 28 April 1938, Hitler denounced the German-Polish Nonaggression Pact of 1934 and Anglo-German Naval Agreement of 1935.[234] He perceived Chamberlain's agreements with East European countries as a British attempt to encircle Germany.[235] He therefore wanted to loosen the diplomatic bonds that hindered German defense efforts. To counter British diplomatic efforts, Hitler looked to Mussolini for the conclusion of a military alliance. He sent Ribbentrop to Milan to arrange the conclusion of a German-Italian alliance in early May.[236] Mussolini was anxious for such an alliance himself because of the Italian invasion of Albania on 7 April 1939.[237] Two weeks later, on 22 May 1939, Ribbentrop and Ciano signed the Pact of Steel, a military alliance treaty drawn up by the Bureau Ribbentrop, in Berlin.[238] Hitler believed this pact to be the answer to Anglo-French policy in Eastern Europe.[239] The next day, on 23 May, Hitler held a military conference, without any Foreign Office representation, to discuss the Polish Question. The Führer told his top military staff, including Göring, that "the Pole is not a fresh enemy. Poland will always be on the side of our adversaries. In spite of treaties of friendship Poland has always been bent on exploiting every opportu-

---

231. Weizsäcker to Moltke, 5 April 1939, *DGFP(D)*, 6:195.
232. As quoted in Weinberg, *The Foreign Policy of Hitler's Germany*, 2:561, n.89.
233. Weizsäcker testimony, 8 June 1948, AMT transcript, OGL 17, Box 136, Folder 13, 7736.
234. Ribbentrop memorandum, 27 April 1939, *BWBB*, 68-70; Ribbentrop memorandum, 28 April 1939, *BWBB*, 32–36; Weizsäcker, 181.
235. Ribbentrop memorandum, 12 April 1939, *DGFP(D)*, 6:228.
236. Ribbentrop memorandum, 18 May 1939, *DGFP(D)*, 6:450-52; Schmidt, 130.
237. MacGregor Knox, *Mussolini Unleashed, 1939-1941: Politics and Strategy in Fascist Italy's Last War* (Cambridge: Cambridge University Press, 1982), 41; H. James Burgwyn, *Italian Foreign Policy in the Interwar Period, 1918-1940* (Westport, CT: Praeger, 1997), 188-91.
238. Ciano, *Ciano's Diplomatic Papers*, 287; German-Italian Pact of Friendship and Alliance, 22 May 1939, *DGFP(D)*, 6:561-64; Kordt testimony, 4 June 1948, AMT transcript, OGL 17, Box 136, Folder 8, 7417; Moseley, 64-68.
239. Ribbentrop testimony, 29 March 1946, *TMWC*, 10:266.

nity against us."[240] The Führer announced his decision "to attack Poland at the first suitable opportunity."[241] Moreover, Hitler told the top military leaders, "we cannot expect a repetition of Czechia. There will be war. Our task is to isolate Poland. Success in isolating her will be decisive."[242]

Having secured an alliance with Italy, Hitler became interested in obtaining an agreement with the Soviet Union concerning the status of East Europe. Despite his anti-Soviet sentiments, the Führer understood that such an understanding would totally isolate Poland from the West, making it unlikely that Britain and France would militarily support the Poles during a German-Polish conflict.[243] Hitler saw the British guarantee to Poland as a bluff, but the added benefit of a German-Soviet pact would guarantee a localized conflict instead of a European war.[244] The idea of a German-Soviet agreement came from Ribbentrop, who was still in Hitler's disfavor over the British reaction to Prague and seeking a way to endear himself to the Führer, in April.[245] The Foreign Minister viewed a German-Soviet understanding as a guaranteed way to diplomatically force the Poles into agreeing to Hitler's demands.[246] He jumped at the opportunity as a way to retain his position as the Führer's top diplomat.[247] Those diplomats in the Foreign Office, such as Weizsäcker and Dirksen, who traditionally had argued for closer German-Soviet relations, supported such an initiative.[248] The German leadership perceived Stalin's dismissal of Maxim Litvinov and appointment of Vyacheslav Molotov as Foreign Commissar as a sign of Soviet interest in a German-Soviet rapprochement.[249] Thus, on 4 May 1939, the Wilhelmstrasse, under Hitler's direction, investigated the possibility of closer relations by recalling Gustav Hilger, the Chief of Economic Affairs at the German

---

240.   Conference minutes, 23 May 1939, *DGFP(D)*, 6:575.

241.   Ibid., 6:576.

242.   Ibid., 6:575.

243.   Hillgruber, 66; Weitz, 208; Anthony Read and David Fisher, *The Deadly Embrace: Hitler, Stalin, and the Nazi-Soviet Pact, 1939-1941* (New York: W.W. Norton, 1988), 75-77.

244.   Weizsäcker, 192.

245.   Wolfgang Michalka, "From the Anti-Comintern to the Euro-Asiatic Bloc: Ribbentrop's Alternate Concept of Hitler's Foreign Policy Programme," in *Aspects of the Third Reich*, ed. H.W. Koch (New York: St. Martin's Press, 1985), 276; Ribbentrop, 109-10; Weitz, 206; Ribbentrop interrogation testimony, 30 August 1945, *NCA*, supplement B, 1186.

246.   Ribbentrop, 110.

247.   Weitz, 208.

248.   Weizsäcker, 186-87; Hill, "The Wilhelmstrasse in the Nazi Era," 568.

249.   Gustav Hilger and Alfred G. Meyer, *The Incompatible Allies: A Memoir-History of German-Soviet Relations, 1918-1941* (New York: Macmillan, 1953), 293; Werner von Tippelskirch to Ribbentrop, 4 May 1939, *NSR*, 2-3.

Embassy in Moscow, to Berlin for consultation with Hitler and Ribbentrop.[250] On 10 May, Hilger answered the Führer's questions concerning the likelihood of a German-Soviet rapprochement at Berchtesgaden. Hilger gave the German leader the impression that Stalin was willing to come to terms.[251]

Hitler, however, hesitated in making a diplomatic move towards the Soviet Union. He waited to find out the results of British and French diplomatic efforts to negotiate a triple alliance with the Soviet Union.[252] Weizsäcker, impatient over the wait, suggested to Ribbentrop that Hilger approach the Soviet Foreign Commissariat to hint at Hitler's desire for closer German-Soviet relations.[253] In the meantime, the Wilhelmstrasse received signals that the Soviet Union was interested in a rapprochement.[254] Therefore, on 29 May 1939, Hitler made the decision to employ the foreign service to pursue closer ties with the Soviet Union.[255] Moscow, nonetheless, showed no immediate interest to begin negotiations.[256] Thus, on 29 July, Ribbentrop directed Count Friedrich Werner von der Schulenburg, the German Ambassador to Moscow (1934-41), to inform Molotov that Germany was ready to take account of "all Soviet interests" in Poland and the Baltic states.[257]

While little diplomatic activity took place between Germany and the Soviet Union, the relations between Germany and Poland were quickly reaching the crisis point. The Wehrmacht, under Hitler's direction, prepared for the invasion of Poland. Tension between the two states increased daily because of Nazi-Polish antagonism in Danzig.[258] On 8 August 1939, Hitler had Ribbentrop protest to Lipski about the Polish stand on Danzig. The Polish Ambassador, however, warned Ribbentrop that any further German interference in Polish-Danzig relations would be considered as an act of aggression against his government.[259] Such

---

250.  Hilger and Meyer, 293.

251.  Ibid.

252.  Weizsäcker to Friedrich Werner von der Schulenburg, 27 May 1939, *NSR*, 9.

253.  Weizsäcker memorandum, 25 May 1939, *DGFP(D)*, 6:586-87.

254.  Ribbentrop to Hitler, 29 May 1939, *NSR*, 10-11.

255.  Ribbentrop memorandum, 29 May 1939, *NSR*, 11; Weizsäcker memorandum, 30 May 1939, *NSR*, 12; Weizsäcker to Schulenburg, 30 May 1939, *NSR*, 15; Weizsäcker to Schulenburg, 30 May 1939, *DGFP(D)*, 6:610.

256.  Geoffrey Roberts, *The Soviet Union and the Origins of the Second World War: Russo-German Relations and the Road to War, 1933-1941* (New York: St. Martin's Press, 1995), 76-80.

257.  Weizsäcker to Schulenburg, 29 July 1939, *DGFP(D)*, 6:1006-9.

258.  Hassell, 53. See also Herbert S. Levine, *Hitler's Free City: The History of the Nazi Party in Danzig, 1925-1939* (Chicago: University of Chicago Press, 1973).

259.  Ribbentrop to Lipski, 9 August 1939, *TMWC*, 41:118-19.

opposition to his diplomatic efforts upset the Foreign Minister. He set his mind on the destruction of Poland.

To discover Mussolini's viewpoint, the Führer requested the Italian Foreign Minister to visit Germany to discuss the German-Polish crisis in early August. Ciano met with Ribbentrop at Salzburg on 11 August. The German Foreign Minister warned his counterpart that the German-Polish situation was "extremely grave, and that, in his opinion, the clash between Germany and Poland is inevitable."[260] Ribbentrop informed Ciano that both Hitler and himself believed that Britain and France were not prepared to fight and therefore would not militarily support Poland, thus the conflict would be kept localized.[261] The next day, on 12 August, Hitler met with Ciano at Berchtesgaden and reemphasized these statements, adding that Germany would achieve a quick victory against Poland. Hitler stated:

> When the moment for the attack on Poland comes—and that moment will come as the result of the outbreak of a serious incident or else because Germany will force Poland to define her position—the German forces will strike simultaneously at the heart of Poland from all points along the frontier where attacks are launched and follow routes well laid down in advance.[262]

Concerning the reaction of the West, Hitler believed:

> France and England will certainly make extremely theatrical anti-German gestures but will not go to war, because their military and moral preparations are not such as to allow them to begin the conflict.[263]

The following day, on 13 August, Hitler again told Ciano that: "I am unshakably convinced that neither England nor France will embark upon a general war."[264] While these German-Italian talks proceeded in southern Germany, British and French diplomats arrived in Moscow to seek an agreement with the Soviet Union. This situation at once worried Hitler because the outcome of such talks

---

260.   Ciano, *Ciano's Diplomatic Papers*, 297. See also Galeazzo Ciano, *The Ciano Diaries, 1939-1943: The Complete, Unabridged Diaries of Count Galeazzo Ciano, Italian Minister for Foreign Affairs, 1936-1943*, ed. Hugh Gibson. introd. Sumner Welles (New York: Doubleday, 1946), 119.

261.   Ciano, *Ciano's Diplomatic Papers*, 297-98. See also Schmidt, 132.

262.   Ciano, *Ciano's Diplomatic Papers*, 300.

263.   Ibid., 301. See also Ciano, *The Ciano Diaries, 1939-1943*, 119; Schmidt, 132.

264.   Schmidt, 132.

could create a significant obstacle to German plans for the invasion of Poland.[265] It looked like the West might be able to block his plans by creating a military bloc encircling Germany. Since July Dirksen had been reporting from London that Britain would standby its promise to Poland.[266] Worried about the outcome of the Moscow talks, Hitler ordered Ribbentrop to seek a rapprochement with the Soviet Union. On 14 August, the Foreign Minister sent a telegram to Molotov, seeking a meeting between the chief diplomats, and calling for friendly cooperation between the two states. He stressed that there were no real conflicts between Germany and the Soviet Union, and offered to settle spheres of influence in Eastern Europe.[267] Such pleas from the German government were sent as the Wilhelmstrasse received warnings from London.[268] These warnings, nevertheless, were highly encouraged by Weizsäcker and the professional diplomats in the Foreign Office as a way to deter Hitler from any warlike action.[269] The Auswärtiges Amt also informed Whitehall of Ribbentrop's move toward the Soviet Union, fearing that a German-Soviet agreement would increase the likelihood of war.[270] But, on 16 August, Stalin, while still talking to the British and French delegates, had Molotov notify Count Schulenburg of his desire to improve German-Soviet relations. He suggested that the two states sign a nonaggression pact.[271] Ribbentrop quickly informed Molotov of Hitler's interest in this proposal.[272] On 18 August, Hitler fearing a possible Soviet agreement with the West, had Ribbentrop seek an immediate meeting with Molotov to conclude such a pact. Hitler considered it essential to clarify German-Soviet relations before Germany invaded Poland.[273]

---

265.  Schulenburg to Ribbentrop, 11 August 1939, *DGFP(D)*, 7:28.

266.  Dirksen, 222. On 13 August 1939, Dirksen arrived in Berlin to warn of the British intention to go to war in support of Poland. However, Hitler and Ribbentrop would not meet with their ambassador to accept such a warning. According to Dirksen, they did not want to hear information contrary to their belief that Britain and France would not fight for the Poles (Dirksen, 228, 231).

267.  Ribbentrop to Schulenburg, 14 August 1939, *NSR*, 50-52; Schulenburg to Ribbentrop, 11 August 1939, *DGFP(D)*, 7:28.

268.  Henderson to Halifax, 16 August 1939, *BWBB*, 115-119.

269.  Ibid.; Weizsäcker, 192.

270.  Kordt, *Nicht aus den Akten*, 311-19; Henderson to Halifax, 16 August 1939, *BWBB*, 115-119; Hill, "The Wilhelmstrasse in the Nazi Era," 568.

271.  Schulenburg to Ribbentrop, 16 August 1939, *DGFP(D)*, 7:76-77. See also Schulenburg to Ribbentrop, 16 August 1939, *DGFP(D)*, 7:87-90.

272.  Ribbentrop to Schulenburg, 16 August 1939, *DGFP(D)*, 7:84-85.

273.  Ribbentrop to Schulenburg, 18 August 1939, *DGFP(D)*, 7:121-23.

Stalin accepted the idea of a quick meeting on 20 August. He sent Hitler a draft of a nonaggression pact,[274] and approved Ribbentrop's trip to Moscow.[275] The Führer consented to the draft that afternoon.[276] On 22 August, Hitler gave his Foreign Minister full powers to negotiate and sign the nonaggression pact with the Soviet Union: an agreement that he had already fully approved.[277] Ribbentrop quickly traveled to Moscow. Once there, he received a telegram from Hitler directing him to ask Stalin to agree to dividing Eastern Europe into German and Soviet spheres of interests.[278] Thus, on 23 August, Ribbentrop and Molotov, in the presence of Stalin, signed the Nazi-Soviet Nonaggression Pact, including an additional secret protocol dividing Eastern Europe into two spheres of interest.[279] The British and French delegation left Moscow empty-handed two days later.[280]

While Ribbentrop was signing the pact with Molotov, Hitler permitted British Ambassador Henderson and the German Foreign Secretary to visit him at Berchtesgaden on 23 August. Henderson handed Hitler a letter from the British Prime Minister declaring that "we are standing by our commitments."[281] Both Henderson and Weizsäcker warned the Führer that Britain would assist the Poles and that Mussolini would not come to the aid of Germany.[282] Commenting on this meeting, Weizsäcker wrote in his memoirs: "My words were spoken into the air. It was clear that Hitler was working for war, and was only uncertain as to whether it could be localised."[283]

274.  Schulenburg to Ribbentrop, 20 August 1939, *DGFP(D)*, 7:150-51.

275.  Schulenburg to Ribbentrop, 20 August 1939, *DGFP(D)*, 7:149-50.

276.  Ribbentrop to Schulenburg, 20 August 1939, *DGFP(D)*, 7:156-57.

277.  Hitler declaration of full diplomatic powers for Ribbentrop, 22 August 1939, *DGFP(D)*, 7:200.

278.  Weizsäcker to Schulenburg, 23 August 1939, *DGFP(D)*, 7:221.

279.  Schmidt, 138; Ribbentrop, 111; Hilger and Meyer, 300-4; Treaty of Nonaggression between Germany and the Union of Soviet Socialist Republics, *DGFP(D)*, 7:245-46. See also Gerhard L. Weinberg, "The Nazi-Soviet Pacts of 1939: A Half Century Later," in *Germany, Hitler, and World War II: Essays in Modern German and World History* (Cambridge: Cambridge University Press, 1995), 168-81.

280.  Schulenburg to Ribbentrop, 25 August 1939, *DGFP(D)*, 7:295.

281.  Chamberlain to Hitler, 22 August 1939, *BWBB*, 125-27; Franz Halder, *The Halder War Diary, 1939-1942*, ed. Charles Burdick and Hans-Adolf Jacobsen (Novato, CA: Presido Press, 1988), 38.

282.  Weizsäcker testimony, 8 June 1948, AMT transcript, OGL 17, Box 136, Folder 14, 7754-755.

283.  Weizsäcker, 204.

Upon his return the next day, Ribbentrop was greeted by an excited Hitler at Berchtesgaden. The Foreign Minister had provided his master the pact that would assure the isolation of Poland, and an easy conquest for Germany. Hitler, according to William Carr, "assumed that the western powers would be so stunned [by the announcement of the Nazi-Soviet Nonaggression Pact] that they would lose all heart for war."[284] Paul Otto Schmidt, who had accompanied Ribbentrop to Moscow, wrote in his memoirs: "By their surprise move in this round of the diplomatic contest, Hitler and Stalin had checkmated England and France."[285] In the midst of the German-Polish crisis the conclusion of the pact provided Ribbentrop great prestige with Hitler, and placed the Foreign Minister's influence with his master at its zenith.[286] Now having achieved Soviet neutrality Hitler was ready to crush the Poles. The German Army was ready to march.[287]

Despite success in achieving an agreement with the Soviet Union, Hitler discovered that the West had not abandoned the Poles. The British Parliament ratified the Anglo-Polish alliance on 25 August 1939.[288] Moments after this announcement, the French Ambassador warned Hitler that France would fight for the Poles.[289] If this was not enough, the Italian Ambassador delivered a message to Hitler from Mussolini declaring that Italy was not ready to fight a war.[290] According to Schmidt, "the letter was a bombshell. He [Hitler] was bitterly disappointed at this sudden…defection of his ally."[291] Now "deeply shaken," the Führer reacted by postponing the invasion of Poland.[292]

At this point the counsel of Ribbentrop, Weizsäcker, Göring, and the General Staff advised Hitler to avoid war because Britain and France would stand by their commitment to Poland.[293] Hitler, nonetheless, quickly regained confidence in his opinion that the West would not intervene, and suddenly decided to risk the possibility of a European war to conquer Poland.[294] Realizing the threat to his

284.  Carr, *Arms, Autarky, and Aggression*, 123.
285.  Schmidt, 138-39.
286.  Carr, *Arms, Autarky, and Aggression*, 116.
287.  Weizsäcker testimony, 8 June 1948, AMT transcript, OGL 17, Box 136, Folder 14, 7755.
288.  Anglo-Polish Mutual Assistance Pact, 25 August 1939, *BWBB*, 49-52.
289.  Schmidt, 145.
290.  Ibid., 146; Weizsäcker, 207.
291.  Schmidt, 146.
292.  Halder, 34-35, 39; Weizsäcker, 205; Ribbentrop, 117; Weizsäcker testimony, 8 June 1948, AMT transcript, OGL 17, Box 136, Folder 14, 7755.
293.  Woermann testimony, 6 July 1948, AMT transcript, OGL 17, Box 140, Folder 7, 1128-129; Dirksen, 226; Ribbentrop, 116-17; Halder, 35.
294.  Ribbentrop interrogation testimony, 10 October 1945, *NCA*, supplement B, 1252; Ciano, *The Ciano Diaries, 1939-1943*, 129.

influence with Hitler, Ribbentrop quickly changed his opinion to match his master's.[295] Weizsäcker complained in his memoirs that Ribbentrop "did not want to take advice from anyone, or to change his views on account of what anyone said."[296] The Foreign Minister, according to Weizsäcker, "did not and would not believe that the Allies would make common cause with Poland."[297] Upset at the Wilhelmstrasse, the Foreign Minister told Weizsäcker and his staff that if they failed to follow Hitler's orders for an aggressive policy than "he would shoot [them] personally in his own office."[298]

Although threatening war, Hitler was still willing to achieve his demands by diplomatic means. On 28 August 1939, the Führer gathered his General Staff together at the Reich Chancellery. According to General Franz Halder, the Chief of the General Staff, Hitler said he was "determined to have [the] eastern question settled one way or another. Minimum demands: Return of Danzig, settling of Corridor question. If minimum demands not satisfied, then war...."[299] The Führer declared that Germany would attack Poland on 1 September, barring any further postponements.[300] That same day Hitler met with the British Ambassador in the presence of Ribbentrop at the Chancellery. The Führer told Sir Nevile Henderson that he had made up his mind on settling the Polish Question once and for all.[301] Henderson informed Hitler that the British government desired the Poles to negotiate with Hitler directly, instead of through London. Henderson believed that the Poles would follow London's advice in this matter.[302]

The following morning Hitler was again somewhat indecisive on what avenue to pursue, diplomatic or military action.[303] In front of the Foreign Secretary, Göring advised the German leader: "Let's drop the 'all-or-nothing' game." To which Hitler replied: "All my life I have played for 'all-or-nothing'."[304] Later that day Hitler met with Henderson and indicated his willingness to talk directly to the Poles if a plenipotentiary arrived in Berlin no later than 30 August.[305]

---

295.  Weizsäcker testimony, 8 June 1948, AMT transcript, OGL 17, Box 136, Folder 14, 7747; Ribbentrop, 117.
296.  Weizsäcker, 192.
297.  Ibid., 193.
298.  Weizsäcker testimony, 8 June 1948, AMT transcript, OGL 17, Box 136, Folder 14, 7747. See also Dirksen, 231; Spitzy, 284.
299.  Halder, 37.
300.  Ibid., 40.
301.  Schmidt memorandum, 29 August 1939, *DGFP(D)*, 7:381-84.
302.  Ribbentrop, 118; Halder, 42.
303.  Weizsäcker, 208.
304.  As quoted in Weizsäcker, 208.
305.  Taylor, *The Origins of the Second World War*, 272; Ribbentrop, 119; Schmidt, 249.

Having been issued an ultimatum, the Polish government rejected the idea of direct talks with Berlin. They began general mobilization on the morning of 30 August.[306] Hitler had half expected the British to pressure the Poles into handing Danzig over to Germany and agreeing to an extraterritorial road and railway through the Polish Corridor.[307] Arriving at Ribbentrop's office after midnight, Ambassador Henderson told the Foreign Minister that there would be no Polish plenipotentiary. Up to this point Ribbentrop had expected to begin negotiations. According to Schmidt, the interpreter, Ribbentrop demanded the immediate arrival of a Polish diplomat with full powers to negotiate a treaty. Becoming extremely upset, the Foreign Minister told Henderson that the situation was "damned serious!"[308] He then read out loud Hitler's demands, drafted by the Wilhelmstrasse in the hope of another Munich type of agreement, rather slowly to the British Ambassador, calling for a return of Danzig to Germany, an extra-territorial road and railway through the Polish Corridor, as well as a plebiscite in the Corridor.[309] Under Hitler's instructions, Ribbentrop refused to provide a copy of the demands to Henderson since they were intended for a Polish envoy and the deadline had already expired.[310] Hitler had issued an ultimatum and would carry through with his threat. Commenting about this meeting, Schmidt told the Nuremberg court:

> The atmosphere during that conference was…charged with electricity. Both participants were extremely nervous. Henderson was very uneasy; and never before, and perhaps only once afterwards, have I seen the Foreign Minister so nervous as he was during that conference.[311]

Having heard Hitler's demands, the British Ambassador, considering them "not unreasonable," immediately went to visit Lipski at his home in Berlin.[312] Now, after Germany's ultimatum to Poland had expired, Henderson found, awoke, and informed Lipski of Hitler's demands at two o'clock in the morning

---

306.   Halder, 42; Ribbentrop, 121; Martin Schliep memorandum, 30 August 1939, *DGFP(D)*, 7:442; Beck to Lipski, 31 August 1939, *DB*, 572.

307.   Halder, 40.

308.   Schmidt, 150-51.

309.   Hassell, 68-72; Kordt, *Nicht aus den Akten*, 234-35; Schmidt, 150, 152; Schmidt memorandum, 31 August 1939, *DGFP(D)*, 7:451-54. Ribbentrop told the International Military Tribunal that Hitler himself had drawn up the document (Ribbentrop testimony, 1 April 1946, *TMWC*, 10:367).

310.   Ribbentrop, 123; Schmidt, 153; Ribbentrop testimony, 29 March 1946, *TMWC*, 10:275.

311.   Schmidt testimony, 28 March 1946, *TMWC*, 10:197. For the British viewpoint of this meeting, see Henderson, 283-97.

312.   Taylor, *The Origins of the Second World War*, 274.

on 31 August.[313] Not authorized with powers to accept these demands, Lipski forwarded them to the Polish Foreign Minister in Warsaw later that morning, but received a negative reply from Beck.[314] Hitler viewed the failure of a Polish envoy to show up in Berlin as a rejection of his demands.[315] Hitler's last minute diplomacy had failed.

The German plan to attack Poland was within hours of being launched. Göring argued against the attack, believing that Britain and France would declare war on Germany.[316] Göring pleaded with Hitler to try once again to diplomatically resolve the Polish Question.[317] But, on the afternoon of the thirty-first, Hitler made the final decision for the attack to proceed.[318] He instructed Ribbentrop of the impending invasion plans.[319] Realizing that the British would never disavow their guarantee to Poland, the Foreign Minister finally got up enough courage to tell Hitler that he believed the British would fulfill their obligations to Poland.[320] However, it was too late! Hitler was already convinced that Britain and France lacked the resolve to fight in aid of Poland.

The German Wehrmacht, including five armies, attacked Poland on 1 September 1939.[321] Within hours the British and French Ambassadors arrived at the Reich Chancellery to hand Ribbentrop ultimatums concerning the unprovoked attack on Poland. Henderson and Coulondre found the Foreign Minister extremely upset over the situation.[322] The following day Britain and France began to mobilize.[323] On 3 September, Henderson arrived at the Chancellery. With instructions to receive the ambassador, Schmidt accepted the British declaration of war. Schmidt entered Hitler's office and read the declaration to both the Führer and his Foreign

313.   Lipski to Beck, 31 August 1939, *DB*, 571.
314.   Beck to Lipski, 31 August 1939, *DB*, 572; Ribbentrop, 118.
315.   German Communique to Britain, 31 March 1939, *TMWC*, 41:121-22.
316.   Weizsäcker, 209.
317.   Hassell, 69.
318.   Ribbentrop testimony, 29 March 1946, *TMWC*, 10:276; Directive No. 1 for the Conduct of War "Case White", 31 August 1939, *HWD*, 3-5.
319.   Ribbentrop testimony, 29 March 1946, *TMWC*, 10:276.
320.   Ibid., 10:275.
321.   Horst Rohde, "Hitler's First Blitzkrieg and Its Consequences for North-East Europe," in *Germany's Initial Conquests in Europe*, vol. II in *Germany and the Second World War*, eds. Klaus A. Maier, Horst Rohde, Bernd Stegemann, and Hans Umbreit, trans. Dean S. McMurray, Ewald Osers, and P.S. Falla (Oxford: Clarendon Press, 1991), 69.
322.   Schmidt, 155.
323.   Ibid., 156.

Minister. Both Hitler and Ribbentrop were surprised at the West declaring war.[324] According to Schmidt:

> [B]oth gentlemen were absolutely silent for about a minute. I could clearly see that this development did not suit them at all. For a while Hitler sat in his chair deep in thought and stared somewhat worriedly into space. Then he broke the silence with a rather abrupt question to the Foreign Minister, saying, "what shall we do now?"[325]

Summing up the crisis, Ulrich von Hassell wrote in his diary on 1 September 1939:

> Hitler and Ribbentrop wanted war with Poland and knowingly took the risk of war with the Western Powers, deluding themselves to varying degrees up to the very last with the belief that the West would remain neutral after all. The Poles, for their part…confident of English and French support, had missed every remaining chance for avoiding war. The Government in London, whose ambassador did everything to keep the peace, gave up the race in the very last days and adopted a kind of devil-may-care attitude. France went through the same stages, only with much more hesitation. Mussolini did all in his power to avoid war.[326]

---

324. Weizsäcker testimony, 8 June 1948, AMT transcript, OGL 17, Box 136, Folder 14, 7755.
325. Schmidt testimony, 10 March 1946, *TMWC*, 10:200.
326. Hassell, 71.

# 8

## *Ribbentrop and the Wilhelmstrasse during the Second World War*

### Ribbentrop and the Foreign Office

The outbreak of war in September 1939 resulted in the demise of Nazi diplomacy and the increased importance of military matters. Directing the Polish Campaign, Adolf Hitler had no time for his Foreign Minister and the Wilhelmstrasse. The Führer would now rely upon his General Staff for military and diplomatic advice in carrying out the war against Poland and its allies.[1] As Ernst von Weizsäcker told the American Military Tribunal at Nuremberg, "Hitler preferred to talk to a soldier about foreign policy rather than to experts."[2]

Hitler's unfavorable disposition towards professional diplomats, of course, was nothing new. He had always despised, and, according to Joachim von Ribbentrop, "hated" the diplomatic corps.[3] Hitler once referred to them as "those sluts."[4] But, now, the Führer was upset at his own Foreign Minister, the Nazi Ribbentrop, because of the British and French declarations of war against Germany on 3 September 1939. Although firmly believing that the West would not intervene in a German-Polish conflict, Hitler, himself, could not help but blame Ribbentrop for the unexpected outcome since, after all, the Foreign Minister was the so-called expert on relations with Britain and France. Key members of the

---

1. Gustav Adolf Steengracht von Moyland testimony, 23 June 1948, AMT transcript, OGL 17, Box 140, Folder 1, 9878.
2. Ernst von Weizsäcker testimony, 8 June 1948, AMT transcript, OGL 17, Box 136, Folder 13, 7703-704.
3. Joachim von Ribbentrop, *The Ribbentrop Memoirs*, trans. Oliver Watson, ed. A. von Ribbentrop (London: Weidenfeld and Nicolson, 1954), 163.
4. As quoted in Michael Bloch, *Ribbentrop* (New York: Crown, 1992), 35.

Nazi inner circle, of which Ribbentrop never belonged, loudly declared the Foreign Minister to blame for the possibility of a European war.[5] However, Hitler, finally realizing the shortcomings of his top diplomat, was forced to keep Ribbentrop on as Foreign Minister since to dismiss the champagne salesman would mean admitting his own miscalculations in diplomacy.[6]

In order to maintain his position in the Third Reich, Ribbentrop needed to take drastic actions to demonstrate his loyalty and usefulness to the Führer. At the onset of the invasion of Poland, the Foreign Minister distanced himself from the professional diplomats at the Foreign Office, whom he also hated for their disloyal service to Hitler and himself.[7] He relied upon the advice and services of his own Secretariat, also known as the Bureau Reichsaussenminister (RAM).[8] This group consisted of Erich Kordt and Paul Otto Schmidt, in addition to former members of the Bureau Ribbentrop, including Walther Hewel, Gustav Adolf Steengracht von Moyland, Franz Sonnleithner, and Rudolf Likus.[9] With this assortment of officials, Ribbentrop procured cars aboard Heinrich Himmler's special train and traveled to the war front to be close to the Führer.[10] Steengracht von Moyland, who had previously worked for Ribbentrop in London (1936-38) and Berlin (1938-39) managed the Foreign Minister's saloon cars.[11] Throughout the Polish Campaign, and for most of the following military campaigns during the Second World War, Ribbentrop and the Bureau RAM utilized this train to keep in close contact with Hitler at his field headquarters.[12] According to Gustav Hilger, who joined this select group of advisers in 1941:

---

5.  Albert Speer, *Spandau: The Secret Diaries*, trans. Richard and Clara Winston (New York: Macmillan, 1976), 142; Joseph Goebbels, *The Goebbels Diaries, 1942-1943*, ed. and trans. Louis P. Locher (New York: Doubleday, 1948), 267; Paul Seabury, "Ribbentrop and the German Foreign Office," *Political Science Quarterly* 66 (December 1951), 545; H.W. Koch, *Aspects of the Third Reich* (New York: St. Martin's Press, 1985), 194; Paul Seabury, *The Wilhelmstrasse: A Study of German Diplomats under the Nazi Regime* (Berkeley and Los Angeles: University of California Press, 1954), 265; Hans-Georg von Studnitz, *While Berlin Burns: The Diaries of Hans-Georg von Studnitz, 1943-1945*, trans. R.H. Stevens (London: Weidenfeld and Nicolson, 1964), 163.

6.  DeWitt C. Poole, "Light on Nazi Foreign Policy," *Foreign Affairs* 25 (October 1946), 153; Speer, *Spandau*, 143; Studnitz, 162-63.

7.  Weizsäcker testimony, 10 June 1948, AMT transcript, OGL 17, Box 137, Folder 2, 8093.

8.  Ibid., AMT transcript, OGL 17, Box 137, Folder 2, 8092.

9.  Dr. Paul Schmidt, *Hitler's Interpreter*, ed. R.H.C. Steed (New York: Macmillan, 1951), 161; Appendix A, *DGFP(D)*, 9:693; Seabury, *The Wilhelmstrasse*, 105-7.

10.  Schmidt, 160; Steengracht von Moyland testimony, 23 June 1948, AMT transcript, OGL 17, Box 138, Folder 16, 9752-754.

11.  Steengracht von Moyland testimony, 23 June 1948, AMT transcript, OGL 17, Box 138, Folder 16, 9752-754.

12.  Ibid; Weizsäcker testimony, 10 June 1948, AMT transcript, OGL 17, Box 137, Folder 2, 8091.

[Ribbentrop] followed Hitler everywhere [in his special train] in order to be close to him at all times. The special train included a parlor car for the minister himself, two dining cars, and no less than eight sleeping cars housing a crew of aides, male and female secretaries, counselors and expert consultants, and a numerous bodyguard responsible for von Ribbentrop's personal safety. The whole thing was very much like a circus which put up its tents here or there just as required, or just as the foreign minister's whims desired.[13]

From this train Ribbentrop directed the operations of the German Foreign Office. Throughout World War II, the Foreign Minister loyally carried out the orders of the Führer as the surest way to remain in Hitler's favor. Baron Gustav Adolf Steengracht von Moyland told the Nuremberg court that "Ribbentrop himself never laid down any policy. He merely executed what Hitler ordered him to do and towards Hitler he was in a sort of trance and he followed all of his orders blindly."[14] To carry out Hitler's orders, Ribbentrop utilized the telephone in his saloon-car to direct the Foreign Office in Berlin on actions to take.[15] During his trial at Nuremberg, Weizsäcker complained of this management technique, stating that Ribbentrop "always wanted to hold all political decisions in his own hands, irrespective of where he happened to be."[16] Moreover, Ribbentrop would not allow Schmidt to provide the Foreign Secretary copies of reports and notes on Hitler's conferences.[17]

The Foreign Minister did not trust the professional diplomats at the Wilhelmstrasse. He appointed National Socialists from the Bureau Ribbentrop to control the activities of the career diplomats. He named Theodor Habicht as the Deputy Director of the Political Department, under Ernst Woermann.[18] But, more importantly, Ribbentrop rapidly promoted Martin Luther to the position of Under State Secretary for Foreign Affairs.[19] From this position, Luther controlled

---

13.   Gustav Hilger and Alfred G. Meyer, *The Incompatible Allies: A Memoir-History of German-Soviet Relations, 1918-1941* (New York: Macmillan, 1953), 294.

14.   Steengracht von Moyland testimony, 23 June 1948, AMT transcript, OGL 17, Box 140, Folder 1, 9878.

15.   Schmidt, 160-61.

16.   Weizsäcker testimony, 10 June 1948, AMT transcript, OGL 17, Box 137, Folder 2, 8097. See also Weizsäcker testimony, 10 June 1948, AMT transcript, OGL 17, Box 137, Folder 2, 8091.

17.   Paul Otto Schmidt testimony, 24 August 1948, AMT transcript, OGL 17, Box 146, Folder 19, 17824-829.

18.   Ernst Woermann testimony, 2 July 1948, AMT transcript, OGL 17, Box 140, Folder 6, 11060.

19.   Weizsäcker, 271.

internal matters at the Wilhelmstrasse, and acquired considerable power over the career diplomats by bugging their offices and telephone calls, and reporting treasonable matters to the Foreign Minister.[20] Weizsäcker, the State Secretary, complained that Luther "made a note of my visitors, tapped my telephone wires, and installed a monitor system in my own study."[21] With aid from Luther, Ribbentrop was preparing to dismiss 150 to 200 of the top officials at the Wilhelmstrasse, including Weizsäcker and Kordt, in early 1940.[22] He planned to replace them with members of the Bureau Ribbentrop, which he disbanded on 1 February 1940.[23] But Hitler denied Ribbentrop his quest to shakeup the Wilhelmstrasse in June 1940. He realized that the expertise of the diplomatic corps might still be needed, while Ribbentrop was useless for most diplomatic requirements other than carrying out instructions.[24]

### Denmark and Norway

Germany and the Soviet Union defeated Poland in October 1939.[25] Meanwhile, in the autumn of 1939, Adolf Hitler and his General Staff formulated plans to attack the West.[26] Having no direct knowledge of such planning, in October, Foreign Secretary Weizsäcker tried to dissuade the Führer from launching an offensive against the West.[27] For numerous reasons Hitler postponed an offensive

20. Steengracht von Moyland, 23 June 1948, AMT transcript, OGL 17, Box 138, Folder 16, 9760-765; Eric Kordt testimony, 4 June 1948, AMT transcript, OGL 17, Box 136, Folder 7, 7347; Weizsäcker testimony, 10 June 1948, AMT transcript, OGL 17, Box 137, Folder 2, 8093-94.

21. Weizsäcker testimony, 10 June 1948, AMT transcript, OGL 17, Box 137, Folder 2, 8093-94.

22. Ibid., 9 June 1948, Box 136, Folder 16, 7891; Kordt testimony, 4 June 1948, AMT transcript, OGL 17, Box 136, Folder 8, 7413; Ernst von Weizsäcker, *Memoirs of Ernst von Weizsäcker*, trans. John Andrews (London: Victor Gollancz, 1951), 242, 271; Schmidt, 255; John Weitz, *Hitler's Diplomat: The Life and Times of Joachim von Ribbentrop* (New York: Ticknor and Fields, 1992), 259.

23. Woermann testimony, 6 July 1948, AMT transcript, OGL 17, Box 140, Folder 7, 11127-1128; Rudolf Hess to Alfred Rosenberg, 30 January 1940, AMT documents, OGL 17, Box 217, Folder 5, NG-1078, 1.

24. Schmidt, 255; Weizsäcker, 242.

25. Horst Rohde, "Hitler's First Blitzkrieg and Its Consequences for North-East Europe," in *Germany's Initial Conquests in Europe*, vol. II in *Germany and the Second World War*, eds. Klaus A. Maier, Horst Rohde, Bernd Stegemann, and Hans Umbreit, trans. Dean S. McMurray, Ewald Osers, and P.S. Falla (Oxford: Clarendon Press, 1991), 67-126.

26. Hitler directive, 9 October 1939, *HWD*, 13; Hitler directive, 18 October 1939, *HWD*, 15; Hitler directive, 20 November 1939, *HWD*, 17.

27. Kordt testimony, 4 June 1948, AMT transcript, OGL 17, Box 136, Folder 8, 7408; Weizsäcker testimony, 9 June 1948, AMT transcript, Box 136, Folder 16, 7886.

through the Low Countries against the British and French forces deploying in France. Even so, the war at sea was active.[28] In this light, Hitler realized the British threat to his northern flank in Scandinavia, and the possible loss of important iron-ore supplies coming from Sweden and shipped via Norwegian ports to Germany.[29]

Hitler was greatly interested in the neutrality of Norway. In December 1939, Alfred Rosenberg arranged for Vidkun Quisling, the leader of the Norwegian Nasjonal Samling Party, to secretly meet with the Führer without the knowledge of the Foreign Office.[30] Quisling, who sought power in Norway, warned Hitler that the West was planning to occupy Norway, and stressed the need for German action to prevent such a move.[31]

Instead of striking directly at Germany, Britain and France made plans to cut off German supplies of iron-ore from Scandinavia. As early as October 1939, the Allies schemed to plant mines in Norwegian coastal waters with the possibility of deploying an expedition force to occupy the iron-ore mines in Sweden.[32] Nevertheless, on 30 November, the Soviet Union attacked Finland, and therefore, temporarily redirected the attention of the Allies from Norway and Sweden further east.[33] By February 1940, however, Britain and France were planning to occupy key ports in Norway.[34]

---

28.    Peter Calvocoressi and Guy Wint, *Total War: Causes and Courses of the Second World War* (London: Allen Lane, 1972), 105-6.

29.    Joachim von Ribbentrop testimony, 30 March 1946, *TMWC*, 10:281; Klaus A. Maier and Bernd Stegemann, "Securing the Northern Flank of Europe," in *Germany's Initial Conquests in Europe*, vol. II in *Germany and the Second World War*, eds. Klaus A. Maier, Horst Rohde, Bernd Stegemann, and Hans Umbreit, trans. Dean S. McMurray, Ewald Osers, and P.S. Falla (Oxford: Clarendon Press, 1991), 185.

30.    Weizsäcker, 228; Weizsäcker testimony, 9 June 1948, AMT transcript, OGL 17, Box 136, Folder 16, 7882-883.

31.    Weizsäcker, 228.

32.    Graham Ross, *The Great Powers and the Decline of the European States System 1914-1945* (London: Longman, 1983), 127-28.

33.    See Max Jakobson, *The Diplomacy of the Winter War: An Account of the Russo-Finnish War, 1939-1940* (Cambridge, MA: Harvard University Press, 1961).

34.    German Foreign Office, *Britain's Designs on Norway: Documents Concerning the Anglo-French Policy of Extending the War*, German Foreign Office White Book No. 4 (New York: German Library of Information, 1940), 5-21; Ross, 128; Eleanor M. Gates, *End of an Affair: The Collapse of the Anglo-French Alliance, 1939-1940* (London: George Allen and Unwin, 1981), 38-43; B.H. Liddell Hart, *History of the Second World War* (New York: G.P. Putnam's Sons, 1970), 54-55.

German military intelligence was well aware of Allied plans for occupying Norway.[35] To prevent the Allies from outflanking Germany and to allow the Third Reich to acquire forward Luftwaffe and naval bases, Hitler and his military staff, under the strong encouragement of Admiral Erich Raeder, the Commander-in-Chief of the German Navy, secretly planned to invade and occupy both Norway and Denmark.[36] Such plans, according to Hitler, were "designed to protect by force of arms the neutrality of the Northern countries."[37] Admiral Wilhelm Canaris, the Head of the German Military Intelligence Service, secretly informed Eric Kordt of such plans, who told his close confederate, Weizsäcker.[38]

Meanwhile, the German General Staff kept planning for an offensive against the buildup of British and French forces along the eastern border of France. Plans called for German forces to attack the Allies through the Low Countries.[39] Ribbentrop became aware of the invasion plans, but Hitler shared no information with his Foreign Minister regarding military details. The Führer, however, told Ribbentrop that Germany needed to conduct a preemptive strike through the Low Countries, which were risking their neutral status by coordinating military efforts with the West, in order to safeguard the Ruhrland from an Allied invasion.[40]

Hitler sent his Foreign Minister to meet Mussolini and Ciano in Rome on 10 March 1940. Ribbentrop informed the Duce of Hitler's plans to attack the West, and defeat France by the fall of 1940.[41]

---

35. Patrick Salmon, "Crimes against Peace: The Case of the Invasion of Norway at the Nuremberg Trials," in *Diplomacy and Intelligence during the Second World War*, ed. Richard Langhorne (Cambridge: Cambridge University Press, 1985), 246, 250.

36. Maier and Stegemann, 190-96.

37. Hitler directive, 1 March 1940, *HWD*, 22-24.

38. Kordt affidavit, 27 September 1947, AMT documents, OGL 17, Box 235, Folder 4, NG-3605, 3.

39. Hitler directive, 18 February 1940, *HWD*, 21-22; P.M.H. Bell, *The Origins of the Second World War in Europe* (London: Longman, 1986), 270.

40. German Foreign Office, *Allied Intrigue in the Low Countries: Further Documents Concerning the Anglo-French Policy of Extending the War*, German Foreign Office White Book No. 5 (New York: German Library of Information, 1940); German Government memorandum to Belgian Government, 9 May 1940, *DGFP(D)*, 9:301-6; Gates, 52-53; Ribbentrop testimony, 30 March 1946, *TMWC*, 10:284; Ribbentrop exhibit 221, *TMWC*, 41:126-27; M. Bargeton to French Foreign Ministry, 9 November 1939, *TMWC*, 41:128; General Maurice Gamelin to French Embassy in London, 13 November 1939, *TMWC*, 41:129-30; Ribbentrop exhibit 243, *TMWC*, 41:136-37.

41. Memorandum, ca. 10 March 1940, IMT documents, OGL 17, Box 195, Folder 9, 2835-PS. See Galeazzo Ciano, *Ciano's Diplomatic Papers: Being a Record of nearly 200 Conversations held during the Years 1936-1942*, ed. Malcolm Muggeridge, trans. Stuart Hood (London: Odhams, 1948), 341.

While preparing for the invasion of the West, German military officials began noting the British Royal Navy's incursions into Norwegian waters on 28 March 1940.[42] Ribbentrop was made aware of this fact by the German Ambassador to Norway the following morning.[43] Wasting little time, on 2 April, Hitler issued an order for the Wehrmacht to invade and occupy Norway and Denmark on the ninth.[44]

Having received such instructions, General Wilhelm Keitel, the Chief of the High Command of the Wehrmacht, drafted a letter to Ribbentrop informing him of the upcoming military action, and requesting the Foreign Minister to coordinate the diplomatic aspect with the military operations planned against Norway and Denmark.[45] The following morning, on 3 April, General Keitel again wrote to Ribbentrop. Distrusting the loyalty of his diplomats, Hitler feared that the Wilhelmstrasse would leak out word of the upcoming invasion to the foreign diplomatic corps in Berlin. Keitel told Ribbentrop: "In accordance with the Führer's specific instructions,…request that the number of persons participating in the preparations be restricted to the fewest possible."[46] To minimize the amount of time that military information would be in the hands of untrustworthy diplomats, both of Keitel's letters were not handed to Ribbentrop until 7 April.[47]

Ribbentrop followed orders and informed only a few key diplomats of Hitler's plans. Weizsäcker, keenly aware of the impending invasion through Kordt and military friends, took leave from Berlin.[48] Ribbentrop had Schmidt and several members of the Languages Division in the Foreign Office secretly prepare and translate notes for the Danish and Norwegian governments at the Hotel Adlon on 8 April.[49] That same day the British Royal Navy began laying mines in Norwegian territorial waters.[50]

As planned, German forces, consisting of nine army divisions, carried out Operation Weserübung and invaded Denmark and Norway on 9 April.[51] The

---

42.    Curt Braüer to Joachim von Ribbentrop, 28 March 1940, *DGFP(D)*, 9:35.

43.    Braüer to Ribbentrop, 28 March 1940, IMT documents, OGL 17, Box 175, Folder 6, D-843.

44.    Salmon, 246; Hitler directive, 2 April 1940, *DGFP(D)*, 9:66-67.

45.    General Wilhelm Keitel to Ribbentrop, 2 April 1940, *DGFP(D)*, 9:68-72.

46.    Keitel to Ribbentrop, 3 April 1940, *DGFP(D)*, 9:72-73.

47.    Ribbentrop, 134-35; Ribbentrop testimony, 30 March 1946, *TMWC*, 10:282.

48.    Weizsäcker testimony, 10 June 1948, AMT transcript, OGL 17, Box 137, Folder 1, 8014-15.

49.    Schmidt, 174-75.

50.    Werner von Grundherr memorandum, 8 April 1940, *DGFP(D)*, 9:98.

51.    Maier and Stegemann, 195. See also Jeremy Black, *World War Two: A Military History* (London: Routledge, 2003), 39-45.

action surprised many of the top diplomats at the Auswärtiges Amt. Ernst Woermann, the Director of the Political Department, knew nothing about the impending invasion.[52] Even the diplomatic experts on Denmark and Norway at the Foreign Office were not aware of Hitler's plans.[53] The invasion of Denmark broke the Dano-German Pact, signed in May 1939.[54] Ribbentrop's task was to deliver diplomatic notes to the Danish and Norwegian Ambassadors that explained Hitler's reasons for the invasion and to request their respective governments not to resist.[55]

## Low Countries and France

On 9 May 1940, as German forces made the last preparations for the attack against the West, Hitler informed Ribbentrop of military matters and requested him to prepare diplomatic notes for the Ambassadors of Belgium, Luxembourg, and The Netherlands. The Foreign Minister immediately called Schmidt and language experts from the Foreign Office to the Presidential Palace to draft and translate the diplomatic notes in complete secrecy from the officials at the Wilhelmstrasse.[56] He told Schmidt that "if news of this offense leaks out, the Führer will have you shot. I shall not be able to save you."[57] It was not until one o'clock in the morning on the tenth that Weizsäcker was informed of Hitler's military plans and Ribbentrop's diplomatic activities planned for later that morning.[58] The entire Foreign Office, with the exception of the Secretariat and the Languages Division, had been kept in the dark about military matters until the last moment.[59]

German forces initiated Hitler's preemptive offensive strike against the Allies through the Low Countries on 10 May 1940. The invasion consisted of 141 German Army Divisions. These forces were equipped with 2,445 tanks and 7,378 artillery pieces. The Luftwaffe had at least 1,736 combat aircraft

---

52.  Woermann testimony, 6 July 1948, AMT transcript, OGL 17, Box 140, Folder 9, 11192.

53.  Weizsäcker testimony, 9 June 1948, AMT transcript, OGL 17, Box 136, Folder 16, 7883.

54.  Maier and Stegemann, 181.

55.  Ribbentrop to Curt Bräuer, 9 April 1940, *DGFP(D)*, 9:103; Danish Foreign Ministry memorandum, 9 April 1940, *NCA*, D-628, 7:98-99.

56.  Schmidt, 175.

57.  Ibid.

58.  Weizsäcker, 233; Weizsäcker testimony, 9 June 1948 AMT transcript, OGL 17, Box 136, Folder 16, 7887.

59.   Woermann testimony, 6 July 1948, AMT transcript, OGL 17, Box 140, Folder 9, 11204-205; Weizsäcker testimony, 10 June 1948, AMT transcript, OGL 17, Box 137, Folder 1, 8028.

available.[60] At the start of the invasion, Hitler had Ribbentrop personally meet with the Belgian, Dutch, and Luxembourgian Ambassadors.[61] Ribbentrop informed the Belgian and Dutch diplomats that their countries had not fulfilled their obligations as neutral countries, and that "they have attempted...to maintain the outward appearance of neutrality, but in practice both countries have shown a one-sided partiality for Germany's opponents and have furthered their designs."[62] He made it plain that Hitler believed a British and French attack through the Low Countries into the Ruhrland to be imminent. Moreover, the Foreign Minister declared:

> [I]n this struggle for existence forced upon the German people by England and France, the Reich Government is not disposed to await idly the attack by England and France and to allow them to carry the war by way of Belgium and the Netherlands into German territory. It has therefore now issued the command to German troops to ensure the neutrality of these countries by all the military means at the disposal of the Reich.[63]

Ribbentrop warned that the Germans would fight if they met any resistance. To the diplomatic representative from Luxembourg, the Foreign Minister only mentioned the necessity for German forces to attack the Allies through his country.[64]

The German blitzkrieg quickly swept through the Low Countries into northeastern France.[65] It defeated the Allied effort resulting in the humiliating withdrawal of British forces from Dunkirk and the capitulation of France on 24 June 1940.[66] With Germany and Britain still at war, Hitler concentrated his efforts on the Battle of Britain during the summer of 1940.[67]

---

60.    Hans Umbreit, "The Battle for Hegemony in Western Europe," in *Germany's Initial Conquests in Europe*, vol. II in *Germany and the Second World War*, eds. Klaus A. Maier, Horst Rohde, Bernd Stegemann, and Hans Umbreit, trans. Dean S. McMurray, Ewald Osers, and P.S. Falla (Oxford: Clarendon Press, 1991), 279.

61.    Ribbentrop, 136-37; Schmidt, 176; German Government memorandum to the Dutch Government, 9 May 1940, *DGFP(D)*, 9:301-6; Weizsäcker testimony, 10 June 1948, AMT transcript, OGL 17, Box 137, Folder 1, 8028.

62.    German Government memorandum to the Dutch Government, 9 May 1940, *DGFP(D)*, 9:301-6.

63.    Ibid.

64.    German Government memorandum to the Luxembourg Government, 9 May 1940, *DGFP(D)*, 9:306-7.

65.    Robert J. Young, *In Command of France: French Foreign Policy and Military Planning, 1933-1940* (Cambridge, MA: Harvard University Press, 1978), 248-57.

66.    See Black, 45-52; Gerhard L. Weinberg, *A World at Arms: A Global History of World War II* (Cambridge: Cambridge University Press, 1994), 122-31.

67.    Liddell Hart, 87-108; Black, 52-56. See also John Lukacs, *The Duel, 10 May-31 July 1940: The Eighty-Day Struggle Between Churchill and Hitler* (New York: Ticknor and Fields, 1991).

## Britain, Yugoslavia, Greece, and the Soviet Union

Meanwhile, Hitler began turning his attention toward his principal enemy, the Soviet Union. Stalin had tread upon Hitler's interests by occupying the German part of Lithuania in June 1940.[68] On 31 July 1940, the Führer's deeply held anti-communist views, combined with increasing German-Soviet tension over territorial disputes in Eastern Europe, prompted him to brief the German General Staff that the Soviet Union must be "smashed" by the spring of 1941.[69]

In September 1940, the Führer sent Ribbentrop to meet with Benito Mussolini to encourage a greater Italian exertion toward defeating Britain. The Duce, however, had other ideas. He preferred to take action in an eastward direction to conquer and expand his power into Yugoslavia and Greece. The German Foreign Minister was overwhelmed by the presence of the Fascist leader, and found it impossible to convince him of concentrating the war effort on Britain.[70]

While he traveled in one direction, Ribbentrop, under Hitler's directions, sent Heinrich Stahmer, a member of the Bureau RAM who was the former Chief of the Far Eastern Section in the Bureau Ribbentrop, as an envoy to Tokyo to arrange a military alliance with Japan.[71] The Führer wanted Japanese military assistance against British forces in the British Empire, as well as to neutralize the United States.[72] Impressed by Germany's victories against most of Europe and desiring to invade French Indochina, the Japanese government sought to join the German-Italian military alliance.[73] With great ease Stahmer achieved success in negotiating the Tripartite Pact (Germany, Italy, and

---

68. Ribbentrop, 145.
69. Extract from General Halder's diary, 31 July 1940, *DGFP(D)*, 10:373; Weizsäcker, 241; Gerhard L. Weinberg, "Germany's Declaration of War on the United States: A New Look," in *World in the Balance: Behind the Scenes of World War II* (Hanover: University of New England Press, 1981), 83; George F. Kennan, *Russia and the West under Lenin and Stalin* (Boston: Little, Brown and Company, 1960), 339-44.
70. Memorandum, 19 September 1940, *NCA*, 1842-PS, 4:477-78.
71. Appendix A, *DGFP(D)*, 11:1241; Appendix C, *DGFP(D)*, 11:1260; Johanna M. Meskill, *Hitler and Japan: The Hollow Alliance* (New York: Atheneum, 1966), 17-18.
72. Heinrich Stahmer and Eugen Ott to Ribbentrop, 10 September 1940, *DGFP(D)*, 11:57-58; Stahmer and Ott to Ribbentrop, 19 September 1940, *DGFP(D)*, 11:123-25; Stahmer and Ott to Ribbentrop, 20 September 1940, *DGFP(D)*, 11:132; Ribbentrop to Hans-Georg von Mackensen, 24 September 1940, *DGFP(D)*, 11:164-65; Schmidt, 224; Gerhard L. Weinberg, "World War II: The Axis, 1939-1942," in *World in the Balance: Behind the Scenes of World War II* (Hanover: University of New England Press, 1981), 18.
73. Ott to Ribbentrop, 3 September 1940, *DGFP(D)*, 11:10.

Japan), signed in Berlin by Ribbentrop, Galeazzo Ciano, and Saburo Kurusu, the Japanese Ambassador to Germany, on 27 September 1940.[74]

In the meantime, territorial squabbles over Bessarabia and Rumania stressed German-Soviet relations during the autumn of 1940.[75] Ribbentrop wanted to avoid a German-Soviet war at all costs. He suggested to Hitler that the Soviet Union join the Tripartite Pact as a way to avoid war.[76] The Führer rejected such an idea, but was willing to discuss German-Soviet territorial interests in Eastern Europe. Hence, on 13 October 1940, Ribbentrop instructed Count Friedrich Werner von der Schulenburg, the German Ambassador to Moscow, to request that Stalin send a diplomatic representative to Berlin to discuss "their interests on a worldwide scale."[77]

Thus, on 12 November 1940, the Soviet Foreign Commissar, Vyacheslav Molotov, arrived in Berlin to discuss matters. During this meeting Ribbentrop suggested that Stalin look southward towards the Indian Ocean instead of the Balkans for expansion.[78] However, Molotov astonished his counterpart by calling for Hitler's recognition of Soviet interests in the Balkans, Soviet bases on the Bosporus and the Dardanelles, Soviet military control of Bulgaria and the entire area of the Straits, as well as a halt to all Germany military activity in Finland.[79] These demands were reaffirmed by Molotov in a statement to the Count Schulenburg in Moscow on 25 November.[80]

Meanwhile, Mussolini had launched an invasion of Greece on 28 October 1940. The short-lived offensive bogged down against Greek resistance within a few days, and Italian forces had dropped back to Albania by 11 November.[81] On 4 November, nevertheless, Hitler had decided to assist the Italians and pull them out of an embarrassing situation by launching a German attack against Greece.[82] To accomplish this the Führer needed Yugoslavia to either remain neutral, or better yet, support the action against Greece. Because of the geographical position of

---

74.    Ribbentrop, 141; Tripartite Pact, 27 September 1940, *DGFP(D)*, 11:204-5.

75.    Vyacheslav Molotov to Friedrich Werner von der Schulenburg, 21 September 1940, *SDFP*, 3:470-74; Ribbentrop, 145-47.

76.    Frau von Ribbentrop affidavit, 5 December 1945, *TMWC*, 41:155-58.

77.    Joseph Stalin to Ribbentrop, 21 October 1940, *SDFP*, 3:474-75; Ribbentrop to Stalin, 13 October 1940, *NSR*, 213.

78.    Ross, 131.

79.    Schmidt, 218; Kennan, *Russia and the West under Lenin and Stalin*, 342.

80.    Molotov to Schulenburg, 25 November 1940, *SDFP*, 3:477-79.

81.    MacGregor Knox, *Mussolini Unleashed, 1939-1941: Politics and Strategy in Fascist Italy's Last War* (Cambridge: Cambridge University Press, 1982), 209.

82.    Martin van Creveld, *Hitler's Strategy, 1940-1941: The Balkan Clue* (Cambridge: Cambridge University Press, 1973), 57-62.

Yugoslavia, Hitler would desperately need the cooperation of Belgrade to carry out any operation aimed at Greece. Hitler therefore met with Aleksandar Cincar-Marković, the Yugoslav Foreign Minister, at Berchtesgaden, on 28 November 1940. In exchange for cooperation with the German effort, the Führer promised the Yugoslav government assistance in acquiring the seaport of Salonika. At the same time, he suggested that Yugoslavia join the Tripartite Pact.[83]

In spite of the Greek-Italian War, the Führer furthered his plans against the Soviet Union. On 18 December 1940, Hitler issued orders for the Wehrmacht to prepare for Operation Barbarossa, designed to "crush Soviet Russia in a quick campaign…even before the conclusion of the war against England."[84] Although the General Staff, according to Barry Leach, shared Hitler's optimism about the task facing them,[85] Ribbentrop urged Hitler to avoid war with the Soviet Union.[86] The Führer brushed aside any such advice and kept his Foreign Minister uninformed about military preparations.[87]

The situation in the Balkans became more serious in early 1941. The British were deploying troops and aircraft to Greece. Realizing this to be the opening of a new front, Hitler hastened to counter British plans. On 21 and 22 January, Hitler and Ribbentrop met Mussolini and Ciano at Salzburg to discuss plans for a German invasion of Greece.[88] Three weeks later, on 14 February, Ribbentrop met the Yugoslav Minister President, Dragiša Cvetković, and the Yugoslav Foreign Minister at Füschl. He strongly suggested that Yugoslavia join the Tripartite Pact and assist in the attack against Greece.[89] Prince Paul, the Regent of Yugoslavia, met with Hitler at Berchtesgaden and discussed politico-military matters on 4 March.[90] The Yugoslav government decided in favor of Hitler's proposals, and joined the Tripartite Pact on 25 March 1941.[91]

---

83.    Schmidt memorandum, 29 November 1940, *DGFP(D)*, 11:728-35.

84.    Hitler directive, 18 December 1940, *DGFP(D)*, 11:899.

85.    Barry A. Leach, *German Strategy against Russia, 1939-1941* (Oxford: Clarendon Press, 1973), 87-89.

86.    Frau von Ribbentrop affidavit, 5 December 1945, *TMWC*, 41:155-58.

87.    Ribbentrop testimony, 2 April 1946, *TMWC*, 10:429; Hitler directive, 18 December 1940, *DGFP(D)*, 11:899.

88.    Ribbentrop, 143; Weizsäcker, 251.

89.    Schmidt memorandum, 15 February 1941, *DGFP(D)*, 12:79-88; Schmidt memorandum, 15 February 1941, *DGFP(D)*, 12:88-96.

90.    Ribbentrop to Mackensen, 5 March 1941, *DGFP(D)*, 12:218-19; Ribbentrop to Viktor von Heeren, 7 March 1941, *DGFP(D)*, 12:230-32.

91.    Heeren to Ribbentrop, 17 March 1941, *DGFP(D)*, 12:303-4; Schmidt memorandum, 25 March 1941, *DGFP(D)*, 12:354-57.

The matter took a significant turn two days later when a group of Yugoslav Army officers, led by General Dušan Simović, overthrew the Cvetković government.[92] That same day, on 27 March, Hitler, who was enraged by such an act against an ally, ordered the Wehrmacht "to smash Yugoslavia militarily and as a state."[93] Hitler told the General Staff and Ribbentrop that this action, combined with the attack against Greece, would delay Operation Barbarossa by about four weeks.[94] According to Weizsäcker, Hitler was personally offended by the putsch: "He decided, on the spur of the moment, to attack Yugoslavia and gave military orders for this within a few hours."[95] To crush Yugoslavia, Hitler sought assistance from his client states. He had Ribbentrop discuss the matter with Döme Sztójay, the Hungarian Ambassador to Berlin, to encourage Hungarian military action against Yugoslavia with the promise of an outlet to the Adriatic as a reward.[96] On 5 April, Hitler instructed Ribbentrop and the Bureau RAM, without the assistance of Weizsäcker and the Foreign Office, to prepare the diplomatic notes to be handed over to the Greek and Yugoslav representatives the following morning.[97]

The German military machine began Operation Punishment, the invasion of Greece and Yugoslavia, on 6 April 1941. Ribbentrop met and explained the reasons for the invasions to the Balkan representatives in Berlin. To the Greek Ambassador the Foreign Minister pointed out the obvious Greek alliance with Britain and acceptance of British forces on Greek soil.[98] He cited the recent putsch by anti-German officers, along with their support for British operations in Greece, as Hitler's reasons for an attack to the Yugoslav representative.[99] The Wehrmacht forced the surrender of Yugoslavia in mid-April,[100] mainland Greece by the end of the month, and captured the island of Crete in May 1941.[101]

---

92.    Heeren to Ribbentrop, 27 March 1941, *DGFP(D)*, 12:368; Heeren memorandum, 3 April 1941, *DGFP(D)*, 12:444-46.

93.    Hitler Conference minutes, 27 March 1941, *DGFP(D)*, 12:373.

94.    Ibid., 12:372; Ribbentrop, 143.

95.    Weizsäcker testimony, 10 June 1948, AMT transcript, OGL 17, Box 137, Folder 1, 8040-41. See also Weizsäcker testimony, 9 June 1948, AMT transcript, OGL 17, Box 136, Folder 16, 7895.

96.    Hewel memorandum, 28 March 1941, IMT documents, OGL 17, Box 195, Folder 5, 2763-PS.

97.    Ribbentrop to Viktor zu Erbach-Schönberg, 5 April 1941, *DGFP(D)*, 12:464-65; Weizsäcker testimony, 9 June 1948, AMT transcript, OGL 17, Box 136, Folder 16, 7895; Weizsäcker testimony, 10 June 1948, AMT transcript, OGL 17, Box 137, Folder 1, 8041.

98.    German Government to Greek Government, *TMWC*, 41:139-42.

99.    German Government to Yugoslav Government, *TMWC*, 41:142-47.

100.    Black, 61.

101.    Ibid., 61-62.

Even though the invasion of the Balkans caused a delay, Hitler continued to plan for German forces to attack the Soviet Union. The fact that Stalin signed a Treaty of Friendship with Yugoslavia during the first week of April 1941 only infuriated the Führer.[102] He would crush the Soviet Union in a surprise attack. In April Hitler informed Ribbentrop of his military plans. The Foreign Minister objected to Hitler's plans; but, realizing the shakiness of his position within the Third Reich, Ribbentrop quickly agreed with his master's reasoning.[103] Ribbentrop described his position in his memoirs:

> I myself at any rate wanted to try one more diplomatic approach to Moscow, but Hitler refused to allow any further *demarche*, and forbade me to talk to anyone about it; no diplomacy, he said, would make him change his mind about Russia's attitude, which was quite clear to him, and it might well deprive him of the weapon of tactical surprise for an attack.[104]

Painfully aware of Hitler's plans by way of confidants in the military, Weizsäcker and the Auswärtiges Amt opposed an invasion of the Soviet Union. The Foreign Office believed that Stalin wanted to avoid a conflict.[105]

Hitler safeguarded the invasion plans from his allies until a week before the attack. Then, on 15 June 1941, Ribbentrop met Ciano in Venice and told the Italian Foreign Minister of Hitler's decision to attack the Soviet Union.[106]

As German forces prepared to attack the Soviet Union, the Foreign Minister, under Hitler's directions, avoided all contact with the Soviet Ambassador, Vladimir Georgievich Dekanozov.[107] On 22 June 1941, as the German military machine invaded the Soviet Union, Ribbentrop had Dekanozov called to a meeting at the former Presidential Palace at four o'clock in the morning. Paul Otto Schmidt related the situation in the Foreign Minister's office in his memoirs:

---

102.  Schulenburg to Ribbentrop, 4 April 1941, *DGFP(D)*, 12:451-52; Weizsäcker, 251.

103.  Seabury, *The Wilhelmstrasse*, 114-15; Weizsäcker, 253; Weizsäcker memorandum, 28 April 1941, *NSR*, 330-34.

104.  Ribbentrop, 152.

105.  Weizsäcker memorandum, 28 April 1941, *NSR*, 333-34; Weizsäcker testimony, 9 June 1948, AMT transcript, OGL 17, Box 136, Folder 16, 7900; Weizsäcker testimony, 10 June 1948, AMT transcript, OGL 17, Box 137, Folder 1, 8048; Schulenburg to Ribbentrop, 24 May 1941, *DGFP(D)*, 12:870. Hitler told Count Schulenburg of the plan to invade the Soviet Union while the ambassador was on leave in Berlin during April 1941 (Hilger and Meyer, 328).

106.  Ciano, *Ciano's Diplomatic Papers*, 446.

107.  Dr. Bruns memorandum, 21 June 1941, *DGFP(D)*, 12:1059; Jasper memorandum, 21 June 1941, *DGFP(D)*, 12:1059; Weizsäcker memorandum, 21 June 1941, *DGFP(D)*, 12:1061-63.

I had never seen Ribbentrop so excited as he was in the five minutes before Dekanosov's (*sic*) arrival. He walked up and down his room like a caged animal. "The Führer is absolutely right to attack Russia now," he said to himself rather than to me; he repeated it again and again as though he wanted somehow to reassure himself. "The Russians would certainly themselves attack us, if we did not do so now." He went on walking up and down the large room in a state of great excitement, his eyes flashing, and kept repeating these words.[108]

Schmidt attributed Ribbentrop's attitude to the fact that the creator of the Nazi-Soviet Pact was now having to destroy his own work.[109] Nevertheless, upon Dekanozov's arrival, the Foreign Minister quickly and politely informed him that "the hostile attitude of the Soviet Government toward Germany and the serious threat that Germany saw in the Russian concentration on the eastern border of Germany, had forced the Reich to [take] military countermeasures."[110] Schmidt believed that Ribbentrop probably thought that this was the beginning of the end for the Third Reich.[111] Initially, however, the attack was a complete tactical surprise along the whole Eastern Front and 3.6 million German, Finnish, and Rumanian troops drove deep into Soviet territory in Operation Barbarossa. They were supported by 3,350 tanks and 1,950 planes.[112]

## Diplomats at War

The swift movements of events and German success after June 1941 threatened Ribbentrop and the Foreign Office with the prospect of becoming obsolete. Hitler established a headquarters, the Wolfsschanze (Wolf's Lair), near Rastenburg in East Prussia. He would spend much of the war at this headquarters to direct German military operations.[113] The Foreign Minister and the Bureau RAM used their special train to follow and stay close to Hitler at the Eastern front.[114] Erich Kordt had been dismissed from the Secretariat and sent to Tokyo.[115] Johann

---

108.  Schmidt, 234.
109.  Ibid.
110.  Schmidt memorandum, 22 June 1941, *DGFP(D)*, 12:1074-75.
111.  Schmidt, 234.
112.  Gerhard L. Weinberg, *Germany and the Soviet Union, 1939-1941* (Leiden: Brill, 1954), 167; Liddell Hart, 164; Read and Fisher, 646; Weinberg, *A World at Arms*, 264-65; John Keegan, *The Second World War* (New York: Viking, 1989), 180-81; Black, 74-75.
113.  Black, 75.
114.  Schmidt, 248-49.
115.  Kordt affidavit, 27 September 1947, AMT documents, OGL 17, Box 235, Folder 4, NG-3605, 4.

Georg Lohmann took his place as Senior Counselor, and others, such as Gustav Hilger, had joined the Bureau RAM.[116] As the war progressed Ribbentrop and diplomacy became less important to the Führer. In fact, the Foreign Minister confided to a subordinate in the Bureau RAM of "the inescapably logical consequence of German world supremacy: Hitler would need no Foreign Minister."[117] During the summer of 1941, Hitler considered plans to reduce the staff of the Foreign Office to the bare minimum.[118] In July 1941, upset at his loss of status, Ribbentrop offered to resign from his post.[119] After Hitler's acceptance, Ribbentrop quickly reconsidered his action and asked for a reinstatement to his position as Foreign Minister, and was granted it.[120] Gustave Gilbert, the psychiatrist at Nuremberg, wrote about this situation that Ribbentrop "panicked at the threat of losing favor…[and after regaining his position] had given his word of honor never to question his [Hitler's] judgment again."[121]

After this incident, Hitler had Ribbentrop concentrate on getting Japan to attack the Soviet Union, British possessions in the Far East, and the United States.[122] But, the Japanese seemed unwilling to launch a strike, especially against the Soviet Union since they had signed a nonaggression pact with Moscow in April 1941.[123] Hitler had pressed Yosuke Matsuoka, the Japanese Foreign Minister, for Japan to strike Singapore and American possessions in the Pacific Region,[124] declaring that "Germany would strike…without delay in case of a conflict between Japan and America, because the strength of the tripartite powers lies in their joint action…."[125] Following the German invasion of the Soviet Union, Ribbentrop cabled Major General Eugen Ott, the German Ambassador to Tokyo (1938-42), and stressed the need for him to do his utmost to get the Japanese to attack the Soviets in Siberia.[126] On 28 November 1941, Ribbentrop told Hiroshi Oshima, the new Japanese Ambassador to Berlin:

---

116.  Hilger and Meyer, 338; Appendix A, *DGFP(D)*, 13:1011.
117.  Seabury, "Ribbentrop and the German Foreign Office," 546.
118.  Weizsäcker, 258; Seabury, *The Wilhelmstrasse*, 112.
119.  Seabury, "Ribbentrop and the German Foreign Office," 546.
120.  Seabury, *The Wilhelmstrasse*, 119.
121.  Gustave M. Gilbert, *The Psychology of Dictatorship* (New York: Ronald, 1950), 201.
122.  Ribbentrop, 159; Weizsäcker, 256; Ribbentrop to German Embassies Abroad, 2 March 1941, *NCA*, 1834-PS, 4:472.
123.  Weizsäcker, 250.
124.  Schmidt memorandum, 31 March 1941, *DGFP(D)*, 12:376-83.
125.  Schmidt memorandum, *NCA*, 1881-PS, 4:524.
126.  Ribbentrop to Ott, 28 June 1941, *DGFP(D)*, 13:40-41; Ribbentrop to Ott, 28 June 1941, *DGFP(D)*, 13:41; Ribbentrop to Ott, 1 July 1941, *DGFP(D)*, 13:61-63; Ribbentrop to Ott, 25 August 1941, *DGFP(D)*, 13:375-79.

It is essential that Japan effect the New Order in East Asia without losing this opportunity. There never has been and probably never will be a time when closer cooperation under the Tripartite Pact is so important. If Japan hesitates at this time, and Germany goes ahead and establishes her European New Order, all the military might of Britain and the United States will be concentrated against Japan.[127]

The German Foreign Minister added that:

[H]e did not believe that Japan could avoid a showdown with the United States, and that the situation could hardly even turn more favorable to Japan than it was now. It was his view that when one was strong, one should take advantage of it. One should not hesitate tackling the Americans right now. It seemed better at any rate to bring a problem to a head at the right moment than to keep putting it off.[128]

Receiving word of the Japanese attack on Pearl Harbor, Hitler and Ribbentrop, both at the Eastern Front, were taken by surprise.[129] The Foreign Minister actually believed that the information was probably enemy propaganda, which had tricked the German Press.[130] Discovering the truth on 8 December, Ribbentrop notified Oshima that Hitler had issued orders for the German Navy to attack American ships.[131] Three days later, on 11 December, Hitler declared war against the United States. Commenting on Hitler's reason for such an action, Schmidt stated in his memoirs, "from what Ribbentrop said at the time I got the impression that, with his inveterate desire for prestige, Hitler, who was expecting an American declaration of war, wanted to get his declaration in first."[132] Germany and the United States were already fighting an undeclared naval war in the Atlantic.[133] In his own memoirs, Ribbentrop described the situation:

As soon as the reports about Pearl Harbor arrived—a complete surprise to us—my first reaction was that we had no contractual obligation to join in the war against the U.S.A. But when I discussed the matter with [Friedrich] Gaus,

127.  Hiroshi Oshima to Japanese Foreign Minister, *NCA*, D-656, 7:160.
128.  Memorandum, 28 November 1941, *DGFP(D)*, 13:868.
129.  Schmidt, 237; Ribbentrop, 159.
130.  Schmidt, 237.
131.  Oshima to Japanese Foreign Ministry, *NCA*, D-657, 7:163.
132.  Schmidt, 237.
133.  Waldo Heinrichs, *Threshold of War: Franklin D. Roosevelt and American Entry into World War II* (New York: Oxford University Press, 1988), 146-220.

the Head of the Legal Department in the Foreign Office, he declared that we could not act in that way and that this argument would in practice mean "the political demise" of the Three-Power Pact. Even so I did give the Führer a sober exposition of the contractual terms, according to which, I held, we were not bound to declare war on the U.S.A. The text of the Pact only provided for our aiding Japan if she were attacked by a third Power. Hitler, however, replied: "The Americans have already opened fire on us, so that a state of war exists even now. Japan will never forget if we do not take the consequences. Besides, soon, and probably at once, we shall be at war with America, for this has been Roosevelt's aim all along.[134]

Even so, Hans Dieckhoff, the German Ambassador to the United States (1937-38), believed that Hitler and Ribbentrop did not take the Americans as a serious threat. In his opinion:

Neither Hitler nor Ribbentrop had any real understanding of the situation in the United States. Hitler counted on the bad experience of the Americans in the First World War [and American neutrality legislation] a sure hindrance to any new American intervention in Europe.[135]

Although successful in getting Japan to attack British and American possessions, Ribbentrop failed to get Tokyo to assist Germany in the war against the Soviet Union. On 9 July 1942, the Foreign Minister pleaded with the Japanese that "if Japan attacked Russia now, it would lead to her final moral collapse;…never again would Japan have such an opportunity as existed at present, to eliminate once and for all the Russian colossus in Eastern Asia.[136] In April 1943, Ribbentrop told the Japanese Ambassador, "that without doubt this year presented the most favorable opportunity for Japan…to attack Russia, which certainly would never again be as weak as she is at the moment."[137] However, he was never able to convince the Japanese to fight a war on two fronts.

Ribbentrop and the Foreign Office lacked an important diplomatic role by 1943. The Auswärtiges Amt went through the motions of foreign policy, maintaining contact with missions abroad and carrying on propaganda and information activities.[138]

---

134. Ribbentrop, 160.
135. As quoted in Poole, 146.
136. Memorandum, 9 July 1942, *NCA*, 2911-PS, 5:580.
137. Memorandum, 18 April 1943, *NCA*, 2929-PS, 5:603.
138. Gordon A. Craig, "Diplomats and Diplomacy during the Second World War," in *The Diplomats, 1939-1979*, eds. G.A. Craig and Francis L. Loewenheim (Princeton: Princeton University Press, 1994), 18.

But, the Third Reich was diplomatically isolated from all but a handful of neutrals and several vassal states. The Wilhelmstrasse maintained diplomatic ties with the neutral powers of Spain, Portugal, Sweden, Switzerland, Iceland, and Turkey, resulting in economic and financial benefits for Nazi Germany.[139] Ribbentrop had gradually lost the stage where he could act out his role as an important statesman. Other diplomats had a low opinion of him. At no time was his position as Foreign Minister secure from opponents. Without repute in Nazi Party circles, Ribbentrop was totally dependent upon Hitler's patronage.[140] Hermann Göring, Heinrich Himmler, Martin Bormann, Joseph Goebbels, and Alfred Rosenberg all viewed Ribbentrop as "haughty, stupid, a fool."[141] In his description of Ribbentrop, Hans-Georg von Studnitz of the Foreign Office Press Department stated:

> The Foreign Minister has put all he possesses on one card — Hitler. A single frown from Führer Headquarters, and his whole world tumbles about his ears. His greatest agony occurs when he has been unable for some considerable time to obtain an audience with Hitler. Over him, as over all the other "paladins," hangs the Damoclean sword of disfavour. But his skin is thinner than that of the others.[142]

For five years Ribbentrop had put up with challenges to his authority as Foreign Minister by members of Hitler's inner circle. He had continually struggled for control of foreign propaganda with Goebbels and the Propaganda Ministry.[143] Slipping from favor during the winter of 1942 and 1943, Ribbentrop was now presented a challenge for control from within the Foreign Office.[144] Martin Luther, Ribbentrop's own hand-picked Under State Secretary for Foreign Affairs (1940-43), tried to overthrow his superior by submitting charges of incompetency. Luther had the support of Heinrich Himmler's Chief of the Secret Service, Walter Schellenberg.[145] He was also strongly connected to the Foreign Office's role in deporting Jews from Germany's satellite countries in Eastern, Western,

139. See Christian Leitz, *Sympathy for the Devil: Neutral Europe and Nazi Germany in World War II* (New York: New York University Press, 2001).

140. Seabury, *The Wilhelmstrasse*, 166.

141. Speer, *Spandau*, 142.

142. Studnitz, 164.

143. Schmidt, 162; Joseph Goebbels, *The Goebbels Diaries, 1939-1941*, ed. and trans. Fred Taylor (New York: G.P. Putnam, 1983), 32, 109, 150, 170, 177, 189-90, 194, 198, 290-91; Goebbels, *The Goebbels Diaries, 1942-1943*, 301, 512, 547; Roger Manvell and Heinrich Fränkel, *Dr. Goebbels: His Life and Death* (New York: Simon and Schuster, 1960), 148.

144. Poole, 153.

145. Craig, "Diplomats and Diplomacy during the Second World War," 18-19.

and Northern Europe to Nazi death camps in Poland.[146] The Foreign Minister discovered the conspiracy, reported it to the Führer, and obtained Luther's banishment to a concentration camp, where Himmler made life easy for his ally.[147]

With such treason coming from the Wilhelmstrasse, Ribbentrop turned hostile against his top Foreign Office officials.[148] He shook up the Wilhelmstrasse by dismissing Ernst von Weizsäcker, Ernst Woermann, and Friedrich Gaus as Foreign Secretary, Director of the Political Department, and Director of the Legal Department. Weizsäcker was reassigned as the German Ambassador to the Vatican while Woermann was sent as the German representative to the Japanese-controlled government in Nanking, China.[149] Ribbentrop appointed the loyal Gustav Adolf Steengracht von Moyland as the Foreign Secretary on 30 March 1943.[150] Moreover, the Foreign Minister employed the Gestapo to search the offices and desks as well as tap the telephone calls of the Wilhelmstrasse to collect evidence of treasonable acts.[151]

Despite losing favor with Hitler, Ribbentrop remained the German Foreign Minister until the last days of the war. Goebbels continually pressed the Führer for Ribbentrop's dismissal, hoping to become the new Foreign Minister himself.[152] Meanwhile, the Allied aerial bombardment of Berlin destroyed much of the Foreign Office. The raid of 11 August 1943 caused severe damage to the Wilhelmstrasse, resulting in Foreign Secretary Steengracht von Moyland and his diplomats to move into twenty-two different buildings scattered across the breadth

---

146.  Donald M. McKale, *Curt Prüfer: German Diplomat from the Kaiser to Hitler* (Kent: Kent State University Press, 1987), 168. See also Christopher R. Browning, "Unterstaatssekretär Martin Luther and the Ribbentrop Foreign Office," *Journal of Contemporary History* 12 (1977), 313-44.

147.  Steengracht von Moyland testimony, 23 June 1948, AMT transcript, OGL 17, Box 138, Folder 16, 9765-766; Seabury, *The Wilhelmstrasse*, 132-33; Speer, *Spandau*, 142. Gustav Hilger wrote that Ribbentrop was "basically ignorant and hardly capable of independent thought, he constantly surrounded himself with experts and idea-men whose brains he could pick whenever it suited him" (Hilger and Meyer, 339).

148.  Ulrich von Hassell, *The Von Hassell Diaries, 1938-1944*, introd. Allen W. Dulles (Garden City: Doubleday, 1947), 270.

149.  Woermann testimony, 2 July 1948, AMT transcript, OGL 17, Box 140, Folder 2, 10848-850; Weizsäcker, 277; Seabury, *The Wilhelmstrasse*, 133.

150.  Steengracht von Moyland testimony, 23 June 1948, AMT transcript, OGL 17, Box 138, Folder 16, 9767, 9771. Joseph Goebbels called Steengracht von Moyland a "mediocre figure," believing him to be "at best a high-grade private secretary" (Goebbels, *The Goebbels Diary, 1942-1943*, 398).

151.  Studnitz, 61.

152.  Joseph Goebbels, *Final Entries, 1945: The Diaries of Joseph Goebbels*, ed. Hugh Trevor-Roper, trans. Richard Barry (New York: G.P. Putnam, 1978), xxiv, xxvi, 228.

of Berlin in order to carry on their diplomatic duties.[153] By the end of the year Allied bombing forced many of the Auswärtiges Amt to leave Berlin and establish offices in the Riesengebirge and Thuringia, the Bodensee, and the neighborhood of Salzburg.[154] Ribbentrop, however, spent most of the time at the Eastern Front close to the Führer,[155] but under constant criticism from Göring.[156] The Soviet advance westwards resulted in Hitler, as well as Ribbentrop, returning to Berlin in late 1944.[157] Allied bombings of the capital city destroyed what was left of the Foreign Office as well as damaged the former Presidential Palace.[158] On 14 April 1945, Foreign Office personnel left the city for the Salzburg area before the arrival of the Soviet Red Army.[159] With the war lost and the Third Reich coming to an end, Hitler finally made the decision to rid himself of Ribbentrop.[160] The Führer appointed Count Lutz Schwerin von Krosigk, the former Finance Minister, as the new German Foreign Minister.[161]

153. Studnitz, 95.
154. Craig, "Diplomats and Diplomacy during the Second World War," 18.
155. Studnitz, 159-60.
156. Manvell and Fränkel, *Dr. Goebbels*, 304; Goebbels, *The Goebbels Diaries, 1942-1943*, 267.
157. Studnitz, 210.
158. Ibid., 241, 251.
159. Hilger and Meyer, 340.
160. Manvell and Fränkel, *Dr. Goebbels*, 316.
161. Seabury, *The Wilhelmstrasse*, 148.

# 9

# *Diplomats on Trial at Nuremberg*

## International Military Tribunal

Towards the end of the war the Allies made plans to round up and try key National Socialists for war crimes. From the very beginning the Allies wanted to indict Adolf Hitler, Heinrich Himmler, Hermann Göring, Joachim von Ribbentrop, and Joseph Goebbels for their crimes against peace.[1] However, Hitler, Himmler, and Goebbels all escaped such a trial by committing suicide in the last days of the Third Reich. This left Göring and Ribbentrop as the top two surviving Nazis to be indicted by the International Military Tribunal at Nuremberg on the charges of conspiracy to wage wars of aggression, crimes against peace, war crimes, and crimes against humanity.[2] Since Hitler, the prime formulator of German foreign policy, was dead, Ribbentrop became the key target for the Allies in condemning the policy that led to war. At the insistence of the French, the International Military Tribunal also indicted two other diplomats, Constantin von Neurath and Franz von Papen, for their part in the conspiracy.[3] Although they disagreed, the British and American officials accepted Neurath and Papen being included as major war criminals in spite of the fact that they did not play key parts in the crisis period that led to war.[4] Both men were being indicted for their diplomatic activities during 1933 to

1. Bradley F. Smith, *The Road to Nuremberg* (New York: Basic Books, 1981), 1979; Bradley F. Smith, *The American Road to Nuremberg: The Documentary Record, 1944-1945* (Stanford: Hoover Institute Press, 1982), 152, 174.
2. International Military Tribunal indictment, *NCA*, 1:13-82.
3. Bradley F. Smith, *Reaching Judgment at Nuremberg* (London: Andre Deutsch, 1977), 68; John L. Heineman, *Hitler's First Foreign Minister: Constantin Freiherr von Neurath, Diplomat and Statesman* (Berkeley: University of California Press, 1979), 220-21.
4. Ann Tusa and John Tusa, *The Nuremberg Trial* (New York: Atheneum, 1983), 92, 94; Heineman, *Hitler's First Foreign Minister*, 224.

1938.[5] Neurath had served as Hitler's first Foreign Minister (1932-38) and Papen as Vice Chancellor (1933-34) and German Ambassador to Austria (1934-38). Including these diplomats, the International Military Tribunal indicted and tried twenty-two major war criminals at Nuremberg during 1945 and 1946.

In planning for the military tribunal, the Allies had picked the conspiracy theme as the best charge to collectively level at a group of Nazi leaders representing different functions within the German government. It was the one charge that they could easily indict the majority of the defendants.[6] With Hitler dead and Ribbentrop having served as his top diplomat during the period of German aggression, the Allies were especially interested in building up a solid case against the former Foreign Minister in order to denounce the aggressive policy that led to world war. Thus, the Allies placed considerable emphasis on Ribbentrop's central role as Foreign Minister when they collected documents to prosecute the war criminals on the conspiracy charge. The importance of convicting Ribbentrop meant that the Allies would spend a considerable effort amassing evidence against him to ensure an absolutely unquestionable conviction.[7] Such a significant effort by the prosecution against him, as well as his own mental deterioration, would make it virtually impossible for Ribbentrop to defend himself during the trial.[8]

Indicted on the conspiracy charge at Nuremberg, Ribbentrop, Neurath, and Papen pleaded not guilty on 21 November 1945. Although hard on Neurath for his actions as Hitler's first Foreign Minister, the prosecution primarily went after Ribbentrop. They produced an enormous amount of documentation to support their argument that Ribbentrop performed a key role in the conspiracy to wage wars of aggression. The prosecution argued that his presence at so many of Hitler's meetings had given Ribbentrop a thorough knowledge of German planning and action, and it was alleged, were enough to prove his complicity.[9]

In his defense, Ribbentrop argued that he had no influence on Hitler's foreign policy. He told the Nuremberg court, "when Hitler gave an order, I always carried out his instructions in accordance with the principles of our authoritarian state."[10] He stressed that Hitler kept diplomatic and military matters separate,

---

5.    Heineman, *Hitler's First Foreign Minister*, 224-25.

6.    Smith, *Reaching Judgment at Nuremberg*, 49; Smith, *Road to Nuremberg*, 51-52, 84, 123, 125; Smith, *The American Road to Nuremberg*, 50.

7.    Smith, *Reaching Judgment at Nuremberg*, 183-84.

8.    Robert E. Conot, *Justice at Nuremberg* (New York: Harper and Row, 1983), 348; Gustave M. Gilbert, *Nuremberg Diary* (London: Eyre and Spottiswoode, 1948), 10, 136.

9.    *TMWC*, 22:530-32; Tusa and Tusa, 299-300.

10.   Joachim von Ribbentrop testimony, 2 April 1946, *TMWC*, 10:416.

resulting in his being kept out of military planning.[11] His argument was supported by Hermann Göring who told the court that Ribbentrop "did not make foreign policy,"[12] and General Wilhelm Keitel, the Chief of the High Command of the Wehrmacht (1938-45), who admitted that the Führer had not authorized him to inform the former Foreign Minister about military plans.[13] To defend himself, Ribbentrop submitted over 300 documents and called several witnesses, including Dr. Paul Otto Schmidt and Gustav Adolf Steengracht von Moyland, in an attempt to prove his lack of influence in foreign relations. The tribunal refused to accept well over half of Ribbentrop's document collection, citing irrelevance and the lack of English translations.[14] Defense witnesses told of Ribbentrop's devotedness and unquestionable loyalty to the Führer. Steengracht von Moyland, the former Foreign Secretary, told the court that Ribbentrop "felt himself personally bound to Hitler, whom he followed with soldierly obedience, and he stood under a certain hypnotic dependence on Hitler."[15] His defense stood on the argument that Hitler was his own Foreign Minister, and Ribbentrop just loyally carried out his master's instructions.[16]

During his own testimony, Ribbentrop, according to many observers, found it beyond his ability to defend himself and Hitler's foreign policy.[17] After the first day of testimony, Neurath and Papen were saying that Ribbentrop's performance and evidence showed that he had no conception of Hitler's policy.[18] Neurath told Gustave Gilbert, the prison psychiatrist: "You can see by the way he talks that he did not have the faintest conception of foreign affairs...."[19] Another defendant, Hjalmar Schacht, stated that "Ribbentrop should be hung for his stupidity; there is no worse crime than stupidity."[20] Even Göring, who had aspired to become Foreign Minister, stated after Ribbentrop's pitiful display that he wished that during his own testimony, which took place before Ribbentrop's, he would have said more about Hitler's foreign policy so as to enlighten the world.[21]

---

11.  Ribbentrop testimony, 1 April 1946, *TMWC*, 10:321.

12.  Hermann Göring testimony, 22 March 1946, *TMWC*, 9:620.

13.  General Wilhelm Keitel testimony, 5 April 1946, *TMWC*, 10:598; Gilbert, *Nuremberg Diary*, 139.

14.  Ribbentrop, 192.

15.  Gustav Adolf Steengracht von Moyland testimony, 26 March 1946, *TMWC*, 10:110.

16.  DeWitt C. Poole, "Light on Nazi Foreign Policy," *Foreign Affairs* 25 (October 1946), 131.

17.  Gilbert, *Nuremberg Diary*, 137-39.

18.  Tusa and Tusa, 303.

19.  Gilbert, *Nuremberg Diary*, 135.

20.  Ibid., 11.

21.  Tusa and Tusa, 303.

In the following days during the cross-examination, Sir David Maxwell-Fyfe, the chief prosecutor against the former Foreign Minister, destroyed what remained of Ribbentrop's case with relative ease.[22] Commenting on Ribbentrop's performance, Papen later wrote:

> When he [Ribbentrop] came under cross-examination, he attempted no measured defence of Hitler's policies, whose most determined advocate he had been for more than twelve years. He revealed himself to the world as what some of us already knew him to be, a husk with no kernel, and an empty facade for a mind.[23]

Thus, as Bradley F. Smith commented on Ribbentrop's trial:

> [W]ith the overwhelming body of evidence against him tailored perfectly to fit the legal categories established by the Tribunal, such as participation in specific war planning, nothing Ribbentrop or his counsel did could conceivably affect the result.[24]

Judgment day came on 30 September 1946. The International Military Tribunal found Ribbentrop and Neurath guilty of conspiracy to wage wars of aggression. The Tribunal acquitted Papen.[25] Ribbentrop was sentenced to death by hanging, and Neurath received a fifteen-year prison sentence at Spandau.[26] The Allies executed Ribbentrop by hanging at Nuremberg on 16 October 1946. Reflecting upon Ribbentrop's trial, Albert Speer, another defendant at Nuremberg, stated:

> Ribbentrop's guilt, that is, did not consist in his having made a policy of war on his own. Rather, he was to blame for using his authority as a supposed cosmopolite to corroborate Hitler's provincial ideas. The war itself was first and last Hitler's idea and work.[27]

---

22.    Ibid., 306-7. See Ribbentrop testimony, 28 March to 2 April 1946, *TMWC*, 10:224-445.

23.    Franz von Papen, *Memoirs*, trans. Brian Connell (New York: E.P. Dutton, 1953), 552.

24.    Smith, *Reaching Judgment at Nuremberg*, 184.

25.    *TMWC*, 22:530-32, 22:570-74; 22:580-82; 22:588-89.

26.    Heineman, *Hitler's First Foreign Minister*, 236-38.

27.    Albert Speer, *Spandau: The Secret Diaries*, trans. Richard and Clara Winston (New York: Macmillan, 1976), 143.

## American Military Tribunal

In addition to the trial of the major war criminals, the Allies planned to try less important Nazis for their part in the conspiracy to wage wars of aggression. The United States Army was responsible for the conduct of such trials in the American Zone of Occupation in Germany. In the last of a series of trials the American Military Tribunal indicted twenty-one defendants in what became known as the Ministries Case, held at Nuremberg, during 1947 to 1949.[28] Eight of the defendants were former officials of the German Foreign Office. Only seven of these men, however, were initially charged with the conspiracy to wage wars of aggression.[29] Gustav Adolf Steengracht von Moyland, a former Foreign Secretary (1943-45) was not indicted on this charge, but on the charges of war crimes and crimes against humanity.[30]

American officials selected Foreign Office defendants based upon their position of authority, involvement in the conspiracy, and their availability for the trial. Dr. Hans-Georg von Mackensen, Neurath's Foreign Secretary (1936-38), had died in an American prison camp in August 1946.[31] The United States Army arrested Ernst von Weizsäcker, Ribbentrop's Foreign Secretary (1938-43), who had stayed at the Vatican for more than a year after the war, in July 1947.[32] He, along with Ernst Woermann, the former Director of the Political Department (1938-43), were the top diplomats indicted on the conspiracy charge. The Tribunal also tried minor diplomatic officials such as Wilhelm Keppler, the State Secretary for Special Duties (1938-45), Edmund Veesenmayer, Keppler's assistant (1938-44), Karl Ritter, Ambassador for Special Duties (1939-45), Otto von Ermannsdorff, the Deputy Director of the Political Department (1941-45), and Ernst Bohle, the Head of the Auslandorganisation (1937-41).[33] Before long, nevertheless, the American Military Tribunal dropped the conspiracy charges against Ermannsdorff and Bohle.[34] Interestingly enough, no former members of the Bureau RAM were indicted for the conspiracy to wage wars of aggression despite the presence of Eric Kordt, Gustav Adolf Steengracht von Moyland, and Paul Otto Schmidt at the trials.

---

28. See Case 11, *NMT*, vols. 12-14; AMT trial transcript, OGL 17, Boxes 136-46; AMT trial evidence documents, OGL 17, Boxes 205-50.
29. *NMT*, 12:20-35. See also *NMT*, 12:419-1330.
30. AMT trial transcript, OGL 17, Box 129, Folder 2, 31.
31. Heineman, *Hitler's First Foreign Minister*, 236.
32. Weizsäcker, 305, 309.
33. *NMT*, 12:14-15.
34. Ibid., 14:323, 14:435.

The diplomats pleaded not guilty to the conspiracy charge. Weizsäcker told the American Military Tribunal that the charge of a diplomatic conspiracy was a figment of the prosecution's imagination.[35] In their defense, the diplomats argued that they had no influence over Hitler's formulation and conduct of foreign affairs. Weizsäcker told the court, "my impression on the rare occasions when I did see Hitler personally was rather that I bored him, probably with my dryness and objectivity."[36] Both Weizsäcker and Woermann told the Tribunal that the Foreign Office lacked influence with both Hitler and Ribbentrop. Ribbentrop relied upon a small select group, mainly his Secretariat, to assist him in the conduct of policy.[37] In their defense, Kordt stressed the opposition to Hitler and Ribbentrop at the Wilhelmstrasse. He told the court how Weizsäcker and the career diplomats went to great lengths, including treason, to keep the European peace. In fact, the Gestapo had executed eleven members of the Foreign Office for their actions.[38] Kordt, the close confident of the Foreign Minister, professed that both Hitler and Ribbentrop greatly disliked professional diplomats, with few exceptions, and thus went to great lengths to bypass the Foreign Office in the formulation and conduct of foreign policy.[39] Schmidt, probably in order to avoid any charges against himself, kept his statements as a defense witness brief and avoided discussing his role in the conduct of Hitler's policy.[40]

In April 1949, the American Military Tribunal announced judgment on the Foreign Office defendants. Weizsäcker, Woermann, and Keppler were found guilty for their part in the conspiracy to wage wars of aggression against Austria, Czechoslovakia, and Poland.[41] The court acquitted Ritter and Veesenmayer.[42] On 13 April, the Tribunal sentenced Weizsäcker and Woermann to seven years in prison while Keppler received a ten-year prison sentence based upon his guilt in the conspiracy as well as crimes against humanity.[43] The defendants immediately filed a motion for the Tribunal to set aside their con-

---

35.  Ernst von Weizsäcker testimony, 8 June 1948, AMT transcript, OGL 17, Box 136, Folder 13, 7703.
36.  Ibid., 8 June 1948, AMT transcript, OGL 17, Box 136, Folder 13, 7718.
37.  Ibid., 11 June 1948, AMT transcript, OGL 17, Box 137, Folder 7, 8274; Ernst Woermann testimony, 6 July 1948, AMT transcript, OGL 17, Box 140, Folder 6, 11037, 11039-40, 11050, 11055-57 and Box 140, Folder 7, 11128.
38.  Eric Kordt testimony, 3 June 1948, AMT transcript, OGL 17, Box 136, Folder 6, 7327.
39.  Ibid., 4 June 1948, AMT transcript, OGL 17, Box 136, Folder 7, 7348-349, 7353.
40.  Paul Otto Schmidt testimony, 24 August 1948, AMT transcript, OGL 17, Box 146, Folder 19, 17819-835.
41.  *NMT*, 14:865; 14:890; 14:951; 14:963-65.
42.  Ibid., 14:865.
43.  Ibid., 14:866-69.

victions.[44] This request for Weizsäcker and Woermann was granted on 12 December 1949.[45] Woermann's prison sentence, however, was not commuted, but reduced from seven to five years because of his conviction for crimes against humanity.[46] Weizsäcker, nonetheless, had his sentence commuted to time served, and he was immediately released, despite the fact that he, too, had been convicted for crimes against humanity.[47] The United States released Woermann in October 1950 and Keppler in January 1951.[48] As for Constantin von Neurath, the Allies released him from Spandau because of poor health in 1954.[49] Ribbentrop, of all the diplomats, was the only one to be held to the full extent of his sentence.

## Conclusion

The International and American Military Tribunals convicted key members of the Wilhelmstrasse for their so-called involvement in the Nazi conspiracy to wage wars of aggression. These diplomats were looked upon as guilty for supporting Adolf Hitler's aggressive foreign policy. Likewise, diplomats, especially those from the losing side, Germany, were held responsible for the outbreak of war in 1914. The international world had come to the point where it would hold diplomats, who were traditionally the promoters of peace, responsible for the plans and actions of their politico-military superiors. In Germany, a nation known for its militarism, the Wilhelmstrasse would take as much, if not more, blame for world wars than the military establishment.

Brandenburg-Prussia had been ruled by several strong individuals who managed their own foreign affairs. The Great Elector, Frederick the Great, and Frederick William IV were all of that mold. Otto von Bismarck continued that tradition for Germany. Beginning with Bismarck, strong German leaders sought to be their own Foreign Minister. German diplomatic success was backed up by a powerful military. Even though the Iron Chancellor created Germany through a combination of diplomatic and military action, the importance of the Army was paramount in achieving this accomplishment. Nonetheless, Bismarck, as Imperial Chancellor and Prussian Foreign Minister, exercised complete control over the activities of the Wilhelmstrasse. He dominated every aspect of German diplo-

---

44.   Ibid., 14:946.
45.   Ibid.
46.   Ibid., 14:865; 14:965.
47.   Ibid., 14:865; 14:1004; Weizsäcker, 310.
48.   *NMT*, 14:965; 14:1002-4.
49.   Heineman, *Hitler's First Foreign Minister*, 238.

macy. Replacing the Iron Chancellor, Emperor William II established his auto-cratic leadership of Germany by the late 1890s. Emulating his predecessor, William II, although heavily under the influence of the military, dominated Ger-man foreign affairs. Under both Bismarck and the Kaiser, the Foreign Office was subservient to the Imperial leadership and served as a mere technical apparatus to carry out foreign policy decisions. Foreign Office officials had little, if any, influ-ence on the formulation of international political policy. This changed after the First World War when Germany lacked an autocratic leader and was militarily weak. The Wilhelmstrasse, especially under Gustav Stresemann, acquired consid-erable influence on the making of foreign policy during the Weimar era. German diplomats were viewed as the experts who could gradually strengthen Germany's weakened international position by negotiating an end to the Versailles restric-tions. Becoming Chancellor of Germany in 1933, Adolf Hitler quickly became a strong leader and rapidly worked to make Germany diplomatically and militarily strong again. Moreover, Hitler sought to carry on the German tradition of an autocratic leader acting as his own Foreign Minister in the style of both Bismarck and William II.

The Führer, like Bismarck and the Kaiser, appointed men to the top diplo-matic post who were loyal and trustworthy, and would not challenge his diplo-matic leadership in the formulation and conduct of foreign policy. Bismarck's foreign secretaries, except for his son Herbert, were no more than administrative experts that ran the day-to-day operations of the Wilhelmstrasse. William II appointed men, with the exception of Chlodwig Hohenlohe-Schillingsfürst and Bernhard von Bülow, to the top diplomatic post that knew little about foreign relations. Leo von Caprivi and Theobald von Bethmann Hollweg both lacked experience in foreign relations. Under the Kaiser's absolute rule, neither Hohen-lohe, Bülow, or Bethmann Hollweg would argue with their master's diplomatic viewpoint, realizing that they could be dismissed as easily as Bismarck had been.

Interestingly enough, neither Bismarck nor William II held the diplomats of the Foreign Office in high esteem. This prejudice was also held by Hitler. Shortly after taking power, Hitler quickly began to bypass his Foreign Minister, Constan-tin von Neurath, and the Auswärtiges Amt by relying upon amateur diplomats to carry out his instructions. Gradually the Führer put faith in the loyal champagne salesman, Joachim von Ribbentrop, to carry out his policy. The inexperienced Ribbentrop unofficially became Hitler's top diplomat, supplanting what little influence Neurath and the Foreign Office had over Hitler's foreign policy. With complete control of the Third Reich, Hitler dismissed Neurath and replaced him with Ribbentrop as the official Foreign Minister in 1938. During the period of crises in Europe in 1938 and 1939, the professional diplomats of the Wilhelm-strasse, as during the time of Bismarck and the Kaiser, had little, if any, influence over the formulation and conduct of foreign policy. Hitler, like his autocratic predecessors, acted as his own Foreign Minister as well as controlled military planning. Although lacking influence over the formulation of foreign policy, Ribbentrop, nonetheless, through his own method of ingratiating himself with the Führer, ultimately swayed Hitler's decisions in the aggressive attempts to fulfill policy objectives that risked a European war. Such influence was evident during the crisis over Czechoslovakia and Poland.

Despite inexperienced leadership in its top post during most of the Wilhelmine and Hitler periods, the German Foreign Office was usually managed by a career diplomat that could supervise both the ministry and the conduct of foreign affairs. Bernhard von Bülow, Alfred von Kiderlen-Wächter, and Gottlieb von Jagow served the Emperor as experienced foreign secretaries who assisted their unskilled superiors. Not only did the seasoned diplomat Neurath serve Hitler as Foreign Minister, with the vain hope of maintaining the influence over the formulation and conduct of foreign policy acquired during the Weimar era, but Bernhard Wilhelm von Bülow, Hans-Georg von Mackensen, and Ernst von Weizsäcker served as highly experienced diplomats in the position of Foreign Secretary during the Third Reich. Even so, the Foreign Office was rife with a trend of insubordination that was rare under Bismarck. In the Kaiser's time, Friedrich von Holstein and Kiderlen-Wächter divided the ranks of the Wilhelmstrasse against their masters. Bülow, and to a much less extent Neurath, opposed Hitler's control over foreign affairs during the early years of the Third Reich. Ernst von Weizsäcker and Ernst Woermann, among others, were unwilling to loyally conduct Nazi foreign policy thereafter. However, it was impossible to resign from the Foreign Office by the late thirties. Eric Kordt told the American Military Tribunal that the career diplomats knew they would be sent to concentration camps because of their knowledge of state secrets.[50] Wilhelmstrasse diplomats, nonetheless, committed treasonable acts in efforts to avoid a European war.[51] For their troubles, the Nuremberg courts tried and convicted Neurath, Weizsäcker, and Woermann for conspiring to wage wars of aggression. Moreover, the courts convicted the amateur Nazi diplomats, Ribbentrop and Wilhelm Keppler, for their parts in the conspiracy. Keppler played a minor role in the annexation of Aus-

---

50.    Eric Kordt testimony, 4 June 1948, AMT transcript, OGL 17, Box 136, Folder 7, 7339-340.
51.    Gordon A. Craig, "Diplomats and Diplomacy during the Second World War," in *The Diplomats, 1939-1979*, eds. G.A. Craig and Francis L. Loewenheim (Princeton: Princeton University Press, 1994), 19.

tria,[52] whereas Ribbentrop served the Führer as the top Nazi diplomat who loyally carried out his master's instructions.

Possessing extreme arrogance, vanity, ambition for status and narrow-mindedness, Ribbentrop was disliked by Hitler's inner circle as well as the international world. He had few friends other than the Führer. He was therefore an easy target for criticism and as a possible scapegoat for the failure of Hitler's foreign policy.[53] His arrogant style of diplomacy had offended the conservative British diplomatic community from the start. It was they who submitted Ribbentrop's name towards the top of their list of persons for trial in the latter stages of the war. Neither Ribbentrop nor the Wilhelmstrasse formulated Nazi foreign policy. The Foreign Minister, nevertheless, had no living friends to support him and plenty of enemies that wanted to convict him for the results of Hitler's foreign policy. Although the prime formulator of foreign relations, Hitler, was dead, Ribbentrop realized at his Nuremberg trial that he would have to take full responsibility for the mistakes of Nazi foreign policy and pay for them with his life.[54]

---

52.    Wilhelm Keppler testimony, 16 July 1948, AMT transcript, OGL 17, Box 142, Folder 2, 12930-931.

53.    H.W. Koch, *Aspects of the Third Reich* (New York: St. Martin's Press, 1985), 194.

54.    Ribbentrop, 180.

# Appendix A

## Chief Ministers and Minister-Presidents of Prussia

## Chancellors of Germany

**Chief Ministers of Prussia**

| | |
|---|---|
| Christian Heinrich Kurt von Haugwitz | 1792-1804 |
| Karl August von Hardenberg | 1804-1806 |
| Christian Heinrich Kurt von Haugwitz | 1806 |
| Karl Friedrich von Beyme | 1806-1807 |
| Karl August von Hardenberg | 1807 |
| Heinrich Friedrich Karl vom Stein | 1807-1808 |
| Karl Friedrich Ferdinand Alexander von Dohna-Schlobitten | 1808-1810 |
| Karl August von Hardenberg | 1810-1822 |
| Otto Karl Friedrich von Voss | 1822-1823 |
| Karl Friedrich Heinrich von Wylich und Lottum | 1823-1841 |
| Ludwig Gustav von Thile | 1841-1848 |

**Minister-Presidents of Prussia**

| | |
|---|---|
| Adolf Heinrich von Arnim-Boitzenburg | 1848 |
| Gottfried Ludolf Camphausen | 1848 |
| Rudolf Ludwig Cäsar von Auerswald | 1848 |
| Ernst von Pfuel | 1848 |
| Friedrich Wilhelm von Brandenburg | 1848-1850 |

| | |
|---|---|
| Otto Theodor von Manteuffel | 1850-1858 |
| Karl Anton von Hohenzollern-Sigmaringen | 1858-1862 |
| Adolf of Hohenlohe-Ingelfingen | 1862 |
| Otto von Bismarck-Schönhausen | 1862-1873 |
| Albrecht von Roon | 1873 |
| Otto von Bismarck-Schönhausen | 1873-1890 |
| Georg Leo von Caprivi | 1890-1892 |
| Botho zu Eulenburg | 1892-1894 |
| Chlodwig zu Hohenlohe-Schillingsfürst | 1894-1900 |
| Bernhard von Bülow | 1900-1909 |
| Theobald von Bethmann Hollweg | 1909-1917 |
| Georg Michaelis | 1917 |
| Georg von Hertling | 1917-1918 |
| Maximilian of Baden | 1918 |
| Friedrich Ebert | 1918 |
| Paul Hirsch | 1918-1920 |
| Otto Braun | 1920-1921 |
| Adam Stegerwald | 1921 |
| Otto Braun | 1921-1925 |
| Wilhelm Marx | 1925 |
| Otto Braun | 1925-1932 |
| Franz von Papen | 1932 |
| Kurt von Schleicher | 1932-1933 |
| Franz von Papen | 1933 |
| Hermann Göring | 1933-1945 |

**Chancellors of the Second Reich**

| | |
|---|---|
| Otto von Bismarck-Schönhausen | 1871-1890 |

| Georg Leo von Caprivi | 1890-1894 |
| Chlodwig zu Hohenlohe-Schillingfürst | 1894-1900 |
| Bernhard von Bülow | 1900-1909 |
| Theobald von Bethmann Hollweg | 1909-1917 |
| Georg Michaelis | 1917 |
| Georg von Hertling | 1917-1918 |
| Maximilian of Baden | 1918 |
| Friedrich Ebert | 1918 |

## Chancellors of the Weimar Republic

| Philipp Scheidemann | 1919 |
| Gustav Bauer | 1919-1920 |
| Hermann Müller-Franken | 1920 |
| Konstantin Fehrenbach | 1920-1921 |
| Joseph Wirth | 1921-1922 |
| Wilhelm Cuno | 1922-1923 |
| Gustav Stresemann | 1923 |
| Wilhelm Marx | 1923-1925 |
| Hans Luther | 1925-1926 |
| Wilhelm Marx | 1926-1928 |
| Hermann Müller-Franken | 1928-1930 |
| Heinrich Brüning | 1930-1932 |
| Franz von Papen | 1932 |
| Kurt von Schleicher | 1932-1933 |

## Chancellors of the Third Reich

| Adolf Hitler | 1933-1945* |

| | |
|---|---|
| Joseph Goebbels | 1945 |
| Lutz Schwerin von Krosigk | 1945 |

*The Office of Reichskanzler (Chancellor) was combined with that of the Reichspräsident in 1934 and called Führer und Reichskanzler. The combined position was separated in Hitler's political testament in 1945.

# APPENDIX B

## *Foreign Ministers*

### Prussian Foreign Ministers

| | |
|---|---|
| August Friedrich Ferdinand Goltz | 1808-1814 |
| Karl August von Hardenburg | 1814-1818 |
| Christian Günther von Bernstorff | 1818-1832 |
| Friedrich von Ancillon | 1832-1837 |
| Heinrich Wilhelm Werther | 1837-1841 |
| Mortimer Maltzan | 1841-1842 |
| Heinrich von Bülow | 1842-1845 |
| Karl Ernst Wilhelm von Canitz und Dallwitz | 1845-1848 |
| Adolf Heinrich von Arnim-Boitzenburg | 1848 |
| Heinrich Alexander von Armin-Suckow | 1848 |
| Alexander von Schleinitz | 1848 |
| Rudolf von Auerswald | 1848 |
| August Hermann von Dönhoff | 1848 |
| Friedrich Wilhelm von Brandenburg | 1848 |
| Franz August Eichmann | 1848-1849 |
| Heinrich Friedrich von Arnim-Heinrichsdorff | 1849-1850 |
| Joseph Maria von Radowitz | 1850 |
| Otto Theodor von Manteuffel | 1850-1858 |
| Alexander von Schleinitz | 1858-1861 |
| Albrecht von Bernstorff | 1861-1862 |
| Otto von Bismarck-Schönhausen | 1862-1890 |
| Georg Leo von Caprivi | 1890-1894 |
| Chlodwig zu Hohenlohe-Schillingfürst | 1894-1900 |

| | |
|---|---|
| Bernhard von Bülow | 1900-1909 |
| Theobald von Bethmann Hollweg | 1909-1917 |
| Georg Michaelis | 1917 |
| Georg von Hertling | 1917-1918 |
| Maximilian of Baden | 1918 |

### Foreign Ministers of Weimar Republic

| | |
|---|---|
| Ulrich von Brockdorff-Rantzau | 1919 |
| Hermann Müller-Franken | 1919-1920 |
| Adolf Köster | 1920 |
| Walter Simons | 1920-1921 |
| Friedrich Rosen | 1921 |
| Joseph Wirth | 1922 |
| Walther Rathenau | 1922 |
| Joseph Wirth | 1922 |
| Friedrich von Rosenberg | 1922-1923 |
| Gustav Stresemann | 1923-1929 |
| Julius Curtius | 1929-1931 |
| Heinrich Brüning | 1931-1932 |
| Konstantin von Neurath | 1932-1938 |

### Foreign Ministers of Third Reich

| | |
|---|---|
| Konstantin von Neurath | 1932-1938 |
| Joachim von Ribbentrop | 1938-1945 |
| Arthur Seyss-Inquart | 1945 |
| Lutz Schwerin von Krosigk | 1945 |

# APPENDIX C

## *State Secretaries for Foreign Affairs*

| | |
|---|---|
| Karl Hermann von Thile | 1862-1872 |
| Hermann von Balan | 1872-1873 |
| Bernhard Ernst von Bülow | 1873-1879 |
| Chlodwig zu Hohenlohe-Schillingsfürst | 1880 |
| Friedrich Wilhelm zu Limburg-Stirum | 1880-1881 |
| Paul von Hatzfeldt-Wildenburg | 1881-1885 |
| Herbert von Bismarck | 1886-1890 |
| Adolf Hermann Marschall von Bieberstein | 1890-1897 |
| Bernhard von Bülow | 1897-1900 |
| Oswald von Richthofen | 1900-1906 |
| Heinrich Leonard von Tschirschky und Bögendorff | 1906-1907 |
| Wilhelm von Schön | 1907-1910 |
| Alfred von Kiderlen-Wächter | 1910-1912 |
| Gottlieb von Jagow | 1913-1916 |
| Alfred Zimmermann | 1916-1917 |
| Richard von Kühlmann | 1917-1918 |
| Paul von Hintze | 1918 |
| Wilhelm Solf | 1918 |
| Ulrich von Brockdorff-Rantzau | 1918-1919 |
| Edgar Haniel von Haimhausen | 1919-1922 |

(Reorganized in 1919 with the creation of an additional post for Wirtschaft)

| | |
|---|---|
| Adolf Boye | 1919-1921 |

| Ernst von Simson | 1921-1922 |
| Ago von Maltzan | 1922-1924 |
| Carl von Schubert | 1924-1930 |
| Bernhard Wilhelm von Bülow | 1930-1936 |
| Hans Dieckhoff | 1936-1937 |
| Hans-Georg von Mackensen | 1937-1938 |
| Ernst von Weizsäcker | 1938-1943 |
| Gustav Adolf Steengracht von Moyland | 1943-1945 |

# *Bibliography*

In researching this study, a wide variety of sources were used to examine the involvement of the German Foreign Office in the Nazi conspiracy to wage wars of aggression. The Nuremberg manuscripts in the Elwyn B. Robinson Department of Special Collections at the University of North Dakota's Chester Fritz Library proved very valuable. The American Military Tribunal collection contains complete trial transcripts and many documents concerning Weizsäcker and other Foreign Office officials not hitherto published. However, the International Military Tribunal documentation concerning Neurath and Ribbentrop is not as complete as in the published ten volume series of *Nazi Conspiracy and Aggression*. The Chester Fritz also possessed complete sets of the *Trial of the Major War Criminals before the International Military Tribunal* (forty-two volumes) and *Trials of War Criminals before the Nuremberg Military Tribunals under Control Council Law No. 10* (fifteen volumes). Of obvious usefulness were the *Documents on German Foreign Policy 1918-1945*, Series C and D. Published memoirs and diaries of important German, British, French, Italian, Polish, and American diplomatic personnel provided insight concerning the activities of the German Foreign Office. Of course, the memoirs of Bismarck, Holstein, William II, Hohenlohe-Schillingsfürst, Bülow, Bethmann Hollweg, Dirksen, Weizsäcker, Papen, Schmidt, Kordt, Spitzy, Meyer, Hilger, Hassell, and the unfortunately, incomplete memoirs of Ribbentrop contributed greatly to my effort.

## I. Primary Sources—Unpublished Works

Trial Transcript. American Military Tribunal. Case 11. The United States versus Weizsäcker, et. al., 1948. Elwyn B. Robinson Department of Special Collections, OGL 17, Boxes 136-146, Chester Fritz Library, University of North Dakota, Grand Forks, North Dakota.

Trial Evidence Documents. American Military Tribunal, Nuremberg, Germany. Elwyn B. Robinson Department of Special Collections, OGL 17, Boxes 205-250, Chester Fritz Library, University of North Dakota, Grand Forks, North Dakota.

Trial Evidence Documents. International Military Tribunal, Trial of the Major War Criminals, 1946. Elywn B. Robinson Department of Special Collections, OGL 17, Boxes 173-204, Chester Fritz Library, University of North Dakota, Grand Forks, North Dakota.

## II. Primary Sources—Published Works

### A. Publications of Documents, Collections, Speeches, etc.

Degras, Jane, editor. *Soviet Documents on Foreign Policy, 1917-1941.* 3 volumes. Oxford: Oxford University Press, 1953; reprint, New York: Octagon, 1978.

France. Ministere des Affaires Etranqeres. *The French Yellow Book: Diplomatic Documents (1938-1939).* New York: Reynal and Hitchcock, 1940.

Geiss, Imanuel, editor. *July 1914, The Outbreak of the First World War: Selected Documents.* New York: Charles Scribner's Sons, 1967.

Germany. Auswärtiges Amt. *Allied Intrigue in the Low Countries: Further Documents Concerning the Anglo-French Policy of Extending the War.* German Foreign Office White Book No. 5. New York: German Library of Information, 1940.

Germany. Auswärtiges Amt. *Bismarck and the Hohenzollern Candidature for the Spanish Throne: The Documents in the German Diplomatic Archives.* Edited and Introduced by Georges Bonnin. Foreword by G.P. Gooch. London: Chatto and Windus, n.d.

Germany. Auswärtiges Amt. *Britain's Designs on Norway: Documents Concerning the Anglo-French Policy of Extending the War.* German Foreign Office White Book No.4. New York: German Library of Information, 1940.

Germany, Auswärtiges Amt. *Akten zur Deutschen Auswärtingen Politik, 1918-1945, Serie A (1918-1925).* 14 volumes. Göttingen: Vandenhoeck and Ruprecht, 1982.

Germany, Auswärtiges Amt. *Akten zur Deutschen Auswärtingen Politik, 1918-1945, Serie B (1925-1933).* 21 volumes. Göttingen: Vandenhoeck and Ruprecht, 1966-83.

Germany, Auswärtiges Amt. *Akten zur Deutschen Auswärtingen Politik, 1918-1945, Series E (1941-1945).* 8 volumes. Göttingen: Vandenhoeck and Ruprecht, 1969-79.

Germany. Auswärtiges Amt. *Die Grosse Politik der Europäischen Kabinette, 1871-1914: Sammlung der diplomatischen Akten des Auswärtigen Amtes.* 40 volumes. Edited by Johannes Lepsius, Albrecht Mendelssohn Bartholdy, and Friedrich Thimme. Berlin: Deutsche Verlagsgesellschaft für Politik, 1922-27.

Germany. Auswärtiges Amt. *Documents on German Foreign Policy 1918-1945, Series C (1933-1937).* 6 volumes. Washington, D.C.: U.S. Government Printing Office, 1957-83.

Germany. Auswärtiges Amt. *Documents on German Foreign Policy 1918-1945, Series D (1937-1941).* 14 volumes. Washington, D.C.: U.S. Government Printing Office, 1949-76.

Germany. Auswärtiges Amt. *Documents on the Events Preceding the Outbreak of the War.* Berlin and New York: German Foreign Office, 1939.

Germany. Auswärtiges Amt. *German Diplomatic Documents, 1871-1914.* Edited and translated by E.T.S. Dugdale. 4 volumes. New York: Harper, 1928-31.

Germany. Auswärtiges Amt. *Nazi-Soviet Relations, 1939-1941: Documents from the Archives of the German Foreign Office.* Washington, D.C.: U.S. Government Printing Office, 1948.

Germany. Auswärtiges Amt. *The German White Paper: Full Text of the Polish Documents Issued by the Berlin Foreign Office.* New York: Howell and Soskin, 1940.

Germany. Nationalversammlung, 1919-20. Untersuchungsausschuss uber die Weltkriegsverantwortlichkeit. *Official German Documents Relating to the World War.* 2 volumes. New York: Oxford University Press, 1923.

Germany (Territory under Allied Occupation, United States Zone). Military Tribunal. *Trials of War Criminals Before the Nuremberg Military Tribunals Under Control Council Law No. 10.* 15 volumes. Washington, D.C.: U.S. Government Printing Office, 1949-53.

Great Britain. Foreign Office. *The British War Blue Book: Documents Concerning German-Polish Relations and the Outbreak of Hostilities between Great Britain and Germany on September 3, 1939.* New York: Farrar and Rinehart, 1939.

Great Britain. Foreign Office. *Documents on British Foreign Policy, 1919-1939, First Series.* 27 volumes. London: Her Majesty's Stationary Office, 1947-86.

Great Britain. Foreign Office. *Documents on British Foreign Policy, 1919-1939, Series 1A.* 7 volumes. London: Her Majesty's Stationary Office, 1966-75.

Great Britain. Foreign Office. *Documents on British Foreign Policy, 1919-1939, Second Series.* 21 volumes. London: Her Majesty's Stationary Office, 1946-84.

Great Britain. Foreign Office. *Documents on British Foreign Policy, 1919-1939, Third Series.* 10 volumes. London: Her Majesty's Stationary Office, 1949-61.

Great Britain. Foreign Office. *Final Report by the Right Honourable Sir Nevile Henderson on the Circumstances Leading to the Termination of His Mission to Berlin, September 20, 1939.* London: His Majesty's Stationary Office, 1939.

Gooch, George P. and Harold W.V. Temperley, editors. *British Documents on the Origins of the War, 1898-1914.* 11 volumes. London: His Majesty's Stationary Office, 1926-28.

Hill, Leonidas E., editor. *Die Weizsäcker-Papiere, 1933-1950.* Frankfurt am Main, Berlin, Vienna: Propylaeen, 1977.

International Military Tribunal. *Trial of the Major War Criminals before the International Military Tribunal, Nuremberg 14 November 1945—1 October 1946.* 42 volumes. Nuremberg, 1947.

Meyer, Henry Cord. *The Long Generation from Empire to Ruin, 1913-1945.* New York: Walker and Company, 1973.

Montgelas, Max and Walther Schucking, editors. *Outbreak of the World War: German Documents Collected by Karl Kautsky.* New York: Oxford University Press, 1924.

Noakes, Jeremy and Geoffrey Pridham, editors. *Documents on Nazism, 1919-1945.* New York: Viking Press, 1974.

Poland. Ministerstwo Spraw Zagranicznych. *The Polish White Book: Official Documents Concerning Polish-German and Polish-Soviet Relations 1933-1939.* New York: Farrar and Rinehart, 1940.

Smith, Bradley F., editor. *The American Road to Nuremberg: The Documentary Record 1944-1945*. Stanford: Hoover Institute Press, 1982.

Smith, Munroe, editor. *The Disclosures from Germany: The Lichnowsky Memorandum. The Reply from Herr von Jagow*. Translated by Munroe Smith. New York: American Association for International Conciliation, 1918.

Snyder, Louis L., editor. *Hitler's Third Reich: A Documentary History*. Chicago: Nelson-Hall, 1981.

United States. Chief of Counsel for the Prosecution of Axis Criminality. *Nazi Conspiracy and Aggression*. 8 volume. and 2 supplements. Washington, D.C.: U.S. Government Printing Office, 1946-48.

## B. Diaries, Memoirs, Collected Papers and Other Works by Key Participants

Bethmann Hollweg, Theobald von. *Reflections on the World War*. Translated by George Young. London: Thorton Butterworth, 1920.

Bismarck, Otto von. *New Chapters of Bismarck's Autobiography*. Translated by Bernard Miall. London: Hodder and Stoughton, 1920.

_____. *The Memoirs*. 2 volumes. Translated by A.J. Butler. New York: Harper and Brothers, 1899; reprint, New York: Howard Fertig, 1966.

Bülow, Bernhard Prince von. *Memoirs of Prince von Bülow*. 4 volumes. Translated by F.A. Voight and Geoffrey Dunlap. Boston: Little, Brown and Company, 1931-32.

Churchill, Winston S. *The Second World War*. 6 volumes. Boston: Houghton Mifflin, 1948-53.

Ciano, Galeazzo. *Ciano's Hidden Diary 1937-1938*. Translated by Andreas Major. Introduction by Malcolm Muggeridge. New York: E.P. Dutton, 1953.

_____. *Ciano's Diplomatic Papers, Being a Record of Nearly 200 Conversations Held During the Years 1936-1942*. Edited by Malcolm Muggeridge. Translated by Stuart Hood. London: Odhams, 1948.

_____. *The Ciano Diaries 1939-1943: The Complete, Unabridged Diaries of Count Galeazzo Ciano, Italian Minister for Foreign Affairs, 1936-1943*. Edited by Hugh Gibson. Introduction by Sumner Welles. New York: Doubleday, 1946.

D'Abernon, Viscount (Edgar). *The Diary of an Ambassador*. 3 volumes. New York: Doubleday and Doran, 1929-30.

Dirksen, Herbert. von. *Moscow, Tokyo, London: Twenty Year's of German Foreign Policy*. Norman, Okla.: Oklahoma University Press, 1952.

Dodd, William E. *Ambassador Dodd's Diary, 1933-1938*. Edited by William E. Dodd, Jr. and Martha Dodd. New York: Harcourt Brace, 1941.

Eden, Anthony (Earl of Avon). *Facing the Dictators, 1923-1938*. Boston: Houghton Mifflin, 1962.

_____. *The Reckoning: The Memoirs of Anthony Eden, Earl of Avon*. Boston: Houghton Mifflin, 1965.

François-Poncet, André. *The Fateful Years: Memoirs of a French Ambassador in Berlin, 1931-1938*. Translated by Jacques LeClercq. New York: Harcourt, 1949.

Gilbert, Gustave M. *Nuremberg Diary*. London: Eyre and Spottiswoode, 1948.

Goebbels, Joseph. *Final Entries 1945: The Diaries of Joseph Goebbels*. Edited by Hugh Trevor-Roper. Translated by Richard Barry. New York: G.P. Putnam's Sons, 1978.

_____. *The Goebbels Diaries 1939-1941*. Edited and Translated by Fred Taylor. New York: G.P. Putnam's Sons, 1983.

_____. *The Goebbels Diaries 1942-1943*. Edited and Translated by Louis P. Locher. New York: Doubleday, 1948.

Grey, (Edward) Viscount of Fallondon. *Twenty-Five Years 1892-1916*. 2 volumes. New York: Frederick A. Stokes, 1925.

Halder, Franz. *The Halder War Diary 1939-1942*. Edited by Charles Burdick and Hans-Adolf Jacobsen. Novato, Calif.: Presido Press, 1988.

Halifax, Lord. *Fullness of Days*. New York: Dodd and Mead, 1957.

Hardenberg, Karl August von. *Karl August von Hardenberg, 1750-1822: Tagebücher und autobiographische Aufzeichnungen*. Edited by Thomas Stamm-Kuhlmann. Munich: Harald Bolt Verlag im R. Oldenbourg Verlag, 2000.

Harvey, Oliver. *The Diplomatic Diaries of Oliver Harvey, 1937-1940*. Edited by John Harvey. London: Collins, 1970.

Hassell, Ulrich von. *The Von Hassell Diaries 1938-1944*. Introduction by Allen W. Dulles. Garden City: Doubleday, 1947.

Henderson, Nevile. *Failure of a Mission: Berlin, 1937-1939*. New York: G.P. Putnam's Sons, 1940.

Hilger, Gustav and Alfred G. Meyer. *The Incompatible Allies: A Memoir-History of German-Soviet Relations 1918-1941*. New York: Macmillan, 1953.

Hitler, Adolf. *Blitzkrieg to Defeat: Hitler's War Directives 1939-1945*. Translated and Edited by Hugh Trevor-Roper. New York: Holt, Rinehart, and Winston, 1964.

_____. *Mein Kampf.* Translated by Ralph Manheim. Boston: Houghton Mifflin, 1943.

_____. *Hitler's Secret Book*. Translated by Salvator Attanasio. Introduction by Telford Taylor. New York: Grove Press, 1962; reprint, New York: Bramhall House, 1986.

_____. Hitler's Secret Conversations 1941-1944. Translated by Norman Cameron and R.H. Stevens. New York: Octagon, 1972.

_____. *The Speeches of Adolf Hitler, April 1922-August 1939*. 2 volumes. Translated and Edited by Norman H. Baynes. London, New York, and Toronto: Oxford University Press, 1942.

Hohenlohe-Schillingsfürst, Prince Chlodwig zu. *Memoirs of Prince Chlodwig of Hohenlohe-Schillingsfürst*. 2 volumes. Edited by Friedrich Curtius. Translated by George W. Chrystal. London: Macmillan, 1906.

Holstein, Friedrich von. *The Holstein Papers: The Memoirs, Diaries and Correspondence of Friedrich von Holstein, 1837-1909*. 4 volumes. Edited by Norman Rich and M.H. Fisher. Cambridge: Cambridge University Press, 1955-63.

Kelley, Douglas M. *22 Cells in Nuremberg: A Psychiatrist Examines the Nazi War Criminals*. New York: Greenberg, 1947.

Kennan, George F. *From Prague After Munich: Diplomatic Papers 1938-1940*. Princeton: Princeton University Press, 1968.

Kordt, Erich. *Nicht aus den Akten: Die Wilhelmstrasse in Frieden und Krieg*. Stuttgart: Deutsche Verlags-Anstalt, 1950.

_____. *Wahn und Wirklichkeit, die Aussenpolitik des Dritten Reiches, Versuch einer Darstellung*. Stuttgart: Union Deutsche Verlagsgesellschaft, 1948.

Lichnowsky, Prince. *Heading for the Abyss: Reminiscences.* Translated by Sefton Delmer. New York: Payson and Clarke, 1928.

Lipski, Jozef. *Diplomat in Berlin 1933-1939: Papers and Memoirs of Jozef Lipski, Ambassador of Poland.* Edited by Waclaw Jedrzejewicz. New York: Columbia University Press, 1968.

Papen, Franz von. *Memoirs.* Translated by Brian Connel. New York: E.P. Dutton, 1953.

Poole, DeWitt C. "Light on Nazi Foreign Policy." *Foreign Affairs* 25 (October 1946): 130-54.

Rauschning, Hermann. *Men of Chaos.* New York: G.P. Putnam's Sons, 1942.

_____. *Voice of Destruction.* New York: G.P. Putnam's Sons, 1940.

Ribbentrop, Joachim von. *The Ribbentrop Memoirs.* Translated by Oliver Watson. Edited by A. von Ribbentrop. Introduction by Allan Bullock. London: Weidenfeld and Nicolson, 1954.

Schmidt, Dr. Paul Otto. *Hitler's Interpreter.* Edited by R.H.C. Steed. New York: Macmillan, 1951.

_____. *Statist auf diplomatischer Bühne, 1923-1945.* Bonn: Athenäum, 1950.

Simon, Sir John. *Retrospect.* London: Hutchinson, 1952.

Speer, Albert. *Inside the Third Reich: Memoirs.* Translated by Richard and Clara Winston. New York: Macmillan, 1970.

_____. *Spandau: The Secret Diaries.* Translated by Richard and Clara Winston. New York: Macmillan, 1976.

Spitzy, Reinhard. *So Haben wir das Reich Verspielt, Bekenntisse eines Illegalen.* Munich: Langen-Muller, 1988; published in English as *How We Squandered the Reich.* Norwich: Michael Russell, 1997.

Stresemann, Gustav. *His Diaries, Letters and Papers.* 3 volumes. Edited and Translated by Eric Sutton. New York: Macmillan, 1935-40.

Studnitz, Hans-Georg von. *While Berlin Burns: The Diary of Hans-Georg von Studnitz 1943-1945.* Translated by R.H. Stevens. London: Weidenfeld and Nicolson, 1964.

Vansittart, Lord. *Bones of Contention.* New York: Knopf, 1945.

_____. *The Mist Procession.* London: Hutchinson, 1958.

Weizsäcker, Ernst von. *Memoirs of Ernst von Weizsäcker.* Translated by John Andrews. Chicago: Henry Regnery, 1951.

Welles, Sumner. *The Time for Decision.* New York: Harper, 1944.

William II. *My Early Life.* New York: George H. Doran, 1926; reprint, New York, AMS, 1971.

_____. *The Kaiser's Memoirs: Wilhelm II, Emperor of Germany 1888-1918.* Translated by Thomas R. Ybarra. New York: Harper and Brothers, 1922; reprint, New York: Howard Fertig, 1976.

Wilson, Hugh. *A Career Diplomat, The Third Chapter: The Third Reich.* Edited by Hugh R. Wilson, Jr. New York: Vantage Press, 1960.

## III. Secondary Sources

Abrams, Lynn. *Bismarck and the German Empire, 1871-1918.* London: Routledge, 1995.

Adams, R.J.Q., editor. *British Appeasement and the Origins of World War II.* Lexington, MA: D.C. Heath, 1994.

_____. *British Politics and Foreign Policy in the Age of Appeasement, 1935-1939.* Stanford: Stanford University Press, 1993.

Adamthwaite, Anthony. *France and the Coming of the Second World War, 1936-1939.* London: Frank Cass, 1977.

_____. *Grandeur and Misery: France's Bid for Power in Europe, 1914-1940.* London: Arnold, 1995.

_____. *The Lost Peace: International Relations in Europe, 1918-1939.* London: Edward Arnold, 1980.

Afflerbach, Holger. *Der Dreibund: Europäische Grossmacht-und Allianzpolitik vor dem Ersten Weltkrieg.* Wien: Böhlau Verlag, 2002.

_____. "Wilhelm II as Supreme Warlord in the First World War." In *The Kaiser: New Research on Wilhelm II's Role in Imperial Germany.* Edited by Annika Mombauer and Wilhelm Deist. Cambridge: Cambridge University Press, 2003.

Albertini, Luigi. *The Origins of the War of 1914.* 3 volumes. London: Oxford University Press, 1957.

Albrecht-Carrié, René. *A Diplomatic History of Europe Since the Congress of Vienna.* London: Methuen, 1958.

Alexander, Martin. *The Republic in Danger: General Maurice Gamelin and the Politics of Defence, 1933-1940.* Cambridge: Cambridge University Press, 1992.

Ambrosius, Lloyd E. "Secret German-American Negotiations during the Paris Peace Conference." *American Studies/Amerikastudien* 24 (1979): 288-309.

Anderson, Eugene N. *The First Moroccan Crisis 1904-1906.* Chicago: University of Chicago Press, 1930; reprint, New York: Archon, 1966.

Anderson, M.S. *The Eastern Question, 1774-1923: A Study in International Relations.* London: Macmillan, 1966.

_____. *The Rise of Modern Diplomacy, 1450-1919.* London: Longman, 1993.

_____. *The War of the Austrian Succession, 1740-1748.* London: Longman, 1995.

Andrew, Christopher. "German World Policy and the Reshaping of the Dual Alliance." *Journal of Contemporary History* 1 (July 1966): 137-51.

_____. *Théophile Delcassé and the Making of the Entente Cordiale: A Reappraisal of French Foreign Policy, 1898-1905.* London: Macmillan, 1968.

Angelow, Jürgen. "Accomplices with Reservations: German Diplomats and the Preparation of the Polish Campaign of September 1939." *Australian Journal of Politics and History* 50 (2004): 372-84.

Asprey, Robert B. *Frederick the Great: The Magnificent Enigma.* New York: Ticknor and Fields, 1986.

_____. *The German High Command at War: Hindenburg and Ludendorff Conduct World War I.* New York: William Morrow, 1991.

Austensen, Roy A. "Austria and the Struggle for Supremacy in Germany, 1848-1864." *The Journal of Modern History* 52 (1980): 195-225.

_____. "Metternich, Austria, and the German Question, 1848-1851." *International History Review* 13 (1991): 21-37.

_____. "The Making of Austria's Prussian Policy, 1848-1852." *The Historical Journal* 22 (1984): 861-76.

Baack, Lawrence J. *Christian Bernstorff and Prussia: Diplomacy and Reform Conservatism, 1818-1832*. New Brunswick: Rutgers University Press, 1980.

Badsey, Stephen. *The Franco-Prussian War, 1870-1871*. Botley: Osprey, 2003.

Baker, V.B. "Appeasement's Ambassador: Sir Nevile Meyrick Henderson." Ph.D. thesis, University of Southwestern Louisiana, 1975.

Bagdasarian, Nicholas der. *The Austro-German Rapprochement, 1870-1879: From the Battle of Sedan to the Dual Alliance*. Rutherford: Fairleigh Dickinson University Press, 1976.

Balfour, Michael. *The Kaiser and His Times*. Boston: Houghton Mifflin, 1964.

Barlow, Ima Christina. *The Agadir Crisis*. Durham: University of North Carolina Press, 1940.

Barclay, David E. *Frederick William IV and the Prussian Monarchy, 1840-1861*. Oxford: Oxford University Press, 1995.

_____. "The Soldiers of an Unsoldierly King: The Military Advisors of Frederick William IV, 1840-1858." *Geschichte als Aufgabe: Festschrift für Otto Büsch*. Edited by Wilhelm Treue. Berlin: Colloquium, 1988.

Barker, Elisabeth. *Churchill and Eden at War*. London: Macmillan, 1978.

Barnett, Correlli. *The Collapse of British Power*. London: Methuen, 1972.

Barraclough, Geoffrey. *From Agadir to Armageddon: Anatomy of a Crisis*. London: Weidenfeld and Nicolson, 1982.

Bartlett, C.J. *Defence and Diplomacy: Britain and the Great Powers, 1815-1914*. Manchester: Manchester University Press, 1993.

_____. *Peace, War and the European Powers, 1814-1914*. New York: St. Martin's Press, 1996.

_____. *The Global Conflict, 1880-1970: The International Rivalry of the Great Powers*. London: Longman, 1984.

Baumgart, Winfried. "Zur Aussenpolitik Friedrich Wilhelms IV, 1840-1858." *Jahrbuch für die Geschichte Mittel-und Ostdeutschlands* 39 (1987): 132-56.

Beckett, Ian F.W. *The Great War, 1914-1918*. London: Longman, 2001.

Bell, P. M. H. *A Certain Eventuality: Britain and the Fall of France*. Farnborough: Saxon House, 1974.

_____. *The Origins of the Second World War in Europe*. London: Longman Group, 1986.

Bennett, Edward W. *German Rearmament and the West, 1932-1933*. Princeton: Princeton University Press, 1979.

_____. *Germany and the Diplomacy of the Financial Crisis, 1931*. Cambridge, MA: Harvard University Press, 1962.

Berg, Manfred. *Gustav Stresemann und die Vereinigten Staaten von Amerika: Weltwirtschaftliche Verflechtung und Revisionspolitik, 1907-1929*. Baden-Baden: Nomos, 1990.

Berghahn, Volker R. *Die Tirpitz-Plan: Genesis und Verfall einer innenpolitischen Krisenstratagie unter Wilhelm II*. Düsseldorf: Droste Verlag, 1971.

_____. *Germany and the Approach of War in 1914*. London: Macmillan, 1973.

_____. *Sarajevo, 28. Juni 1914: Der Untergang des alten Europa*. Munich: Deutscher Taschenbuch, 1999.

_____ and Martin Kitchen, editors. *Germany in the Age of Total War*. London: Croom Helm, 1991.

Bessel, Richard. *Germany after the First World War*. Oxford: Clarendon Press, 1993.

Biewer, Ludwig. "The History of the German Foreign Office: An Overview." Berlin: Auswärtigen Amt, ca. 2005.

Billinger, Robert D., Jr. "The War Scare of 1831 and Prussian-South German Plans for the End of Austrian Dominance in Germany." *Central European History* 9 (1976): 203-19.

_____. "They Sing the Best Songs Badly: Metternich, Frederick William IV, and the German Confederation during the War Scare of 1840." In *Deutscher Bund und deutsche Frage, 1815-1866*. Edited by Helmut Rümpler. Munich: R. Oldenbourg, 1990.

Birnbaum, Karl E. *Peace Moves and U-Boat Warfare: A Study of Imperial Germany's Policy Towards the United States, April 18, 1916-January 9, 1917*. Hamden: Archon Books, 1970.

Bloch, Michael. *Ribbentrop*. New York: Crown, 1992.

Boemeke, Manfred F., Gerald D. Feldman, and Elisabeth Glaser, editors. *The Treaty of Versailles: A Reassessment after 75 Years*. Cambridge: Cambridge University Press, 1998.

Bolen, Claude C. *Kiderlen-Wächter and German Foreign Policy*. Durham: Duke University Press, 1940.

Bond, Brian. *British Military Policy between Two World Wars*. Oxford: Clarendon Press, 1980.

_____. *France and Belgium, 1939-1940*. Newark: University of Delaware Press, 1979.

Boog, Horst, Jürgen Förster, Joachim Hoffman, Ernst Klink, Rolf-Dieter Müller, and Gerd R. Ueberschär, editors. *The Attack on the Soviet Union*. Volume IV in *Germany and the Second World War*. Translated by Dean S. McMurry, Ewald Osers, and Louise Wilmott. Oxford: Oxford University Press, 2001.

_____, Werner Rahn, Reinhard Stumpf, and Bernd Wegner, editors. *The Global War*. Volume VI in *Germany and the Second World War*. Translated by Ewald Osers, John Brownjohn, Patricia Crampton, and Louise Willmot. Oxford: Oxford University Press, 2001.

Borries. Kurt. *Preussen im Krimkrieg (1853-1856)*. Stuttgart: W. Kolhammer, 1930.

Bosworth, Richard J.B. *Italy and the Approach of the First World War*. London: Macmillan, 1983.

_____. *Italy, The Least of the Great Powers: Italian Foreign Policy Before the First World War*. Cambridge: Cambridge University Press, 1979.

_____. *Mussolini*. London: Arnold, 2002.

Bourne, Kenneth. *The Foreign Policy of Victorian England, 1830-1902*. Oxford: Clarendon Press, 1970.

Boyce, Robert, editor. *French Foreign and Defence Policy, 1918-1940: The Decline and Fall of a Great Power*. London: Routledge, 1998.

Bridge, F.R. *From Sadowa to Sarajevo: The Foreign Policy of Austria-Hungary, 1866-1914*. London: Routledge and Kegan Paul, 1972.

_____. *Great Britain and Austria-Hungary, 1906-1914: A Diplomatic History*. London: Weidenfeld and Nicolson, 1972.

_____. *The Habsburg Monarchy among the Great Powers, 1815-1918.* New York: Berg, 1990.

_____ and Roger Bullen. *The Great Powers and the European States System, 1815-1914.* London: Longman, 1980.

_____ and Roger Bullen. *The Great Powers and the European States System, 1814-1914.* Second edition. London: Longman, 2005.

Brook-Shepherd, Gordon. *The Anschluss: The First Full Account of the Success that went to Hitler's Head—The 1938 Rape of Austria.* Philadelphia: Lippincott, 1963.

Brose, Eric Dorn. *The Kaiser's Army: The Politics of Military Technology during the Machine Age, 1897-1918.* Oxford: Oxford University Press, 2001.

Brown, Anthony Cave. *"C": The Secret Life of Sir Stewart Menzies, Spymaster to Winston Churchill.* New York: Macmillan, 1987.

Browning, Christopher R. "Unterstaatssekretär Martin Luther and the Ribbentrop Foreign Office." *Journal of Contemporary History* 12 (1977): 313-44.

Bucholz, Arden. *Moltke and the German Wars, 1864-1871.* London: Palgrave, 2001.

_____. *Moltke, Schlieffen, and Prussian War Planning.* New York: Berg, 1991.

Bullock, Alan. *Hitler: A Study in Tyranny.* London: Odhams Press, 1952.

_____. *Hitler and Stalin: Parallel Lives.* New York: Alfred A. Knopf, 1992.

Burgwyn, H. James. *Italian Foreign Policy in the Interwar Period, 1918-1940.* Westport, CT: Praeger, 1997.

Butler, J.R.M. *Lord Lothian, 1882-1940.* London: Macmillan, 1960.

Calvocoressi, Peter and Guy Wint. *Total War: Causes and Courses of the Second World War.* London: Allen Lane, 1972.

Canis, Konrad. *Bismarck und Waldersee: Die Aussenpolitischen Krisenerscheinungen und das Verhalten des Generalstabes 1882 bis 1890.* Berlin: Akademie-Verlag, 1980.

_____. *Bismarcks Aussenpolitik, 1870-1890: Aufstieg und Gefährdung.* Paderborn: Schöningh, 2004.

_____. *Von Bismarck zur Weltpolitik: Deutsche Aussenpolitik 1890 bis 1902*. Berlin: Akademie-Verlag, 1999.

Carr, E.H. *German-Soviet Relations, 1919-1939: Between the Two World Wars*. Baltimore: Johns Hopkins University Press, 1951.

Carr, William. *Arms, Autarky and Aggression: A Study in German Foreign Policy, 1933-1939*. London: Edward Arnold, 1972.

_____. *Hitler: A Study in Personality and Politics*. London: Edward Arnold, 1978.

_____. *Schleswig-Holstein, 1815-1848: A Study in National Conflict*. Manchester: Manchester University Press, 1963.

_____. *The Origins of the Wars of German Unification*. London: Longman, 1991.

Carroll, E. Malcolm. *Germany and the Great Powers, 1866-1914: A Study in Public Opinion and Foreign Policy*. Hamden, CT: Archon, 1966.

Carsten, F.L. *The Reichswehr and Politics, 1918 to 1933*. Oxford: Clarendon Press, 1966.

Cassels, Alan. *Mussolini's Early Diplomacy*. Princeton: Princeton University Press, 1970.

Cecil, Lamar. *Albert Ballin: Business and Politics in Imperial Germany, 1888-1914*. Princeton: Princeton University Press, 1967.

_____. "History as Family Chronicle: Kaiser Wilhelm II and the Dynastic Roots of the Anglo-German Antagonism." In *Kaiser Wilhelm II: New Interpretations*. Edited by Rohn C.G. Röhl and Nicolaus Sombart. Cambridge: Cambridge University Press, 1982.

_____. *The German Diplomatic Service, 1871-1914*. Princeton: Princeton University Press, 1976.

_____. *Wilhelm II*. 2 volumes. Chapel Hill: University of North Carolina Press, 1989-96.

Cecil, Robert. *Hitler's Decision to Invade Russia 1941*. New York: David McKay, 1975.

Chamberlain, Muriel E. *"Pax Britannica"? British Foreign Policy, 1789-1914*. London: Longman, 1988.

Charmley, John. *Chamberlain and the Lost Peace.* London: Hodder and Stoughton, 1989.

_____. *Churchill, the End of Glory: A Political Biography.* New York: Harcourt and Brace, 1993.

Chickering, Roger. *Imperial Germany and the Great War, 1914-1918.* Second edition. Cambridge: Cambridge University Press, 2004.

Cienciala, Anna M. *Poland and the Western Powers 1938-1939.* London: Routledge and Kegan Paul, 1968.

Citino, Robert M. *The Evolution of Blitzkrieg Tactics: Germany Defends Itself against Poland, 1918-1933.* New York: Greenwood Press, 1987.

Clark Chester Wells. "Bismarck, Russia, and the Origins of the War of 1870." *Journal of Modern History* 14 (1942).

_____. *Francis Joseph and Bismarck Before 1866: The Diplomacy of Austria Before the War of 1866.* Cambridge, MA: Harvard University Press, 1934.

Clark, Christopher. *Kaiser Wilhelm.* London: Longman, 2000.

Clarke, J. Calvitt. *Russia and Italy Against Hitler: The Bolshevik-Fascist Rapprochement of the 1930s.* New York: Greenwood Press, 1991.

Clingan, C. Edmund. *Finance from Kaiser to Führer: Budget Politics in Germany, 1912-1934.* Westport, CT: Greenwood Press, 2001.

Cockett, Richard. *Twilight of Truth: Chamberlain, Appeasement and the Manipulation of the Press.* New York: St. Martin's Press, 1989.

Colvin, Ian. *None So Blind: A British Diplomatic View of the Origin of World War II.* New York: Harcourt, Brace, and World, 1965.

_____. *The Chamberlain Cabinet.* New York: Taplinger, 1971.

Conot, Robert E. *Justice at Nuremberg.* New York: Harper and Row, 1983.

Cornebise, Alfred E. *The Weimar Crisis: Cuno's Germany and the Ruhr Occupation.* Washington, D.C.: University Press of America, 1977.

Coverdale, John F. *Italian Intervention in the Spanish Civil War.* Princeton: Princeton University Press, 1975.

Cowie, R.B. "Nevile Henderson and the Chamberlain Government: A Case Study in Democratic Foreign Policy, 1937-1939." Ph.D. diss., Bowling Green State University, 1970.

Cowling, Maurice. *The Impact of Hitler: British Politics and British Policy, 1933-1940*. Chicago: University of Chicago Press, 1975.

Craig, Andrew W. "The Limits of Success: Joachim von Ribbentrop and German Relations with Great Britain, 1934-1939." Ph.D. diss., Bowling Green State University, 1982.

Craig, Gordon. "Bismarck and his Ambassadors: The Problem of Discipline." Chapter in *War, Politics, and Diplomacy, Selected Essays*. London: Weidenfeld and Nicolson, 1966.

_____. "Diplomats and Diplomacy during the Second World War." In *The Diplomats, 1939-1979*. Edited by G.A. Craig and Francis L. Loewenheim. Princeton: Princeton University Press, 1994.

_____. *From Bismarck to Adenauer: Aspects of German Statecraft*. Baltimore: Johns Hopkins Press, 1958.

_____. *Germany 1866-1945*. New York: Oxford University Press, 1978.

_____. "The German Foreign Office from Neurath to Ribbentrop." In *The Diplomats 1919-1939*. Edited by Gordon A. Craig and Felix Gilbert. Princeton: Princeton University Press, 1953.

_____. *The Politics of the Prussian Army, 1640-1945*. Oxford: Oxford University Press, 1966.

_____. "The Professional Diplomat and His Problems, 1919-39." In *War, Politics, and Diplomacy, Selected Essays*. London: Weidenfeld and Nicolson, 1966.

_____. "The Revolution in War and Diplomacy, 1914-1939." In *War, Politics, and Diplomacy, Selected Essays*. London: Weidenfeld and Nicolson, 1966.

_____. "The World War I Alliance of the Central Powers in Retrospect: The Military Cohesion of the Alliance." *The Journal of Modern History* 37 (1966): 336-44.

_____. "Totalitarian Approaches to Diplomatic Negotiation." In *War, Politics, and Diplomacy, Selected Essays*. London: Weidenfeld and Nicolson, 1966.

_____. *War, Politics, and Diplomacy: Selected Essays*. London: Weidenfeld and Nicolson, 1966.

_____ and Alexander L. George. *Force and Statecraft: Diplomatic Problems of Our Time*. Oxford: Oxford University Press, 1983.

_____ and Felix Gilbert. *The Diplomats 1919-1938*. Princeton: Princeton University Press, 1953.

Crampton, R.J. "The Decline of the Concert of Europe in the Balkans, 1913-1914." *Slavonic and East European Review* 52 (1974): 393-419.

_____. *The Hollow Detente: Anglo-German Relations in the Balkans, 1911-1914*. Atlantic Highlands: Humanities Press, 1980.

Crankshaw, Edward. *Bismarck*. New York: Viking Press, 1981.

Creveld, Martin van. *Hitler's Strategy 1940-1941: The Balkan Clue*. Cambridge: Cambridge University Press, 1973.

Dallek, Robert. *Franklin D. Roosevelt and American Foreign Policy, 1932-1945*. New York: Oxford University Press, 1979.

Davidson, Eugene. *The Trial of the Germans: An Account of the Twenty-Two Defendants Before the International Military Tribunal at Nuremberg*. New York: Collier, 1966.

Davies, Norman. *White Eagle, Red Star: The Polish-Soviet War, 1919-1920*. New York: St. Martin's Press, 1972.

Deakin, Frederick W. *The Brutal Friendship: Mussolini, Hitler, and the Fall of Italian Fascism*. New York: Harper and Row, 1962.

Debo, Richard K. *Revolution and Survival: The Foreign Policy of Soviet Russia, 1917-1918*. Toronto: University of Toronto Press, 1979.

_____. *Survival and Consolidation: The Foreign Policy of Soviet Russia, 1918-1921*. Montreal: McGill-Queen's University Press, 1992.

Dedijer, Vladimir. *The Road to Sarajevo*. New York: Simon and Schuster, 1966.

Deist, Wilhelm. "Kaiser Wilhelm II in the Context of His Military and Naval Entourage." In *Kaiser Wilhelm II: New Interpretations*. Edited by Rohn C.G. Röhl and Nicolaus Sombart. Cambridge: Cambridge University Press, 1982.

_____. "The Rearmament of the Wehrmacht." In *The Buildup of German Aggression*. Volume I in *Germany and the Second World War*. Edited by W. Deist, M. Messerschmidt, H.-E. Volkmann, and W. Wette. Translated by

P.S. Falla, Dean S. McMurry, and Ewald Osers. Oxford: Clarendon Press, 1990.

_____. "The Road to Ideological War: Germany, 1918-1945." In *The Making of Strategy: Rulers, States, and War*. Edited by Williamson Murray, Macgregor Knox, and Alvin Berstein. Cambridge: Cambridge University Press, 1994.

_____. *The Wehrmacht and German Rearmament*. Toronto: University of Toronto Press, 1982.

_____. Manfred Messerschmidt, Hans-Erich Volkmann, and Wolfram Wette, editors. *The Buildup of German Aggression*. Volume I in *Germany and the Second World War*. Translated by P.S. Falla, Dean S. McMurry, and Ewald Osers. Oxford: Clarendon Press, 1990.

Deutsch, Harold C. *Hitler and His Generals: The Hidden Crisis, January-June 1938*. Minneapolis: University of Minnesota Press, 1974.

_____. *The Conspiracy against Hitler in the Twilight War*. Minneapolis: University of Minnesota Press, 1968.

Dockhorn, Robert. "The Wilhelmstrasse and the Search for a New Diplomatic Order, 1926-1930." Ph.D. Dissertation, University of Wisconsin, 1972.

Dockrill, Michael L. *Diplomacy and World War: Studies in British Foreign Policy, 1890-1951*. Cambridge: Cambridge University Press, 2002.

_____ and J. Douglas Goold. *Peace without Promise: Britain and the Peace Conferences, 1919-1923*. London: Batsford, 1981.

_____ and John Fisher. *The Paris Peace Conference 1919: Peace Without Victory?* Basingstoke: Palgrave, 2001.

Dorn, Walter L. "The Prussian Bureaucracy in the Eighteenth Century." *Political Science Quarterly* 46/47 (1931): 402-43, 75-94, 259-73.

Dorwart, Reinhold August. *The Administrative Reforms of Frederick William I of Prussia*. Cambridge, MA: Harvard University Press, 1953.

Döscher, Hans-Jürgen, *Das Auswärtiges Amt im Dretten Reich: Diplomatie im Schatten der Endlösung*. Berlin: Siedler, 1986.

Doss, Kurt. "The History of the German Foreign Office." Chapter in *The Times Survey of Foreign Ministries of the World*. Edited by Zara Steiner. London: Times, 1982.

Doughty, Robert A. "The Illusion of Security, France, 1919-1940." In *The Making of Strategy: Rulers, States, and War*. Edited by Williamson Murray, Macgregor Knox, and Alvin Berstein. Cambridge: Cambridge University Press, 1994.

Douglas, Roy. *The Advent of War 1939-40*. London: Macmillan, 1978.

Duffy, Christopher. *Frederick the Great: A Military Life*. London: Routledge and Kegan Paul, 1985.

_____. *The Army of Frederick the Great*. Newton Abbot: David and Charles, 1974.

Dupuy, Trevor N. *A Genius for War: The German Army and General Staff, 1807-1945*. Fairfax, VA: Hero, 1984.

Dwyer, Philip G., editor. *Modern Prussian History, 1830-1947*. London: Longman, 2001.

_____. "Prussia and the Armed Neutrality: The Invasion of Hanover in 1801." *The International History Review* 15 (1993): 661-87.

_____. "Prussia and the Second Armed Neutrality, 1799-1801." Ph.D. diss., University of Western Australia at Perth, 1992.

_____. *The Impact of Napoleon: Prussian High Politics, Foreign Policy and the Crisis of the Executive, 1797-1806*. Cambridge: Cambridge University Press, 1997.

_____. "The Politics of Prussian Neutrality, 1795-1806." *German History* 12 (1994): 351-74.

_____, editor. *The Rise of Prussia, 1700-1830*. London: Longman, 2000.

_____. "The Two Faces of Prussian Foreign Policy: Karl August von Hardenberg as Minister for Foreign Affairs, 1804-1815." In *"Freier Gebrauch der Krafte": Eine Bestandsaufnahme der Hardenberg-Forschung*. Edited by Thomas Stamm-Kuhlmann. Munich: Oldenbourg Verlag, 2001.

_____. "Two Definitions of Neutrality: Prussia, the European States-System and the French Invasion of Hanover in 1803." *International History Review* 19 (August 1997): 522-40.

Dyck, Harvey Leonard. "German-Soviet Relations and the Anglo-Soviet Break, 1927." *Slavic Review* 25 (1966): 67-83.

_____. *Weimar Germany and Soviet Russia 1926-1933: A Study in Diplomatic Instability*. New York: Columbia University Press, 1966.

Echard, William E. *Napoleon III and the Concert of Europe*. Baton Rouge: Louisiana State University Press, 1983.

Emmerson, James T. *The Rhineland Crisis 7 March 1936: A Study in Multilateral Diplomacy*. London: Maurice Temple Smith, 1977.

Ergang, Robert. *The Potsdam Führer: Frederick William I, Father of Prussian Militarism*. New York: Columbia University Press, 1941.

Evans, R.J.W. and Hartmut Pogge von Strandmann, editors. *The Coming of the First World War*. Second edition. Oxford: Clarendon Press, 1990.

Eyck, Erich. *A History of the Weimar Republic*. 2 volumes. Translated by Harlon P. Hanson and Robert G.L. Waite. Cambridge, MA: Harvard University Press, 1962-63.

_____. *Bismarck and the German Empire*. London: George Allen and Unwin, 1950.

Eyck, Frank. *The Frankfurt Parliament, 1848-1849*. New York: St. Martin's Press, 1968.

Falls, Cyril. *The Great War*. New York: G.P. Putnam's Sons, 1959.

Farrar, Lancelot L., Jr. *Arrogance and Anxiety: The Ambivalence of German Power, 1848-1914*. Iowa City: University of Iowa Press, 1981.

_____. *Divide and Conquer: German Efforts to Conclude a Separate Peace, 1914-1918*. Boulder, CO: East European Quarterly, 1978.

_____. "Impotence of Omnipotence: The Paralysis of the European Great Power System, 1871-1914." *International Review of History and Political Science* (February 1972): 13-44.

_____. "Opening to the West: German Efforts to Conclude a Separate Peace with England, July 1917-March 1918." *Canadian Journal of History* 10 (April 1975): 73-90.

_____. "Peace Through Exhaustion: German Diplomatic Motivations for the Verdun Campaign." *Revue internationale d'histoire militaire* 32 (1972-75): 477-94.

_____. "The Limits of Choice: July 1914 Reconsidered." *Journal of Conflict Resolution* (March 1972): 1-23.

_____. *The Short-War Illusion: German Policy, Strategy and Domestic Affairs, August to December 1914.* Foreword by James Joll. Santa Barbara: ABC Clio, 1973.

_____. "The Short-War Illusion: The Dilemma of German Military Strategy, August-December, 1914." *Militärgeschichtliche Mitteilungen Der Monat* (October 1972): 39-52.

Feiling, Keith. *The Life of Neville Chamberlain.* London: Lowe and Brydone; reprint, Hamden, Connecticut: Archon, 1970.

Felix, David. *Walther Rathenau and the Weimar Republic: The Politics of Reparations.* Baltimore: Johns Hopkins Press, 1971.

Ferguson, Niall. "Germany and the Origins of the First World War: New Perspectives." *Historical Journal* 35 (1992): 725-52.

_____. *The Pity of War.* New York: Basic Books, 1998.

Ferris, John Robert. *Men, Money, and Diplomacy: The Evolution of British Strategic Foreign Policy, 1919-1926.* Ithaca: Cornell University Press, 1989.

Fesser, Gerd. *Der Traum vom Platz an der Sonne: Deutsche "Weltpolitik" 1897-1914.* Bremen: Donat, 1996.

_____. *Reichskanzler Bernhard Fürst von Bülow: Eine Biographie.* Berlin: Deutscher Verlag der Wissenschaften, 1991.

Fest, Joachim C. *Hitler.* Translated by Richard and Clara Winston. London: Weidenfeld and Nicolson, 1973.

_____. *The Face of the Third Reich: Portraits of Nazi Leadership.* Translated by Michael Bullock. New York: Pantheon, 1970.

Feuchtwanger, Edgar J. *Bismarck.* London: Routledge, 2002.

_____. *From Weimar to Hitler: Germany, 1918-1933.* Second edition. New York: St. Martin's Press, 1993.

Fiddick, Thomas C. *Russia's Retreat from Poland, 1920: From Permanent Revolution to Peaceful Coexistence.* New York: St. Martin's Press, 1990.

Fink, Carole. "European Politics and Security at the Genoa Conference of 1922." In *German Nationalism and the European Response, 1890-1945.* Edited by Carole Fink, Isabel V. Hull, and Macgregor Knox. Norman: University of Oklahoma Press, 1985.

_____*The Genoa Conference: European Diplomacy, 1921-1922*. Chapel Hill: University of North Carolina Press, 1984.

_____, Axel Frohn, and Jurgen Heideking, editors. *Genoa, Rapallo, and European Reconstruction in 1922*. Cambridge: Cambridge University Press, 1991.

Fischer, Fritz. *Germany's Aims in the First World War*. Introductions by Hajo Holborn and James Joll. New York: W.W. Norton, 1967.

_____. "Kaiser Wilhelm und die Gestaltung der deutschen Politik von 1914." In *Der Ort Kaiser Wilhelm II in der deutschen Geschichte*. Edited by J.C.G. Röhl. Munich: Oldenbourg, 1991.

_____. "The Foreign Policy of Imperial Germany and the Outbreak of the First World War." In *Escape into War?: The Foreign Policy of Imperial Germany*. Edited by Gregor Schöllgen. Oxford: Berg, 1990.

_____. *War of Illusions: German Policies from 1911 to 1914*. Translated by Marian Jackson. Foreword by Alan Bullock. London: Chatto and Windus, 1975.

Foley, Robert T. *German Strategy and the Path to Verdun: Erich von Falkenhayn and the Development of Attrition, 1870-1916*. Cambridge: Cambridge University Press, 2004.

Ford, Guy Stanton. *Hanover and Prussia, 1796-1803: A Study in Neutrality*. New York: AMS Press, 1967.

Ford, Franklin L. "The Voice in the Wilderness: Robert Coulondre." Chapter in *The Diplomats 1919-1939*. Edited by Gordon A. Craig and Felix Gilbert. Princeton: Princeton University Press, 1953.

_____. "Three Observers in Berlin: Rumbold, Dodd, and François-Poncet." Chapter in *The Diplomats 1919-1939*. Edited by Gordon A. Craig and Felix Gilbert. Princeton: Princeton University Press, 1953.

Forsbach, Ralf. *Alfred von Kiderlen-Wächter (1852-1912): Ein Diplomatenleben im Kaiserreich*. 2 volumes. Göttingen: Vandenhoeck and Ruprecht, 1997.

Förster, Jürgen and Evan Mawdsley. "Hitler and Stalin in Perspective: Secret Speeches on the Eve of Barbarossa." *War in History* 11 (January 2004): 61-103.

Förster, S., W.J. Mommsen, and R. Robinson, editors. *Bismarck, Europe and Africa: The Berlin Conference of 1884-1885 and the Onset of Partition.* Oxford: Oxford University Press, 1989.

Fox, John P. "Alfred Rosenberg in London." *Contemporary Review* 213 (July 1968): 6-11.

_____. *Germany and the Far Eastern Crisis 1931-1938: A Study in Diplomacy and Ideology.* Oxford: Oxford University Press, 1982.

Frank, Elke. "The Wilhelmstrasse during the Third Reich: Changes in Its Organizational Structure and Personnel Policies." Ph.D. diss., Harvard University, 1963.

French, David. *British Strategy and War Aims, 1914-1916.* London: George Allen and Unwin, 1986.

Freund, Gerald. *Unholy Alliance: Russian-German Relations from the Treaty of Brest-Litovsk to the Treaty of Berlin.* New York: Harcourt, Brace, and Company, 1957.

Frey, Linda S. and Marsha L. Frey. *Frederick I: The Man and His Times.* Boulder: East European Monographs, 1984.

_____. *The History of Diplomatic Immunity.* Columbus: Ohio State University Press, 1999.

Friedjung, Heinrich. *The Struggle for Supremacy in Germany, 1859-1866.* Translated by A.J.P. Taylor and W.L. McElwee. London: Macmillan, 1935.

Friese, Christian. *Russland und Preussen von Krimkrieg bix zum polnischen Aufstand.* Berlin: Ost-Europa Verlag, 1931.

Fuller, Joseph Vincent. *Bismarck's Diplomacy at Its Zenith.* Cambridge: Harvard University Press, 1922.

Fuller, William C., Jr. *Civil-Military Relations in Imperial Russia, 1881-1914.* Princeton: Princeton University Press, 1985.

Gall, Lothar. *Bismarck: The White Revolutionary.* 2 volumes. Translated by J.A. Underwood. London: George Allen and Unwin, 1986.

Gasiorowski, Zygmunt J. "Stresemann and Poland after Locarno." *Journal of Central European History* 18 (1958): 292-317.

_____. "Stresemann and Poland before Locarno." *Journal of Central European History* 18 (1958): 25-47.

_____. "The German-Polish Nonaggression Pact of 1934." *Journal of Central European Affairs* 15 (April 1955): 3-29.

_____. "The Russian Overture to Germany of December 1924." *The Journal of Modern History* 30 (1958): 99-117.

Gates, Eleanor M. *End of an Affair: The Collapse of the Anglo-French Alliance 1939-40.* London: George Allen and Unwin, 1981.

Gatzke, Hans, editor. *European Diplomacy Between Two Wars, 1919-1939.* Chicago: Quadrangle, 1972.

_____. *Germany's Drive to the West: A Study of Germany's War Aims during the First World War.* Baltimore: Johns Hopkins University Press, 1950.

_____. "Russo-German Military Collaboration during the Weimar Republic." *American Historical Review* 63 (1958): 565-97.

_____. *Stresemann and the Rearmament of Germany.* Baltimore: Johns Hopkins Press, 1954.

Gehl, Jürgen. *Austria, Germany, and the Anschluss 1931-1938.* London: Oxford University Press, 1963.

Geiss, Imanuel. *Das Deutsche Reich und die Vorgeschichte des Ersten Weltkriegs.* Munich: Hanser, 1983.

_____. *Der lange Weg in die Katastrophe: Die Vorgeschichte des Ersten Weltkrieges, 1815-1914.* Munich: Piper, 1991.

_____. *German Foreign Policy 1971-1914.* London: Routledge and Kegan Paul, 1976.

_____. "The German Version of Imperialism, 1898-1914: Weltpolitik." In *Escape into War?: The Foreign Policy of Imperial Germany.* Edited by Gregor Schöllgen. Oxford: Berg, 1990.

_____. "The Outbreak of the First World War and German War Aims." *Journal of Contemporary History* 1 (July 1966): 75-91.

Gilbert, Felix. "Ciano and His Ambassadors." In *The Diplomats 1919-1939.* Edited by Gordon A. Craig and Felix Gilbert. Princeton: Princeton University Press, 1953.

_____. "Two British Ambassadors: Perth and Henderson." In *The Diplomats 1919-1939.* Edited by Gordon A. Craig and Felix Gilbert. Princeton: Princeton University Press, 1953.

Gilbert, G.M. *The Psychology of Dictatorship*. New York: Ronald, 1950.

Gilbert, Martin. *Churchill, A Life*. New York: Henry Holt and Company, 1991.

_____. *The First World War: A Complete History*. New York: Henry Holt, 1994.

_____ and Richard Gott. *The Appeasers*. Boston: Houghton Mifflin, 1963.

Goda, Norman J.W. "A.J.P. Taylor, Adolf Hitler, and the Origins of the Second World War." *The International History Review* 23 (March 2001): 97-124.

Goerlitz, Walter. *History of the German General Staff, 1657-1945*. New York: Praeger, 1953.

Goldstein, Erik. *The First World War Peace Settlements, 1919-1925*. London: Longman, 2002.

_____. *Winning the Peace: British Diplomatic Strategy, Peace Planning, and the Paris Peace Conference, 1916-1920*. Oxford: Clarendon Press, 1991.

Gooch, George Peabody. *Before the War: Studies in Diplomacy*. 2 volumes. New York: Russell and Russell, 1938.

_____. "Kiderlen-Wächter." *Cambridge Historical Journal* 5 (1936): 178-92.

Gooch, John. *The Plans of War: The General Staff and British Military Strategy, c. 1900-1916*. London: Routledge and Kegan Paul, 1974.

_____. "The Weary Titan: Strategy and Policy in Great Britain, 1890-1918." In *The Making of Strategy: Rulers, States, and War*. Edited by Williamson Murray, Macgregor Knox, and Alvin Berstein. Cambridge: Cambridge University Press, 1994.

Gordon, Harold J. *The Reichswehr and the German Republic, 1919-1926*. Princeton: Princeton University Press, 1957.

Gottlieb, W.W. *Studies in Secret Diplomacy during the First World War*. London: George Allen and Unwin, 1957.

Grathwol, Robert P. *Stresemann and the DNVP: Reconciliation or Revenge in German Foreign Policy 1924-1928*. Lawrence: Regents Press of Kansas, 1980.

Grenville, J.A.S. *Europe Reshaped, 1848-1878*. New York: Cornell University Press, 1980.

_____. "Imperial Germany and Britain: From Cooperation to War." In *Das gestörte Gleichgewicht: Deutschland als Problem britischer Sicherheit im 19. und 20. Jahrhundert.* Edited by Adolf M. Birke and Marie-Luise Recke. Munich: Saur, 1990.

_____. *Lord Salisbury and Foreign Policy: The Close of the Nineteenth Century.* London: Athlone Press, 1964.

Grupp, Peter. *Deutsche Aussenpolitik im Schatten von Versailles, 1918-1920.* Paderborn: Schöningh, 1988.

Guinn, Paul. *British Strategy and Politics 1914 to 1918.* Oxford: Clarendon Press, 1965.

Gunsburg, Jeffrey A. *Divided and Conquered: The French High Command and the Defeat of the West, 1940.* Westport: Greenwood Press, 1979.

Gutsche, W. *Aufstieg und Fall eines kaiserlichen Reichkanzlers: Theobald von Bethmann Hollweg, 1856-1921.* Berlin: Akademie-Verlag, 1973.

Haigh, Robert H. *The Rise and Rise of the Third Reich: Nazi Foreign Policy, 1933-1939.* Sheffield: Sheffield Hallam University Press, 2001.

_____, David S. Morris, and A.R. Peters. *German-Soviet Relations in the Weimar Era: Friendship from Necessity.* Totowa, NJ: Barnes and Noble, 1985.

_____. *Soviet Foreign Policy, the League of Nations and Europe, 1919-1939.* Aldershot: Gower, 1986.

_____. *The Years of Triumph? German Diplomatic and Military Policy, 1933-1941.* Totowa, NJ: Barnes and Noble, 1986.

Hale, Oron James. *Germany and the Diplomatic Revolution: A Study in the Diplomacy of the Press, 1904-1906.* London: Oxford University Press, 1931.

Hall, Richard C. *The Balkan Wars, 1912-1913: Prelude to the First World War.* London: Routledge, 2000.

Haller, Johannes. *Philip Eulenburg: The Kaiser's Friend.* 2 volumes. Translated by Ethel Colburn Mayne. New York: Alfred A. Knopf, 1930.

Halperin, S. William. "Bismarck and the Italian Envoy in Berlin on the Eve of the Franco-Prussian War." *Journal of Modern History* 33 (1961).

_____. "The Origins of the Franco-Prussian War Revisited: Bismarck and the Hohenzollern Candidature," *The Journal of Modern History* 45 (1973): 83-91.

_____. "Visconti-Venosta and the Diplomatic Crisis of July 1870." *Journal of Modern History* 31 (1959): 295-309.

Hamilton, Richard F. and Holger H. Herwig. *Decisions for War, 1914-1917.* Cambridge: Cambridge University Press, 2004.

_____, editors. *The Origins of World War I.* Cambridge: Cambridge University Press, 2003.

Haslam, Jonathan. *Soviet Foreign Policy, 1930-1933: The Impact of the Depression.* Basingstoke: Macmillan, 1983.

_____. *The Soviet Union and the Struggle for Collective Security in Europe, 1933-1939.* Basingstoke: Macmillan, 1984.

Haupts, Leo. *Graf Brockdorff-Rantzau: Diplomat und Minister im Kaiserreich und der Republik.* Göttingen: Muster-Schmidt, 1984.

Hayne, M.B. *The French Foreign Office and the Origins of the First World War, 1898-1914.* Oxford: Clarendon Press, 1993.

Heineman, John L. "Constantin Freiherr von Neurath as Foreign Minister, 1932-1935: A Study of a Conservative Civil Servant and Germany's Foreign Policy." Ph.D. thesis, Cornell University, 1965.

_____. "Constantin von Neurath and German Policy at the London Economic Conference of 1933: Background to the Resignation of Alfred Hugenberg." *The Journal of Modern History,* 41 (June 1969): 160-88.

_____. *Hitler's First Foreign Minister: Constantin Freiherr von Neurath, Diplomat and Statesman.* Berkeley: University of California Press, 1979.

Helbrich, Wolfgang J. "Between Stresemann and Hitler: The Foreign Policy of the Brüning Government." *World Politics* 12 (October, 1959): 24-44.

Helmreich, Ernst Christian. *The Diplomacy of the Balkan Wars, 1912-1913.* Cambridge, MA: Harvard University Press, 1938.

Henig, Ruth, editor. *The League of Nations.* New York: Barnes and Noble, 1975.

_____. *The Origins of the First World War.* Second edition. London: Routledge, 1993.

_____. *The Origins of the Second World War, 1933-1939*. London: Methuen, 1985.

_____. *The Weimar Republic, 1919-1933*. London: Routledge, 1998.

_____. *Versailles and After, 1919-1933*. Second edition. London: Routledge, 1995.

Herman, J. "The Paris Embassy of Sir Eric Phipps, 1937-1939." Ph.D. thesis, London School of Economics and Political Science, 1996.

Herrmann, David G. *The Arming of Europe and the Making of the First World War*. Princeton: Princeton University Press, 1996.

Herwig, Holger H. "Germany and the 'Short-War' Illusion: Toward a New Interpretation?" *The Journal of Military History* 66 (July 2002): 681-94.

_____. *"Luxury" Fleet: The Imperial German Navy, 1888-1918*. London: Ashfield Press, 1980.

_____. "Strategic Uncertainties of a Nation-State: Prussia-Germany, 1871-1918." In *The Making of Strategy: Rulers, States, and War*. Edited by Williamson Murray, Macgregor Knox, and Alvin Berstein. Cambridge: Cambridge University Press, 1994.

_____. *The First World War: Germany and Austria-Hungary, 1914-1918*. London: Arnold, 1997.

_____. *The Outbreak of World War I: Causes and Responsibilities*. Sixth edition. Boston: Houghton Mifflin, 1997.

Hewitson, Mark. "German and France before the First World War: A Reassessment of Wilhelmine Foreign Policy." *English Historical Review* 115 (2000).

_____. *Germany and the Causes of the First World War*. New York: Berg, 2004.

Hiden, John. *Germany and Europe 1919-1939*. London: Longman Group, 1977.

_____ and T. Lane, editors. *The Baltic and the Outbreak of the Second World War*. Cambridge: Cambridge University Press, 1992.

Hildebrand, Klaus. "Between Alliance and Antagonism: The Problem of Bilateral Normality in British-German Relations in the Nineteenth Century (1870-1914)." In *German Foreign Policy from Bismarck to Adenauer: The Limits of Statecraft*. Translated by Louise Willmot. London: Unwin Hyman, 1989.

_____. *Das vergangene Reich: Deutsche Aussenpolitik von Bismarck bis Hitler, 1871-1945*. Stuttgart: Deutches Verlags-Anstalt, 1995.

_____, *Deutsche Aussenpolitik, 1871-1918*. Munich: Oldenbourg, 1989.

_____. *German Foreign Policy from Bismarck to Adenauer: The Limits of Statecraft*. Translated by Louise Willmot. London: Unwin Hyman, 1989.

_____. "Hitler's Policy towards France until 1936." Chapter in *German Foreign Policy from Bismarck to Adenauer: The Limits of Statecraft*. Translated by Louise Willmot. London: Unwin Hyman, 1989.

_____. "Lord Clarendon, Bismarck and the Problem of European Disarmament, 1870: Possibilities and Limitations in British-Prussian Relations on the Eve of the Franco-Prussian War." In *German Foreign Policy from Bismarck to Adenauer: The Limits of Statecraft*. Translated by Louise Willmot. London: Unwin Hyman, 1989.

_____. "Opportunities and Limits of German Foreign Policy in the Bismarckian Era, 1871-1890: 'A System of Stopgaps'?" In *Escape into War?: The Foreign Policy of Imperial Germany*. Edited by Gregor Schöllgen. Oxford: Berg, 1990.

_____. "The Crisis of July 1914: The European Security Dilemma: Observations on the Outbreak of the First World War." In *German Foreign Policy from Bismarck to Adenauer: The Limits of Statecraft*. Translated by Louise Willmot. London: Unwin Hyman, 1989.

_____. *The Foreign Policy of the Third Reich*. Translated by Anthony Fothergill. Berkeley: University of California Press, 1973.

_____. *The Third Reich*. Translated by P.S. Falla. London: George Allen and Unwin, 1984.

Hill, Leonidas E. "The Wilhelmstrasse in the Nazi Era." *Political Science Quarterly* 82 (December 1967).

_____. "Three Crises, 1938-39." *Journal of Contemporary History* 3 (January 1969): 113-44.

Hillgruber, Andreas. *Bismarcks Aussenpolitik*. Freiburg: Rombach, 1972.

_____. *Germany and the Two World Wars*. Translated by William C. Kirby. Cambridge, MA: Harvard University Press, 1981.

_____. "Hitler's Strategy and Politics in the Second World War." Chapter in *Politics and Strategy in the Second World War*. Manhattan: Kansas State University, 1976.

_____. "The Historical Significance of the First World War: A Seminal Catastrophe." In *Escape into War?: The Foreign Policy of Imperial Germany*. Edited by Gregor Schöllgen. Oxford: Berg, 1990.

Himmer, Robert. "Rathenau, Russia, and Rapallo." *Central European History* 9 (1976): 146-83.

Hinsley, F.H., editor. *British Foreign Policy under Sir Edward Grey*. Cambridge: Cambridge University Press, 1977.

Hochman, Jiri. *The Soviet Union and the Failure of Collective Security, 1934-1938*. Ithaca: Cornell University Press, 1984.

Holborn, Hajo. *A History of Modern Germany*. 3 volumes. New York: Alfred A. Knopf, 1959-69.

_____. "Diplomats and Diplomacy in the Early Weimar Republic." Chapter in *The Diplomats 1919-1939*. Edited by Gordon A. Craig and Felix Gilbert. Princeton: Princeton University Press, 1953.

Holmes, Richard. *The Road to Sedan: The French Army, 1866-1870*. London: Royal Historical Society, 1984.

Horn, D.B. *Frederick the Great and the Rise of Prussia*. London: English Universities Press, 1964.

Howard, Christopher. *Splendid Isolation*. London: Macmillan, 1967.

Howard, Michael. *The Continental Commitment: The Dilemma of British Defence Policy in the Era of the Two World Wars*. London: Temple Smith, 1972.

_____. *The Franco-Prussian War: The German Invasion of France, 1870-1871*. London: Rupert Hart-Davis, 1961.

Hubatsch, Walther. *Frederick the Great: Absolutism and Administration*. London: Thames and Hudson, 1973.

Hughes, Judith M. *To the Maginot Line: The Politics of French Military Preparation in the 1920's*. Cambridge, MA: Harvard University Press, 1971.

Hunt, Barry and Adrian Preston, editors. *War Aims and Strategic Policy in the Great War, 1914-1918*. London: Croom Helm, 1977.

Irving, David. *Göring: A Biography*. New York: William Morrow, 1989.

_____. *The War Path: Hitler's Germany 1933-1939*. New York: Viking, 1978.

Jäckel, Eberhard. *Hitler in History*. Hanover: University of New England Press, 1984.

_____. *Hitler's Weltanschauung: A Blueprint for Power*. Translated by Herbert Arnold. Middletown: Wesleyan University Press, 1972.

Jacobsen, Hans-Adolf. *Nationalsozialistische Aussenpolitik 1933-1938*. Frankfurt am Main: Alfred Metzner, 1968.

Jacobson, Jon. *Locarno Diplomacy: Germany and the West 1925-1929*. Princeton: Princeton University Press, 1972.

_____. *When the Soviet Union Entered World Politics*. Berkeley: University of California Press, 1994.

Jaffe, Lorna S. *The Decision to Disarm Germany: British Policy towards Post-War German Disarmament, 1914-1919*. Boston: Allen and Unwin, 1985.

Jakobson, Max. *The Diplomacy of the Winter War: An Account of the Russo-Finnish War, 1939-1940*. Cambridge, MA: Harvard University Press, 1961.

Jarausch, Konrad H. *The Enigmatic Chancellor: Bethmann Hollweg and the Hubris of Imperial Germany*. New Haven: Yale University Press, 1973.

_____. "The Illusion of Limited War: Chancellor Bethmann Hollweg's Calculated Risk, July 1914." *Central European History* 2 (March 1969): 48-76.

Jelavich, Barbara. *The Habsburg Empire in European Affairs, 1814-1918*. Hamden, CT: Archon, 1975.

_____. *St. Petersburg and Moscow: Tsarist and Soviet Foreign Policy, 1814-1974*. Bloomington: Indiana University Press, 1974.

Johnson, Hubert C. *Frederick the Great and His Officials*. New Haven: Yale University Press, 1975.

Joll, James. *The Origins of the First World War*. London: Longman, 1984.

Jones, Raymond A. *The British Diplomatic Service, 1815-1914*. Gerrards Cross: Colin Smythe, 1983.

_____. *The Nineteenth-Century Foreign Office: An Administrative History*. London: Weidenfeld and Nicolson, 1971.

Kaiser, David E. *Economic Diplomacy and the Origins of the Second World War: Germany, Britain, France, and Eastern Europe, 1930-1939.* Princeton: Princeton University Press, 1980.

_____. "Germany and the Origins of the First World War." *The Journal of Modern History* 55 (1983): 442-74.

Keegan, John. *The First World War.* New York: Alfred A. Knopf, 1999.

Keeton, Edward D. *Briand's Locarno Policy: French Economics, Politics, and Diplomacy, 1925-1929.* New York: Garland, 1987.

Keiger, John F. *France and the Origins of the First World War.* London: Macmillan, 1983.

Kelly, T.L. "Appeasement: The Ploy that Failed: Henderson, Chamberlain, the Foreign Office and Anglo-German Relations, 1937-1939." Ph.D. diss., University of Alabama, 1979.

Kennan, George F. *Russia and the West under Lenin and Stalin.* Boston: Little, Brown and Company, 1960.

_____. *The Decline of Bismarck's European Order: Franco-Russian Relations, 1875-1990.* Princeton: Princeton University Press, 1979.

_____. *The Fateful Alliance: France, Russia, and the Coming of the First World War.* New York: Pantheon, 1984.

Kennedy, Greg. "Becoming Dependent on the Kindness of Strangers: Britain's Strategic Foreign Policy, Naval Arms Limitation and the Soviet Factor, 1935-1937." *War in History* 11 (January 2004): 34-60.

Kennedy, Paul M. "German World Policy and the Alliance Negotiations with England, 1897-1900." *The Journal of Modern History* 40 (December 1973): 605-25.

_____. "The First World War and the International Power System." *International Security* 9 (1984): 7-40.

_____. *The Rise of the Anglo-German Antagonism 1860-1914.* London: George Allen and Unwin, 1980.

_____. "The Kaiser and German Weltpolitik: Reflexions on Wilhelm II's Place in the Making of German Foreign Policy." In *Kaiser Wilhelm II: New Interpretations.* Edited by John C.G. Röhl and Nicholaus Sombart. Cambridge: Cambridge University Press, 1982.

_____, editor. *The War Plans of the Great Powers, 1880-1914*. Foreword by Fritz Fischer. London: George Allen and Unwin, 1979.

_____. "Tirpitz, England and the Second Navy Law of 1900: A Strategical Critique." *Mariner's Mirror* 2 (1970): 33-57.

Kent, George O. *Arnim and Bismarck*. Oxford: Clarendon Press, 1968.

_____. *Bismarck and His Times*. Carbondale: Southern Illinois University Press, 1978.

Kent, Marian, editor. *The Great Powers and the End of the Ottoman Empire*. London: George Allen and Unwin, 1984.

Kershaw, Ian. *Hitler*. 2 volumes. New York: W.W. Norton, 1999-2000.

_____. "1933: Continuity or Break in German History?" *History Today* 33 (January 1933).

_____. *The Nazi Dictatorship: Problems and Perspectives of Interpretation*. Fourth edition. London: Arnold, 2000.

Kessler, Count Harry. *Walther Rathenau: His Life and Work*. Translated by W.D. Robson-Scott and Lawrence Hyde. New York: Harcourt, Brace and World, 1930; reprint, New York: Howard Fertig, 1969.

Kimmich, Christoph M., editor. *German Foreign Policy, 1918-1945: A Guide to Research and Research Materials*. Revised edition. Wilmington: Scholarly Resources, 1991.

_____. *Germany and the League of Nations*. Chicago: University of Chicago Press, 1976.

_____. *The Free City: Danzig and German Foreign Policy, 1919-1934*. New Haven: Yale University Press, 1968.

Kindermann, Gottfried-Karl. *Hitler's Defeat in Austria, 1933-1934: Europe's First Containment of Nazi Expansionism*. Translated by Sonia Brough and David Taylor. London: C. Hurst, 1988.

Kitchen, Martin. *A Military History of Germany from the Eighteenth Century to the Present Day*. London: Weidenfeld and Nicolson, 1975.

_____. *Europe Between the Wars: A Political History*. London: Longman, 1988.

_____. *The German Officer Corps, 1890-1914*. Oxford: Clarendon Press, 1968.

_____. *The Silent Dictatorship: The Politics of the German High Command under Hindenburg and Ludendorff, 1916-1918*. New York: Holmes and Meier, 1976.

Klein, Fritz. "Between Compiègne and Versailles: The Germans on the Way from a Misunderstood Defeat to an Unwanted Peace." In *The Treaty of Versailles: A Reassessment after 75 Years*. Edited by Manfred F. Boemeke, Gerald D. Feldman, and Elisabeth Glaser. Cambridge: Cambridge University Press, 1998.

Knox, Macgregor. *Mussolini Unleashed 1939-1941: Politics and Strategy in Fascist Italy's Last War*. Cambridge: Cambridge University Press, 1982.

Koch, H.W. *A History of Prussia*. New York: Dorset, 1978.

_____, editor. *Aspects of the Third Reich*. New York: St. Martin's Press, 1985.

_____, editor. *The Origins of the First World War: Great Power Rivalry and German War Aims*. Second edition. London: Macmillan, 1984.

Kolb, Eberhard. *The Weimar Republic*. Translated by P.S. Falla. London: Unwin Hyman, 1988.

Kollman, Eric C. "Walter Rathenau and German Foreign Policy." *The Journal of Modern History* 24 (1952): 127-42.

Korbel, Josef. *Poland between East and West: Soviet and German Diplomacy toward Poland, 1919-1933*. Princeton: Princeton University Press, 1963.

Kroener, Bernhard R., Rolf-Dieter Muller, and Hans Umbreit, editors. *Organization and Mobilization of the German Sphere of Power. Part I: Wartime Administration, Economy, and Manpower Resources, 1939-1941*. Volume V in *Germany and the Second World War*. Translated by Bernhard R. Kroener, Rolf-Dieter Muller, and Hans Umbreit. Oxford: Oxford University Press, 2003.

_____, editors. *Organization and Mobilization of the German Sphere of Power. Part II: Wartime Administration, Economy, and Manpower Resources, 1942-1944/45*. Volume V in *Germany and the Second World War*. Translated by Derry Cook-Radmore, Ewald Osers, Barry Smerin and Barbara Wilson. Oxford: Oxford University Press, 2003.

Krüger, Peter. "A Rainy Day, April 1922: The Rapallo Treaty and the Cloudy Perspective for German Foreign Policy." In *Genoa, Rapallo, and European*

*Reconstruction in 1922.* Edited by Carole Fink and others. Cambridge: Cambridge University Press, 1991.

_____. *Deutschland und die Reparationen, 1918-19: Die Genesis des Reparationsproblems in Deutschland zwischen Waffenstillstand und Versailler Friedensschluss.* Stuttgart: Deutsche Verlags-Anhalt, 1973.

_____. "Das Reparationsproblem der Weimarer Republik in fragwürdiger Sicht: Kritische Überlegungen zur neuesten Forschung." *Vierteljahrshefte für Zeitgeschichte* 29 (1981): 21-47.

_____. *Die Aussenpolitik der Republik von Weimar.* Darmstadt: Wissenschaftliche Buchgesellschaft, 1985.

_____. "Die Reparationen und das Scheitern einer deutschen Verständigungspolitik auf der Pariser Friedenkonferenz im Jahre 1919." *Historische Zeitschrift* 221 (1975): 326-72.

_____. *Versailles: Deutsche Aussenpolitik zwischen Revisionismus und Friedenssicherung.* Munich: Deutscher Taschenbuch Verlag, 1986.

Lahme, Rainer. *Deutsche Aussenpolitik, 1890-1894: Von der Gleichgewichtspolitik Bismarcks zur Allianzstrategie Caprivis.* Göttingen: Vandenhoeck and Ruprecht, 1990.

Lambi, Ivo Nikolai. *The Navy and German Power Politics, 1862-1914.* Boston: George Allen and Unwin, 1984.

Langer, William L. *European Alliances and Alignments, 1871-1890.* Second edition. New York: Alfred A. Knopf, 1950.

_____. *The Diplomacy of Imperialism, 1890-1902.* 2 volumes. New York: Alfred A. Knopf, 1935.

Langhorne, Richard, editor. *Diplomacy and Intelligence during the Second World War: Essays in Honour of F.H. Hinsley.* Cambridge: Cambridge University Press, 1985.

_____. *The Collapse of the Concert of Europe: International Politics, 1890-1914.* London: Macmillan, 1981.

_____. "The Naval Question in Anglo-German Relations, 1912-1914." *Historical Journal* 14 (1971): 359-70.

_____ and Keith Hamilton. *The Practice of Diplomacy: Its Evolution, Theory and Administration.* London: Routledge, 1995.

Laqueur, Walter. *Stalin: The Glasnost Revelations.* New York: Charles Scribner, 1990.

Laue, Theodore H. von. "Soviet Diplomacy: G.V. Chicherin, People's Commissar for Foreign Affairs, 1918-1930." In *The Diplomats, 1919-1939.* Edited by Gordon A. Craig and Felix Gilbert. Princeton: Princeton University Press, 1963.

Leach, Barry A. *German Strategy against Russia 1939-1941.* Oxford: Clarendon Press, 1973.

Leaman, J. "The Treaty of Non-Aggression between Germany and the USSR, August 1939: Old Myths, New Myths, and Reinterpretations." *German History* 12 (1994).

Lebnow, Richard Ned. "Agency versus Structure in A.J.P. Taylor's Origins of the First World War." *The International History Review* 23 (March 2001): 51-72.

Lee, Dwight E. *Europe's Crucial Years: The Diplomatic Background of World War I, 1902-1914.* Hanover: University Press of New England, 1974.

Lee, Marshal. "Disarmament and Security: The German Security Proposals in the League of Nations, 1926-1930: A Study in Revisionist Aims in an International Organisation." *Militärgeschichtliche Mitteilungen* 1 (1979): 35-45.

_____. "The German Attempt to Reform the League: The Failure of German League of Nations Policy, 1930-1932." *Francia: Forschung zur Westeuropäischen Geschichte* 5 (1977): 473-90.

_____ and Wolfgang Michalka. *German Foreign Policy, 1917-1933: Continuity or Break?* Leamington Spa: Berg, 1987.

Leffler, Melvyn P. *The Elusive Quest: America's Pursuit of European Stability and French Security, 1919-1933.* Chapel Hill: University of North Carolina Press, 1979.

Leitz, Christian. *Nazi Foreign Policy, 1933-1941: The Road to Global War.* London: Routledge, 2003.

_____. *Nazi Germany and Neutral Europe during the Second World War.* Manchester: Manchester University Press, 2001.

Lentin, Antony. *Lloyd George and the Lost Peace: From Versailles to Hitler, 1919-1940.* Oxford: Davenant Press, 2004.

_____. *Lloyd George, Woodrow Wilson and the Guilt of Germany*. Leicester: Leicester University Press, 1984.

Leonhard, Wolfgang. *Betrayal: The Hitler-Stalin Pact of 1939*. Translated by Richard D. Bosley. New York: St. Martin's Press, 1989.

Lerman, Katharine. *Bismarck*. London: Longman, 2004.

_____. *The Chancellor as Courtier: Bernhard von Bülow and the Governance of Germany, 1900-1909*. Cambridge: Cambridge University Press, 1990.

_____. "The Decisive Relationship: Kaiser Wilhelm II and Chancellor Bernhard von Bülow, 1900-1905." In *Kaiser Wilhelm II: New Interpretations*. Edited by Rohn C.G. Röhl and Nicolaus Sombart. Cambridge: Cambridge University Press, 1982.

Levine, Herbert S. *Hitler's Free City: The History of the Nazi Party in Danzig, 1925-1939*. Chicago: University of Chicago Press, 1973.

Liddell Hart, Basil. H. *History of the First World War*. London: Cassell, 1970.

_____. *History of the Second World War*. New York: G. P. Putnam's Sons, 1970.

Lieven, Dominic C.B. *Nicholas II: Twilight of the Empire*. New York: St. Martin's Press, 1993.

_____. *Russia and the Origins of the First World War*. London: Macmillan, 1983.

Lord, Robert Howard. "Bismarck and Russia in 1863." *The American Historical Review* 29 (October 1923/July 1924).

_____. *The Origins of the War of 1870: New Documents from the German Archives*. Cambridge, MA: Harvard University Press, 1924.

Louis, William Roger. *Great Britain and Germany's Lost Colonies, 1914-1919*. Oxford: Clarendon Press, 1967.

Lovin, Clifford R. *A School for Diplomats: The Paris Peace Conference of 1919*. Lanham: University Press of America, 1997.

Lowe, C.J. *The Reluctant Imperialists: British Foreign Policy, 1878-1902*. 2 volumes. London: Routledge and Kegan Paul, 1967.

_____ and M.L. Dockrill. *The Mirage of Power*. 3 volumes. London: Routledge and Kegan Paul, 1972.

_____ and F. Marzari. *Italian Foreign Policy 1870-1940*. London: Routledge and Kegan Paul, 1975.

Lowe, John. *Britain and Foreign Affairs, 1815-1885: Europe and Overseas*. London: Routledge, 1998.

_____. *The Great Powers, Imperialism, and the German Problem, 1865-1925*. London: Routledge, 1994.

Loynd, Bruce D. "Bismarck and Napoleon III: The Diplomacy of the German Crisis of 1866." Ph.D. dissertation, University of California at Santa Barbara, 1974.

Luckau, Alma. *The German Delegation at the Paris Peace Conference*. New York: Columbia University Press, 1941.

MacDonald, C.A. *The United States, Britain and Appeasement, 1936-1939*. London: Macmillan, 1981.

Macfie, A.L. *The Eastern Question, 1774-1923*. Revised edition. London: Longman, 1996.

Mack Smith, Denis. *Mussolini*. London: Weidenfeld and Nicolson, 1981.

_____. *Mussolini's Roman Empire*. London and New York: Longman, 1976.

Maier, Klaus A., Horst Rohde, Bernd Stegemann, and Hans Umbreit, editors. *Germany's Initial Conquests in Europe*. Volume II in *Germany and the Second World War*. Translated by Dean S. McMurray, Ewald Osers, and P.S. Falla. Oxford: Clarendon Press, 1991.

Maiolo, Joseph A. *The Royal Navy and Nazi Germany, 1933-1939: A Study in Appeasement and the Origins of the Second World War*. London: Macmillan, 1998.

Manvell, Roger and Heinrich Fränkel. *Dr. Goebbels: His Life and Death*. New York: Simon and Schuster, 1960.

_____. *Göring*. New York: Simon and Schuster, 1962.

Marks, Sally. "Behind the Scenes at the Paris Peace Conference of 1919." *Journal of British Studies* 9 (1970): 154-80.

_____. *The Illusion of Peace: International Relations in Europe 1918-1933*. London: Macmillan, 1986.

Marrow, Ian. "The Foreign Policy of Prince von Bülow, 1898-1909." *Cambridge Historical Journal* 4 (1932): 63-93.

Martel, Gordon. *Imperial Diplomacy: Rosebery and the Failure of Foreign Policy.* Kingston: McGill-Queen's University Press, 1986.

_____, editor. *The Origins of the Second World War Reconsidered: The A.J.P. Taylor Debate After Twenty-Five Years.* Boston: Allen and Unwin, 1986.

Massie, Robert K. *Dreadnought: Britain, Germany, and the Coming of the Great War.* New York: Random House, 1991.

Maurer, John H. *The Outbreak of the First World War: Strategic Planning, Crisis Decision Making, and Deterrence Failure.* Westport, CT: Praeger, 1995.

Mawdsley, Evan. "Crossing the Rubicon: Soviet Plans for Offensive War in 1940-1941." *The International History Review* 25 (December 2003): 818–65.

May, Ernest R. *Imperial Democracy: The Emergence of America as a Great Power.* New York: Harcourt, Brace, and World, 1961.

Mayer, Arno J. *Politics and Diplomacy of Peacemaking: Containment and Counter-revolution at Versailles, 1918-1919.* New York: Alfred A. Knopf, 1969.

Mayer, S.L. "Anglo-German Rivalry at the Algeciras Conference." In *Britain and Germany in Africa: Imperial Rivalry and Colonial Rule.* Edited by Prosser Gifford and William Roger Louis. New Haven: Yale University Press, 1967.

McDonald, David MacLaren. *United Government and Foreign Policy in Russia, 1900-1914.* Cambridge, MA: Harvard University Press, 1992.

McDonough, Frank. *The Origins of the First and Second World Wars.* Cambridge: Cambridge University Press, 1997.

McDougall, Walter A. *France's Rhineland Diplomacy, 1914-1924: The Last Bid for a Balance of Power in Europe.* Princeton: Princeton University Press, 1978.

McKay, Derek. *The Great Elector.* London: Longman, 2001.

_____. "Small-Power Diplomacy in the Age of Louis XIV: The Foreign Policy of the Great Elector during the 1660s and 1670s." In *Royal and Republican Sovereignty in Early Modern Europe: Essays in Memory of Rag-*

*nhild Hatton*. Edited by Robert Oresko, G.C. Gibbs, and H.M. Scott. Cambridge: Cambridge University Press, 1997.

McLean, Roderick R. "Dreams of a German Empire: Wilhelm II and the Treaty of Björkö of 1905." In *The Kaiser: New Research on Wilhelm II's Role in Imperial Germany*. Edited by Annika Mombauer and Wilhelm Deist. Cambridge: Cambridge University Press, 2003.

_____. *Royalty and Diplomacy in Europe, 1890-1914*. Cambridge: Cambridge University Press, 2001.

McMillan, James F. *Napoleon III*. London: Longman, 1991.

McSherry, James E. *Stalin, Hitler and Europe, 1933-1941*. 2 volumes. New York: World Publishing, 1968-70.

Medlicott, W.N. *Bismarck and Modern Germany*. London: English Universities Press, 1965.

_____. *Bismarck, Gladstone, and the Concert of Europe*. London: Athlone Press, 1956.

_____. *British Foreign Policy since Versailles, 1919-1963*. Second edition. London: Methuen, 1968.

_____. *Britain and Germany: The Search for Agreement 1930-1937*. London: Weidenfeld and Nicolson, 1969.

_____. *The Congress of Berlin and After: A Diplomatic History of the Near Eastern Settlement, 1878-1880*. London: Methuen, 1938.

Menning, Bruce W. *Bayonets before Bullets: The Imperial Russian Army, 1861-1914*. Bloomington: Indiana University Press, 1992.

_____. "Pieces of the Puzzle: The Role of Iu. N. Danilov and M.V. Alekseev in Russian War Planning before 1914." *The International History Review* 25 (December 2003): 775-798.

Meskill, Johanna M. *Hitler and Japan: The Hollow Alliance*. New York: Atheneum, 1966.

Messerschmidt, Manfred. "Foreign Policy and Preparation for War." In *The Buildup of German Aggression*. Volume I in *Germany and the Second World War*. Edited by W. Deist, M. Messerschmidt, H.-E. Volkmann, and W. Wette. Translated by P.S. Falla, Dean S. McMurry, and Ewald Osers. Oxford: Clarendon Press, 1990.

Michalka, Wolfgang. "Conflicts Within the German Leadership on the Objectives and Tactics of German Foreign Policy, 1933-9." Chapter in *The Fascist Challenge and the Policy of Appeasement*. Edited by Wolfgang J. Mommsen and Lothar Kettenacker. London: George Allen and Unwin, 1983.

_____. "From the Anti-Comintern to the Euro-Asiatic Bloc: Ribbentrop's Alternate Concept of Hitler's Foreign Policy Programme." Chapter in *Aspects of the Third Reich*. Edited by H.W. Koch. New York: St. Martin's Press, 1985.

_____. *Ribbentrop und die deutsche Weltpolitik 1933-1940: Aussenpolitische Konzeptionen und Entscheidunsprozze in Dritten Reich*. Munich: Wilhelm Fink, 1980.

Middlemas, Keith. *Diplomacy of Illusion: The British Government and Germany, 1937-1939*. London: Weidenfeld and Nicolson, 1972; reprint, Aldershot: Gregg, 1991.

Miller, Stephen E., Sean M. Lynn-Jones, and Stephen Van Everla. *Military Strategy and the Origins of the First World War*. Revised and expanded edition. Princeton: Princeton University Press, 1991.

Millman, Richard. *Britain and the Eastern Question, 1875-1878*. Oxford: Clarendon Press, 1979.

_____. *British Foreign Policy and the Coming of the Franco-Prussian War*. Oxford: Clarendon Press, 1965.

Mombauer, Annika. "A Reluctant Military Leader? Helmuth von Moltke and the July Crisis of 1914." *War in History* 6 (November 1999): 417-46.

_____. *Helmuth von Moltke and the Origins of the First World War*. Cambridge: Cambridge University Press, 2001.

Mommsen, Wolfgang J. "Domestic Factors in German Foreign Policy Before 1914." *Central European History* 6 (March 1973).

_____. *Grossmachtstellung und Weltpolitik, 1870-1914: Die Aussenpolitik des Deutschen Reiches*. Frankfurt-am-Main: Propyläen, 1993.

_____ and Lothar Kettenacker, editors. *The Fascist Challenge and the Policy of Appeasement*. London: George Allen and Unwin, 1983.

Monger, George. *The End of Isolation: British Foreign Policy, 1900-1907*. London: Thomas Nelson and Sons, 1963; reprint, Westport, CT: Greenwood Press, 1976.

Moore, Anthony. *The Army of Brandenburg-Prussia, 1685 to 1715*. Upton: Gosling Press, 1992.

Morley, James W., editor. *Deterrent Diplomacy: Japan, Germany, and the USSR 1935-1940*. New York: Columbia University Press, 1976.

Morris, A.J.A. *The Scaremongers: The Advocacy of War and Rearmament, 1896-1914*. London: Routledge and Kegan Paul, 1984.

Morris, Warren B. *The Road to Olmültz: The Career of Joseph Maria von Radowitz*. New York: Revisionist Press, 1976.

Moseley, Ray. *Mussolini's Shadow: The Double Life of Count Galeazzo Ciano*. New Haven: Yale University Press, 1999.

Moses, John A. *The Politics of Illusion: The Fischer Controversy in German Historiography*. London: Prior, 1975.

Mosse, Werner E. *The European Powers and the German Question, 1848-1871: With Special Reference to England and Russia*. Cambridge: Cambridge University Press, 1968.

Murphy, David T. "Prussian Aims for the Zollervein, 1828-1833." *The Historian* 53 (1991): 258-302.

Murray, Williamson. *The Change in the European Balance of Power, 1938-1939: The Path to Ruin*. Princeton: Princeton University Press, 1984.

_____. "The Collapse of Empire: British Strategy, 1919-1945." In *The Making of Strategy: Rulers, States, and War*. Edited by Williamson Murray, Macgregor Knox, and Alvin Berstein. Cambridge: Cambridge University Press, 1994.

Namier, Lewis. *Diplomatic Prelude, 1938-1939*. New York: Macmillan, 1948.

_____. *Europe in Decay*. London: Macmillan, 1950.

_____. *In The Nazi Era*. London: Macmillan, 1952.

Nelson, K.L. *Victors Divided: America and the Allies in Germany, 1918-1923*. Berkeley: University of California Press, 1975.

Néré, J. *The Foreign Policy of France from 1914 to 1945*. London: Routledge and Kegan Paul, 1975.

Neville, Peter. *Appeasing Hitler: The Diplomacy of Sir Nevile Henderson, 1937-1939*. Basingstoke: Macmillan, 2000.

Newman, Simon. *March 1939: The British Guarantee to Poland*. Oxford: Oxford University Press, 1976.

Newton, Douglas. *British Policy and the Weimar Republic, 1918-1919*. Oxford: Clarendon Press, 1997.

Nicholls, A.J. *Weimar and the Rise of Hitler*. Second edition. New York: St. Martin's Press, 1979.

Nichols, J. Alden. *Germany after Bismarck: The Caprivi Era, 1890-1894*. Cambridge, MA: Harvard University Press, 1958.

_____. *The Year of the Three Kaisers: Bismarck and the German Succession, 1887-88*. Urbana: University of Illinois Press, 1987.

Nicolson, Harold. *Curzon, The Last Phase, 1919-1925: A Study in Post-War Diplomacy*. Boston: Houghton Mifflin, 1934.

_____. *Diplomacy*. Second edition. Oxford: Oxford University Press, 1950.

_____. *Sir Arthur Nicolson, Bart., First Lord Carnock: A Study in the Old Diplomacy*. London: Constable, 1930.

_____. *The Evolution of Diplomatic Method*. London: Constable, 1954.

Nish, Ian. *Japanese Foreign Policy 1869-1942: Kasumigaseki to Miyakezaka*. London: Routledge and Kegan Paul, 1977.

_____. *Japanese Foreign Policy in the Interwar Period*. Westport, CT: Praeger, 2002.

Northedge, F. S. *The Troubled Giant: Britain Among the Great Powers 1916-1939*. London: G. Bell and Sons, 1966.

Nowak, Karl Friedrich. *Germany's Road to Ruin*. Translated by E.W. Dickes. London: Longmans, 1932.

O'Connor, Timothy Edward. *Diplomacy and Revolution: G.V. Chicherin and Soviet Foreign Affairs, 1918-1930*. Ames: Iowa State University Press, 1988.

Offner, Arnold A. *American Appeasement: United States Foreign Policy and Germany, 1933-1938*. Cambridge, MA: Harvard University Press, 1969.

Oncken, Hermann. *Napoleon III and the Rhine: The Origin of the War of 1870-1871*. Introduction by Ferdinand Schevill. Translated by Edwin H. Zeydel. New York: Alfred A. Knopf, 1928; reprint, New York: Russell and Russell, 1967.

Oppel, Bernard F. "The Waning of a Traditional Alliance: Russia and Germany after the Portsmouth Peace Conference." *Central European History* 5 (December 1972): 318-29.

Padfield, Peter. *The Great Naval Race: Anglo-German Naval Rivalry, 1900-1914*. London: Hart-Davis, MacGibbon, 1974.

Paine, S.C.M. *The Sino-Japanese War of 1894-1895: Perceptions, Power and Primacy*. Cambridge: Cambridge University Press, 2003.

Palmer, Alan. *Alexander I: Tsar of War and Peace*. London: Weidenfeld and Nicolson, 1974.

_____. *Bismarck*. New York: Charles Scribner's Sons, 1976.

_____. *Metternich*. London: Weidenfeld and Nicolson, 1972.

_____. *The Chancelleries of Europe*. London: George Allen and Unwin, 1983.

_____. *The Kaiser: Warlord of the Second Reich*. New York: Charles Scribner's Sons, 1978.

Paret, Peter. *Yorck and the Era of Prussian Reform, 1807-1815*. Princeton: Princeton University Press, 1966.

Parker, R.A.C. *Chamberlain and Appeasement: British Policy and the Coming of the Second World War*. New York: St. Martin's Press, 1993.

Payne, Stanley G. *A History of Fascism, 1914-1945*. Madison: University of Wisconsin Press, 1995.

Peters, A.R. *Anthony Eden at the Foreign Office, 1931-1938*. New York: St. Martin's Press, 1986.

Pflanze, Otto. *Bismarck and the Development of Germany*. 3 volumes. Princeton: Princeton University Press, 1990.

Pinson, Koppel S. *Modern Germany: Its History and Civilization*. Second edition. New York: Macmillan, 1966.

Polonsky, Antony. *The Little Dictators: The History of Eastern Europe since 1918*. London: Routledge and Kegan Paul, 1975.

Pommerin, Reiner. "Germany's Reaction to the Globalisation of International Relations, 1890-1898: A Different Course." In *Escape into War?: The Foreign Policy of Imperial Germany*. Edited by Gregor Schöllgen. Oxford: Berg, 1990.

Porch, Douglas. *The March to the Marne: The French Army, 1871-1914*. Cambridge: Cambridge University Press, 1981.

Post, Gaines Jr. *Dilemmas of Appeasement: British Deterrence and Defense, 1934-1937*. Ithaca: Cornell University Press, 1993.

_____. *The Civil-Military Fabric of Weimar Foreign Policy*. Princeton: Princeton University Press, 1973.

Pottinger, E. Ann. *Napoleon III and the German Crisis, 1865-1866*. Cambridge, MA: Harvard University Press, 1966.

Prażmowska, Anita J. *Britain, Poland and the Eastern Front, 1939*. Cambridge: Cambridge University Press, 1987.

_____. *Eastern Europe and the Origins of the Second World War*. New York: St. Martin's Press, 2000.

_____. "Poland's Foreign Policy: September 1938-1939." *Historical Journal* 29 (1986).

Presseisen, Ernst L. *Germany and Japan: A Study in Totalitarian Diplomacy, 1933-1941*. The Hague: Martinus Nijhoff, 1958.

Price, Roger. *Napoleon III and the Second Empire*. London: Routledge, 1997.

Ragsdale, Hugh. *The Soviets, the Munich Crisis, and the Coming of World War II*. Cambridge: Cambridge University Press, 2004.

Ratliff, William G. *Faithful to the Fatherland: Julius Curtius and Weimar Foreign Policy*. New York: Peter Lang, 1990.

Read, Anthony and David Fisher. *The Deadly Embrace: Hitler, Stalin, and the Nazi-Soviet Pact 1939-1941*. New York: W.W. Norton, 1988.

Retallack, James. *Germany in the Age of Kaiser Wilhelm II*. London: Macmillan, 1996.

Reynolds, David. *Britannia Overruled: British World Policy and World Power in the Twentieth Century*. London: Longman, 1991.

Rhodes, Benjamin D. *United States Foreign Policy in the Interwar Period, 1918-1941: The Golden Age of American Diplomatic and Military Complacency.* Westport, CT: Praeger, 2001.

Rice, William C., Jr. "The Uncertain Alliance: A Study of the German Foreign Ministry Liaison Staff at General Headquarters during the First World War." Ph.D. diss., Johns Hopkins University, 1986.

Rich, Norman. *Friedrich von Holstein.* 2 volumes. Cambridge: Cambridge University Press, 1965.

_____. *Great Power Diplomacy, 1814-1914.* New York: McGraw-Hill, 1992.

_____. *Great Power Diplomacy Since 1914.* Boston: McGraw-Hill, 2003.

_____. "Hitler's Foreign Policy." Chapter in *The Origins of the Second World War Reconsidered: The A.J.P. Taylor Debate After Twenty-Five Years.* Edited by Gordon Martel. Boston: Allen and Unwin, 1986.

_____. *Hitler's War Aims.* 2 volumes. New York: W. W. Norton, 1973-74.

Riekhoff, Harald von. *German-Polish Relations, 1918-1933.* Baltimore: Johns Hopkins University Press, 1971.

Ritter, Gerhard. *The Schlieffen Plan: Critique of a Myth.* New York: Praeger, 1958.

_____. *The Sword and the Scepter: The Problem of Militarism in Germany.* 4 volumes. Translated by Heinz Norden. Coral Gables: University of Miami Press, 1969-71.

Roberts, Geoffrey. "A Soviet Bid for Coexistence with Nazi Germany, 1935-1937: The Kandelaki Affair." *International History Review* 16 (August 1994): 466-90.

_____. *The Soviet Union and the Origins of the Second World War: Russo-German Relations and the Road to War, 1933-1941.* New York: St. Martin's Press, 1995.

_____. *The Unholy Alliance: Stalin's Pact with Hitler.* London: Tauris, 1989.

Robertson, Esmonde M. *Hitler's Pre-War Policy and Military Plans 1933-1939.* New York: Citadel Press, 1963.

_____. "Mussolini and the Rhineland." *European Studies Review* 7 (1977): 409-35.

_____. *Mussolini as Empire-Builder: Europe and Africa, 1932-1936*. London: Macmillan, 1977.

_____, editor. *The Origins of the Second World War: Historical Interpretations*. London: Macmillan, 1971.

Robins, Keith. *Sir Edward Grey: A Biography of Lord Grey of Fallodon*. London: Cassell, 1971.

Röhl, John C.G. "Admiral von Müller and the Approach of War, 1911-1914." *Historical Journal* 12 (1969): 651-73.

_____. *Germany Without Bismarck: The Crisis of Government in the Second Reich, 1890-1900*. London: Batsford, 1967.

_____. *1914: Delusion or Design? The Testimony of Two German Diplomats*. London: Elek, 1973.

_____. *The Kaiser and His Court: Wilhelm II and the Government of Germany*. Cambridge: Cambridge University Press, 1994.

_____. *Wilhelm II: The Kaiser's Personal Monarchy, 1888-1900*. Translated by Sheila de Bellaigue. Cambridge: Cambridge University Press, 2004.

_____. *Young Wilhelm: The Kaiser's Early Life, 1859-1888*. Cambridge: Cambridge University Press, 1998.

Rolo, P.J.V. *Entente Cordiale: The Origins and Negotiations of the Anglo-French Agreements of 8 April 1904*. London: Macmillan, 1969.

Roosen, William J. *The Age of Louis XIV: The Rise of Modern Diplomacy*. Cambridge, MA: Schenkman, 1976.

Ross, Graham. *The Great Powers and the Decline of the European States System 1914-1945*. London: Longman, 1983.

Rothenberg, Gunther E. *The Army of Francis Joseph*. West Lafayette: Purdue University Press, 1976.

Rothwell, Victor. *Britain War Aims and Peace Diplomacy, 1914-1918*. Oxford: Clarendon Press, 1971.

Salmon, Patrick. "Crimes against Peace: The Case of the Invasion of Norway at the Nuremberg Trials." Chapter in *Diplomacy and Intelligence during the*

*Second World War.* Edited by Richard Langhorne. Cambridge: Cambridge University Press, 1985.

Sasse, Heinz. "Zur Geschichte des Auswärtingen Amts." *Mitteilungsblatt der Vereinigung der Angestellen des Auswärtiges Dienstes* 4 (1960): 105-18.

Schevill, Ferdinand. *The Great Elector.* Chicago: University of Chicago Press, 1947.

Schmidt, Gustav. "Contradictory Postures and Conflicting Objectives: The July Crisis." In *Escape into War?: The Foreign Policy of Imperial Germany.* Edited by Gregor Schöllgen. Oxford: Berg, 1990.

Schmitt, Bernadotte E. *The Annexation of Bosnia, 1908-1909.* Cambridge: Cambridge University Press, 1937.

Schöllgen, Gregor, editor. *Escape into War? The Foreign Policy of Imperial Germany.* Oxford: Berg, 1990.

_____. "Germany's Foreign Policy in the Age of Imperialism: A Vicious Circle?" In *Escape into War?: The Foreign Policy of Imperial Germany.* Edited by Gregor Schöllgen. Oxford: Berg, 1990.

Schorske, Carl E. "Two German Ambassadors: Dirksen and Schulenburg," In *The Diplomats 1919-1939.* Edited by Gordon A. Craig and Felix Gilbert. Princeton: Princeton University Press, 1953.

Schreiber, Gerhard, Bernd Stegemann, and Detlef Vogel, editors. *The Mediterranean, South-East Europe, and North Africa, 1939-1941.* Volume III in *Germany and the Second World War.* Translated by Dean S. McMurray, Ewald Osers, and Louise Wilmott. Oxford: Oxford University Press, 1995.

Schroeder, Paul W. *The Transformation of European Politics, 1763-1848.* Oxford: Clarendon Press, 1994.

Schüddekopf, Otto-Ernst. "German Foreign Policy between Compiègne and Versailles." *Journal of Canadian History* 4 (April 1969): 181-97.

Schuker, Stephen A. *The End of French Predominance in Europe: The Financial Crisis of 1924 and the Adoption of the Dawes Plan.* Chapel Hill: University of North Carolina Press, 1976.

Schwabe, Klaus. "Germany's Peace Aims and the Domestic and International Constraints." In *The Treaty of Versailles: A Reassessment after 75 Years.* Edited by Manfred F. Boemeke, Gerald D. Feldman, and Elisabeth Glaser. Cambridge: Cambridge University Press, 1998.

_____. *Woodrow Wilson, Revolutionary Germany, and Peacemaking, 1918-1919: Missionary Diplomacy and the Realities of Power*. Chapel Hill: University of North Carolina Press, 1985.

Schwarz, Dr. Paul. *This Man Ribbentrop*. New York: Julian Messner, 1943.

Schwoerer, Lois G. "Lord Halifax's Visit to Germany, November 1937." *The Historian* 32 (May 1970): 353-75.

Scott, Hamish M. "Aping the Great Powers: Frederick the Great and the Defence of Prussia's International Position, 1763-1786." *German History* 12 (1994).

_____. "Prussia's Emergence as a European Great Power, 1740-1763." In *The Rise of Prussia, 1700-1830*. Edited by Philip G. Dwyer. London: Longman, 2000.

_____. "Prussia's Royal Foreign Minister: Frederick the Great and the Administration of Prussian Diplomacy." In *Royal and Republican Sovereignty in Early Modern Europe*. Edited by Robert Oresko, G.C. Gibbs, and H.M. Scott. Cambridge: Cambridge University Press, 1997.

_____. *The Birth of a Great Power System, 1740-1815*. Harlow: Pearson, 2006.

_____. *The Emergence of the Eastern Powers, 1756-1775*. Cambridge: Cambridge University Press, 2001.

Scott, I. "The Making of the Triple Alliance, 1882." *East European Quarterly* 12 (1978): 339-423.

Scott, William Evans. *Alliance against Hitler: The Origins of the Franco-Soviet Pact*. Durham: Duke University Press, 1962.

Seabury, Paul. *The Wilhelmstrasse: A Study of German Diplomats under the Nazi Regime*. Berkeley: University of California Press, 1954.

_____. "Ribbentrop and the German Foreign Office." *Political Science Quarterly* 66 (December 1951): 532-55.

Senn, Alfred E. *The Great Powers, Lithuania, and the Vilna Question 1920-1928*. Leiden: Brill, 1966.

Shanafelt, Gary W. *The Secret Enemy: Austria-Hungary and the German Alliance, 1914-1918*. New York: Columbia University Press, 1985.

Shanahan, William O. *Prussian Military Reforms, 1786-1813*. New York: Columbia University Press, 1945.

Sharp, Alan. *The Versailles Settlement: Peacekeeping in Paris, 1919.* Basingstoke: Macmillan Educational, 1991.

Shay, Robert Paul, Jr. *British Rearmament in the Thirties: Politics and Profits.* Princeton: Princeton University Press, 1977.

Sheehan, James J. *German History 1776-1866.* Oxford: Oxford University Press, 1989.

Shirer, William L. *The Rise and Fall of the Third Reich: A History of Nazi Germany.* London: Secker and Warburg, 1959.

Shore, Zachary. *What Hitler Knew: The Battle for Information in Nazi Foreign Policy.* New York: Oxford University Press, 2003.

Shorrock, William I. *From Ally to Enemy: The Enigma of Fascist Italy in French Diplomacy, 1920-1940.* Kent: Kent State University Press, 1988.

Showalter, Dennis. "From Deterrence to Doomsday Machine: The German Way of War, 1890-1914." *The Journal of Military History* 64 (July 2000): 679-710.

_____. *Railroads and Rifles: Soldiers, Technology, and the Unification of Germany.* Hamden, CT: Archon, 1975.

_____. "The Prussian Landwehr and Its Critics, 1813-1819." *Central European History* 4 (1971): 3-33.

_____. *The Wars of Frederick the Great.* London: Longman, 1996.

_____. *The Wars of German Unification.* London: Arnold, 2004.

Silberstein, Gerard E. *The Troubled Alliance: German-Austrian Relations 1914 to 1917.* Lexington: University Press of Kentucky, 1982.

Silverman, Dan P. *Reconstructing Europe after the Great War.* Cambridge, MA: Harvard University Press, 1982.

Simms, Brendan. *The Impact of Napoleon: Prussian High Politics, Foreign Policy, and the Crisis of the Executive, 1797-1806.* Cambridge: Cambridge University Press, 1997.

_____. *The Struggle for Mastery in Germany, 1779-1850.* Basingstoke: Macmillan, 1998.

Singer, Donald L. "German Diplomats at Nuremberg: A Study of the Foreign Office Defendants of the Ministries Case." Ph.D. diss., American University, 1981.

Sked, Alan, editor. *Europe's Balance of Power, 1815-1848*. London: Macmillan, 1979.

Smelser, Ronald M. "Nazi Dynamics, German Foreign Policy and Appeasement." Chapter in *The Fascist Challenge and the Policy of Appeasement*. Edited by Wolfgang J. Mommsen and Lothar Kettenacker. London: George Allen and Unwin, 1983.

_____. *The Sudeten Problem, 1933-1938: Volkstumspolitik and the Formulation of Nazi Foreign Policy*. Middletown: Wesleyan University Press, 1975.

Smith, Bradley F. *Reaching Judgment at Nuremberg*. London: Andre Deutsch, 1977.

_____. *The Road to Nuremberg*. New York: Basic Books, 1981.

Snell, John L. *Illusion and Necessity: The Diplomacy of Global War, 1939-1945*. Boston: Houghton Mifflin, 1963.

Snyder, Jack. *The Ideology of the Offensive: Military Decision Making and the Disasters of 1914*. Ithaca: Cornell University Press, 1984.

Snyder, Louis L. *Diplomacy in Iron: The Life of Herbert von Bismarck*. Malabar, Florida: Krieger, 1985.

_____. *Encyclopedia of the Third Reich*. New York: Paragon House, 1976.

Sondhaus, Lawrence. *Naval Warfare, 1815-1914*. London: Routledge, 2001.

_____. *Preparing for Weltpolitik: German Sea Power before the Tirpitz Era*. Annapolis: Naval Institute Press, 1997.

_____. "Schwarzenberg, Austria, and the German Question, 1848-1851." *International History Review* 13 (1991): 1-20.

Steefel, Lawrence D. *Bismarck, the Hohenzollern Candidacy, and the Origins of the Franco-German War of 1870*. Cambridge, MA: Harvard University Press, 1962.

_____. *The Schleswig-Holstein Question*. Cambridge, MA: Harvard University Press, 1932.

Steinberg, Jonathan. "Germany and the Russo-Japanese War." *American Historical Review* 75 (December 1970): 1965-86.

_____. "The German Background to Anglo-German Relations, 1905-1914." In *British Foreign Policy under Sir Edward Grey*. Edited by F.H. Hinsley. Cambridge: Cambridge University Press, 1977.

_____. "The Kaiser and the British: The State Visit to Windsor, November 1907." In *Kaiser Wilhelm II: New Interpretations*. Edited by Rohn C.G. Röhl and Nicolaus Sombart. Cambridge: Cambridge University Press, 1982.

_____. *Yesterday's Deterrent: Tirpitz and the Birth of the German Battle Fleet*. New York: Macmillan, 1965.

Steiner, Zara S. *Britain and the Origins of the First World War*. New York: St. Martin's Press, 1977.

_____. *The Foreign Office and Foreign Policy, 1898-1914*. Cambridge: Cambridge University Press, 1969.

_____. *The Lights that Failed: European International History, 1919-1933*. Oxford: Oxford University Press, 2005.

_____, editor. *The Times Survey of Foreign Ministries of the World*. London: Times, 1982.

_____ and Keith Neilson. *Britain and the Origins of the First World War*. Second edition. Basingstoke: Palgrave Macmillan, 2003.

Stern, Fritz. "Bethmann Hollweg and the War: The Limits of Responsibility." In *The Responsibility of Power: Historical Essays in Honor of Hans Holborn*. Edited by Leonard Krieger and Fritz Stern. Garden City: Doubleday, 1967.

Stevenson, David. *Armaments and the Coming of War: Europe, 1904-1914*. Oxford: Clarendon Press, 1996.

_____. *French War Aims against Germany, 1914-1919*. Oxford: Clarendon Press, 1982.

_____. *The First World War and International Politics*. Oxford: Oxford University Press, 1988.

Stibbe, Matthew. "Wilhelm II and the Decision in Favour of Unrestricted Submarine Warfare in January 1917." In *The Kaiser: New Research on Wilhelm II's Role in Imperial Germany*. Edited by Annika Mombauer and Wilhelm Deist. Cambridge: Cambridge University Press, 2003.

_____. *The Outbreak of the First World War*. New York: St. Martin's Press, 1997.

Stine, J.E. "Frederick William III and the Decline of the Prussian Army, 1786-1797." Ph.D. diss., University of South Carolina, 1980.

Stoakes, Geoffrey. *Hitler and the Quest for World Domination: Nazi Ideology and Foreign Policy in the 1920s*. Leamington Spa: Berg, 1986.

Stone, David R. *Hammer and Rifle: The Militarization of the Soviet Union, 1926-1933*. Lawrence: University Press of Kansas, 2000.

_____. "The Prospect of War? Lev Trotskii, the Soviet Army, and the German Revolution in 1923." *The International History Review* 25 (December 2003): 799-817.

Stone, Norman. "Moltke-Conrad: Relations between the Austro-Hungarian and German General Staffs, 1909-1914." *Historical Journal* 9 (1966): 201-28.

Strachan, Hew. *The Outbreak of the First World War*. New York: Oxford University Press, 2004.

Suval, S. *The Anschluss Question in the Weimar Era: A Study of Nationalism in Germany and Austria, 1918-1922*. Baltimore: Johns Hopkins University Press, 1974.

Taffs, Winifred. *Ambassador to Bismarck: Lord Odo Russell, First Baron Ampthill*. London: Frederick Muller, 1938.

_____. "The War Scare of 1875." *Slavonic Review* 9 (1930-31): 335-49, 632-49.

Taylor, A.J.P. *Bismarck: The Man and the Statesman*. London: Hamish Hamilton, 1955.

_____. *Germany's First Bid for Colonies, 1884-1885: A Move in Bismarck's European Policy*. New York: W.W. Norton, 1970.

_____. *The First World War*. London: Hamish Hamilton, 1963.

_____. *The Origins of the Second World War*. London: Hamish Hamilton, 1961.

_____. *The Struggle for Mastery in Europe, 1848-1918*. Oxford: Oxford University Press, 1954.

_____. *War by Time-Table: How the First World War Began*. New York: American Heritage, 1969.

Taylor, Telford. *Munich: The Price of Peace*. London: Hodder and Stoughton, 1979.

Thaden, Edward C. *Russia and the Balkan Alliance of 1912*. University Park: Pennsylvania State University Press, 1965.

Thorne, Christopher. *The Approach of War 1938-1939*. London: Macmillan, 1967.

Toscano, Mario. *The Origins of the Pact of Steel*. Baltimore: Johns Hopkins University Press, 1964.

Trachtenberg, Marc. *Reparation in World Politics: France and European Economic Diplomacy, 1916-1923*. New York: Columbia University Press, 1980.

Trumpener, Ulrich. *Germany and the Ottoman Empire, 1914-1918*. Princeton: Princeton University Press, 1968.

Tuchman, Barbara W. *The Guns of August*. New York: Macmillan, 1962.

_____. *The Zimmermann Telegram*. New York: Macmillan, 1958.

Tucker, Spencer C. *The Great War, 1914-1918*. Bloomington: Indiana University Press, 1998.

Tunstall, Graydon A. *Planning for War against Russia and Serbia: Austro-Hungarian and German Military Strategies, 1871-1914*. Boulder, CO: Social Science Monographs, 1993.

Turner, Henry Ashby Jr. *Stresemann and the Politics of the Weimar Republic*. Princeton: Princeton University Press, 1963.

Turner, L.C.F. *Origins of the First World War*. London: Edward Arnold, 1970.

_____. "The Russian Mobilization in 1914." *Journal of Contemporary History* 3 (October 1968): 65-88.

Tusa, Ann and John Tusa. *The Nuremberg Trial*. New York: Atheneum, 1983.

Ulam, Adam B. *Expansion and Coexistence: Soviet Foreign Policy, 1917-1973*. Second edition, New York: Praeger, 1974.

Uldricks, Teddy J. *Diplomacy and Ideology: The Origins of Soviet Foreign Relations, 1917-1930*. London: Sage Publications, 1979.

_____. "Russia and Europe: Diplomacy, Revolution, and Economic Development in the 1920s." *International History Review* 1 (January 1979): 55-83.

_____. "Stalin and Nazi Germany." *Slavic Review* 36 (1977): 599-603.

_____. "The Soviet Diplomatic Corps in the Cicerin Era." *Jahrbücher für Geschichte Osteuropas* 23 (1975): 213-24.

Vital, David. "Czechoslovakia and the Powers, September 1938." *Journal of Contemporary History* 1 (October 1966): 37-67.

Vogel, Barbara. *Deutsche Russlandpolitik: Das Scheitern der deutschen Weltpolitik unter Bülow, 1900-1906.* Dusseldorf: Bertelsmann Universitätsverlag, 1973.

Waddington, Geoffrey T. "The Career and Political Views of Joachim von Ribbentrop, 1932-1938, with Special Reference to Anglo-German Relations." Ph.D. diss., University of Leeds, 1987.

Waller, Bruce. *Bismarck at the Crossroads: The Reorientation of German Foreign Policy after the Congress of Berlin, 1878-1880.* London: Athlone Press, 1974.

Walworth, Arthur. *America's Moment, 1918: American Diplomacy at the End of World War I.* New York: Norton, 1977.

Wandycz, Piotr S. *France and Her Eastern Allies, 1919-1925: French-Czechoslovak-Polish Relations from the Paris Peace Conference to Locarno.* Minneapolis: University of Minnesota Press, 1962.

_____. *The Twilight of French Eastern Alliances, 1926-1936: French-Czechoslovak-Polish Relations from Locarno to the Remilitarization of the Rhineland.* Princeton: Princeton University Press, 1988.

Wargelin, Clifford F. "A High Price for Bread: The First Treaty of Brest-Litovsk and the Break-Up of Austria-Hungary, 1917-1918." *The International History Review* 19 (November 1997): 757-88.

Watt, D.C, *How War Came: The Immediate Origins of the Second World War, 1938-1939.* London: Heinemann, 1989.

_____. "The Anglo-German Naval Agreement of 1935: An Interim Judgement." *The Journal of Modern History* 28 (June 1956): 155-75.

_____. "The German Diplomats and the Nazi Leaders 1933-1939." *Journal of Central European Affairs* 15 (July 1955): 148-60.

_____. "The Initiation of the Negotiations Leading to the Nazi-Soviet Pact: A Historical Problem." Chapter in *Essays in Honour of E.H. Carr*. Edited by C. Abransky. Hamden: Archon Books, 1974.

_____. "The Rome-Berlin Axis, 1936-1940: Myth and Reality." *Review of Politics* 22 (October 1960): 519-43.

_____. *Too Serious a Business: European Armed Forces and the Approach of the Second World War*. Berkeley: University of California Press, 1975.

Watt, Richard M. *Bitter Glory: Poland and its Fate, 1918-1939*. New York: Simon and Schuster, 1982.

_____. *The King's Depart: The Tragedy of Germany: Versailles and the German Revolution*. New York: Simon and Schuster, 1968.

Wawro, Geoffrey. *The Austro-Prussian War: Austria's War with Prussia and Italy in 1866*. Cambridge: Cambridge University Press, 1996.

_____. *The Franco-Prussian War: The German Conquest of France in 1870-1871*. Cambridge: Cambridge University Press, 2003.

_____. *Warfare and Society in Europe, 1792-1914*. London: Routledge, 2000.

Weber, Frank G. *Eagles on the Crescent: Germany, Austria, and the Diplomacy of the Turkish Alliance, 1914-1918*. Ithaca: Cornell University Press, 1970.

Weinberg, Gerhard L. "A Proposed Compromise over Danzig in 1939?" *Journal of Central European Affairs* 14 (January 1955): 334-38.

_____. *A World at Arms: A Global History of World War II*. Cambridge: Cambridge University Press, 1994.

_____. *Germany and the Soviet Union 1939-1941*. Leiden: Brill, 1954.

_____. *Germany, Hitler, and World War II: Essays in Modern German and World History*. Cambridge: Cambridge University Press, 1995.

_____. "Germany's Declaration of War on the United States: A New Look." Chapter in *World in the Balance: Behind the Scenes of World War II*. Hanover: University Press of New England, 1981.

_____. "Hitler's Image of the United States." Chapter in *World in the Balance: Behind the Scenes of World War II*. Hanover : University Press of New England, 1981.

_____. *The Foreign Policy of Hitler's Germany.* 2 volumes. Chicago: University of Chicago Press, 1970-80.

_____. "The Defeat of Germany in 1918 and the European Balance of Power." *Central European History* 2 (September 1969): 248-60; reprinted in *Germany, Hitler, and World War II: Essays in Modern German and World History.* Cambridge: Cambridge University Press, 1995.

_____. "The May Crisis of 1938." *Journal of Modern History* 29 (September 1957): 213-25.

_____. *World in the Balance: Behind the Scenes of World War II.* Hanover: University Press of New England, 1981.

Weitz, John. *Hitler's Diplomat: The Life and Times of Joachim von Ribbentrop.* New York: Ticknor and Fields, 1992.

Wengst, Udo. *Graf Brockdorff-Rantzau und die aussenpolitischen Anfänge der Weimarer Republik.* Frankfurt am Main: Peter Lang, 1973.

Wetzel, David. *A Duel of Giants: Bismarck, Napoleon III, and the Origins of the Franco-Prussian War.* Madison: University of Wisconsin Press, 2001.

Wheeler-Bennett, John W. *Brest-Litovsk: The Forgotten Peace, March 1918.* London: Macmillan, 1963.

_____. *The Nemesis of Power: The German Army in Politics.* London: Macmillan, 1954.

White, John Albert. *Transition to Global Rivalry: Alliance Diplomacy and the Quadruple Entente, 1895-1907.* Cambridge: Cambridge University Press, 1995.

White, Jonathan R. *The Prussian Army, 1640-1871.* Lanham: University Press of America, 1996.

Williamson, Samuel R., Jr. *Austria-Hungary and the Origins of the First World War.* New York: St. Martin's Press, 1991.

_____. *The Politics of Grand Strategy: Britain and France Prepare for War, 1904-1914.* Cambridge, MA: Harvard University Press, 1969.

Willis, Edward F. *Prince Lichnowsky Ambassador of Peace: A Study of Prewar Diplomacy 1912-1914.* Berkeley: University of California Press, 1942.

Willis, J. *Prologue to Nuremberg: The Politics and Diplomacy of Punishing War Criminals of the First World War.* Westport, CT: Greenwood Press, 1982.

Wilson, Keith M. *The Policy of the Entente: Essays on the Determinants of British Foreign Policy, 1904-1914.* Cambridge: Cambridge University Press, 1985.

_____, editor. *British Foreign Secretaries and Foreign Policy: From Crimean War to First World War.* London: Croom Helm, 1987.

_____, editor. *Decisions for War, 1914.* London: University College London Press, 1995.

Wilson, Peter H. *German Armies, War and German Politics, 1648-1806.* London: University College London Press, 1998.

Winzen, Peter. *Bülows Weltmachtkonzept: Untersuchungen zur Frühphase seiner Aussenpolitik, 1897-1901.* Boppard am Rhein: Boldt, 1973.

_____. *Das Kaiserreich am Abgrund: Die Daily-Telegraph Affäre und das Hale Interview von 1908.* Stuttgart: Franz Steiner Verlag, 2002.

_____. *Reichskanzler Bernhard Fürst von Bülow: Weltmachtstratege ohne Fortune, Wegbereiter der Grossen Katastrophe.* Göttingen: Muster-Schmidt, 2003.

Wiskemann, Elizabeth. *The Rome-Berlin Axis: A History of the Relations Between Hitler and Mussolini.* Second edition. London: Collins, 1966.

Wittgens, Herman J. "The German Foreign Office Campaign against the Versailles Treaty: An Examination of the Activities of the Kriegsschuldreferat in the United States." Ph.D. Dissertation, University of Washington, 1970.

Wollstein, Günter. *Theobald von Bethmann Hollweg: Letzter Erbe Bismarcks, Erstes Opfer der Dlochstosslegende.* Göttingen: Muster-Schmidt, 1995.

Wolter, Heinz. *Bismarcks Aussenpolitik, 1871-1881: Aussenpolitische Grundlinien von der Reichsgründung bis zum Dreikaiserbündnis.* Berlin: Akademie-Verlag, 1983.

Woodward, E.L. *British Foreign Policy in the Second World War.* 5 volumes. London: Her Majesty's Stationery Office, 1970-76.

Wright, J. "Stresemann and Locarno." *Contemporary European History* 42 (1995): 109-31.

Young, Robert J. *France and the Origins of the Second World War.* New York: St. Martin's Press, 1996.

_____. *In Command of France: French Foreign Policy and Military Planning, 1933-1940*. Cambridge, MA: Harvard University Press, 1978.

Young, William. *International Politics and Warfare in the Age of Louis XIV and Peter the Great: A Guide to the Historical Literature*. Lincoln: iUniverse, 2004.

_____. "The Wilhelmstrasse and the Nazi Conspiracy to Wage Wars of Aggression: An Investigation into the Continuity of German Foreign Office Influence on the Formulation of Foreign Policy, 1871-1945." M.A. thesis, University of North Dakota, 1993.

Zeman, Z.A.B. *A Diplomatic History of the First World War*. London: Weidenfeld and Nicolson, 1971.

Ziemke, Earl F. "Strategy for Class War: The Soviet Union, 1917-1941." In *The Making of Strategy: Rulers, States, and War*. Edited by Williamson Murray, Macgregor Knox, and Alvin Berstein. Cambridge: Cambridge University Press, 1994.

Zimmermann, Ludwig. *Deutsche Aussenpolitik in der Ära der Weimarer Republik*. Göttingen: Musterschmidt, 1958.

# *About the Author*

Dr. William Young is the Associate Director of International Programs and Lecturer in History at the University of North Dakota. He holds doctoral and master's degrees in history from the University of North Dakota, a master's degree in international relations from the School of International Relations at the University of Southern California, and bachelor's degrees from the University of Maryland and University of the State of New York. Dr. Young is a former historian for the United States Air Force History Program. He is the author of forty-two volumes of Air Force history as well as numerous special studies and monographs. He is a three-time recipient of the Air Force Historian of the Year Award. His military assignments included thirteen years in the United Kingdom, Germany, The Netherlands, and Saudi Arabia. Dr. Young is the author of *International Politics and Warfare in the Age of Louis XIV and Peter the Great* (2004) and *European War and Diplomacy, 1337-1815* (2003). He also contributed articles to *Magill's Guide to Military History* (2001), *America in the Fifties* (2005), and *America in the Seventies* (2005). He is married to Patricia Young, and they live in Grand Forks, North Dakota.

# *Index*

978-0-595-40706-◄
0-595-40706-4

Printed in Great Britain
by Amazon